How the Soviet Union Is Governed

How the Soviet Union Is Governed

Jerry F. Hough and Merle Fainsod

An extensively revised and enlarged edition by Jerry F. Hough of Merle Fainsod's *How Russia Is Ruled*

105239

Harvard University Press
Cambridge, Massachusetts
    and
London, England

Copyright © 1953, 1963, 1979 by the President
and Fellows of Harvard College

10   9   8   7   6

This book is printed on acid-free paper, and its binding materials have
been chosen for strength and durability.

Printed in the United States of America

Library of Congress Cataloging in Publication Data

Hough, Jerry F., 1935–
  How the Soviet Union is governed.

  "An extensively revised and enlarged edition by Jerry F. Hough of
Merle Fainsod's How Russia is ruled."
  Includes bibliographical references and index.
  1. Russia—Politics and government—1917–   I.   Fainsod, Merle,
1907–1972, joint author.   II.   Fainsod, Merle, 1907–1972.   How Russia
is ruled.   III.   Title.
JN6531.F3   1979   320.9′47′08   78-22047
ISBN 0-674-41030-0

Preface

I was fortunate enough to attend Harvard in the mid-1950s when the evolution of the Soviet system was a central intellectual issue. Merle Fainsod and Barrington Moore (together with Zbigniew Brzezinski) were dominant figures in that intellectual analysis and Fainsod and Moore were teaching courses explaining the Soviet political system. It has seemed to me that my research and writing since then have been an attempt to work through in my own mind the reasons for my attraction to the very different perceptions of Fainsod and Moore and for my partial disagreement with Brzezinski. Barrington Moore clearly had the greater impact upon my comparative perspective (and, therefore, upon my labeling of phenomena), but I have always considered myself very much a Fainsodian in my sense of how the Soviet system actually works, how its institutions interact, and how social forces affect its political process. For this reason I felt it a great honor indeed to be asked by the publisher to revise *How Russia Is Ruled*.

In view of the nature of this revised edition, I believe I ought to explain in some detail what I have tried to do. First, the historical happenings of the last fifteen years and the latest statistics have been included to enable me to describe institutions in present-day terms. Second, I have tried to incorporate changes in historical interpretation based on the immense amount of scholarly work published since the 1960s. In the case of the most important scholarly debates, I have tried to outline the opposing positions (often including Fainsod's) before presenting my own views on the question.

The most significant change, however, has been in the organization and focus of the book. Merle Fainsod's study was organized historically within each chapter. The original 1953 text of this pathmarking book was revised

v

comparatively little in the 1963 edition, as the major change embraced the addition of new sections on the developments in the post-Stalin period to each chapter. I felt chapters in this edition would have become unwieldy if I supplemented them once more. Instead, I rearranged much of the material of the earlier editions to yield a historical section, organized chronologically, and I added a new institutional and policymaking section.

The change in organization has been accompanied by a partial change in focus. In the first edition of his book, Fainsod concentrated upon the techniques that the Bolsheviks—and then Stalin—had used to gain control of the Russian political system and their ability to maintain control. The policymaking process in the Soviet Union was discussed primarily in short sections within chapters mainly concerned with different questions.

Yet the analysis of how the Soviet government worked was extremely sophisticated, even at that early stage of the study of a closed system, and the contemporary scholar is impressed by the extent to which even the 1953 edition emphasized the importance of social forces at key junctures in Soviet history, the presence of cleavages behind the "totalitarian façade" (one of Fainsod's favorite phrases), and the consistency with which the bureaucratic units tried to evade central controls and pursue their own interests.

In particular, Fainsod did not define totalitarianism as a movement to transform society, but rather as the leader's drive for political control, one that had led "Stalinism [to emerge] in the conservative garb of the party of tradition and order." He wrote not of atomization of society, but of "family circles"; he pointed to the rising technical expertise among the younger party leaders. Moreover, he did not see the party apparatus as the center of policy initiation and the government as the passive executor of policy, but he understood the implications of Stalin pitting the party, governmental, and police hierarchies against one another.

This extensively revised and enlarged edition follows Fainsod in trying to explain how the Soviet Union has been controlled. It begins by asking why the old regime collapsed and how the Bolsheviks gathered sufficient support to seize the reins of power and win a long civil war. It explores how Stalin consolidated his power and raises the question: In a century in which peasant guerrilla action has often been so successful, how did Stalin manage to pull off collectivization? It ends with a discussion of the factors that contribute to a continuation of the existing political system or that could theoretically lead to a change in it.

However, this edition increases very substantially the amount of attention given to aspects of the political process: How policy is formed and how the Soviet Union is governed. It supplements the analysis of Lenin's struggle against the various oppositions with more discussion of the beginnings of bureaucratic struggle; it expands the analysis of Stalin's rise to power with more analysis of the economic debates of the 1920s; it brings together and amplifies much of Fainsod's description of the policy process of the Stalin period.

The explanation of the policy process becomes strongest in the second half of the book. Whenever possible, I have tried to analyze the alignments and interrelationships among institutions, and I devote an entire chapter to the power relationships, variously defined, throughout the political system. The reasons for the relative shift of emphasis are several. First, the growing openness of the Soviet political system permits scholars to write more today about questions that analysts of two decades ago would have wanted to discuss had more information been available. Second, the mechanisms of control—and the degree to which they are successful—have been the central question of Soviet studies for three decades. Because the policy process has been studied less, a greater contribution to scholarship can be made by devoting more attention to this subject. Third, research and writing about western governments has centered on the policy process and the factors associated with responsiveness in political systems, and meaningful comparative political science requires that a conscious attempt be made to ask the same questions about the Soviet Union.

Awareness of focus or level of analysis is absolutely crucial in political research. Scholars such as David Easton correctly insist that a political system may be analyzed from different perspectives (for example, the political community, the regime or political institutions, the actual governmental leaders) and that the political process has many different "parts" to it—the inputs (which include both supports and demands), the outputs (the decisions and their impact upon the population), the "black box" of policymaking itself. Too often scholars have not been fully aware of these levels or aspects of political systems. Thus scholarly debates have occurred over artificial differences as questions that are not really comparable have been posed, and black-and-white comparisons of political systems have sometimes been made on criteria or definitions that are not comparable.

The problems that are embedded in comparing different political systems need to be kept clearly in mind as this work is viewed as a revision of Fainsod's book. In certain cases there are differences between the two studies in substantive interpretation. In many other instances, what may seem to be shifts in view are often no more than answers to very different questions. Fainsod was greatly interested in how the system as a whole, the regime as a whole, was maintained, and in the politics that revolved around that process. I am much more frequently interested in the question: Given the existence of the system, how are within-system questions decided? Given the ultimate structure of power and the dominance of the party leadership, what is the structure of influence and of responsiveness to social forces? Both sets of questions are, in my opinion, important (and I try to give my answers to both), but what is most crucial is that one person's answers to one set of questions not be compared with another person's answers to the other set. In the United States the process of maintaining the fundamentals of the political, economic, and social system involves rather different politics from that dealing with within-system questions, for example, tax credits for college tuition, the building of the neutron bomb, the nature of health insurance; the difference in political process that deals with structural fundamentals, or within-system demands, holds true also for the Soviet Union.

It should be emphasized once more that the choice of focus for this book, as well as all specific interpretations, are my responsibility alone, and the partial change in title re-emphasizes that fact. Merle Fainsod had begun thinking about a third edition of *How Russia Is Ruled* and he had apparently concluded that an extensive revision was required, but at the time of his death he left almost nothing to indicate the direction of his thinking. Even if I had wanted to be guided by his interpretations, there would have been no way for me to find such assistance. In practice, I think it raises far fewer questions of propriety if I make no pretense of modifying my judgments to correspond with what I think might have been his. In fact, on the one question on which Fainsod is known to have been considering revisions—the relationship of Stalin to his lieutenants and especially Kirov in 1934—I have essentially retained the interpretation of the first two editions of *How Russia Is Ruled* because I personally find it convincing.

As is customary in publishing, I have been allowed to use the words of the earlier editions of *How Russia Is Ruled* verbatim and without attribution, and most of the early part of this volume was, in fact, written by Merle Fainsod. However, I also wanted to explore the western scholarly debates on the major historical issues, and Fainsod's position was often a key one in the debates. In these discussions, Fainsod's words from his editions of *How Russia Is Ruled* have frequently been placed in quotation marks so that his views could be considered explicitly. In addition, quotation marks were also used at points where, in my opinion, Fainsod's interpretations have sometimes been misunderstood and where it seemed useful to clarify the situation.

The practice of occasionally placing quotation marks around material from the editions of *How Russia Is Ruled* may further help in reminding the reader of the locus of responsibility for the mistakes and interpretations in this book. Yet, if there can be no pretense of writing a book with precisely the same views that Merle Fainsod would have held, it is at least possible to try to aspire to the type of thoroughness represented in his work. Presumably

there will be further editions of this newly published edition, and I hope
that readers will take the time to point out errors, omissions, or mistakes in
interpretation so that a future work will be a closer approximation to the
standard that Fainsod set.

In the best of all possible worlds, it would be desirable if the Soviet
Union, too, decided that any meaningful improvement in international relations depended ultimately upon a more sophisticated American understanding of Soviet reality. It is completely natural that many interpretations in this
book will be unacceptable to Soviet scholars (although not so natural that they
may feel it necessary to denounce them as "bourgeois falsifications"). It is
also completely natural that future editions of this book will continue to
advance interpretations that will in all probability prevent its being published
in a Russian-language edition in the Soviet Union. Nevertheless, there are
far too many places in this version where it has been necessary to end with an
admission of ignorance—and often on questions where there seems no Soviet
self-interest in maintaining a policy of secrecy. Considering the importance of
American elite and mass opinion in shaping American foreign policy, the
information policy of the Soviet Union does not seem to serve the nation's own
interests.

Ultimately the only excuse for publishing this new book must be the
hope that it provides a framework for analysis of the Soviet political system
that is as sophisticated and comprehensive as possible. In that happy circum-
stance, Merle Fainsod's great work will live as a monument to the level of
carefulness in research required of us all.

Contents

Tables

The Development of the Soviet System

1 | The Origins of Bolshevism

A<small>N ACUTE OBSERVER</small> of Russian society in the late nineteenth and early twentieth centuries might have found the potential for revolution in every corner of the realm. Had he predicted that it would be the Bolsheviks who would ultimately inherit the tsar's diadem, most of his contemporaries would probably have dismissed him as mad. Until 1917, the tiny handful of revolutionaries who followed the Bolshevik banner appeared to be swallowed in the vastness of Russia. Lenin, in a speech before a socialist youth meeting in Zurich on January 22, 1917, expressed strong doubts that he would "live to see the decisive battles of this coming revolution."[1] The sudden rise of Bolshevism from insignificance to total power was as great a shock to the Bolshevik leaders as it was to those whom Bolshevism displaced.

Yet, the triumph of Bolshevism should not be treated as a mere accident. It is a shallow view of Russian history that sees Bolshevism as an alien element grafted on the Russian body politic by a handful of power-lusting conspirators without roots in the past. Bolshevism as a movement was an indigenous response to the environment of tsarist absolutism from which it emerged; its success is to be explained by its appeals to the deeper forces of social unrest that produced the collapse of the tsarist regime—by its ability to harness the surge of revolutionary energy that it played only a relatively minor role in creating.

The Seedbed of Revolution

In retrospect, the observer is always impressed by historical continuity, and the flow of events seems inexorable. No political movement can be suc-

3

cessful without representing the interests of important social forces and without appealing to important national symbols and traditions. No governmental policy can be enacted without being favored by some social group or groups. Since social forces generally develop slowly and have a partial impact upon events before becoming dominant, few major political developments can occur that do not have historical antecedents. Consequently, when history is written (particularly with the benefit of historical perspective of some distance), it is easy and natural to show the links with the past—to interpret events either as the culmination of some powerful trend or as the repetition of earlier themes and motifs.

In writing history in terms of antecedents and traditions, however, we forget that historical traditions and antecedents are always multifaceted and ambiguous and that many stories of inexorable development could have been written if only the final outcome had been a different one. Thus, if Russia had fitfully evolved into a constitutional monarchy during the twentieth century, scholars would have pointed to the liberation of the serfs, the development of local institutions of partial self-rule, the development of "company" trade unions, the establishment of the duma (consultative parliament), and the legalization of parties after the 1905 revolution as steps in the inevitable democratization of Russia in the wake of industrialization. They would have pointed to the commune or mir in the village—a collective that made such important decisions as distribution of land among the peasants of a village—as a body that gave the Russian peasants long experience in democratic give-and-take.

Similarly, if Lenin's Bolsheviks had seized power but the political system had become increasingly open and liberal after the Civil War—or even if the policies of the 1920s had not been cut short—scholars would have pointed to the democratic elements within Marxist thought, to the transformations taking place within all social-democratic parties at this time, to Lenin's utopian and democratic statements in *State and Revolution* and elsewhere. They would have emphasized the conflicts within the party during 1917 and before. Even if they had noted authoritarian strains within Bolshevism, they would have attributed these to the requirements of revolutionary action against a police state and/or would have remarked about the inevitable impact of the assumption of power upon any party's doctrinaire assumptions.

Or, if—and this was probably the most likely outcome of all—a military dictatorship had been established in Russia as it was in a number of other eastern European countries after World War I, then we would have read of Russian political developments being the inevitable product of a conservative political tradition or a conservative national character. Instead of having innumerable studies of the Russian socialist movement and various minor figures in it, we would have had countless studies of the military in the tsarist system (today the subject is almost totally neglected), and these would have undoubtedly shown the military's hand in most of the policies of the late tsarist period, the ideologies and career patterns within the military, and so forth.

While the story would be much neater and more satisfying if the Bolshevik revolution were treated as the foreordained product of earlier Russian history, an exclusive focus upon the prerevolutionary antecedents or analogies leads to an unwarranted neglect of the complexities of history. Nevertheless, at a minimum it seems safe to say that the Russian political system was virtually certain to undergo some very drastic change in the first half of the twentieth century, whatever the nature of that change might have proved to be. Russia was beginning to industrialize rapidly, and one need not be a Marxist to argue that that development was posing an enormous challenge to a political system that relied upon a divine-right-of-kings argument as its legitimating ideology, that rested primarily upon a declining landowning nobility as its foremost social support, and that (by the test of war) was proving ineffective in maintaining the position of the nation vis-à-vis its major competitors.

The center of the Russian political system prior to World War I was a tsar-emperor whose conception of the plenitude of autocratic power dated back to the fifteenth century.[2] The more the moral authority of the system was shaken by defeat in war, the more insistently the tsar clung to the substance as well as the semblance of his power. Nicholas II, forced to convoke a consultative parliament after the 1905 revolution, nevertheless proclaimed that "the Supreme, Autocratic power belongs to the All-Russian Emperor" and repeated the ancient formula: "Obedience to his authority, not only for wrath but also for conscience sake, is ordained by God Himself."[3] The words of Nicholas II rang like an atavistic echo of Ivan the Terrible, who pronounced that the "Rulers of Russia have not been accountable to anyone, but have been free to reward or chastise their subjects,"[4] or of Peter the Great who wrote, "The autocratic monarch has to give an account of his acts to no one on earth, but has a power and authority to rule his states and lands as a Christian sovereign according to his own will and judgment."[5]

The society that the tsar ruled differed enormously from western Europe of that day. The technological revolution that gave such powerful impetus to English (and later American and western European) industrial productivity in the late eighteenth and early nineteenth centuries had been slow to penetrate Russia.[6] The population was overwhelmingly peasant, and prior to 1861 it was a peasantry largely locked in serfdom or employed as state peasants—in either case, a peasantry that was bound to land which it did not own.[7] The social-political elite centered on a number of great social families whose estrangement from society was symbolized by the fact that many used French as their normal language of discourse early in the century. A broader elite would include the rest of the hereditary nobility (estimated at 131,000 men outside Poland in 1858–1859, though many were quite impoverished),[8] the state bureaucracy (organized in a rigid rank system but very small in relation to its western European counterparts), and the clergy of the Russian Orthodox Church, the official state church.

In the nineteenth century, however, Russia was beginning to undergo major change. In 1815, after the Napoleonic invasion had been repelled, the tsar had been able to march victoriously through the streets of Paris, but when Russia became embroiled in war with England in 1853, it suffered a humiliating defeat on its own territory in the Crimea. The defeat in the Crimean War was eventually followed by an increase in antiregime political activity, but more immediately, it awakened a concern within the government itself about the increasing gap between the economic performance of Russia and that of western Europe.

The most dramatic action to emerge from this policy reexamination was an 1861 proclamation by Tsar Alexander II that emancipated the serfs,[9] but from the peasants' point of view the agricultural reform was incomplete. Half of the private land was retained by its previous owners, and the other half was transferred to the village commune or mir which owned it and allocated it among the peasants for their use. Moreover, the peasants were obligated to make large redemption payments for the land they received.

A second set of actions attempted to prepare the way for industrial development. The state invested considerable funds of its own for this purpose, and through a system of concessions, subsidies, and guarantees, it moved to create favorable conditions for industrial investment by both domestic and foreign capital. During the 1860s and 1870s, capital flowed chiefly into railroads and banking, 9,395 miles of railroad lines being opened from 1866 to 1875, compared with 2,338 miles for all the years up to 1866.

Although the economic depression that spread from Europe to Russia in 1873 and continued with minor interruption until the nineties administered a sharp setback to the rate of industrial growth, Russia entered upon a decade of intensive industrialization during the 1890s. This expansion was actively promoted by the government, especially Count Witte, Minister of Finance from 1892 to 1903.[10] Between 1891 and 1900, 14,121 miles of railroad were added (much of it in the Trans-Siberian Railroad linking European Russia with Vladivostok on the Pacific). Oil production increased 132 percent, pig iron 190 percent, coal 131 percent, and cotton manufactures 76 percent.[11]

The sharp industrial advance of the nineties was interrupted by the severe commercial crisis of 1900–1903 and the revolutionary disturbances of 1905–1907, but by 1909 progress was resumed.[12] While Russia was a major industrial power when compared with a number of European countries, it remained backward by the standards of the foremost. Coal production amounted to 36 million tons in 1913, compared with the German production of 190.1 million tons and the United States total of 517.1 million tons. The Russian pig-iron production of 4.6 million tons was far below the 16.8 million tons produced in Germany and the 31.5 million tons in the United States.[13] The machinery industries were in the most rudimentary stage of development, and almost all machinery was imported. Nevertheless, the overall rate of growth in the years prior to World War I was striking indeed, particularly in the textile, metallurgical, and mining industries.

In addition to emancipating the serfs and beginning to encourage industrial development, Alexander II instituted a series of other reforms as well. The Zemstvo Statute of 1864 created a system of rural self-government (the zemstvos) that opened the way to popular participation (especially by those with higher status) in such aspects of local government as education, health, and sanitation.[14] In the same year, a judicial reform introduced trial by jury in criminal cases, election of justices of the peace by zemstvo and town assemblies, and removal of judges only for judicial misconduct. In addition to encouraging the expansion of lower level education by the zemstvos, the government also began to increase the size of the higher education network by more direct means.[15]

As is so often the case when an autocratic regime attempts to industrialize and modernize its country, the results of the reform program were mixed—particularly from the point of view of the regime. As was to be true in the Soviet Union in the mid-twentieth century, the agricultural sector posed the most serious problems. The collective ownership of land by the commune led to the carving of the land of a village into a crazy-quilt network of strips, which could be shifted from peasant to peasant in a general redistribution. This system provided little incentive and little opportunity for the most rational improvement of agricultural productivity. The redemption payments proved beyond the ability of the peasants to pay in full, and problems were multiplied by a large increase in rural population and in the number of mouths to feed.[16] The agricultural difficulties came to a head in 1891–1892 when several years of drought and resulting poor harvests tipped the increasingly precarious balance sufficiently to produce a serious famine.[17] A decade later in the wake of a further crop failure, peasant disorders broke out in Kursk, Poltava, and Kharkov provinces. The movement gave every evidence of being spontaneous; as a rule, villagers simply banded together to seize grain to feed themselves and their animals.

Many of the problems of the tsarist regime stemmed not so much from the failure of policies as from their success or partial success. The judicial reforms produced such an independent judiciary that in 1878 a jury acquitted Vera Zasulich, who shot the governor of St. Petersburg for ordering the flogging of a student revolutionary. (In the wake of such independence, much of the judicial reform was abolished.) The health program was a significant factor in the agricultural problems, for it was sufficiently successful to have the usual impact in a developing nation—a lowering of the mortality rate with the birth rate remaining high. The result was a sharp rise in population with overcrowding both in the city and country.

But perhaps worst of all, the successes in the industrial and educational realms expanded those social groups that were least likely to find tsarism congenial, that were most likely to want change in the political system and/or governmental policy. One such group was the bourgeoisie—the business leaders. The lateness of industrial development, the important role played by foreign capital, the dependence of the internal business community upon governmental subsidies—all these factors interfered with the development of a strong and self-reliant business class. Nevertheless, although business leaders often turned to the government for protection against strikes and revolutionary demand for social change, a number of them showed signs of restlessness and self-assertiveness in the years before World War I. Employer associations became quite common, and among their various functions they served as a sounding board for political aspirations. Within the revolutionary spectrum, even those industrialists desiring institutional change were a conservative element who hoped for little more than a constitutional monarchy; but from the tsar's point of view this demand was hardly conservative.

A second group created by the industrialization program was the industrial proletariat. As is typical in the developmental process, many of the workers were peasants who had just arrived from the village—and often returned to the village for part of the year. While the link with the village remained a characteristic feature of Russian industrial development into the Soviet period, a proletariat with its own "factory genealogy" began to appear, as more and more persons settled permanently in the cities. The enlarging nucleus of "true" proletarians tended to develop class consciousness and to take leadership in articulating the grievances of their fellow workers, as the fresh arrivals brought with them the backwardness of the village and a passive endurance of the misery of their lot.

In the early phase of industrialization, labor exploitation was at its worst. Wages were miserably low and were frequently reduced by fines pocketed by the factory owners. Sanitary conditions in the factories were unsatisfactory, and workers were often crowded together in huge factory barracks without distinction as to age and sex. The government made some effort to ameliorate conditions. Attempts were made to regulate child labor, and in 1897 the work day of adults was limited to eleven and a half hours and night work to ten hours. The regime gradually introduced social-benefits legislation, but as in so many other fields the concessions were belated and largely extorted under pressure. Advances were interrupted by retreats, and enforcement was uncertain. The credit that might have accrued to the autocracy was dissipated by the impression it left of intransigent opposition to the very reforms which it was reluctantly sponsoring.

Finally, the regime's educational programs helped to create a new professional and white collar stratum. The number of those in higher education rose from 3,000 in the early 1850s to 25,000 in the early 1890s and 77,000 in 1914, and a Soviet historian has recently estimated that the number of those with professional training rose from 20,000 to 85,000 between 1860 and 1900.[18] A number of these persons came to conceive of themselves as an "intelligentsia" —as a group that by its very nature was obligated to stand in opposition to the tsarist system. The institutions of higher education in particular became the scene of such persistent student unrest that "the very word 'student' would finally become synonymous with revolutionist,"[19] and the ability of the radicals to win acceptance of a politicized definition of an *intelligent* was itself an important step in building opposition.

The oppositionist intelligentsia tended to speak of a gap between "state" and "society" and to describe the bureaucracy as one of the dead hands of the tsarist regime hindering innovation. Yet, it was in the bureaucracy that a large proportion of those with professional training found employment. The impact of the bureaucracy varied from person to person, but this institution came to include many who absorbed professional norms of service and reform and who must have felt special frustration when some court favorite was permitted to interfere with a line of action they thought necessary.[20]

The Rise of the Revolutionary Movement

One can trace many precursors of the revolutionary movement that eventually overthrew the tsar—the peasant uprisings under Pugachev, a lone radical named Radishchev at the end of the eighteenth century, the abortive Decembrist revolt in 1825 by army officers affected by their exposure to western ideas during the Napoleonic campaign, the gathering disillusionment expressed in the golden age of Russian literature in the first half of the nineteenth century. Fundamentally, though, the first great upsurge of political unrest occurred in the 1860s in the wake of the defeat inflicted during the Crimean War and the subsequent attempts of the regime to institute partial reform.

The radicals of the 1860s and 1870s were later called Narodniki or Populists by their Marxist opponents, but this ex post facto label conveys the sense of a movement much more unified than was actually the case.[21] The revolutionaries of this period usually did focus upon the peasant—as was, of course, natural in a country with so little industrial development. They did tend to idealize the village as an embodiment of cooperative fellowship, and they hoped for an anarchist socialism that could be built on this institution. They did give great attention to Marx, translating his works into Russian and attempting to use his negative picture of western European capitalism as an example of a development that Russia should avoid. But beyond this, there were major differences in the vague images they had of Russia's future.

The Russian radicals were even less united on tactics than they were on program. Some quickly moved into terrorist activity. A secret organization *Zemlia i Volia* (Land and Freedom) planned a peasant rising for the summer of 1863, but nothing came of it, and a number of the leaders were executed. An attempt was made to assassinate the tsar in April 1866 but this also failed. A much larger segment of the intelligentsia eschewed terrorist tactics, feeling that it was the obligation of the intelligentsia to go out into the villages to help awaken the peasant masses. The result was the famous movement of "going to the people" from the summer of 1872 to the summer of 1874, as students, teachers, lawyers, physicians, officers, and "repentant noblemen" swarmed into the countryside in a veritable crusade.

What happened is depicted in unforgettable fashion in Turgenev's *Virgin Soil*. The "dark forces" of the village could make nothing of the invaders. Most of the intelligentsia did not know how to talk to the people when they met them, and the peasants could not understand what they were driving at. Some of the missionaries were confused with antichrist, and many were turned over to the police. The authorities took a very dim view of revolutionary propaganda being conducted in the countryside, and they staged a number of mass trials of those involved.[22]

For the intelligentsia, the experience of peasant distrust was sobering and disillusioning. Some of them digested the lesson and settled down in the countryside to undertake the long, disagreeable task of overcoming suspicion and proving their usefulness. The work of the zemstvos in the fields of education and medicine—which could not have been done without the devoted work of the rural intelligentsia—forms one of the brightest pages of Russian history. Yet, the response of many of the intelligentsia was to flock back to the towns and cities to torture their consciences in endless conversation.

Those who remained active in revolutionary activity became increasingly dedicated to terror. The triumph of the extremists found expression in the organization in 1879 of *Narodnaia Volia* (People's Will), perhaps the first tactically unified and tightly organized Russian revolutionary party.[23]

While the Narodnaia Volia actually depicted the proletariat as the vanguard of the Russian revolutionary movement in its 1879 program and did conduct work among the workers,[24] its aim was a constituent assembly composed overwhelmingly of peasant representatives who could be trusted to put a program of agrarian socialism into effect. Its members turned to terror, hoping through a series of key assassinations to intimidate the government into concessions, to arouse the people, and perhaps to seize power at the center.

From the fall of 1879 to the spring of 1881, the terrorists waged a relentless duel with the government, with liberal society showing some sympathy or tolerance. Despite the imposition of martial law, the Narodnaia Volia managed to kill a number of important officials, and finally in March 1881 it accomplished its chief aim—the assassination of Alexander II. Instead of ushering in a constituent assembly, however, the revolutionists only succeeded in putting a more repressive ruler into power. The peasants were deaf to the revolutionary signal, and after a short-lived panic in court circles, reaction consolidated its hold. The revolutionary groups were smashed by the authorities, as the new tsar increased the powers of the police.[25]

Brief western synopses of Russian history usually treat the crushing of the Narodnaia Volia as a turning point in the history of the revolutionary movement. They often suggest that the revolutionary movement now swung in a more orthodox Marxist direction, recognizing the inevitability of a capitalist development for Russia and the need for the revolution to be built upon an urban base. The narrative centers on Georgii Plekhanov, a man who by 1879 had broken with the organizers of Narodnaia Volia because of his doubts about terror, and who fled abroad in 1881 to avoid the roundup of all revolutionaries that occurred in the wake of the assassination of Alexander II.[26]

Plekhanov abandoned the old faith in the peasantry (whose "political indifference and intellectual backwardness" he now called "the main bulwark of absolutism"), and he placed his trust instead in the workers:

> The historic role of the proletariat is as revolutionary as the historic role of the *muzhik* [peasant] is conservative. The muzhiks have been the support of oriental despotism for thousands of years. The proletariat in a comparatively short space of time has shaken the "foundations" of western European society.[27]

In 1883 Plekhanov joined with Paul Akselrod, Leo Deutsch, and Vera Zasulich in establishing the first Russian Marxist organization, the group known as *Osvobozhdenie truda* (The Emancipation of Labor).

It is tidy to see the formation of the Emancipation of Labor group as the beginning of the end for the Populists and for concern with the peasants and to trace a direct line from it to the Marxist upsurge in the 1890s and then to the rise of Lenin and the Bolshevik revolution, but any neatly drawn narrative of this type has serious shortcomings. In the first place, the old radical focus upon the peasantry scarcely disappeared from the Russian scene in the 1880s and the 1890s. While 1881 was a turning point in the sense that the increased police repression and the disillusionment about the consequences of the assassination of the tsar drove many revolutionaries into a despairing passivity, the revolutionaries had always been a tiny activist element in a much broader spectrum of antiregime opinion, and a decline in activism did not mean an end to thought. In a peasant country, the peasants were not likely to be ignored by those thinking of the future, and, in fact, they were not. Thus, it is hardly surprising that when formal political parties were established at the turn of the century, one of the most prominent was the Socialist Revolutionary party (the SR's)—a peasant-oriented socialist party which at the beginning even adopted the terrorist tactics of its predecessors. Moreover, even leaving aside the SR's, Lenin's image of revolution came to involve a heavy dependence upon peasant revolutionary action.

In the second place, the Emancipation of Labor group was a tiny one—really only three people after the first two years—and there is little evidence that the works it produced in Switzerland were even known in Russia until the mid-1890s.[28] In actual practice, Marxism became an important movement only after the famine of 1891–1892 and the doubt it cast upon the performance of the system. By this time, the massive industrialization program provided powerful support to the Marxist proposition that Russia was embarked on an irreversible course of capitalist development. In addition, the Marxists' ability to propagate their views was facilitated by the government's decision to permit many of their works to be published legally—a policy based on a desire to weaken the Marxists' radical opponents, who were considered more revolutionary and terroristic. It was during this period that Plekhanov's works—sometimes published legally under a pseudonym—began reaching a Russian audience.

Marxism did enjoy great success in winning adherents in the nineties, but this fact is partly explained by the great diversity in the views that came to fit under the Marxist umbrella at this point. Because Russia was essentially at the beginning of its capitalist stage—at the beginning of its period of rapid industrialization—Marxism could be attractive not only to those who looked forward to a proletarian revolution at some time in the future but also to those who saw that in immediate terms it first implied the need for an attack on "feudalism" (and the tsarist political system) and a promotion of industrial development.

Thus, for many during this period of Legal Marxism (the phrase refers to the government's censorship policy), "Marxist" was hardly more than a generic name for the protagonists of the industrial development which appeared in full triumph. Peter Struve, a future liberal leader who counted himself a Marxist at this time and who played a key role in promoting Marxism with his "Critical Remarks on the Problem of the Economic Development of Russia" (1894), could end this work with the appeal, "Let us recognize our backwardness in culture and let us take our lessons from capitalism."[29] For still others, Marxism meant little more than "bread and butter" trade unionism. (Lenin labeled such people "Economists," and he applied the term to leading opponents who—with some justification—berated him for misrepresentation of their views.)[30]

There were, of course, also Marxists who were anxious that the revolutionary thrust of Marxism not be diluted—a concern that only intensified after 1898 when one of the leading German Marxists, Eduard Bernstein, called upon his party to formally accept the possibility of a peaceful road to socialism. Plekhanov was one of the most insistent critics of any kind of revisionism, and among the younger revolutionaries who held to this position was a young group headed by Vladimir Ilich Ulianov (or Lenin, to use the pseudonym he came to adopt). After three years of exile for revolutionary activity, Lenin had emigrated to Switzerland to establish a newspaper (*Iskra*) to promote orthodox Marxist views in cooperation with two contemporaries (Iulii Martov and Alexander Potresov) and with Plekhanov and other members of the Emancipation of Labor group. It was out of a conflict within this *Iskra* group that the Bolshevik party arose.

Lenin and the Dilemmas of Marxism in Russia

Thousands of pages have been written in English alone about the split within the *Iskra* group (and the orthodox Russian Marxist movement) in 1903, and the issue remains crucial in the continuing scholarly debate on the origins of the political system that existed under Stalin and afterwards. Many explanations for this event have been advanced, but none is wholly satisfying. Personal jealousies and differences in personal style surely combined in a complex manner with subtle differences in views about history and the revolution, views that the leading protagonists themselves may not have been able to articulate at the time.

Perhaps one useful way of at least putting the formation of the Bolshevik party in perspective is to recall that a person who wanted to be an orthodox Marxist in Russia at the turn of the century faced a number of difficulties. One of these problems was common to all European Marxists. Marx's *The Communist Manifesto* had been written in 1848, infused with the revolutionary optimism of the time; by 1900 a full fifty years had passed. Not only had the socialist revolution failed to occur, but the workers' economic position seemed to be improving and their political attitudes seemed to be becoming less revolutionary as well. In western Europe a number of Marxists were beginning to wonder if revolution was inevitable or even necessary to achieve socialist goals, and anyone who disagreed needed to explain the delay in the revolution and to suggest why and how the future would be different.

An orthodox Marxist in Russia faced a further and in many ways more severe problem. Marxism, as has often been noted, is a multifaceted doctrine. On the one hand, Marx's analysis purported to be completely scientific. As Engels stated at his friend's grave, Marx believed that he had discovered the laws of historical development in the same sense that Darwin had discovered the laws of evolution.[31] According to Marx, these laws dictated both that a society's political, ideological, and moral superstructure are shaped in the most fundamental manner by its basic economic relationships, and also that history inexorably evolves toward the establishment of a communist society. Feudalism inevitably is replaced by capitalism, which (after making a major contribution to industrial development) inevitably is plagued by increasingly severe business depressions and lowering standards of living and then is inevitably overthrown by the working class, who establish first a socialist and then a communist system.

As noted, the broad appeal of Marxism in the 1890s and early 1900s in Russia stemmed in large part from its scientific claims. First, it seemed to be accurate in its predictions about the rise of capitalism in the country, and, second, it was suggesting that the tsarist political system was the anachronistic (and soon-to-be-replaced) superstructure of a feudal system that was disappearing. Not only was Marxism a useful ideology for those wanting to modernize Russia, but also its claim to be scientific seemed increasingly validated by the Russian experience.

Marxism was, however, always more than a science; it was also a moralistic attack upon a capitalist system that it saw as repressive, unjust, and repulsive. One might have thought that Marx's own analysis would have led him to treat the capitalists as tragic heroes—men who made a great contribution to mankind by conquering nature in the industrial revolution, men whose exploitation of the workers was absolutely dictated by laws of the market which they could not control, men who were ultimately doomed by the inner mechanisms of the system that had created them. But this is scarcely how Marx described the bourgeoisie or how he felt about them. As the American reformer Carl Schurz recalled, "I remember most distinctly the cutting disdain with which he pronounced the word 'bourgeois'; and as a 'bourgeois,' that is, as a detestable example of the deepest mental and moral degeneracy, he denounced everyone that dared to oppose his opinion."[32]

In western Europe, the dual nature of Marxism posed few problems, and, indeed, was an advantage. Even the analytical side of Marxism had always posited that capitalism would be overthrown, not that it would wither away, and hence that individuals would have to come forward to persuade the workers of the need to revolt. The moralistic side of Marxism provided some of the emotional incentive for this development to occur. In Russia, on the other hand, a real conflict arose. If a Marxist assumed that Russia was essentially making the transition from feudalism to capitalism and that capitalism would survive even half as long as it had in western Europe, then he was choosing to enter dangerous underground work—or go into exile— in order to install a system that he believed exploitative and morally disgusting. He must try to persuade the workers to join their natural class enemy, the businessmen, in establishing a constitutional democracy that Marx had depicted as no more than an undemocratic, repressive screen for rule by the business class.

There are many ways to summarize the position of Vladimir Ilich Ulianov, but perhaps the most useful is to say that for him—as for the Russian revolutionaries of the 1860s and 1870s, and probably for Marx himself— the moralistic side of Marxism seemed the crucial one. Lenin passed through a number of stages in his intellectual development,[33] and, like any major thinker, he was not always consistent in the positions he took over time. Nevertheless, with the exception of a period in the 1890s and a few brief periods thereafter, Lenin was renowned among the Russian Marxists for the strength of his antipathy to the bourgeoisie and their political representatives (the liberals) and for the extent to which he avoided meaningful political collaboration with them. When Lenin first visited Plekhanov in Switzerland in 1895, the latter observed, "You turn your behind to the liberals, but we our face."[34] Lenin seemed to take the reproach to heart for a few years, but it was a characterization that could have been made at almost any time from 1901 until November 1917. The corollary was a real reluctance for Lenin to accept in a meaningful way the idea that there would be a prolonged period of capitalist rule.

Those disposed toward probing the psychological roots of attitudes could advance—and have advanced—a number of explanations for Lenin's aversion to cooperation with the liberals.[35] His wife, Nadezhda Krupskaia, suggested that the explanation could be found in an incident in Lenin's youth. He had been born in 1870 in the Volga town of Simbirsk (now Ulianovsk), the son of a highly respected provincial education official. When Vladimir was fifteen, his father died, and when he was seventeen, his favorite brother, Alexander, became involved in a plot to assassinate the tsar, but was caught and executed. According to Krupskaia, the impact of this event was traumatic:

Vladimir Ilich once told me how "society" reacted to the arrest of his older brother. All their acquaintances forsook the Ulianov family. Even an old teacher who constantly came to play chess in the evenings ceased to come. At that time there still was no railroad from Simbirsk [to St. Petersburg], and Vladimir Ilich's mother had to go by coach to Syzran in order to reach St. Petersburg where her son was imprisoned. Vladimir Ilich was sent to seek a traveling companion, but no one wanted to go with the mother of an arrested man. According to Vladimir Ilich, this universal cowardice produced a very strong impression on him. This youthful experience undoubtedly placed its stamp on Vladimir Ilich's relation to "society," to the liberals. He early learned the value of any liberal chatter.[36]

Whatever the reasons for Lenin's attitudes—and we should surely be very cautious in our judgments about his subconscious psychological drives, especially since we also need to explain his brother's entry into revolutionary activity— it has been fashionable for western scholars to argue that they led Lenin to break with orthodox Marxism, to move toward a seizure of power that was grossly premature in terms of Marx's theory of historical development, and therefore to embrace the dictatorial measures that would be required. This argument certainly is a reasonable one, but we should at least recognize that no one in Russia of the time could be a completely orthodox Marxist in both analytical and normative terms. While a Russian Marxist could try to straddle and to evade the dilemma (as all of them did), he essentially had to abandon either the notion of a universal pattern of development or the moralistic revulsion toward the capitalists and all their works. Lenin's response was at least one of the logical ones to an extremely severe dilemma. Even his ultimate insistence upon single-party dictatorship instead of constitutional democracy was quite compatible with the Marxist belief that a constitutional democracy in a capitalist system was not democratic in any case.

Whether the acceptance of a prolonged capitalist stage as predetermined or the acceptance of the moralistic condemnation of capitalism and the exhortation to overthrow it at once was really the "more" correct Marxist response to the Russian dilemma seems rather pointless to discuss at length. (But, given the extremely widespread tendency to deny the Marxist label to Lenin, it should perhaps be mentioned that in the 1879–1881 period Marx and Engels did support the Narodnaia Volia in its terroristic attack on the tsar, did suggest that Russia might avoid the capitalist stage, and were very cool toward Plekhanov's efforts to undercut the Narodnaia Volia.)[37] For our purposes, the most important point to note is that a decision to conduct a proletarian revolution before the strong industrial base was created meant that many of the preconditions that Marx had foreseen for the communist society had not been met. It was to be a problem to which Communist theorists had to return after the revolution.

Lenin's Conception of the Party

In 1917 Lenin needed to explain how a proletarian revolution could occur at such an early stage of Russian industrial development; in 1900 the more pressing problem was to explain why it was so late in occurring in western Europe. The so-called Revisionists were increasingly contending that Marx's basic argument was flawed—that the revolution had not occurred because there was no real need for it, that the workers' position was improving and could improve even more as they used the universal suffrage that they were being accorded. The orthodox Marxists were under severe pressure to counter the Revisionist line of analysis and to indicate why a revolutionary upsurge was likely in the future.

Lenin's first comprehensive attempt to explain the tardiness of the European revolution came in a 1902 pamphlet, *What Is To Be Done?* Beginning this work with a savage attack upon the Russian Economists and the Revisionists in general, Lenin was very forthright in his basic explanation for the failure of the European revolution to have occurred: "The history of all countries shows that the working class by its own strength is able to achieve only trade union consciousness—that is, the conviction that it is necessary to unite into unions, to lead a struggle with the owners, to seek laws from the government that are necessary for the workers."[38] This sentence from *What Is To Be Done?* is the Lenin statement most widely cited in western scholarly literature, and it certainly is not torn out of context, for it was repeated a number of times in different forms. Moreover, because Lenin believed that anything which retarded the development of the revolution was supportive of the capitalists and their system, one logical conclusion followed from his analysis and he did not hesitate to draw it: "The *spontaneous* development of the workers' movement leads precisely to its subordination to bourgeois ideology . . . Any submission to the spontaneity of the workers' movement . . . means . . . a *strengthening of the influence of bourgeois ideology on the workers.*"[39]

Lenin's answer to the question of his own title was that major changes were needed in the socialist movement, particularly in Russia. Since "the workers [by themselves] *cannot have* Social-Democratic consciousness, . . . it can be introduced only from without . . . [that is, from] representatives of the propertied classes, the intelligentsia."[40] This task, he contended, the intelligentsia were performing poorly: "No one has doubted that the force of the contemporary movement is the awakening of the masses (chiefly, the industrial proletariat), and its weakness is that the leader-revolutionaries do not have enough consciousness and initiative." Not only were many Marxists falling into one form of revisionism or another, but their efforts were being dissipated by their "cottage industry methods" (*kustarnichestvo*)—by the concentration of their efforts on unconnected study circles for small groups of workers.[41]

In Lenin's view, what the Russian Marxists needed to do was to organize —to create (as he wrote in two letters in August 1902) "a very conspiratorial and tight nucleus of professional revolutionaries" and to engage in "more daring, more important, more *united,* more centralized work."[42]

> The organization of the revolutionary social-democratic party unavoidably should be *of a different type* than the organization of the workers for [economic] struggle. The organization of workers should be, in the first place, vocational in structure; in the second place, it should be as broad as possible ... By contrast, the organization of revolutionaries should embrace, first of all and chiefly, people whose profession consists of revolutionary activity . . . It is indispensable that this organization should not be very wide and that it should be as conspiratorial as possible."[43]

While Lenin wrote in general terms in *What Is To Be Done?* about the necessity for centralization in the organization, it was in his "Letter to a Comrade on Our Organizational Tasks," written seven months later in September 1902, that he spelled out his proposal with the greatest clarity:

> In the ideological and practical *leadership* of the movement and revolutionary struggle, there must be *as much centralization* as *possible* . . . The newspaper [*Iskra*] can and should be the *ideological* leader of the party, and should develop the theoretical truths, the tactical problems, the general organizational ideas, the general tasks of the whole party in this or that moment. The direct *practical* leader of the movement can be only a special central group (let's call it a Central Committee) which communicates *personally* with all [local] committees, which includes all the best revolutionary forces of all Russian Social-Democrats, and which is in charge of all general party affairs such as distribution of literature, publication of leaflets, distribution of personnel, assignment of the management of special undertakings to various persons and groups, preparation of all-Russian demonstrations and uprisings . . .
> [In the localities, there should be a committee which] should lead *all* sides of the local movement and manage *all* local institutions, forces,

and resources of the party . . . When we have a central organ [newspaper] and a Central Committee, new committees should be formed only with their participation and agreement. The number of members of the committee should not be very great, if possible . . . [but] if it turns out that there are fairly many members and it is dangerous for them to meet often, then perhaps there would be assigned from the committee a special, very small (let's say about five persons or even less) *managerial* group which should definitely include the secretary and the persons most capable to be the practical managers of all work as a whole . . .

The factory group or the factory committee . . . should consist of a very small number of *revolutionaries* who receive *directly from the [local] committee* the mission and authority to lead all social-democratic work in the factory. All members of the factory committee should look on themselves as agents of the committee, obligated to subordinate themselves to all its orders, obligated to observe all "laws and customs" of that "active army" in which they have entered and from which they do not have the right to leave in time of war without permission of the command . . .

So far as *informing* the party center about the movement is concerned . . . so far as *responsibility* before the party is concerned, we need *as much decentralization as possible* . . . The party should always have exact data not only about the activity of each group, but also *as complete data about their composition as possible* . . . When the centralization is carried through to completion and we have a central organ and a Central Committee, then there will be a possibility for the tiniest group to turn to them—and there will be the possibility not only of an appeal, but of an established practice of regular information to the central organ and the Central Committee. This will remove the possibility of a chance failure in the composition of this or that local committee . . . For the center . . . to actually direct the orchestra, it needs to know who plays which violin and where, who plays a false note and why (when the music begins to grate on the ear), and how and where it is necessary to transfer someone to correct the dissonance.[44]

In developing his conception of the proper revolutionary organization, Lenin instinctively thought of the early Russian revolutionary tradition, of which both his brother and his associate Plekhanov were such an intimate part. The very name of his seminal pamphlet was taken from the title of Chernyshevsky's novel, *What Is To Be Done?* which featured Rakhmetov, a professional revolutionary who devotes the whole of his life to the revolutionary cause, and his works were filled with tributes to the famous revolutionaries of the seventies. He referred to the "magnificent organization" of the Zemlia i Volia of the seventies "which should serve us all as a model," while his condemnation of Marxist revolutionary activity in the 1890s was based in part on the argument that "with our cottage industry methods we debased the prestige of the revolutionary in Russia."[45]

Because of his concentration upon the revolutionary organizations of the Russian past, because of his preoccupation with the problem of establishing a network of agents (a word he much liked)[46] who would handle the illegal smuggling of *Iskra* into Russia and its distribution there, Lenin was slow to adjust to the western conception of a party. In *What Is To Be Done?* he spoke of an "organization of revolutionaries" more than of a "party," and sometimes he seemed to imply that party membership would be limited to the full-time revolutionaries. If this was indeed Lenin's conception of the party in February 1902, however, he had already abandoned it by September of that year. In his "Letter to a Comrade on our Organizational Tasks," he distinguished between "the network of executive agents" and members of less conspiratorial groups and circles who need not—but could—become party members.[47]

At the Second Party Congress in August 1903, Lenin explicitly denied in open debate that he was thinking of an extremely narrow party. "It is not necessary to think that the party organizations should consist only of professional revolutionaries. We need the most different organizations of all kinds, ranks, and hues [within the party], beginning with the extremely narrow and conspiratorial and ending with the extremely wide and free— *lose Organisationen.*"[48] He spelled out this point more fully in his May 1904 history of the congress ("One Step Forward, Two Steps Backward"), ridiculing the charge of one speaker that he (Lenin) would not permit into the party those "tens of workers who [simply] distribute literature and lead oral agitation." "On the contrary," he said, "I have already cited the place from 'Letter to a Comrade' which shows that precisely the inclusion of all such workers in the organizations (in hundreds, not in tens) is both necessary and indispensable. Moreover, very, very many of these organizations can and should enter the party." He went so far as to argue that "for purposes of supervision the Central Committee can intentionally include in the party, in certain conditions, a not quite reliable organization which is capable of work in order to test it, in order to try *to direct* it on the path of truth."[49] And, in practice, as will be seen, when the revolutionary upsurges of 1905 and 1917 respectively increased the appeal of the party, large numbers were, in fact, admitted—most of them clearly not professional revolutionaries.

To a person with a modern western perspective, the type of party that Lenin was proposing still had several distinctive features in addition to the conspiratorial inner core of revolutionaries. First, of course, there was the repeated concern about "the firmness, the durability, the purity of our party"

—the repeated worry about "straggling, swaying, and opportunism," about "diffusion and unsteadiness"—the repeated scorn directed toward "chatterboxes" and the "game of democracy" played by émigré politicians.[50] However wide party membership was to be, it was to be limited to those who were willing to submit themselves to party discipline. Organizations and committees could use the party label only if the Central Committee confirmed their respective right to do so, and, as Lenin made clear, the right of expulsion was to be a real one.[51] The *Iskra* group had been formed to rescue Marxism from the very broad definition that it had had in the 1890s, to present a clearly defined orthodox Marxist program in the face of growing revisionism, and Lenin often seemed obsessed with fears about a return to the nineties. As he wrote in his notes during the debate at the Second Party Congress, "the strength and authority of the Central Committee, firmness and purity of the party—this is the essence of the matter. [Otherwise], Struve will organize and enter the party."[52]

A second distinctive characteristic of Lenin's conception of a party was his insistence that its members be active. His formal requirement for entry into the party was not only support of the party program and payment of dues but also "personal participation in one of the party organizations." A party member need not be a professional revolutionary, but he or she must be willing to do some work—at least distribute leaflets, lead a worker's circle or trade union group, or the like. One reason for this attitude was, of course, Lenin's belief that much work was needed if the workers' "trade union consciousness" was to be overcome. Another seems to have been an understanding of the psychological truth that organizations (political or otherwise) which make demands upon their members, which treat membership as a privilege, can sometimes have greater appeal than those which do not. He was determined to restore the lost "prestige of the revolutionary," and he emphasized the need "to raise the status and significance of a party member higher and higher and higher."[53]

The Creation of the Bolsheviks

At least on the surface, it was the question of the definition of a party member and Lenin's insistence upon activity as a condition of membership that broke up the *Iskra* group in 1903 and that eventually led to the formation of the Bolshevik party (the name adopted by Lenin's followers). Yet, this explanation surely is too simplified. The split during the Second Party Congress was an enormous surprise to those involved—even to Lenin and his wife[54]—and in many respects the reasons for it remain puzzling today.

The association of Lenin, Martov, and Potresov with the Emancipation of Labor group was designed, as the name *Iskra* (Spark) implied, to set off a conflagration in Russia, but it also produced many internal sparks as well. Plekhanov was forty-three years of age in 1900 while Lenin was thirty, and in the history of a revolutionary movement thirteen years can be a long time. The older man had often had difficult relations with younger disciples who had visited him in the 1890s,[55] and his relationship with Lenin was no different (Lenin has provided a vivid account of the early conflicts in his "How the Spark was Nearly Extinguished.")[56]

Nevertheless, the quarrels were composed and the newspaper was successfully published, first weekly and then twice a week. Lenin and Martov directed the production of the paper in Munich, London, and then briefly Geneva, while the other editors (notably Plekhanov) often handled their responsibilities by mail from other cities. Together with his wife, Nadezhda Krupskaia, Lenin was in charge of recruiting agents to smuggle *Iskra* into Russia, and he conducted a substantial correspondence with Social Democrats inside the country as he tried to put together a network of revolutionary committees to promote the *Iskra* line.

Determined to build a party around their newspaper, the *Iskra* group called for the convening of a congress of Russian Social Democrats in Brussels in the summer of 1903—formally the Second Party Congress, although the first was an 1898 meeting of but nine delegates which had little real meaning. Forty-three voting delegates (who exercised a total of 51 votes) assembled in July, together with fourteen nonvoting delegates. Partly through Lenin's skillful preparatory work,[57] 33 of the votes belonged to the *Iskra* faction. The remaining 18 were in the hands of a collection of Bundists (members of the All-Jewish Workers' Union of Russia and Poland), Economists, and miscellaneous uncommitted representatives, whom the Iskraites contemptuously described as "The Bog" because they wallowed in a quagmire of uncertainty.

The *Iskra* group appeared to be in full control of the congress. They named the presidium and easily pushed through their draft program and various resolutions on tactics. *Iskra* was recognized as the central organ of the party, and the editors stood firm against an attack on the centralized nature of the party organization.

When the congress turned to the party rules, however, the Iskraites were no longer united. The initial issue was posed by the definition of party membership in paragraph one of the rules. Lenin's draft reflects his demand that a member be active: "A party member is one who accepts its program and who supports the party both financially and by personal participation in one of the party organizations." Martov's formulation defined a party member as "one who accepts its programs, supports the party financially, and renders it regular personal assistance under the leadership of one of its organizations." In Martov's view, "the more widely spread is the title of party member, the better. We can only rejoice if each striker, each demonstrator can state himself a party member when he answers for his actions." He believed that his formulation would permit a broader party.[58]

To many of the delegates, the difference in shading between the two drafts appeared slight, particularly since Lenin emphasized that he was not suggesting the limitation of party membership to professional revolutionaries and since Martov was opposing any notion of a federated party.[59] Indeed, four days before the debate on paragraph one, Martov had said that he differed with Lenin on "only two questions" on the party rules, and these two did not include the definition of a party member.[60] During the debate itself, Lenin had said, "I do not at all consider our difference so essential that the life or death of the party depends on it."[61] Yet, within a few days, the congress was featured by shouting and a refusal of Martov to serve on the editorial board of Iskra.

The explanation for an outcome seemingly so out of proportion to the significance of the issue being discussed is to be found in developments taking place off the floor of the congress. The Iskra delegates were meeting in a private caucus, and they had broken into a "hard" majority led by Lenin and a "soft" minority led by Martov. The central issue was a proposal by Lenin that the editorial board of Iskra be reduced from six to three—Lenin, Plekhanov, and Martov, with Akselrod, Zasulich, and Potresov being dropped. Akselrod and Zasulich were "agitated in the extreme,"[62] and Martov (but, strangely, not Plekhanov) also became much disturbed by the suggestion. The heat of the exchange in the caucus is indicated by Lenin's later acknowledgment of the nature of his own behavior there:

Of course, in discussions of candidates at the congress, it was impossible not to refer to certain personal qualities; it was impossible not to express one's approval or disapproval, particularly in an unofficial and intimate meeting . . . Comrade Martov bitterly complained about the sharpness of my disapproval. Lenin was in a rage, to use his phrase. Sure. He [Lenin] slammed the door. True. By his conduct (at the second or third session of the Iskra organization), he angered the members who remained at the meeting. True.[63]

The most mysterious aspect of Lenin's role at the Second Party Congress is the reason for his insistence on a change in the editorial board. His own explanation was that Akselrod, Zasulich, and Potresov had not been doing their share of the work (by his own count, the 45 issues of Iskra had included 39 articles by Martov, 32 by himself, 24 by Plekhanov, 8 by Potresov, 6 by

Zasulich, and 4 by Akselrod),[64] and he argued that a smaller board would be more effective. He further suggested that Akselrod and Zasulich tended to vote—or might tend to vote—with Plekhanov for reasons of friendship.

Such feelings are quite understandable, but the move made little political sense. It hardly promoted the dominance of *Iskra* and its line to repudiate half of the editorial board that was being hailed and legitimated at the congress. And, if the real question was control of *Iskra* vis-à-vis Plekhanov, it made even less political sense to seek a three-man board that not only forced Plekhanov to humiliate his two long-time associates but also antagonized the potential swing vote, Martov. Apparently Martov had originally agreed with the smaller editorial board, but had retreated in the face of Akselrod's and Zasulich's strong objections.[65] This change simply produced a feeling of betrayal in Lenin and a surge of rage rather than any rethinking of the new political situation. On the face of it at least, a man who was to be renowned for his political acumen was showing astonishing political insensitivity.

Although there surely were semisuppressed political differences that help to explain the conflict, although Lenin clearly was thinking of the problems of control and influence, we should guard against the tendency to see the events at the Second Party Congress solely in light of later developments and especially against the tendency to treat Lenin as no more than a coldly rational seeker of power. Lenin was a man of passion as well as of calculation —a man whose strong conviction about the validity of his judgment was coupled with a quickness to take offense and a tendency toward real pettiness in his immediate response to perceived enemies.

Moreover, Lenin was far from alone in possessing these characteristics. His associates too were often difficult men whose programmatic divergences with him frequently followed the outset of conflict instead of preceding it.[66] Conventional men seldom enter underground political work that risks prison and exile, and the artificiality of life in émigré political circles only intensifies any tendency toward conflict. A quarter of a century later Krupskaia was to describe the situation very well:

> In former times the so-called "exile histories" occurred very frequently in exile. There was nothing to do, and a squabble, mutual suspicion, an inaccurate statement of facts, and accusations back and forth of the blackest thoughts and actions would begin around some incident that often was insignificant. These "exile histories" engulfed people, drained their nervous energy, and made it impossible for them to work for a long time.[67]

Whatever the causes of the conflicts at the Second Party Congress, they quickly led to an irreparable split. Lenin had a majority within the *Iskra* faction, but most of the non-Iskraites supported Martov's definition of a party member, and it triumphed by a vote of 28 to 22. (The fact that Martov's margin of victory came from the nonorthodox delegates only added to Lenin's rage.) In subsequent sessions of the congress, however, the five delegates of the Bund withdrew when the congress rejected the Bundist claim to be the sole representative of the Jewish proletariat. Their departure was followed by the withdrawal of the delegates from the League of Russian Social Democrats, an Economist-dominated organization, which the congress voted to dissolve on Lenin's motion. With the exit of these two groups, Martov lost his majority, and Lenin's *Iskra* group proceeded to elect the three-man editorial board and the three-man Central Committee that Lenin wanted. It was this triumph which became the basis for Lenin calling his caucus the Bolsheviks (the majority men) and his opponents the Mensheviks (the minority men). The unexpected reversal of their victory, of course, only added to the bitterness of the Mensheviks, and Martov refused to serve on the *Iskra* editorial board unless the original editors were restored to it.

After the congress, the conflict between the Bolsheviks and Mensheviks escalated sharply. The latter moved toward an acceptance of the very Economist attack on Lenin's "hypercentralism" and on his *What Is To Be Done?* which they had rejected earlier. Trotsky, who had happily acknowledged at the congress that "our rules represent 'organizational nonconfidence' of the party toward its parts, that is, supervision (*kontrol'*) over all local, district, national and other organizations," now charged that in Lenin's view "the organization of the party takes place of the party itself; the Central Committee takes the place of the organization; and finally the dictator takes the place of the Central Committee."[68] Lenin, in turn, began treating the Mensheviks as if they were little more orthodox than those he called Economists.

While the congress left Lenin and Plekhanov in charge of *Iskra* and Lenin in charge of the Central Committee inside Russia, the Bolsheviks' victory was short-lived. Within three months Plekhanov was eager to heal the breach with his old associates. He acceded to Martov's conditions and insisted on the restoration of the original *Iskra* board. Lenin promptly resigned, and at one stroke *Iskra* was transformed into an organ of Menshevism. Differences now began to develop in the Bolshevik Central Committee in Russia, as a majority group emerged that advocated a policy of conciliation toward the Mensheviks. Three Mensheviks were coopted into the Central Committee, and in the summer of 1904 this strategic power position, which Lenin had regarded as impregnable, passed over to the opposition. After all his careful planning and apparent triumph, Lenin was left isolated and alone, betrayed by his own nominees in Russia, alienated from the leading figures of the emigration, and the chief target of abuse in the party organ which he had been primarily instrumental in establishing.

After a temporary fit of utter discouragement,[69] Lenin rallied and began once more to gather his forces. The remnants of the faithful in the emigration were welded into a fighting organization. Connections were reestablished with the lower party committees in Russia, and a new body, the Bureau of the Committee of the Majority, was established to coordinate the work of Lenin's supporters. Toward the end of 1904 a new paper, *Vpered* (Forward), was founded as the organ of the bureau. A second effort to capture control of the party organization was now in the full tide of preparation. But this time the Mensheviks were wary and refused to attend the so-called Third Congress of the Social Democratic Labor Party, which assembled on Lenin's initiative in London in May 1905. The Mensheviks met separately in Geneva.

The Revolution of 1905 and Its Aftermath

While the Russian Marxist émigrés squabbled in Geneva—generally to the disgust of other European Marxists and the puzzlement of Marxists inside Russia—the mood inside Russia moved in a more radical direction. The severe commercial crisis of 1900–1903 was associated with a rise of labor unrest, while in 1902 peasant disorders erupted in Kursk, Poltava, and Kharkov provinces in the wake of a crop failure. Then in February 1904 war broke out with Japan, as the latter attacked the Russian fleet in Port Arthur, and over the next eighteen months that war went increasingly badly for Russia. The final result was the first defeat of a European power by an Asian one in modern times.

With the Russo-Japanese War came the Revolution of 1905. In 1904 many of those active in the middle class had already increased their agitation for reform, but by early 1905 the workers and peasants were also in a state of high unrest. The year 1905 witnessed the greatest strike movement in Russian history, as practically every worker was involved at some point during that year. While the eight-hour working day figured very largely in the workers' economic demands, political strikes became commonplace, and many workingmen joined with the radical intelligentsia in calling for the abolition of the autocracy and the convocation of a constituent assembly to establish a democratic republic. In the wake of the peace treaty with Japan in August 1905, the political crisis deepened, and in St. Petersburg an elected workers' council (or, in Russian, soviet) moved from strike leadership to the assumption of many governmental functions.

Unrest consumed the countryside as well. The rural disturbances began deep in Kursk province in the black-soil region in February 1905, and rapidly extended to neighboring provinces. Initially, the peasants confined their defiance to illicit timber cutting and pasturing and to rent and labor strikes, but as the disorders spread, the peasants became bolder. The disturbances became more violent and reached a climax in November 1905. Looting, burning, and land seizures were common, and the local authorities showed themselves impotent in the face of the anarchic violence. During the winter there was a lull, but in the spring the peasants returned to the attack, and it was not until the end of the summer of 1906 that the revolt began to show signs of exhausting itself.

In the initial panic inspired by general strikes and land seizures, the tsar and his advisers prepared to make large-scale concessions. A commission was set up to draft labor legislation. The tsar promised a representative assembly, though the first proposal incorporated in the Imperial Manifesto of August 6, 1905, limited the functions of the duma (as it was called) to that of an advisory body which could merely discuss laws, the budget, and the report of the state auditor. As the popular disorders continued, wider concessions were offered. The Manifesto of October 17, 1905, promised universal suffrage, freedom of speech, assembly, conscience, and organization. It pledged that no law would become effective without the approval of the duma and gave assurances that the duma would have authority to investigate the legality of all actions of governmental authorities. The October Manifesto was supplemented by measures designed to placate the peasantry. The redemption payments which peasants were still making for the land they received when serfdom was abolished were at first reduced and then canceled. Purchase of land through peasant land banks was facilitated.

The policy of concessions paid rich dividends. The revolutionary tide began to ebb, and the solid ranks of the opposition were broken. The rural gentry and the wealthier merchants and manufacturers rallied around the government as a symbol of law and order, while an uprising of Moscow workers in December alienated liberals and moderates who sought to direct the energies of the nation into constitutional channels. Once the moment of supreme danger had passed, however, the autocracy began to qualify its concessions. The Fundamental Law promulgated by the tsar on April 23, 1906, sought to make the duma as innocuous a legislative body as possible. The electoral law provided for the representation of workers, peasants, and intellectuals as well as the landed gentry, but the latter were heavily overrepresented. Although the class character of the suffrage provisions was designed to dilute the force of the opposition to autocracy, the first electoral campaign yielded a great victory for the opposition in general and the Kadets (Constitutional Democrats) in particular. For the first time, organized legal political parties assumed a role on the Russian political stage.

The history of the dumas is largely a record of the frustration of parliamentary hopes. The first duma (1906) was quickly dissolved after a bitter struggle in which the Kadet majority refused to bow before the will of the government. The second duma (1907), with strengthened radical representation, proved even less tractable than its predecessor, and it too was soon dissolved. Repression replaced concession as the reactionary "ruling spheres" around the throne consolidated their dominant position. The new electoral law proclaimed on the occasion of the dissolution of the second duma greatly increased the influence of the wealthier categories of the electorate, and the composition of the third and fourth dumas reflected their increased power. The reconstruction of the duma provided a pliant and accommodating majority for the government, and the third duma was permitted to serve out its full term (1907–1912). The elections to the fourth duma (1912–1916) resulted in a victory for the conservative nationalist groups, but even these groups were pushed into opposition to the government by the incompetence of the autocracy in grappling with the problems presented by the First World War.

Despite the government's measures to restrict the effectiveness of the duma and to emasculate its representative character, it was far from a meaningless institution. Owing largely to its initiative, and in the face of the deep-rooted opposition of the Ministry of Public Instruction, the expenditures for education grew steadily from 44 million rubles in 1906 to 214 million rubles in 1917. On the eve of the war in 1914, 8 million pupils, or approximately half of the eligible child population, were enrolled in primary schools.[70] Under pressure from the duma, the civil rights of peasants were equalized with those of other citizens. Even though the duma became increasingly conservative over the years, it remained a sounding board of ameliorative reform.

The most important policy change after the Revolution of 1905 came in the agricultural sphere, and it was associated not with the duma, but with the tsar's prime minister, P. A. Stolypin. Agrarian policy in the past had been directed at maintaining the peasant mir, with its system of mutual responsibilities and periodic redistributions of land, for it was assumed that the mir nurtured conservatism in the villages. The agrarian disorders challenged this assumption, and now the landholding nobility denounced the mir as "based upon socialistic foundations" and as "the nursery of socialist bacilli."[71] The First Congress of Representatives of the Nobles' Assemblies, meeting in St. Petersburg in May 1906, called on the government to break up the mir into private peasant holdings. "The strengthening of property-rights among the peasants," stated the "Most Humble Address" which they forwarded to the tsar, "will increase their attachment to that which is their own, and their respect for that which belongs to others."[72]

This program won acceptance from the government and became the basis of Stolypin's agrarian reforms which were incorporated in a ukaz of November 6, 1906, and approved by the third duma in 1910. The objective of the Stolypin reform was to create a class of trustworthy small proprietors who could be counted on to provide a bulwark against revolution. Prime Minister Stolypin supplied an unforgettable statement of his purposes in an address to the third duma. "The government," he said, "has placed its wager, not on the needy and the drunken, but on the sturdy and the strong— on the sturdy individual proprietor who is called upon to play a part in the reconstruction of our Tsardom on strong monarchical foundations."[73] By January 1, 1916, a total of 2,478,000 householders in European Russia owning an area of 45.6 million acres left the communes and became private owners, and whether in response to this change or not, the years prior to World War I were ones of great improvement in agricultural production.[74]

The Marxists After the Revolution of 1905

The 1905 revolution caught the Bolsheviks and Menshiviks by surprise, and its first effect was to bring them closer together. Responding to the élan of the uprising, Mensheviks became more militant and Bolsheviks seemed to abandon their distrust of uncontrolled mass organization. As Lenin put it, "The rising tide of revolution drove . . . differences into the background . . . In place of the old differences there arose unity of views."[75] Joint committees were formed in many cities, and finally a Joint Central Committee was created, on a basis of equal representation, to summon a "unity" congress. Both parties were flooded with new members for whom the old quarrels were ancient history and the practical tasks of the moment were paramount. The misgivings of the leaders were swept aside in a widespread yearning for unity.

With the onset of the period of reaction and repression, the divisions came to the fore once more. By this time the leaders had had more of an opportunity to think through and to articulate their positions, and differences were beginning to emerge on the shape and pace of the revolution. The Menshevik wing saw the arrival of socialism in Russia as the climax of a long process of development. The Menshevik response to the relative industrial backwardness of Russia was to preach the postponement of the socialist revolution until industrial backwardness had been overcome. Impressed by the weakness of the Russian industrial proletariat, the Mensheviks concluded that a socialist Russia was a matter of the distant future and that the immediate task was to clear the way for a bourgeois, middle-class revolution. They saw their first charge as good Marxists to help the bourgeoisie to carry out its own historical responsibilities. They were therefore prepared to conclude alliances with liberal bourgeois forces who opposed the autocracy and to join them in fighting for such limited objectives as universal suffrage, constitutional liberties, and enlightened social legislation. Meanwhile, they awaited the further growth of capitalism in Russia to establish the conditions for a successful socialist revolution.

At the opposite extreme from the Menshevik conception was the theory of "permanent revolution" developed by Parvus and adopted by Trotsky during and after the 1905 revolution.[76] For Parvus and Trotsky, the industrial backwardness of Russia was a political asset rather than a liability. As a result of backwardness and the large role played by state capitalism, the Russian middle class was weak and incapable of doing the job of its analogues in western Europe. According to Parvus and Trotsky, the bourgeois revolution in Russia could be made only by the proletariat. Once the proletariat was in power, its responsibility was to hold on to power and keep the revolution going "in permanence" until a socialist order was established both at home and abroad. (The Russian revolution, Trotsky thought, would ignite a series of socialist revolutions in the West.) The two Russian revolutions—bourgeois-democratic and proletarian-socialist—would be combined, or telescoped, into one. The working class would assert its hegemony from the outset and leap directly from industrial backwardness into socialism. Implicit in the Trotsky-Parvus formula was a clear commitment to the theory of minority dictatorship for Russia, for an industrial proletariat which was still relatively tiny in numbers would be called upon to impose its will and direction on the vast majority of the population.

The verbal premises from which Lenin started seemed indistinguishable from the Menshevik tenets, but his position was much closer in spirit to Trotsky than to the Mensheviks. Like the latter, Lenin denounced the populists and anarchists for thinking that "Russia can avoid capitalist development . . . In such countries as Russia the working class suffers not so much from capitalism as from insufficiencies in the development of capitalism. The working class has *an unconditional interest* in the widest, freest, and quickest development of capitalism."[77]

Yet, in practice, Lenin continued "to turn his back on the bourgeois liberals," men he continued to see as a weak and unreliable reed. Like Trotsky, he came to believe that the proletariat (and particularly the party of the proletariat) would have to take leadership in completing the bourgeois revolution, but his answer to the problem of a still small proletariat was an alliance with the peasantry. In Marxist terms, the peasants were a petty bourgeois element, a relatively conservative element, and, as has been seen, the rise of the Marxist movement had involved an attack upon the faith of the 1860s and 1870s in the revolutionary potential of the peasant. Especially after the peasant unrest from 1902 to 1906, Lenin saw their role in different terms. In his essay on "Two Tactics," he declared:

Those who really understand the role of the peasantry in a victorious Russian revolution would not be capable of saying that the sweep of the revolution would be diminished if the bourgeoisie recoiled from it. For, as a matter of fact, the Russian revolution will begin to assume its real sweep . . . only when the bourgeoisie recoils from it and when the masses of the peasantry come out as active revolutionaries side-by-side with the proletariat.[78]

Lenin's growing appreciation of the possible role of the peasantry in the revolution was reflected in the very language he came to use to describe the stages of the revolution. The first stage would be a "revolutionary-democratic dictatorship of the proletariat and the peasantry." In overthrowing the tsarist system and establishing the new regime, "the proletariat must carry the democratic revolution to completion by allying with the mass of the peasantry, in order to crush by force the resistance of the autocracy and to paralyze the instability of the bourgeoisie." The second stage—the socialist revolution—would involve an alliance between the proletariat and the village poor. "The proletariat must accomplish the socialist revolution by allying to itself the mass of the semiproletarian elements of the population [for example, the hired hands] in order to crush by force the resistance of the bourgeoisie and to paralyze the instability of the peasantry and the petty bourgeoisie."[79]

Lenin was not very specific about the timing of this second socialist revolution in relation to the first (the overthrow of the tsar), but when the excitement of the 1905 revolution mounted, we sometimes find him speaking the language of Trotsky: "From the democratic revolution we shall at once, and just in accordance with the measure of our strength, the strength of the class-conscious and organized proletariat, begin to pass to the socialist revolution. We stand for uninterrupted revolution. We shall not stop half way."[80] When the tsar was actually overthrown in March 1917, Lenin did, indeed, "stand for uninterrupted revolution," but the shock that this position produced among his top lieutenants testifies to the lack of clarity in his earlier statements of intention.

With more formal doctrinal differences developing between the Bolsheviks and the Mensheviks on such questions as the nature of the revolution and the role of the peasant in it (the Mensheviks called Lenin's view non-Marxist), with the Mensheviks tending to accept even more fully the notion of an open party when the tsarist political system became less restrictive, it is not surprising that the two Marxist factions moved toward a formal break. Various attempts at unity in the years after the Revolution of 1905 failed, and Lenin finally insisted on an open and irrevocable rupture. A rump conference was called for January 1912 in Prague. It assumed the title of the Sixth Party Congress, and it elected a new "pure" Bolshevik Central Committee from which even those Bolsheviks who tended toward accommodation with the Mensheviks were excluded. Then in October 1913 the Bolsheviks in the duma formally ended their association with the Mensheviks and formed a separate parliamentary group.

Meanwhile, however, conflicts were also taking place within the Bolsheviks and the Mensheviks themselves. Conflicts over whether to boycott the duma, over whether to seek peace with the Mensheviks (and on what terms), and over various abstract (and seemingly little-important) philosophical questions were only the most prominent of those that wracked the Bolsheviks. Lenin tolerated disagreements on these questions as long as the heretics were enrolled in his camp, but they became intolerable when his control of the party faction was challenged. In the summer of 1909, a number of these heresies were declared incompatible with membership in the Bolsheviks, and it was subsequent to this that the Central Committee was cleansed of those who still leaned toward reconciliation with the Mensheviks. The history of the party in these years of disappointment between 1906 and World War I is a tangled one,[81] and even more than had been the case earlier, this period lends credence to Krupskaia's observations about exile politics.

Probably more important than the political strife among the émigré politicians, however, were the developments within Russia itself. No subject is more difficult to discuss, for no public opinion polls were being taken, and the conditions of police repression made even the basic figures on party membership difficult to collect. Moreover, the situation in Russia was always in flux. An extrapolation from a Soviet biographical directory of persons active in the Social Democratic movement prior to 1905 suggests that some 12,000 persons became members between 1898 and 1905—"for a revolutionary underground movement, a large number of persons."[82] Nevertheless, in March 1905, after the first wave of unrest had occurred, a leading Bolshevik in St. Petersburg told a meeting of those thinking of an actual uprising that his group could provide only a few hundred persons for such an event in the national capital.[83] Clearly people were moving in and out of political activity, and throughout this period the Bolshevik-Menshevik split in exile often did not extend into local committees.

The broad outlines of party development inside Russia are still at least generally visible. It is obvious, for example, that the 1905 revolution did produce a large increase in the size of both the Bolsheviks and Mensheviks, and, according to the estimate of David Lane, each faction grew to some 40,000 members.[84] In elections to the 1907 duma, the vote in the workers' sections (curia) went overwhelmingly to the Social Democrats (98 of 145 electors), and the Bolsheviks received much more support than the Mensheviks among the *Russian* working class. (The Mensheviks, as throughout the 1903–1917 period, did better in the non-Russian south of the country.)[85]

After 1907, both Menshevik and Bolshevik segments of the party underwent a serious crisis. Party membership crumbled away, and even Bolshevik vigilance could not prevent the secret agents of the police from penetrating the underground hierarchy and rising to high places in the party apparatus. "In 1908," notes the Bolshevik historian Popov, "the Party membership numbered not tens and hundreds of thousands, as formerly, but a few hundreds, or, at best, thousands."[86] The plight of the Moscow organization was not atypical. From the end of 1908 to the end of 1909, membership declined from 500 to 150; in the next year the organization was completely destroyed when it fell under the control of a police spy.[87]

Beginning in 1910–1911, workers' unrest began to rise once more, and according to official statistics, the number of strikes rose from 446 in 1911 to 2,032 in 1912 and 3,534 in 1914. Party membership may have remained low because of police repression and other factors, but as the workers became more militant, their allegiance was given to the Bolsheviks rather than the Mensheviks, particularly in Russia proper. In fact, as the Menshevik leaders wrote in despair in their letters, as other contemporary sources testified, the Bolsheviks even began winning control of trade unions (especially in Moscow and St. Petersburg) that had been Menshevik strongholds. Perhaps the Bolsheviks, by virtue of their conspiratorial traditions and tight discipline, made a better adjustment than the Mensheviks to the rigors of illegal existence, but Leopold Haimson has made a convincing case that the major explanation lies in the relative strength of the Bolshevik appeals—in their radicalism, their intolerance toward the status quo, and (others might add) their authoritarianism.[88]

Western scholars have argued much about the probable future course of Russian history had World War I not intervened. Most have tended to assume that the Stolypin reforms would have stabilized the peasantry, that the fruits of rapid industrialization would have satisfied the industrial workers, and that the middle classes would have succeeded in moving Russia toward a constitutional democracy. Haimson, acutely aware of the radicalism of the Russian industrial workers, is much more skeptical and, given the history of many countries in "transition" in the twentieth century and the scale of the social problems, one certainly should not lightly assume that a smooth Russian evolution was probable in the best of circumstances.

In either case, the argument is a moot one, for World War I did intervene. At the outset, its impact upon the Bolsheviks was very negative. Lenin treated the war as an "imperialist" one stemming from a fight among capitalist powers for colonies rather than one over legitimate national interests.[89] He argued that the workers of all countries (including Russia) should withhold their support from the war effort. This position not only was unpopular among many Russian workers but also provoked the tsarist government to the most vigorous repression of a party it now considered treasonous.

In the long run, however, the impact of the war was of a different character. After a major defeat in 1915, the eastern front was stabilized (indeed, there was a successful Russian offensive in 1916), but the Russian losses were very heavy. Moreover, the governmental management of the war and the economy was the subject of severe criticism. Symptomatic of the problem is the fact that Russia had four premiers between July 1914 and February 1917, six ministers of internal affairs, three ministers of foreign affairs, four ministers of war, and four ministers of agriculture.[90]

Russian defeat in the Crimean War had been followed by the instability of the 1860s, and defeat in the Russo-Japanese War by the 1905 revolution. With unsatisfactory performance in World War I came the final collapse of the tsarist system in March 1917. The following month Lenin returned to Russia as he had briefly in 1906—but now there was no government authority with strong legitimacy, there was a public opinion angry at a war that had not ended, and Lenin was returning as the national leader who had been the most consistent opponent of the war from the beginning.

The Prerevolutionary Legacy

Western scholars have devoted enormous time to the study of the revolutionary movement in Russia prior to 1917 and especially to the development of Lenin's line of thought. Ultimately, the reason for this attention has been a desire to understand the roots and dynamism of the system that emerged in Russia after 1917. The basic conclusion that the scholarly community has tended to draw from this examination was well summarized in the first two editions of *How Russia Is Ruled*:

> The early organizational history of Bolshevism, which has been briefly summarized here, holds more than historical interest. The experience of the formative years left an ineradicable stamp on the character and future development of the party. It implanted the germinating conception of the monolithic and totalitarian party. The elitism which was so deeply engrained in Lenin, the theory of the party as a dedicated revolutionary order, the tradition of highly centralized leadership, the tightening regimen of party discipline, the absolutism of the party line, the intolerance of disagreement and compromise, the manipulatory attitude toward mass organization, the subordination of means to ends, and the drive for total

power—all these patterns of behavior which crystallized in the early years were destined to exercise a continuing influence on the code by which the party lived and the course of action which it pursued.[91]

Those holding this view generally emphasized the very close parallels between the party organization described in *What Is To Be Done* and the party structure that evolved after the revolution. They argued that Lenin's expressions of scorn for "chatterboxes" and his insistence upon the removal of "opportunists" and "renegades" from the party had their logical consequences in the outlawing of factions in the party in 1921 and the bloodless purge of 1921–1924—a purge that resulted in the expulsion of perhaps half the members of the party and was a precedent for even more drastic actions by Stalin after Lenin's death. They suggested that a low opinion of the workers' "trade union consciousness" before the revolution foreshadowed a willingness to override mass opinion after the revolution.

This judgment was always a somewhat controversial one, particularly among Trotsky and his followers, who wrote much in the West after his exile in 1928 and who treated dictatorial developments under Stalin as the result of an overthrow of Lenin's "living party" by the bureaucrats. In recent years a number of other scholars have challenged more directly the line of analysis associated with Merle Fainsod and the majority of western scholars. In the words of Moshe Lewin:

> Leninist doctrine did not originally envisage a monolithic state, nor even a strictly monolithic party; the dictatorship of the party *over* the proletariat was never part of Lenin's plans . . . It is not true that the concentration of power that reached its apogee with the Stalinist regime was the result of the ideas and splits of 1903–1904. It is in the history of a later period, in the events that followed the Revolution and the way in which they molded theory, that its origin is to be found.[92]

A debate on historical origins and roots of any development can, of course, never be resolved. An assertion or line of analysis made at one point of time can never be said with assurance to describe a person's frame of mind fifteen, twenty, or twenty-five years later when the events to be explained take place. Trotsky moved from a strong defense of Lenin's centralized party in 1903 to a denunciation of it in 1904 (as did Martov), but he (although not Martov) returned to the party in 1917 and gained the reputation of being one of the strong centralizers in the postrevolutionary regime. The famous German Marxist Karl Kautsky is quoted in *What Is To Be Done?* as describing working-class consciousness in terms almost indistinguishable from

Lenin's,[93] but by the time of the Bolshevik revolution he was a leading Revisionist. And, of course, in more recent years, Americans have seen the evolution in views of the radical Marxists of the mid-1960s that occurred in the following decade. One has to acknowledge the possibility that Lenin too underwent changes in his assumptions.

Those who attack the more conventional interpretation of the prerevolutionary legacy are clearly on firmest ground when they try to keep prerevolutionary developments in some perspective. Lenin's analysis of working-class consciousness was, after all, no more than a frank recognition of an obvious fact (the history of all countries *had* shown that the working class was not developing a consciousness of the need to revolt). Unless a Marxist were going to join the Revisionists in abandoning the concept of a socialist revolution, he *had* to believe that the workers were wrong and that consciousness of the need for revolution would have to be brought from without. Likewise, Lenin's conception of the party organization—in particular, his frequent use of the word "agents"—was almost the only reasonable one for an émigré organization that was intent on smuggling an illegal newspaper into Russia, having it distributed under conditions of police suppression, and receiving financial support in return. Small wonder that the men who became Mensheviks criticized *What Is To Be Done?* only in retrospect. Finally, of course, when the break between the Bolsheviks and Mensheviks did occur, we also surely would be wrong to forget that we are reading about an émigré politics that has the tensions discussed by Krupskaia.

It is perhaps even more important to remember that for all of Lenin's language about a centralized party, for all the schisms that took place prior to the revolution, the Bolshevik faction and then the Bolshevik party before November 1917 had little resemblance to the party of *What Is To Be Done?* and "Letter to a Comrade." From the beginning, Lenin complained about the unreliability of the party's "agents" and the difficulty of receiving any information from Russia.[94] Inside Russia, the party seemed always to be in flux— in large part because of the police, but also because local Marxists often had their own views about the meaningfulness of various arguments made in emigration. Moreover, even abroad Lenin often tolerated more diversity than the history of the schisms suggests.[95]

If the newer reinterpretation of the Bolshevik revolutionary heritage is limited largely to the points of the last two paragraphs, then it seems a valuable corrective to any generalization which, in the abstract, may convey to readers a more single-minded image of Lenin and his party than the confusion and ambivalence of the times warrant. If, however, the critics are denying that Lenin was a very determined and self-confident man, that he seemed to have an enormous faith in the efficacy of organization, that his relations with political associates were often rocky, that he lacked the instincts of a broker politician in dealing with those leaders outside his group, and that he had a very orthodox Marxist view of the undemocratic nature of "bourgeois [constitutional] democracy" (and placed little value in its institutions), then they seem on much more shaky ground in their denial of the "conventional wisdom." At a minimum there is the need for a detailed and convincing biography of Lenin that documents these points. It does not now exist.

Even if a softer picture of Lenin were to emerge, there still is the party inside Russia to consider. Obviously many of the members remained only for a short time and/or were relatively inactive, but the party contained a core of the "committeemen" (*komitetchiki*) who were professional revolutionaries and who stayed with the party through a number of arrests. Particularly after 1905, they could have chosen other political paths, but there was something in Bolshevism that attracted them. In many cases it may simply have been the extremism of the program and the promise of the withering away of the state. (In 1917 one does, indeed, find a number of anarchists in the party.) However, the very reluctance to cooperate and compromise, the dogmatism in the rejection of "opportunism" and opponents, the image of a strong organization in which membership is a privilege—these features of the party image may also have proved unconsciously attractive in many cases. Unlike the émigrés in Switzerland, the komitetchiki had little exposure to the West and to a political system other than the tsarist autocracy, and it would not be surprising if many were more Leninist than Lenin himself. It is not only the personality and philosophy of Lenin that leads one to speak of the stamp of the experience of the formative years on the future development of the party.

2 | The Road to Power

O N NO OTHER major event in recent Russian history is there so much general agreement among leading western specialists as there is on the Revolution of 1917. Although there are some differences in emphasis and some variation in interpretation on narrower points, the same general picture emerges from the magnificent and long-standard *The Russian Revolution* written by William Henry Chamberlin in the 1930s, from *How Russia Is Ruled* in the early 1950s, and from the more recent work of such scholars as Robert Daniels, John Keep, and Alex Rabinowitch.[1] The educated population in the United States also holds a common view of the Bolshevik revolution, one that is shared by many scholars (including a number in Russian and Soviet studies). Such unexpected consensus would be the source of great rejoicing were it not for one unfortunate fact—namely, that in almost all important respects the consensus of the educated public is radically different from that of those who study the revolution.

In the image of the educated public and many scholars, two revolutions occurred in Russia in 1917—a democratic revolution in March (or February, according to the Russian calendar of the time)[2] and a Communist coup d'etat that overthrew the democratic regime in November (or October, by the old calendar). The Bolsheviks succeeded, it is believed, not because of popular support (their 25 percent vote in the Constituent Assembly election of November 1917 is often cited), but because of their "organizational weapon."[3] The Bolshevik success is attributed to the "fact" that the party of *What Is To Be Done?* had the unity of views, the military discipline, the narrow elite membership, and the great conspiratorial leader needed for seizing the levers of power in a time of chaos and indecisive governmental leadership.

Scholars studying the revolution more seriously, however, have tended to see only one revolution in Russia in 1917—a continuing surge of unrest that overthrew the tsar in March and that, with short periods of abatement, grew in intensity as the year wore on.[4] It was a time of conflict, breakdown of authority, polarization of opinion of a type observed more recently in Chile. These scholars would say that the party was, indeed, fairly well organized in comparative terms, but they find the Bolsheviks of 1917 to be a much-divided mass party quite unlike that depicted in *What Is To Be Done?* In their explanations of the Bolshevik success, they emphasize much more the nature of the Bolshevik program. While acknowledging the failure of the party to win majority support, these scholars would argue that the Bolsheviks did have a program that won the support of half of the inhabitants of Russian cities and the soldiers stationed near the major urban centers and that satisfied the basic desires of the peasantry. In this view, the Bolsheviks won because they were the only party whose radicalism really matched the spirit of the urban majority and the army. Indeed, if the Bolshevik victory is dated by the successful completion of the Civil War in 1921 rather than by the seizure of power in November 1917 (in many ways, the most reasonable viewpoint), then one should no doubt give more attention to the millions of peasants who joined the Red army of the Communists instead of their opponents, the Whites.

The contrast between the specialists' view of the revolution and that of the nonspecialist has created a serious problem for western understanding of the Soviet experience. If the social forces that produced the Bolshevik revolution are neglected, as they often are in generalizations about the Soviet system, the new regime inevitably assumes the appearance of a totally alien agent that has grafted itself, like a tumor, onto a helpless organism. The ability of the regime to survive such shocks as collectivization, the Great Purge, and World War II becomes quite incomprehensible, except perhaps in terms of some almost mystical and superhuman totalitarian control. Moreover, of course, if Communist movements in general are seen in light of the nonspecialist's image of the Bolshevik revolution, we may be led into a fundamental misunderstanding of the dynamics of Communist movements in the Third World, sometimes with unfortunate consequences in the foreign policy realm.

The Collapse of the Autocracy and the Dual Power

The revolution to which all the revolutionary parties had looked forward for years took them all by surprise in early 1917. The collapse of the Romanov autocracy occurred with a catastrophic suddenness which stunned even those who had done most to bring it about. The dynasty had survived the 1905 revolution because in the hour of decision it could still count on the allegiance of the army, the police, the bureaucracy, the majority of the landed gentry, and the leading figures of the business and financial world. By 1917 these sources of support were melting away. Grand Duke Alexander Mikhailovich was not far wrong when he wrote to the tsar in February of that year, "Strange though it may be, the government itself is the organ that is preparing the revolution."[5] The war—with its vast losses in men, territory, and resources, its revelation of impotence, incompetence, and degeneration in the highest court circles, its mounting weariness, its deprivations and hunger—stretched loyalty to tsardom to the final breaking point.

In an immediate sense, the collapse of the tsarist regime began with demonstrations by women in Petrograd on the occasion of the socialists' International Women's Day on March 8, 1917 (February 23 by the old calendar). The women's protest against living conditions and especially against the recent imposition of bread rationing was soon joined by male workers and students, and the demonstration widened into a general strike. The revolutionaries continued their efforts to shift public anger from tsarist policies to the institutions of tsarism itself. However, large parts of the population had poured into the streets before in similar protest strikes (the two most recent in October 1916 and January 1917), and at first neither the government nor the revolutionaries seem to have believed that these "bread riots" were any more serious in their implications than previous ones.

The decisive step toward revolution was taken on March 11 when the government ordered the troops to disperse the crowds by firing on them. The bloody results of the first such incident created deep revulsion among many of the soldiers, and mutiny began to spread to the units of the Petrograd garrison. The soldiers increasingly turned against the officers attempting to organize crowd control, and the officers themselves increasingly abandoned their units in the face of soldier hostility. The power was in the streets, but it was still formless, anarchic, and without clear direction. The fate of the revolution turned on who would rush in to fill the vacuum of leadership which had been created.

Out of the chaos of the early days two centers of initiative began to take shape. On March 12 a miscellaneous group of left-wing duma deputies, members of the labor group of the War Industries Committee, and representatives of trade unions and cooperatives met to discuss the formation of a Soviet of Workers' and Soldiers' Deputies, to be modeled on its 1905 prototype. They constituted a Temporary Executive Committee and invited delegates from factories and regiments to assemble that same evening in the Tauride Palace to organize the soviet. A meeting of some 250 delegates of doubtful mandate did, in fact, convene, and it elected an Executive Committee essentially composed of the temporary committee.[6]

In the absence of any other authority, the Petrograd soviet quickly assumed such governmental functions as the regulation of the food supply and the organization of a workers' militia as a temporary substitute for the police. Perhaps the most famous of its early decrees was Order Number One (March 14) which, in effect, transferred control of the military forces to elected committees of soldiers and sailors by entrusting them with the disposition of all forms of arms. The same decree was also designed to make the armed forces subject to the paramount jurisdiction of the soviet. Nevertheless, the members of the soviet gave no indication of any eagerness to proclaim themselves the supreme rulers. They groped their way in the confusion, assumed authority by default, and took such action as the moods of the marching soldiers and workers seemed to dictate.

Meanwhile, a number of the more conservative leaders of the duma also moved to take advantage of the disorder and to create the type of constitutional monarchy they had been seeking previously. Their first hope was to persuade the tsar to establish a cabinet responsible to the duma, but the tsar's response was to dissolve the duma. The duma leaders then attempted to preserve the monarchy by securing the abdication of Nicholas II in favor of his son or his brother Michael. This dream exploded when Michael, in whose favor Nicholas II soon did abdicate, refused the throne. With the more radical soviet beginning to function, nothing was left except to establish a provisional government. As one of the duma leaders put it, "If we don't take power, others will take it, those who have already elected some scoundrels in the factories."[7]

No government with any pretense to authority could be formed at this juncture without the support, or at least the acquiescence, of the soviet. The duma leaders consequently negotiated an arrangement with representatives of the soviet by which the latter agreed to give conditional support to a provisional government, provided that it met certain conditions designed to guarantee the establishment of civil liberties and democratic institutions.[8] The First Provisional Government, which was headed by Prince G. E. Lvov, the head of the Union of Zemstvos, was predominantly Kadet and Octobrist in composition. An effort to broaden the political base of the cabinet by including several soviet leaders met with a rebuff. The only member of the soviet in the cabinet was the Socialist Revolutionary Alexander Kerensky, who, despite a resolution of the Soviet Executive Committee against the participation of its members in the new government, accepted the portfolio of Minister of Justice.

Thus began the system of dual power (*dvoevlastie*). The formal authority was vested in a cabinet supported by a relatively narrow stratum of articulate society, while much of the actual power of veto and decision reposed in the Petrograd soviet, which, although elected by the factories and army units of the capital alone, came to act as if it was a national body. As War Minister Guchkov wrote on March 22, 1917,

> The Provisional Government possesses no real power and its orders are executed only in so far as this is permitted by the Soviet of Workers' and Soldiers' Deputies, which holds in its hands the most important elements of actual power, such as troops, railroads, postal and telegraphic service. It is possible to say directly that the Provisional Government exists only while this is permitted by the Soviet of Workers' and Soldiers' Deputies. Especially in the military department it is possible now only to issue orders which do not basically conflict with the decisions of the above-mentioned Soviet.[9]

The soviet Executive Committee in turn promised support only "in the measure in which the newborn government will act in the direction of fulfilling its obligations and struggling decisively with the old government."[10] The arrangement between the Provisional Government and the soviet was a fragile truce rather than a solid agreement.

Few more difficult arrangements can be imagined than the one which was, in fact, instituted. Not only were two centers of governmental authority established, each led by men of different views and of different constituencies, but the center that was recognized as the formal government felt it had no authority to deal with the major problems that had led to the fall of the government. It was, after all, a *provisional* government, a temporary government (in what is probably a better translation than Provisional Government for the Russian *Vremennoe pravitel'stvo*). Its leaders thought that their major mandate was limited to the calling of a constituent assembly ("constitutional convention" would be a more meaningful translation for an American) and that only the democratically elected institutions that would emerge under the new constitution could appropriately introduce major policy change. In principle, it was an admirable decision; in practice, the question was whether the population was in a mood to wait.

The Bolsheviks and the Dual Power

On the eve of the Revolution of March 1917, the total membership of the Bolshevik party was generously estimated as 23,600.[11] Lenin was marooned in Switzerland and out of touch with his adherents in Russia. Oppressed by the staleness of émigré life, he immersed himself in a ceaseless round of literary and political activity, editing the journal *Sotsial-Demokrat* with Zinoviev, carrying on polemics with other socialists, working on his treatise on imperialism, and participating in a series of meetings and conferences with antiwar socialists at which he called for the transformation of the war among the nations into an international civil war.

The forces of the party inside Russia were scattered and disorganized, for the antiwar program of the Bolsheviks made them the special target of regime repression. Most of the better-known Bolshevik leaders like Kamenev and Stalin languished in prison or in Siberian exile. Such remnants of the Bolshevik underground organization as survived functioned under the general supervision of the Russian Bureau of the Central Committee, which was then located in Petrograd.

During the early days and weeks of the revolution, the Bolsheviks played a minor role. Whether because they had lost much of their support during the war or simply because their strong candidates were in exile or in prison, the party did very poorly in the first elections to the soviets—the Mensheviks and Socialist Revolutionaries winning a heavy preponderance of the seats.[12] During the general euphoria in the wake of the revolution, sectarian political distinctions tended to be obliterated as far as the rank-and-file were concerned, and the Bolshevik leadership in Petrograd responded to this mass mood by pursuing a relatively conciliatory policy toward other left-wing parties in the soviet. While the first manifesto issued by the Petrograd leaders called for the creation of a provisional revolutionary government,[13] and the Provisional Government itself was subsequently denounced as "a class government of the bourgeoisie and the large landlords,"[14] the Bolsheviks did not demand that the soviet take power. Instead, as a Bolshevik resolution submitted to the soviet phrased it, "The Soviet of Workers' and Soldiers' Deputies must reserve for itself complete freedom of action in the selection of means of realizing the fundamental demands of the revolutionary people, and in particular in the selection of means of influencing the Provisional Government."[15]

On March 25 Kamenev, Stalin, and Muranov returned from Siberian exile, and their assumption of the direction of the party in Petrograd only served to reinforce the policy of conciliation and compromise. Kamenev, in an article published in *Pravda* on March 28, took a position on the war with which many Mensheviks and SR's would have fully agreed. He wrote:

Our slogan is—pressure on the Provisional Government with the aim of forcing it openly, before world democracy, and immediately to come forth with an attempt to induce all the belligerent countries forthwith to start negotiations concerning the means of stopping the World War.

Up to that time, however, each remains at his post.[16]

Kamenev was by no means alone. His position reflected the dominant view of the party leadership in Petrograd at that time.

Meanwhile, Lenin, still in Zurich, was plotting a different course. In a letter to one of his supporters on March 16, he wrote, "We, of course, retain our opposition to the defense of the fatherland."[17] The next day, he wrote again,

> In my opinion, our main task is to guard against getting entangled in foolish attempts at "unity" with the social-patriots . . . and to continue the work of *our own* party in a consistently *international* spirit.
>
> Our immediate task is . . . to prepare the seizure of power by the *Soviets of Workers' Deputies.* Only this power can give bread, *peace,* and freedom.[18]

Within a week of the establishment of the dual power, Lenin had set forth the slogan that would bring Bolshevism to power—"bread, peace, and freedom"—and he had enunciated total support for the soviet as the legitimate governing body, while renouncing cooperation with the political leaders who had established the soviet. Then, as later, "All Power to the Soviets" was a slogan directed against the leaders of the soviet, not made in support of them, and it meant in practice all power to the Bolsheviks.

Lenin, however, was still abroad, physically separated from Russia by countries with which Russia was engaged in war. The Germans finally agreed to permit Lenin, Zinoviev, Krupskaia, and a number of other revolutionaries to travel across Germany to neutral Sweden, and on April 16 Lenin arrived at the Finland Railroad Station in Petrograd.[19] A sizable group assembled to greet the Bolshevik leader, but the welcoming speech of the president of the soviet, Chkheidze, was a cool one: "Comrade Lenin, in the name of the Petrograd Soviet of Workers' and Soldiers' Deputies, we welcome you to Russia. But we suppose that the main problem of the revolutionary democracy is the defense of our Revolution against any attacks on it, whether from without or from within. We suppose that for this end not disunion but consolidation of the ranks of the whole democracy is necessary. We hope that you will pursue these objectives along with us."[20]

It was to be a vain hope. Lenin's plan of campaign had already matured, and cooperation with Chkheidze and other leaders of the soviet had no place in it. His first words to Kamenev were a sharp rebuke for the tone of *Pravda*. In speeches delivered to his own followers on his first two days in Russia, he demanded a complete break with the old line of "revolutionary defensism" and a repudiation of the Provisional Government. He called for "a republic of Soviets of Workers, Agricultural Laborers, and Peasants Deputies throughout the land, from top to bottom . . . abolition of the police, the army, the bureaucracy," and an arrangement by which all officials were "to be elected and to be subject to recall at any time, their salaries not to exceed the average wage of a competent worker." He proposed "confiscation of all landlords' lands, nationalization of all land and placing of it under the oversight of the local soviets of agricultural workers and peasant deputies . . . immediate merger of all banks in the country into one general national bank which the Soviet of Workers' Deputies should oversee . . . not the introduction of socialism as our immediate task, but transition only to oversight (*kontrol'*) of social production and distribution of goods . . . immediate calling of a party congress . . . changing the party program . . . changing the name of the party . . . [and] rebuilding of the International."[21]

Lenin's radicalism was at first almost completely unacceptable to his own party. At a meeting of the Petrograd committee of the party, his theses were rejected by 13 votes to 2, with one abstention.[22] Kamenev, in an article in *Pravda* entitled "Our Differences," referred to these theses as Lenin's "*personal* opinion." "As regards Comrade Lenin's general line," he wrote, "it appears to us unacceptable inasmuch as it proceeds from the assumption that the bourgeois-democratic revolution *has been completed* and it builds on the immediate transformation of this revolution into a Socialist revolution."[23]

The controversy between Lenin and Kamenev exposed a deep fissure within Bolshevik ranks which was to continue right up to the seizure of power, and even beyond. To Bolsheviks of Kamenev's persuasion, Russia was simply not ripe for a socialist revolution. Like the Mensheviks and like Lenin up to the 1905 revolution, these Bolsheviks made a sharp demarcation between the successive stages of bourgeois-democratic and socialist revolution. The first stage had to be completed before one could embark on the second, and the tactics suitable for the first stage excluded a Bolshevik coup d'etat and the assumption of supreme power. In the perspective of Kamenev and his followers, the Russian revolution still had to run a long bourgeois course. The agrarian revolution had to be completed. The bourgeois-democratic revolution would culminate in the establishment of a revolutionary dictatorship of the proletariat and the peasantry, and only then would the socialist revolution become the order of the day.

To Lenin this perspective was now anathema. "Our doctrine," he quoted

Marx, "is not a dogma, but a guide to action."[24] "The peculiarity of the present situation in Russia," Lenin declared, "is that it represents a *transition* from the first stage of the revolution, which, because of the inadequate organization and insufficient class-consciousness of the proletariat, led to the assumption of power by the bourgeoisie—to its second stage which should place power in the hands of the proletariat and the poorest strata of the peasantry."[25] "To that extent," Lenin insisted, "the bourgeois, or the bourgeois-democratic, revolution in Russia is *completed*."[26] Kamenev's use of the formula of "the revolutionary-democratic dictatorship of the proletariat and peasantry" seemed to him "antiquated." "The Soviet of Workers' and Soldiers' Deputies—here," Lenin argued, "you have 'revolutionary-democratic dictatorship of the proletariat and peasantry' already realized in life." "Theory, my friend," Lenin goaded Kamenev, "is grey, but green is the eternal tree of life." The orthodox theory of the Old Bolsheviks that "the rule of the proletariat and peasantry, their dictatorship, can and must follow the rule of the bourgeoisie" had to be discarded as no longer corresponding with "living reality."[27]

Instead, Lenin offered his conception of dual power: "alongside of the Provisional Government, the government of the *bourgeoisie,* there has developed *another,* as yet weak, embryonic, but undoubtedly real and growing government—the Soviets of Workers' and Soldiers' Deputies."[28] To Lenin it appeared incontrovertible that such a combination could not endure. "There *can be no* two powers in a state."[29] For the moment, the two powers were interlocked; the Provisional Government rested on the support of the soviet, and the soviet yielded such support because it was still under the spell of petty bourgeois delusions implanted by the SR and Menshevik leaders of the soviet. These delusions had to be destroyed if the Provisional Government were to be overthrown. "The only way it can and must be overthrown," Lenin insisted, "is by winning over the majority in the soviets."[30]

Despite the opposition of Kamenev and others whom Lenin described contemptuously as Old Bolsheviks, Lenin carried the day. His program was approved first at the Petrograd City Conference of the Party, which took place from April 27 to May 5, 1917, and then at the even more important All-Russian Conference of the Party (described in party histories as the April Conference), which lasted from May 7 to May 12, 1917. The resolutions adopted by the conference represented a great personal triumph for Lenin, a reaffirmation of the leading role of the man who had, after all, created the party, but in many respects it was a natural triumph. The Bolshevik party had always been the most radical of the parties, it had always been the one least inclined to cooperation with middle-class and moderate working-class parties, and its most radical members were rapidly returning to active political life from

exile. In the first two months after the March revolution the size of the party
rose sharply,[31] and if these new members had been at all moderate in their
inclinations, one would have thought that they would have been drawn to
the parties of the Provisional Government and the soviet. Only if public
opinion as a whole had been increasingly receptive of the new regime would
Lenin's arguments have failed to strike a very responsive chord within the
party, and, in actuality, the movement of public opinion was in the other
direction.

The End of the Honeymoon

The first weeks after the revolution were marked by a general feeling of
revolutionary exaltation, but this period soon drew to a close. The major
problem undermining the legitimacy of the political leadership was the war,
and only six weeks after the revolution it had already produced a major crisis.
The Executive Committee of the soviet, while pledging its support of the
war, also emphasized the need for peace, and, in line with this policy, it called
for a peace without annexation and indemnities. The Provisional Government and particularly Foreign Minister Miliukov, on the other hand, were
loathe to abandon the agreements with the Allies that would grant Con-
stantinople to Russia after the war, and they saw the continuation of the war
as vital in maintaining Russia's honor and its position as a great power.

The crisis came on May 3 when Miliukov, intent on reassuring the Allies
about Russian intentions, emphasized the government's determination to
carry on the war to "a decisive end." Miliukov wrote of fulfilling "obligations
undertaken toward her Allies" and of the need for "guarantees and sanctions"
to be imposed after the war, and he made no attempt to appease the soviet
by incorporating any of its language into the note. The result was a storm of
protest not only in the soviet, but also in the streets. Soldiers, sailors, and
workers marched through Petrograd under banners bearing such inscriptions
as "Down with the war."

Public reaction to the Miliukov note had important political consequences. Coming at a crucial juncture in Lenin's struggle for the adoption
of his April Theses by the Bolsheviks, the demonstrations were a clear sign
of the depth of popular discontent, and they must have strengthened Lenin's
hand vis-à-vis the more moderate Bolsheviks. The demonstrations also produced a major change within the Provisional Government. The government
issued "an explanation" which was designed to square its war aims with the
views of the leaders of the soviet, but Guchkov, the Minister of War, and then
Miliukov felt compelled to resign. After protracted negotiations with the
leaders of the soviet, in which the Executive Committee finally agreed to
a coalition regime, Prince Lvov announced a new cabinet on May 18 which

included ten liberals and six socialists—three SR's (including Kerensky as Minister of War), two Mensheviks, and one Populist-Socialist.

With the creation of the coalition, the moderate socialist parties that had dominated the soviet also assumed major responsibility for the actions of the Provisional Government. This ensured an exit from the immediate crisis, but the moderate socialists were now in a position in which they too inevitably would become a target for mass frustration and dissatisfaction if policy did not change.

In fact, the war policy did not change. Despite the many warning signs, the new coalition government believed that the restructuring of the government would transform public attitudes toward the war and that a successful offensive would rekindle patriotic ardor and re-establish national unity. (Chamberlin suggests that the desire to legitimate an offensive had actually been the main reason that the Kadets had moved toward a coalition government with the socialists in the first place.)[32] A large-scale offensive was launched on July 1 on the Galician front, but after achieving some success in the early days, it turned into an utter debacle. By July 24 the Russians had given up the main town which they had occupied in Galicia (Tarnopol) without a struggle, and the army retreated in disarray even though it was no longer under German attack. Subsequent events (for example, the fall of well-defended Riga almost without a fight on September 2) indicated that the Russian army had virtually ceased to function.

There were many explanations for the collapse of the Russian army—the ineffectiveness of the war operation, the Bolshevik propaganda, the events in the countryside, and so forth—but no small part was played by the attitude of the moderate socialists themselves:

> If one looks through any typical resolution passed by the Menshevik and Socialist Revolutionary majority [of the soviet] one finds an utterly negative characterization of the War as imperialistic, a demand that it be stopped as quickly as possible and an unobstrusive phrase or two, inserted at Kerensky's urgent demand, suggesting, with dubious logic and no emotional appeal whatever, that, pending a general peace, it would be a good thing if the Russian soldiers would continue to fight ... It is not surprising that the average soldier who was literate enough to read through a Soviet pronouncement on the War reached the conclusion that there was nothing worth risking his life for and voted very decisively against the continuance of the conflict by refusing to obey orders to advance, by running away to his native village and, in extreme cases, by killing his commanding officer.[33]

The war was not, however, the only problem facing the moderate political leaders in 1917. Russia was an overwhelmingly peasant country, and the peasants were becoming increasingly dissatisfied with the failure of the political authorities to satisfy their wants. The "dark people," as the peasants were sometimes called, had relatively little outlet for the expression of their views, and it is quite likely that a very high proportion of them had the passive, fatalistic attitude toward politics that is widespread in peasant society throughout the world. Nevertheless, there was at least an active minority among them who were expressing grievances and demanding change. These demands, as reflected in early petitions of peasant assemblies, were varied, but 31 percent of the petitions called for the seizure of state and crown lands and large estates, and another 20 percent called for seizure of state and crown lands alone.[34] It was this desire that Lenin tried to exploit when he included "land" along with "bread" and "peace" in his famous slogan.

In the first weeks after the revolution, the situation in the countryside remained fairly quiescent, but as the new government failed to develop and enact a land reform program, the peasants began to act on their own. When their first cautious use of meadows and water on landed estates went unpunished, they became progressively bolder. The situation in Smolensk gubernia seems typical:

> Peasants disorders in Smolensk were slower to develop, but once launched they gathered a momentum that rivaled the violence of the urban workers . . . By May there were reports of peasants sending their cattle to feed on estate meadows. By June they were occupying the meadows. Landowners sought vainly to collect fees from them and addressed complaints to the guberniya commissars representing the Provisional Government. In July the Kerensky regime appointed land committees to impose orderly legal processes on the encroachments of the peasants. The land committees in turn established mediation chambers to adjudicate disputes between peasants and landowners. The mediation chambers ruled that the owners whose land had been occupied by the peasants were entitled to just compensations, but there was no way to enforce these decisions. The peasants proceeded to detach more land from the estates and by the end of July they were already harvesting the land which they had seized . . . As peasant land seizures became epidemic, there were mounting demands from property owners that the guberniya land committee take action . . . But these appeals were in vain . . . The peasant hunger for land could not be denied.[35]

While the land issue can be treated in isolation, in practice it became closely intertwined with the question of the war. The army was always predominantly a peasant army, and many (23 percent) of the first peasant petitions after the revolution contained references to a "quick and just peace"—a demand that was almost never found in the first workers' petitions.[36] As the seizure of land became more widespread, awareness of the social base of the army could add a special bitterness to the peasant unhappiness at the government's failure to endorse land redistribution. "When we take the land from the Kulaks, it's Anarchy. When they take our sons, it's Patriotism."[37]

Yet, the link between the land and war issues went far deeper than the village discontent about the loss of its young men. There was no practical way to carry out land reform while the war was going on, for, in the words of Oliver Radkey, "to distribute the land while the most virile element in the village was at the front would have brought the soldier-peasants home like locusts to a grainfield."[38] Indeed, the rising problem of desertion was already stimulated by rumors of illegal land seizure, for those at the front naturally feared that they were being deprived of their share of the fruits of the revolution. Moreover, of course, the arrival back in the village of battle-experienced and disgruntled deserters, often with rifles in hand, did nothing to promote social peace there.

As the summer progressed, peasant dissatisfaction was reflected not only in a rising number of violent incidents but also in growing radicalism of the peasant delegates. At the National Congress of Soviets of Peasant Deputies, held in Petrograd from May 17 to June 17, the Bolsheviks mustered an insignificant minority of 14 out of a total of 1,115 delegates.[39] The congress was dominated by the SR's, who wrote the resolutions and elected a heavy majority of the Executive Committee. By late summer, however, the SR party itself divided into a right and left wing, the former still giving support to the Provisional Government while the latter called for the transfer of power to a government "responsible to the soviets." At the meeting of the council of the SR party in late August 1917, the left wing mobilized 35 votes to 54 for the right-wing majority. The next month the left wing captured control of the party's strategically important Petrograd committee. In November the left was to break away to form an independent party and even to join the Bolsheviks in a coalition which did much to sustain the latter's regime in its early precarious days.[40]

Among the urban workers the level of dissatisfaction was also rising rapidly. Immediately after the revolution, the workers elected relatively moderate socialists to the soviets,[41] and their own demands, as expressed in their petitions, centered on such nonrevolutionary concerns as the eight-hour day.[42] The Mensheviks were elected to the leadership of the rapidly expanding trade union network.[43]

However, the economic problems that had produced the February riots did not disappear with the revolution. Supply difficulties continued, and prices rose still higher. The only things that had changed were the expectations of the workers and the nature of the political leaders on whom blame could be placed. The workers tended to believe in the existence of large war profits and demanded large wage increases, if for no other reason than to meet the inflation; the owners considered the wage demands wildly excessive and unpatriotic in time of war, thinking that the workers should consider a decline in living standards inevitable in such conditions and the assumption of sacrifices praiseworthy. The situation worsened with the periodic shutting-down of many factories. While the owners usually attributed such actions to supply difficulties, many of the workers—rightly or wrongly—thought them a deliberate tactic in the struggle to hold down wages.

There are a number of indicators of the rise of discontent among the workers in the late spring and early summer of 1917. One is a rise in the number of strikes: from 141 in March to 231 in April to 298 in May to 402 in June in a sample of provinces.[44] Another is the rise in the number of Bolsheviks among deputies to the soviets in the largest cities. At the First All-Russian Congress of Soviets, which met in Petrograd on June 16, the Bolsheviks were in the definite minority. Of the 777 delegates who declared their political affiliations, 285 were SR's, 247 Mensheviks, 105 Bolsheviks, and the rest belonged to various minor parties and groupings. Even this figure overstates Bolshevik strength, for the 313 delegates who did not specify their party affiliation were scarcely likely to be Bolsheviks.[45] However, as early as June 13, the Workers' Section of the Petrograd soviet, by a vote of 173 to 144 passed a resolution endorsing the Bolshevik formula of "All Power to the Soviets."[46] In the July-August elections to the city dumas—elections held after the July repression and giving the franchise to citizens of all classes —the Bolsheviks received only 7.5 percent of the vote in 50 guberniia cities and 2.2 percent of the vote in 418 small towns, but in Petrograd they received 33.5 percent of the vote on August 20 as compared with 20 percent of the vote of the borough dumas in the capital in May-June.[47]

The dissatisfaction among the Petrograd workers—and particularly among the soldiers of the Petrograd garrison—came to a head in a second major wave of unrest which swept the capital in July. Well before the July offensive had collapsed, the government had decided to transfer troops around Petrograd to the front to support the offensive, and this action in itself had provoked a strong reaction. The First Machine Gun Regiment, two-thirds of whose members were to be transferred, became the center of a movement first for a mass demonstration and then for the overthrow of the Provisional Government.

As unrest spread, the Bolshevik Central Committee found itself in an awkward position. Their slogan "All Power to the Soviets" had been taken up by many soldiers and was supported by a number of workers. To a considerable extent this development was being encouraged by the Petrograd committee of the party and especially by the party's Military Organization, which was responsible for developing support in the army and which was, of course, in tune with radical military opinion. The Central Committee felt a seizure of power premature, and at first it tried to prevent street action. When that proved impossible, the Central Committee issued a call for "a peaceful organized demonstration."

The movement of July 16–18 quickly got out of control. Masses of soldiers and workers poured through the streets shooting aimlessly, breaking into houses and stores, and looting their contents. For two days both the government and the soviet were powerless to deal with the rioting mobs; order began to be restored only on July 18, when reliable troops were brought in to patrol the streets of the capital. The government moved to repress the Bolsheviks, whom it blamed for the unrest, and momentarily the tide of public opinion seemed to turn in reaction against extreme radicalism.[48]

The Bolsheviks in the Late Spring and Early Summer

During the July Days, there were observable "very real differences in outlook and policy between the Bolshevik [city] committee and the party Central Committee . . . [and] apparently uncoordinated but by no means insignificant activities of the Bolshevik Military Organization during this time,"[49] and this was but one manifestation of the diversity within the party in 1917. The Bolsheviks had been formed in 1903 at least ostensibly because of a disagreement within the Social Democratic party over the structure of the party and the definition of a party member, but, after the March revolution, no effort was made to follow a restrictive membership policy. The "flooding of the party by new members" was so precipitous that the leadership itself had only a rough idea of the size of the organization. By the party's Sixth Congress (August 8–16) it was estimated that the membership had risen to 200,000 persons, and Soviet historians now speak of 240,000 members at that time—approximately a tenfold increase in five months.[50] "The new recruits who formed the party base were frequently illiterate, sometimes turbulent, badly disciplined, and unreliable."[51]

As Fainsod wrote in 1953, "the Bolshevik Party of 1917 was far from being the monolithic organization of which Lenin had dreamed in 1903 . . . The authority of the party leadership rested largely on its capacity to persuade and convince rather than to direct and dictate. In 1917, agitation and propaganda were the keys to party leadership; many who emerged from the ranks to become leaders in this period were precisely those who showed themselves gifted agitators and propagandists. If some semblance of order and homogeneity was imposed on the heterogeneous elements that flocked to the Bolshevik banner, it was due less to the perfection of the organizational instrument than to the party leadership's ability to articulate slogans and improvise tactics which rallied the support of the rank and file. It is symptomatic of this stage of development in Lenin's career that, under the influence of the revolutionary ferment, he temporarily abandoned the distrust of mass spontaneity which characterized so much of his earlier outlook. 'Do not be afraid,' he now cried, 'of the initiative and independence of the masses.' The transformation of the Bolshevik Party from a small conspiratorial band into a mass revolutionary organization was a visible expression of this change of outlook."[52]

The sheer mass of the fresh forces which inundated the party in 1917 carried an implied threat of swamping the old leadership, but Lenin, as always, strove to ensure that control of the organization which he had created would not gravitate into other hands. At the Sixth Congress in August, a left-wing group called the *Mezhraiontsy,* which numbered some 4,000 persons and included such well-known figures as Trotsky and Lunacharsky, merged with the Bolsheviks, but except for a few of these recruits, the Central Committee elected in August was constituted almost entirely of the seasoned underground veterans and exiles who had been in the party from prerevolutionary days. Of the 171 delegates at the Sixth Congress who answered a questionnaire, 149 stated that they had begun work in the Bolshevik organization in 1914 or before (81 by 1906).[53]

The Central Committee as a body devoted itself chiefly to broad policy and tactical matters, with most of its energies being concentrated on developments in the capital. The guidance it provided for the party was exerted largely through *Pravda* and other party publications. An attempt was made to maintain communications with the local party units, to dispatch workers where needed, and to arrange visits to and from the center, but responsibility for such organizational work was concentrated in the hands of one man— Lenin's faithful lieutenant, Sverdlov. Not surprisingly, communications with the peripheral areas remained tenuous and adventitious, and the amount of real Central Committee control very slight.

While relationships between the Central Committee in Petrograd and adjoining party organizations in the Baltic, in Finland, in Moscow, and in the capital itself were fairly close, even they could be marked by considerable turbulence. In Petrograd, the Central Committee had difficulty in maintaining complete control over the city committee and the Military Organization. In Moscow, there was a sharp cleavage between the more cautious leaders of the Moscow party organization and the radicals controlling the Moscow regional party bureau that theoretically supervised it.[54] And even the Central Committee itself, while fundamentally quite loyal to Lenin, included a number of men, including Kamenev, who originally had opposed Lenin's April Theses and who often retained a more cautious view than Lenin of the immediate revolutionary prospects—a fact that was to be manifested with great clarity in the fall when the Bolshevik leader began calling for seizure of power.[55]

The Kornilov Affair and Its Aftermath

Whatever the Bolshevik responsibility for the demonstrations of July 16–18, the government laid the blame at the party's door and moved to counterattack. The Ministry of Justice released documents of doubtful authenticity which purportedly proved that Lenin was a German spy, and these documents were used as justification for repression of the party. On the morning of the eighteenth, the offices of *Pravda* were raided and a newly established Bolshevik printing plant destroyed. The next day, an order was issued for the arrest of Lenin, Zinoviev, and Kamenev. Lenin and Zinoviev succeeded in avoiding arrest by going into hiding, but during the next few weeks Kamenev and many lesser Bolsheviks were apprehended and imprisoned, along with Trotsky and Lunacharsky who associated themselves with the Bolshevik position. Some of the more turbulent regiments were dissolved, and on July 25 the death penalty at the front was restored.

The display of firmness by the Provisional Government was more fictive than real. To be sure, several prominent Bolsheviks were confined to prison, but they were released in mid-September in the face of a threat from the right. The second level of the party apparatus remained largely intact, and Lenin continued to make some effort to direct its operations from his various hideouts. Agitators were still at work in the factories and garrisons, with the Petrograd and the Baltic fleet remaining Bolshevik strongholds. The repression of the party did not prevent the sub rosa convening of the Sixth Congress in August, and it registered a striking increase in party membership. The party continued to flourish, its roots of support still intact.

The dilemma of the Provisional Government and its Menshevik and SR supporters was severe. In the foreign policy realm the failure of the Galician offensive and the continuing reluctance to withdraw from the war meant that they could offer the country neither victory nor peace. In the internal policy realm, they faced the familiar problem of a change in perspective once they assumed office. Thus, "the Menshevik Minister of Labor . . . who started out with promises to extract all the War profits from the capitalists, was appealing to the workers in July to reduce their wage demands and increase their output."[56] The result, not surprisingly in the circumstances, was simply a feeling by the workers that there had been a sellout.

In the face of growing Bolshevik support and the increasing radicalism of the peasants, workers, and soldiers—and given the moderate socialists' unwillingness to sign a separate peace and to initiate land reform before the establishment of a legally elected government—the natural course of action for the moderate socialists was closer cooperation with the more moderate elements within the middle class, the landlords, and the army. (The only potential truly effective counterpoise to Bolshevik power was the officer corps and such loyal regiments as it could command.) Some effort was, indeed, made to pursue such a course. In the wake of the July Days, Kerensky replaced Prince Lvov as head of the Provisional Government, and he chose a cabinet in which socialists held a small majority, but socialists who were on the right wings of their respective parties. Lavr Kornilov, a man reputed to be strong-willed and tough, was appointed Commander-in-Chief of the armed forces, and a national conference was called for August 25 to 28 in Moscow to bring together representatives of every class, profession, and shade of opinion in Russia except Bolshevism in a show of national unity. As a gesture to the right, it was given essentially equal representation with the left, despite its much smaller base in the population as a whole.

The attempt to rally the anti-Bolshevik forces behind the Provisional Government proved a fiasco, and the Moscow conference itself provided the most dramatic evidence of the failure. To begin with, the absence of the Bolsheviks gave all references to national unity a somewhat specious ring, but, even more important, there was a deep chasm separating those who did attend. "A stranger quite ignorant of the Russian language would have had little difficulty in sensing the spirit of the Moscow Conference; when the Left burst into applause the Right was stonily silent, and vice versa."[57] The "moderate" socialists were, after all, still socialists, and they were associated with the creation of the soviet and the turmoil and radicalism that had been linked with it from the start. They could never bring themselves to abandon the essence of the revolution as they saw it (even if this had been possible without complete loss of their constituency), and the middle and upper classes could never accept them and what they represented.

Even in the month before the Moscow Conference, mutual suspicion and tension had been developing in the relationship between Kerensky and his new Commander-in-Chief, Kornilov.[58] Disturbed by the lack of discipline within the army and the industrial plants, believing it encouraged by the indecisiveness of the government, and apparently seeing no significant difference between the moderate socialists and the Bolsheviks, Kornilov manifested little spirit of deference to his political superiors. As early as August

19 or 20, he had positioned troop units within easy striking distance of Petrograd and Moscow, and rumors of an attempted coup began circulating.

When Kornilov arrived in Moscow on August 26 for the Moscow "unity" conference, the nature of his reception dramatized the gulf between the left and the right:

> A guard of honor, recruited from the military schools of the city, was drawn up at the station and met the Commander-in-Chief with bands playing and banners flying; deputations from a number of conservative groups and military organizations were waiting to welcome Kornilov as he stepped out of his car . . . The well known Cadet orator Rodichev pronounced a speech of welcome, ending: "We believe that at the head of the revived Russian army you will lead Russia to victory over the enemy and that the slogan 'long live General Kornilov'—now a slogan of hope—will become a cry of people's triumph. Save Russia and the grateful people will crown you." There were loud hurrahs and Kornilov was showered with flowers. Later he proceeded to the Chapel of the Iberian Virgin, the most famous shrine in Moscow, which Tsars habitually visited before their coronation, and prayed before its reputedly wonder-working ikon.[59]

In early September the conflict between Kerensky and Kornilov moved to its conclusion. Through a man whom he thought to be an intermediary from Kerensky, Kornilov demanded the imposition of martial law in Petrograd, the resignation of the cabinet, and the transfer of all military and civil authority to the Commander-in-Chief. On September 9 Kerensky demanded Kornilov's resignation. Kornilov ignored the order and, in a mood of high confidence, gave the word for the "promenade" to proceed to Petrograd. However, difficulties quickly developed—railroad workers sabotaged trains carrying the troops of the expedition; telegraph operators refused to dispatch the messages of the staff; agitators penetrated Kornilov's picked divisions and, without too great difficulty, persuaded them not to fight against the legal government. By September 14, the coup had collapsed without the firing of a shot, and Kornilov and a number of his associates were under arrest.

The collapse of the Kornilov expedition marked an important turning point in the revolution. It revealed the emptiness of the power of the generals and the weakness of the appeal of traditional conservatism. When troops regarded by the general staff as its most reliable support were no longer willing to obey the commands of their officers, it became patently clear that the officer corps had lost the power to determine the destiny of the Russian revolution. With the strength of the Bolsheviks continuing to grow, Kerensky must have wondered if the troops would be any more obedient if there were a repetition of the July Days or a direct attempt by the Bolsheviks to stage a coup d'etat.

Without question, the main beneficiary of the victory over Kornilov was the Bolshevik party. At the height of the Kornilov crisis, the Central Executive Committee of the Soviets, on the initiative of the Mensheviks, created a Committee for Struggle with Counterrevolution in which Bolsheviks, Mensheviks, and SR's were represented by three members each. The Bolsheviks who had been imprisoned in July were released, and the government authorized the issuing of arms to workers' units within the factories—the so-called Red Guard. After the crisis had passed, the government attempted to recall these weapons, but this decision could not be enforced.

In political terms, the Kornilov affair completed the polarization of opinion that had been developing since mid-summer, at least in the most important cities. In the frequent re-elections of deputies to the soviet, the Bolsheviks were steadily increasing their representation. On September 13, in a poorly attended session, the Petrograd soviet passed a Bolshevik resolution for the first time, but on September 22 there was no room for doubt: by 519 to 414, with 67 abstentions, the deputies voted a resolution of no confidence in the Menshevik-Socialist Revolutionary leadership of the body. On October 8 Trotsky was elected president of the Petrograd soviet. In Moscow, the soviet passed a Bolshevik resolution on September 18, and soon Bolsheviks were elected chairmen of both the city and the provincial soviet. Indeed, in Moscow the Bolsheviks even won 51 percent of the vote in elections to the borough dumas—elections in which (unlike those to the soviets) the middle class was fully enfranchised—whereas in June they had received but 11 percent of the vote in similar elections. The vote of the Kadets had been holding steady, but that of the Mensheviks and the Socialist Revolutionaries was declining precipitously. Conditions in the provinces were more varied, but here too Bolshevik influence was on the rise, and in a number of provincial capitals the party gained a majority position in the soviet.[60]

When the rise in Bolshevik support in September is analyzed more closely, it is in the attitude of the soldiers that the change turns out to have been the most dramatic. The Bolshevik support among the workers had been increasing gradually and fairly steadily during the spring and summer, but the Galician offensive, the reimposition of the death penalty at the front, and the fact that Kornilov had been appointed by Kerensky seem to have coalesced in producing a major impact on the views of those in uniform. The change within the Moscow garrison from 70 percent support for the SR's in the June elections to 90 percent support for the Bolsheviks in the September elections was surely greater than normal, but it is indicative of the extremes which the shift in the soldiers' mood could reach.[61]

With the Bolsheviks coming to dominate the urban left, one might have thought that the other social forces would unite around the Provisional Government, but such was not to be the case. After the Kornilov affair, the officer corps spared no love for Kerensky. In any case, its support had become an asset of dubious value by this time, and the determination of Kerensky and the moderate socialist leaders to carry on with the war was hardly calculated to make them very popular with the rank-and-file in the army or navy. Many Kadets of the right hardly scrupled to conceal their distaste for Kerensky. They gave him grudging and reluctant support only because Bolshevism appeared to them so much the greater evil. Nor were the Mensheviks united in their approval of the Provisional Government. A substantial group of Menshevik internationalists led by Martov was sharply critical of Kerensky's foreign policy, and the backing which they extended was at best wavering and hesitant.

The situation within the SR party was, if anything, even more critical. On September 13 Chernov, the Minister of Agriculture and one of the foremost of the SR leaders, resigned from the government in protest against the postponement of a land settlement. As has been seen, the left-wing SR's, who moved close to the Bolsheviks on many issues, were gaining strength, and in September they came to dominate the Petrograd organization of the party. Conditions within the SR's reflected the deepening discontent in the countryside. Faced with the autumn upswing of peasant violence and land seizures, Kerensky countered on September 21 by issuing a military order forbidding the peasants to take other people's land or property and threatening them with dire legal penalties if they persisted. Since there was no power capable of enforcing the order, the peasants paid no attention to it. Its only effect was to serve as an irritant and to drive the peasants into the arms of the Left SR's and, sometimes, into the arms of the Bolsheviks, who were willing to bless what the peasants in any case were determined to do.

Toward the end of September, Kerensky made a last desperate effort to cement the coalition which was so obviously falling apart. On September 27, the so-called Democratic Conference assembled in Petrograd; the twelve-hundred-odd delegates represented soviets, cooperatives, trade unions, and municipal and county dumas. The conference first passed a resolution to exclude Kadets from the coalition, and then added a final touch of absurdity to the proceedings by overwhelmingly defeating the formula of "coalition without the Kadets." When SR orator Minor made his plea for a coalition government with the warning that otherwise "we will begin to cut to pieces," voices from the floor inquired, "Whom?" Minor's reply, "We will cut each other to pieces,"[62] had more than a touch of prophetic vision.

The Question of Insurrection

In the aftermath of the July Days, Lenin had abandoned the slogan "All Power to the Soviets." If nothing else, it generated confusion in the chaos of July, for it appealed for the transfer of power to an institution whose leaders were repudiating the appeal and were themselves moving into the Provisional Government. In July, Lenin called directly for "the passing of power into the hands of the proletariat, supported by the poorest peasantry," and he abandoned the idea of a peaceful revolution through the mechanism of the elected soviets. In practice, however, this change in tactics had little real meaning, for Lenin went into hiding in Finland at this time, and he spent much of August not in the organization of a revolutionary overthrow, but in the writing of political theory (notably his *State and Revolution*).

At the time of the Kornilov affair, Lenin toyed with the idea of cooperation with the other socialist parties,[63] but with Kornilov's collapse and the movement of the Bolsheviks toward majorities in the Moscow and Petrograd soviets, Lenin revived his call for "All Power to the Soviets." But now it had an urgent meaning. In two letters dated September 25–27 and September 26–27 respectively (less than two weeks after Kornilov's arrest), Lenin, still in hiding, wrote the Central Committee demanding an immediate seizure of power. The first letter's opening sentence was as blunt as it could be: "Having obtained a majority in the Soviets of Workers' and Soldiers' Deputies of both capitals, the Bolsheviks can and *must* take state power into its own hands." He left no doubt about the type of seizure of power he had in mind—an "armed uprising in Petrograd and in Moscow . . . an overthrow of the government."[64] In his second letter Lenin spelled out what he meant by giving an "illustration" of what had to be done:

> Without losing a minute, we must organize a *staff* of insurrectionary detachments; distribute our forces; move the loyal regiments to the most important points; surround the Alexander Theater [site of the Democratic Conference]; occupy the Peter and Paul Fortress; arrest the general staff and the government; send against the military cadets and the Wild Division such detachments as will die rather than allow the enemy to move to the centers of the city. We must mobilize the armed workers, call them to the desperate last battle, occupy the telegraph and telephone stations at once, place *our* revolutionary staff at the central telephone station, connect it by telephone with all the plants, all the regiments, all the points of armed uprising, etc.[65]

Lenin was quite conscious that only two months before he had refused to take advantage of the July riots and to attempt an overthrow of the government, but he argued that the situation had changed. Now the Bolsheviks had or were moving toward a majority in the soviets of the big cities. Now the Chernov resignation as Minister of Agriculture had accentuated the unwillingness of the government to engage in land reform. And, perhaps most important, "despite the fact that Petrograd was momentarily in our hands [in July] . . . we would not have been able to hold power, for the army and the provinces, before the *Kornilov affair,* could have marched and would have marched on Petrograd. Now the situation is quite different."[66] Once in power, he argued, the providing of peace, land, and an end to the governmental "vacillation that torments the people" would solidify the party's support among the population. And, once in power, of course, the Bolsheviks' position would be further solidified by the world revolution that their victory would stimulate.[67]

The Central Committee took up Lenin's letters at its meeting on September 28.[68] They exploded like bombshells. Some four years later, Bukharin, at an evening of reminiscences, described the meeting of the group:

> We all gasped. Nobody had posed the question so abruptly . . . At first all were bewildered. Afterwards, having talked it over, we made a decision. Perhaps that was the sole case in the history of our party when the Central Committee unanimously decided to burn a letter of Lenin . . . Although we believed unconditionally that in Petersburg and Moscow we should succeed in seizing the power, we assumed that in the provinces we could not yet hold out.[69]

The actual minutes of the meeting of the Central Committee are more laconic and provide a somewhat contradictory version of the affair. They merely record that by a vote of 6 to 4, with 6 abstentions, the committee voted to preserve only one copy of the letters. Kamenev, as in earlier days, emerged as one of the leaders of the opposition to Lenin, and, surprisingly, he was joined by Zinoviev, Lenin's closest associate in exile. Kamenev's resolution, which proposed an outright repudiation of the conclusions contained in Lenin's letters, failed of approval. The vote was not recorded.[70]

The opposition to Lenin within the Central Committee came from two directions. One group—that associated with Kamenev and Zinoviev—believed that it would be impossible for the Bolsheviks to maintain themselves in power as a single governing party after a coup d'etat, and they spoke of postponing any thought of governmental power until after the Constituent Assembly had met. Even after the Bolshevik revolution had succeeded in transferring "all power to the soviets," this group thought that the Bolsheviks should enter into a coalition with other socialist parties in leading the soviet.

A second group within the Central Committee, which essentially was led by Trotsky, seemed more optimistic about the possibility of Bolshevik rule, but at a minimum they believed that any seizure of power should be timed to coincide with an overdue Congress of Soviets so that it could be properly legitimated in the eyes of the workers. They wanted to maneuver events so any armed action would assume the appearance of a defense of the soviets against attack by the Provisional Government or rightest forces, and they may actually have wanted little more than the overthrow of the Provisional Government by the soviets.[71] From this point of view, it was crucial that a new Congress of Soviets (that is, a convention of delegates from soviets throughout the country) be convened, and, after considerable Bolshevik pressure, on October 6 the All-Russian Central Executive Committee of the soviets agreed to call one for November 2.[72]

As November 2 and the convening of the Congress of Soviets became a target date to which a hesitant Central Committee could postpone all meaningful revolutionary action, Lenin became more and more impatient. He noted in his diary on October 6, "Not all is well at the 'parliamentary' top of our party . . . At the top of our party there is wavering which can become *ruinous*."[73] By October 12 he seemed frantic. In a letter to the Central Committee in which almost every sentence of the crucial section contained underlined words, he asserted that, "To wait for the Congress of Soviets is *complete idiocy* or *complete treason* . . . This means to wait *weeks,* but weeks and even days now decide *everything* . . . 'Struggle for the congress' means *to ruin the revolution* . . . It is my urgent conviction that if we 'wait' for the Congress of Soviets and let the present moment pass, we are *ruining* the revolution." He tried to shock the party leaders into action by offering his resignation from the Central Committee, while leaving himself "freedom of agitation in *the lower* levels of the party and the party congress."[74] In fact, he did follow up his implied threat of war against the Central Committee by firing a volley of letters at the Petrograd and Moscow committees and the Bolshevik participants in a Northern Regional Congress of Soviets.[75]

The nature of Lenin's thought processes at this time are not altogether clear, and, in actuality, they may well have not been very clearheaded. In the first place, his decision to remain in hiding in Finland for six weeks after the Kornilov affair is very puzzling. To be sure, there still was an arrest warrant out against him, and there was a Central Committee decree ordering (or sanctioning) him to remain in hiding. Nevertheless, Bolshevik leaders were functioning openly in Petrograd, and one would have thought that the depth of Lenin's irritation with the Central Committee and the strength of his conviction that everything depended on immediate action would have overcome all caution and all scruples about the Central Committee decree. (After all, he was threatening to resign from the Central Committee and was appealing to lower organizations against it.)

In the second place, the reasons for Lenin's extreme impatience are also puzzling. That he would think it necessary to strike before the election to the Constituent Assembly with its heavy peasant vote is quite understandable, but the "waiting for weeks" of which he spoke when referring to the forthcoming Congress of Soviets was but a wait of two and a half weeks (actually three when the session was later postponed for five days by the Provisional Government). This was hardly an inordinate length of time for a party that had made no concrete plans for an uprising. It would also be readily understandable if Lenin had been talking about a coup on the very eve of the Congress (as, in fact, occurred) so that it could be legitimated by a Congress that was faced with a fait accompli. However, Lenin was demanding immediate action.

The major reason that Lenin gave for urgency was the fear that the Provisional Government would be expecting action at the time of the Congress and would use the Cossacks to prevent it.[76] Yet, since all the newspapers were filled with rumors of an impending Bolshevik coup (and, not surprisingly, since Lenin's letters were being widely read to Bolshevik gatherings in Petrograd as he demanded), there could not be much surprise in any case. Moreover, if the Provisional Government had military force that could suppress a Bolshevik coup in the capital, the party was very unlikely to be able to retain power for long, regardless of the timing of its seizure of power. (The expectation of a Bolshevik coup followed quickly by a successful right-wing counterattack was widespread, including, of course, among the more cautious members of the Party Central Committee.) Perhaps Lenin did not realize how far the Bolshevization of the province soviets had progressed and perhaps he feared that he would not have a majority in the Congress of Soviets, but at least in his letters he wrote as if he believed that there would even be a Bolshevik–Left SR majority in the Constituent Assembly. Perhaps, as Daniels suggests, Lenin simply "was against the 'constitutional illusion' of using the Congress of Soviets to get power—he positively did not want it that way."[77]

On October 20 Lenin finally decided to return to Petrograd in disguise, and he went into hiding in an apartment in a northern section of the capital. He fired off two more letters calling for revolution and pressed the point with party leaders he met. Then, on October 23 the Petrograd City Conference, at Lenin's initiative, passed a resolution which "insistently" requested "the Central Committee to take all measures for the leadership of the inevitable insurrection of the workers, soldiers, and peasants,"[78] and that night Lenin met with the Central Committee to try to force through a decision. The minutes of that meeting are very brief, but they indicate that Lenin reproached his colleagues for "a certain indifference toward the question of uprising" and argued the case for insurrection once more.[79] His argument was powerful enough to induce ten of the twelve committee members present (Zinoviev and Kamenev voted against) to put "the armed uprising on the agenda." "Recognizing therefore," the resolution read, "that an armed uprising is inevitable and the time perfectly ripe for action, the Central Committee proposes to all the organizations of the party to act accordingly and to discuss and decide from this point of view all the practical questions." The issue, however, was still not finally resolved, for no mention was made of a date—not even of the crucial question of the timing of the uprising in relationship to the Congress of Soviets.[80]

Kamenev and Zinoviev remained adamant in their opposition to the Central Committee's decision. Following the example set by Lenin earlier, on October 24 they sent a letter to the Petrograd and Moscow city committees, the Moscow and Finnish regional committees, and the Bolshevik factions of the All-Russian Executive Committee of the soviets and of the Northern Regional Congress of Soviets, in which they stated the case for postponement of the insurrection. Their stubborn opposition was again made manifest at a meeting of the Central Committee on October 29 which key leaders of the Petrograd party organization also attended. At this meeting, Lenin's resolution calling for the most energetic preparation of the armed uprising carried by a vote of 19 to 2, with 4 abstentions. The lack of unanimity in the group was more sharply brought out by the vote on Zinoviev's resolution, which stated: "Without delaying the reconnoitering preparatory steps, it is considered that such uprisings are inadmissable until a conference [is held] with the Bolshevik deputies to the Congress of Soviets." This time the vote was 6 for and 15 against, with 3 abstaining. At the conclusion of the meeting, Kamenev announced his resignation from the Central Committee with a warning that the party had embarked on the road to disaster.[81]

On October 31 in response to Menshevik rumors about his position, Kamenev published a statement in *Novaia zhizn'*, a nonparty paper of the left, in which, speaking in his own name and in that of Zinoviev, he declared himself "against any attempt to take the initiative of an armed uprising."[82] The hint in the declaration that the party had taken its stand for insurrection, and the violation of party discipline involved in the disclosure, sent Lenin into a towering rage. In an angry letter addressed to party members that same day, he demanded the immediate expulsion of Kamenev and Zinoviev from the party. "I say outright that I do not consider them comrades any longer, and that I will fight with all my power both in the Central Committee and at the congress to expel them both from the party."[83]

The following day, in another letter to the Central Committee, Lenin again reiterated his demand for the expulsion of the "strikebreakers" from the party,[84] and the issue came to a head at a meeting of the Central Committee on November 2. With Lenin absent and Stalin trying to play the role of peacemaker, the Central Committee ratified Kamenev's resignation from the Central Committee by a vote of five to three with Stalin in the minority, but it refused to expel Zinoviev and Kamenev from the party. At the same time, the Central Committee voted to impose on the two leaders "the obligation not to make any statements against the decision of the C.C. and the line of work laid out by it."[85] Kamenev and Zinoviev suppressed their dissatisfaction and refrained from further outbursts against the uprising. A last-minute truce was arranged, and Kamenev reappeared as a member of the Central Committee at its meeting of November 6.[86] At the moment of insurrection, the unity of the top command was at least temporarily restored.

While the battle raged in the Central Committee, preparations for the uprising were beginning to go forward. The military forces on which the Bolsheviks relied were (1) the Red Guard recruited from factory workers; (2) the sailors of Kronstadt and the Baltic fleet; and (3) the units of the Petrograd garrison which were favorably inclined. Of these, the most dependable was the workers' Red Guard, approximately 20,000 strong. Compared with professional soldiers, they were poorly trained and equipped, but what they lacked in arms they made up in morale and dedication to the Bolshevik cause. The sailors were unruly and undisciplined, but their fighting spirit was high, and they too could be counted on to play an active role in the insurrection. Bolshevik influence in the fleet was strong, though it had to dispute for supremacy with units of the Left SR's and anarchists. The most dubious quantity was the Petrograd garrison. While the major part of the troops could probably be depended on not to oppose the insurrection, they could not be relied on to give it vigorous support. The struggle to gain control of the garrison constituted the last stage preparatory to the insurrection itself.

The preparation for the insurrection was greatly facilitated by two steps taken by the Provisional Government. First, in the face of the advancing Germans, the cabinet began discussing the transfer of the government to Moscow. This discussion, leaked to the press on October 19, was interpreted —and not wholly incorrectly—as also motivated by a desire to remove the Provisional Government from dependence upon the Petrograd soviet and the revolutionary forces associated with it. Then on October 22, the army headquarters ordered that one-third of the Petrograd garrison units prepare for transfer to the front, a step which had also been taken on the eve of the Kornilov affair and which therefore not only angered the garrison but also raised fears of a new military coup.[87]

In these circumstances the Bolsheviks were able to raise the cry of danger to the soviet and to appeal for military actions of self-defense. On October 22 they pushed a resolution through the Petrograd soviet which authorized "the Executive Committee to organize a revolutionary committee of defense, which would concentrate in its hands all information relating to the defense of Petrograd and its approaches, would take measures to arm the workers, and thus would assure the revolutionary defense of Petrograd and the safety of the people from the attack which is openly being prepared by military and civilian Kornilovites."[88] On October 29 the committee—the Military Revolutionary Committee—was actually created, and on November 2 it held its first meeting. In practice, the core of the committee was composed only of Bolsheviks and sympathetic Left SR's—in fact, in significant part of members of the Bolshevik Military Organization. "Fundamentally the [Military Revolutionary Committee] operation was the work of the Bolshevik Military Organization, and in unguarded moments it was still referred to as such."[89]

The Military Revolutionary Committee served as the staff of the revolution. From November 3 to 5 it worked to assign commissars to the various combat units of the garrison, as well as to the arsenals. The acceptance by a unit or arsenal of a commissar meant that the unit would not move nor the arsenal distribute arms without the commissar's (and ultimately therefore the Military Revolutionary Committee's) permission; it meant that that unit or arsenal was no longer at the disposal of the Provisional Government. The process was not always a smooth one, for kernels of resistance developed. For example, the Bolshevik commissar was unable to establish his authority in the important Fortress of Peter and Paul which commanded the Winter Palace, but on the afternoon of November 5, this obstacle was overcome when Trotsky appealed to the soldiers of the fortress. With this peaceful surrender went a prize of 100,000 rifles, no mean contribution to future success.

On the evening of the fifth, the Provisional Government made a belated attempt to fight back. The decision was made to close the Bolshevik newspapers, *Rabochii put'* and *Soldat,* to initiate criminal proceedings against the members of the Military Revolutionary Committee, to arrest leading Bolsheviks, and to summon reliable military units from the environs of Petrograd. The first tests of strength augured badly for the government. The Bolshevik printing plants were raided by government troops at 5:30 A.M. on November 6 and copies of the newspapers confiscated; by eleven o'clock that morning the newspapers reappeared. The government ordered the cruiser *Aurora,* manned by a Bolshevik crew and moored in the Neva uncomfortably close to the Winter Palace, to put to sea on a training cruise; the order was effectively countermanded by the Military Revolutionary Committee.

On the morning of the sixth, Kerensky proclaimed a state of insurrection in Petrograd, and asked for unqualified support in suppressing the Bolsheviks. After prolonged debate, the Pre-Parliament (a representative body created by Kerensky after the Kornilov affair and boycotted by the Bolsheviks) adopted a resolution of Martov, now a Menshevik internationalist, by the close vote of 113 to 102, with 26 abstentions. (The Kadets and Cossack delegates were in opposition.) The resolution condemned the insurrection, but it pointed the finger of responsibility at Kerensky by calling on him "first of all, to pass immediately a decree transferring the land to the land committees and to take a decisive stand on foreign policy, proposing to the Allies that they announce the conditions of peace and begin negotiations."[90] A delegation headed by the Menshevik leader Dan called on Kerensky to plead for quick action in the spirit of the resolution. According to Dan's account, "our conversation did not last very long. Kerensky gave the impression of a man completely enervated and worn out. To every argument he replied with irritation, saying finally with disdain that the government did not need any of our advice, that this was not the time to talk but to act."[91]

While the Bolsheviks essentially had control of the military force of Petrograd by November 5, it is by no means clear that they knew what they were going to do with it. Incredibly, Lenin himself, after three days of intense concern over the Zinoviev-Kamenev question (and a meeting with the leaders of the Bolshevik Military Organization on October 31), essentially dropped out of the picture from November 1 to late in the evening of November 6. In response to the Kamenev letter, the Central Executive Committee had postponed the Congress of Soviets until November 7, thereby giving the Bolsheviks a renewed opportunity to strike before the congress. However, Lenin wrote no appeals for insurrection during this period, only a single short article on the peasants and a note to Sverdlov on November 4 or 5 objecting vigorously to the Central Committee compromise on the Zinoviev-Kamenev question (a note that implies he was not being kept in touch on top party questions); he attended neither the Central Committee session November 2 nor that held on the morning of the sixth (the very day before the opening of the Congress of Soviets); he apparently met with no party leaders privately. "By all appearances," Daniels argues, "Lenin had lost hope that an insurrection could still be launched before the Congress of Soviets . . . Feeling politically and physically isolated [he] seems to have lapsed into a state of a real depression."[92]

The major figure in organizing day-to-day operations during this week seems to have been Trotsky, but the exact nature of his role is shrouded in mystery and controversy. After Stalin's rise to power, Trotsky disappeared from discussions of the revolution (at least in any favorable context), and even in recent years traditional Soviet historians have quite improbably contended that "he did not take any part at all in working out the plan of the uprising."[93] Trotsky himself, on the other hand, wrote much and often about these days, and he did little to minimize his role. For example, he claimed that he served as the chairman of the Military Revolutionary Committee, and while this may be true, Daniels correctly points out that "no available documentation supports this."[94] A year after the revolution, Stalin expressed what seems to have been a widespread contemporary judgment when he stated, "All the work of the practical organization of the insurrection proceeded under the immediate direction of the chairman of the Petrograd Soviet, Comrade Trotsky. It can be said with assurance that for the quick shift of the garrison to the side of the soviet and the bold insurrectionary work of the [Military Revolutionary Committee] the Party is indebted firstly and mainly to Comrade Trotsky."[95] Most western historians (but not Daniels) accept this judgment.

The point that really seems uncertain is whether Trotsky (and most other leading Central Committee members) were really planning an insurrection before the congress or whether, as Stalin told a group of Bolshevik delegates on November 6, they were still simply trying "to concentrate our forces."[96] Certainly the Central Committee members were talking publicly about the Congress of Soviets peacefully voting to transfer "all power to the soviets" (a point that concerned their Left SR allies) and the concrete steps they were taking, other than arming the Red Guard and placing commissars with veto power in the key locations, were reactions to the Provisional Government's attempts to suppress them. Trotsky claimed after the fact that this posture was a deliberate screen to hide the Central Committee's true intentions, but there are grounds for maintaining doubts.

At a minimum, one can say that the Central Committee successfully hid from its leader any intention to conduct an immediate insurrection. On November 6, after hearing a report on the Central Committee session held in the morning, Lenin twice sought permission of the Central Committee to come to the Bolshevik headquarters in Smolny, but was refused. In the evening he took up his pen, again, demanding in the strongest language that the seizure of power take place that night: "We must, come what may, arrest the government this evening or in the early morning hours of the night . . . It is impossible to wait!! We may lose everything!! . . . It would be ruin or a formality to wait for the wavering voting of [November 7] . . . It would be a crime for revolutionaries, to let pass the moment, knowing that *the salvation of the revolution* depends on them."[97]

Finally around 10:30 in the evening, Lenin took the step that one would have expected earlier. He sat out on foot for Smolny with his bodyguard. After his arrival at midnight, the Bolshevik forces moved quickly to seize the strong points of the capital—the telephone office, the state bank, the central post office, the railroad station on the Moscow line, the treasury. The cruiser *Aurora* anchored at the Nikolaevsky bridge, not far from the Winter Palace, the seat of the Provisional Government. Resistance was virtually nominal, and the seizures were accomplished with almost no bloodshed. The military support on which the Provisional Government counted simply melted away.

At 10 o'clock on the morning of the seventh, Lenin issued a proclamation declaring that "the Provisional Government has been overthrown" and ending with the words "Long live the revolution of the workers, soldiers, and peasants!"[98] Nevertheless, the Winter Palace remained in the hands of the Provisional Government. The Congress of Soviets was scheduled for noon, and Lenin wanted to announce the fall of the Winter Palace and the arrest of the ministers at the opening of the session. The session was postponed until evening, as Lenin once again raged at his subordinates trying to produce action. It was not until after midnight (that is, in the early morning of the eighth), after the Congress of Soviets was in session, that the Winter Palace was finally taken. Its defenders too had essentially given up without a struggle when the *Aurora* fired a few blanks at the palace.

At the Second All-Russian Congress of Soviets itself, there were approximately 650 delegates in attendance. The Bolsheviks claimed 390 of the delegates and with the help of the Left SR's quickly asserted control over the proceedings. Confronted with a fait accompli, the Mensheviks and SR's of the right and center left the session in order to disassociate themselves with the seizure of power. The congress concluded its first day's business by issuing a proclamation announcing its assumption of supreme power, transferring all local authority to the soviets, and appealing to the country to defeat all efforts of Kerensky and other "Kornilovists" to return to power. With a sure revolutionary instinct for the issues that would attract maximum support for the Bolsheviks, the proclamation promised:

> The Soviet Authority will at once propose a democratic peace to all nations and an immediate armistice on all fronts. It will safeguard the transfer without compensation of all land . . . to the peasant committees; it will defend the soldiers' rights, introducing a complete democratization of the army, it will establish workers' control over industry, it will insure the convocation of the Constituent Assembly on the date set; it will supply the cities with bread and the villages with articles of first necessity, and

it will secure to all nationalities inhabiting Russia the right of self-determination.[99]

The next day Lenin made his first appearance at the congress and was received with a tumultuous ovation. After the applause died down, he quickly assumed the reins of leadership with nine fateful words, "We shall now proceed to construct the socialist order."[100] With Lenin presenting the main reports, the congress approved the important decrees on peace and on land and then concluded its work by entrusting the power of government to the newly created cabinet, which was called the Council of People's Commissars.[101] The Council of People's Commissars—or Sovnarkom, as it quickly became known—was exclusively Bolshevik in composition: its membership included Lenin as Chairman, Trotsky as Commissar (Minister) of Foreign Affairs, Rykov as Commissar of the Interior, Lunacharsky as Commissar of Education, and Stalin as Commissar of Nationalities. The hour of triumph had finally come. Lenin rarely indulged in introspection or backward glances, but at that moment he paused in wonder and confided to Trotsky, "You know . . . from persecution and a life underground, to come so suddenly into power . . . *Es schwindelt* (intoxicating)."[102]

Of course, in actuality, the struggle was far from over. In Petrograd itself the major military battle took place on November 11 and 12 when Kerensky (who had escaped on November 7) sent a group of 700 Cossack troops to overthrow the Bolsheviks and when a group of military cadets attempted a counterrevolution from within the city. The garrison declared its neutrality, but the Red Guard and a Bolshevik troop of several thousand repelled the attack. Even then the problem of restoring order was a difficult one, for the storming of the Winter Palace had included an attack upon its wine cellar and this successful operation was followed by many similar ones in coming days.[103] It was also necessary to establish the Bolshevik regime in the country as a whole—a task that turned out to be simple in some cities but more difficult in others.[104] (For example, the Bolsheviks lost approximately 500 men in the seizure of power in Moscow.) And ultimately, to secure the country, the Bolsheviks had to fight a three-year Civil War, rebuilding in the process an army that had disintegrated during 1917.

Reasons for the Bolshevik Success in 1917

In the brief period of eight months, a tiny band of underground revolutionaries, numbering fewer than 25,000 men on the eve of the March revolution, had gained sufficient support to catapult themselves into a governing authority over nearly 150,000,000 people. The success of the Bolsheviks can be explained on many levels. In one sense, of course, the crucial factor was the revolutionary mood of the time and the way in which the Bolsheviks' opponents responded—or failed to respond—to it. If the Provisional Government had been able to withdraw from the war and carry through a land settlement satisfactory to the peasantry, it is highly doubtful that the Bolsheviks could have been so successful.

Yet, to state this alternative, so plausibly reinforced by hindsight, is to miss the tragic imperatives of 1917. Each of the parties which maneuvered for ascendancy in the months between March and November was the prisoner of its own illusions, its own interests, and its own visions of the future. To a Kadet leader like Miliukov it was inconceivable that Russia could betray her allies and her own national interests by suing for a separate peace; consequently, it was all too easy to believe that his own sense of patriotic exaltation and dedication were shared by soldiers, workers, and peasants who had lost their taste for war. To SR's of the right like Kerensky, who in a measure shared Miliukov's illusions, the successful prosecution of the war was paramount, with the agenda of economic reforms to be postponed until properly constituted legal bodies could be assembled to deal with them. To SR's of the center and left, who were much closer to the aspirations and expectations of the villages, land reform brooked no delay. Frustrated by the procrastinations of the Provisional Government, the Left SR's were thrown into the arms of the Bolsheviks. For Mensheviks of all shades, still loyal to the orthodox Marxist two-stage panorama of capitalist development, the socialist revolution had to be postponed until the bourgeois-democratic revolution was completed. They were left with a program of the establishment of a bourgeois order they described in the harshest of terms and a policy of conducting legal opposition to it—hardly a program for which the wretched and disinherited could develop more than qualified enthusiasm.

Until the arrival of Lenin from exile, the Bolsheviks too were prisoners of ancient formulas. They oriented their policies on a perspective not very different from that of Menshevism. Lenin reversed this course and set the party on the road to the conquest of power. With an unswerving faith in his goal and a readiness to take any measures whatever to realize it, Lenin, frequently over bitter opposition, managed to transform the party into an instrument that carried out his will.

Despite all its divisions and disorganization, despite all the lack of real direction given to the organization of the revolution in the provinces, despite the fact that "there was little systematic about Bolshevik Party organization during this period,"[105] the party still had a sense of discipline that was relatively greater than that of its rivals. On October 30, when a debate on the insurrection broke out at a meeting of Petrograd borough leaders, Sverdlov could say, "The decision of the Central Committee on the uprisings has been made . . . We have not gathered to set aside a decision of the Central Committee, but to consider how we ought to carry it out."[106] It was an appeal that was peculiarly effective to men who had accepted the principle of "democratic centralism" in joining the party. The Central Committee certainly felt that it had the right to debate Lenin's proposals and to disagree with them (as it clearly did, according to the principles of democratic centralism), and the continued presence of a man like Kamenev in the Central Committee despite his opposition to Lenin since April indicates a willingness to maintain a diversity of views within that body. Even the two "strikebreakers" returned to party discipline with the "compromise" of November 2 and Kamenev at least was present at the planning sessions through the night of November 6–7.

Nevertheless, as Fainsod emphasized, the success of the Bolsheviks is to be explained not nearly so much by their discipline as by Lenin's "remarkable talent as a revolutionary strategist . . . [his] unerring sense for the deeply felt dissatisfactions of the masses and a genius for finding the slogans to catalyze grievances into revolutionary energy."

Except for his insistence on striking at the right moment, Lenin had relatively little to do with the actual mechanics of the insurrection. His great contribution was to set the stage for insurrection by identifying Bolshevism with the major forces of mass discontent in Russian society. Lenin did not create the war-weariness which permeated the army and the nation: the material was at hand; his task was to exploit it. With one word —peace—Lenin and the Bolsheviks fused it into a revolutionary amalgam. The land-hunger of the peasants was an ancient grievance of which all parties were aware. The SR's built their ascendancy in the villages on the promise to satisfy it, but, while they temporized, Lenin stole their program from under their noses . . . With one word—land—Lenin insured the neutrality of the villages . . . With two slogans—bread and workers' control —Lenin captured the allegiance of substantial sections of the industrial workers from the Mensheviks.[107]

The nature of the Bolshevik support—and the limitations on it—were clearly revealed in the elections to the Constituent Assembly, which were held (on the whole) on November 25 to 27—three weeks after the uprising in Petrograd. All parties participated in the election, and the vote was generally free—a fact attested to by the 25 percent vote that the Bolsheviks received.

While the Bolsheviks were not a majoritarian movement, they did have important pockets of strength.[108] They claimed that they were the party of the proletariat, and it was a claim that they could generally substantiate. The Mensheviks received only 3 percent of the vote in Moscow and Petrograd, and only 1.5 percent of the total vote outside of the Transcaucasus (where they were strong) and a district in which voters were compelled to vote for the Menshevik candidate.[109] In Petrograd and Moscow, the Bolsheviks received 45 percent and 48 percent of the vote respectively, but the Kadets—the party of the middle class and the bourgeoisie—were their major competition here, receiving 26 percent and 35 percent of the vote respectively in the two metropolises.[110]

The Bolsheviks also had strong support among a number of the army units. The Baltic fleet remained a Bolshevik center (63 percent of the vote), as did the army units at the western front (67 percent of the vote) and at the northern front (56 percent of it). In a pattern that was repeated in the peasant vote, the Bolshevik vote declined sharply in units more distant from the metropolitan centers where they had had much less opportunity to present their case. The Bolsheviks received only 30 percent of the vote at the southwest front and only 15 percent of the vote at the Rumanian front, which was the most remote of all. Similarly, the sailors of the Black Sea fleet presented only 20 percent of their votes to Lenin's party.[111]

The picture in the countryside is more mixed. The SR's "won" the election in that they received 38 percent of the total vote, and the bulk of this support came from the peasants. In remote rural areas such as Siberia and the Central Black-Earth region (for example, Kursk and Voronezh), their vote exceeded 75 percent of the total, but in the central and western provinces, where peasant families had more contact with the cities and the army units, the Bolsheviks garnered a substantial number of peasant votes. The latter won 43 percent of the vote in the eleven central and northwest Russian guberniias, and actually carried the rural guberniia of Smolensk with 55 percent of the vote and rural Belorussia with 59 percent. It is hard to avoid the conclusion that the Bolshevik program had strong support among the Russian peasantry whenever the latter were exposed to it in a substantial way.[112]

Social revolution is seldom a matter of winning majority support. In all revolutions there are large numbers who are uninterested, and in the Russian provinces in particular "what emerges," to quote Fainsod, "is a picture of utmost confusion in which passivity and apathy played a much larger role than is commonly assumed."[113] Revolutions are made by active minorities who tap groundswells of discontent, and this the Bolsheviks were able to do; they are successful when the military force supporting the old regime melts away or defects, and this too the Bolsheviks were able to achieve. Russia of 1917 had much in common with the disorder and polarization of the last months of the Allende regime in Chile, but in Chile the soldiers carried out the orders of the "Chilean Kornilov." In Russia they did not, and the war and the war-weariness were surely crucial in this respect.

As William Chamberlin emphasized many years ago, the essence of Lenin's great insight in September and October was an understanding of the meaning of the failure of the Kornilov affair:

> There is no period in Lenin's life when his stature as a leader and his capacity to grasp accurately the basic facts of a new and changing political situation appear so vividly as in the few weeks which elapsed between the Kornilov affair and the Bolshevik stroke for power. He recognized immediately that Kornilov's defeat was Bolshevism's opportunity . . . Living in hiding . . . it was only natural that his judgment should be faulty in connection with some of the details of the projected uprising . . . He seems to have been precipitate with his suggestion that the uprising should have begun at the time of the Democratic Conference, and in his single-track insistence on the organization of insurrection at the earliest possible moment he was somewhat too contemptuous of the expediency of linking up the uprising with the meeting of the Second Congress of Soviets, with its assured Bolshevik majority. But these were minor miscalculations of detail, which could be and were corrected in the development of the action. Lenin's indisputable claim to greatness as a revolutionary leader lies in the fact that he realized immediately after the collapse of Kornilov that the time for action had come, that he drove home this view . . . and that he never relaxed his pressure on the Party Central Committee . . . until the opposition was crushed and the Party organization had swung into line behind his proposals.[114]

To repeat a crucial point, however, the real test of the Bolsheviks came not in November, but in the coming three years. They had to demonstrate an ability to rule that no one expected this group of fractious extremists to have; they had to build an army from a war-weary population after having promised peace; they had to win a Civil War while extracting grain by force from peasants in the countryside, while attempting to reinstitute authority relations in the army and the factory, and while ending the wildly free politics of 1917 and emasculating the soviets in whose name they came to power. It was in 1917–1921 that the Bolshevik revolution was really won.

3 | The Establishment of the Soviet Regime

THE COUP D'ETAT of November 7, 1917, transformed the Bolsheviks at one stroke from a revolutionary party into a governing party. In assuming the responsibilities of governance, the Bolsheviks had to define their relationship to other parties and to the organs of state power which they inherited or hoped to create, but the Marxist intellectual armory offered little precise guidance for revolutionaries come to power. The brief quotations from Marx and Engels, which Lenin assembled in his pamphlet *State and Revolution* during the period he was in hiding in August and September 1917, left much to be desired as a blueprint for the construction of the socialist state.

Lenin's views of the future, too, were not always clearly discernible in the slogans he espoused. In speaking of democracy, of the transfer of all power to the soviets, of workers' control, and so forth, he may sometimes have created the impression that he was advocating a more fully developed system of institutions based on western notions of democracy, but the scorn that he heaped on "bourgeois democracy," on "parliamentarism," and the like pointed in a different direction.

As early as 1905, Lenin asserted that "the decisive victory of the revolution over tsarism" could be achieved only after the creation of "a revolutionary-democratic dictatorship of the proletariat and peasantry." His image of such a regime at that point was that it would be very limited in its goals:

This will, of course, not be a socialist but a democratic dictatorship. It will not be able to affect (without a whole series of intermediary steps of revolutionary development) the bases of capitalism. It will be able, in the best case, to introduce a basic redistribution of land for the use of the peasantry, to establish consistent and full democratism right up to the national level . . . [and] to lay the basis for a serious improvement of the position of the workers' conditions and a raising of their living standards.[1]

But even with such a limited vision of the role of the revolutionary-democratic dictatorship, Lenin was quite frank about its character. "Such a victory will be precisely a dictatorship—that is, it will unavoidably rest on military force, on the armed masses, on an uprising, and not on some 'legal' or 'peaceful path' through created institutions. It can only be a dictatorship, [for] without a dictatorship it is impossible to break the resistance [of the landlords, the important bourgeoisie, and tsarism] and to repel counterrevolution."[2]

A dozen years later in *State and Revolution*, written after tsarism had already been overthrown, Lenin vigorously defended such Marxian concepts as the withering away of the state, but he warned that the promises for the final stage of "communism" would not be realized immediately. The withering away of the state, he asserted, would "obviously" be "a lengthy process," and he treated the adoption of the principle "From each according to his ability, to each according to his needs" as a matter for the rather distant future. Such developments, Lenin said, "presuppose not the present productivity of labor *and not the present* ordinary run of people, who . . . are capable of damaging the stocks of public wealth 'just for fun' and of demanding the impossible."[3]

We are not utopians, we do not indulge in "dreams" of dispensing *at once* with all administration, with all subordination. These anarchist dreams . . . are totally alien to Marxism, and, as a matter of fact, serve only to postpone the socialist revolution until people are different. No, we want the socialist revolution with people as they are now, with people who cannot dispense with subordination, control, and "foremen and book-keepers."[4]

So far as the short and the intermediate term were concerned (that which was described as the stage of "socialism"), Lenin in *State and Revolution* drew on Marx's conception of the dictatorship of the proletariat in describing the character of state power in the transitional period between capitalism and communism. Following Marx and Engels, he turned to the experience of the Paris Commune to illustrate the nature of the dictatorship of the proletariat in action.[5] For Lenin, the Commune demonstrated that "the working class cannot simply seize the available ready machinery of the state and set it going for its own ends": it must "shatter the bureaucratic and military machine."

While acknowledging that the dictatorship of the proletariat would entail "a series of restrictions on the freedom of the oppressors . . . the capitalists" and insisting that "their resistance must be crushed by force," Lenin contended in *State and Revolution* that this phase of history would "simultaneously" mean an "immense expansion of democracy . . . for the poor . . . for the people." In praising the Commune, he listed those of its features which would be embodied in the dictatorship of the proletariat: the abolition of the old army and the old police, the payment of workers' wages to officials, the organization of the Commune into "a working corporation, legislative and executive at the same time," the election of delegates, the filling of all administrative and judicial posts on the basis of universal suffrage and recall. On the other hand, the attacks on "parliamentarism"—which presumably meant the clash of parties in the legislature and competition among them in elections—suggested the nonwestern meaning of some of these phrases. The "commune state" would represent the incarnation of the interests of the proletariat. The power of the state would be used to prepare the way for the eventual emergence of a classless Communist society in which class repression would be replaced by voluntary cooperation.

> Under socialism, much of "primitive" democracy will inevitably revive, since for the first time in the history of civilized societies the *mass* of the population will be raised to *independent* participation not only in voting and elections, but in *day-to-day administration.* Under socialism *all* will administer in turn and will quickly become accustomed to nobody administering . . .
>
> A beginning can and must be made at once . . . *We ourselves, the workers,* will organize large-scale production on the basis of what capitalism has already created, establishing strict, iron discipline supported by the state power of the armed workers. We will reduce the role of the state officials to that of simply carrying out our instructions as responsible, revocable, modestly paid "foremen and bookkeepers" (of course, with the aid of technicians of all sorts, types, and degrees).[6]

The problem, however, was that Marx had visualized the proletarian revolution as the culmination of a long process of industrialization in the course of which the working class became the preponderant element in society. Thus, for Marx, the dictatorship of the proletariat implied majority rule. While Lenin talked in *State and Revolution* about a dictatorship of the proletariat explicitly in these terms, the Russian industrial proletariat was a small minority in an overwhelmingly agrarian country. To exercise power in the name of the proletariat was to impose the rule of the few on the many; the dictatorship of the Russian proletariat was by definition a minority dictatorship. To make the problem more complex, the industrial working class was itself divided in its political loyalties. Most followed the leadership of the Bolsheviks, but others gave their allegiance to the Mensheviks and even to the Socialist Revolutionaries, whose main strength was with the peasantry.

One-Party Rule versus Coalition Government

After their seizure of power, the Bolsheviks immediately faced a difficult choice. Marx and Lenin had talked of a "dictatorship of the proletariat," not a "dictatorship of the party," and the question was—how was the proletariat to be represented and how were decisions to be taken in party-political terms? For the Bolsheviks to try to govern alone as a party was to bear the stigma of a minority dictatorship and to cement the strength of the opposition. To share power with other parties and to await the judgment of a constituent assembly based on popular elections was to risk losing the fruits of the insurrection. The path of dictatorship led irrevocably in the direction of civil war, the suppression of the opposition, and invocation of terror. The path of coalition and constitutionalism meant compromise, concession, and the abdication of supreme power.

Within the bosom of Bolshevism, two conflicting patterns of thought struggled for ascendance on this question. The majority group, led by Lenin and Trotsky, pronounced in favor of a party dictatorship, though they expressed a reluctant willingness to admit representatives of other socialist parties into the government, provided the hegemony of the Bolsheviks was safeguarded. The minority, led by Kamenev and Zinoviev, advocated a coalition of the parties in the soviet, an agreement to share power with the Mensheviks and SR's in order to broaden the base of support for the new regime.

The position of the Leninist majority was sharply expressed in the interparty negotiations on the composition of the new government after the uprising of November 7. Under Lenin's leadership, the party Central Committee instructed its negotiators to insist on "a majority in the Central Executive Committee [TsIK], a majority in the government, and [the acceptance of] our [Bolshevik] program." Trotsky went even further and at a meeting of the Central Committee on November 14, 1917, asserted, "We should have 75 percent."[7] Lenin's deep-rooted skepticism toward coalition came out even more sharply at a session of the Petrograd committee of the party held on the same day: "As for conciliation," he said, "I cannot even speak about that seriously . . . Our present slogan is: No compromise: i.e., for a homogeneous Bolshevik Government."[8]

Meanwhile, the minority led by Kamenev and Zinoviev sought to escape the grim logic of one-party dictatorship. Frustrated in the Central Committee, they insisted on airing their views outside. Despite Lenin's effort to silence them by invoking the threat of party discipline, the minority persisted in demanding a coalition. On November 17, 1917, they took the unprecedented step of using the forum of the Central Executive Committee of the Congress of Soviets to move the repeal of the press decree of November 9, which the Bolshevik Council of People's Commissars was using to suppress hostile newspapers. When this motion was defeated, the minority representatives resigned from the Council of People's Commissars and the Central Committee of the party. Five of the fourteen members of the council joined in the following statement which was read to the Central Executive Committee on November 17:

We take the stand that it is necessary to form a socialist government of all parties in the soviet. We believe that only the formation of such a government can preserve the fruits of the heroic struggle of the working class and the revolutionary army in the October-November days.

We deem the alternative to be a purely Bolshevik government which can maintain itself only by means of political terror. The Council of People's Commissars has chosen such a path. We cannot and will not accept it. We can see that it will lead to the withdrawal of mass proletarian organizations from the leadership of political life and to the establishment of an irresponsible regime and to the ruin of the revolution and the country. We cannot assume responsibility for such a policy, and, therefore, we give up the name of People's Commissars.[9]

At the same time, five members of the twenty-one-man party Central Committee—Kamenev, Zinoviev, Rykov, Miliutin, and Nogin—issued a declaration announcing their resignation. They charged that "the leading group of the Central Committee . . . has firmly decided not to permit the formation of a government of the parties in the soviet and to insist on a purely Bolshevik government . . . regardless of the sacrifices to the workers and soldiers." The statement continued:

We cannot assume responsibility for this ruinous policy of the Central Committee, carried out against the will of a large part of the proletariat and soldiers who are most eager for an early cessation of blood-shedding by the different wings of the democracy.

We resign therefore from membership in the Central Committee in order to have the right to express our opinion openly to the masses of workers and soldiers and to ask them to support our slogan: Long live the government of the parties in the soviet! For an immediate understanding on these terms.[10]

Although all the signers of this statement soon recanted and resumed positions of responsibility in the party and government, the views they expressed at this juncture revealed a significant crisis in Bolshevik ranks. In *What Is To Be Done?* Lenin had written of a tightly organized action party in which those of like views joined together to achieve what was historically necessary and desirable. As this and many subsequent issues were to indicate, the party that came to power in 1917 was far less monolithic than Lenin's words of 1902 suggested.

The Dissolution of the Constituent Assembly

Simultaneously with the question of the composition of the government, the Bolsheviks had to decide the fate of the Constituent Assembly. The Provisional Government explicitly had been provisional, and in the days before the seizure of power, the Bolsheviks had launched bitter attacks against the Kerensky government for its delay in calling a constituent assembly—a constitutional convention. As a result of this and other pressure, the Kerensky government had—well before the Bolshevik revolution—fixed November 25, 1917, as the day for holding elections to the assembly.

Once the Bolsheviks were in power, they faced the question of whether to hold elections and, if so, whether to permit the Constituent Assembly to assemble and complete its work. The Bolsheviks found themselves in a curious dilemma. They had attacked the Provisional Government so sharply for its dilatory tactics that it did not appear politically expedient to cancel or even delay the elections. They had, however, no intention of depositing their newly won power in a hostile Constituent Assembly. Lenin advocated postponement of the election, but, after a very warm intraparty discussion, other counsel prevailed. The decision to proceed with the elections was approved, recognizing, as one Bolshevik put it, that if the Constituent Assembly turned out to be refractory, "we may have to dissolve it with bayonets."

The elections were held in an atmosphere of relative freedom, and the Bolsheviks received but one-quarter of the votes. On January 18, 1918, the first and only meeting of the Constituent Assembly took place at the Tauride Palace in Petrograd. The palace was heavily guarded and surrounded by trustworthy Bolshevik sailors and Red Guards. The Bolshevik bloc failed to gain control of the proceedings. With the aid of their allies, the Left SR's, the

Bolsheviks were able to muster only 136 votes, while the Right SR's commanded 237 votes on the crucial motion to make their program the order of the day.[11] The Bolsheviks and Left SR's then withdrew from the assembly, leaving the rest of the delegates to continue their talk until far into the night. At five in the morning, a sailor who headed the guard of the palace approached the chairman of the assembly and requested the delegates to leave the hall "because the guard is tired."[12]

The delegates dispersed, presumably to meet again the next day. The next session was never held. On January 19, 1918, the Central Executive Committee of the Soviets, which was dominated by the Bolsheviks, issued a decree dissolving the Constituent Assembly on the ground that it served as a cover for "the bourgeois counter-revolution in its efforts to crush the power of the Soviets."[13] The delegates who sought to reassemble on the nineteenth were not allowed to enter the palace.

When criticized for dissolving the assembly, Lenin replied:

Those who remind us of the time when we also stood for the Constituent Assembly and rebuke us for now "dispersing" it don't have a grain of sense in their heads, only pompous and empty phrases. For, as compared with tsarism and the Kerensky republic, the Constituent Assembly at one time seemed to us better than their notorious organs of power; but with their establishment the Soviets, being revolutionary organizations of all the people, of course, became immeasurably superior to all the parliaments in the world . . . All power to the Soviets we said then, and for this we are fighting . . . The Constituent Assembly which failed to recognize the power of the people, is now dispersed by the will of the Soviet power . . . All power to the Soviets! And we shall crush the saboteurs.[14]

When some of his own followers encountered difficulty in following the argument, Lenin warned:

Every attempt, direct or indirect, to consider the question of the Constituent Assembly from a formal, legal point of view, within the framework of ordinary bourgeois democracy, ignoring the class struggle and civil war, is a betrayal of the cause of the proletariat, and the adoption of the bourgeois standpoint. It is the bounden duty of revolutionary Social Democracy to warn all and sundry against this error, into which a few Bolshevik leaders, who have been unable to appreciate the significance of the October uprising and the tasks of the dictatorship of the proletariat, have fallen.[15]

The Consolidation of Single-Party Dictatorship

With the dissolution of the Constituent Assembly on January 22, 1918, the Bolshevik break with the bourgeois legal order was complete. However, the Bolsheviks still faced the problem of legitimating their rule, and, unlike traditional dictatorial groups, they attempted to do so through the use of democratic forms. Supreme governing authority was formally assumed by the Third All-Russian Congress of Soviets. At the closing session of the congress on January 31, the assembled delegates unanimously approved a proposal to abandon the designation of Provisional Workers' and Peasants' Government and to refer to the supreme power henceforth as the Workers' and Peasants' Government of the Russian Soviet Republic.[16]

By resolution, the Russian Socialist Soviet Republic was declared to be a "federation of Soviet republics founded on the principle of a free union of the peoples of Russia." Its highest organ was defined as the All-Russian Congress of Soviets. The Congress of Soviets was to choose a Central Executive Committee (VTsIK in its Russian abbreviation) which was to be vested with legislative power between sessions of the Congress of Soviets. Despite the designation "executive," the Central Executive Committee had two hundred and then three hundred members, and it really became more the equivalent of the parliament in the governmental structure.

The executive branch of government was organized into people's commissarists (a total of eighteen in 1918, including a people's commissariat for foreign affairs, one for internal affairs, one for finance, and so forth), and it was supervised by a Council of People's Commissars (Sovnarkom). At least in legal terms, the government was parliamentary in nature, for the Council of People's Commissars was to be "elected or dismissed in whole or in part" by either the Congress of Soviets or the Central Executive Committee. "All local matters" were to be settled exclusively by the local soviets, but higher soviets reserved the right "to regulate affairs between the local soviets and to settle differences that may arise between them."[17]

The Central Executive Committee was charged with the task of drafting a constitution in accordance with these principles for submission to the next Congress of Soviets. On April 1, 1918, it designated a committee of fifteen, including two Left SR's and one Maximalist, to prepare the final document.[18] The presence of the non-Bolsheviks on the committee and the relative looseness of party discipline in this period guaranteed that on this issue too there would be vigorous debate. The basic conflicts were between those who pressed for a strengthening of central power and others who wished to safeguard the autonomy of the local soviets; between some who favored a concentration of legislative and executive powers in the supreme organs of government and others who sought their separation and delimitation; between some who urged a syndicalist solution based on autonomous trade union federations and those who rejected syndicalism in favor of political centralization; between those who supported a form of federalism built on nationality divisions and others who advocated the establishment of federal republics organized around economic interests; and between some who pressed for equal representation of the peasantry and industrial workers and those who sought to safeguard the hegemony of the industrial proletariat by guaranteeing it a preferred electoral position.

Under the influence of its Bolshevik leadership (including Stalin, who played a major role in the deliberations), the luxuriant debate in the committee was brought under control, and the basic lines of Bolshevik policy were impressed on the constitutional draft. They involved subordinating the local soviets to centralized authority, safeguarding the concentration of legislative and executive power in the supreme governmental organs, repudiating the syndicalist deviation, organizing the federal republic on nationality lines, and recognizing the industrial working class as the principal supporting pillar of the regime.

Although the Soviet constitution placed supreme legislative power in the Congress of Soviets and the Central Executive Committee and named the Council of the People's Commissars as the country's cabinet, party theory was quite explicit in asserting that the ultimate political authority was to reside in the party. In March 1919, the Eighth Party Congress formalized an already existing policy when it declared that "the Russian Communist party should master for itself undivided political supremacy in the soviets and practical supervision over all their work." The formation of "party fractions" in all soviets was said to be "absolutely indispensable" for this purpose. "All party members who work in the given soviet organizations should enter these fractions . . . which are subject to the strictest party discipline." As printed in *Pravda,* the resolution further specified that "these fractions are unconditionally subordinate to the corresponding party organizations"—that is to the extraparliamentary party organs in the territorial unit in which the soviet was located.[19]

Despite the fact that the leading personnel in the Central Executive Committee and especially in the Council of People's Commissars were party members (and Lenin was Chairman of the Council of People's Commissars), the major policy decisions were taken not in these bodies—or even in their party fractions—but in the major institutions of the Communist party. As Zinoviev stated in the discussion at the Eighth Party Congress, "Fundamental questions of policy, international and domestic, must be decided by the central committee of our party."[20] This statement accurately reflected the decision-making process which had, in fact, existed prior to the congress, but after the congress, power flowed to another party institution created at that time, an inner committee of the Central Committee which was termed the Politburo.

Establishment of Control in the Civil War

The determination of the Leninist majority to ensure Bolshevik hegemony pushed inexorably in the direction of single-party dictatorship. The actual suppression of opposition parties did not, however, take place at once, but proceeded by slow stages. The attack began with a Council of People's Commissars proclamation on December 11, 1917, declaring the Kadet party "an organization of counterrevolutionary conspirators" and an "enemy of the people."[21] On the same day an order was issued to arrest leading members of the Kadet party and to hand them over to the revolutionary tribunal. "We have made a modest beginning," commented Trotsky.[22]

At first, the Bolsheviks moved cautiously in dealing with their socialist rivals. The Socialist Revolutionaries and the Mensheviks had nominal representation in the Central Executive Committee, and for a brief period from December 22, 1917 to March 15, 1918, three Left SR's held portfolios in the Council of People's Commissars. Opposition newspapers continued to appear, but they were subjected to harassment in the form of suspensions and the cutting-off of newsprint. Then on December 31, 1917, the Cheka (secret police) ordered the arrest of a number of important Right SR and Menshevik leaders,[23] and on June 14, 1918, the Central Executive Committee issued a decree excluding both parties from its ranks on the ground that they were engaged in alleged counterrevolutionary and anti-Soviet activities.

This meant that the Left SR's were the only major group remaining in the Central Executive Committee aside from the dominant Bolshevik majority. By this time, relations between the Bolsheviks and the Left SR's had reached a stage of extreme tension as the result of the opposition of the Left SR's to the peace treaty with Germany and to the confiscatory requisition policy that was being adopted to supply grain to the cities. On July 6, 1918, two Left SR's assassinated the German ambassador in the hope of forcing a breach with the Germans. The abortive Left SR uprising which followed prepared the way for the elimination of this last vestige of effective opposition to Bolshevik one-party rule. Most of the Left SR delegates to the Fifth All-Russian Congress of Soviets were arrested, and thirteen were shot. In reprisal, the Left SR's turned the weapon of political terror against the Bolsheviks. On August 20, 1918, the head of the Petrograd Cheka was assassinated, and Lenin was seriously wounded. The Cheka replied in kind, and the Red

Terror assumed a mass character. By the autumn of 1918, all non-Communist political organizations had been rendered practically impotent, though some continued to exist in a precarious limbo of quasi-legality.

More serious a problem for the regime than the suppression of opposition parties was the establishment of basic control in the areas outside central Russia. The Germans already controlled much of the western Russian empire at the time of the revolution, and it obtained more territory before the party leadership finally signed a peace treaty (the Treaty of Brest-Litovsk) in March 1918. With this treaty, the Bolsheviks had acknowledged the loss of 34 percent of Russia's population, 32 percent of her agricultural land, 54 percent of her industry, and 89 percent of her coal mines. The Baltic States, Belorussia, and the Ukraine were essentially under German domination, and Finland had become independent. When Germany collapsed in late 1918, these territories became a political and military vacuum.

Other parts of the Russian empire also came under the control of non-Communist (White) armies, of Allied troops (at first at least, ostensibly attempting to maintain a second front against the Germans), or of indigenous forces. In the summer of 1918, aided by the revolt of a Czechoslovak brigade which had been fighting on the Russian side in World War I, White forces controlled most of the Urals, Siberia, and even the Upper Volga region, while other Whites, basing themselves upon the Cossacks, were the dominant force in much of the Caucasus. Control of the Transcaucasus was largely divided between the Germans and the Turks, while Central Asia, except for the major city of Tashkent, was "ruled" by a number of different non-Communist regimes.[24]

Thus, the fate of the Bolshevik regime came to depend upon an ability to win military battles in a three-year civil war with the forces of the White generals, the Allied intervention armies, and rebellious anti-Bolshevik nationalist movements in the borderlands. To accomplish this task, the new regime had the task of creating a reliable army—a problem all the more complicated because the collapse of the Russian army had been a key element in the success of the revolution in 1917. The early Red army was a sorry one from a professional point of view. Discipline within the units was virtually nonexistent, and the units themselves were responsible to the local soviets, whose interests often conflicted with those of the center.

In March 1918 Leon Trotsky was designated People's Commissar for War and entrusted with the responsibility of reorganizing the military establishment. In order to guarantee a supply of trained manpower for the army, Trotsky strongly supported the introduction of compulsory military training and conscription. By the end of 1918, 800,000 were enrolled in the

. Red army, and at its peak in 1920, the army numbered five and a half million men.

Perhaps the most important of Trotsky's reforms was his insistence that the Red army have a corps of trained military commanders. Since there were few trained Bolsheviks to fill the higher command and staff posts, Trotsky believed that the Red army had to enlist the knowledge of officers of the tsarist army. From June 1918 to August 1920, more than 48,000 were either drafted or volunteered for the Red army, and they were supported by nearly 215,000 former tsarist noncommissioned officers.[25]

With insurrection and counterrevolution on a whole circle of fluid fronts, the effectiveness of the Red army varied according to the strength its opponents could muster. Confronted with opposing force, the Bolsheviks imposed rule when the means were available and granted independence when no alternative solution was feasible. After the Bolsheviks had recognized the independence of Finland on December 31, 1917, Soviet military forces combined with Finnish Red Guards to capture Helsinki and establish a Finnish Socialist Workers' Government on January 28, 1918. A treaty of friendship was concluded by the new Soviet regime with that government on March 1, 1918, but the attempt to seize power encountered unanticipated resistance. The Bolsheviks were driven out, and the independence of Finland was finally confirmed by a peace treaty in 1920. The experience in the Baltic states was broadly parallel. Local military forces enjoying British and Allied aid succeeded in driving the Soviet armies beyond the frontier, and in 1920 treaties were concluded recognizing the independence of Latvia, Estonia, and Lithuania.[26]

In other areas the Bolsheviks were more successful. Soon after the end of World War I in November 1918, Soviet troops occupied Belorussia, expelled the government which had been established by the Germans, and proclaimed a provisional Belorussian Socialist Soviet Republic on January 1, 1919. While the Red army saw action on all fronts in 1919, its major successes came in the Volga and Urals regions against the White general, Kolchak. By the end of the year the Red army occupied most of Siberia. (Kolchak fell into Bolshevik hands and was executed in February 1920.) The extreme far east remained under the control of the Japanese and their puppet regime for some time, and Soviet sovereignty over all of Siberia was not completed until October 1922 when Japanese troops were withdrawn from Vladivostok and the Maritime Province.

The battle against the White forces in the south (led by General Denikin) was given lower priority through most of 1919, but in October a Denikin offensive approached Moscow itself. A counterattack was launched and the Red army moved south quickly. The Ukraine was captured and a Communist regime established. In May 1920, however, the Bolshevik position in the Ukraine was threatened once more—this time by an offensive of the Polish army from the west. The Poles captured the Ukrainian capital of Kiev and attempted to establish an independent Ukraine, but they in turn were repelled. By August the Red army was at the gates of Warsaw, with the Bolshevik leadership hopeful that the Communist revolution would sweep Poland and even western Europe. When these hopes proved illusory and the Red army was driven back, an armistice signed in October ended the last major battle of the Civil War.

The year 1920 also witnessed the establishment of the Bolshevik rule in the Transcaucasus and Central Asia. The retreat of the German and Turkish armies from the former area after the end of World War I left a vacuum which the British temporarily filled. With the withdrawal of the British forces toward the end of 1919, the independent Transcaucasian republics were left face-to-face with Soviet Russian power. The Bolshevik leadership wasted little time. In the spring of 1920, a Communist revolutionary committee was established in Azerbaidzhan, requested the aid of the Red army, and quickly received it. Much the same pattern was followed in Armenia in December 1920 and in Georgia in February 1921. The establishment of Soviet ascendancy in Central Asia was a more complex process, for guerrilla groups (the Basmachi) were very successful in resisting the Red army. It was not until the fall of 1922 that Soviet authority was basically established in most of Central Asia, and minor missions of Red army pacification continued to be necessary over the next few years.[27]

Under the pressure of the Civil War, the Bolshevik leadership made an effort to distinguish between "loyal" Mensheviks and SR's, who supported the Soviet government in its struggle against the Whites and "disloyal" elements, who gave their support to the counterrevolution. On November 30, 1918, the loyal Mensheviks were readmitted to the Central Executive Committee, and this action was followed on February 25, 1919, by the reinstatement of SR's who were prepared to repudiate "external and internal counterrevolution." But Bolshevik toleration was based solely on expediency and the good behavior of the "captive" representatives of the minority parties. Lenin contemptuously said of them at the Eighth Party Congress, "We say . . . 'You are not a serious enemy. Our enemy is the bourgeoisie. But if you march with it, then we shall have to apply to you too the measures of the proletarian dictatorship.' "[28]

Despite Cheka arrests and persecutions, the Mensheviks as late as 1920 continued to elect delegates to local soviets, to control important trade unions, and to participate, though without voting rights, in the All-Russian Congress of Soviets. Nevertheless, the position of the minority parties became more and more unenviable during the Civil War years. While Menshevik and SR party conferences took place occasionally and their newspapers and manifestoes made sporadic appearances, their activities were subjected to constant harassment and interference.

With the end of the Civil War, the policy of contingent toleration of opposition groups was abandoned. No formal decree was issued dissolving the minority parties, but the signal for extinction was given by Lenin himself in May 1921, when he proclaimed: "We shall keep the Mensheviks and SR's, whether open or disguised as 'nonparty,' in prison." After a revolt by sailors at the Kronstadt garrison in Petrograd in March 1921, this condition came close to total realization. The fiction of a legal opposition was completely abandoned. Kadets, Mensheviks, and SR's were arrested in large numbers and exiled to the far north, Siberia, and Central Asia. Some avoided arrest and won temporary absolution by writing to Bolshevik papers renouncing connections with the outlawed groups. By 1921–1922, almost all opposition political activity had been driven underground, and the consolidation of the one-party dictatorship was virtually completed.

It should be noted, however, that the Bolshevik problem went far beyond the winning of military victories or the suppression of other parties. Despite the most strenuous efforts of the leadership to impose central direction on the course of events, the first years of Soviet power were a period when the spontaneous and anarchic forces of the revolution had their way. The flood of decrees from the center bore little relation to the actual sequence of developments in the localities. The breakdown of supplies and communications, the shifting lines of battle, and the initial inexperience of the new regime combined to create a situation in which authority was dispersed and broken into fragments. The capacity to lead was tested by the ability to extemporize an effective response to the crisis of the moment. Ad hoc improvisation became the order of the day.

The creation of an administrative system that would carry out central orders turned out to be enormously difficult. Trusted Bolsheviks held the strategic positions at the top of the administrative pyramid, but the lower levels of the bureaucracy were still composed predominantly of old regime carryovers whose knowledge made them indispensable and whose skills frequently enabled them to determine the policies of the institutions with which they were connected. As Lenin was later to observe in his political report to the Eleventh Party Congress in March 1922,

Suppose we take Moscow with its 4,700 responsible Communists, and suppose we take that huge bureaucratic machine, that huge pile—who is directing whom? I doubt very much whether it can truthfully be said that the Communists are directing this pile. To tell the truth, they are not doing the directing, they are being directed.[29]

What was true of Moscow was infinitely truer of the periphery. Localism flourished, and the effectiveness of Communist controls decreased in direct relationship to the distance from the great urban centers. The Red army was far from being the monolithic machine which Trotsky sought to make it. The top command encountered the greatest difficulty in enforcing its authority on the armies in the field, and guerrilla units loosely attached to the army fought their own war in their own way. The Cheka was a law unto itself. While it served the purposes of the party leadership by striking terror into the hearts of the class enemy, it also became the refuge of all sorts of adventurers and scoundrels who used their untrammeled power to commit acts of pilfering and pillage for their own personal advantage. The people's commissariats often had tenuous connections with their subordinate units, and in many key policy areas (for example, education) the republican commissariats conducted policies of considerable diversity. Within the party itself, the problem of establishing a well-functioning apparatus was so great that the leadership did not even have an accurate count of party membership until 1922.

The Regime, the Population, and the Economy

Ultimately, victory in the Civil War depended on the development of a sense of legitimacy for the regime—or at least one of relative tolerance—among the populace, and a number of factors contributed to such a development. The Bolsheviks had, of course, come to power in November 1917 with solid popular support among the workers, and the new regime did bring important symbolic rewards to this group. The political system was officially termed a "dictatorship of the proletariat," and it was the face of the worker (together with that of the peasant), or of the hammer and sickle which symbolized them, that appeared on postage stamps, on the front pages of newspapers, on posters, and so forth. So far as could be judged in a faltering economy, the revolution had also produced a major reduction in wage inegalitarianism in the factory, while "workers' control" often meant a greater participation of the worker and the trade union in industrial decision-making.

For other groups, too, the Bolsheviks represented at least a tolerable alternative. Lenin had promised peace, and the regime had indeed quickly withdrawn from World War I; he had promised land, and, whatever the repugnance of private property to the Bolsheviks, the regime had been glad to sanction the seizure of the landlords' land.[30] The presence of foreign interventionist armies on Russian soil aroused patriotic sentiments which the Bolsheviks were able to use for their own purposes. The reactionary character of the policies espoused by the White generals had antagonized many who bore no love for the Bolsheviks but reluctantly embraced their cause because a restorationist regime appeared even more unpalatable. And, of course, the Civil War also ensured that many of the most hostile opponents of Bolshevism would not be in the country in 1921—some because they did not survive, others because they left for exile with the withdrawing Allied armies.

Perhaps even more important as a source of support, as Adam Ulam has emphasized, the Bolsheviks had a doctrine with many appeals to a country in the early stages of industrialization. For those who saw industrial development as the answer to personal dreams or to dreams of national independence and glory, Marxism included, above all, "an intense cult of technology and a conviction of the historical necessity and blessings of industrialism." While the ultimate promise of Marxism was "anarchism pure and simple . . . the most violent protest against industrialism," its immediate message was that "industrialism is necessary and must be submitted to."[31] "Communism," Lenin would say, "equals socialism plus electrification." Those who yearned for westernization and modernization thought the promise of electrification exciting enough by itself.

Indeed, even during the days of the desperate struggle for survival, the Bolsheviks seemed to demonstrate their dedication to modernity. The initial reaction of the intelligentsia to the Bolsheviks was one of great suspicion, but the regime strove to correct the situation:

> The result of [the Commissariat of Enlightenment's] first contacts with the artistic and literary world was not, in the normal sense, the establishment of an administration, but of a framework of cooperation with disparate and mutually intolerant groups. [The People's Commissar] Lunacharsky's policy was one of open-handed goodwill, subject only to the qualification that he had little to offer except employment, arbitration and small bonuses to individuals in particular need. His policy was to open channels of communication with the literary and artistic intelligentsia, to encourage equally all groups which were sympathetic or accommodating in their attitude to the Soviet government, and to outmaneuver those which showed it blatant hostility.[32]

As a result, the Civil War period was an era of considerable cultural and social experimentation. The overthrow of the old regime was accompanied by a relatively unfettered ferment of literary and artistic productivity and by a number of educational innovations, many based in one way or another on the ideas of John Dewey that were fashionable then in the progressive circles of the West. There was a new emphasis on the emancipation of women and the authority of youth. The right to divorce was instituted, and traditional moral values were frequently challenged. For many the revolt against the old order overshadowed the consolidation of the new. Amidst the grimness of the ruins of the Civil War, the rebels against the old society often whipped themselves into fits of great enthusiasm, played out roles of heroic adventures, sometimes tasted the heady wine of power, and found it good.

The basic problem for the regime was that the symbolic rewards and the promises for the future were coupled with a severe deterioration in the functioning of the economy. The Bolsheviks had promised "bread" in addition to "land" and "peace," and on that promise they were not delivering. During the first months of the revolution, Lenin tried to confine nationalization to the commanding industrial heights and to smooth the transition from the old order to the new by utilizing the managerial skills of former capitalists and bourgeois specialists. These efforts quickly revealed themselves as abortive. Capitalists and managers abandoned their plants in large numbers, and many others were driven out by workers intent on revenging past grievances.

In the first surge of revolutionary spontaneity, the working classes often assumed that the factories now belonged to them, and they sought to operate them for their own account and in their own interest. The results were usually disastrous. Lacking managerial talent and technical skill and unable to impose discipline on their own members, the factory committees frequently brought their enterprises to a standstill. Their problems were, of course, greatly accentuated by the chaos and disorganization of war and revolution. Failures of communication and transport, as well as shortages of raw materials, led to work stoppages, and industrial breakdowns were contagious and cumulative. The entire industrial life of Russia threatened to grind to a halt.

The Bolshevik leadership exerted every effort to revive production, to restore labor discipline, and to organize industry to serve military needs. A Supreme Council of the National Economy (Vesenkha or VSNKh) with local branches was established to provide the framework for central direction of the economy. On June 28, 1918, virtually every important branch of industrial life was nationalized, though Lenin still sought to preserve a distinction between those enterprises to be run by state administrators and others to continue operation under their former owners for state account. Spurred on by Lenin, the Central Council of Trade Unions issued a regulation on April 3, 1918, which empowered trade union commissions to fix productivity norms, approved the use of piece-rates and bonuses to raise the productivity of labor, and invoked the sanction of expulsion from the union for violators of labor discipline.[33] After the nationalization decree, the "workers' state," in theory at least, became the main employer. In January 1920 the Council of People's Commissars drew what it conceived to be the logical inference by introducing universal labor service and transforming military units into labor armies.[34]

As the Civil War pursued its difficult course, Lenin turned again and again to his favorite recipes for raising productive efficiency—centralized control, one-man management, and the employment of bourgeois specialists to provide technical and managerial advice. Each of these measures met strong resistance from elements in the party, but Lenin continued to urge their adoption, and his views won increasing acceptance. The Supreme Council of the National Economy gradually expanded its authority and began to master the syndicalist and localist tendencies which prevailed in industrial management. It imposed central priorities to ensure supplies for the army and closed down poorly run factories in order to concentrate production in the most efficient enterprises. At Lenin's insistence, large numbers of bourgeois specialists and technicians were incorporated into the industrial bureaucracy.

Despite Lenin's strenuous efforts to improve the administrative efficiency of the nationalized enterprises, industrial disorganization was endemic. The ravages of world war, revolution, and civil war could not be overcome by mere administrative expedients. The cities suffered from cold and hunger; the workers abandoned the factories in large numbers. Supplies were cut off; industrial production declined catastrophically. In practice, the army and the industrial labor force were supplied by a process of desperate improvisation. The output of those factories that continued to operate was reserved almost entirely for the Red army. Such food and consumer goods as remained were available, theoretically, for distribution to the town population, at fixed prices under a system of differential rationing which favored workers performing assignments of vital urgency to the war effort. In practice, shortages became so extreme as to render price and rationing controls meaningless. Money lost all value. Workers had to be paid in kind, and a rapidly expanding black market largely displaced the official channels of trade. The egalitarian aspirations of the revolution were made real by the egalitarianism of universal sacrifice.

The situation in the countryside was no better. The disorder of the urban economy made an orderly, incentive-based acquisition of food goods very difficult, and the regime was forced to rely upon a policy of compulsory requisitioning to feed the army and the cities. In short, Soviet authorities were driven to seize grain wherever they could lay hands on it. In Lenin's words, "we actually took from the peasants all the surplus grain and sometimes not only surplus grain, but part of the grain the peasant required for food, for the purpose of meeting the requirements of the army and of sustaining the workers."[35] Little distinction was made among different social strata of the peasantry in carrying out the requisition policy. Although this policy may have saved the Soviet regime from defeat, many of its consequences were less than happy. The response of the peasants to the confiscation was what might be expected. Peasants reduced their plantings to meet only their consumption needs, did their utmost to conceal their reserves from the requisitioning authorities, and occasionally responded to seizures by violent attacks on the food collectors. Thus, not only were peasants alienated by this policy but also a sharp decline in production ensued.

By the winter of 1920–1921, the Civil War had essentially ended, and perhaps for this reason the resentments of the workers and peasants about the standard of living now came to a head. The lessening of the danger of the landowners' return removed one source of restraint upon peasant action, and the end of military action meant the demobilization of the soldiers (over 2.5 million of them by early 1921)[36] and the return to the village of men who had been trained for military action and were impatient for the fruits of their fighting. The countryside witnessed a sharp growth in the number of marauding bands and a swelling tide of sporadic peasant risings, 118 in February 1921 by police count.[37]

Increasingly the workers' response to worsening conditions was to turn to strikes, demonstrations, and protest meetings. Sparked at least in part by a governmental announcement that the bread ration would be cut by a third, the workers of Moscow and Petrograd became dangerously active and militant in February. Their demands and resolutions first focused on economic grievances, but toward the end of the month they began to include political demands as well. Then in March 1921 the major naval base at Kronstadt near Petrograd, one of the earliest bastions of Bolshevik strength, revolted. The sailors called for economic reform, but political questions were at the center of their program. They had no desire to establish a constitutional democracy in which the parties of all classes would be represented, but they were equally adamant in damning the complete Bolshevik domination of the soviets. The first two points of their resolution read as follows: "1. In view of the fact that the present soviets do not express the will of the workers and peasants, immediately to hold new elections by secret ballot, with freedom to carry on agitation beforehand for all workers and peasants; 2. To give freedom of speech and press to workers and peasants, to anarchists and left socialist parties."[38]

The Bolsheviks' first response to the peasant uprisings, the urban demonstrations, and the Kronstadt revolt was suppression; their long-term response was a major change in economic policy. At the Tenth Party Congress in March 1921, Lenin announced a series of measures which collectively became known as the New Economic Policy (NEP). The most important reversal of policy was the abandonment of forced requisitions in favor of a tax in kind which left the peasants free to dispose of such surpluses as remained after the tax assessment had been met. The "peasant Brest-Litovsk," as David Riazanov called it,[39] sought to guarantee the party a new breathing space. As Lenin said at the Tenth Party Congress, "only an agreement with the peasantry can save the socialist revolution in Russia until the revolution has occurred in other countries.[40]

The tax in kind represented a determined effort to win back the favor of the peasantry. In order to persuade the peasants to part with their surpluses, incentives had to be provided in the form of increased supplies of consumer goods. This made a revival of industrial production imperative. Over the next months the regime moved to restore private trade and to permit the establishment of small private industries and industrial cooperatives, in the hope that they would most readily increase the flow of consumer goods. New enterprises were promised freedom from nationalization. Small enterprises that had been nationalized were leased to their former owners or industrial artels (producers' cooperatives) for fixed terms with the provision that rentals were to be paid in the form of a definite proportion of the output of the enterprise. The Soviet leadership sought to attract foreign capital by offering "concessions" to capitalist entrepeneurs, but the bait proved unalluring and in all but a few cases negotiations collapsed.

The so-called "commanding heights" of large-scale industry remained under state administration, though even these enterprises, organized in the form of trusts, were to be operated on commercial principles with substantial freedom to buy and sell on the open market and with the obligation to operate on a basis of profitability. In actuality, the "commanding heights" (which included all heavy industry, the transportation system, and the central banking system) did dominate the industrial scene, employing 84 percent of the industrial labor force. However, so far as the consumer was concerned, much of the tone of NEP was set by the private sector. Although small in size, the private industries constituted 88.5 percent of the total number of enterprises, and the trade network was virtually all private.[41] The symbol of the era became the so-called Nepmen who arose to carry on the functions of buying and selling, sometimes through private trading concerns of their own, sometimes concealed as cooperatives, and not infrequently as official agents of the state trading organizations themselves.

The initial recuperative effects of NEP policies fortified the position of the party leadership. With the introduction of the tax in kind (eventually replaced by a straight money tax), peasant disorders died down; and after the disastrous harvest of 1921, a steady improvement in agricultural production was evident. Inflation became an enormous problem for several years (for example, the price of the cheapest stamp rose from 35 kopecks in 1920 to 1 ruble in 1921 and 5,000 rubles in 1922), but a marked revival of light industry took place, and consumer goods became more plentiful. Although there was considerable unemployment and worker dissatisfaction, a modicum of relief was provided by unemployment benefits and the perceptible improvement in economic conditions generally.

Nevertheless, the new Soviet state faced a dilemma for which there was no easy resolution. However firmly it controlled the instruments of state power, it remained a "dictatorship of the proletariat" in an overwhelmingly peasant country. It might conceivably have transformed itself into a peasant government by shaping its policy around peasant demands, but the socialist and industrial orientation of communism well-nigh precluded such a transformation. Indeed, both the logic of long-term survival and the dogmas of ideology dictated a program of industrialization, and, given the resistance to foreign investment, the most obvious source of investment capital seemed— particularly to a Marxist—to be the peasantry. It was not until after Lenin's death that the party leadership faced up to this dilemma.

Party Conflicts in the Civil War

Thus far the Bolsheviks have been treated largely as a single unit—a treatment which corresponds to popular stereotypes of them. We have become accustomed to a Communist party in the Soviet Union which strives to present a monolithic face to the Soviet people and to the outside world— a party which elects its leaders unanimously and which brooks not the slightest open criticism of them in print, a party whose members in the national and local legislatures and in the party congresses vote unanimously for all laws and decisions proposed by the leadership. Yet, we should not think that a one-party system necessarily must have these characteristics. Theoretically at least, one could imagine a one-party system in which quite open factionalism and criticism of the leader and his policies were permitted.

Indeed, in the early years, political life within the Communist party was quite unlike that which has prevailed since the 1920s. Despite all of Lenin's talk in *What Is To Be Done?* about a disciplined action party whose members already agreed on fundamentals, the Bolshevik party contained many types of members at the time of the revolution. For some, the authoritarian bent of the party and the relative rigidity of Bolshevik ideology surely was psychologically attractive. However, the Bolshevik party also was attractive to undisciplined anarchists, syndicalists, and radicals of all types simply because it was the most left-wing of the major parties. Moreover, as the Mensheviks moved in a less revolutionary direction in 1917, the Bolshevik party remained the only home for an "orthodox Marxist," and, as the only party to favor withdrawal from the war, it must also have picked up some members for whom the peace issue was most salient. And, of course, once the party became the country's ruling party, it drew many persons who simply wanted to partici-pate in political life—or who hoped for material rewards. The rise in party membership to 576,000 persons in early 1921 undoubtedly reflected more than appeals of ideology.[42]

In addition to divisions stemming from the diversity of values among those who joined the party, the jobs that Communists were assigned pro-duced further diversity. The party leaders began to notice—often to their surprise and consternation—that the members had begun to acquire separate occupational identities and policy views. In the words of Bukharin in 1921,

> The party as it existed earlier when there was a single psychology and a single ideology has split into a variety of separate columns representing somewhat different outlooks. Military workers, trade union workers, and party workers proper have organized together among themselves. This process of specialization has reached extraordinary proportions . . . This specialization has split our party, which was earlier psychologically united in a single whole, into a series of groupings with different psychological tendencies.[43]

As Jeremy Azrael has noted, the situation with respect to the industrial managers was typical: "The red directors did not cease to be committed Com-munist [but] they did develop a policy orientation that differed markedly from that of other party members who were caught up in the 'logic' of other vocations. The resultant disagreements were often quite severe."[44]

As a result, the middle level politics of the Communist system came to be featured by the type of bureaucratic and institutional conflict familiar to observers of the western political scene. For example, in the educational sphere a wide range of persons debated educational theory. Such institu-tions as the Russian and the Ukrainian Commissariats of Enlightenment (which supervised education) came to adopt differing positions on key issues, as did, indeed, the Moscow and Petrograd offices within the Russian com-missariat itself. The Komsomol (the youth organization) developed its own perspective as well. When other interests—notably the trade unions and the economic managers—were affected by educational policy in areas such as technical-vocational education for teenagers and young adults, they too became involved—and in ways quite predictable from a knowledge of their institutional interests.[45]

The political struggles in such realms as education generally took place below the level of the Central Committee and the Politburo, but the Bolshevik leadership was no more monolithic than the bureaucratic units or the rank-and-file members. After the first conflict over a coalition government, the most dramatic and drastic division within the top Bolshevik leaders arose a few months after the revolution on the question of war or peace. Soon after the seizure of power, an armistice had quickly been arranged with the Germans, but the Germans demanded that a formal treaty be signed, with lines of demarcation leaving them in control of most of the western borderlines of the old Russian empire.

The Bolsheviks had to decide whether to accept the harsh German conditions, and the leadership broke into three distinct groups. Lenin argued for the signing of a separate peace, regardless of the terms. Believing that the Russian army was in no condition to fight, he contended that it would be "adventurous" to base policy on the assumption that the revolution "will happen in the next half year (or some such short time)." On the other hand, the left within the party, led by Bukharin, strongly felt that a "shameful" peace treaty (particularly one formally acknowledging German subjugation of the peoples of eastern Europe) would hopelessly compromise the cause of revolution. They thought that the Bolshevik regime could not survive without revolution abroad in any case, and they called for "revolutionary war"— "a holy war against militarism and imperialism"—one in which German soldiers would be loathe to fire their weapons against fellow workers and would be stimulated into revolution. Trotsky advocated a middle position of "No war, no peace." He doubted whether the army could fight a revolutionary war, but he agreed with the left about the peace treaty. If the Russians simply declared an end to the war, Trotsky argued, there would be peace without a humiliating treaty, for the Germans would be afraid to renew their attack, lest their own soldiers and workers revolt.[46]

When the debate about peace came to a head in late January, the atmosphere was highly emotional. One left-wing member of the Central Committee, Karl Radek, went so far as to tell Lenin, "If there were five hundred courageous men in Petrograd, we would put you in prison."[47] At a major meeting on January 21 attended by Central Committee members and another forty-five party leaders, Lenin's position received only 15 votes, as against 16 for Trotsky's, and 32 for Bukharin's. In desperation, Lenin struck a compromise with Trotsky, agreeing to give "No war, no peace" a trial, and on

January 22 this formula was approved by the Central Committee by a narrow 9 to 7 vote.

After a few more weeks of negotiations with the Germans, the Bolsheviks did, in fact, proclaim the war at an end, and they left the peace talks. Unfortunately, the Germans were not deterred, and on February 18 they launched their attack. The Russian troops put up no resistance,[48] but even the success of the German attack did not end the division within the party leadership. Although Trotsky reluctantly changed his vote to give Lenin a 6 to 5 victory on the evening of February 18, the Germans now responded with tougher conditions: the Soviet government was to withdraw its army from the Ukraine, Livonia, and Estonia. Despite the seemingly inexorable German advance, the Central Committee split once more. Only on February 23, when Lenin threatened to resign, did Trotsky, while still objecting, agree to abstain. Lenin's motion carried 7 to 4, with 4 abstentions. That evening the Central Executive Committee approved the terms, this time 116 to 84, but once more the number of Bolshevik abstentions exceeded the margin of victory. Even with Lenin issuing the bluntest ultimatum on the most important issue of the day, he could not obtain a majority in the top organs of the party that he had created.

No sanctions were invoked against Lenin's opponents on the Brest-Litovsk question, and both Bukharin and Trotsky remained among the most important party leaders. The Leninists did seek to reduce the strength of the left Communists by working against them in the local organizations, and Lenin's personal authority carried even more weight for the rank-and-file than it had for the leadership.[49] In addition, when the Civil War broke out in earnest in May 1918, the various party factions themselves patched over many of their differences to unite in face of the common danger.

Nevertheless, as the military fortunes of the Bolsheviks improved, high-level opposition to Lenin's policies emerged once more. The most persistent of these opponents—again including many of the same left Communists who had opposed Lenin over the Brest-Litovsk peace—repeatedly objected to his efforts to re-establish both central political control and authority relations in institutions such as the army and the factory. They harked back to the utopian, libertarian, democratic elements of the ideology, and would gladly have accepted Robert Daniels' characterization of them as the "conscience of the revolution."[50]

While the same people generally were involved in charging excessive centralization and bureaucratic control in different contexts, Lenin's opponents on a number of issues came to be labeled separate "oppositions." The first, which emerged at the Eighth Party Congress in March 1919, was called the Military Opposition. It was sharply critical of the policy of employing former tsarist officers as military specialists in the Red army and of restoring the discipline and symbols of authority (for example, the salute, the obligatory use of the "Comrade commander" form of address, separate living quarters and orderlies for officers) that the socialists had been attacking since Order Number One of the Soviet in 1917.[51] The latter policy was all the more galling because the officers—the specialists—were generally thought to be of bourgeois class origin in contrast to the worker and peasant soldiers they commanded.

In a test vote at the party congress, the resolution of the Military Opposition mobilized 95 votes to 174 for the majority. Again, no effort was made to invoke party discipline against the opponents. The issue was submitted to a conciliation commission on which both majority and minority were represented, and the resulting resolution, which made some slight concessions to the opposition, was unanimously affirmed by the congress.[52]

At the Ninth Party Congress in March 1920, the major opposition, called the Democratic Centralists, focused its attack on concentration of power in the center. Its leader described the Leninist Central Committee as a "small handful of party oligarchs," and other members complained that the Central Committee "was banning those who hold deviant views." Several were quite specific, speaking of the dispatching of oppositionists to distant places as a "system of exile." (The Ukraine was mentioned as one place to which "those comrades who for any reason are not agreeable to Moscow are exiled.")[53]

Lenin's reply was evasive. It was the task of the Central Committee to distribute the forces of the party. "Of course," he conceded, "if the Central Committee had banned the opposition before the congress, this would be an inadmissible matter." "Perhaps," he admitted, "mistakes have been made." But, he concluded, "whatever Central Committee you choose to elect, it cannot desist from distributing forces."[54] At the Ninth Congress, Lenin was apparently still on the defensive against charges of repressing the opposition. The disciplining of oppositionists took the relatively mild form of transfer of work assignments from the center to the periphery, and even such actions were not openly acknowledged.

During the summer and autumn of 1920, it was the issue of democracy in the industrial realm that came to the fore and that became the center of the so-called Workers' Opposition. The Workers' Opposition, under the leadership of Madame Kollontai and Alexander Shliapnikov, the first People's Commissar for Labor, called for collegial organs rather than one-man management in industrial administration, for increased reliance on the proletariat in decision-making, and, in particular, for autonomy of the trade unions and a dominant role for them in industrial administration. The Workers' Opposition went so far as to demand that the Communists in the trade unions should be bound by the directives of higher trade union bodies rather than those of the party organs in the territories in which they were located. As had been the case in the debates over the military, the fact that many of the administrators were "bourgeois specialists" added special emotional force to the Workers' Opposition program. Indeed, the opposition did gather considerable rank-and-file support, especially in the trade unions, but it found itself greatly handicapped in its bid for power by its failure to attract any of the first-rank leaders of the party.

In the trade union discussion which raged in the party in 1920 and 1921, three platforms vied for support. At the opposite extreme from the Workers' Opposition's conception of semiautonomous trade unions which controlled and managed industry as representatives of the workers was Trotsky's proposal that labor be militarized and that the trade unions be united with the state in fulfilling the tasks of plan fulfillment. Trotsky believed that the answer to the growing economic difficulties lay in the same type of discipline and organization that he had used in building the Red army:

> If we seriously speak of planned economy, which is to acquire its unity of purpose from the center, when labor forces are assigned in accordance with the economic plan at the given stage of development, the working masses cannot be wandering all over Russia. They must be thrown here and there, appointed, commanded, just like soldiers.
>
> The young socialist state requires trade unions, not for a struggle for better conditions of labor . . . but to organize the working class for the ends of production, to educate, discipline . . . to exercise authority hand in hand with the state in order to lead the workers into the framework of a single economic plan.[55]

Once again the Central Committee was deeply divided, and Lenin moved to an intermediate position. (Earlier he had shown sympathy for Trotsky's ideas on the subject.) He and nine other members of the Central Committee offered an intermediate program designed to preserve a degree of autonomy for the trade unions while denying them direct responsibility for economic administration and emphasizing their educational role. Lenin explicitly rejected Trotsky's contention that the workers did not need trade unions to protect them from their own state: "Our present state is such that the entire organized proletariat must defend itself; we must use these workers' organizations for the defense of the workers from their state and for the defense by the workers of our state."[56] In the crucial vote at the Tenth Party Congress in March 1921, Lenin's platform carried by an overwhelming majority. Although the Workers' Opposition was able to mobilize but 18 votes, compared with 50 for Trotsky's motion and 336 for Lenin's,[57] the vote was far from reflecting the real strength of the Workers' Opposition among the party rank and file. Lenin was genuinely alarmed by the dissension, and his anxiety was deepened by the Kronstadt mutiny which broke out on the eve of the congress.

This time Lenin was ready to invoke stern measures. In a pamphlet called *The Party Crisis,* he first rebuked Trotsky for factionalism, and then turned his main fire against the Workers' Opposition. He denounced its program as out of bounds: "Of course it is permissible (especially before a congress) for different groups to organize in blocs (and so is it to canvass for votes). But it must be done within the limits of communism (and not syndicalism.)"[58]

In discussions at the Tenth Congress, the Workers' Opposition showed no disposition to give ground. In the eyes of Shliapnikov, the platforms of Lenin and Trotsky were equally reprehensible; both were "economic militarizers." In the event of defeat at the congress, the leaders of the Workers' Opposition proclaimed that there would be no retreat; they would remain within the party, fight for their point of view, "save the party and correct its line." To Lenin this was the last straw.

> Comrades, it is necessary to talk not only about words, but about their content as well. You cannot trick us with words like "freedom of criticism." When we said that the party showed symptoms of disease, we meant that this deserves threefold attention; undoubtedly, the disease is there: Help us to heal this disease. Tell us how you can heal it. We have spent a good deal of time in discussion, and I must say that now it is a great deal better to "discuss with rifles" than with the theses offered by the opposition. We need no opposition now, comrades, it is not the time! Either on this side, or on that, with a rifle, but not with the opposition . . . And I think that the party congress will have to draw that conclusion too . . . that the time has come to put an end to the opposition, to put a lid on it; we have had enough of opposition now![59]

The outburst was a prelude to more drastic action. The resolution which the Tenth Party Congress adopted "On the Syndicalist and Anarchist Deviation in Our Party" condemned the ideas of the Workers' Opposition as "a complete rupture with Marxism and communism," called for "an unswerving and systematic ideological struggle against these ideas," and declared "the propagating of these ideas as being incompatible with membership in the Russian Communist party."[60] Lenin, however, still expressed a hope that the oppositionists could be salvaged for the party. "A deviation," he explained to the congress, "is not a fully formed movement. A deviation is something that can be corrected. People have strayed a little from the path or are beginning to stray, but it is still possible to correct it."[61] When members of the Workers' Opposition who had been re-elected to the Central Committee offered to resign, the resignations were not accepted. Instead, they were called upon to submit to party discipline.

The Antifactionalism Rule

Nonetheless, the Tenth Party Congress marks an important dividing point in party policy toward opposition, for the Resolution on the Workers' Opposition was supplemented by an even more important Resolution on Party Unity. "All class-conscious workers must clearly realize," said the Resolution on Party Unity, "the perniciousness and impermissibility of factionalism of any kind, for no matter how the representatives of individual groups may desire to safeguard party unity, in practice factionalism inevitably leads to the weakening of team work and to intensified and repeated attempts by the enemies of the party, who have fastened themselves onto it because it is the governing party, to widen the cleavage and to use it for counterrevolutionary purposes." The resolution continued:

> In the practical struggle against factionalism, every organization of the party must take strict measures to prevent any factional actions whatsoever . . . Every analysis of the general line of the party, estimate of its practical experience, verification of the fulfillment of its decisions, study of methods of rectifying errors, etc., must under no circumstances be submitted for preliminary discussion to groups formed on the basis of any sort of "platform" etc., but must be exclusively submitted for discussion directly to all members of the party . . .
>
> The congress therefore hereby declares dissolved and orders the immediate dissolution of all groups without exception that have been formed on the basis of one platform or another (such as the Workers' Opposition group, the Democratic Centralism group, and so on). Nonobservance of this decision of the congress shall entail absolute and immediate expulsion from the party.[62]

These statements were followed by the famous Point Seven which remained unpublished until, on the motion of Stalin, it was released for general circulation at the Thirteenth Party Conference in January 1924, just before Lenin's death. The Tenth Congress' decision to keep Point Seven secret revealed an understandable reluctance to document the growing power of the central party machine. Point Seven provided:

In order to ensure strict discipline within the party and in all Soviet work and to secure the maximum unanimity in removing all factionalism, the congress authorizes the Central Committee, in cases of breach of discipline or of a revival or toleration of factionalism, to apply all party penalties, including expulsion, and in regard to members of the Central Committee to reduce them to the status of alternate members and even, as an extreme measure, to expel them from the party. A necessary condition for the application of such an extreme measure to members of the Central Committee, alternate members of the Central Committee, and members of the Control Commission is the convocation of a plenary session of the Central Committee, to which all alternate members of the Central Committee and all members of the Control Commission shall be invited. If such a general assembly of the most responsible leaders of the party, by a two-thirds majority deems it necessary to reduce a member of the Central Committee to the status of alternate member, or to expel him from the party, the measure shall be put into effect immediately.[63]

Despite the ban on factionalism, leaders of the Workers' Opposition continued their agitation against the line of the Central Committee. On August 9, 1921, Lenin, in accordance with Point Seven, convened a meeting of the plenary session of the Central Committee to consider the expulsion of Shliapnikov from the committee and the party. The motion failed by one vote to secure the necessary two-thirds majority, and Shliapnikov escaped with a stern censure and a threat that the matter would be reopened if he continued to violate party discipline.[64]

Just before the Eleventh Party Congress met in March 1922, the opposition made a desperate and pathetic bid for the support of foreign Communists by filing an appeal with the Enlarged Plenary Session of the Executive Committee of the Communist International (the Comintern). "The Declaration of the Twenty-Two," as this document came to be known, echoes the familiar grievances of the Workers' Opposition. It was submitted without the consent of the Party Central Committee or the Russian delegation to the Communist International. The Comintern, not unexpectedly, replied with a resolution affirming its faith in the Russian party leadership. The problem of dealing with the dissenters was shifted back to the Eleventh Congress of the Party, which appointed a commission to recommend the appropriate penalties.

At the Eleventh Congress, a rapidly thinning but still determined band of Workers' Oppositionists returned to the fray. Shliapnikov complained that "since the time the Tenth Party Congress sent me into the Central Committee as whip of the Workers' Opposition, that committee has often sat in judgment upon me." He declared that "Comrade Frunze brought up the possibility of convincing me with machine guns that he was in the right,"[65] and he designated both Lenin and Frunze as machine gunners. Madame Kollontai accused the party leadership of suppressing thought and of inadequate attention to the welfare of the workers.[66]

Lenin's reply was to insist on the continued necessity of iron party discipline. The NEP, he pointed out, was a period of retreat:

> During a retreat . . . discipline must be more conscious and a hundred times more necessary . . . Under such circumstances a few panic-stricken voices are enough to cause a stampede. The danger is enormous. When a real army is in retreat, machine guns are set up, and when an orderly retreat degenerates into a disorderly one, the command is given, "Fire!" And quite right.
>
> If, during an incredibly difficult retreat, when everything depends on preserving good order, anyone spreads panic—even for the best of motives —the slightest breach of discipline must be punished severely, sternly, ruthlessly.[67]

The veiled threat of "machine guns" was explained away by Lenin in his concluding speech as directed against Mensheviks, SR's, and their ilk; oppositionists, he made clear, would be dealt with through "party measures of discipline."[68] The commission appointed to adjudicate the affair of the Twenty-Two brought in a recommendation that Kollontai, Shliapnikov, and three others be expelled from the party. The congress concurred in the expulsion of two of the relative newcomers to the party, but it could not steel itself to expel such Old Bolsheviks as Kollontai and Shliapnikov. It contented itself with a stern warning to them that the Central Committee would resort to expulsion in the event of further antiparty activities on their part.[69]

Lenin and the Nature of the Postrevolutionary Party and Society

The Eleventh Congress was the last in which Lenin participated. Hit by a stroke in May 1922, partially paralyzed by a second one in December 1922, effectively removed from public life by a third in March 1923, Lenin died on January 21, 1924. By the time of his death, he had had the opportunity to conduct a historic revolution, to lead the victorious side in a civil war, and to consolidate the position of a new regime on what seemed to be a solid footing. He had not, however, had any real opportunity to demonstrate what he would do with power once he could seriously turn his attention to the construction of the type of society he desired.

For this reason, one of the great unanswered questions of Soviet studies must be the relationship of Lenin and Leninism to the type of party and society which developed after his death. Were the great industrialization and collectivization drives of 1928–1929—and the terror and purges of later years as well—the logical culmination of Lenin's basic line of thought and the system which he created? Or did Stalin represent a fundamental break with the past? These, like all other "what if" questions on important subjects, have provoked a lively debate, with the entire range of possible answers receiving support.

In the past, probably the dominant interpretation of the relationship of Stalin to Leninism has been that expressed in (and, of course, to some extent created by) the first two editions of this book. This interpretation did not hold Lenin responsible for the worst excesses of the Stalin era: "[Lenin's] intolerance of opposition in principle was tempered by a practical realization that differences of view within the Party were unavoidable and that the function of a Party leader was to persuade first and to invoke sanctions only as a last resort. Thus he cajoled, argued, and even pleaded with his Party opponents before he confronted the necessity of declaring open war on them. Despite violent threats and tirades, the most dramatic penalty which he imposed on dissenters was expulsion from the Party, and even this penalty was rarely utilized against Party members of any prominence who had rendered distinguished services in the past. If on occasion Lenin seemed to equate dissent with treason, he still shrank from drawing the practical consequences, at least so far as intra-Party struggles were concerned."

Although the more radical "opposition's" were subject to increasing repression, the reader of the first two editions was reminded that "Party leadership was still visualized as collegial. Lenin, to be sure, was recognized as *primus inter pares* within the Politburo, but his authority derived from his stature rather than his position in the Bolshevik hierarchy. Though the climate of decision was one of tightening discipline, discussion and debate were still active and vigorous in the leading Party organs, and the tradition of collective consultation and leadership was maintained."

Yet in this view, Lenin was basically quite authoritarian in his approach and in his theories. "As long as he remained active, his influence was clearly exerted in the strengthening of Party discipline and consolidation of the hold of the central machinery on the Party. The Party faction was anathema to him, and in the Resolution on Party Unity, which he had drafted for the Tenth Congress, he did everything in his power to destroy the embryonic development of a two- or multi-faction system within the framework of the single-party dictatorship. He could find a place for criticism in his organizational scheme only if it presented no political challenge to the Party leadership and if it was 'practical' criticism which served to improve the efficiency of the Party machine . . . The body of precedents which he created steered a course toward the outlawing of all opposition. However much practice meliorated theory with Lenin, he was responsible for the germinating conception on the basis of which all intra-Party opposition came to be extinguished."[70]

The viewpoint expressed in these lines is still quite widespread, and some scholars seem willing to go further. Thus, one biographer of Lenin concludes, "As with the cult of personality, so with mass terror and compulsion, [Lenin's] own psychology made inevitable the future and more brutal development under his successor. That the Communist should consider the human cost of social engineering was for Lenin almost unthinkable." In this view, "had he not been stricken in 1922, it is not improbable that the NEP would have ended sooner than it did."[71] Another scholar has suggested that while Stalin "did not possess . . . the ear for the music of humaneness which Lenin had retained, however unwillingly," he "was indeed the perfect Leninist:"

> Two traits stood out in the history of Russian communism as shaped by Lenin. The first was the boundless will to advance the country (not as an accidental base of world revolution but as Russia—Holy Russia) to a position of global pre-eminence . . . The other trait was a fanatical reliance on organization . . . He who could give vigor to these Leninist traits and advance them with the same monstrous impatience which Lenin had shown almost to the end of his career would be his true heir . . . [Stalin's] rise to power . . . [marked] the high summer of fruition for the most dynamic and emotion-charged element of Bolshevism.[72]

Since the mid-1960s, however, the prevailing interpretation of Lenin has been vigorously attacked from the opposite point of view as well. For example, Moshe Lewin, the foremost western specialist on party policy on the Soviet countryside in the 1920s and the 1930s, has contended that Lenin was relatively nonauthoritarian in character, even in his early years:

> Leninist doctrine did not originally envisage a monolithic state, nor even a strictly monolithic party; the dictatorship of the Party over the proletariat was never part of Lenin's plans, it was the completely unforeseen culmination of a series of unforeseen circumstances . . . Once peace had been reestablished with internal victory, Lenin set about underpinning political power by the acquisition of an economic infrastructure and the raising of the cultural level of the cadres and of the people—beginning

with the problem of illiteracy. Lenin knew that in the situation in which his regime found itself, the political preceded the economic, but . . . he was not resigned to using political power as sole lever for too long a period.[73]

The major thrust of this argument, however, rests upon an analysis of five articles which Lenin dictated in January and February 1923 between his second and third strokes: "Pages from a Diary," "On Cooperation," "Our Revolution," "How We Should Reorganize Rabkrin," and "Better Fewer, and Better." Stephen Cohen in his biography of Bukharin sees these articles taken together as representing "a remarkable about-face . . . a profound change in Lenin's thinking," while Moshe Lewin terms them "Lenin's second *What Is To Be Done?*"[74]

In this view, Lenin had at the end concluded that NEP was not merely a temporary retreat, but could be a long-term evolutionary path to full socialist and Communist development. "Lenin's second *What Is To Be Done* pleads for caution, moderation, and patience. Lenin has not abandoned the use of constraint in the defense of the regime, but for purposes of construction all haste is forbidden."[75] To quote Lenin,

> We are forced to admit a radical change in our entire view of socialism. This radical change consists of the fact that earlier we placed, and had to place, the main emphasis on the political struggle, on revolution, on conquering power, etc. Now the main emphasis is being changed to such an extent that it is being shifted to peaceful organizational "cultural" work.[76]

Lewin in particular suggests that Lenin was thinking not simply about gradualism in any socialist transformation of the countryside, but also about political moderation as well. "The use of constraint—let alone terror—is ostensibly excluded in establishing the foundations of a new society . . . Lenin no longer described force as the 'midwife of a new society.' " Lewin concludes that "it is reasonable to believe . . . that if Lenin had not been finally incapacitated in March, 'the final structure of the Soviet Union would have been quite different from that which Stalin ultimately gave it.' A similar hypothesis may be offered concerning the whole structure of the Soviet regime."[77]

What is to be said about this conflict in analysis? Ultimately, of course, we cannot know, and the surest conclusion is that voiced in 1954 by E. H. Carr:

> While Lenin had appeared in 1922 to voice the demand for a resumption of the march towards socialism, his last injunction was to keep the link with the peasantry in being at all costs. So long as the compromise

held, all was well. But, in any crisis which made the existing compromise unavoidable without further concessions to one side or the other, any course of action could be supported by appropriate quotations from the fountain-head.[78]

Nevertheless, if we are to engage in speculation—and the temptation is always overwhelming—then the basic conclusion of the third edition of this book on this point will not differ greatly from that of earlier editions. The continuing debate within the leadership and even within the party press at the end of Lenin's life, as well as Lenin's continuing reluctance to deal harshly with party dissidents, is a fact, but it must be balanced against the trend in policy toward opposition. It is extremely difficult to imagine that Lenin would have followed Stalin's policy of mass executions, but the imminent debates on the pattern of industrialization provided ample opportunity for major disagreements within the party and the party leadership. It is easy to imagine that Lenin would have characterized persistent opponents on these questions as "oppositions," as "factions," and that he would have dealt with them as he did with the Workers' Opposition.

It is also quite possible that Lenin would have felt compelled to take strong action against the well-to-do peasants if he were faced with the same dilemmas, the same posing of the question, with which his successors had to grapple shortly after his death. In the abstract, NEP could be seen as a natural, long-term road to socialism, but in the short-run, it led not to the disappearance of classes in the countryside, but to a strengthening of the position of the efficient (and, therefore, relatively better-off) peasant vis-à-vis the inefficient (and, therefore, poorer) one. In 1923, Lenin wrote about the peasantry in general, but as the class consequences of policy became clearer, he might have reacted more negatively—as, indeed, did his widow. Moreover, in his last articles Lenin also showed much concern about the international position of the Soviet Union, and, as we shall see, such a concern was to be a powerful justification for drastic rates of industrialization.

The basic doubt that arises about Lenin's last five articles concerns their timing. Lenin's most democratic and tolerant statements emanated from periods when he was essentially incapacitated (for example, *State and Revolution* when he had to hide from the police in 1917 and the articles written in 1923 when he was bedridden).[79] When he was active, Lenin's concern was the policy outcome, and even when he was on his death-bed, it was to Trotsky —the strongest advocate of industrialization and planning—that he turned for assistance in getting his ideas enacted.

The unanswerable question about the course of Soviet history had Lenin lived is not, however, the only one to ask. For our purposes the more important question is the present and future course of Soviet history and the relationship of the Leninist heritage to them. From this perspective it is, of course, important that Stalin did draw upon certain strains in Lenin's thought, for this meant that institutions were developed over the years that acquired strong vested interests in these strains. If we talk of interest groups in the Soviet system, let us not forget that political action can create such groups as well as reflect their views and that it is through such an "institutionalization" of policy that the evil men do (and perhaps even the good) lives after them.

Yet, if the contemporary impact of Leninism is to be fully appreciated, the newer critics are surely right in emphasizing the ambiguities in Lenin's views. Present-day Soviet citizens who are concerned about the direction of the development of Soviet society and who seek guidance from Lenin's vision of the future (or who simply seek legitimization for their policy suggestions) will find themes in State and Revolution and in Lenin's "last testament" that are quite at odds with the actual course of Soviet history in the past. Indeed, those who since Stalin's death have successfully been pushing some democratization and liberalization in society, as well as a more egalitarian distribution of income, may already have been drawing upon some of these themes.

What is particularly striking about Lenin's doctrine from the point of view of the contemporary Soviet scene is the extent to which his justifications for repression were time-limited. Lenin was profoundly pessimistic about "the present ordinary run of people" and about the level of their awareness of their own long-term interests, and he showed great concern about the stability of the new system. Both of these attitudes were a significant part of the motivation for the type of political system that he developed. And, of course, it should not be forgotten that the stability of the regime was, in fact, in question during Lenin's lifetime and that the population to which he was referring was scarcely fifty years from serfdom and had a literacy rate of under 50 percent.

Much has changed since Lenin's death. The Soviet Union is one of the two great superpowers instead of a country whose performance in the Russo-Japanese War and World War I was so pathetic. The educational level of the Soviet population—and the degree to which that population has become accustomed to industrial society—has increased substantially. The industrial base (a matter of great import, given the frame of mind at the time) has to a considerable extent been constructed.

In these circumstances it would be surprising if the following argument were not heard: Lenin was right about the need for political repression in the conditions of his time. Now, however, the "consciousness" of the worker has been raised in a major way; any popular preference for immediate economic gains is not as historically anachronistic at a higher stage of industrial development; the party is no longer in a state of retreat in which "a few panic-stricken voices are enough to cause a stampede." The time has come to remember Lenin's words: "Of course it is permissible (especially before a congress) for different groups to organize in blocs (and so is it to canvass for votes). But it must be done within the limits of communism (and not syndicalism.)"

In short, if we accept Karl Mannheim's distinction between ideology (a set of ideas that buttresses the status quo) and utopia (a set of ideas that undercuts it),[80] it is vital to remember that Leninism contains elements that can serve both ideological and utopian functions at the present time and in the future. Soviet political development in the coming years is not likely to revolve around a struggle between the proponents and opponents of Lenin's views. Rather, the central protagonists will all be supporters of Lenin, and the key question will be—Which Lenin is most relevant for the late 1970s and 1980s?

4 | The Choices and Struggles of the 1920s

THE 1920s were a watershed in the history of the Soviet Union. Lenin by necessity was occupied with the immediate concerns of survival, but his successors had to decide the fundamental questions of the structure of the new society. Were the policies of NEP to be a rather short "temporary retreat" as Lenin originally stated, or were they to constitute the defining feature of society for some time to come, as Lenin seemed to suggest in his last articles? Was the antifactionalism rule merely to be a temporary response to the emergencies of the early years, or was it a signal that the democratic elements in democratic centralism were to be continually reduced over the years?

The basic answers to these questions were furnished in two interrelated dramas that were played out in the mid and late 1920s. One of these dramas was a free-ranging controversy on both NEP and party structure which raged within the party and even within the printed media. The other—more subtle, but perhaps more crucial—was the struggle to succeed Lenin as the leader of the party and the country. The policy debate and the struggle for power were closely intertwined, but whether the outcome of the debate was determined by the outcome of the struggle for power or vice versa is a question that scholars still debate.

Actors in the Struggle for Power

By the mid-1920s those who entered the Communist party before the revolution were sometimes called the "Old Bolsheviks." Yet, as is typical in revolutionary movements, the leaders of the Bolshevik party were quite young in comparison with the leaders of more established nations. When he

110

suffered his first stroke in 1922, Lenin was referred to as "the old man," but he was then only fifty-two years old. The average age of the other twenty-six voting members of the Central Committee elected at the Eleventh Party Congress in April 1922 was thirty-eight, while that of the dozen most important supporters of Stalin in his rise to power was thirty-three at that time.[1] The signers of the Declaration of the Forty-Six (generally considered the core of Trotsky's support) were an average of thirty-five years in age.[2]

With one exception, the members of the Politburo who were most deeply involved in the struggle for power—Nikolai I. Bukharin, Lev B. Kamenev, Aleksei I. Rykov, Joseph V. Stalin, Mikhail P. Tomsky, Lev (Leon) Trotsky, and Grigorii E. Zinoviev—were of a somewhat different "generation" than their supporters. Bukharin was but thirty-four in 1922, but the other six were all born between 1879 and 1883 and hence were five to nine years older. Small though the gap in age was, it meant the difference between being a teenager or an experienced revolutionary at the time of the 1905 revolution.

Among the contenders for power, the most prominent and flamboyant was Leon Trotsky. Trotsky had been a member of Lenin's original *Iskra* group, but he broke with Lenin soon after the Second Party Congress and played an independent role in émigré Russian revolutionary politics for nearly fifteen years. In the summer of 1917, Trotsky wholeheartedly joined the Bolsheviks and became Lenin's intimate associate and supporter. When the party leader was forced into hiding, it fell to Trotsky to function as a major organizer of the revolution in Petrograd. After the revolution he was appointed the first People's Commissar for Foreign Affairs and then, after the Treaty of Brest-Litovsk, the People's Commissar for War. In the latter capacity, he was instrumental in transforming the Red army into an effective fighting unit. Moreover, he repeatedly was at the center of the major political disputes of the Lenin period.

In a secret evaluation of the major Politburo figures made while he was gravely ill, Lenin spoke of Trotsky's "exceptional abilities," adding that "personally he is perhaps the most able man in the present central committee."[3] Trotsky's eloquence in both spoken and written communication was even less in doubt, and he entered the leadership struggle with the record of having been both Lenin's right-hand man in leading the revolution and the organizer of the victorious army in the Civil War. Moreover, he had been the man to whom Lenin had turned in his last days when he sought an ally in imposing his will on events.

Nevertheless, Trotsky had major weaknesses as a prospective leader. First, of course, his late entry into the party, his early vitriolic exchanges with Lenin, and his later conflicts with the Soviet leader provided an enemy with extremely convenient weapons in any future polemical exchange. Second, he was a Jew—a point whose significance is sometimes not emphasized by present-day scholars, but which was keenly felt at the time and which was to become an even larger handicap when hundreds of thousands of workers were enrolled in the party soon after Lenin's death.[4] Indeed, Trotsky was a Jew who "was the most western and least specifically Russian" of all the party leaders—a man who "showed particular zest in dwelling on the nullity of the Russian contribution to civilization."[5] Third, the fact that he expressed this latter attitude was perhaps symptomatic of a further and even greater problem: a real lack of political sensitivity. Trotsky had taken strong and antagonizing positions on many issues (for example, vis-à-vis the trade unions and the workers in the 1920 debates), and he had made many enemies. At the time, analogies often were drawn between the French and Russian revolutions, and even the Bolsheviks sometimes worried about the possibility of Bonapartism or a conservative Thermidor. With his forceful personality and his connection with the army, Trotsky was the easiest to picture as a potential Bolshevik Napoleon.

A second major contender for the post-Lenin leadership, Joseph Stalin, is particularly difficult to discuss, for judgments about the Stalin of 1922 were quickly colored by knowledge of his later career. In addition, Stalin was the least accessible of the major party leaders to outsiders. For example, he never gave an interview to a foreign newsman before Lenin's death.[6]

Evaluations of the Stalin of the Lenin period are quite varied. By many criteria—heroic revolutionary past, oral eloquence, theoretical contributions in Marxism—Stalin was the "least illustrious" of the major Politburo members, and he often has been depicted in that fashion in the West.[7] In many ways the impression that his early career makes upon the westerner is summarized in a much-quoted statement by Nikolai Sukhanov, one of the best participant-reporters of the Bolshevik revolution: Stalin "produced—and not only on me—the impression of a gray blur, looming up now and then dimly and not leaving any trace. There is really nothing more to be said about him."[8] This image was not limited to non-Communists. At the Twelfth Party Congress in 1923, groups throughout the country sent greetings to the congress. "In almost every message tributes were paid to Lenin and Trotsky. Only now and then did the greetings refer to Zinoviev and Kamenev, and Stalin's name was hardly mentioned."[9]

Yet, the fact remains that, as Sukhanov stated in the sentence immediately before the famous one cited above, Stalin was "one of the most central figures of the Bolshevik Party."[10] In April 1917, he was one of nine persons elected a voting member of the Central Committee, and immediately after the revolution, he was one of four Central Committee members (in practice, one of three together with Lenin and Trotsky) who were made responsible for deciding urgent questions that could not wait for Central Committee meetings. In 1919 he was one of five men named a voting member of the new Politburo, and then Lenin called him and Trotsky "the two outstanding leaders of the present central committee" in his last evaluation of his subordinates, a document traditionally called his testament.[11] What the inconsistencies between this record and Stalin's reputation may demonstrate is that, again to quote from Sukhanov, "'influence' in these exalted and irresponsible spheres, remote from the people and alien to publicity, is so capricious (*prikhotlivyi*)" that outsiders find it hard to judge its nature and source.[12] Particularly in a person who has not yet reached the top, one of the indispensable characteristics of real political greatness may be the ability not to give the impression of excessive political greatness.[13]

Unlike many of the most prominent Old Bolsheviks, Stalin had spent his prerevolutionary career almost exclusively inside Russia, and his major theoretical work in his early years, *Marxism and the Nationality Question*, obviously was of primary relevance for party work inside Russia, specifically in borderlands such as his native Georgia. After the revolution, Stalin continued to serve as the leadership's top specialist in nationality problems (and hence also on constitution drafting). His original governmental post was that of People's Commissar for Nationality Affairs, but in 1919 he also became People's Commissar for State Control. (In 1920, the name of the latter institution was changed to the People's Commissarist for Workers' and Peasants' Inspection or Rabkrin for short.)

Nevertheless, Stalin's major role in the Lenin period must have been more basic than his governmental responsibilities imply. In the early years, he seems to have been, in Trotsky's words, Lenin's "chief-of-staff or . . . clerk on responsible missions"[14]—apparently a role not unlike that of head of the White House staff. Without challenging its factual accuracy, Trotsky quotes a report by one of Stalin's assistants, Pestkovsky: "Lenin could not get along without Stalin even for a single day . . . In the course of a day, he would call Stalin out an endless number of times, or would appear in our office and lead him away. Most of the day Stalin spent with Lenin."[15] After Sverdlov's death in 1919 and the establishment of an Orgburo to handle party organizational questions, Stalin was placed in charge of supervision of the lower party and governmental machinery, and his earlier role seems to have changed. (In many ways Molotov's role in this period seems close to what Trotsky had described for Stalin, but conceivably Molotov was working under Stalin's direction.)[16] In any case Stalin clearly became the dominant member of the Orgburo, and he was the natural candidate for the post of General Secretary of the Central Committee when it was created in April 1922.

As a potential successor to Lenin, Stalin had both advantages and disadvantages. The fact that he was non-Russian was a shortcoming, but at least he was not a Jew, and he was a Georgian who had opposed Georgian nationalism and who seemed to identify himself strongly with Russia. (Indeed, at times he seemed to talk like a Slavophile opposing westernizers when he scornfully referred to party leaders who had spent much of their prerevolutionary career in exile in western Europe.) In any case, Stalin did have great experience in dealing with the non-Russian nationalities, one of the most crucial questions in a multinational country,[17] and from the Russian point of view a non-Russian with the "right" attitudes might be better than a Russian for this job.

Another advantage possessed by Stalin was that he, alone among the top leaders, had never had a major public conflict with Lenin either before or after the revolution.[18] For this reason by itself, "he has strong grounds for claiming to be Lenin's political heir."[19] Stalin's most important advantage in the struggle for power, however, was his institutional base—and his ability to use it. The leader of any institution engaged in personnel selection and in constant correspondence with local officials—institutions such as the Orgburo and the Secretariat—has an immense number of contacts and a real opportunity to build a political machine. Stalin was aware of this possibility.

Stalin's major potential difficulty in the struggle for succession arose from concern about his personality. Certainly it would be wrong to exaggerate Stalin's problem in this respect, for his home seems to have been a social center during the early 1920s,[20] and a Soviet scholar has asserted privately that he was the Politburo's toastmaster (*tamada*) during this period. A western correspondent even reported in 1922 that "within the Communist party, Stalin's personality gives him special influence. His way of life, his sobriety, and his intense industry, in which his wife, who was formerly his secretary, joins him, have attracted to him an almost religious adherence from the faithful."[21] Yet, there was also a darker side to Stalin's personality. The correspondent just cited also mentioned his "fierceness" and his reputation for being "ruthless," and she quoted the words of one "devoted Bolshevik": "A savage man . . . a bloody man. You have to have swords like him in a revolution but I don't like that fact, nor like him."[22] How widespread this feeling was is hard to judge, but clearly Stalin had had a history of difficult relations with various party associates in his earlier life.[23]

From Stalin's point of view, the most dangerous fact about his personality was that at the end of 1922 it had begun to disturb Lenin seriously. Perhaps Lenin was merely chafing at the medical restrictions imposed on him and was directing his frustration at Stalin whom the Politburo had given the unappetizing task of enforcing them,[24] but whatever the reason, his judgment became harsh indeed. In his testament on his colleagues, written on December 23, 1922, Lenin referred to Stalin's "boundless power" and admitted not being "sure that he will always manage to use this power with sufficient caution." Ten days later Lenin added a postscript:

> Stalin is too rude, and this fault, fully tolerable in our midst and in the relations among us Communists, becomes intolerable in the office of general secretary. Therefore I propose to the comrades that they devise a way of shifting Stalin from this position and appointing to it another man who in all other respects falls on the other side of the scale from Comrade Stalin, namely, more tolerant, more loyal, more polite and more considerate of comrades, less capricious, and so forth.[25]

Apparently Lenin was thinking of delivering this proposal to the Twelfth Party Congress in the spring of 1923, but he was incapacitated by that time and the letter was not opened until after his death. It should not be forgotten, however, that Lenin was capable not only of quick anger but also of quick reconciliation (as in the case of Kamenev and Zinoviev in November 1917), and it is quite conceivable that this judgment of Stalin would not have been a final one.

The two other most prominent candidates to succeed Lenin—Grigorii Zinoviev and Lev Kamenev—were closely linked in the struggle for power, "a Castor and Pollux" in Isaac Deutscher's phrase.[26] Of the two, Zinoviev had the reputation of being the more ambitious, the one willing to provide political leadership, while Kamenev was considered the junior partner— "Zinoviev's *alter ego* . . . [his] shadow,"[27] a skilled administrator who was "unreservedly under the influence of his political friend Zinoviev."[28]

Grigorii Zinoviev was born in 1883 of a Jewish dairy farmer. A clerk and a teacher while a teenager, he quickly entered revolutionary work, but actually spent little time inside Russia. He worked continuously with Lenin, serving as "Lenin's principal collaborator in the latter's activities abroad" throughout the decade prior to the revolution.[29] Apparently the only major occassion on which Zinoviev opposed Lenin was in the latter's determination to launch a socialist revolution in 1917, but, as has been seen, that opposition became both major and dramatic. Together with Kamenev, he not only voted against Lenin's proposed coup d'etat but even disclosed the intention in the nonparty press. Immediately after the revolution, he was one of the five to resign from the Central Committee on the issue of a coalition government.

Upon returning to the party leadership, Zinoviev had two major responsibilities during the Lenin period. One was the party leadership (literally

the chairmanship of the soviet) in Petrograd. The other was handling relations with left-wing foreigners, a duty which flowed naturally from his extensive work and contacts in western Europe before the revolution and which
was of special importance at a time when the leadership thought revolution
in western Europe to be vital for the survival of the regime. This latter role
became formalized in 1919 when the Communist International (Comintern)
was formed, for Zinoviev was named chairman of its executive committee.
In March 1919 he was elected one of the three candidate members of the
new Politburo, and in 1921 he was promoted to full membership.

Like Zinoviev, Lev Kamenev was born in 1883 of Jewish parents, but
his father was a railroad engineer with some technological education.
Kamenev studied briefly at Moscow University before moving into revolutionary work. His prerevolutionary career alternated between Russia and
emigration abroad, the last three years before the revolution being spent
in exile in Siberia. Although Kamenev was to be linked with Zinoviev as
a leader of the Left Opposition, his early political career was almost exclusively on the right wing of the Bolshevik party. In 1910, in opposition to
Lenin, he sought the reunification of the Bolsheviks and the Mensheviks;
in 1915 and early 1917 he supported the defense of Russia in contrast to
Lenin's total rejection of the war; in the spring of 1917 he was the last major
Bolshevik to accept Lenin's April Theses calling for revolutionary action
against the Provisional Government. Then, of course, Kamenev joined Zinoviev in opposing both the revolution and the establishment of a one-party
government.

After the revolution, Kamenev became chairman of the Moscow soviet—
the party leader in Moscow—and during the Lenin period he also held a
number of administrative posts in the Council of People's Commissars and
in the Council of Labor and Defense. In 1919 he was named a full member
of the party Politburo at a time when Zinoviev was but a candidate member,
and, in 1922, at the time of Lenin's illness, he became the First Deputy Chairman of the Council of People's Commissars, actually chairing both this body
and the Politburo in Lenin's absence.

When Lenin first became ill, top political leadership passed to a troika
composed of Stalin, Zinoviev, and Kamenev. Zinoviev was formally recognized to be the senior member of the troika, and he was chosen to give the
main political reports at the Twelfth and Thirteenth Party Congresses in
1923 and 1924. His considerable oratorical skills and international experience
complemented Kamenev's domestic governmental experience nicely, and,
of course, the two controlled the party organizations in the country's two
largest cities. Yet, in retrospect, the pair really was never completely credible
as a ruling duumvirate. Both were Jews, and both had opposed the historical

decision to carry out the revolution. (This latter fact was the only one mentioned about the two men in Lenin's testament, and it was accompanied by the rather ambiguous remark, "This was, of course, no accident, but neither can blame be laid upon them personally.")[30] Moreover, the personal reputation of Zinoviev appears to have been exceedingly poor,[31] and at the Tenth Party Congress in 1921 (the last at which the votes in the elections to the Central Committee were announced) he ranked eighteenth in the voting and Kamenev was twentieth.[32]

The last major leader mentioned in Lenin's testament was Nikolai Bukharin, the editor of *Pravda* and (in Lenin's words) "the party's most valuable and biggest theoretician."[33] Born in 1888 with a schoolteacher father, Bukharin was the youngest member of the top Bolshevik leadership. He had not joined the party until 1906, and, like Kamenev, had had a bit of exposure to Moscow University before moving full-time into revolutionary work. When he went into exile in 1911 at the age of twenty-three, he quickly became a major Bolshevik theorist. His book, *Imperialism and the World Economy*, foreshadowed (and apparently influenced) Lenin's more famous work on the subject written several months later, and in 1916 he wrote a piece, "Toward a Theory of the Imperialist State," which provided many of the core arguments of Lenin's *State and Revolution*.[34]

Upon returning to Russia in 1917, Bukharin, unlike many of the others who centered their activities in the capital of Petrograd, became one of the Bolshevik leaders in Moscow, specifically the leader of the important (and predominantly young) left wing of the party there. After the revolution, he occupied a similar political position. As has been seen, he led the "revolutionary war" group in the Brest-Litovsk debates, and he strongly supported the economic measures of war communism. Nevertheless, despite his stand on the left throughout the Civil War period, Brest-Litovsk was the last of the left-wing oppositions in which he became involved. Instead, he gained recognition as the main-line theorist of the party. He served as chief editor of *Pravda*; provided general supervision to the press, youth affairs, and propaganda activities; in general, was the de facto deputy chairman of the Comintern; and wrote popularizing as well as serious treatises on the relationship of Marxism to the new regime.

Several of Bukharin's most famous works—for example, *The Economics of the Transition Period* and especially *The ABC of Communism*—embodied the mood of war communism, "a militant optimism invigorated by the belief that 'what Marx prophesied is being fulfilled under our very eyes.' "[35] By 1922, however, his views were undergoing radical change. He accepted the necessity of NEP, and, at least as E. H. Carr has seen it, "Bukharin went characteristically further than his master. Having readjusted his ideas with his usual theoretical consistency, he found himself henceforth on the extreme Right of the party."[36] In the mid-1920s he was to become the foremost proponent of the view that Lenin's last five articles defined the correct path to socialism.

In retrospect, Bukharin's comprehensive and highly visible defense of NEP made him appear the logical alternative to the man who overturned these policies, but it is not at all clear that Bukharin had the look of a potential leader at the time. True, he was an ethnic Russian, but he was very young—thirty-four years of age in 1922 compared, for example, with a forty-three-year-old Stalin. Moreover, his reputation had been made as a theorist, and he was devoid of major administrative experience either as a party or governmental leader. Perhaps most significant of all, he had been elected a candidate member of the Politburo in 1919, but he remained at that level at the time of Lenin's death five years later, even though three other leaders (Zinoviev, Rykov, and Tomsky) had risen to full membership in that period.

Indeed, even Bukharin's work as a theorist between 1918 and 1924 had largely been one of defending policy rather than initiating it, and consistency had not been his trademark. In 1920, well before he had made the major move to the right, Lenin had characterized him as "soft": "It is one of the qualities we love him for and cannot help loving him for. We know more than once he has been called in jest 'soft wax.' It appears that any 'unprincipled' person, any 'demogogue' can make an impression on this soft wax.'"[37] This reputation may well have been unfair,[38] but repeatedly in the 1920s Bukharin was to be treated—even by his supporters—as more lovable than tough. There is no worse reputation for an aspirant to the leadership of a nation.

From a number of perspectives, one might have thought that the strongest candidate for the leadership position would have been Mikhail Tomsky, the chairman of the trade union organization. In a dictatorship of the proletariat, his post had made him the representative of the proletariat in the most immediate sense, and he himself was the only top Bolshevik who had actually been an industrial worker—and for a decade at that. Given the tendency of the workers to think that NEP disproportionately benefited the peasantry, Tomsky might have been a reassuring figure, and the mass enrollment of production workers into the party in 1924 and 1925 seemingly would have given him a major base of support within the party. Yet, Tomsky (although a full member of the Politburo) apparently was never taken seriously as a major party leader, and for this reason he remains a shadowy figure in most histories of the period.

Tomsky was born in 1880 and at the age of thirteen followed his father into factory work. (He was a lithographer by trade.) While other contenders had entered party work in their teens, Tomsky did not join the party until the age of twenty-four. Even earlier, however, he had been active in trade union work, and he continued that association throughout his career. Except for attendance at several conferences abroad, he remained inside Russia throughout the tsarist period.

During 1917 Tomsky worked in the Metal Workers' Trade Union, and apparently did not play a major role in the revolution. In January 1918 he became the top official in the trade union movement as a whole (the chairman of the All-Russian Central Council of Trade Unions), but he was not elected a member of the party Central Committee until March 1919. While Tomsky was generally the leader of the less militant forces within the trade unions during the Civil War (in opposition to Shliapnikov who led the left wing),[39] even right-wing trade union leaders took positions on industrial management and the role of the trade unions that Lenin found inadmissible. In the wake of the trade union controversies of 1920–1921, Tomsky was removed from the chairmanship and sent to Central Asia on party work. Upon his return later in the year, he was only given the number two position in the trade union.

Adjusting himself to the more restricted role of the trade unions defined by the Tenth Party Congress, Tomsky was once more named trade union chairman, and in 1922 he was elected a full member of the party Politburo. He entered the struggle for power as the trusted leader of a major national institution, but it was an institution that had been denied the primary role in economic management and whose leadership was far more responsible to the party leadership than to the union rank-and-file. It was a fragile base of power.[40]

The final major actor in the struggle for power, Aleksei Rykov, was in many respects the most natural successor to Lenin if NEP was actually to be the wave of the Soviet future, and, in fact, he did assume Lenin's position as Chairman of the Council of People's Commissars in 1924. Rykov was an ethnic Russian and had been the party's top economic administrator since the revolution. He was enthusiastic in his support for the economic philosophy and policies of NEP—especially the policies toward the peasant that lay at the heart of NEP—but, as befit his position as top industrial administrator, he also was a strong supporter of industrialization.

Rykov was born in 1881 into a peasant family, and he spent most of his prerevolutionary career inside Russia. Like Kamenev, he consistently was on the right wing of the party. Before the revolution, he had favored reconciliation with the Mensheviks, and immediately after the revolution he was one of the five Central Committee members to resign on the question of coalition government. In Stephen Cohen's words, "he was a not uncommon type among early Bolsheviks, a Marxist whose real political cause had been anti-czarism, and whose socialism related to the 'toilers' [that is, the peasants] rather than just the proletariat."[41]

Soon after the revolution, in February 1918, Rykov returned to the government as Chairman of the Supreme Economic Council. Although apparently not enthralled with the party's peasant policy at the time, he administered war communism loyally. His precise post changed occasionally during Lenin's lifetime (for example, in 1921 he became Deputy Chairman of the Council of People's Commissars), but Rykov and Kamenev essentially served as the top two governmental administrators under Lenin, with Rykov concentrating more on economic-industrial administration. He was not re-elected to the Central Committee until April 1920, but he became a full member of the Politburo in April 1922.

As had been the case with Tomsky and Kamenev, Rykov does not seem to have been considered a serious candidate to succeed Lenin. Lenin did not mention him in his testament, and journalists of the time usually described him as an administrator rather than a political leader—an overtired administrator absorbed in detail, at that. The actual meaning of this latter reputation is not clear. It is striking that those most often seen as political leaders—Trotsky, Zinoviev, and Bukharin—were men who had stayed abroad until 1917. Those who had returned to Russia or remained there—Stalin, Kamenev, Rykov, and Tomsky—were looked upon as administrators of one type or the other. Perhaps political leadership was being equated too much with theorizing or even the émigré style of activity, and conceivably Rykov, like Stalin, (or like Anwar Sadat, to take a contemporary leader who came to power with a similar reputation) would have made a very effective political leader if circumstances had been different.

It is also possible, on the other hand, that the treatment of Rykov—and especially Lenin's choice of the hard-line industrializer Piatakov rather than Rykov as the economic administrator to discuss in the testament—reflects the conscious or unconscious judgment of the time that the type of Bolshevism, the type of policies, with which Rykov was identified really did not represent the central core of the party. It is possible, in other words, that the treatment of Rykov reflected the concern of the majority of party influentials about a conservative Thermidor and their dedication to rapid industrialization, even if this entailed difficulties with the peasantry.

The Issue of the Party Apparatus

The first dramatic issue in the struggle for power involved not the policies toward the peasantry and industrial development, but the degree of democracy within the party. "Democracy" had, of course, been a perennial issue for the various party oppositions, but in the past it usually had centered on the relationship between the party and the institutions supposed to be elected by the population (for example, the soviets and the trade unions), the relationship between the rank-and-file citizens and their direct administrative superiors (for example, soldiers vis-à-vis commanders or workers vis-à-vis plant managers), or, less so, the relationship between the central party organs and those in the territorial units (for example, the degree of independence for the Ukrainian party organization).

Now one of the more minor issues of the past came to the fore—the relationship between those Communists who worked full-time in the party apparatus and those Communists who worked in other institutions. This time, paradoxically, it was Trotsky, the very symbol of centralization and discipline, who spoke out in the name of democracy, first raising the question in a muted manner at the Eleventh Party Congress in March-April 1922. In his opening statement to the congress, Lenin had criticized the relationship between the Politburo and the Council of People's Commissars, complaining that too many decisions were being appealed from the governmental cabinet to the party one, but Trotsky, together with Zinoviev, used this criticism to attack the relationship of party and economic officials in the provinces. In Zinoviev's words, "we should introduce such a division of labor in our party that we don't have to direct policy with the help of resolutions of the provincial party committees (gubkomy) . . . If there are splendid officials in the provincial party committee who understand economic questions well, then it is necessary to send them to the economic organs."[42]

Zinoviev soon abandoned the issue of the role of the party apparatus when he entered into alliance with Stalin after Lenin's first stroke, but Trotsky returned to it with increasing insistence. In the fall of 1922 he raised the question with Lenin himself, contending that control by the party apparatus was a key explanation for the bureaucratism that worried Lenin at this time. Trotsky gained the impression that Lenin had agreed to an alliance against the apparatus,[43] but any such hope was thwarted by the deterioration in Lenin's health. In early 1923 Trotsky (now in conjunction with Rykov) tried to achieve his aims through a reorganization of the central party organs, but instead it was Stalin's plan (an enlargement of the Central Committee—in practice, by the election of a number of party secretaries to it) that won.

By early fall of 1923, Trotsky was moving toward open denunciation, and on October 8 he sent a letter to the Central Committee expressing his feelings clearly:

> The bureaucratization of the party apparatus has developed to unheard-of proportions . . . There has been created a stratum of party workers, entering into the apparatus of the government of the party, who

completely renounce their own party opinion, at least the open expression of it, as though assuming that the secretarial hierarchy is the apparatus which creates party opinion and party decisions. Beneath this stratum . . . there lies the broad mass of the party, before whom every decision stands in the form of a summons or a command.[44]

A week later, the charge of party apparatus domination was echoed in the Declaration of the Forty-Six. "Nowadays," the declaration asserted, "it is not the party, not its broad masses, who promote and choose members of the provincial committees and of the central committee of the RKP. On the contrary the secretarial hierarchy of the party to an ever greater extent recruits the membership of conferences and congresses, who are becoming to an even greater extent the executive assemblies of this hierarchy."[45] In December, Trotsky himself took the issue to the party as a whole. He contended that the apparatus was trying to ensure that the "leadership of the party gives way to administration by its executive organs (committee, bureau, secretariat, etc.)" and that "as this regime becomes consolidated, all affairs are concentrated in the hands of a small group, sometimes only of a secretary who appoints, removes, gives the instructions, inflicts the penalties, etc."[46]

Trotsky's assertions could simply be dismissed as the outsider's perennial complaint about the natural state of affairs in any large-scale organization. The full-time official in any organization has an obvious advantage in decision-making, and the rise in the role of the full-time party officials, of the party Secretariat, could be interpreted in these terms. In the words of E. H. Carr, "concentration of power at the centre everywhere distinguishes modern mass parties from the small elite parties of the past; and, within the central authority, the elected organ meeting periodically tends to lose power to the permanent bureaucratic machinery staffed by appointment."[47]

This argument has validity on one level, but it overlooks the fact that Trotsky's complaints were directed at a very fundamental change that was occurring in the Soviet political system. In most countries, the concentration of "power at the centre" flows into the hands of the parliamentary party officials, not those of the extraparliamentary organization. The real leaders of the British Conservative and Labour parties are the members of Parliament in the cabinet and shadow cabinet. The "presidents" of the respective parties—those who supervise the party's staff—are, like the chairmen of the Democratic and Republican National Committees in the United States, primarily concerned with fund-raising and intraparty administration, and they have relatively little impact on policy.

The same pattern prevailed in the Soviet Union during the Lenin period. Power quickly did come to be exercised by party leaders at the top, but, as in the West, it was the parliamentary leaders who exercised it—those party members who occupied positions outside the party apparatus. Lenin himself was Chairman of the Council of People's Commissars (that is, leader of the government), and, as shown in table 1, Stalin was the only party secretary to be elected a full member of the Politburo after Lenin's last party congress (the Eleventh) and he also held governmental positions. (One

Table 1   *Members of the Politburo, April 1922*

MEMBER	YEAR OF BIRTH	YEAR OF PARTY ENTRY	POSITION
L. B. Kamenev	1883	1901	Deputy Chairman of the Council of People's Commissars and Chairman of the Moscow soviet
V. I. Lenin	1870	1893	Chairman of the Council of People's Commissars
A. I. Rykov	1881	1899	Deputy Chairman of the Council of People's Commissars
I. V. Stalin	1879	1898	General Secretary of the Central Committee, People's Commissar for Nationalities, People's Commissar for Workers'-Peasants' Inspection (Rabkrin)
M. P. Tomsky	1880	1904	Chairman of the Trade Union Council
L. D. Trotsky	1879	1917	People's Commissar for War
G. E. Zinoviev	1883	1901	Chairman of the Comintern and Chairman of the Petrograd soviet
AVERAGE	1879	1902	
Candidate members			
N. I. Bukharin	1888	1906	Editor of *Pravda*
M. I. Kalinin	1875	1898	Chairman of the Central Executive Committee
V. M. Molotov	1890	1906	Secretary of the Central Committee

Source: Borys Levytsky, *The Soviet Political Elite* (Stanford, The Hoover Institution on War, Revolution, and Peace, 1970), pp. 745–747.

additional secretary was a candidate member of the Politburo.) Similarly, with one possible exception,[48] no head of a Central Committee department was made a voting member of the Central Committee, and only two regional party officials (the chairman of the Caucasian Bureau and the secretary of the Moscow organization) were included among the twenty-seven members. Four Ukrainian officials—the chairman of the Central Executive Committee, the chairman of the Council of People's Commissars, the commander of the army, and the head of the Donets Coal Industry Administration—were elected full members of the Central Committee at this time, but the first secretary of the Ukrainian party organization was only a candidate member.

It was this situation—the subservience of the extraparliamentary organization to the parliamentary or governmental Communists—that Trotsky believed to be eroding in the last years of Lenin's life. If he had been among the extraparliamentary leaders, his attitude might well have been different, for, when he was in power, Trotsky was far better known for his authoritarian ways and proposals than for his democratic leanings. However, in 1922 and 1923 Trotsky was not in the Secretariat, and surely the heart of his concern was a fear that the rise in power of the officials of the party Secretariat meant a rise in power of the leader of the Secretariat, his arch-rival Joseph Stalin.

Development of the Party Apparatus

The party apparatus about which Trotsky was complaining had its origins well before the Bolshevik revolution. Bolshevism from the beginning was characterized by an emphasis on organizational solidarity and discipline as a necessary basis for successful revolutionary action, and this principle found expression in an underground organization of local committees which formed the basis of Lenin's revolutionary machine. The committeemen of the underground—the komitetchiki (of whom Stalin was one)—were the prototypes of the men of the postrevolutionary apparatus—the *apparatchiki*. During the march to power in 1917 when the party was flooded with new members, the party organization itself remained in the hands of the komitetchiki, and these seasoned workers of the underground maintained a firm grip on the rapidly expanding local party organization.

With the party's seizure of power in November 1917 and the assumption of governing responsibilities, the system of regionally based party committees was retained, and many of the committeemen of the underground tended to gravitate into the apparatus, to become local and regional party secretaries, and to concern themselves with problems of internal party management.[49] (With much of the country in the hands of the Whites, many of the committeemen were, of course, compelled to continue an underground role.) In those areas under Bolshevik control, the real party leader in the provinces seems to have been (as was the case of Zinoviev and Kamenev in Petrograd and Moscow, respectively) the chairman of the soviet rather than the party secretary. As late as 1919 at least, the Central Committee secretary, Krestinsky, reported that the regional party committees were "in practice, the agitation departments of the local soviets."[50]

Until early 1919, the central official with primary responsibility for party organization was Iakov Sverdlov, veteran committeeman of prerevolutionary days, whose rich and varied experience in the underground gave him a wideranging acquaintance among the committeemen. The fact that Sverdlov was simultaneously Chairman of the Central Executive Committee and thus responsible for supervision both of the local soviets and the lower party apparatus reduced any tendency toward major conflict between the two sets of institutions. When Sverdlov suddenly died in March 1919, however, the situation changed. He had functioned largely without staff, and the only complete record of transactions was in his head. His death meant that the party had lost not only a respected member of the Central Committee but also its record office and central secretarial apparatus as well.

Sverdlov's death posed the problem of regularizing and rationalizing the central machinery of the party, and the Eighth Congress addressed itself to this task. In order to provide for the direction of the party's wide- ranging activities, the Central Committee was instructed to create three new organs: (1) a Political Bureau (Politburo), to be composed of five members of the Central Committee; (2) an Organizational Bureau (Orgburo), also to be composed of five Central Committee members; and (3) a Secretariat, to consist of one responsible Secretary, who had to be a member of the Orgburo, and five technical secretaries, to be chosen from among experienced party officials.

The Politburo was charged with the responsibility of deciding all questions requiring immediate action; from the outset it became the top policy-determining organ of the party. Lenin, Trotsky, Stalin, Kamenev, and Krestinsky were its first members, and Bukharin, Kalinin, and Zinoviev were added as candidate (nonvoting) members. During the debates at the Eighth Congress, the objection was raised that the creation of the Politburo involved the demotion of the rest of the Central Committee into second-class party leaders. In order to blunt the force of this charge, the Politburo was required to deliver regular reports on its actions to the Central Committee, and members of the Central Committee who were not members of the Politburo were given the right to attend and participate in Politburo sessions with a consultative, though not a deciding, vote.

The Orgburo was authorized "to direct all the organizational work of the party."[51] It was to meet at least three times a week and, like the Politburo, was required to render biweekly reports to the Central Committee. Two members of the Politburo, Krestinsky and Stalin, were also named to work in the Orgburo. The assignment of Stalin to the Orgburo was to have momentous significance. Unlike some of his more intellectually scintillating associates in the Politburo who spurned internal party management, he was quick to realize the crucial importance of the party apparatus in deciding the issue of supremacy within the party. The Orgburo became his first base of operations in building his own machine.

The authority of the Secretariat was not defined by the Eighth Congress. Its powers evolved in practice. The first responsible Secretary, Krestinsky, was a lawyer-journalist who had joined the party in 1903 and had served in 1917 as chairman of the Ekaterinburg and Ural regional party committees. Even though he was the only person to sit on the Politburo, Orgburo, and Secretariat in the period 1919–1921 (a point usually glossed over in discussions of Stalin's rise to power), Krestinsky made no effort to construct an independent power base of his own. The Secretariat remained subservient to the Politburo and Orgburo to the extent that Lenin hardly discussed this institution in describing the interlocking responsibilities of the three organs at the Ninth Party Congress in March 1920. The Secretary really seems to have functioned as a secretary.

> During the year under review the current daily work of the Central Committee was conducted by the two bodies elected at the Plenum of the Central Committee: the Organizational Bureau . . . and the Political Bureau . . . In order to achieve coordination and consistency in the decisions of these two bodies, the Secretary acted as a member of both. The practice which emerged was for the Orgburo, as its main and proper function, to distribute the forces of the party while the function of the Politburo was to deal with policy questions. It goes without saying that this distribution is to a certain extent artificial; it is obvious that no policy can be carried out in practice without finding expression in appointments and transfers. Consequently, every organizational question assumes a political significance; and the practice was established that the request of a single member of the Central Committee was sufficient to have any question for any reason whatsoever examined as a political question. Any attempt to divide the functions of the Central Committee in another way would hardly have achieved its purpose.

> This method of conducting business was productive of extremely good results: no difficulties have arisen between the two bureaus on any occasion. The work of these bodies has on the whole proceeded harmoniously, and practical fulfillment was facilitated by the presence of the Secretary

. . . It must be emphasized from the very outset, so as to remove all mis-understanding, that only the corporate decisions of the Central Committee adopted in the Orgburo or the Politburo or in the Plenum of the Central Committee—exclusively such matters were carried out by the Secretary of the Central Committee of the party.[52]

At the Ninth Congress, a resolution was passed to "strengthen" the Secretariat by adding to it two members of the Central Committee who would devote all their time to its work. However, all three of the secretaries aligned themselves with Trotsky against Lenin in the bitter trade union discussion of 1920–1921, and their secretarial careers were quickly terminated. At the Tenth Congress in 1921, they were replaced by Molotov, Iaroslavsky, and V. Mikhailov, the first two of which were among the staunchest supporters of Stalin in his rise to supremacy in the party. As a result of this action, Stalin emerged as the dominant specialist on intraparty organizational questions. He was the only member of the Politburo who also served on the Orgburo and, as such, became its unquestioned leader. Through his ascendancy in the Orgburo, he began in effect to direct the work of the Secretariat. The announcement on April 4, 1922, of his appointment to the post of General Secretary registered a de facto authority which had already been achieved.

The Central Committee Secretariat was, of course, far more than the several men who were given the title of "secretary." From 1919 to 1921 its staff increased from 30 to 602 persons (plus an additional contingent of 140 guards and messengers),[53] and by 1926 this number had risen to 767.[54] These officials were organized into a series of specialized sections with the name of *otdel* (usually translated "department.") The most important of the departments was the Records and Assignment Department (Uchraspred), really the personnel department. A second major department was the organization-instruction department, which served as an investigatory agency and a conveyor of the instructions of central organs to the local party organs. The third major department was the agitation-propaganda department, which supervised ideological work. In addition, departments were established to direct party work in the press and among women, respectively, and subunits (*sektsiia*) were formed to supervise specialized ideological work among national minorities.[55]

Even the staff of the Central Committee Secretariat was but the tip of the apparatus-iceberg. Party organizations had been placed in each republic and province, as well as in subdivisions within them, and each of these party organizations had its own staff, which on a smaller scale was structured along the lines of its central counterpart. General statements about the proportion of party members to party officials suggest some 25,000–27,000 apparatchiki in 1924–1925,[56] but a list submitted to the Twelfth Party Conference in August 1922 included 15,325 responsible workers—325 in the center and regional bureaus, 2,000 at the provincial or guberniia level, 8,000 at the county level, and 5,000 in the larger industrial centers.[57]

The Secretariat, Personnel Selection, and Intraparty Democracy

The Secretariat began, as we have seen, as a secretarial organization, and its first officials seem to have made no effort to use it as a base for personal political power. The party leadership agreed that its first duty was the direction of ideological work among the population and the establishment of basic order in the structure and organization of the party. It was not until 1922 that the Secretariat finally succeeded in establishing a system which provided it with a list of party members or even a reliable count on their number. Similar problems were encountered in ensuring that local party organizations send regular reports to the center.

In another type of political system, the officials of the Secretariat might never have acquired a major policy role, but Lenin's insistence upon democratic centralism had profound organizational implications. The party rules of the time proclaimed that "the discussion of all disputable questions of party life is completely free until the decision is taken," and they called for the election of local party officials and of delegates to the party congress. Yet, at the same time, they also declared that "the foremost obligation of all party members and all party organizations is the strictest party discipline. The decisions of the party centers should be executed quickly and exactly."[58]

But how was this latter obligation to be enforced given the election of local party officials? Would not such elections give the party officials every incentive to respond to local pressures rather than central ones? For example, a Ukrainian party official who tried to enforce a central decree that was considered contrary to republican interests might find himself replaced by a party official with different views. The obvious answer to this dilemma was to demand that local party officials be responsible to the center—that they be selected by the center and replaceable by it. In practice, the local secretaries often were elected from below in the early years, but the principle of central control of personnel was quickly established. Membership in the party meant being at the party's complete disposition, and members could be summoned when needed and assigned wherever their services were required.

As has been seen, when members of the Civil War oppositions complained that the Central Committee had begun to use its power over the assignment of party members to ban "those who hold deviant views," Lenin did not acknowledge that dissidents had been punished (except, maybe, where there had been a few "mistakes"), but he insisted that "whatever Central Committee you choose to elect, it cannot desist from distributing forces." Moreover, it was freely acknowledged that if local elected officials were quite hostile to central preferences, the center would intervene. When the Democratic Centralists gained control of the Ukrainian party organization in 1920, the Central Committee in Moscow simply dismissed the Ukrainian Central Committee elected at the Ukrainian party congress and appointed a new one.[59] Precisely the same procedure was followed in 1921 when the Workers' Opposition gained control of the party organization in the Russian province of Samara (now Kuibyshev).[60]

The basic role of the Orgburo (and of the Secretariat which was to serve as its staff) was to create smoother responsiveness of the local party organizations to central directives and to prevent the necessity of the type of drastic action taken in the Ukraine and in Samara. During the Civil War period, the central apparatus had had to concern itself almost exclusively with so-called mass mobilizations: quotas assessed on local party organization when party workers were needed in quantity for particular assignments. Shortly after the end of the Civil War, mass mobilizations were abandoned in favor of individual assignments,[61] and the role of the Records and Assignment Department (the department which handled the staff work for this responsibility) was described in the following terms:

> The detailed and attentive accounting of the commanding cadres to the party; reassignment of party forces to strengthen the most important provincial organizations; selection of organizers for party work, review of the leaders of oblast, guberniia, and uezd organizations and to a certain extent secretaries of cells; replacements of workers who [do] not measure up to the standards set forth by the Party Congress.[62]

In making individual assignments, the Records and Assignment Department concentrated first on filling party posts. The party rules officially proclaimed that lower secretaries, while elected from below, had to be "confirmed" (that is, approved by) higher-standing organizations.[63] In practice, the higher-standing organizations usually made "recommendations" to the election meetings, and these "recommendations" usually were mandatory.

Personnel decisions with respect to the highest party positions came under the jurisdiction of the Orgburo, although in such cases the Secretariat did the necessary staff work and made suggestions. At lower levels the authority of the Secretariat was more extensive. The department's report to the Twelfth Party Congress in April 1923 indicated that more than 10,000 assignments had been made in the preceding year, half of them involving so-called responsible officials.[64] During 1922, thirty-seven guberniia secretaries were removed or transferred by the central party apparatus, and forty-two new "recommendations" were made for the post of secretary.[65]

Not all personnel selection was centralized in the higher party apparatus. Responsibility for lesser posts was delegated to lower levels in the hierarchy and these levels did not hesitate to intervene. In late 1923 or early 1924, Bukharin (then a supporter of the Politburo majority) described the "election" of secretaries of the party cells in the various places of work:

> To judge by the Moscow organization, the secretaries of the party cells are usually appointed by the district committee . . . Normally the putting of the question to a vote takes place in a set pattern. They come and ask the meeting, "Who is against?" and since people more or less fear to speak out against, the individual in question finds himself elected secretary of the bureau of the cell.

Bukharin added that "the same thing can be observed in somewhat modified form in all the other stages of the party hierarchy as well."[66]

Stalin, in his organizational report to the Twelfth Congress, made no effort to conceal the range of the work of the party apparatus. He praised the leading role played by the provincial party organs, pointedly stating that eight months earlier (that is, a few months after Trotsky's and Zinoviev's "victory" on the question at the Eleventh Congress) they had overcome their confusion and had gotten to their feet. So far as the Records and Assignment Department was concerned, he acknowledged that it was "acquiring huge significance." He further revealed that its staff was being expanded by the addition of a deputy head who would specialize in personnel selection for the economic organs and the soviets. (The department in the localities was also to have such a deputy head.)[67]

Officially, of course, the Secretariat became involved in personnel selection only to ensure that officials "measure up to the standards set forth by the party congress." If such had been the case, the other Politburo members would have had little objection (at least until the Secretariat began interfering with appointments in the governmental apparatus they supervised). The conception of a centralized action party had been an important element of the Bolshevik party since its beginning, and Old Bolsheviks occupying key policy positions in Moscow must have been much attracted to the idea of a party which could and would carry out the policy they decided.

The essential problem which disturbed Trotsky and his supporters was that the lower party organizations did not simply execute central decisions; they also elected delegates to the party congress—the highest policy organ in the country, the institution that elected the Central Committee. Given this fact, the danger of selection of secretaries from above was, first, that political loyalty to the central official in charge of personnel selection might become a criterion in selection and removal of local secretaries and, second, that selection of delegates to the party congress might become as controlled as the selection of secretaries, a natural development in any system with a strong political machine. In such circumstances, there was every likelihood that most delegates coming to the party congress would be beholden to the man who supervised selection of party secretaries—namely, the General Secretary, Joseph Stalin.

In 1923 Trotsky charged that the Twelfth Party Congress of that year had, in fact, been packed in just such a manner. "Very many members of the party, by no means the worst," Trotsky wrote on October 8, have "felt the greatest alarm at the methods and procedures by dint of which the twelfth party congress was constituted." He did not mention, but without doubt acutely remembered, that 55.1 percent of the voting delegates to that congress were full-time party officials (in contrast to 24.8 percent only two years earlier at the Tenth Congress in 1921).[68]

Trotsky did, indeed, have cause for alarm. Mikoian reports in his memoirs that as early as January 1922—on the eve of the Eleventh Party Congress—Stalin was already striving to prevent Trotsky supporters from being elected delegates to the congress, and, according to Mikoian, he was doing this as a defensive action against Trotsky at the behest of Lenin. (Perhaps Lenin was concerned about an analoge with the Tenth Congress conflict with Trotsky on the trade union issue.)

The conditions in which the preparation for the Eleventh Congress is taking place, Stalin said [to me privately], are fundamentally different from those on the eve of the Tenth Congress. No disagreements or open groups or political platforms are visible on the horizon. The Central Committee does not give great significance to the fact that Shliapnikov and a narrow group of his supporters, who are isolated from the masses, are secretly engaged in group work. He and his group do not pose a serious danger now, and, if anything of an antiparty nature arises, than it will quickly fail.

[Now] the chief danger can come from Trotsky and his supporters, but they still are not making any noise. There are not any visible disagreements that can have an effect on the party. Of course, anything can be expected from Trotsky . . . [and] one can suppose that he will adopt the . . . tactic of coming to the congress without disagreements and without platforms and manifesting a spirit of complete unity.

... If in such circumstances relatively many former Trotskyists will be elected to the Central Committee, then this will represent a danger for the further work of the Central Committee. Then Trotsky can raise his head, provoke disagreements in the Central Committee, and, relying on his supporters, complicate the work of the Central Committee in many ways ... For this reason, Stalin said, we are concerned about the kind of delegates who will come to the forthcoming party congress and whether there will be many Trotskyists among them.

... In this connection Siberia worries us. There are still fairly many Trotskyists there. They enjoy a certain confidence and influence in their organizations, and for this reason, there is the danger that many of them will be among the elected delegates to the congress. "That is why," he said in conclusion, "Lenin entrusted me to call you in, to tell you about the situation, and if you share this view about conditions in the party, to ask you to go to Lashevich in Novo-Nikolaevsk [the name at that time of the present Novosibirsk] in order to transmit to him everything that I have told you in the name of Lenin."

Without hesitation, I [Mikoian] stated that I agreed to set out for Siberia on this assignment.[69]

Trotsky's 1923 complaints had little impact upon events—or at least little of value to him. In December 1923 the Politburo did pass a resolution reaffirming the principles of party democracy. It flatly declared that the right of higher party organs to confirm party secretaries should not be transformed into a right of appointment, and it even vaguely pledged to "examine the advisability" of retaining the right at all.[70] However, a few days later Trotsky attempted—unwisely, even his friends and supporters acknowledged[71]—to solidify his interpretation of the resolution by writing a letter about party democracy which quickly was published in *Pravda*. In this letter, which has been quoted earlier, Trotsky condemned any tendency toward the concentration of all affairs "in the hands of a small group, sometimes only of a secretary who appoints, removes, gives the instructions inflicts the penalties, etc.," and he even went further to suggest that such a situation benefitted long-time party members at the expense of young people.[72]

Whether genuinely annoyed at what they considered a breach of faith on Trotsky's part, whether alarmed at the response which Trotsky's charges received at opposition meetings in Moscow and elsewhere, or whether simply happy to have been given a good pretext, the other Politburo members launched a large-scale attack upon Trotsky. Zinoviev demanded Trotsky's immediate arrest, but Stalin counseled caution. It was "inconceivable," Stalin said in an article in *Pravda,* to eliminate Trotsky from the leadership of the party.[73] "We did not agree with Zinoviev and Kamenev," he revealed to the Fourteenth Party Congress, "because we knew that a policy of chopping off [heads] is fraught with great dangers for the party, that the method of chopping off and bloodletting—and they did demand blood—is dangerous, infectious: today you chop off one [head], tomorrow another, the day after a third—what in the end will be left of the party?"[74]

While appearing as the apostle of moderation and restraint, Stalin did not hesitate to press home the charge that Trotsky and his supporters were guilty of the crime of factionalism. In his attack on Trotsky in January 1924 Stalin wrapped himself in the mantle of Leninism and, as the loyal pupil of Lenin, accused Trotsky and his associates of violating the Resolution on Party Unity which Lenin himself had drafted. Trotsky, he insisted, sought to place himself above the party and its Central Committee; the factional freedom which he claimed could only lead to the destruction of the party.[75] "The opposition," Stalin declared, "expressed the temper, moods, and aspirations of the nonproletarian elements in and outside the party. The opposition, itself unconscious of it, unshackles a petty bourgeois element. The factional work of the opposition is water on the mill of those who wish to weaken and overthrow the dictatorship of the proletariat. I said that yesterday, and today I reaffirm it."[76] The resolution adopted by the conference called upon the party to wage "a systematic and energetic battle" against Trotskyism as a "petty bourgeois deviation in the party."[77]

At the Thirteenth Party Congress in May 1924, Trotsky was not even elected a voting delegate. His attack upon the party apparatus' control of the congresses had had little impact, for the proportion of full-time party officials among the voting delegates rose to 65.3 percent and the proportion of such officials among the voting members of the Central Committee rose to 38 percent (from 32 percent in 1923, 26 percent in 1922, and 20 percent in 1921).[78] The Secretariat also took steps to remove or transfer Trotsky's supporters from strategic party and governmental posts, and in January 1925 Trotsky himself was removed from his post of People's Commissar for War.

The Economic Debate

The open debate on the party Secretariat quickly came to an end. Trotsky's pamphlets on the subject were soon withdrawn from circulation, and the pages of *Pravda* were temporarily closed to fundamental criticism of the role of the party apparatus. In 1926–1927 the issue was raised again with the publication of the opposition's theses, but the major debates of the rest of the decade really centered on social-economic issues. These were not academic discussions, but involved the top members of the Politburo and were closely associated with the political fate of these men.

In discussing the 1920s, westerners have often described the economic debate and the concurrent struggle for power in rather schematic terms. On the one hand, it is said, the left (notably Trotsky, Zinoviev, and Kamenev) favored rapid industrialization and centralized planning—even if this meant extraction of the necessary investment capital from the peasant and an end to the agricultural policies of NEP. On the other hand, the right (notably Bukharin, Rykov, and Tomsky) insisted on the central importance of the "alliance" (smychka) with the peasants—even if this meant a long-term continuation of NEP and gradual industrialization with an emphasis on the consumers' goods industry. Stalin, it is said, was a cynical Machiavellian interested only in his own power. He is supposed to have first allied himself with the right in order to defeat the Left Opposition in the Politburo, then to have stolen the latter's program so that he could condemn his erstwhile allies as a Right Opposition and remove them from the seats of power.

This schematic summary, like most others of a similar type, has elements of truth in it, but it leaves a very misleading impression of the NEP period and almost surely constitutes too harsh a judgment of Stalin. The crucial fact to remember about the 1920s is that, as the following chronology makes clear, economic conditions changed radically from year to year.

1921	Near economic collapse
Winter of 1921–1922	Famine in the countryside
1922 and much of 1923	Runaway inflation
1923	Gradual stabilization of prices through governmental actions (including tight money)
Summer of 1923	Worker strikes over wage payment difficulties produced by the tight money policy
1923 and 1924	Rapid revival of industry
1924	Drought and partial crop failure
1924 and 1925	Drought-produced explosion of agricultural prices (an attempt to cut down grain prices in late 1924 led to hoarding and a low level of marketings)
Winter 1924–1925	Weather conditions that suggested a second straight poor harvest
1925	In practice, an excellent harvest, but lower grain sales than anticipated and the resulting end to prospects for large grain exports

1925 and 1926	First real emergence of the need for new industrial investment rather than reconstruction of existing plant
1926	Excellent grain harvest *and* marketing
1926–1927	Growing indications that agricultural prosperity was being accompanied by an increase in class stratification among the peasants
1927	Reasonably good harvest, but very sharp decline in grain marketings at end of year
Spring and summer 1927	Bread lines and beginnings of bread rationing
1928	Decline of production of the types of grain eaten by humans and renewed marketing problems

Given these rapidly changing circumstances, it would have been foolish for any Soviet leader to advocate the same short-term policy at all times, and, in practice, none of them did so. At the beginning of the decade, all of the major leaders, at least so far as can be judged from the record now, agreed on the necessity of the New Economic Policy. (If there had been doubts, the Kronstadt revolt resolved them.) The famine that occurred in the countryside during the winter of 1921–1922 further dampened any inclination to challenge the need for agricultural recovery or the concessions that had been made to the peasants.

With the excellent harvest of 1922, however, new problems arose. Agricultural production in that year approximated the average prewar level, but the recovery of industry was very slow and that of heavy industry almost nonexistent. Not surprisingly, this imbalance did produce a debate—one which, to a large extent, began as an institutional one. The State Planning Commission (Gosplan) favored state subsidies to heavy industry to correct the situation—partly, no doubt, because such a policy implied greater planning and hence a greater role for the planning organs. The heavy industry administrators, of course, had no objection to such subsidies. On the other hand, the People's Commissariat for Finance opposed this policy, fearing that subsidies would mean either an unbalanced budget (and hence an undercutting of the campaign to end runaway inflation) or the sacrifice of the proagricultural policy (and agriculture provided the export grain that was the source of foreign currency.)[79]

With the exception of Trotsky, the Politburo strongly supported the position of the People's Commissariat for Finance (scarcely a surprising fact considering the severity of the inflation), and even Trotsky's opposition was not very intense or focused. Trotsky was deeply committed to the principle of planning in general and to the strengthening of Gosplan in particular, and (as might be expected of a Commissar for War), he favored rapid expansion of industry, especially of the heavy industry that was important for the military. Yet, Trotsky also favored a stable currency,[80] and he was not disposed to attack agricultural policy. While the strikes of the summer of 1923 provided the occasion for some criticism of economic policy (and the coining of the phrase 'scissors crisis," which plays a far larger role in western literature on the Soviet Union than its brief existence in the Soviet Union would suggest), the rapid industrial recovery of 1923–1924 muted the industrialization debate for a short period. In practice, while Trotsky was accused of "neglecting the peasants," neither his attack upon the leadership nor their campaign against him in these years really touched on economic issues.[81] Instead, the argument centered first on the issue of party organization and then moved increasingly to an unedifying exchange of misleading and irrelevant charges about each other's historical record.

The economic debate really began in earnest in late 1924. Not only had both agricultural and industrial recovery finally reached levels which required policymakers to face up to real alternatives, but, in addition, one of the early critics, E. A. Preobrazhensky (probably the leading figure behind the Declaration of the Forty-Six) sharpened his position and thereby created the conditions for meaningful counterattack and debate.[82]

The debate began with a paper entitled "The Fundamental Law of Socialist Accumulation," which Preobrazhensky presented in August 1924— a paper that squarely faced the problem of the "premature revolution." The socialist revolution, Marx had said, would come at an advanced stage of capitalist development—a state at which the capitalists had already performed the historically necessary and beneficial (although painful) task of building an industrial base out of the sweat of the population. The revolution would occur at a time when the economy would produce more than could be purchased by the population—at least given the wage level that the capitalist system provided. In reality, of course, the Bolshevik revolution in Russia had taken place during the early stages of industrialization, and the "primitive capitalist accumulation" (as Marx called this process of building the industrial base) had not occurred. The country did not have the industrial capacity to distribute "each according to his needs," for needs far outstripped production.

Preobrazhensky argued that the process of "primitive accumulation" was an inevitable one and that, as a consequence, the socialist regime would be compelled to follow a policy of "primitive socialist accumulation." As under capitalism, the population would not receive the full value of their labor, for a significant portion of it would be "expropriated" for the purposes of capital investment. Given the agricultural nature of the economy, this meant, in practice, the financing of industrialization largely through the difference between the value of agricultural produce and the value of the consumer goods and machinery the peasants received in exchange. While taxation was one way to achieve this aim, Preobrazhensky thought that artificially low agricultural prices (or artificially high industrial goods prices) were the "politically more advantageous" method of doing so.

Whatever the means of "primitive socialist accumulation" (and in Preobrazhensky's analysis, the word "primitive" in no way implied any meaning of "crude" in the sense of forced collectivization), Preobrazhensky insisted that the need for it was an iron law:

> The more economically backward, petty bourgeois and peasant in character is the country making the transition to a socialist organization of production, the smaller is the legacy which the proletariat of the country in question receives at the moment of the socialist revolution to build up its own socialist accumulation, and the more in proportion this socialist accumulation will be obliged to rely on the expropriation of the surplus production of pre-socialist forms of the economy.[83]

Perhaps because he simply felt the need to "rebuild and reassert Bolshevism as a coherent ideology" in the new conditions of NEP,[84] perhaps because Preobrazhensky's link with Trotsky made his article "a godsend to the leaders of the campaign against Trotsky,"[85] but perhaps also because the leadership was on the verge of an even more conciliatory policy toward the peasants in an attempt to prevent a second straight bad harvest in 1925,[86] Bukharin was moved to mount a sharp and basic attack against the Preobrazhensky position. As he did so over the next two years he developed a comprehensive analysis of NEP as the proper transitory road to socialism rather than merely a retreat.

Stephen Cohen has suggested that Bukharin's rejection of the Preobrazhensky arguments rested not only on political and economic grounds, but also in significant part upon ethical considerations—a distaste for the tone of Preobrazhensky's line of analysis and for the thought that socialism and capitalism might be somewhat similar in their exploitative nature.[87] Overtly, however, the analysis was phrased essentially in political and economic terms. In his 1924 paper Preobrazhensky had frankly recognized that his position would be politically unpopular with the peasants if understood by them: "I do not speak here of the difficulties of a political nature which arise from the mutual relations of the working class and the peasantry and made it often obligatory to speak of equivalent exchange, though that is even more utopian under the socialization of large-scale industry than under the rule of monopoly capitalism."[88] Bukharin, on the other hand, thought that these political difficulties could not be brushed aside so easily. He had no faith that an exploitative policy could be hidden from the peasants against whom it was directed, and he was very pessimistic about the consequences of peasant dissatisfaction. "A proletariat dictatorship which is in a state of war with the peasantry," he declared, "can in no way be strong."[89]

Bukharin argued that the "alliance with the peasant" was also essential for economic reasons. He believed that, rather than there being a conflict between industrial growth and peasant prosperity, the former depended upon the latter. In the first place, rural prosperity would provide the effective demand for industrial goods and therefore for industrial growth. ("The greater the buying powers of the peasantry, the faster our industry develops.") In the second place, a prosperous peasantry would provide investment funds both through a progressive income tax and through voluntary savings.[90]

Bukharin's analysis was developed at a time when the leadership was concerned about the implications of the poor 1924 harvest and when the ambitious peasants were complaining about their dilemma: "You call on us to improve our cultivation, to mechanize it. We shall grow, our revenues will grow, we shall have more horses, cattle, and machines, and what will you do? The representative of the executive committee of the department answers: 'We shall dekulakize you.' "[91] ("Kulak" was the pejorative term for a well-to-do peasant.) In April 1925, the regime moved to answer these objections and to create conditions for the efficient peasants to produce more. It lowered agricultural taxes and (within limits) legalized the hiring of labor and the leasing of land by those peasants who wished to do so.

The 1925 concessions to the peasants were approved by the entire Politburo, but it was Bukharin who defended them most vociferously:

> The well-to-do top layer of the peasantry—the kulak and in part the middle peasant—is at present afraid to accumulate . . . If the peasant wants to put up an iron roof tomorrow he will be denounced and that will be the end of him. If the peasant buys a machine, he does it "so that the communists may not see." The technical improvement of agriculture is enveloped in a kind of conspiracy . . . Our policy in relation to the countryside should develop in the direction of removing, and in part abolishing many restrictions which put the brake on the growth of the well-to-do and kulak farm. To the peasants, to all the peasants, we must say: Enrich yourselves, develop your farms, and do not fear that constraint will be put on you.[92]

Throughout the 1922–1925 period, Zinoviev and Kamenev had been leading supporters of the regime's agricultural policy, and Zinoviev in particular had responded to the poor harvest of 1924 with a call for more concessions to the peasants—for the party "to turn its face to the countryside." As E. H. Carr has written, "if anyone in January 1925 had been acute enough to predict an imminent break between Stalin and Zinoviev on [the agricultural issue], he would almost certainly have seen in Zinoviev the prospective champion of a peasant policy and Stalin as its opponent."[93]

In the early summer of 1925, however, Zinoviev and Kamenev came out in opposition to the agricultural policy which they had been supporting earlier in the year. They centered their attack upon Bukharin's slogan "Enrich yourselves" and upon the attitude toward the rich peasant (the kulak) which it implied. Zinoviev now asserted that "the kulak in the countryside is more dangerous, far more dangerous, than the nepman in the town," and Kamenev expressed concern about the "social content" of the excellent 1925 harvest (that is, the amount produced by well-to-do peasants).[94] They began characterizing NEP as a period of "state capitalism" and began emphasizing that it should be no more than a temporary retreat.

Western accounts of the mid-1920s often imply—and sometimes flatly state—that Stalin moved to the right in this period in order to have an issue with which to defeat the left. In reality, Stalin himself was moving to the left at this time. Like the other leaders, he did support the 1925 agricultural policy, but he never associated himself with the extremes of Bukharin's language—particularly the latter's "Enrich yourselves" slogan. Furthermore, in the spring and summer of 1925, the General Secretary, together with Rykov, also began to emphasize the need for industrial growth, citing several statements by Lenin about the importance of "heavy industry." (Stalin generally used the phrase "metal industry" at the time: "heavy industry" was so new that it was enclosed in quotation marks.)[95] Indeed, Stalin and Rykov did not limit themselves to verbal statements in favor of the metal industry, for the leadership began to increase the actual amount of industrial investment sharply. The control (or plan figures) for the 1925–1926 fiscal year which Gosplan prepared forecast an industrial growth of 33 percent.[96]

If Stalin is to be attacked for Machiavellianism in 1925, it should not be for a cynical move to the right (at least not in domestic policy), but for a deliberate inconsistency between his industrial and agricultural policies—for failing to acknowledge how he was planning to finance rapid industrial growth. Yet on balance, such a charge probably is not fair. Preobrazhensky had seen a sharp conflict between the interests of industrial development and those of the peasants, but in 1923–1925 industry had, in practice, grown very rapidly at a time when price policy was favorable toward agriculture. (Industrial production increased by 48 percent during the 1924–1925 fiscal year.)[97] As Stalin himself noted in a speech, the extent of the recovery had caught the planners by surprise,[98] and it was not illogical for a politician with little responsibility for economic decision-making to assume that the problem of financing industrial investment might not be as difficult as some had stated.

Moreover, it would be quite natural—almost instinctive—for any politician to think that if a contradiction did, indeed, exist between agricultural policy and the plans for industrial investment, there would be plenty of time to change the former when—and if—difficulties arose. (This is, as we shall see, precisely what happened.) And, perhaps, as will be discussed shortly, there actually may not have been that much contradiction between agricultural and industrial policies in the mid-1920s—a point that a number of leading western scholars have begun to suggest, but that Stalin himself apparently did not suspect by the time of the crucial decisions at the end of the decade.

Stalin's Consolidation of Power

In actuality, what seems to have occurred in 1925 was not some move to the right on Stalin's part, but an attempt by Zinoviev and Kamenev to adopt left policies for political reasons—and not a very consistent attempt at that. While Kamenev and Zinoviev did differ with Bukharin on the peasant question, it is difficult to avoid the conclusion that they launched their attack on agricultural policy as a desperate effort to stave off political defeat at Stalin's hands rather than as a result of deep policy differences with the Politburo majority.

For over a year Stalin had been undercutting the position of his partners in the troika. The selection of Rykov as Chairman of the Council of People's Commissars marked a de facto demotion for Kamenev, for the latter had actually been filling this post during Lenin's illness. Then during the following months Stalin subtly began to criticize his presumed associates in various ways.[99] Even his espousal of "socialism in one country" in late 1924, while later seen as the keystone of his argument with Trotsky, was perhaps more of an immediate thrust at Zinoviev as head of the Comintern. (It surely is significant that Trotsky did not criticize the slogan until 1926, while Zinoviev began attacking it within a matter of months.)[100] Of even more importance, Stalin managed to gain control of Kamenev's Moscow organization in the fall of 1924,[101] and in early 1925 he gave signs of wanting both to reduce Zinoviev's domination of Comintern affairs and to take over his stronghold in Leningrad (the new name for Petrograd).

These actions of Stalin, more than any policy differences, seem to have driven Zinoviev and Kamenev into opposition. The immediate occasion for their decision was a June 1925 letter which Lenin's widow, Krupskaia, wrote to denounce the favoritism shown the kulak and Bukharin's defense of this policy. The suspicion of the kulak was becoming quite strong, and, particularly given Krupskaia's support, Zinoviev and Kamenev must have believed the issue an ideal one on which to mobilize party opinion against the leadership.

Even though Zinoviev's and Kamenev's charges were given added credibility by the procurement difficulties after the excellent 1925 harvest, their opposition proved unsuccessful. They were given a full opportunity to develop their differences with Stalin at the Fourteenth Party Congress in December 1925, but they now found themselves in much the same position as Trotsky at the Thirteenth Congress. As the chief executioners of Trotsky at that Congress, they had led the call for party unity and suppression of factionalism. Now, like Trotsky, they were in the position of appearing to challenge the very slogans which they had earlier defended. "When there is a majority for Zinoviev," Mikoian remarked at the Fourteenth Congress, "he is for iron discipline, for subordination. When he has no majority . . . he is against it."[102]

When Kamenev climaxed a long speech with a personal attack on Stalin and the whole theory of vesting supreme power in a *vozhd* or leader, the congress dissolved into a noisy uproar. Stalin's supporters shouted "Stalin! Stalin!" while the Leningrad delegation shouted back, "Long live the Central Committee of our party! . . . The party above all!"[103] With that demonstration, less than two years after Lenin's death, the Stalin cult was launched. The outcome of the Fourteenth Congress was an overwhelming victory for Stalin. The opposition could muster but 65 votes as against 559 for the leadership. The Central Committee elected at the congress (now raised to sixty-three voting members) demoted Kamenev to candidate membership in the Politburo, and within a month he was removed from his position as Deputy Chairman of the Council of People's Commissars.

Even at this stage, Stalin's final destruction of the Left Opposition was a gradual one. Immediately after the congress, he sent a team of supporters to Leningrad to purge the party leadership of Zinoviev's followers, and they succeeded in this aim, installing one of Stalin's supporters, Sergei Kirov, as the Leningrad first secretary. With this base of power gone, Zinoviev and Kamenev had little except their prestige and oratory left to sustain them. At this low point in their fortunes, they joined forces with Trotsky in the hope of staging a recovery, but the decision came too late. In April 1926 Zinoviev was removed from the Politburo, and in October Trotsky lost his membership and Kamenev his candidate membership. All remained members of the

Central Committee for the next year, but in October 1927 Trotsky and Zinoviev were expelled from this body and none of the oppositionists retained their membership in the Central Committee elected in December at the Fifteenth Party Congress.

The two-year campaign against the Left Opposition was not accompanied by any movement of economic policy in a rightward direction. On the contrary, investments in government-planned industry rose steadily and rapidly: 811 million rubles in the 1925–1926 fiscal year, 1,068 million in 1926–1927, 1,304 million in 1927–1928, 1,679 million in 1928–1929.[104] On the agricultural front, the Fifteenth Congress spoke in general terms of the desirability of collectivization, and it raised taxes on the well-to-do peasant and limited the amount of land that could be leased. Even earlier, state procurement prices—particularly those for grain—had been cut sharply.

While economic policy was moving leftward, it (for the first time in several years) did not produce the desired results in 1927. The 1927 harvest, like that in 1926, was an excellent one, but the grain marketings of 1926 were not repeated in 1927. By the fall, consumer goods were in short supply, and grain marketings dropped precipitously. Bukharin and others called for a reversal in the grain price policy in order to solve the latter problem (they might also have called for an increase in consumer goods prices to solve the former one). Stalin's response, however, was the use of threats and administrative actions against the kulaks who were thought to be hoarding the grain. "Free markets were closed, private traders thrown out, peasants ordered to deliver grain and punished as criminals if they failed to do so."[105]

The grain collection campaign of January-February 1928 was admittedly marked by "excesses," and Rykov, Bukharin, and Tomsky became increasingly alarmed at reports of unrest in the countryside. By the summer of 1928, Bukharin and Stalin were no longer on speaking terms, and the former was in desperate contact with Kamenev in an unsuccessful attempt to limit Stalin. By October the leadership was denouncing the "right deviation"—but without giving names. By December, Stalin had taken over the institutional sources of support of the right.

While struggling with the Right Opposition, Stalin continued—indeed, intensified—the industrialization program that he had been espousing since 1925. Production in planned industry had risen 26.3 percent in the 1927–1928 fiscal year, and as the regime strove to compile its First Five-Year Plan in 1927 and 1928, the projected rate of industrial investment within it was increasing steadily. By the end of 1928 the Supreme Economic Council was advocating a 50 percent rise for the 1929–1930 fiscal year. Despite Gosplan's strenuous objection to this proposal as too extreme, the Politburo in April 1929 approved a plan that was even more ambitious.[106]

As the debate on industrial investment raged, the problem of grain procurements worsened rather than improved. Neither the decisions of the Fifteenth Congress nor the procurements campaign of early 1928 nor the continuing low prices did much to induce the peasants to increase grain production and marketings, particularly since livestock prices were high and it was profitable to produce grain and fodder for their animals (or even to buy bread in the cities to feed them). As a consequence, the winter of 1928–1929 was marked by yet another procurements crisis, this one severe enough to lead to the introduction of bread rationing in the cities. With growing unrest in the countryside, the 1929 harvest looked even worse.

Stalin's response to this procurement crisis was even harsher than to that of 1927–1928. On the one hand, he completed the rout of the Right Opposition, who had continued to call for higher grain prices and moderation in the rate of increase of industrial development. Bukharin was removed from the leadership of the Comintern in April 1929, and in June Tomsky lost his position as head of the trade union. In November the Central Committee expelled Bukharin from the Politburo, and he, together with Tomsky and Rykov, capitulated with a statement to *Pravda* "recognizing our mistakes."[107] Even this self-abasement did not suffice. At the Sixteenth Party Congress (June 26 to July 13, 1930), Tomsky was dropped from the Politburo. Toward the end of December, Rykov was also removed from that body, as well as from his position as chairman of the Council of People's Commissars.

At the same time Stalin acted to "solve" the problems of grain marketings and of "primitive socialist accumulation" by means more drastic than the leaders of the left had ever publicly proposed—the forced collectivization of the Soviet countryside. As early as February 1928, Stalin had stated (in an unpublished speech) that "in order to put grain procurements on a satisfactory basis other measures are required . . . I have in mind the formation of collective farms and state farms." In June of that year he had spoken of "tribute" from the peasants and of the need to "industrialize the country with the help of internal accumulation."[108] In the winter of 1929–1930, he revealed what those words were to mean.

The Explanation for Stalin's Victory

As on the relationship between Leninism and Stalinism, there has been scholarly debate on the reasons Stalin emerged as ruler of Russia by 1929. To some extent, the two debates overlap and center on the nature of the party and the Soviet system as a whole. Was one-man rule of the Stalin type inevitable given the nature of the Communist party and the ideology of the time, or did Stalin simply take advantage of circumstances to conduct a veritable cout d'etat over the party as a collective? Nevertheless, there is a narrower question to analyze—the emergence of Stalin personally as the leader rather than the emergence of dictatorial rule in general.

From what has been seen in the early discussion of the strengths and weaknesses of the various contenders and in the later analysis of the history of the 1920s, it is obvious that no single factor will explain Stalin's rise to power. The General Secretary's victory was facilitated by a number of his personal characteristics (particularly in contrast to those of his opponents), by his strategic position in the Central Committee Secretariat, by his skill in dealing with his opponents in a piecemeal fashion and in using the anti-faction rule in labeling them as "deviations," by the caution and patience he displayed before challenging the norms of collective rule, by his ability to identify himself with a number of strong strains in Bolshevism (notably those of nationalism and a dedication to industrial development), and by the lack of political astuteness shown by most of his opponents.

The question is the relative weight to be accorded these various factors. With (at least to some extent) the exception of Barrington Moore, the fore-most scholars of the 1950s emphasized the importance of Stalin's position as General Secretary. E. H. Carr expressed the point in a particularly stark form when he stated that "the victory of Stalin . . . was a triumph, not of reason, but of organization,"[109] but Merle Fainsod was scarcely less strong in his emphasis upon "the power of the party's bureaucratic phalanx," "the disciplined battalions of the apparatus," and the fact that "the Stalinist machine was so solidly entrenched in all the key positions in the party apparatus as to be virtually impervious to attack."[110]

The basic argument of this position, as has been seen, is that the principle of democratic centralism of the party had a fatal flaw so far as its democratic elements were concerned. The desire for a disciplined party apparatus required selection and supervision of lower party officials from above, but—especially in view of the prohibition against factions—these lower officials themselves were in a position to control the selection of delegates to the party congresses. Since the party congress selected the Central Committee which in turn selected the Politburo and the General Secretary, the man charged with supervising the party apparatus (the General Secretary) had the opportunity to build a machine which could dominate not only the congresses but also the Central Committee and the Politburo. In this view, such a "circular flow of power" was the crucial element in the history of the 1920s. It gave Stalin the ability to have the Central Committee increased from a voting membership of twenty-seven in 1922 to one of seventy-one in 1927, to place his supporters among the new members, and to thereby guar-antee that the Central Committee would make the changes in the Politburo that he desired.[111]

No contemporary western scholar is inclined to say that these "organizational factors" were an insignificant factor in Stalin's rise to power, but some contend that their importance was exaggerated in the past. Robert Tucker, for example, suggests that "without minimizing the force of these [organizational] considerations . . . they do not suffice to explain the events of that period." "A would-be party chief had to develop a politically persuasive program and be convincing in his way of presenting it in higher party circles."[112] Tucker does not make the point, but it could be argued that only some 45 percent of the voting members of the 1927 Central Committee were party officials, and that Stalin's industrialization program was particularly attractive to the growing number of economic administrators on the Central Committee.[113] (They totaled nearly 20 percent of the voting members in 1927.)

Stephen Cohen seems to go even further in questioning the importance of Stalin's control of the apparatus, for he calls into question the control itself:

> Machine politics alone did not account for Stalin's triumph . . . The Central Committee . . . ratified an outcome already decided by a smaller, informal group of senior Central Committee members—an oligarchy of 20 to 30 influentials made up of high party leaders and heads of the most important Central Committee delegations . . . As administrators and politicians, they were often associated with the general secretary. Most of them, however, were not his mindless political creatures . . . By April 1929 these influentials had chosen Stalin and formed his essential majority in the high leadership. They did so, it seems clear, less because of his bureaucratic power than because they preferred his leadership and policies . . . The salient political fact of 1928–29 was a growing climate of high party opinion impatient with the Right's cautionary sermons and receptive to Stalin's assiduous cultivation of Bolshevism's heroic tradition.[114]

To some extent, the debate about Stalin's victory is a moot one. Any person with the intention, the skill, and the strategic location to build a political machine usually will also have the intention and skill to present a program that is politically sound. That this latter intention and skill is a necessary part of building a machine is, of course, a vital fact to keep in mind. If we forget that the strongest political machine ultimately rests on the self-interest and loyalty of the leader's subordinates, we may not be sensitive to the possibility that machines can and do collapse. (This "we" may include the leader of a machine—for example, Khrushchev—as well as those who study it.) Moreover, we may fail to see the multiplicity of supports for a successful leader and may fail to explain convincingly how a leader such as Stalin could not only win in 1929 but also still be in power in 1935, let alone 1938.

Nevertheless, while Stalin was politically astute in his program (at least until 1929), this edition of *How Russia Is Ruled* will continue to emphasize the importance of the "circular flow of power." It surely is true, as Cohen suggests, that the 1928 Central Committee contained twenty to thirty influentials who could have overthrown Stalin if they had acted in concert, but it was Stalin who had had the major role in determining who these oligarchs would be (including the economic administrators among them) and what views would be prevalent among them. An effort by a few of them to organize a concerted attack against the General Secretary could have led to the same consequences suffered by the more illustrious oppositionists and deviationists within the Politburo who made a similar attempt.

Given Stalin's organizational position, given a moderately intelligent program on his part (and the extreme industrialization program of 1929 scarcely seems the most intelligent from a political point of view), it seems to me that none of his opponents really were in a position after the Twelfth Congress in 1923 to put together a program or a coalition that could have defeated him. On his fiftieth birthday on December 21, 1929—a time at which he was launching his great transformation of Soviet society—Stalin was hailed in *Pravda* as "the truest and most dedicated pupil and associate of Lenin," "the leader (*vozhd*) of the party of the proletariat," "the leader of the class struggle," "the real leader of industrialization," "the leader of the Comintern," "the most important theoretician of Leninism," "the closest and dearest friend of the Red army," and so forth. In the words of A. S. Bubnov, the RSFSR People's Commissar of Enlightenment, "Stalin is an entire epoch in the history of our party."[115] He had little of the appearance of a man who had just been chosen by an oligarchy a relatively short time ago. One would think that the agricultural disasters of the First Five-Year Plan would have raised some questions about the quality of his leadership and perhaps eroded some of his support, but these developments are relevant for our understanding of how Stalin maintained power in the 1930s, not how and when he gained it in the 1920s.

5 | The Years of Transformation and Petrification

THE STALIN PERIOD has become the neglected orphan of political scientists studying the Soviet Union. Many innovative studies have emerged on the 1920s, and examination of the post-Stalin scene continues. The intervening quarter of a century has been left largely to several major historians, economists, and journalists who have been re-exploring the early industrialization drive or retelling the horrors of the purges, and even these studies deal not with the Stalin period as a whole but with the first third of it.[1]

Indeed, if the early 1930s are excluded, it is probable that understanding of the Stalin era actually has deteriorated rather than improved over the last decade. The first great flowering of western scholarship on the Soviet Union occurred in the late 1940s and early 1950s, and, of course, it concentrated on the political system of the day. In practice, it did so with considerable skill and subtlety. As time passed, however, this analysis of the late Stalin period became less applicable to the current Soviet scene, new literature arose which demanded to be read, and young scholars began to return less frequently to the earlier work. They criticized the applicability of the totalitarian model to current Soviet reality, but in the process they tended to assume that the model was an adequate representation of the Stalin system. While at times dismissing Soviet studies of the Stalin era as "cold war scholarship," they themselves often adopted an image of that era which comes closer to deserving that appelation than does the literature they criticize.

In fact, the Stalin period was a complex one, and the various characterizations made of it seldom apply to all of its subperiods. The years that are most appropriately described as a revolutionary transformation of society

147

(the late twenties and early thirties) were not years of terror within the party or even of unquestioned one-man dictation on every question. The years in which Stalin's rule was most unchallenged (the postwar period) were more a time of stagnation and rigidity than of the remaking of society—although, to be sure, the rigidity in maintaining a high level of investment ensured the rapid continuation of the type of societal change always produced by industrialization and urbanization. Finally, one-fifth of the period was occupied by World War II—when the relationship between the party and the population deviated significantly from the stereotypes about the Stalin period as a whole.

The Great Transformation

The end of the 1920s featured the liquidation of NEP and the initiation of a radically new phase in the development of the Soviet system. The new policy represented a determined effort to destroy the petty bourgeois peasant revolution which had been achieved in 1917 and to seize the positions which the peasantry had occupied during NEP. It launched the Soviet Union on a course of industrialization which transformed it into a first-class military power. It was also accompanied by the emergence and consolidation of a regime which ruthlessly crushed any trace of political dissent and tried to subordinate every form of social organization to its own purpose.

The change in the basic policy line did not occur at once, for hints of the end of NEP emerged as early as 1927. The first great change in atmosphere took place in the foreign policy realm. The 1920s had been a period of establishing diplomatic relations with most of the western powers, but these relations often proved to be rocky in nature. In late May 1927 Great Britain severed diplomatic relations altogether, and in October France demanded the recall of the Soviet ambassador in Paris. The result, whether reflective of genuine leadership concern or contrived by it for domestic purposes, was a major press campaign stressing the dangers of imminent war. A widespread war scare spread through the population as a whole,[2] and the political implications and uses of this development were not ignored. "The Bolsheviks used the war scare against the Trotsky Opposition," wrote a friendly journalist. " 'Look at these traitors,' they said in effect, 'who undermine the party while the capitalists threaten from without.' "[3] But, of course, it was the right for whom the war scare should have been even more ominous.

After the Fifteenth Party Congress in December 1927, the storm clouds of impending internal strife gathered more quickly in the face of the shortfall in grain purchases. In January 1928 Stalin personally and openly identified himself with the need for harsh emergency action. Traveling to Siberia by train, he demanded that local officials seize grain being hoarded and that they deal ruthlessly with kulak sabotage. The mood in the countryside changed radically.[4]

Then in March the press announced the discovery of a counterrevolutionary group—composed largely of technical specialists—which allegedly was engaged in sabotage in the coal fields near Shakhty.[5] If the war scare emphasized the severity of the international class danger and the grain collection campaign the danger from class enemies in the countryside, the Shakhty affair, with its six-week trial, dramatically focused attention on the enemy among the "bourgeois specialists" and the non-Communist intelligentsia. Those who had been angered by the positions of privilege held by these people or who simply wanted a distinctive Communist culture found that the Shakhty affair provided welcome legitimization for a general "cultural revolution" (kul'-turnaia revoliutsiia)—for "class war on the cultural front."

The cultural revolution in the Soviet Union had, on a somewhat lesser scale, much the same spirit as its Chinese counterpart four decades later. Individual specialists often were harassed by local forces; purges were conducted within the bureaucracy and the universities; culture became politicized as the radical figures in the various cultural realms were unleashed to launch frontal attacks upon the established cultural authorities (the People's Commissariat of Enlightenment, which supervised education and the arts, as well as the non-Communist intelligentsia); and many utopians took advantage of the situation to push forward their pet projects. In the education realm the main lesson drawn from the Shakhty affair was the need for creation of a new Soviet or proletarian intelligentsia, and the decision was taken to expand the higher education system enormously and to attract a far larger proportion of students of proletarian background into it. The Komsomol were encouraged to undertake a large-scale and boisterous campaign to liquidate illiteracy among the population and to promote universal primary education.[6]

With the cultural revolution, the rapidly quickening pace of industrialization, and then collectivization, the first years of the Five-Year Plan marked a return to the military traditions of the Civil War period and war communism. In the words of Merle Fainsod, "the Plan opened up an exhilarating period of struggle and combat, a leap forward into the New Jerusalem . . . The air was electric with positions to be stormed, class enemies to be destroyed, and fortresses to be built . . . The last remnants of private capitalism and the old 'bourgeois culture' appeared to be headed for extinction."[7]

As the Five-Year Plan gathered momentum, it was, of course, the countryside that received the brunt of the attack. While only 4.1 percent of the peasant households had entered collective farms, or kolkhozes, voluntarily by October 1929, the Politburo decided at this time to launch a mass collectivization drive. After Stalin had written in Pravda in early November about "the great turn" and "a radical change within the peasantry itself," the Central Committee met that month to endorse his program. It called for the mobilization of 25,000 urban workers (the famous 25,000ers) to spearhead the drive. In the deliberations going on behind the scenes, Stalin pushed for greater speed. On 27 December—six days after he had been glorified in *Pravda* on his fiftieth birthday—he gave the final public signal. The kulaks were to be liquidated as a class, and the expropriation of their property was sanctioned.[8]

When the Kremlin insisted that speed was necessary, the whole machinery of the party and government was mobilized to force the peasants to join. Detailed instructions were drawn up (including, for example, a prohibition against the dekulakization of families of Red army soldiers or officers), but in practice the campaign was featured by great confusion and disorganization. The conditions near Smolensk were probably quite typical:

> Despite apparently precise directives and instructions, many raion and village authorities went their own way, interpreting the kulak category broadly to embrace middle and even poor peasants who were opposed to collectivization [and] evicting kulak families with Red army connections . . . Excesses were commonplace. According to [a secret police report of February 28, 1930] certain members of the workers' brigades and officials of lower echelons of the party-soviet apparatus deprived members of kulak and middle peasant households of their clothing and warm underwear (directly from the body), "confiscated" headwear from children's heads, and removed shoes from people's feet. The perpetrators divided the "confiscated" goods among themselves; the food they found was eaten on the spot; the alcohol they uncovered was consumed immediately, resulting in drunken orgies.[9]

The use of pressure tactics yielded a quick statistical triumph. On paper at least, the proportion of peasant households enrolled in collective farms mounted to 58.1 percent in March 1930. But as reports accumulated that the peasants were slaughtering their cattle and draft animals in order to avoid confiscation and that they were often refusing to contribute their labor to the new collective farms, the leaders of the regime began to realize that they had won a Pyrrhic victory. On March 2, 1930, Stalin again reversed course with the publication of his famous article, "Dizziness from Success."[10] In this and subsequent pronouncements, he blamed misguided local party and Soviet authorities for forcing the pace of collectivization. Stalin's article was interpreted by many peasants as permission to withdraw from the kolkhozes, and the mass exodus which followed reduced the percentages of peasant households in collective farms from 58.1 in March to 23.6 in June.[11]

Despite this setback, the campaign for collectivization was resumed in the fall of 1930. This time more subtle means of "persuasion" were combined with the old reliance on force and threats. Discriminatory taxation was imposed on individual peasants, while those who joined the collective farms were offered certain forms of tax alleviation as well as the advantages of sharing in the credits, machinery, seed grain, and other privileges and preferences. The regime was now adamant, and efforts to avoid collectivization were increasingly hazardous and difficult. By the middle of 1931, 52.7 percent of all peasant households had been collectivized. The proportion increased steadily over the following years, amounting to 71.4 percent in 1934 and 89.6 percent in 1936. (The percentage of crop area collectivized rose more quickly, reaching, for example, 87.4 percent as early as 1934.)[12]

To ensure that grain would be collected and delivered to the state, the party moved to establish machine-tractor stations (the MTS) to carry out this task. Like collectivization itself, the creation of the MTS was an incremental process. (As late as December 1934, the kolkhozes served by the MTS possessed only 63.9 percent of the sown area of all kolkhozes, and often even this service was nominal in character.)[13] However, in the system which gradually developed, all farm machinery was centralized in the hands of the MTS, and the MTS (rather than the kolkhozes) then conducted the farm operations which utilized machinery. Since grain was the foremost product subject to mechanized work at the time, the state was in a position to solve the grain procurement problem simply by retaining the necessary grain harvested by the MTS and by paying whatever price it desired.

Gradual though the collectivization program was in some respects, its costs were enormous. The level of grain production, which had been rising during the 1920s became essentially static after 1928. Some 73 to 76 million tons of grain a year had been produced in the 1925–26 to 1927–28 period, but the average annual production of grain was no more than 73.6 million tons in the years 1928–1932, 72.9 million tons in 1933–1937, and 77.9 million tons in 1938–1940.[14] The impact of collectivization upon the country's livestock was nothing short of devastating, for a high percentage of peasants slaughtered their animals rather than give them to the kolkhoz. The number of cattle in the country declined from 70.5 million in 1928 to 52.5 million in 1930 to 38.4 million in 1933, while that of pigs decreased from 26 million to 12.1 million in these years.[15]

The human costs of collectivization were also extremely high. Homes and land were defended, "terroristic" acts taken against Soviet and kolkhoz officials, and guerrilla bands formed, and the regime responded ruthlessly. Many peasants died during the formation of the kolkhozes, and others were sent to camps or to exile in Siberia or the north where a number failed to survive. Still another group perished in the famine of 1932–1933. In talking with Churchill in one of their wartime meetings, Stalin stated that the period of collectivization had been more stressful than World War II, that it had been a "terrible struggle,"[16] and this assertion is quite easy to believe.

The scale of the "war" in the countryside and number of casualties are difficult to gauge. Soviet historians have published a number of books and articles with figures on peasant resistance and guerrilla activity in specific areas and specific periods: 200 groups in Moscow region in 1930, 32 underground organizations and 190 kulak groups (with 3,000 members) in Lower Volga Territory at the beginning of 1930, 76 counterrevolutionary organizations and 411 groups (with 6,259 participants) uncovered in the North Caucasus from April to August 1930, and so forth.[17]

A comprehensive, overall picture of the peasant resistance does not emerge from Soviet literature, but by the second half of 1930 the regime apparently began to have success in its efforts to bring it under control. One major tool was the exile of kulak and other resisting peasant families. Soviet historians have now concluded that nearly 300,000 families were exiled to distant regions during the collectivization drive, with the average family containing some four members. By the beginning of 1935, there were 1,085,000 exiles (including members of their families), 640,000 of them in special settlements connected with industrial, construction, or transportation work and 445,000 in special collective farms. Approximately 50 percent of the exiles were living in the Urals, and another 40 percent divided among western Siberia, the Northern Territory (in European Russia), and Kazakhstan.[18]

Soviet historians have not published statistics on the number who died during collectivization, but westerners have ventured estimates which sometimes run into the tens of millions. When checked against available census data, however, the more extreme figures cannot be sustained and a smaller—but still horrifying—number emerges. If we take age distribution data from the 1926 census and attempt to project the number of citizens who should (on the basis of "normal" mortality rates) be found in the appropriately older categories thirteen years later at the time of the 1939 census, the results can be compared with the actual 1939 data and the number of "excess" deaths (at least among those already born in 1926) can be estimated. Employing this methodology, Frank Lorimer concluded that there were some 4.5 to 5.5 million "excess" deaths (or emigrants) between 1926 and 1939.[19] To obtain collectivization casualties, we must reduce this figure by the number of Central Asian nomads who moved into Sinkiang to avoid collectivization (and they may be in the hundreds of thousands) and by the number of those who died because of overcrowding in the cities and then the Great Purge. Nevertheless, the largest portion of deaths—maybe some 3.5 million in all—were almost surely the direct or indirect result of collectivization, most probably the product of the famine of 1932–1933.[20]

While western scholars have emphasized the high cost of collectivization and its horrors, they have also tended to argue in the past that, despite the costs, it at least did achieve the most important goals set for it by Stalin. Forced collectivization was launched in 1928–1929, all scholars agree, not simply because of a desire to build socialism or a belief that it would increase production immediately, but because it was seen as a solution to the 1928–1929 difficulties with grain marketings. Net marketings in the 1926–27 fiscal year had been 10.3 million tons, but had fallen to 8.3 million tons both in 1927–28 and 1928–29. Exports had decreased from 2.5 million tons to .4 million tons to .1 million tons in these years.[21] These figures rose to new heights after 1929, and even in the famine years they were well above the precollectivization level (see table 2).

In addition, a great many of the most influential scholars in the Soviet field held a set of essentially Marxist assumptions about the need for "primitive accumulation" in the early stages of industrial development. They accepted that rapid industrialization (unless financed by foreign investment) requires a "squeeze" on the peasant in some form or another, and hence they found the heart of Preobrazhensky's argument generally compelling. The more rapid the industrialization, the greater need, they assumed, for pressure on peasant incomes, either through price policy, taxation, or perhaps forced requisition from peasants in collective farms. Thus, Alec Nove concluded in the early 1960s that there clearly were "excessive excesses" in the 1930s which were attributable to Stalin personally, but he still argued "once the decision to move fast [on industrialization] was taken, this had very radical consequences. In 1928 any practicable Bolshevik programme would have been harsh and unpopular."[22]

In this respect, too, the collectivization program was generally seen as successful in providing the necessary capital for industrial development. The extraordinary rates of growth projected in the First Five-Year Plan period were not achieved, but industry did grow rapidly by any standard. Unfortunately, the rate of growth is difficult to pinpoint precisely, for in the early stages of industrialization the figures vary enormously with the method of calculation used, and there really is no objective way to solve the problem.[23] However, most of the statistics on actual (as opposed to ruble) production are reasonably accurate, and they are quite clear in their implications. Thus, for example, the amount of oil produced rose from 11.6 million tons in 1928 to 31.1 million tons in 1940 to 70.8 million tons in 1955; that of coal from 35.5 million tons to 165.9 million to 389.0 million in these years; that of steel from 4.3 million tons to 18.3 million to 45.3 million; that of electrical energy from 5.0 billion kilowatt-hours to 48.3 billion to 170.2 billion. Light industry rose much more slowly, but the production of cotton cloth, for instance,

Table 2 *Grain marketings and exports, 1928–1940 (in millions of tons)*

MARKETINGS AND EXPORTS	1928/29[a]	1929/30[a]	1930/31[a]	1931/32[a]	1932/33[a]	1933–37[b]	1938–40[b]
Gross marketings	15.7	19.5	22.6	23.7	19.4	27.5	32.8
Net marketings	8.3	10.2	17.9	18.8	13.7	—	—
Exports	.1	1.3	5.8	4.5	1.8	—	—

Source: Jerzy F. Karcz, "From Stalin to Brezhnev: Soviet Agricultural Policy in Historical Perspective," in James R. Millar, ed., *The Soviet Rural Community* (Urbana, University of Illinois Press, 1971), p. 44; Lazar Volin, *A Century of Russian Agriculture* (Cambridge, Mass., Harvard University Press, 1970), p. 250.
[a] Fiscal year.
[b] Average.

increased from 2.7 billion square meters in 1928 to 4.0 billion in 1940 to 5.9 billion in 1955.[24]

The industrialization program was even more spectacularly successful in terms of its military consequences. Russian performance in both the Russo-Japanese War and World War I had been highly unsuccessful, but a half-century later the Soviet Union was one of the two acknowledged superpowers —the first country to send a man into space. Most striking of all was Soviet performance in World War II. Unable to cope with a German threat in World War I while allied with powerful partners, the Soviet Union had to deal with a stronger German attack in World War II with relatively little outside help in the early period of the war, and it emerged victorious—but just barely so. In 1931 Stalin had said, "We lag from the advanced countries by 50 to 100 years. We must make up this distance in 10 years. Either we do this or they crush us." Hitler's attack came ten years and three months after this speech, and many who questioned the pace of industrial development must have wondered whether the outcome would have been the same with a slower rate of industrial growth—and, therefore, without something like collectivization.

In recent years this widely accepted view has been subject to increasing challenge. One already mentioned line of analysis contends that the grain-marketing problem was the result not of kulak hoarding (except, perhaps, on a very short-term basis as the peasants anticipated a rise in grain prices), but of an imbalance between grain and livestock prices that was solvable without Draconian action. A more radical analysis—that of James Millar—has suggested that, historically, industrialization never had been financed in any country through turning the terms of trade against the countryside, that Soviet industrialization too was not financed through a "squeezing" of the peasants, and that especially in the crucial First Five-Year Plan period "rapid industrialization actually took place . . . without any net accumulation from agriculture—in fact, with a net outflow to agriculture."[25] The rise in market-ings is simply attributed to the decline in the amount of grain that the countryside needed to consume because of the lower number of animals and people to feed,[26] but these developments—particularly the slaughter of the cattle—are seen as having an adverse impact on industrialization that continued for years.

There is no evidence whatsoever to indicate that the peasants would have withdrawn from the market even had the terms of trade been turned against them, and there is no evidence that the terms of trade even had to be turned against them. Collectivization was not necessary for the industrialization drive, and it was not optimal either. It was instead a disaster just like a hurricane or any other natural disaster. Economically, no one gained from collectivization, including those promoting rapid industrial development.[27]

In a very important book on a key Soviet industry, David Granick has shown that industrial investment itself did not have the immediate consequences that were foreseen. Because of the regime's predeliction for giant projects, much of the investment had little return in the First Five-Year Plan, for it was frozen in projects that could not be completed for years. Instead of becoming more capital-intensive as anticipated, industry actually became more labor-intensive.[28]

To the extent that the revisionist case is true, and it is a strong one, it raises more questions than it answers. If the traditional explanations for the very rapid industrial growth in the Soviet Union in the early 1930s are wrong, then what were its "sources"? Was it perhaps utilization of the urban unemployed, or, even, the drawing of women into the labor force by providing job opportunities for those who wanted to work and forcing others to work by lowering the real wages of their husbands?[29] (The number of women workers and white collar employees rose from 2,795,000 in 1928 to 6,720,000 in 1933 to 13,190,000 in 1940—24, 30, and 39 percent of the total employment in each year, respectively.)[30] Or perhaps was there even something crucial in the whole "great leap forward" spirit of the time? Since the question lies at the center of the discussion of the "Soviet model of industrialization," it deserves the most serious continued study and debate.

Stalin, Kirov, and the Great Retreat

By all indications Stalin was at the height of his power in December 1929. Whatever his previous relationship to the party oligarchs, he had succeeded in defeating the last remaining full members of Lenin's Politburo, and he had pushed through an industrialization program considerably more radical than a consensus of his supporters would have produced. His fiftieth birthday was marked by the launching not only of the cult of personality but also of a veritable war against the peasantry.

Of course, no governmental system consists of one-man rule in pure terms, and the Soviet Union of the early 1930s was no exception. As Stalin's opponents and their supporters were removed from top positions, they had to be replaced—and they were, frequently by men who had worked in the party apparatus under Stalin. In 1934, eight of ten voting members of the Politburo were working or had worked in the party apparatus under Stalin, at least 63 percent of the voting members of the Central Committee. The top elite, as represented in the Central Committee voting membership, were in the prime of their life (only 20 percent were over fifty years of age, less than 3 percent over sixty), but almost all of them had been in the party since before the revolution. Those in the Politburo were in their mid to late forties on the average, with an average length of party membership of over a quarter century (see table 3).

Table 3 *Members of the Politburo, February 1934*

Member	Year of birth	Year of party entry	Position
A. A. Andreev	1895	1914	People's Commissar of Railroads
L. M. Kaganovich	1893	1911	Secretary of the Central Committee and the Moscow party organization
M. I. Kalinin	1875	1898	Chairman of the Central Executive Committee
S. M. Kirov	1886	1904	Secretary of the Central Committee and the Leningrad party organization
S. V. Kosior	1889	1907	General Secretary of the Ukrainian party organization
V. V. Kuibyshev	1888	1904	First Deputy Chairman of the Council of People's Commissars
V. M. Molotov	1890	1906	Chairman of the Council of People's Commissars
G. K. Ordzhonikidze	1886	1903	People's Commissar for Heavy Industry
I. V. Stalin	1879	1898	General Secretary of the Central Committee
K. E. Voroshilov	1881	1903	People's Commissar for Defense
AVERAGE	1886	1905	

continued

Table 3—Continued

Member	Year of birth	Year of party entry	Position
Candidate member			
V. Ia. Chubar	1891	1907	Chairman of the Ukrainian Council of People's Commissars
A. I. Mikoian	1895	1915	People's Commissar for the Food Industry
G. I. Petrovsky	1878	1897	Chairman of the Ukrainian Central Executive Committee
P. P. Postyshev	1887	1904	Second secretary of the Ukrainian party organization and first secretary of the Kiev party organization
Ia. E. Rudzutak	1887	1905	Deputy Chairman of the Council of People's Commissars

Source: Borys Levytsky, *The Soviet Political Elite* (Stanford, The Hoover Institution on War, Revolution, and Peace, 1970), pp. 745–747.

The relationship of these top officials to Stalin in the early 1930s has been a subject of some controversy. Few suggest that they resisted the early collectivization-industrialization drive in any meaningful, concerted manner, but by 1934 Stalin's five years of open rule must have raised serious questions about his program and leadership. Collectivization had been carried to near completion, but it had resulted in the decimation of the livestock herd and in 1932–1933 a major famine. The industrialization program had achieved impressive results, but, nevertheless, the targets of the First Five-Year Plan had not even been approached.

Foreign policy had been perhaps the greatest disaster of all. One part of the strident line initiated in 1928 had been a series of Comintern resolutions and directives condemning cooperation between foreign Communist parties and the non-Communist left. As a consequence, the German Communist party had been instructed not to enter into any joint efforts with the socialist and center parties to block Hitler's rise to power, even though

Hitler's stated foreign policy goals were highly threatening to the Soviet Union. Indeed, the German Communists had been ordered to direct their main attack against the socialists (the "social fascists," they were always called at the time), and Comintern journals had hailed Hitler's assumption of power as tearing the democratic "veil" from the bourgeois dictatorship and paving the way for revolution. By 1934, however, it was abundantly clear that a Communist revolution was far from imminent in Germany and that Hitler posed a major and growing foreign policy danger. Since Japan had in 1931 occupied Manchuria on the eastern flank of the Soviet Union and seemed determined to continue an aggressive foreign policy, the old conceptions of a capitalist encirclement were beginning to assume a very concrete and ominous meaning.

A number of westerners—largely following the lead of Boris Nicolaevsky—have argued that in response to these developments a major opposition to Stalin began to develop within the top party leadership, one that advocated a more conciliatory internal policy in particular. Such opposition is supposed to have been led in the Politburo and Central Committee sessions by Sergei Kirov, first secretary of the Leningrad party organization, and it is said to have inflicted "a severe defeat on Stalin" at the Seventeenth Party Congress in January 1934 and to have forced "an abrupt change in course" at that time.[31]

This view of Politburo relationships has gained support in recent years,[32] but we scarcely should accept it as proved—or, in some of its central features, as even probable. To be sure, some aspects of the analysis must be essentially accurate. Certainly a number of persons, including prominent party leaders, must have had doubts and questions about the internal and foreign policies followed during the period of the First Five-Year Plan. Certainly some must have expressed these doubts, and quite probably some of them at least tentatively raised the possibility of a change in leadership.[33] But it is a long, long jump from such suppositions to the contention that there was strong Politburo opposition to Stalin that inflicted a major defeat on him at the Seventeenth Party Congress.

In the first place, even the exact nature of Kirov's policy views and the extent of his popularity within the party should not be considered a closed subject. Judging by the stenographic report of the Seventeenth Party Congress, Kirov was, indeed, warmly greeted and his speech very well received, but the ovations for Molotov and Kaganovich—the presumed conservatives on the Politburo—were reported as being more substantial.[34] As for Kirov's views, Nicolaevsky in his "Letter of an Old Bolshevik" asserts that Kirov "was a 100 percent supporter of the general line, and distinguished himself during its operation by great energy and inflexibility."[35] Kirov may well have opposed the execution of political opponents (a point on which all rumors agree), and he may have been one of the moderates in his policy advice (although there is no evidence on this point in either direction). However, such a position would hardly lead Kirov into opposition in 1934, for by that time, as will be discussed shortly, policy was already moving along such lines. In fact, both the "Letter of an Old Bolshevik" and Roy Medvedev in his more recent *Let History Judge* agree that Kirov was resisting any notion of a change in leadership.

In the second place, the evidence of any significant action directed against Stalin at the Seventeenth Party Congress is really quite weak. The "Letter of an Old Bolshevik" itself stated that "whereas formerly all forms of opposition had been opposition *against* Stalin and for his removal from the post of Party chief, there was now no longer any question of such removal . . . Everyone emphasized tirelessly his devotion to Stalin. It was rather *a fight for influence over Stalin,* a fight for his soul, so to speak."[36] If there is convincing evidence of more than this type of struggle (which surely takes place in all dictatorships at all times), it is hard to imagine why it did not emerge in the Khrushchev era, for Khrushchev was extremely eager to distinguish between the correctness of the party line prior to 1934 and the illegitimacy of many of Stalin's actions thereafter.

In the third place, the evidence that Stalin suffered a defeat at the Seventeenth Congress is weakest of all. Roy Medvedev reports the undocumented recollection of one participant that 270 delegates (22 percent of the total) voted against Stalin's election to the Central Committee in the secret ballot at the end of the congress,[37] but, as he also reports, the actual result of the "significant change" in the Central Committee membership at the time was a strengthening of Stalin's position:

> The XVIIth Congress removed many people who were unsuitable to Stalin, and, on the other hand, some top officials of the NKVD (V. A. Balitskii, E. G. Evdokimov) were for the first time elected to the Central Committee. L. Z. Mekhlis was also elected, although he had not even been a delegate at the previous Congress. N. I. Ezhov became a member of the Central Committee and G. G. Iagoda was promoted from candidate to full membership.[38]

It is true that Kirov was elected a secretary of the Central Committee at the congress—a decision that some see as threatening to Stalin—but during 1934 it was Stalin who was pushing Kirov to move to full-time work in the Secretariat in Moscow and Kirov who was resisting. The latter suggested to

Stalin that he be permitted to remain in Leningrad until the end of the Second Five-Year Plan—three years hence in 1937![39]

The greatest problem in the contention that Stalin was defeated by a "conciliatory opposition" at the Seventeenth Party Congress, aside from lack of any positive evidence for its existence, is that there was little need for such an opposition to arise. Well before the congress, the party leadership—with Stalin leading the way in his speeches—had already begun a Great Retreat from the industrial, agricultural, and cultural policies of the First Five-Year Plan.[40] While maintaining and tightening controls on freedom of expression, the leadership had been changing policy in directions desired by more traditional elements of the population. Only in foreign policy can one find evidence of a policy of the First Five-Year Plan in obvious "need" of major reversal. The reversal of that policy actually did begin during the congress as the French Communists were encouraged for the first time to cooperate with the moderates in resisting a right-wing general strike, but one would have thought that the threat of a fascist coup in France, coupled with Hitler's moves over the previous year (including recent talks with Poland), would have been sufficient in itself to convince Stalin.[41]

The first dramatic policy change had occurred in June 1931—two and a half years before the Seventeenth Party Congress—when Stalin himself boldly announced a reversal of posture toward the old intelligentsia:

> We must change our policy toward the old technical intelligentsia . . . Our attitude toward them must be expressed mainly in a policy of enlisting them and taking care of them . . . It would be wrong and undialectical to continue our former policy under the new, changed conditions. It would be stupid and unwise to regard practically every expert and engineer of the old school as an undetected criminal and wrecker. We have always regarded and still regard "expert-baiting" as a harmful and disgraceful phenomenon.[42]

The employment of the old intelligentsia was viewed as a stopgap expedient; the major long-term task was the education of a new Soviet-trained intelligentsia. Unlike the leadership of countries such as India that have permitted the education of far too many lawyers for the economy to absorb, the Soviet regime had invested its funds in new technical institutes from the outset of the industrialization drive.[43] Now it began to emphasize the incentives for the bright and the talented to enter these institutes and to move into managerial work. In his June 1931 speech Stalin denounced "the leftist practice of wage equalization," and wage policy gave some indications of following the lines he advocated.[44] Not only were engineering-managerial personnel given preference over workers, but the wage differentials between skilled and unskilled workers seem to have widened and output in excess of fixed norms was paid at progressively increasing rates as well. Actual wage trends may not have been affected by Stalin's speech as much as westerners have assumed,[45] but at a minimum that speech reassured the Soviet public about the rewards to be gained from acquiring skills, and that assurance may have been more important than the details of policy.

The authority of administrative officials was also strengthened in both real and symbolic terms. Managerial prerogatives were reinforced, and the penalties that could be imposed on absentees gradually increased.[46] The managers continued to operate within a system of party, trade union, central, and employee controls, but greater emphasis was placed upon the requirement (embodied in the principle of one-man management) that direct orders to subordinates be carried out without appeal.[47] After-the-fact protest to the party and trade unions remained legitimate, but higher pressure for plan fulfillment often led the latter institutions to forgive a successful manager many improprieties or even illegalities. In practice, the managers gained considerable discretion vis-à-vis central directives as long as the major goals assigned to them were fulfilled.[48]

The status of administrative officials was increased along with their pay and power. In many organizations—for example, the railways, the coal and iron ore industries, the Ministry of Foreign Affairs, and the Procuracy (the prosecutor's office)—officials were given uniforms or insignia that depicted status. ("The main reason stated for this innovation was its importance in improving discipline and increasing the authority of those in positions of responsibility.")[49] In general, the intelligentsia (particularly the technical intelligentsia) came to be called "the best sons of the Soviet people." Fiction writers increasingly turned to them rather than to the workers as the heroes of their works. The children of engineers and technicians were no longer discriminated against in college admission, and the specialists themselves were welcomed into the party for the first time. Only 1.2 percent of those specialists employed in the economy had been party members in 1928, but this figure rose to 20.5 percent of the much larger number of specialists in January 1941.[50]

The policy changes with respect to the technical intelligentsia and the managers had their counterparts in almost all policy areas, as the Communist militants were repudiated and/or brought under control in field after field and as those who had been under sharpest attack during the cultural revolution often returned to gradual favor. A real effort was made to create (in the words of Merle Fainsod) "an identification of Communist rule with the forces of tradition and respectability,"[51] and many of the values of the old intelligentsia came to be embraced by a leadership determined to be "cultured" (kul'turnyi).

In the educational sphere, for example, a series of Central Committee decrees beginning in the summer of 1931 broke with the child-centered school and the experimentalism of the 1920s and the First Five-Year Plan period. They emphasized the teaching of fundamentals, the establishment of discipline in the schools, and the raising of academic standards (even if the latter meant admissions on the basis of qualifications rather than class origin).[52] Family policy, which earlier had combined attacks on the bourgeois family with appeals for parental responsibility, moved toward unambiguous support of a strong family unit. Parents were made legally responsible for the delinquent acts of their children and could be fined for child neglect.[53]

Similarly, in literature the radical writers organization, RAPP, was abolished in 1932 and the non-Communist Gorky, who finally returned permanently to the Soviet Union in 1931, rose to a predominant position. In science the Communist Academy steadily lost in power vis-à-vis the more traditional Academy of Sciences. In the legal realm, talk of a withering away of the state and law ceased, and individual accountability for crimes and other shortcomings was reaffirmed while the prestige of legal institutions was reestablished. Even the Orthodox Church and the believer were defended from the excesses perpetrated by the Komsomol and the League of the Godless during the initial stages of the First Five-Year Plan.

Finally, Stalin increasingly sought to identify himself and his policy with the Russian past and the cause of Russian patriotism. As early as the 1920s, his espousal of "socialism in one country" had demonstrated a sensitivity to the appeals of this issue and a willingness to utilize it. The war scare of 1927–1928 further helped to link the industrialization drive with the need for national defense, but in February 1931 Stalin made this link even more explicit in an emotional statement made to a conference of economic managers:

Sometimes people ask whether it is not possible to slow the pace somewhat, to hold back the movement. No, comrades, that is impossible! It is impossible to reduce the pace. On the contrary, it should be increased as much as is within our power . . . To reduce the pace means to lag. And the laggards are beaten. But we do not want to be beaten. No, we do not want it! The history of old Russia consisted, among other things, of being beaten continuously for her backwardness. The Mongol khans beat her. The Turkish beys beat her. The Swedish feudal lords beat her. The Polish-Lithuanian landlords beat her. The Anglo-French capitalists beat her.

The Japanese barons beat her. All beat her because of her backwardness—because of military backwardness, of cultural backwardness, of governmental backwardness, of industrial backwardness, of agricultural backwardness. They beat her because it was profitable and could be done without punishment . . . Do you want for our socialist fatherland to be beaten and lose its independence? If you don't want this, you should in the shortest time liquidate its backwardness . . . We lag behind the advanced countries by 50 to 100 years. We must make up this distance in 10 years. Either we do this or they crush us.[54]

As the alarm about Hitler's rise rapidly grew after 1933, the emphasis upon Russian patriotism increased proportionately, as in a *Pravda* editorial of June 9, 1934. "The cry 'For the fatherland,' " *Pravda* declared, "kindles the flame of heroism, the flame of creative initiative in all fields, in all realms of our rich, our many-sided life . . . The defense of the fatherland is the supreme law . . . For its honor, glory, might, and prosperity."[55] After 1934 the leading Marxist historian, Pokrovsky, who emphasized the role of classes in Russian history and depicted the former ruling classes and their political representatives in the darkest hues, was repudiated. The new history celebrated tsarist military victories and territorial expansion, taught pride in Russia's achievements, and hailed the accomplishments of her great men, despite their unfortunate class background. Peter the Great and eventually even Ivan the Terrible were refurbished as Soviet heroes and presented as far-sighted patriots and great statesmen whose despotic measures were justified by the constructive ends they served.

While much of the Great Retreat represented an attempt to restore traditional symbols of authority and to curb the ideological militants who were causing offense to the respectable, an effort to move toward a partial reconciliation with the mass of the population was also involved. Despite Stalin's insistence that the pace not be slackened, the Second Five-Year Plan, which began in 1933, was, in fact, more realistic than its predecessor, and it did, in fact, produce an improvement in living conditions.

At the same time, the regime also sought a partial accommodation with the peasantry. In 1932 the peasant's right to a private plot was formally recognized for the first time, as was the right to own limited numbers of animals; in January 1933 the procurement system was changed so that the kolkhozes had fixed obligations based on acreage rather than being subject to largely arbitrary requisitions. Then in May 1933 a secret circular signed by Stalin and Molotov ordered the end to mass deportations in the countryside, and collective farm chairmen came, on the whole, to be nonparty peasants chosen from within the village.[56] In practice, the recognition of the private plot meant that collectivization was to remain rather partial in nature, being limited for decades largely to the production of grain and technical crops such as cotton. Thus, in 1937, a year in which the socialist sector of agriculture did particularly well, the private sector provided 52 percent of the country's potatoes and vegetables, 71 percent of its meat, 57 percent of its fruit, and 71 percent of its milk.[57]

It is conceivable that there was an opposition at the Seventeenth Party Congress which was demanding a more conciliatory policy toward the population, but the men in question were those who had supported Stalin in the struggle with the right in 1928–1929 and it really is easier to imagine them believing that the retreat had gone too far. It is also conceivable, of course, that the new policy line really represented the views of the opposition rather than of Stalin—that Stalin had, in fact, been defeated by a more moderate group within the Politburo, but simply a year or two earlier than usually indicated.[58] The difficulty with this line of analysis, however, is that almost none of the policy changes initiated in the early 1930s were reversed after the Great Purge of 1937–1938, even though Stalin presumably was then in a position to do so if he wished.

The explanation for the Great Retreat emphasized by Fainsod was that there had been a growing recognition by the leadership (above all, Stalin) of the "imperatives of industrialization." The First Five-Year Plan had been marked by "tremendous labor turnover and absenteeism," by "large-scale social disorganization and crime waves," by schools in which "discipline was lax" and "traditional subjects were not taught." The changes in policy were a response to these problems:

> Industrialization imposed its own imperatives . . . After the first burst of grandiose intoxication had exhausted itself, it became evident that industrialization presented the challenge of a new discipline which had to be patiently mastered . . . Incentives had to be provided to stimulate production and habits of order and precision instilled to assure quality production. The educational system had to be remodeled to indoctrinate students in the values of efficiency and conscious discipline and to produce officers as well as the soldiers and "noncoms" of the new labor army. Sanctions had to be invoked to keep workers on their jobs and to prevent absence, tardiness, or "labor-flitting." The large-scale organizational requirements of industrialization appeared to call for the reinforcement of authority, the focusing of responsibility, a hierarchical structure that capitalized the values of specialization and division of labor, accounting regulation that ensured precise control, and a system of income distribution that provided incentives for increased production and efficiency.[59]

Of course, the exact nature of the "imperatives" of industrialization really are not certain, and many political leaders in developing nations have not seen the type of actions described here as imperative. Nevertheless, if we speak of the imperatives of a successful industrialization drive, the position has much logic to it. In motivational terms, it does tend to correspond with the historical fact that many of the changes were, indeed, pushed by the officials of the major industrial organs—VSNKh (Vesenkha or the Supreme Economic Council) and its successor, the People's Commissariat for Heavy Industry—and that many were publicly defended as necessary for the industrialization drive.[60]

A second possible explanation for the Great Retreat—by no means incompatible with the first and also presented in partial terms by Merle Fainsod —is that Stalin did not highly value the chaos associated with continuous revolution and that his "formula for rule" rested far less on a full-scale attempt to remake man and society than some variants of the totalitarian model have suggested. As he moved to consolidate his power, Stalin may have felt that many of the traditional pillars of support for non-Communist systems would be more solid and congenial bases of support for his own system than the enthusiasm of the Communist militants. The Communist party had always' had an appeal to many who were dedicated to modernization and industrialization (issues intimately linked with that of national dignity and independence), and Stalin scarcely can have been unaware of the possible political advantage in policies favorable to the administrative-professional personnel spearheading the industrialization-modernization drive.

Stalin's Formula of Rule

Westerners discussing Stalin's ability to maintain himself in power for a quarter of a century often have emphasized his use of force, terror, and indoctrination, and such factors surely should be given prominence in any analysis of the Stalin period. The industrialization-collectivization program was not achieved without increasing resort to compulsion. The relative cultural freedom of NEP was quickly suppressed, and the debates in the press were sharply restricted. The regime moved to deny the people access to any alternative by cutting them off from the outside world and from each other, and it tried to saturate them with a monolithic stream of agitation and propaganda stressing the superiority of the Soviet system and the virtue of its leaders. The history of the Communist party and the Soviet period was rewritten, with Stalin portrayed as a hero of legendary proportions and his former Politburo colleagues completely denigrated. Finally, of course, Stalin eventually sought to create a milieu of pervasive insecurity based on ever-present fear of the informer and the labor camp.

In his dealings with his major subordinates, Stalin did not limit himself to efforts to prevent the rise of political opposition. He also sought to protect himself from excessive reliance upon one individual or institution for information and advice in a given policy area. At times he used specific individuals for these purposes. (For example, the journalist Boris Steiger became so well known to the diplomatic community as a check on the veracity of the reports of the People's Commissariat for Foreign Affairs that the diplomats came to use him as a reliable independent channel of communication to the top.)[61] More important, Stalin also attempted to institutionalize a varied flow of information by organizing his subordinates into competing party and administrative hierarchies with overlapping responsibilities.

The Stalin period has often been treated in the West as one in which the state apparatus came to dominate the party apparatus, but this is accurate in a partial sense at best. It is true that Soviet ideology with respect to the state underwent profound change. The theory of the withering away of the state was all but repudiated, and the state superstructure was exalted as a creative source of initiative and direction in Soviet society. It is also true that many of the most powerful officials in the Stalin period were the economic managers (khoziaistvenniki) and that many of the products of the party apparatus who rose to top positions in the early 1930s did so by moving into government posts. (As a consequence of these two developments, only 40 percent of Politburo and Central Committee voting members elected in 1934 still worked in the party apparatus at that time.)

Nevertheless, prior to 1934 the Central Committee apparatus was not organized in such a way as to facilitate its participation in the policy process, and, in practice, it seemed to have relatively little role in policy formulation in the 1920s and perhaps even in the First Five-Year Plan.[62] In 1934 this situation changed. The organization-instruction department and the assignment department were abolished, and the Central Committee apparatus now was divided into nine departments which corresponded to branches or groups of agencies: (1) agriculture, (2) industry, (3) transport, (4) planning-finance-trade, (5) political-administrative, (6) leading party organs, (7) culture and propagation of Leninism, (8) special department, and (9) foreign department.[63] Each of these departments had subsections which corresponded to more specialized branches of industry and administration, and the following year the culture and propagation of Leninism department was formally divided into five separate departments: (1) party propaganda and agitation, (2) press and publishing, (3) schools, (4) cultural-educational work, and (5) science.[64]

In 1939 there was a partial return to the pre-1934 structure of the Central Committee apparatus, for a personnel administration and an organization-instruction department were reconstituted under different names, and a number of the specialized departments were abolished. However, the agriculture and the school departments remained, as did a propaganda-agitation administration which supervised science, culture, and the media of communications as well, and the personnel and organization-instruction units were subdivided along branch lines. In 1948 there was a complete return to the principles of the 1934 structure, and these arrangements (with some differentiation and expansion) have been retained until the present time.[65]

While a number of possible explanations can be advanced for the various reorganizations of the Central Committee apparatus, the branch type of organization, which in compact form duplicated the structure of the governmental institutions, provided a particularly convenient check upon the ministries. In particular, it provided a convenient second source of information on policy questions that might arise and a convenient staff instrument for drafting legislation of relevance to more than one ministry. By institutionalizing rivalry in policy formulation, Stalin evidently believed that he could minimize distortion and concealment in the information flowing to him.

It would be easy to describe Stalin's formula of rule solely in terms of mechanisms by which he sought to instill fear, insecurity, and suspicion among the administrative elite as well as the population as a whole, but such an interpretation would represent a very one-sided distortion. Force and terror must be applied by real people, and at least to a limited degree they must be accepted by real people. Dissatisfied peasants can engage in guerrilla warfare, dissatisfied urban dwellers can pour out into the streets, and regimes can collapse almost overnight if the police and the army refuse to fire and melt away into the population. That these events did not occur must also be explained.

For this reason, the use of the appeals of patriotism and the accommodation to key values in the population (particularly among the managerial-professional personnel) obviously must be seen as key positive elements in Stalin's formula of rule, whether they were originally so intended or not. Perhaps even more important as a source of support was the possibility of upward mobility that the industrialization drive opened to the young, the talented, the ambitious—precisely those groups within the population who must be at the core of any successful revolutionary action. Perhaps the best indicator of the scale of mobility in these years is provided by the figures on Communist party membership. The period 1924–1932 saw an enormous expansion in the size of the party—from 472,000 members and candidates in 1924 to 3,555,338 in 1933. Some 43 percent of the party members at the latter date were employed in white collar occupations of one type or another, but only 8 percent of the members had been in such occupations at the time of their admission into the party. From January 1930 to October 1933 alone, 666,000 worker-Communists had moved into soviet, administrative, or political work or had returned to an educational institution to receive the training that would qualify them for such work in the future.[66] Moreover, upward mobility was not limited to those entering white collar jobs. The number of workers increased from 8.7 million in 1928 to 17.8 million in 1932 to 23.7 million in 1940.[67] For most of the peasants and children of peasants streaming into the city (and there were 16.6 million of them from 1929 through 1935),[68] these jobs represented upward mobility just as much as the technical-managerial ones.

The most spectacular mobility was enjoyed by those who crowded into the new technical institutes in the late 1920s and the early 1930s and who emerged to become the engineers and industrial managers of the future—and the political leaders as well. The bulk of these students were not young high school graduates (indeed, for several years after 1930 there formally was *no* direct access to college through the secondary school) but persons who had left school, sometimes without finishing, and had become minor local officials, political activists, or simply industrial workers. A number were party members and still others joined the party while in the institute.[69]

The young adults who returned to college during the First Five-Year Plan came to provide a substantial proportion of the top political-administrative elite in the years from 1940 into the 1970s. One of the older students, for example, was Nikita Khrushchev, who was directed to the Industrial Academy in Moscow in 1929 at the age of thirty-three after a decade of lower party work. While Khrushchev served as party secretary at the Academy and may have been a student only in a minimal sense, this clearly was not true in other cases. Leonid Brezhnev had risen to the post of deputy head of a regional agriculture administration before going to the Dneprodzerzhinsk Metallurgical Institute in 1931 at the age of twenty-five. Aleksei Kosygin was twenty-six and a minor trade official when he entered the Leningrad Textile Institute in 1930. Andrei Kirilenko (the number two man in the Secretariat in the Brezhnev era) had been working for four years as an electrician before spending a year in Komsomol and trade union work and enrolling in the Novocherkassk Aviation Institute when he was twenty-four years old. In 1957 —when this group of students was in its early and mid-fifties on the average— some 45 percent of all USSR ministers had entered college at the beginning of the five-year plans, after working for some years in some relatively minor job or jobs.

There is a tendency for upward mobility to be associated with acceptance of the basic political system in any country, and there is every indication that this link was present in the Soviet Union for this group that Milovan Djilas pejoratively called "the New Class." Entry into the party (soon to become virtually compulsory for those seeking administrative work) gave added reason for concern about the personal consequences of an anti-Communist revolt. Moreover, the industrializing-modernizing ideology of the party, coupled with the expansion of job opportunities provided by the industrialization drive, helped to create within this group the sense of self-confidence, the sense of legitimacy of their own position, that can be crucial in identifying the upwardly mobile with a regime.[70] In the words of the best study of Soviet management published in the Stalin era,

> These young engineers [of the early and mid-1930s] were a restless element, inclined toward experimentation, record-breaking, "speed-up." They brought *elan* into the plants, a sense that people somehow become embodied in the gigantic recovery of the new revolutionary country through work in which they submerge themselves completely. Confident of advance, but largely not conscious careerists, they saw their rise as a natural consequence of the development of the young country.[71]

The Great Purge

The mid-1930s featured a growing generational problem in the Soviet Union. The products of the educational expansion of the First Five-Year Plan period were streaming into the economy, men who already were in their early thirties, who in large numbers were party members, who had work experience (often of an administrative-political nature) before college, and who now had a technical education not possessed by their superiors. (In 1928, 89.3 percent of the directors of state enterprises were party members, and only 2.8 percent of these party directors had a higher education, 78.6 percent only an elementary school education.)[72] Yet, the superiors themselves were but in their mid-forties. Were men of long party standing, of considerable organizational ability, and in many cases with pre-1917 revolutionary experience to be pushed, disgruntled, into lower work, or were the new graduates to wait twenty years, also disgruntled, for less well-educated superiors to retire?

Whether this generational problem was a key factor in the decision or not, it was dramatically "solved" in 1936–1938, as Stalin launched a widespread and lethal purge of the top officials in both the state and party apparatuses. A total of 1,108 of the 1,966 delegates to the Seventeenth Party Congress in 1934 and 98 of the 139 voting and candidate members of the Central Committee elected at that congress perished in this period—the overwhelming majority of them shot. The Great Purge reached into all levels of the administrative system, decimating the Old Bolsheviks in the process. This too was part of the formula by which Stalin maintained his rule.

Terror had always been an officially acknowledged aspect of the Soviet political system. The regime was called a dictatorship of the proletariat, and there was no pretense about the need to suppress counterrevolutionary activity and those who engaged in it. The Cheka had been created immediately after the revolution for this purpose, and even after the end of the Civil War, Lenin had insisted with reference to the Criminal Code, "The Courts must not do away with terror; to promise such a thing would be either to fool ourselves or other people."[73]

During NEP the operations of the OGPU (as the successor to the Cheka was called) reflected the dominant preoccupations of the party leadership. Particular attention was devoted to checking on church activities, persons of unfavorable social origins, and former members of opposition parties. As the struggle of the Trotsky opposition mounted in intensity, the OGPU concerned itself with nonconformity and deviation within the party itself. However, its direct impact on the masses of Soviet citizens was still slight, and the relatively few oppositionists who were confined in OGPU prisons were still treated with comparative humanity.[74]

With the abandonment of the NEP and the decision to proceed with a program of rapid industrialization and agricultural collectivization, the OGPU began to play a much more prominent role. Its energies were concentrated on three targets: the Nepmen or private traders, who had been permitted to flourish under the NEP; the old intelligentsia, who were made the scapegoats for early failures and difficulties in the industrialization drive; and the peasants who offered active or passive opposition to the collectivization program. The mass incidence of OGPU arrests during the period of the First Five-Year Plan was most widely felt in the countryside, and the great majority of those deported became wards of the OGPU.[75]

In July 1934 the OGPU was merged into the People's Commissariat of Internal Affairs (NKVD), the commissariat that had been responsible for routine police and fire protection (among other duties). Particularly since the statute creating the new NKVD appeared to restrict its judicial powers, some observers tended to view the reorganization as an effort to impose limits on the arbitrary authority of the secret police.[76] On December 1, 1934, however, a young Communist called Nikolaev assassinated Sergei Kirov in Leningrad, and his shot signaled the inauguration of an unparalleled campaign of repression and lawlessness run wild.

The circumstances surrounding the Kirov assassination remain obscure. In 1956 and again in 1961 Khrushchev insinuated that Stalin was responsible for the act, and several scholars have supported this proposition openly.[77] Others find the charge quite implausible, and see the assassination merely fueling Stalin's suspicions and pushing him in a repressive direction.[78] (The suicide of his wife two years earlier could also be seen as an important event in his psychological development during these years.) In either case Zinoviev had had a long association with Leningrad, Kirov had been the man who had been sent to Leningrad to impose central control on the Leningrad organization, and officially his assassin was alleged to be a member of an "underground counter-revolutionary terrorist group . . . consisting of former members of the Zinoviev opposition."[79]

The concentrated power of the NKVD was now directed toward uprooting all actual or potential opposition in the party. For the first time the party felt the full brunt of the terror. More than a hundred persons who had been arrested prior to Kirov's death as "counterrevolutionaries" were promptly handed over to military commissions of the Supreme Court of the USSR for trial, were found guilty of preparing and carrying out terrorist acts, and were instantly shot. Nikolaev and thirteen alleged accomplices were quickly tried and executed, and then in January 1935 Zinoviev, Kamenev, and seventeen leading associates were brought to trial for complicity. Zinoviev received a ten-year sentence, Kamenev one of five years, and those of the other defendants ranged between. In the spring of 1935, thousands of Leningrad inhabitants who were suspected of harboring opposition sentiments were arrested and deported to Siberia.[80]

During 1935 the proportions of the purge were still relatively restricted. An old-fashioned purge or cleansing of the party had already been going on prior to Kirov's death, party membership declining from 3,555,338 on January 1, 1933, to 2,358,714 on January 1, 1935. This purge had little to do with Stalin's suspicions or his desire to suppress opposition, but was undoubtedly part of the general Great Retreat from the exuberances and excesses of the First Five-Year Plan period. (Membership had more than doubled from 1,677,910 on January 1, 1930, to 3,555,338 on January 1, 1933.) Rigby has convincingly contended that "the great majority were removed either because they made unscrupulous use of their party membership to secure personal benefits, were immoral or undisciplined in their person lives or at their job, or simply failed to participate in party activities."[81] While the Central Committee twice in 1935 called for further action to purify the party, the rate of decline in membership actually became less. The party decreased in size by 282,000 in 1935 and by only 95,000 in 1936.

The Great Purge reached its climax in the period 1936–1938. Its most dramatic external manifestation was the series of show trials in the course of which every trace of Old Bolshevik opposition leadership was officially discredited and exterminated. Paradoxically, just two months after the Central Committee had approved a new constitution and at the same time that the press was engaged in extensive public discussion about its guarantees of individual freedom,[82] the first of the great public trials took place in August 1936.[83] Zinoviev, Kamenev, and fourteen associates were charged with organizing a clandestine terrorist center under instructions from Trotsky, with accomplishing the murder of Kirov, and with preparing similar attempts against the lives of other party leaders. All sixteen confessed and were executed. In the course of the trial, the testimony of the accused compromised many other members of the Bolshevik Old Guard—members of the former Right Opposition as well as those of the Left. A wave of new arrests followed. On August 23, 1936, Tomsky, hounded by a sense of impending doom, committed suicide.

In September 1936 the head of the NKVD, Iagoda, was replaced by Ezhov, who had been the party secretary in charge of personnel selection, and the worst period of the purge—the so-called *Ezhovshchina*—was initiated. The most dramatic events of these years were two additional show trials of former oppositionists. In January 1937 came the Trial of the Seventeen, the so-called Anti-Soviet Trotskyite Center, which included such prominent figures as Piatakov, Radek, and Sokolnikov. This time the accused were charged with plotting the forcible overthrow of the Soviet government with the aid of Germany and Japan, with planning the restoration of capitalism in the USSR, and with carrying on espionage, wrecking, diversive, and terrorist activities on behalf of foreign states. The trial was arranged to demonstrate that Trotsky was the *eminence grise* who inspired, organized, and directed all these activities, and the prisoners in the dock fought for their lives by playing their assigned role.

The slaughter of the Old Guard continued with the Trial of the Twenty-One, the so-called Anti-Soviet Bloc of Rights and Trotskyites, in March 1938. Among the accused were Bukharin, Rykov, and Krestinsky, all former members of the Politburo, as well as Iagoda, the former head of the NKVD. The indictment against them embraced the usual combination of treason, espionage, diversion, terrorism, and wrecking. Members of the bloc headed by Bukharin and Rykov were alleged to have spied for foreign powers from the earlier days of the revolution (for example, Bukharin's espousal of "revolutionary war" at the time of Brest-Litovsk was interpreted in these terms), to have entered into secret agreement with the Nazis and the Japanese to dismember the Soviet Union, to have planned the assassination of Stalin and the rest of the Politburo, and to have organized innumerable acts of sabotage and diversion in order to wreck the economic and political power of the country. Some of the defendants (for example, Bukharin) resisted some of the more specific charges, but, as a whole, they poured out their guilt and confessed to deeds of which they were patently incapable.[84]

However, if the trials and executions of many of the most important figures of the Lenin era and the twenties provided the highest drama of the Ezhovshchina, the terror at this time was directed, first and foremost, at those who had supported Stalin in his rise to power and who occupied the major posts in the party and governmental hierarchy. The purge swept out in ever-widening circles and resulted in wholesale removals and arrests of leading officials in the union republics, secretaries of the party, Komsomol, and trade union apparatus, heads of industrial trusts and enterprises, and leading writers, scholars, engineers, and scientists. Whole categories of Soviet citizens found themselves singled out for arrest because of their "objective characteristics." Old Bolsheviks, Red Partisans, foreign Communists of German, Austrian, and Polish extraction, Soviet citizens who had been abroad or had relations with foreign countries or foreigners and "repressed elements" were highly likely to be caught up in the NKVD web of wholesale imprisonment.

No sphere of Soviet life, however lofty, was left untouched. Among the purged Stalinists were three former members of the Politburo (Rudzutak, Chubar, and S. V. Kosior) and two candidate members (Postyshev and Eikhe). A fourth Politburo member, Ordzhonikidze, committed suicide, and a third candidate member, Petrovsky, was removed in disgrace but not executed. As we have seen, 70 percent of the Central Committee members died in the purge, and no major institution was spared. So far as can be judged, some 80 percent of the members of the Council of People's Commissars and an even larger percent of the regional (*obkom* and *kraikom*) secretaries were labeled "enemies of the people" (*vragi naroda*) and perished. The senior officers corps of the armed forces suffered severely. According to one count, 3 of the 5 marshals, 3 of the 4 first-rank army commanders, all 12 of the second-rank army commanders, 60 of the 67 corps commanders, 136 of the 199 division commanders, and 221 of the 397 brigade commanders were arrested.[85]

The arrests mounted rapidly. The arrest of an important figure was followed by the seizure of the entourage which surrounded him. The apprehension of members of the entourage led to the imprisonment of their friends and acquaintances. The chain of involvements and associates threatened to encompass entire strata of society. Fear of arrest, exhortations to vigilance, and perverted ambition unleashed new floods of denunciations, which generated their own avalanche of cumulative interrogations, and detentions.

As the fury of the Ezhovshchina mounted, Stalin and his intimates finally became alarmed. Evidence accumulated that the purge was overreaching itself and that much talent sorely needed by the regime was being irretrievably lost. The first signal of a change of policy was given in a resolution of the January 1938 plenum of the party Central Committee. A new culprit was criticized—the Communist-careerists who sought to make capital out of the purge by securing promotions through denunciations of their superiors. These careerists, the resolution charged, were primarily responsible for sowing suspicion and insecurity within party ranks and for decimating the party cadres.[86] The immediate effect of this resolution was to produce a new purge of the so-called careerists, but in late July 1938 Ezhov's sun began to set when Beria took over as his deputy. By the end of the year it was the turn of Ezhov and his collaborators to play the role of scapegoat for the excesses of the purge, and a wave of arrests spread through the NKVD organization. "Prisoners were released by the thousands, and many were restored to their old positions or even promoted."[87]

As the dust began to clear—and the whole period 1939–1941 was one of high but nonlethal turnover as the fresh appointees were being tested out—a new generation was staffing the upper levels of the Soviet administrative system. In 1934 the average regional party first secretary in the RSFSR had joined the party in 1912–1913, the average people's commissar in 1910. In 1939 the regional secretaries had entered the party in 1923 on the average, the people's commissars in 1919 (1921, if we exclude three prominent holdover commissars).[88] Many of those who had been sent to college during the First Five-Year Plan period received spectacular promotions during this period. Kosygin graduated from a textile industry institute in 1935 and was People's Commissar of the Textile Industry in 1939; Brezhnev graduated in the same year and was regional secretary (but not the first secretary) in Dnepropetrovsk in 1939; Kirilenko graduated in 1936 and was second secretary of the Zaporozhe regional committee by the end of the decade; D. F. Ustinov (appointed Minister of Defense in 1976) had graduated in 1934 and became People's Commissar for Armaments in 1941. These four men averaged thirty-four years of age in 1940. They were perhaps three or four years younger than than the average occupant of such posts, but their biographies could be duplicated many times over.

While we know much about the Great Purge and its consequences, a number of mysteries still remain. One which fascinated an earlier generation was the reason that many of the great figures of Bolshevism confessed in open court to the most awful crimes, crimes of which they were innocent. One popular explanation was given in Arthur Koestler's novel, *Darkness at Noon* —namely that the logic of Leninism drove these men to make one final sacrifice for the party.[89] The evidence of the last two decades, however, suggests a simpler explanation—torture, threat of additional torture, threat of reprisals to family, perhaps promises of leniency.

Other mysteries still are no closer to resolution. One is the basic question of the number of deaths that occurred during the Great Purge. As in the case of collectivization, some extremely high estimates have been advanced by westerners. Boris Nicolaevsky, for example, put the number of deaths at "more than half a million Communists who held responsible posts in the regime, and no fewer than 10 million non-Communists,"[90] while Robert Conquest put the number of executions at a million persons ("a minimal estimate") and the number of deaths in the camps in 1937–1938 at another 2 million.[91] (He further estimated that a total of 12 million persons died in the camps in the 1936–1950 period.)

There is, however, a real problem in reconciling such figures with available census data. In the first place, we presumably must work within the limit of 4–5 million "excess" deaths between 1926 and 1939 as calculated by Lorimer, most of which probably should be attributed directly or indirectly to collectivization. (Camp deaths after 1939 are, of course, another matter.) In the second place, all seem to agree that most of those who died were between the ages of thirty and fifty-five, and most (maybe 90 percent) were men.[92] A disproportionate number must also have lived in urban areas. Yet, in 1939 there were but 21 million men in these age groups, and perhaps only 7 million of them lived in urban areas. Surely we don't want to hypothesize 3 million executions or prison deaths in 1937–1938 or anything like this figure, or we are assuming most improbable percentages of men dying. In the third place, one distinguished Soviet demographer, B. Ts. Urlanis, has published a history of the "generation" born in 1906, and his mortality figures for the late 1930s suggest very few purge deaths for that cohort during this period—perhaps as few as a thousand[93] (see table 4). The 1906 group was but thirty-

Table 4   *1934–1939 deaths among Soviet citizens born in 1906*

Year	Men	Women	Total
1934	10,000	9,000	19,000
1935	9,000	8,000	17,000
1936	9,300	8,100	17,400
1937	9,600	8,000	17,600
1938	9,600	8,000	17,600
1939	9,500	7,500	17,000

Source: B. B. Ts. Urlanis, *Istoriia odnogo pokoleniia* (Moscow, Mysl', 1968), pp. 200–205. See pp. 227 and 229 for figures on the cause of death among urban members of the group from 1935 to 1938.

two years of age in 1938 and almost surely suffered much less than older groups, but if Urlanis' data is accurate, the number of deaths in the purge would certainly be placed in the hundreds of thousands rather than in excess of a million. A figure in the low hundreds of thousands seems much more probable than one in the high hundreds of thousands, and even George Kennan's estimate of "tens of thousands" is quite conceivable, maybe even probable.[94]

Some persons seem instinctively to object to these figures on the ground that the Great Purge was so horrible that the number of deaths cannot have been so "low." We must not become so insensitive to the value of human life, however, that we dismiss tens of thousands of deaths as insignificant and need to exagerate the number by ten, twenty, thirty, forty times to touch our feelings of horror.

Of course, the most important question about the purge is why it took place at all. Even if the execution of the former oppositionists is seen as reasonably explicable, why did Stalin liquidate so many loyal supporters, in particular since this action decimated the military and administrative hierarchies that seemed vital for the achievement of his major policy aims (especially given the growing danger of war)?

A number of explanations for the purge have been suggested. Some scholars argue, as has been seen, that the "loyal supporters" were not all that loyal and that Stalin acted to maintain his position against the type of opposition that supposedly appeared at the Seventeenth Congress. At least in one place, George Kennan extends this argument to hypothesize that Stalin felt a need to remove potential opposition to future foreign policy moves he was considering (specifically, the possibility of a pact with Hitler).[95] Others would refer generally to "the role of terror in Stalin's formula of government" "The insecurity of the masses must be supplemented by the insecurity of the governing elite . . . The too strongly entrenched official with an independent base of power is by definition a threat to the dictator's total sway."[96] In addition, one might add the desire to utilize the newly trained products of the engineering institutes in administrative posts and a fear that a peaceful purge would leave far too large a pool of discontents with organizational experience.

Nevertheless, Riasanovsky is surely right in saying that "there was madness in Stalin's method."[97] In retrospect, the purge succeeded in solidifying Stalin's control and in installing an administrative elite that was much too insecure to challenge him in the future. However, success should not make us forget that the policy was not without its risks and that in the short run it must have increased rather than decreased the danger that Stalin would be overthrown or assassinated. While rational calculation was no doubt part of the purge, excessive and unnatural suspicion must have been another part, and, of course, the ever-widening spread of the denunciations as a result of lower level fear and ambition added to the irrationality.

The Rigidity and Petrification of the Postwar Years

During World War II major changes occurred in the Soviet political process. Except for the Central Committee, the leading party institutions continued to function. (The Politburo, Orgburo, and Secretariat met over two hundred times during this period, and it is said that "the chief questions of the war were decided" at these sessions.)[98] Nevertheless, new state agencies were created and played a major role in the administration of both the war and the economy. The most important of these—particularly for management of the economy and of supply to the front—was the State Defense Committee. At first, the State Defense Committee was a small inner bureau of the Politburo consisting of Stalin (its chairman), Molotov (its deputy chairman), Beria, Malenkov, and Voroshilov, but it was later expanded to include Kaganovich (the Commissar for Railroads), Mikoian (the Deputy Chairman of the Council of People's Commissars for trade), Bulganin (Deputy Commissar for Defense), and Voznesensky (the Chairman of Gosplan). The decisions of the State Defense Committee were obligatory for all institutions in the Soviet Union (including the lower party apparatus). A second major new institution was the Supreme Headquarters, which directed actual military operations and became the location of Stalin's personal office.[99]

While a period of war obviously is one of great strain—particularly when it is waged on a country's soil and some 20 million citizens die in the process— the relationship between the regime and population took on a rather different and accommodating character during the war. The war was the crucial time of test for the new administrative echelon which had risen during the purge and then was in its thirties and early forties, and it must have been a period of growing self-confidence for this group. While wartime decisions had the force of martial law, the difficult nature of communications during the war necessitated an unusual amount of real delegation of authority away from Moscow. Indeed, most of the people's commissariats were actually transferred to eastern provinces early in the war.[100]

Perhaps in response to the tendency of significant elements of the Soviet population to tolerate German conquest too readily in the first stages of war,[101] the leadership also moved toward a reconciliation with lower strata of the population and even more with the values important to nonelite elements of society. Take, for example, the policy of recruitment of new party members. From January 1933 through 1937, almost no one had been admitted into the party, and even when party membership rose rapidly between January 1, 1938 and January 1, 1941 (from 1,900,000 to 3,900,000 persons), the new recruits were drawn primarily from the "best people" of the new administrative-professional strata. Only 24 percent of those entering the party from 1937 through June 1941 were workers, and probably less than 10 percent were peasants.[102] During the war, however, 5,319,000 men and women were admitted as candidate members, and an unknown additional number became party members at the front without passing through the candidate stage. Thirty-two percent of the wartime admissions were classified as workers and 25 percent as peasants.[103]

The leadership also moved to mute some of the more antagonistic ideological themes (although it certainly would be wrong to assume that propaganda in support of the Soviet system or socialism was abandoned). In large part, the war was treated as one for Russia's survival rather than for socialism's, and the nationalism theme that had been growing in regime propaganda since the mid-1930s became even stronger. The war was called not World War II, but the Great Patriotic War, the Great Fatherland War, and a National War of Liberation. At the same time some attempt was also made at partial reconciliation with the Russion Orthodox Church, and the reestablishment of the Moscow Patriarchy was permitted. Western correspondents reported that the citizens themselves were allowed to speak out more freely than they had since the 1920s.[104]

At the conclusion of the war many hoped that these wartime trends would continue, and in certain respects their hopes were realized. During the postwar years the administrative-professional stratum was not subjected to another Great Purge, the industrial managers in particular often being given long tenure in their positions.[105] The yearning of the stratum for more "normalcy" and for greater legitimization of "middle-class values" was also partially accommodated.[106] Nevertheless, even the administrative-technical stratum was scarcely guaranteed security from arbitrary secret police action, and other groups fared much less well.

It was the peasant who seemed to bear the brunt of the continuing high rate of investment. At the end of the war rumors were rife in the villages (and were apparently tolerated by the regime) that the kolkhoz system would be fundamentally revised in the postwar period. However, in practice, agricultural policy moved in the direction of tightening rather than loosening of control over all kolkhoz activities. In September 1946, a Central Committee and Council of Ministers resolution denounced illegal wartime expansion of private plots, and in October a special Council on Kolkhoz Affairs was established to put an end to these abuses and to restore order on the collective-farm front.[107] As a result of its activity, *Pravda* asserted, some 14 million acres of illegally appropriated land were restored to the kolkhozes.[108]

Not only was the Council on Kolkhoz Affairs added to the array of agencies already supervising the farm, but the farm chairmen themselves no longer were peasants as had been the case since the mid 1930s. Instead the new chairman was usually a returnee from the war, and he "brought from the war strictness and discipline. He decided to overcome the savage devastation with a desperate attack, as he had recently taken enemy entrenchments. His ears sometimes became deaf to the innumerable human complaints and requests which he could in no way satisfy. The word 'give' became the most frequent in his lexicon."[109]

In 1950 the leadership began to change the nature of the kolkhoz itself, making its management more remote from the village than it had been previously. The kolkhozes were merged into larger units (their number declined from 252,000 to 97,000 between 1950 and 1952),[110] and the basic work unit within the kolkhoz—the *zveno* or team of some ten persons (really a unit of extended family size)—was denounced as leading to "the splitting of a single large-scale collective unit into small cells," the "shaking [of] the very foundations of large-scale collective socialist agriculture."[111] The much larger brigade was endorsed as the basic work unit.

Most important of all, the peasants received few fruits from their labor. Indeed, an important change in grain collection policy disadvantaged the peasants even more than in the past. Grain collections in 1952 were slightly smaller than in 1940, but in 1952, 68 percent took the form of payment for machine-tractor station work (that is, were deliveries for which the farms received no payments) as against 47 percent in 1940. Moreover, the planned payments to the MTS and obligatory deliveries to the state were higher than actual payments and deliveries, and hence the farms were continually in arrears on past payments. As Khrushchev frankly recognized (and complained) after Stalin's death, the regime could thus appropriate any extra grain the kolkhoz might produce.[112] Even in a fairly good year (1952) the average monthly earnings of a collective farmer were only 13 rubles (in new rubles) compared with some 67 rubles for employees in other branches of the economy.[113]

The situation of the industrial worker was mixed. The severe labor laws of 1940 remained on the books, but they seem to have lost most of their force as the postwar period wore on.[114] The average monthly wages of those employed elsewhere than in the kolkhozes rose from 33 rubles in 1940 to 48 rubles in 1946, 64 rubles in 1950, and 72 rubles in 1955. (The figures for industrial workers were 32 rubles in 1940 and 69 rubles in 1950.) Nevertheless, inflation ate into these gains and Soviet scholars put 1950 real income at the 1940 level.[115] The status differentials between workers and administrative-technical personnel introduced in the 1930s were not only maintained, but even strengthened somewhat.[116]

It was for the intelligentsia, however, that the postwar years were most threatening of all. The last years of the war were marked by a re-emphasis upon ideological themes, and throughout the postwar era ideology was defined in increasingly rigid and simplified terms. After five years during which World War II was defined as one between the aggressors and the peace-loving nations (including such countries as the United States and Great Britain), Stalin signaled the return to classic formulations in February 1946, when he stated without qualification that "the war arose as the inevitable result of world economic and political forces on the base of monopoly capitalism."[117] This view became embodied in the Two-Camp foreign policy followed in the last years of Stalin's life. The capitalist and socialist camps were said to be inexorably hostile to each other, and any country not in the socialist camp was declared to be in the capitalist one. The newly independent Asian countries which proclaimed their neutrality in the cold war were denounced as capitalist tools and treated as implacable enemies.

In the summer of 1946 the Central Committee issued four decisions on literature, the theater, and the motion pictures—all emphasizing the need for more "partyness" (*partiinost'*) and signifying the tightening of ideological control over the arts.[118] The ideological campaign has often been called the Zhdanovshchina in "honor" of Andrei Zhdanov, a secretary of the Central Committee who was its leading spokesman.[119] The Zhdanovshchina had many themes, but a central one, which fitted well with the growing hostility toward the West in international affairs, was an increasing transformation of the nationalism of the war years into an ugly xenophobia. Internationalism and cosmopolitanism became supreme sins, and nothing was denounced more harshly than any "spirit of servility toward everything foreign."[120] All inventions (even games such as baseball) were said to have originated in Russia, and intellectuals who tried to study—let alone praise—the West or to use western concepts, methodologies, or contemporary artistic forms were particularly suspect. The distrust of outsiders extended to Russian Jews (especially after the creation of the state of Israel), and between 1948 and 1953 many prominent Jews disappeared from view, some actually executed.

The suppression of deviation among intellectuals was a gradual process, and it was by no means a thoroughgoing one. In literature, for example, Harold Swayze reports that even at the height of the Zhdanovshchina in 1948, "certain discontented writers pointed quite boldly to symptoms of a decline in Soviet letters, and their criticism implied that official prescriptions of content and method in literary works were a cause of the unsatisfactory state of affairs. Some writers even went beyond this, and in doing so they threatened to raise the whole question of the nature of the control system." The most outspoken critics soon had to recant, but the years after 1949 "witnessed a certain moderation of the stringency in cultural affairs." In 1951 a number of literary specialists continued to speak out. "While paying ample tribute to the principle of *partiinost'*, [they] seemed to be endeavoring to win the acceptance of a less restrictive attitude toward the nature of the political functions of art." These men were attacked by more orthodox literary spokesmen, "but the party, contrary to its usual practice, did not interfere in these controversies by issuing decrees or running editorials in *Pravda* or *Bolshevik*."[121]

However, the intellectual repression in other spheres (especially in the scholarly world) did seem to be intensifying in Stalin's last years. Stalin himself intervened decisively in scholarly conflicts in esoteric fields such as genetics, linguistics, and psychology. When the decision to write a new textbook on political economy in 1951 opened the door for major behind-the-scenes debate among economists, the Soviet leader responded the following year with his "The Economic Problems of Socialism," which reasserted orthodoxy and condemned "some comrades" for engaging in revisionism. The last months of Stalin's life were marked by widespread public recantations by the economists.[122] Westerners had a strong tendency to see this repression as the result of an imposition of a Marxist-Leninist strait jacket on intellectual life, but while the congealing orthodoxy was expressed in ideological terms, its contents could be very non-Marxist. In genetics, support was given to a nonparty figure (Lysenko) whose views had not been considered the most Marxist in the 1920s and who emerged victorious largely because his agronomical views fitted well with regime priorities;[123] in linguistics, Stalin actually supported the position that played down economic factors; in psychology, the non-Communist Pavlov was deified.[124]

The most ominous development of the period was the announcement on January 13, 1953 that a number of Kremlin doctors (most with Jewish names) had been arrested for conspiring to destroy the health of Soviet officials and for having caused the death of key leaders (including Zhdanov in 1948).[125] Accompanying the announcement of the "doctors' plot" was a campaign for "vigilance." In one especially notable article in the leading journal, *Kommunist,* Frol Kozlov, second secretary of the Leningrad obkom and soon to be a major figure in the Khrushchev era, called for "political vigilance" in party admissions and in the preservation of party-state secrets. In the course of this article he referred favorably to the Central Committee's letter after Kirov's murder, to the 1935–1936 exchange of party documents, and to Stalin's speech to the February 1937 plenary session of the Central Committee (which ushered in the bloody phase of the purge of Soviet officialdom).[126] Khrushchev later suggested convincingly that certain Politburo members—notably Molotov and Mikoian—were in serious personal danger as Stalin's life drew to a close,[127] and others such as Beria should surely be added to the list. Indeed, it is possible that a major political purge was impending.

The first major western scholarly effort to understand the Soviet Union came to fruition precisely in these years when intellectual repression seemed to be intensifying. The totalitarian model articulated at this time embodied the type of repressive system toward which the Soviet Union seemed to be evolving, but it is conceivable that these predictions were overdrawn. Just as the Zhdanovshchina was followed by a very partial relaxation in the literary realm, so perhaps the attack against the scholars would not have been carried to its extreme conclusion. The selection of A. M. Rumiantsev (the noted liberal spokesman of the early post-Khrushchev period) as head of the science and education department of the Central Committee in 1952 might be given more attention and importance than it normally has.

Nevertheless, whatever the future would have brought had Stalin lived (and many of the signs were ominous), the major result of the continuing intellectual repression for the policy process was the closing of a whole series of policy matters to public debate. Even many questions which an outsider might have thought quite nonsensitive—for example, the replacement of steam locomotives by diesels such as was occurring in the West—became taboo in nature. Growing restrictions on economic research, let alone the continuation of the prohibition on sociological work, meant that many policy questions were never even raised because the necessary data were not generated.

The explanation for the increasingly severe limitations placed even on "nonsensitive" public debate in the postwar years is not altogether clear. A very simplified interpretation might treat it as an attempt by Stalin to create a monopoly for himself in policy initiative and final decision-making. This may essentially be true, but a large portion of Stalin's motivation seems to have been a desire not to orchestrate policy in accordance with some personal vision, but to avoid the need to make major policy choices at all. There were very few striking policy innovations taken in these years, and in one policy area after another one gains the clear impression of petrification. The actual pattern of decisions seems to support Khrushchev's view in his memoirs: "The government virtually ceased to exist . . . Everyone in the orchestra was playing on his own instrument anytime he felt like it, and there was no direction from the conductor."[128] Or, at least this view seems true if one adds that each player was (in fear of his life) still trying to play as the conductor had wanted him to play in the past.

The Policy Process of the Late Stalin Period

To the extent that important policy choices were avoided rather than faced, it may seem inappropriate to talk about a policy process, but, of course, decisions actually were made. Stalin clearly occupied a dominant role in Soviet decision-making: at any time he could make a decision or change one—or even kill any other decision-maker. However, Stalin should not be seen as an isolated policymaker who issued directives without consultation. On the contrary, Khrushchev reported, Stalin "suffered terribly from loneliness [and] he needed people around him all the time."[129]

The image of top Soviet policymaking which emerges from Khrushchev's memoirs is one in which personal considerations were extremely important. Business was conducted in significant part during dinners at Stalin's dacha—dinners which lasted from 8:00 P.M. until early morning, and influence depended upon who was invited. Malenkov, Beria, and Khrushchev were the inner core of the confidants, with Bulganin usually joining them. Others attended, but even Politburo members did so only on Stalin's sufferance. (In fact, at the end Molotov and Mikoian were denied entrance, and Voroshilov was almost never invited.)[130]

It is difficult to be sure about the freedom of the policy debates, let alone the patterns of influence, within the top ruling circle. Khrushchev suggested—with almost no elaboration on this point—that "we were supposed to talk intimately and freely,"[131] and Milovan Djilas asserts that this did seem to be the case at dinners which he attended early in the postwar period. The dinners, he found, were marked by an "atmosphere of cordiality and informality," and featured "rambling conversation" that "touched on the most serious political and even philosophical subjects." "At these dinners the Soviet leaders were at their closest, most intimate with one another. Everyone would tell the news from his baliwick, whom he had met that day, what plans he was making . . . An uninstructed visitor might hardly have detected any difference between Stalin and the rest." Djilas hastened to add, however, that a difference did exist. Stalin's "opinion was carefully noted. No one opposed him very hard. It all rather resembled a patriarchal family with a crochety head whose foibles always caused the home folks to be apprehensive."[132]

Despite the fear in which Politburo members lived (as Bulganin once said to Khrushchev, "it has happened sometimes that a man goes to Stalin at his invitation as a friend . . . when he sits with Stalin, he does not know where he will be sent next, home or to jail"),[133] Politburo members did, in fact, push forward their policy ideas. Agricultural policy, for example, was clearly one on which Politburo members were not united, and differences among Khrushchev, Malenkov, Andreev, and possibly Beria were apparent even at the time.[134] Djilas' statement that "no one opposed [Stalin] very hard" clearly indicates that even the views of the Soviet leader could be opposed with an intensity less than "very hard," and the memoirs of World War II generals contain many examples of such disagreement with Stalin, even by sub-Politburo figures.[135]

In one striking case involving a most fundamental ideological and foreign policy question, a dispute between Stalin and Politburo members actually broke into public view in an oblique manner. As Fainsod noted,[136] the question of the validity of Lenin's doctrine of the inevitability of war was raised in the last years of Stalin's life. This was one of the revisions of doctrine denounced by Stalin in his 1952 "The Economic Problems of Socialism," but in this article he revealed that the view which he repudiated had found some support among his party colleagues:

> Some comrades affirm that, in consequence of the development of new international conditions after the second world war, wars among capitalist countries have ceased to be inevitable. They consider that the contradictions between the camp of socialism and the camp of capitalism are greater than the contradictions among capitalist countries, that the United States of America has made other capitalist countries sufficiently subservient to itself to prevent them from going to war with one another.[137]

In Stalin's view, "these comrades are mistaken . . . The inevitability of wars among the capitalist countries remains." "Yet, Malenkov, in his report to the Nineteenth Congress, was less categorical. He confined himself to the observation that 'the contradictions which today rend the imperialist camp *may* lead to war between one capitalist state and another.' "[138] (The italics are Fainsod's.) Observing that the views which Stalin criticized quickly became official doctrine after his death, Robert Tucker has suggested that the "some comrades" of Stalin's article included not only Malenkov but also a large proportion of the entire Politburo, and that Stalin's comment indicates the type of opposition (or at least disagreement) that Stalin frequently encountered behind the scenes.[139] This almost surely is correct.

While much top policymaking took place informally at Stalin's dacha or at his vacation retreat near the Black Sea, there also was more formal discussion of policy alternatives in specialized subgroups of the Politburo or in ad hoc commissions. Khrushchev reported that there were "quintets," "sextets," septets," and "novenaries" formed within the Politburo, each containing persons whose responsibilities were directly relevant to that particular policy area.[140] He also reported on a commission formed to draft a resolution on agriculture. (Such commissions apparently were—and are—the usual mechanism for the drafting of "legislation," and this case is interesting both in showing that a commission did not hesitate to present ideas of its own that did not flow from Stalin and, of course, in reminding us that Stalin still did have final authority.)

> When [Stalin] was once told during a discussion that our situation was a difficult one and that the livestock situation was especially bad, a commission was formed and charged with drafting a resolution entitled "Means Toward Further Development of Livestock Raising on Collective and State Farms." We worked out this draft. Of course, our proposals did not contain all possibilities, but we did chart ways in which livestock raising on the collective and state farms could be improved. We proposed then to raise the prices of animal products to create material incentives for the collective farmers and MTS and state farm workers in the development of livestock. But our draft was not accepted and in February 1953 was laid aside entirely."[141]

Despite the unquestioned importance of contact with Stalin as a source of political influence in the Soviet Union—and despite the particular advantage enjoyed by key Politburo members in this respect—the Soviet political process under Stalin was not limited to Politburo members. In the first place, as Fainsod argued in 1953, Kremlin figures surely had personal followings at lower levels in the hierarchy and they too were part of the political struggle.

> The phenomenon of the personal entourage . . . [continues] to form an essential ingredient in the informal life of the Party . . . The testimony of Soviet emigres provides abundant indication that Soviet careers are still made by clinging to the coattails of the great lords of Communism and that cliques rise and fall in the Soviet hierarchy depending on the fortunes of their patrons. The recent fate of the Zhdanov entourage furnishes a dramatic example . . . The death of Zhdanov on August 31, 1948, was followed by a ruthless purge of his dependents in the apparatus . . . [an action which] gave every surface evidence of being Malenkov-inspired. By installing his own henchmen in these key vacancies, Malenkov consolidated his control of the Party apparatus and emerged as the most powerful of Stalin's lieutenants.[142]

Some scholars seemed to suggest that political conflict in the Stalin period was based almost exclusively on such personalistic cliques, but Fainsod's "conflict theory"—his "group theory" of Soviet politics—centered far more on "the fluid play of bureaucratic politics that underlies the monolithic totalitarian façade,"—on "the frequently camouflaged processes of bureaucratic representation and manipulation":[143]

> Behind the totalitarian façade, the struggle of the elite formations of Soviet society for power and influence continues to find expression. The Party apparatus, the police, the army, and the administrative bureaucracy vie with one another for preferment, and the local and departmental interests of different sections of the bureaucracy exercise their counterinfluence on the Party . . . These organizations cannot be dismissed as mere robots . . . They are power structures in their own right . . .
>
> Each of [the apparat's] specialized parts manifests the characteristics of bureaucracy everywhere. It seeks to transmute skill into influence and power. It views every decision from the vantage point of its own particular interests, and it strives to defend and expand the area of its own dominion. Behind the monolithic façade of totalitarianism, the plural pressures of professional bureaucratic power continue to find dynamic expression . . . Bureaucratic representation . . . expresses itself in a struggle for preferential advantage. Because each part of the bureaucracy operates with an eye to the feasibility of the demands which are made on it, it becomes an unwitting spokesman for the claims of that sector of Soviet life for which it is responsible . . .
>
> Each bureaucratic group is constantly engaged in an effort to mobilize as much political support as it can muster, right up to the member of the Party [Politburo] responsible for its performance . . . The planning experts, whose precise calculus is supposed to define the tasks of the bureaucracy, are not divorced from the play of bureaucratic politics. Indeed, Gosplan is a focal point around which the battle for special treatment rages.[144]

Of course, Fainsod also emphasized the pressure from above in the Soviet system and the network of controls established to ensure administrative responsiveness to the center. Yet, even here he stressed that the control system was based on the principle of conflict: "The ruling group . . . pits one bureaucracy against another and relies on the rivalry between them to enforce its demands on both. It depends heavily on the separately organized Party and police hierarchies to control administration, and it supplements this type of surveillance and pressure by planning, financial, personnel, legal, and investigatory controls which are built into the administrative structure."[145]

The policy conflict in the late Stalin era was not limited to struggle between major bureaucracies. Scholars often expressed their opinions on policy alternatives, even at times conducting social experiments to gather evidence on the question at hand. Consider one of the most sensitive questions of the Stalin period: the machine-tractor stations and their relationship to the kolkhozes. In the late 1940s Soviet economists, including V. G. Venzher, were able to conduct "extensive experiments" in Krasnodar region on the effects of abolishing the MTS. These were not short-term experiments but lasted for several years. (Robert Miller states that in an interview with Venzher he "received the impression that such relatively radical experiments on a small, semisecret basis were fairly common even under Stalin.") In March 1951, Venzher published an article suggesting that technology must be introduced into the kolkhoz sector not only through the MTS but also through the kolkhozes themselves. In this article he did not advocate the sale of tractors and agricultural machinery to the kolkhozes, but when Stalin called for suggestions for the economics textbook, Venzher and his wife "submitted a number of letters proposing the abolition of the MTS and the sale of MTS equipment to the kolkhozes."[146] The fact that Venzher was one of those condemned in the criticisms of 1952–1953 and was forced to recant may indicate that such an involvement in the policy process was coming to an end, but we are discussing what occurred in the Stalin period, not what might—or might not—have occurred if Stalin had lived.

In a limited way, bureaucratic and nonbureaucratic actors were sometimes even able to make policy proposals (although seldom the argumentation behind these proposals) to a broader public through the press. Take, for example, a number of proposals that appeared in *Pravda* and *Izvestiia* during the month of December 1951.[147] An engineer argued for an improvement in the way the production of skis was organized; an academician called for a substantial improvement in the condition of the Central Station of Young Technicians; the Belorussian party first secretary demanded that the Committee on the Arts and the Ministry of Movies be more responsive to the republic's needs (including the need for a new movie studio); a doctor of technical science asked that all scholarly journals print the date of submission on articles they publish; a district educational official proposed that the number of district school inspectors be made proportionate to the number of schools in the district; the chairman of the Tadzhikistan Council of Ministers called for narrower rows in cotton planting and complained that the USSR Ministry of Cotton opposed this innovation.[148]

Although many of the foregoing policy suggestions were rather restricted in scope, others had more far-reaching implications and, in fact, involved a cautious, collective attack on many of the defects in economic administration and planning that were to lie at the center of post-Stalin economic reforms and debates. Thus, an article on the Kazakhstan party congress reported that the chairman of the Kazakh Council of Ministers spoke about "the urgent problems in creating a reliable feed base for agriculture," while an article written by the Leningrad obkom secretary specializing in agriculture appealed for more mechanization of orchard work. An obkom first secretary asserted that the MTS section agronomists each should, so far as possible, be assigned to serve an individual kolkhoz and actually be attached to it. The head of a store complained that the crockery factories, with the agreement of the Ministry of Trade, shipped all dishes in one predetermined assortment (an assortment that included many more tea cups than the consumers wanted), and he asked that the shipments vary in response to consumer demand. Both the head of construction of the Great Turkmen Canal and the director of the giant Leningrad plant Elektrosila demanded that the scientific institutes render the construction and industrial enterprises more consistent and concrete help in solving specific problems, but an academician praised the existing level of cooperation between scientific institutes and industrial plants and stated that the scientists should concentrate on "big" theoretical and economic problems. His suggestion for improving the contact between science and industry was to increase the number of conferences at which scientists could report their results to industrial administrators.[149]

Such were the proposals that appeared in only two Soviet newspapers in one rather typical month in 1951. During the following year, the regime called for extensive discussion of drafts of the new Five-Year Plan and new party rules that were to be approved at the Nineteenth Party Congress, and for a short period the flow of printed suggestions increased enormously.[150] After the Congress, despite the vigilance campaigns, policy proposals did not disappear from the press. In January and February 1953, Pravda carried, among others, an appeal by a kolkhoz chairman for a change in the pay scales for those employed in animal husbandry, a Central Asian official's outline of steps needed for an increase in cotton production, and a party official's demand that the Ministry of Agriculture solve "the basic problems of mechanizing feed procurement and organizing the feed base in the proper way."[151] Moreover, throughout the Stalin period (and the post-Stalin period for that matter) the debate in the specialized journals was much greater than in Pravda and Izvestiia.

The situation with respect to local decision-making was much more complex. On the one hand, the degree of autonomy for any policymaking at that level was much less than in the center, and post-Stalin commentators suggested that many local administrators had emulated the General Secretary in their highhandedness. On the other hand, many "administrative" decisions made in the localities were very analogous in their scope and impact to the run-of-the-mill decisions made by state and local governments in the United States. As a technique for controlling local administrators, the regime put great emphasis on "criticism and self-criticism" (*kritika* and *samokritika*) both by administrators and by the citizenry, and a good deal of criticism was permitted. In 1951, Alex Inkeles wrote, "It has indeed been remarked that in the United States one criticizes the President but little else, whereas in the Soviet Union one never criticizes Stalin or his policy but does criticize virtually everything else. This generalization is certainly too broad, but it represents an element of reality."[152] Moreover, to the extent that the regime was serious about controlling its local administrators, the criticism permitted must sometimes have been translated into citizen influence on local decisions, at least within the limits of the budget and higher objectives.

There must have been great variation in the pattern of influence from place to place and from decision to decision, but the general role of the local soviets was described by Fainsod in 1953 in the following terms:

> At lower levels of the governmental hierarachy, the soviets discharge an important function in ensuring large-scale participation in community activities. In the winter elections of 1947–48, approximately 1,600,000 deputies were chosen to serve in local soviets. In addition, many soviets follow the practice of organizing groups of *aktivs* who are available to assist the soviet members in carrying out their responsibilities. While actual administrative assignments are reserved for the *ispolkoms* or executive committees of the soviets rather than ordinary soviet deputies or members of the *aktiv*, the latter are drawn into a consideration of communal plans and activities, even if it be only in the form of passive attendance at meetings at which reports are rendered by the chairman and members of the *ispolkom*. Ordinarily, however, both deputies and members of the *aktiv* are expected to take the lead in checking the execution of work assignments by soviet officials, in mobilizing voluntary labor for civic improvements, and in serving as agitators among the masses to spread devotion to soviet goals. Since a substantial part of the work plans of local soviets is concerned with the maintenance and expansion of communal services and involves such everyday needs of the electorate as housing, sanitation, transportation, and recreation, interest in the activities of local soviets is not too difficult to arouse. Party-directed participation at this level of government builds on a genuine concern with common requirements.[153]

Of course, none of these quotations or statements should be taken to deny either the centralized nature of the Soviet political system of the time or the repression and rigidity of the regime. Yet, if we are to understand correctly the nature and the degree of the change that occurred in the Soviet Union after 1953, if we are to understand the Soviet Union in comparative terms, it is vital that we be aware of the real life that words such as "centralized," "repressive," and "rigid" hide, even in the late Stalin era. Otherwise when we observe real life at a later time or in a different setting, we may exaggerate the degree of change, the degree of difference that is involved.

6 | The Revitalization of the System

THE GREAT tour de force of Stalinism was the construction of a political system which combined the revolutionary and authoritarian heritage of Leninism, the traditional nationalism of tsarism, the stabilizing equilibrium of conservative social institutions, the dynamics of rapid industrialization, and the terror apparatus of a full-blown police state. The patrimony Stalin handed on to his successors was in some respects impressive. Under his leadership, the Soviet Union had become a leading industrial and military power in the space of a few decades. The success of the industrialization drive had been ensured by massive investments in the expansion of elementary and higher education, in the emphasis placed on the training of engineers, technicians, and scientists, in the reorganization of the incentive system to reward the skills essential to the production process, and in the prestigious place accorded the new industrial elite in Soviet society. But forced-draft industrialization on the Soviet model also exacted its toll. Its costs under Stalin could be measured in the millions who were consigned to forced-labor camps, in mass purges and the denial of human rights, and in the chronic shortages of food, consumer goods, and housing which accompanied the industrialization drive.

Stalin's death left a legacy of suppressed aspirations with which his successors had to reckon. First, there was widespread desire for improvement in the standard of living—for more food and consumer goods, better housing, more leisure, and more adequate provision for old age and other disabilities. The most disadvantaged groups were the collective farmers and the unskilled and semiskilled workers, but the pressure for higher living standards extended well beyond these groups into the middle and even relatively privileged strata.

192

Any such economic improvement clearly depended in turn upon a radical change in the agricultural sphere. Despite a large increase in the size of the population, the number of cattle in the Soviet Union in 1953 was below that of 1916 and well below that of 1928. Grain production was below the 1940 level.[1]

Second, there was an equally widespread yearning for greater security, for a life of stable expectations, for liberation from the threat of the concentration camp and the numbing uncertainties of constant surveillance and denunciation. In the last weeks before Stalin's death, the Soviet air was heavy with a sense of impending doom. The announcement of the arrest of the Kremlin doctors on January 13, 1953, evoked grim memories of the earlier "doctors' plot" during the Great Purge and seemed to portend its repetition on a mass scale.[2] As Khrushchev later revealed, even the members of Stalin's innermost circle feared for their lives.[3] It is not hard to imagine how the lieutenants yearned for firm ground under their feet and, in this yearning, mirrored the fears and hopes of every bureaucrat in the hierarchy. Perhaps not altogether paradoxically, the resentment against Stalin's system of calculated insecurity was most intense among those who had the most to lose as a result of arbitrary arrest and removal.

Third, there was the desire for greater freedom, not necessarily freedom in the western political sense, but freedom to use one's talents and capacities, freedom to perform one's function without fearing the consequences, freedom to travel outside Soviet boundaries, and freedom to transcend the Stalinist doctrinal rigidities in thinking and writing about Soviet realities. Suppressed though these aspirations were during the Stalinist era, they were nevertheless fermenting behind the façade of Stalinist ideological conformity. Understandably, these aspirations found their sharpest focus in the new Soviet intelligentsia who were coming into positions of responsibility and influence during the latter part of Stalin's regime. Their dreams of greater autonomy did not necessarily involve an overt challenge to the ruling ideology; for many of those who harbored thoughts of greater independence and authority remained loyal to the Soviet system and envisaged such developments as strengthening a regime of which, after all, they were an integral part.

With Stalin's death, his successors had to make a host of difficult decisions on how to handle these aspirations. There was the immediate need to achieve an orderly transfer of power and to set forces in motion that would launch the new regime on a stable course. There was the issue of succession which could not be evaded and which was already implicit in the parceling out of appointments and powers within twenty-four hours after the release of the news of Stalin's demise. But above all was the question of Stalinism. How could the leadership break out of the dysfunctional immobilism of the late

Stalin period without relaxing its controls over the populace and officialdom to the point of placing its authority in peril? How much could it afford to dare and how much should it?

The Contenders for Power

Immediately after Stalin's death, the enlarged Presidium elected at the Nineteenth Congress was abolished, and the inner bureau of that body, with Molotov and Mikoian added, was constituted as a new Presidium of ten voting members (and four candidates). The relative lack of information about the personalities and views of these men makes it difficult to describe them in the same detail as the contenders in the 1920s, but a good deal still is known about them.

In sociological terms—and to a considerable extent in political terms as well—the full members of the 1953 Presidium (as the former Politburo continued to be called until 1966) can be divided into several major groups.[4] Four of the ten were Old Bolsheviks who had joined the party before the revolution and had been close supporters of Stalin in his rise to power in the 1920s: Viacheslav M. Molotov, Lazar M. Kaganovich, Kliment E. Voroshilov, and Anastas I. Mikoian. Despite their enormous political longevity, they (except for Voroshilov who was seventy-two years old) were only in their late fifties and early sixties at the time of Stalin's death, and in that sense at least, all of them except for Voroshilov were viable contenders.

Another five members of the Presidium—Lavrentii P. Beria, Georgii M. Malenkov, Mikhail G. Pervukhin, Mikhail Z. Saburov, and, to a considerable extent, Nikolai A. Bulganin—were of a different generation. Eleven years younger on the average than the Old Bolsheviks, these men did not join the party until after the March revolution—in Malenkov's and Saburov's cases, not until 1920—and they did not become voting members of the Politburo until after World War II. Also unlike the Old Bolsheviks, four of the five younger Presidium members were products of engineering institutes, and the fifth (Bulganin) had a decade of administrative work in an important Moscow heavy industry factory.

In many ways the tenth Presidium member, Nikita S. Khrushchev, was a transitional figure. His age—fifty-nine in 1953—was closer to that of the Old Bolsheviks than to that of Malenkov, Beria, Pervukhin, and Saburov, and, like the former group, he became a full Politburo member before the war. Yet, Khrushchev was not elected to the Politburo until 1939, and he was more a harbinger of the new generation than a representative of the old. He had been the first Politburo member who had entered the party after the revolution (he became a member in 1918). He was also the first Politburo member to have received higher education after the revolution—and education directly related to industrial management at that—but it is perhaps symbolic of the transitional nature of his career that he went to the Industrial Academy for only two years and probably was absorbed by his duties as party secretary there.

The senior member of the Presidium in terms of tenure (and also, by all accounts, the most conservative) was V. M. Molotov.[5] Elected a secretary of the Central Committee and a candidate member of the Politburo in 1921, he had been Stalin's closest associate in the prewar period. When Rykov lost his position as Chairman of the Council of People's Commissars in 1930, Molotov was chosen as his successor, and he served as the country's "prime minister" throughout the decade of rapid industrialization, collectivization, and the Great Purge.

In 1939, as Stalin moved toward abandoning the attempt to ally with the West against Hitler, he removed the symbol of that policy—M. M. Litvinov, the People's Commissar for Foreign Affairs—and replaced him with Molotov. Molotov held this post for two years in conjunction with the chairmanship of the Council of People's Commissars, and then for eight years in conjunction with the deputy chairmanship after Stalin took over the chairmanship. In 1949 he relinquished the foreign affairs ministry, remaining as first deputy chairman of what then was called the Council of Ministers. However, whatever his title, Molotov was Stalin's top lieutenant for foreign policy throughout most of the 1930s and 1940s. In the last year or two of Stalin's life, he seemed to lose favor with the dictator and was not named to the inner bureau of the Presidium after the Nineteenth Party Congress.

Lazar Kaganovich had the reputation of being the troubleshooter of the Politburo in the Stalin period. He had been head of the organization-instruction department of the Central Committee in 1922 (and a Central Committee secretary in 1924), and, as such, he played a major role in Stalin's consolidation of control of the party apparatus. Then came a succession of political and administrative posts in a wide range of policy spheres, giving the impression that he was being rushed from breach to breach to repair breakdowns and introduce order where chaos had prevailed.

Kaganovich's troubleshooting career began in the Ukraine, and in his tenure as first secretary of its party organization from 1925 to 1928 he attracted nationwide attention for his energetic leadership of the construction of the Dnepro Hydroelectric Station. As secretary of the Moscow organization between 1930 and 1935, his most dramatic achievement was the building of the Moscow subway. At the same time he was Central Committee secretary and, together with Molotov and perhaps Voroshilov, was one of Stalin's top two or three lieutenants. In 1933 he was temporarily shifted to the critical agricultural front, and was largely responsible for organizing the political sections of the machine-tractor stations through which the disintegrating collective farm structure was salvaged and restored. In 1935 he became People's Commissar of Railroads and applied similar techniques to improve the efficiency of the Soviet Union's overloaded and poorly functioning transportation network. Then when Ordzhonikidze died in 1937, Kaganovich succeeded him as Commissar for Heavy Industry. When oil production began to lag, he was given the assignment of putting the oil industry on its feet. In 1938 he returned to the railroads, and during the war, as a member of the State Committee for Defense, was responsible for all wartime transportation.

After World War II, Kaganovich was put in charge of a newly created Ministry of Building Materials. When the 1946 drought created an emergency in the Ukraine, he was dispatched to replace Khrushchev as first secretary and to lead the work of reconstruction. In December 1947 he returned to Moscow, where as one of the deputy chairmen of the Council of Ministers he apparently continued to exercise major supervisory authority over the group of ministers concerned with transportation and heavy industry. Kaganovich's talents as an administrator made him an important figure in the Politburo, but during the postwar period he no longer occupied the outstanding position which he had attained in the early thirties.

Kliment Voroshilov is the most shadowy figure among the Presidium members of 1953. Essentially the same age as Stalin, he had been an outstanding military leader during the Civil War and was closely associated with Stalin in the defense of Tsaritsyn (later renamed Stalingrad). After the Civil War he commanded the North Caucasus Military District and then the Moscow Military District before being appointed People's Commissar for Military and Naval Affairs in 1925. He retained this portfolio (renamed several times) until 1940 when the Finnish War turned into a debacle. His role in World War II seems not to have been a great one, and, although he became Deputy Chairman of the Council of Ministers in 1946, responsibility for the military sphere was given to another member of the Politburo—Nikolai Bulganin, the new Minister of Defense. From 1947 to 1951 he served as Chairman of the Bureau of Culture under the Council of Ministers (a bureau that ceased to exist in 1951), and he was responsible for education, culture, and science. It may be that he was more a symbol of victory in the Civil War than a dominant figure in decision-making, even in the sphere he headed, and in Stalin's last year he too was falling into disfavor.[6]

The fourth Old Bolshevik, Anastas Mikoian, was not as old as the other three in any sense.[7] He was five years younger than even Molotov and Kaganovich and had joined the party a decade later (see table 5). While a strong supporter of Stalin in the 1920s (he spearheaded the counterattack to Zinoviev and Trotsky's attempt in 1922 at the Eleventh Party Congress to limit the

Table 5 *Members of the Presidium, March 1953*

Member[a]	Year of Birth	Year of Party Entry	Position
G. M. Malenkov	1902	1920	Chairman of the Council of Ministers
L. P. Beria	1899	1917	First Deputy Chairman of the Council of Ministers and Minister of Internal Affairs
V. M. Molotov	1890	1906	First Deputy Chairman of the Council of Ministers and Minister of Foreign Affairs
K. E. Voroshilov	1881	1903	Chairman of the Presidium of the Supreme Soviet
N. S. Khrushchev	1894	1918	Secretary of the Central Committee
N. A. Bulganin	1895	1917	First Deputy Chairman of the Council of Ministers and Minister of Defense
L. M. Kaganovich	1889	1905	First Deputy Chairman of the Council of Ministers
A. I. Mikoian	1895	1915	Deputy Chairman of the Council of Ministers and Minister of Internal and Foreign Trade
M. Z. Saburov	1900	1920	Minister of the Machinery Industry
M. G. Pervukhin	1904	1919	Minister of Electric Power Stations and the Electrical Industry
AVERAGE	1895	1914	
Candidate members			
N. M. Shvernik	1888	1905	Chairman of the All-Union Central Council of Trade Unions
P. K. Ponomarenko	1902	1925	Minister of Culture

continued

Table 5—Continued

Member[a]	Year of Birth	Year of Party Entry	Position
L. G. Melnikov	1906	1928	First secretary of the Ukrainian Central Committee
M. D. Bagirov	1896	1917	First secretary of the Azerbaidzhan Central Committee

Source: *Pravda*, March 7, 1953, p. 1.

[a] Members and candidate members are listed in the rank order of the official announcement.

authority of the provincial party organs), Mikoian was one of the provincial secretaries of the period—not, like Molotov, a person involved in selecting them. Although he became a candidate member of the Politburo in 1925 and People's Commissar for Domestic and Foreign Trade in 1926, he did not become a full member of the Politburo until 1935.

Mikoian's precise post changed over the years, but, whatever his title, he, as the Politburo's Armenian, was its major specialist on the stereotypical occupation of the Armenian—trade, both domestic and foreign. In 1930 he became People's Commissar for Supplies, in 1934 People's Commissar for the Food Industry. In 1937 he was named Deputy Chairman of the Council of People's Commissars, a position he held until 1953 (after 1946, of course, his title became Deputy Chairman of the Council of Ministers). From 1938 to 1949 he simultaneously served as People's Commissar—then Minister— for Foreign Trade, but throughout the period continued to bear general responsibility for domestic trade as well. Perhaps as befits a man whose posts had given him special familiarity with the plight of the consumer, as well as with the advantages to be gained from foreign trade, Mikoian was to be the only one of the Old Bolsheviks to take a more liberal political line after Stalin's death.

The other Presidium members—while alike in their postrevolutionary entry into the party, their postwar entry into the Politburo (with the exception of Khrushchev), and their engineering background (with the exception of Bulganin)—were men of very differing stature. Malenkov, Beria, and Khrushchev had been Stalin's three most powerful subordinates during his last years, essentially supervising the state, police, and party apparatuses respectively, and Bulganin as superviser of the military was also a man of considerable standing. Pervukhin and Saburov, on the other hand, had not entered the

Politburo until 1952 and clearly were on a lesser level than their colleagues.

Judging from the fact that he had given the Central Committee report to the Nineteenth Party Congress (and on the basis of his other activities as well), Georgii Malenkov seemed to be Stalin's chosen heir apparent at the time of the dictator's death.[8] At fifty-one, he was one of the youngest members of the Presidium, and, in contrast to such men as Molotov and (earlier) Zhdanov, he had the reputation of being pragmatic and flexible rather than a rigid ideologue.

Malenkov's political career dated from the Civil War, when as a teenager he entered the party and served in the army as a political worker. Between 1922 and 1925 he attended the Higher Technical School in Moscow and also held the post of secretary of the school's party organization. In 1925 he joined the apparatus of the Party Central Committee and became a member of Stalin's personal secretariat. Between 1930 and 1934, he headed the organization-instruction department of the Moscow regional party organization, and from 1934 to 1939 he directed the leading party organs department of the Central Committee Secretariat. (As such, he had a major role in the placement of party personnel and in the supervision of local party organizations during the height of the Great Purge.) In 1939 he became one of the secretaries of the Central Committee, in which position he apparently continued to direct the personnel activities of the party. In 1941 he was made a candidate member of the Politburo.

During World War II Malenkov began assuming governmental responsibilities in addition to those in the party apparatus. He played a crucial role as a member of the State Committee for Defense, his major assignments including responsibility for aircraft production and the chairmanship of the Committee for the Economic Rehabilitation of Liberated Areas. In 1946 he moved from the Secretariat to become a Deputy Chairman of the Council of Ministers, and, although he was elected a full member of the Politburo in that year, his prestige seemed to suffer a temporary eclipse as that of Andrei Zhdanov rose.[9]

With the illness and death of Zhdanov in 1948, Malenkov returned to full favor. Now serving both as Deputy Chairman of the Council of Ministers and secretary of the party Central Committee, he supervised the party apparatus from late 1948 to early 1950. This period saw not only the infamous Leningrad Affair in which top officials from Zhdanov's Leningrad were executed, but also a change of first secretary in thirty-five of the fifty-eight regional party committees in the Russian Republic. Malenkov's hand in these changes is suggested by the fact that only 20 percent of the new secretaries were in equivalent or better posts at the end of Khrushchev's purge of the party apparatus in 1954 and 1955. (By contrast, 56 percent of the persons elected regional first secretary in the RSFSR in 1951 and 1952 remained in an equivalent or higher position seven years later.) However, in 1950, with the naming of Khrushchev as a Central Committee secretary, Malenkov's responsibilities seemed to shift from supervision of the party apparatus to that of the state machinery and the economy—and even, to some extent, foreign policy. From all appearances, he was Stalin's first deputy on major policy matters.

Like Malenkov and most of Stalin's top subordinates, Nikita Khrushchev began his career in the party apparatus, but, unlike most of them, he had never moved into governmental work.[10] After joining the party in 1918 at the relatively advanced age of twenty-four, he had participated in the Civil War in fairly low level political and military work. Upon the conclusion of the war, he enrolled in a Rabfak or Workers' Faculty, which provided elementary and secondary schooling for adult workers. Khrushchev then entered party work in Stalino and Kiev in the Ukraine, at which time he may well have attracted the attention of Kaganovich while the latter was the Ukrainian first secretary.

In any case in 1929 (one year after Kaganovich's return to Moscow to be first secretary there), Khrushchev was sent to the Industrial Academy for training as a future industrial executive. At the same time he acted as party secretary in the Academy, a relatively important position in that period. In 1931 he moved into more general party work in Moscow: first as borough party secretary, then second secretary of the city party committee, then its first secretary, then second secretary of the regional committee. (It is worth noting that while Khrushchev was working in the city committee, Malenkov was head of the organization-instruction department of the regional committee, and Bulganin was chairman of the Moscow soviet—all of them working under Kaganovich's general supervision.) In 1935 Khrushchev succeeded Kaganovich as the combined first secretary of the Moscow regional and city committee, but in 1938 he was shifted to the first secretaryship in the Ukraine and soon became a full Politburo member. From 1938 to 1949, except for nine months in 1947 when he was temporarily replaced by Kaganovich, Khrushchev was first secretary of the Ukrainian party organization. (In the nine-month interlude, he was demoted to the chairmanship of the Ukrainian Council of Ministers, again, as in the early 1930s, serving as Kaganovich's deputy.)

In December 1949 Khrushchev was returned to Moscow as first secretary of the regional committee (which at the time had responsibility for the capital as well) and as one of the secretaries of the Central Committee. In retrospect, there is considerable evidence that, in this latter capacity, Khrushchev replaced Malenkov as the Central Committee secretary in charge of personnel selection in the provinces. The prominent personnel changes of the post-Stalin era—the move of industrial officials into major party work and of experienced rural officials into the post of kolkhoz chairman (an enlarged kolkhoz at that)—date from 1950,[11] and, as has been noted, the regional party first secretaries selected in 1951 and 1952 (unlike those selected in 1948-1949 when Malenkov clearly was the personnel secretary) had a high political survival rate in the Khrushchev era of the mid and late 1950's. Finally, it was Khrushchev who was chosen to give the report at the Nineteenth Congress on changes in party rules—a duty generally given to the person charged with supervision of the party apparatus.

The third powerful figure among the postrevolutionary Bolsheviks, Lavrentii Beria, had had a career which featured a rather unusual combination of party and secret police work.[12] In 1921, after participation in the Civil War, Beria began to work for the Cheka. During the next ten years he rose rapidly in the secret police hierarchy, ultimately coming to head both the Georgian and the Transcaucasian police. In 1931 he was transferred to party work, and for the following seven years served as first secretary of the Georgian and Transcaucasian party organizations, an assignment of special sensitivity because of Stalin's ties to the area.

In 1938 Beria returned to police work, and soon succeeded Ezhov as the USSR People's Commissar for Internal Affairs (NKVD). The following year he was made a candidate member of the Politburo, but, like Malenkov, he was denied promotion to full membership until 1946. Whether actually holding the post of secret police chief or of First Deputy Chairman of the Council of Ministers, Beria was the Politburo specialist on the police and terror apparatus in the last fifteen years of the Stalin period. Because of the security aspects involved, Beria also provided general supervision to the Soviet atomic energy developments; because of the foreign responsibilities of the security ministry, he also must have been involved in foreign policy questions, especially those concerning eastern Europe.

Beria remains a rather enigmatic figure in Soviet history. He was arrested within four months of Stalin's death and was blamed for the worst police excesses of the Stalin era. He was depicted as a terrible man—a rapist of hundreds of young girls and women, a person who played up to and intensified Stalin's most morbid suspicions and then had a gleeful "housewarming" over Stalin's corpse.[13] Yet, it remains true that he became head of the NKVD when Stalin was moving to end the Great Purge—not begin it—and the foreign, nationality, and domestic policies with which he seemed associated in 1953 were nearly always of a liberalizing nature. Beria may well have been the supreme opportunist, but it is at least conceivable that a somewhat different picture of him will emerge as the archives open and Soviet scholars can discuss the 1940s and 1950s more freely.

In contrast to Khrushchev, Malenkov, and Beria, the other three younger Presidium members had never worked in the party apparatus. Nikolai Bulganin began his career as an officer in the Cheka, but he transferred to economic work in 1922. During the next decade, he made his reputation as a talented industrial administrator, rising to the directorship of the important electric equipment plant Elektrozavod in Moscow. From 1931 to 1937 Bulganin served as chairman of the Moscow soviet—a post which brought him into close contact with the Moscow party secretaries of the time, first Kaganovich and then Khrushchev. In 1938 he became chairman of the State Bank.

During World War II, Bulganin served as political commissar of the Moscow front. In 1944 he was named Deputy People's Commissar for Defense and in 1946 (with the change in the name of the commissariat) First Deputy Minister of the Armed Forces. In 1947 he became Minister of the Armed Forces, Deputy Chairman of the Council of Ministers, and a candidate member of the Politburo. His promotion to full Politburo membership followed the next year. While Bulganin relinquished his ministerial portfolio to Marshall Vasilevsky in 1949, he continued to play a major role in supervising and coordinating defense and the defense industry as Deputy Chairman of the Council of Ministers.

Mikhail Pervukhin was even more a specialist in industrial management. Graduating as an electrical engineer, he rose in the 1930s in the electric power energy industry. He became head of a power station but during the purge quickly was promoted to be deputy head of the Moscow Electrical Power Administrative Bureau, then head of the USSR Main Electrical Power Administration, then Deputy Commissar and soon First Deputy People's Commissar for Heavy Industry. (All of this took place in little over a year's time.) In 1939 he was designated People's Commissar for Electric Power Stations and the Electrical Industry. From 1940 to 1942 he served as Deputy Chairman of the Council of People's Commissars and from 1943 to 1950 as People's Commissar and then Minister of the Chemical Industry. In 1950, he became a Deputy Chairman of the Council of Ministers, providing general supervision to the industries that he had already led. He became a member of the party Politburo (or, more accurately, Presidium) only in 1952 when that body was expanded to twenty-five men.

Mikhail Saburov represented that group of Russians who left school early (in his case at thirteen) and who worked in industry and low level political work before being sent to an engineering institute during the First Five-Year Plan period. Upon graduation in 1933, he, like Pervukhin, had an orderly progression of lower industrial jobs (in his case at a major machinery plant) but in the period 1938–1941 he was propelled upward from the post of head of the machinery department of the USSR Gosplan to that of the institution's

First Deputy Chairman and finally its Chairman. From 1944 to early 1947 Saburov served as a special agent of the State Defense Committee and then as deputy head of the Soviet Military Administration in Germany. In 1947 he became Deputy Chairman of the Council of Ministers, and two years later he returned to the chairmanship of Gosplan, this time as Vosnesensky's replacement. Again like Pervukhin, he was named to the party Presidium for the first time only in 1952.

Our knowledge of the personalities and reputations of the various contenders for power in the 1950s really is too incomplete to warrant a confident or reliable analysis of the advantages and disadvantages each faced. To the extent that the top party leadership and the broader party elite felt the necessity for some reform, the Old Bolsheviks may well have seemed too old in psychological, if not physical terms—too conservative, too tied to the Stalin past. To the extent that only party work generally trains a rising official in the supervision of all phases of life—industry, agriculture, education, ideological work, and so forth—Presidium members such as Bulganin, and particularly Saburov and Pervukhin may have seemed too narrow in their preparation for the top leadership. To the extent that the police was feared and the leadership desired a scapegoat for past policies, Beria was in a most vulnerable position, and to the extent that the leadership feared for their own safety, both he and Malenkov (with his background as head of the leading party organs department during the purge and his role in the Leningrad affair) may have seemed particularly worrisome contenders.

On many of these questions Nikita Khrushchev was much better placed. He had been Moscow first secretary during the height of the purge, and his hands could not have been clean, but his post during this period—and his relationship to Stalin then—was not as central as that of many of the others. His personality, his rather jovial nature, his uncouth manners, his rough peasant proverbs and jokes—all of these may have given him a less threatening appearance, and the transitional nature of his career may have increased his acceptability to both younger and older groups within the Presidium.

Most important, Khrushchev had experience and expertise that were uniquely broad in comparison to the other Presidium members. Except for the short-lived Beria, he was the Presidium member with the most experience supervising a non-Russian area of the country. (Kaganovich was the only other member with such a background, and most of that was in the 1920s.) Moreover, Khrushchev had served in the military during the war and was associated with the great victories at Stalingrad and Kursk, as well as the liberation of Kiev. He had industrial education and in his work in both Moscow and the Ukraine had a great deal of experience in supervising industrial centers, but he had developed such a taste for agricultural questions

that Stalin once called him a "regular Ukrainian agronomist."[14] Not only
was Khrushchev better acquainted with agriculture than were other Presidium members, also he was a man with ideas for reform in this realm of
society—surely the one realm in which the need for change was apparent to
nearly all Presidium members.

Finally, of course, Khrushchev had a not inconsiderable power base—
perhaps an extremely strong one. If selection of delegates to the party congress
was to be a significant factor in determining the ultimate outcome, as it had
been in the 1920s (and as it should have been according to the party rules),
Khrushchev had the advantages of having headed the Ukrainian organization until 1949 and then the Moscow organization until 1953—organizations
that were to select exactly 25 percent of the voting delegates to the Twentieth
Party Congress in 1956.[15] In addition, he had also been working as Central
Committee secretary in the period immediately prior to Stalin's death, apparently supervising the national party apparatus. This latter experience
may have provided him with far more than expertise as the various contenders strove to develop support in the succession period—a hypothesis
supported by the political longevity of most of the men selected as regional
party secretary in 1951 and 1952.

The Thaw and the Politburo Struggles of the Mid-Fifties

The most famous novel of the immediate post-Stalin period was Ilya
Ehrenburg's *The Thaw*.[16] This book focused on the downfall of a highhanded
production-oriented plant manager who during the course of the novel
lost both his job and his wife. The manager had used housing funds to obtain
a new foundry which he thought vital for the plan fulfillment that both
the center and the local party officials were demanding and praising. Then
a major winter storm destroyed much of the old housing, and the plant
manager was removed in disgrace. The novel ended with the onset of the
spring thaw, the beginning of new housing construction, and a sharp improvement in the mood of the sympathetic characters.

In itself, *The Thaw* was not a very distinguished novel, but its theme
of the conflict between the values of industrial development and other values
was a central one, and its title became the symbol for a political process that
Ehrenberg and many readers believed to be occurring and that they hoped
would lead to a true spring and summer. In many ways the word "thaw"
does serve as an apt characterization for the breakup of the frozen rigidities
of the Stalin period that took place in the first few years after Stalin's death.

The first response of Stalin's lieutenants to the crisis of his death on
March 5, 1953, was to submerge their differences and to rally the forces of
national unity around the party and the government. Malenkov and Beria

apparently took the lead in forming the new government,[17] and it featured Malenkov in the posts of both Chairman of the Council of Ministers and Secretary of the Central Committee. *Pravda* gave him special prominence, moving him, for example, to the center of the stage with Stalin and Mao in a doctored photograph from which all other Presidium figures were excluded.[18]

On March 21, however, *Pravda* carried an announcement that a plenary session of the Central Committee had voted on March 14 "to grant the request . . . of Malenkov to be released from the duties of Secretary of the party Central Committee." This decision, which left Khrushchev the only Presidium member in the Secretariat and made him the de facto First Secretary (as the General Secretary was called from 1952 to 1966), meant that no one of Stalin's former colleagues had the strength to assume immediately the position of undisputed leadership which Stalin commanded.

In retrospect, the removal of Malenkov from the Secretariat was the key event in the post-Stalin succession crisis, for Khrushchev now was in a position to strengthen his power base. As we examine the steps Khrushchev took over the next few years to consolidate his position, we must never forget this first crucial decision of his colleagues. Possibly the power base that he had the opportunity to build in the Central Committee prior to 1953 was an important factor in this decision, but it seems far more likely that the main explanations are to be found in his personality, his policy positions, the knowledge and expertises he had developed in his various career experiences, and, of course, the fears his rivals provoked.[19]

In March 1953 Khrushchev's consolidation of power lay in the future, and the leadership presented a united front to the outside world. If the later testimony of Khrushchev and his associates is to be believed, Kaganovich and especially Molotov were very doubtful about the need for reform, but the rest of the leadership seem, in fact, to have agreed upon a policy of concessions designed to win popular support.

The most important step in the inauguration of a thaw was the repudiation of the worst aspects of Stalinist terror. On April 3, 1953, the Kremlin doctors who had been arrested in January were released as guiltless; a *Pravda* editorial three days later promised that all cases of official "highhandedness and lawlessness" would be severely punished and that the legal rights of the Soviet citizenry would henceforth be safeguarded. In July the drive to bring the secret police under control received dramatic expression in the arrest of Lavrentii Beria. Khrushchev claimed in his memoirs that he was the organizing force behind this decision,[20] but in any case Beria was charged with "trying to set the Ministry of Internal Affairs above the party and government and to employ the agencies of the MVD, both in the center and localities, against the party and its leadership, against the government of the USSR."[21] Six months later the secret police chief and six other high police officials were executed. (At least another fifteen of Beria's collaborators—including M. D. Bagirov, first secretary of the Azerbaidzhan party organization and a candidate member of the Presidium—suffered the same fate over the next three years.)

With Beria's removal came the reversal of a number of policies with which the secret police had been associated. Many prisoners were released from the forced-labor camps; the Special Board of the Ministry of Internal Affairs was abolished; many persons condemned as "enemies of the people" during and after the Great Purge were rehabilitated (frequently posthumously); the definition of political crimes was sharply narrowed.[22] Then at the Twentieth Party Congress in 1956, as will be discussed shortly, Khrushchev moved to a more open break with the Stalinist past by denouncing the Soviet dictator himself in the sharpest terms.

At the same time that the power of the police was being curbed, the new leaders also moved to identify themselves with the improvement of living standards and a relaxation of tension in the world arena. Here there seemed to be a division of labor and even a difference of priorities between Khrushchev and Malenkov. As early as April 1, 1953, a substantial cut in retail prices was announced, and by July the columns of all Soviet newspapers began to fill with articles promising more consumer goods, increased housing, better restaurant facilities, and closer attention to workers' grievances. However, the consumer goods campaign came to be linked to Malenkov more specifically when he gave the major address to a Supreme Soviet session on the subject in August and elaborated government plans to expand the production of such goods and to supply more housing.

Malenkov also seemed to associate himself closely with a more moderate foreign policy toward the West and a movement away from some of the rigidities of the Two-Camp doctrine. In April 1953 the Soviet Union took the initiative in resuming the negotiations for an armistice to put an end to the Korean War, and the conclusion of the armistice itself on July 27 dramatized the regime's search for a detente in foreign affairs. Instead of treating any future war as one which the Soviet Union inevitably would win because of the superiority of its economic-social system, Malenkov publicly declared that nuclear war would spell "the destruction of world civilization," and he called for an improvement in relations with the United States through a process of patient negotiations.[23]

The Soviet Union also sought a more light-handed control over the Communist Bloc. Pressure was put upon the leaders in eastern Europe to follow the Soviet example in its various steps to reduce terror and improve living standards, and the Soviet Union in turn tried to be less stringent in the demands it made upon these leaders. The most exploitative aspects of economic relations with east Europe were changed, and most of the concessions the Soviet Union had gained in China from the Yalta Agreement were abandoned.

While Malenkov identified himself with consumer goods production and a new trend in foreign policy, Khrushchev placed his emphasis upon agriculture and seems to have been given a relatively free hand to develop policy in this realm. Although Malenkov's August 8, 1953, speech to the Supreme Soviet already had announced a break with the agricultural policies of the old regime, Khrushchev pre-empted the issue with a dramatic speech to a plenary session of the Central Committee in September. He described the situation in the countryside in frank terms, telling the population for the first time the facts about the level of grain output and the number of livestock.

The line laid down by Khrushchev and approved by the Central Committee followed in the main the program which Malenkov had already announced. Payments for agricultural products were increased to stimulate output, and a substantial rise was planned for capital investment in agriculture. Khrushchev also called for an intensive effort to train personnel in needed agricultural skills, to redirect agricultural specialists from office jobs to production assignments, and to strengthen administrative and party controls in the countryside.

When the 1953 grain harvest was even lower than that of 1952, Khrushchev unfolded a grandiose program to open up and cultivate so-called virgin lands in Kazakhstan, Siberia, the northern Caucasus, the Volga, and the eastern regions.[24] The program as originally announced called for 32 million new acres, but by 1960 it had expanded to more than 101 million acres—an amount equal to more than one-third of all the grain area in Russia in 1953 and considerably in excess of the total wheat area cultivated in the United States.

When the number of livestock failed to increase significantly between January 1953 and January 1955, Khrushchev then launched a crash program for the expansion of corn acreage in order to bolster the lagging feed supply and to provide a more adequate feed base for animal husbandry. Even regions that were totally inappropriate for corn production were ordered to plant it, and Khrushchev spoke so much about the subject that some Muscovites labeled him a "corn-man." Throughout the rest of the decade the party leader again and again personally identified himself with the agricultural sphere, sponsoring a series of reorganizations and programs which, he hoped, would provide the final solution to this most knotty of all Soviet problems.

Although Khrushchev was endorsing large-scale expenditures in agriculture and justifying them in terms of a better life for the Soviet citizen, he could be much cooler in his public reaction to the initiatives associated with Malenkov. Rather than speaking of the destruction of world civilization in a nuclear war, he delivered a fiery speech in Czechoslovakia in 1954 that not only boasted of Soviet leadership in developing the hydrogen bomb but also asserted that a nuclear war would mean the end of capitalism.[25] He accused reactionary capitalist circles of seeking a way out of their difficulties "by the preparation of a new war" and stressed the aggressive intentions of the imperialist camp. Similar views were expressed in a series of speeches delivered by Molotov, Kaganovich, Voroshilov, and Bulganin.

At least in late 1954 and early 1955 Khrushchev also took a harder line on the issue of consumer goods production. "In connection with the measures taken lately to increase output of consumer goods," Khrushchev said in January 1955, "some comrades have confused the question of the pace of development of heavy and light industry in our country . . . These pseudo-theoreticians try to claim that at some stage of socialist construction the development of heavy industry ceases to be the main task and that light industry can and should overtake all other branches of industry. This is profoundly incorrect reasoning, alien to the spirit of Marxism-Leninism—nothing but slander of our party. This is a belching of the rightest deviation, a regurgitation of views hostile to Leninism, views which Rykov, Bukharin, and their ilk once preached."[26]

The conflict with Malenkov came to a head in late 1954, and the conflict rose to full visibility with the appearance of a curious pair of editorials on December 21, 1954. *Izvestiia*, the organ of the government and presumably of Malenkov, called for the increased production of consumer goods; *Pravda*, the organ of the Central Committee and presumably more responsive to the First Secretary, summoned "the Soviet people to direct their main attention to fulfilling the plans for the further growth of heavy industry."

The issue was raised again at the meeting of the Central Committee. Khrushchev's published speech (which was quoted above) named no names, but its intent was unmistakable. The question of Malenkov's position must have been discussed more frankly in private, for on February 7, 1955, he "resigned" as Chairman of the Council of Ministers. The letter which was read for him acknowledged his administrative "inexperience" and his past "guilt and responsibility for the unsatisfactory state of affairs in agriculture." It praised the new agricultural reforms which, it was said, were "based upon the only correct foundation—the further all-around development of heavy industry—and only the realization of this program will provide the necessary conditions for a real increase in the production of all necessary consumer goods."[27] To the initiated, this devious Aesopian language suggested a capitulation which closed the debate.

In defeating Malenkov, Khrushchev gave the impression of having chosen his issues carefully in order to build a winning coalition. This reassertion of the priority of heavy industry and armaments drew the support of the armed forces, as well as the more conservative members of the Presidium. On other issues—for example, agriculture and de-Stalinization—the alignments were different, for in these cases Khrushchev often occupied the position of innovator and received the support of other elements within the Presidium. Thus, Khrushchev was able to emerge as a centrist who could denounce both the "rightism" of Malenkov and the "dogmatism" of the conservatives.

The resignation of Malenkov opened the way to a reconstruction of the top leadership. On Khrushchev's nomination, Bulganin replaced Malenkov as Chairman of the Council of Ministers, and he in turn yielded his post as Minister of Defense to Marshal Zhukov. (Apparently at this time—or shortly thereafter—Khrushchev secretly was named Commander-in-Chief of the armed forces.)[28] Malenkov retained his post in the party Presidium, but was demoted to the position of Deputy Chairman of the Council of Ministers and Minister of Power Stations. At the July 1955 session of the Central Committee, two new members were elected to the Presidium: A. I. Kirichenko, first secretary of the Ukrainian Party Central Committee, and M. A. Suslov, a Central Committee secretary with broad responsibilities in the realm of ideology, foreign policy, and, judging by his speech at the Twentieth Party Congress in 1956, also supervision of the party apparatus.

Although many westerners have labeled Suslov as a conservative and have seen his election to the Presidium as a counterbalance to Kirichenko, both of the new members did support Khrushchev in his crucial showdown with his opponents in 1957. It is very probable that from the beginning Suslov was one of the spearheads against the ideological and foreign policy positions being advanced by Molotov and that he was serving as Khrushchev's "second secretary" during this period. The fact that he had taught in the Industry Academy in 1930 when Khrushchev was party secretary there may have created a tie between the two men that went back a quarter of a century.

In any case, Khrushchev lost little time in moving against the two leading conservatives on the Presidium. In March 1955 Kaganovich's authority in the industrial sphere was diluted when Mikoian, Pervukhin, and Saburov joined him as first deputy chairmen of the Council of Ministers. In May 1955 he was designated Chairman of the State Committee for Labor and Wages, a quite minor position in the Soviet government.

At the July 1955 session of the Central Committee, Molotov was marked as the next candidate for demotion and disgrace. Khrushchev's victory over Malenkov had not been followed by any reversal in the foreign policy realm. A new peace treaty was signed which recognized the independence and neutrality of Austria, and Khrushchev and Bulganin traveled to Geneva to meet President Eisenhower, the first time any top Soviet leader had ever visited the West.[29] Efforts were made to court the neutral countries in the Third World, often with the use of rather substantial amounts of foreign aid. All of these actions involved a repudiation of Stalinist foreign policy with which Molotov was closely associated and which he apparently still approved. The July 1955 Central Committee session dealt explicitly with policy toward Tito and Yugoslavia. As was subsequently revealed, Khrushchev favored reconciliation and an effort to recapture Tito for the Soviet cause; Molotov opposed such concessions as unnecessary and dangerous to bloc unity.[30] Molotov's views found little support in the Central Committee and, from that point on, his influence sharply declined.

In September 1955 the party's theoretical journal, *Kommunist,* administered an added blow to Molotov's prestige as a theorist when it published a strange letter of recantation signed by him. He acknowledged that in a speech delivered some seven months earlier he had committed a major ideological error in describing the Soviet Union as having constructed only "the foundations of a socialist society," instead of adhering to the orthodox formula that the Soviet Union had already achieved socialism and was now building communism.

Changes in the Political Process

The thaw of the first post-Stalin years extended not only to the content of policy but also to the process by which policy was made. First, of course, the major institutions of the Communist party and the government began to operate on a more regular basis once more. One of the first decrees of the new government ordered governmental agencies to conduct their work during normal business hours, and this denoted that the leadership too would not be making its decisions at dinners that extended through the night. (With Stalin and the Politburo doing most of their work at night, other governmental officials had had to be on call as well.)

The party Presidium apparently began meeting on a once-a-week basis, and the Central Committee too began to be convened fairly frequently—six times between March 1953 and February 1956. Even before its crucial role in June 1957, the Central Committee meeting in plenary session may well have exercised a decisive impact on the Politburo conflicts. In addition, the Supreme Soviet, while still a minor institution, was convened twice a year instead of once as in the recent past.

Although the Soviet political-administrative system remained highly centralized, steps were taken to increase the authority of the union republics somewhat. By the end of 1956 (before the creation of the *sovnarkhozes* or regional economic councils) about 15,000 industrial enterprises formerly administered by the central government were reporting to the republics. By that time the enterprises under the jurisdiction of the republican Councils of Ministers accounted for 55 percent of all industrial production, as compared to 31 percent in 1953.[31] Another indication of the apparent increase in central trust of the non-Russian nationalities was the background of the men chosen as the republican party secretaries in charge of personnel selection and "organizational questions" (including supervision of the police). In the late Stalin era this official in the non-Slavic republics almost invariably was a Russian, and a Russian brought in from the outside at that. (He usually was named the second secretary.) By late 1956, however, the organizational secretary was a man of local nationality in eight of the fourteen republics.[32]

An even more important political change was a loosening of the restrictions on the discussion of societal defects and of possible policy alternatives that might correct them—and, thereby, a change in the basic process by which policy was actually influenced and formulated. Paradoxically, the issue was first raised most directly in the area of highest sensitivity, that of military theory. In September 1953, Major General N. Talensky, the editor of the journal *Voennaia mysl'* (Military Thought) questioned the adequacy of the traditional notion that surprise attacks (even surprise atomic attacks) could never be a decisive factor in the winning of a war. At the end of his article, Talensky called for a general exploration of this theoretical problem in the pages of his journal, and, in fact, subsequent issues did publish a number of articles on the subject, some criticizing his position, others defending it. While *Voennaia mysl'* was a journal aimed solely at officers, the debate soon was "extended to other military journals, which were intended for all ranks."[33]

Even after opening the pages of their journal to differing opinions on the nature of war, the editors of *Voennaia mysl'* still felt compelled in March 1955 to call for a radical improvement in the general quality of debate on military theory:

Military scientific work in the armed forces still lags. For too long our military scientific cadres have confined themselves to repeating truths long and well-known—to the detriment of the situation and to the detriment of the investigation of a number of urgent new problems . . . In a number of cases discussions, which are one of the effective instruments for the development of military theory, are on secondary problems, proceed sluggishly, drag out . . . If we are talking about the reasons which cause the backwardness in the development of our military science in general, the chief of these is the *fear* to say something new, or to say something different from what has already been said by one or another authority . . . In the postwar years hardly a single significant work in the sphere of military theory was published . . . Such a pernicious style in military scientific work leads to marking time and hinders correct understanding. As historical conditions change, many propositions once completely justified no longer meet the requirements of a new situation.[34]

Such an attitude with respect to military theory certainly would be expected to extend to domestic policy questions as well and, in actuality, it did. Indeed, although the discussion of military strategy was limited largely to military journals—and, therefore, in practice, was read almost exclusively by those in the military, the analogous widening of the freedom of public discussion of domestic matters was not limited to specialists' media, but occurred in the general newspapers such as *Pravda* and *Izvestiia* as well. The May 1955 plenary session of the Central Committee marked an important stage in the legitimization of criticism in industry (and in freedom to mention western achievements in this realm), and then in 1956–1958 a series of important laws (pension legislation, industrial reorganization, abolition of the machine-tractor stations, educational reform) were accompanied by month-long formal "debates" in the mass press. The significant fact about this development was not so much that it resulted in a major change in the legislation in question (although at times the resulting legislation did deviate from the original proposal), but that it signaled the opening of these general policy areas to regular, albeit still restricted, public criticism and suggestions for policy change.

The relaxing of restraints on policy debate was also greatly facilitated by a gradual easing of censorship on factual data about Soviet society. While the first postwar statistical handbook had to wait until 1956 and the first postwar census until 1959, the trend toward frankness was unmistakable. Fiction writers depicting societal and personal problems benefitted from this decision as much as those writing descriptive articles and books. In 1956 particularly, there was a striking increase in the type of literature that would not have been permitted a few years earlier.[35]

The thaw of the mid-1950s did not, of course, lead to a complete transformation of the Soviet political system nor to a total change in policy. Censorship remained in force, and, particularly after the Polish and Hungarian revolts and the flowering of dissident literature in the Soviet Union in 1956, the de-Stalinization program was kept within strict boundaries. The KGB (the new name for the secret police) continued to be active, subjecting the politically suspect to careful surveillance and relying as of old on networks of informers to report disloyal utterances or conduct.

The Twentieth Party Congress and the Antiparty Group

Despite their various humiliations, Malenkov, Molotov, and Kaganovich all remained on the party Presidium, where they nursed their grievances and hopes of revenge. However, the Twentieth Party Congress marked a further stage in Khrushchev's battle against them. Already before the Congress, the first secretary had been replaced in seven of the fourteen union republics and in forty-one of sixty-nine RSFSR regions in the period since the death of Stalin.[36] (The first secretary had been changed in twelve of the remaining twenty-eight regions in 1952.) The hand of Khrushchev in many of these changes was dramatically suggested by the fact that three of the republican first secretaries and six of the regional secretaries were former subordinates of his in the Ukraine. As a consequence of these developments, 25 percent of the voting delegates to the Twentieth Congress were selected from Khrushchev's old strongholds in Moscow and the Ukraine, 13 percent from areas with first secretaries who had come from the Ukraine, and 37 percent from other areas in which a change of first secretary had occurred since Stalin's death.[37]

At the Congress itself, even the opening sessions gave evidence of Khrushchev's rise to greater prominence. Khrushchev was given the assignment of delivering the main Central Committee report, and in his discussion of foreign policy he had the self-confidence to announce revisions in some of the most central doctrines of Marx and Lenin. He renounced Lenin's doctrine that war among capitalist states was inevitable, and he abandoned the old image of a capitalist encirclement of the Soviet Union. He proclaimed the possibility of a peaceful overthrow of capitalist systems and of different roads to socialism after the revolution.

The most striking event of the Twentieth Congress was a secret speech given by Khrushchev at the conclusion of the congress. In this speech the First Secretary portrayed Stalin as a murderer and provided a lurid bill of particulars. He praised Stalin's services during the revolution and Civil War, his struggles against Trotskyites, Bukharinites, and bourgeois nationalists, and his contributions to industrialization and collectivization, but argued that the situation changed after the Seventeenth Party Congress in 1934. Stalin was condemned for the murder of thousands of honest, innocent Communists during the Great Purge; for the weakening of the Red army as the result of the liquidation of Tukhachevsky and other high-ranking officers on the basis of slanderous and unjustified charges; for his failure to take necessary defensive measures against the Nazi attack; for his inept interference with the Red army high command during the war; for his responsibility in the mass deportation of nationality groups whose loyalties aroused his suspicion; for his fabrication of the Leningrad Affair in which Voznesensky and other high party officials lost their lives; and for his final responsibility for the completely falsified "doctors' plot."[38] The latter-day Stalin was portrayed as a morbidly suspicious man who suffered from a persecution phobia, saw enemies and spies in his closest associates, and demanded servility and obsequiousness from all who served him.

The motives which inspired Khrushchev to make these sensational disclosures are still subject to debate. His own subsequent explanation stressed his anxiety to "preclude the possibility of such phenomena in the future" and his desire to restore Leninist "norms" in the party.[39] Yet, if we assume, as in the light of later events we must, that Khrushchev was determined to consolidate his own authority, his secret speech can also be read as an effort to discredit his major opponents in the Presidium. In the process of attacking Stalin, he made a studied effort to disassociate himself from responsibility for Stalin's excesses. Other senior members of the Presidium, he pointed out, worked much more closely with Stalin, and he especially singled out Malenkov, Molotov, and Kaganovich as tarred with the brush of their master's misdeeds. He attempted somewhat lamely to demonstrate that he and Bulganin had opposed Stalin's outrages. Even though the explanations were labored, their intent was clear. Khrushchev was seeking to demonstrate that the party had nothing to fear from him but that it had a great deal to fear from those who had been more intimately involved in Stalin's crimes.

The thrust of Khrushchev's motivation may well be best indicated by the source of the opposition to it. At the Twentieth Congress itself Kaganovich confessed that the decision to embark on a struggle against the cult of the individual was "no easy question."[40] Khrushchev later testified that "Molotov, Kaganovich, Malenkov, Voroshilov, and others categorically objected to this proposal [of the secret speech]. In answer to their objections, they were told that if they continued to oppose the raising of this question, the delegates to the party congress would be asked to decide the matter. We had no doubt that the congress would favor discussion of the question. Only then did they agree, and the question of the cult of the individual was presented to the Twentieth Party Congress."[41]

The Twentieth Party Congress was followed by a series of actions that further strengthened Khrushchev's position. More than a third of the Central Committee members—54 of 133—and more than half of the candidate members—76 of 122—named at the end of the congress were newly elected, and, in numerous instances, their elevation was directly traceable to earlier association with Khrushchev. Over 45 percent of the new voting members had been in the Ukraine, at the Stalingrad front, or in lower party or governmental work in Moscow under Khrushchev's direct supervision. No changes occurred among the full members of the Presidium, but the five new candidate members who were selected appeared to owe their appointments to Khrushchev. Khrushchev also assumed personal command of the Russian party organization. A special Russian Republic Bureau of the Central Committee was established with him as chairman and with its membership dominated by his entourage.

The Twentieth Party Congress was followed by a series of blows directed at the Stalinist Old Guard. On June 2, 1956, Shepilov replaced Molotov as Minister of Foreign Affairs, and the latter was moved to the lesser post of Minister of State Control. On June 9, Kaganovich was "relieved" of his chairmanship of the State Committee on Labor and Wages and his designation in September as Minister of the Building Materials Industry relegated him to a still more minor post. By mid-1956 Khrushchev loomed as the most powerful figure in the Presidium, with no competitor on the horizon to offer a serious challenge.

But appearances were deceptive. The shock of Khrushchev's revelations about Stalin at the Twentieth Party Congress released a series of wholly unintended consequences. Unrest in Poland and a full-fledged uprising in Hungary in October appeared for a time to threaten the Soviet satellite system with disintegration. All this gave powerful ammunition to Khrushchev's Presidium opponents who could now argue that Khrushchev had placed the entire Soviet bloc in jeopardy. During this period, evidence accumulated that Khrushchev was in trouble. The delegation that was hastily dispatched to Warsaw on October 19, 1956, to discuss "topical problems" with the Polish Politburo included Molotov and Kaganovich, as well as Khrushchev and Mikoian—a juxtaposition which seemed to point to a new balance of forces in the Presidium. The break with Tito which followed the Hungarian events served to discredit Khrushchev's policy of reconciliation with Yugoslavia to which Molotov had been bitterly opposed.

Increasing difficulties on the industrial front, which were complicated by the need to buttress the shaky satellite economies, contributed to the undermining of Khrushchev's leadership. The Central Committee met in December 1956 and at this session lowered the industrial targets and reorganized the planning machinery. The powers of the State Economic Commission, which was charged with current planning, were greatly broadened. Pervukhin was designated chairman of the commission and became something of an "overlord of overlords," exercising primary responsibility for the operation of the national economy. The members of the Presidium who had an interest in restraining Khrushchev rallied behind the reorganization. The scheme was approved by the Supreme Soviet on February 12, 1957.

On the very next day Khrushchev launched a counterattack. Appearing before a specially summoned session of the Central Committee, he offered a plan which was designed to emasculate the Economic Commission, abolish most of the central industrial ministries, and devolve many of their operational responsibilities on new regional economic councils (sovnarkhozes). Khrushchev's scheme was clearly calculated to weaken the power of his ministerial opponents and to enlist support from republican and regional officials, who now would be in a position to supervise the intermediate industrial administrators and to force them to take regional interests more into account.

Why was Khrushchev prepared to throw down the gage to his opponents in February when he was not willing to do so in December? The answer must be speculative, but certain considerations appear to be relevant. By February, far more than in December, the unrest in the satellite empire appeared to be under control and less of a threatening factor. The bountiful harvest in the virgin lands provided a vindication of Khrushchev's agricultural program. Perhaps most important of all, Khrushchev's readiness to act indicated a belief that he now had devised a program which could rally the Central Committee membership to his banner. There were nineteen central industrial administrators among the voting members of the Central Committee, compared with seventy republican state and party officials and regional party secretaries—53 percent of the voting membership—who would benefit from industrial reorganization directly.

From this point on, Khrushchev moved swiftly to consolidate his position. The public discussion of what were referred to as "Comrade Khrushchev's theses" and the ensuing debate in the Supreme Soviet were organized to create the impression that they enjoyed overwhelming support, though an occasional hint came through of the opposition they were encountering in the industrial ministries. Most significant of all, not a single member of the party Presidium other than Khrushchev spoke out in favor of the reorganization, either in the press or during the Supreme Soviet session that enacted the law. Nevertheless, on May 10, 1957, the Supreme Soviet did approve Khrushchev's proposals with minor modifications (notably retention of state committees in various defense industries, though with responsibility for coordinating technical policy rather than administering plants directly). One of Khrushchev's rather minor subordinates in the Central Committee apparatus —I. I. Kuzmin, head of the machinery industry department—was installed as Gosplan chairman and First Deputy Chairman of the USSR Council of Ministers, the top industrial administrator in the country.

It was at this point that Khrushchev's opponents in the Presidium combined in one major effort to overthrow him. The timing of their action for June 1957 is most mysterious, for the one policy on which all seem to have agreed was industrial reorganization. If—as must have occurred—Khrushchev had been able to overcome a Presidium majority on this issue in February by appealing to the Central Committee, it is difficult to understand why the Presidium members thought the outcome would be any different in June when the question was Khrushchev's personal position and, presumably, a wide range of his policies, including industrial reorganization. One of Khrushchev's supporters later suggested that Khrushchev was beginning to raise the question of the criminal responsibility of major Presidium members for the deaths in the purges,[42] and, if so, the reaction of the Presidium majority may have been a defensive one of desperation.

Whatever their motivation, Khrushchev's opponents met regularly in Bulganin's office, and by June they were ready to act.[43] Khrushchev found himself in a minority, being supported by only three of the other ten full members (Mikoian, Suslov, and Kirichenko). However, the effort to unseat the First Secretary misfired. During the crucial phase of the conflict, the Presidium was in almost continuous session from June 18 to June 21. Khrushchev's opponents called for his resignation from the first secretaryship and pressed for an immediate public announcement of changes in the leadership in order to confront the Central Committee with a fait accompli. Khrushchev refused and demanded that a meeting of the Central Committee be immediately convened to resolve the issue. As he later revealed to the Twenty-Second Party Congress, "I told them that . . . it was the plenum of the Central Committee that had elected me, and it should therefore be the plenum that made the decision."[44]

Khrushchev initiated action to bring the weight of the Central Committee into the scale. Except for Shepilov, his support among the candidate members of the Presidium remained firm. As word circulated of the Presidium crisis, Khrushchev's followers in the Central Committee who were then in Moscow rallied to his support and sought to intercede in the Presidium discussions. According to one of them, "instructions were given not to admit the members of the Central Committee to the Kremlin, and many of them had to use literally illegal means in making their way to where the Central Committee's Presidium was in session."[45] A debate ensued in the Presidium as to whether they should be received. The majority sought to make Voroshilov or Bulganin the point of contact in the hope of overawing the unwelcome group and warding off Central Committee intervention. Khrushchev would not agree, and finally Khrushchev and his ally Mikoian, as well as Voroshilov and Bulganin, were authorized to receive the assembled Central

Committee members. What transpired in these discussions is not on record, except that the representatives filed the following statement:

> We, members of the Central Committee, have learned that the Central Committee Presidium is in continuous session. We are also aware that you are discussing the question of the leadership of the Central Committee and of the Secretariat. Matters of such importance for our whole party cannot be concealed from the members of the plenum of the Central Committee. In view of this, we members of the Central Committee urgently request that a plenary session of the Central Committee be called and this matter submitted to it for discussion. We, as members of the Central Committee, may not stand aloof from the question of our party's leadership.[46]

By this time, members of the Central Committee were descending on Moscow from the provinces in large numbers. The Presidium majority was left with no alternative except to accede to the demand for a meeting. At least on the question of the leadership, the plenary session was dominated by Khrushchev's supporters. Of the 309 voting and nonvoting members of the Central Committee and Auditing Commission, 215 requested the floor to speak on Khrushchev's behalf.[47] In the face of this overwhelming show of strength, the Presidium majority found itself isolated, and some of its members, such as Voroshilov, Pervukhin, and possibly others, turned against their fellow conspirators in the course of the discussion. Nevertheless, the Central Committee session lasted for eight days, and it would be fascinating to know just what was discussed. It is possible that the fate of Khrushchev's opponents and even their criminal responsibility for the Great Purge were also on the agenda and that the outcome was more of a compromise than appeared on the surface.

The resolution of the Central Committee condemning the opposition revealed no hesitation. It limited its fire to Malenkov, Kaganovich, Molotov, and Shepilov, "who joined them," and termed these men an "antiparty group." The group was accused of having used "antiparty, factional methods in an attempt to change the composition of the party's leading bodies" and of having fought the party line on a number of issues, including industrial reorganization, agricultural policy, and foreign policy.[48] All four lost their governmental posts and their membership in both the Central Committee and the Presidium. The fact that the conspiracy had wider ramifications could be inferred from the fact that Saburov was also dropped from the Presidium and that Pervukhin was demoted to candidate membership.

Information about the other members of the anti-party group came out more slowly. Bulganin retained both his seat on the party Presidium and his position as Chairman of the Council of Ministers. Although his public role as a government spokesman declined greatly, he was not replaced as Chairman until March 27, 1958, not ousted from the Presidium until September 5, 1958, and not formally linked with the antiparty group until November 14, 1958. Although Voroshilov's resignation as Chairman of the Presidium of the Supreme Soviet and his "retirement" from the party Presidium came in July 1960, his full-scale participation was not officially confirmed until the Twenty-Second Congress in October 1961. His statement of recantation, which "for health reasons" was read by a proxy, was a pathetic tale of an old man who "had been led astray."[49]

The reconstruction of the membership of the Presidium which followed the June 1957 plenum represented a striking triumph for Khrushchev. The Presidium was enlarged to fifteen members. Marshal Zhukov was promoted from candidate to full membership, an action which seemed to imply that the Marshal had given full support to Khrushchev in the struggle against the antiparty group. The other new members of the Presidium—Aristov, Beliaev, Brezhnev, Furtseva, Ignatov, Kozlov, Kuusinen, and Shvernik—had all rallied to Khrushchev's support in his bid for supremacy and were appropriately rewarded. The victory was also one for the Central Committee Secretariat. In 1953 only one of the ten full members of the Presidium was a party secretary; in July 1957, nine of the fifteen voting members were full-time Central Committee employees and this figure rose to ten of fifteen in December (see table 6).

The next stage in the consolidation of Khrushchev's authority involved a settling of accounts with Zhukov. Only four months after he had been named a full member of the Presidium, Zhukov was removed not only from the Presidium but also from his position as Minister of Defense and his membership in the Central Committee. The Central Committee resolution published at the time accused the marshal of "pursuing a policy of curtailing the work of party organizations, political agencies, and Military Councils and of eliminating the leadership and control of the party, its Central Committee, and the government over the army and navy." Zhukov was also denounced for "surrounding himself with sycophants and flatterers" who, with his encouragement, promoted a personality cult. He was finally described "as a politically deficient figure, disposed to adventurism both in his understanding of the major tasks of the Soviet Union's foreign policy and in his leadership of the Ministry of Defense."[50] Many of these charges were dubious, but Khrushchev clearly was removing a strong-willed man who might be a potential threat.[51]

By the opening of the Twenty-First Congress in January 1959 Khrushchev's position seemed quite supreme. In April 1958 he had become the

Table 6   *Members of the Presidium, December 1957*

MEMBER[a]	YEAR OF BIRTH	YEAR OF PARTY ENTRY	POSITION
N. S. Khrushchev	1894	1918	First Secretary of the Central Committee
A. B. Aristov	1903	1921	Secretary of the Central Committee and deputy chairman of the Central Committee Bureau for the RSFSR
L. I. Brezhnev	1906	1931	Secretary of the Central Committee
E. A. Furtseva	1910	1930	Secretary of the Central Committee
N. G. Ignatov	1901	1924	Secretary of the Central Committee
A. I. Kirichenko[b]	1908	1930	Secretary of the Central Committee
O. V. Kuusinen	1881	1904	Secretary of the Central Committee
N. A. Mukhitdinov	1917	1942	Secretary of the Central Committee
M. A. Suslov	1902	1921	Secretary of the Central Committee
N. M. Shvernik	1888	1905	Chairman of the Control Commission
N. I. Beliaev	1903	1921	First secretary of the Kazakhstan Central Committee
K. E. Voroshilov	1881	1903	Chairman of the Presidium of the Supreme Soviet
N. A. Bulganin	1895	1917	Chairman of the USSR Council of Ministers
A. I. Mikoian	1895	1915	First Deputy Chairman of the USSR Council of Ministers
F. R. Kozlov	1908	1926	Chairman of the RSFSR Council of Ministers
AVERAGE	1899	1921	

Table 6—Continued

MEMBER[a]	YEAR OF BIRTH	YEAR OF PARTY ENTRY	POSITION
Candidate member			
P. N. Pospelov	1898	1916	Secretary of the Central Committee
Ia. E. Kalnberzin	1893	1917	First secretary of the Latvian Central Committee
A. P. Kirilenko	1906	1931	First secretary of the Sverdlovsk Obkom
K. T. Mazurov	1914	1940	First secretary of the Belorussian Central Committee
V. P. Mzhavanadze	1902	1927	First secretary of the Georgian Central Committee
A. N. Kosygin	1904	1927	Deputy Chairman of the USSR Council of Ministers
M. G. Pervukhin[c]	1904	1919	Chairman of the State Committee for Foreign Economic Ties
D. S. Korotchenko	1894	1918	Chairman of the Presidium of the Ukrainian Supreme Soviet

Source: *Pravda,* July 9, 1957, p. 2; November 3, 1957, p. 1; December 19, 1957, p. 1.

a Candidate members are listed in the rank order of the official announcement.

b Kirichenko was first secretary of the Ukrainian Central Committee until December, hence that office is not represented on this membership list. His successor. N. V. Podgorny, became a candidate member in 1958 and a full member in 1960.

c Pervukhin's position would not normally warrant membership, but he retained a candidate membership as an aftermath of the antiparty group.

Chairman of the Council of Ministers in addition to being the Party's First Secretary and the Chairman of the Bureau of the Central Committee for the RSFSR. At the Twenty-First Congress, delegate after delegate joined in praising his "Leninist firmness," "profound practical knowledge," "fatherly solicitude," and "tireless energy," and offered effusive thanks for the personal guidance and initiative which Khrushchev had supplied in every sector of

Soviet life from foreign policy and the development of guided missiles to cotton growing in Tadzhikistan. If these genuflections were still a far cry from the heights of self-glorification which the Stalin cult achieved, they left little doubt that Khrushchev was by far the foremost political figure in the Soviet Union.

The Ambiguities of Policy in the Khrushchev Period

With the reshaping of the Presidium, Khrushchev was able to pursue his policies more freely, and many of the features of the man emerged more clearly. The First Secretary had already shown his boldness in launching the Virgin Lands program, in risking the secret speech on Stalin, and in replacing the industrial ministries with the sovnarkhozes; after 1957 his enthusiasm and willingness to take drastic action continued. He abolished the machine-tractor stations in 1958 and had their machinery sold to the collective farms; he pushed through educational reform aimed at giving working-class and peasant children greater access to higher education and exposing all children to work situations; he undertook a radical reorganization of the party and governmental apparatus, splitting it into separate urban and rural hier-archies at the regional level and below. He spoke of a transition to communism and a withering away of the state and promised that the Soviet Union soon would catch up with American standards of living.

In Khrushchev, one had the impression of a man who took Marxism-Leninism seriously. The attack on Stalin undercut one of the major legiti-mating figures for the regime, but as a substitute Khrushchev increased the emphasis given to Lenin. Many of the institutional reforms of the Khrushchev period—for example, the creation of sovnarkhozes and the combined Party-State Control Committee in 1962—involved the reestablishment of bodies that had counterparts in the Lenin period. His educational and wage policies bespoke a real concern with achieving the social goals of Marxism; his strong insistence upon increased popular participation in political life suggested a dedication to democratization as he (and Lenin) conceived it.

Above all, Khrushchev seemed to be imbued with the spirit of the First Five-Year Plan period. Some of his specific proposals reflected the more utopian ideas that were circulating at that time, but, more important, Khrushchev seemed convinced of the possibility of a "great leap forward," a great breakthrough. When he pushed an economic program—for example, expansion of the chemical industry or goals for food production—his original projections were impossibly high. When he saw a problem, his first instinct was a total solution (in education, to place all children in boarding schools away from parental influence and to force all high school graduates to work several years before college), or at least a frontal assault (in foreign policy, ultimatums on the western presence in Berlin and the placing of missiles in Cuba). He treated each reorganization—and there was one almost every year —as a panacea, and when it failed to achieve a miracle, the result was not disillusionment about the effort, but a search for a new panacea.

Yet, despite Khrushchev's victory over the antiparty group, the programs that he espoused were not completely enacted, and policy in the 1957–1964 period often was ambiguous in character. For example, the creation of the sovnarkhozes was clearly one of Khrushchev's major initiatives. This step was repeatedly justified as increasing the powers of the localities, and, in fact, the sovnarkhozes did greatly expand the authority of local party organs, especially party and governmental institutions at the republican level. Then in December 1957, the Ukrainian Aleksei Kirichenko was moved from first secretary of the Ukrainian Central Committee into the Central Committee Secretariat and given responsibility for personnel and organizational questions—an appointment that apparently signified greater toleration for other types of diversity within the republics.

Khrushchev had also always strongly emphasized the need for central planning and for the maintenance of strong discipline and centralization within the party, but within a short time even the limited trend toward decentralization seemed to be reversed. In 1959 the party first secretary in Azerbaidzhan was removed, one of the major issues being the results of the autonomy in the educational realm,[52] and in Latvia a major purge of a number of top officials accused of nationalism was carried out. (In the latter case, the major issue was opposition to expansion of heavy industry because of its association in the republic with the immigration of Russian skilled labor).[53] In 1960 Kirichenko was removed from the Secretariat in disgrace, and he was replaced by a Great Russian, Frol Kozlov, who reputedly was much more of a hard-liner on these questions. It is symptomatic of the change in mood that the number of organizational secretaries in the republics who were of the local nationality declined from eleven in July 1959 to five in October 1961 and four in January 1963.[54]

At the same time the principles of economic management endorsed by Khrushchev were also gradually eroded. As early as the summer of 1958, the ability of the sovnarkhozes to shift capital investment funds was severely restricted,[55] and in 1960 republic-level sovnarkhozes were created in the RSFSR, the Ukraine, and Kazakhstan to coordinate the activities of the oblast-level regional councils located within them. (Eighty-nine of the 101 sovnarkhozes in existence at the time were affected.) In May 1961 further steps were taken to check localism by establishing new coordinating councils to develop long-term plans for the integrated economic development of some nineteen large "natural" regions, the new councils being superimposed on the existing institutions.

Then in November 1962 the original regions were abolished and replaced by forty-two large regions encompassing several oblasts each. (The nineteen superregions created in 1961 continued to exist, but their powers remained restricted.) At the same time the sovnarkhozes were deprived of their control over construction, new designs, and new technology. Construction work was to be carried out by independent building organizations which were subordinated not to the sovnarkhozes but to the USSR State Committee for Construction; control over the introduction of new technology and design was vested in fourteen central state committees. (For example, there was a state committee for ferrous and non-ferrous metallurgy, one for light industry, one for the chemical industry, and so forth.)

The exact relationship among the planning organs, the state committees, the republican sovnarkhozes, and the lower sovnarkhozes is quite unclear—and there is much evidence that it also was not clear or satisfying to those working within the system at the time. The confusion was heightened by the fact that the 1962 industrial reorganization was accompanied by an even more major reorganization of the local party and governmental organs—the division of most of the lower apparatus into two completely independent industrial and agricultural units (really urban and rural ones). All important regions were given both an industrial regional party committee and soviet, with subordinate units in the cities and counties, which supervised nearly all the population in the cities and in rural industry and construction, and an agricultural regional party committee and soviet, which supervised most of the rural citizenry and institutions, together with those in the city that were closely related to agriculture (for example, agricultural research institutes and the food processing industry). Each of these institutions had independent staff, and thus a given region would have two party first secretaries and two chairmen of the executive committees of the soviet. This reorganization was defended largely on the grounds that it would facilitate detailed local party supervision of the economy—and particularly industry—but it is typical of the inconsistency of the period that it was severely undercut by the simultaneous amalgamation of the economic regions, which removed the sovnarkhoz officials from subordination to the party regional committee and thereby weakened the possibility of the new party organs to supervise them.[56] In addition, a new Party-State Control Committee was established with broad checking responsibilities.

Similar ambivalence in policy—as well as deviation from Khrushchev's statements—is observable in almost every other policy area as well. In the economic realm, for example, there were great disparities between grandiose Khrushchevian pronouncements and modest deeds. Despite Khrushchev's 1955 insistence upon the priority of heavy industry, consumer interests came to be very much in the forefront of his public pronouncements by 1956. In May 1957 he launched a campaign to catch up with the United States in the per capita production of meat, milk, and butter. In July of the same year he promised "to liquidate the housing shortage in the course of ten to twelve years."[57] In the spring of 1958 he initiated a program to raise the production of chemicals and synthetics—measures that promised a substantial increase in the supply of modern fabrics and chemical fertilizer.

Some of Khrushchev's statements seemed to imply an even heavier commitment to the consumer, and they suggested the need to engage in political struggle to achieve this commitment. In May 1961 at the British Fair in Moscow, Khrushchev declared in a statement which was not reproduced in the Soviet press: "Soviet heavy industry is considered built. Therefore, in the future, light and heavy industry will develop at the same pace."[58] Four months earlier at a Central Committee plenary session on agriculture, he had registered a verbal complaint indicating that others did not hold this view: "Some of our comrades have developed an appetite to give the country more metal. That is a praiseworthy desire, providing no harm is done to other branches of the national economy. But if more metal is produced while other branches lag, their expansion will be slowed down. Thus, not enough bread, butter, and other food items will be produced. This will be a one-sided development."[59]

It would be wrong to suggest that these promises of a better life had no meaning, for, in fact, the standard of living of the Soviet citizenry did register significant improvement when compared with the Stalinist days. Total income of the agricultural population rose from 18.6 billion rubles in 1953 to 32.3 billion rubles in 1964, while the number of agricultural workers declined by some 10 percent in that period.[60] Progress was also visible on the industrial front. The harsh criminal penalties previously used to enforce labor discipline were abandoned, and the work week was reduced from forty-eight hours to forty-six in 1956 and to forty-one in 1960. The average wage of workers and employees (excluding kolkhozniks) rose from some sixty-seven rubles per month in 1952 to ninety-one rubles in 1964,[61] the increase being disproportionately great among lower income groups.

Nevertheless, the improvement in living conditions and even the programs adopted were far from what Khrushchev had advocated and promised. The figures for the seven-year plan for 1959–1965, which were published in November 1958, were much less consumer oriented than the preceding Sixth

Five-Year Plan. Capital investment in agriculture lagged much behind investment in heavy industry, and the banner harvest of 1958 was followed by a series of mediocre harvests. Instead of the United States being equalled in livestock production, shortages were widely reported. (In June 1962 the price of meat was raised 30 percent and the price of butter 25 percent.) The goals in Khrushchev's pet chemical program were not met, and although the Soviet leader called for a 1970 chemical fertilizer plan of 100 million tons in a memorandum to the Presidium in July 1963, the plan established in December provided for only 70-80 million tons.[62]

Similarly in the realm of education, Khrushchev proposed a number of radical changes in 1958: a comprehensive boarding school system, the replacement of the full-time secondary school with evening and correspondence schools for students who would combine their education with work; the admission of persons into higher education only after a period of full-time work after graduation from secondary school; a combination of study and work in the first years of higher education. Subsequent to this proposal, important changes were, in fact, made in the amount of polytechnical training and physical labor in the educational process and in the preference given to full-time employees in college admission. Many of the central features of Khrushchev's plan were never enacted, however. The old secondary school was not abolished (in practice, it was expanded from ten to eleven years so that the additional polytechnical education could be accommodated without loss to the rest of the curriculum), and the possibility of a student moving directly from secondary school to college was retained.[63] Moreover, the new educational policies of 1958, like the policies involving the sovnarkhozes, tended to be gradually and often inconsistently eroded as the years passed.[64]

On questions associated with "Soviet democracy," Khrushchev continually supported causes such as the extension of the powers of the union republics, the rejuvenation of the soviets and the trade unions, the drawing of larger numbers of people into governmental activity and into the party itself, the development of the initiative and publicmindedness of the citizenry. This theme became especially pronounced with the drafting of a new party program in 1961, when Khrushchev declared that the Soviet Union had moved from the stage of socialism into the stage of the construction of communism and that this would have a profound impact upon the political system.

In particular, Khrushchev asserted, the state was entering a new phase; now, instead of being a "dictatorship of the proletariat" as it had for over forty years, it had become an "all-people's state," and it would continue to evolve even further in a democratic direction. The new Party Program promised that the organs of state power "will gradually be transformed into organs of public self-government." The role of the soviets, "which combines the features of a government body and a social organization," was to expand, and "local soviets will make final decisions on all questions of local significance." In order to provide for more mass participation in the work of the soviets, the program proclaimed that "it is desirable that at least one third of the total number of deputies to a soviet should be elected anew each year," and to guard against abuses of authority by government officials, it advised that "the leading officials of the union, republic, and local bodies should be elected to their offices, as a rule, for not more than three consecutive terms." The program also promised that the role of other "social" organizations was to be heightened, and it spoke of the beginning of the withering away of the state as Marx had foreseen. "Bodies in charge of planning, accounting, economic management, and cultural advancement . . . will lose their political character and will become organs of public self-government."[65]

In many ways these aspects of Khrushchev's program did seem to be reflected in the policy of the period. The official statistics showed a major expansion of the number of persons enrolled in various types of political participation (see table 11 of Chapter 8), and membership in the party itself increased 47 percent between 1957 and 1964, in contrast with 18 percent between 1950 and 1957. Many citizens were appointed voluntary, part-time officials of local soviet, party, and trade union organs, and even wholly volunteer departments were created in many of these institutions to supplement the departments with paid staff. While these developments were cited as evidence of the democratization of Soviet society, there was even a major symbol of the "withering away of the state": the transformation of the State Committee for Physical Culture and Sports into a "social organization" supervising the institutions in this area.

In addition, the regime also seemed to be encouraging greater and freer communication among citizens and between them and government. A Central Committee decree demanded more attention to letters from citizens, and, in practice, the number of such letters to newspapers did increase.[66] The trend toward more open policy debates continued (for example, many aspects of the economy became the subject of debate), and sociological research was seriously encouraged for the first time in thirty years. Even writers were encouraged by Khrushchev in 1959 to think that the leadership would like them to govern their own affairs, and at times the First Secretary intervened personally to ensure the publication of an unorthodox work (for example, Alexander Solzhenitsyn's novel of life in a forced labor camp, *One Day in the Life of Ivan Denisovich*).

Nevertheless, this policy was scarcely a consistent one. The principles of socialist realism and partiinost' remained supreme in literature, and the laws against slandering the Soviet system continued to be enforced. In recent years, some have suggested that the suppression of dissidents began only with the Brezhnev era and that Khrushchev "relied on persuasion," but if one reads the biographies of the dissidents, this notion soon disappears. These biographies clearly demonstrate that arrests, jail, and confinement to mental asylums were part of the Khrushchev years as well.[67]

The inconsistencies were especially noticeable in literary policy. Khrushchev's conciliatory statements to the Writers' Congress in 1959 were sandwiched between a 1958 decision not to publish Boris Pasternak's *Doctor Zhivago* and a late 1959 decision to tighten controls again. (For example, beginning in January 1960, the circulation permitted the liberal literary journal *Novyi mir* was cut from 140,000 copies an issue to 90,000.)[68] By 1962, however, policy was flowing once more in the other direction. Throughout that year the liberal writers won a series of victories, culminating in the publication of *One Day in the Life of Ivan Denisovich* in November.[69]

On December 1, 1962, however, Khrushchev and four Presidium members visited an art exhibition which contained some abstract and semiabstract work. Khrushchev seemed to explode in anger, and in the aftermath a drastic change occurred in the cultural atmosphere. In the words of one leading authority on the subject, the regime "launched an enormous public campaign to bring writers and artists more closely to heel . . . [a] campaign waged on a vaster and more threatening scale than anything of its kind since the Stalin era."[70] Scarcely eight months later, after a plenary session of the Central Committee in July 1963, the policy trend seemed to reverse itself again. The work of leading liberal writers was published once more; circulation of *Novyi mir* was raised to 113,000 copies an issue—a restoration of nearly half of the 1960 reduction.

In the realm of foreign and military policy, the pattern was less one of contradiction between policy and Khrushchevian statements than one of sharp alternation between movement toward detente with the West and other actions certain to produce confrontation. In 1955 Khrushchev was involved in a peace treaty with Austria, reconciliation with Yugoslavia, and a summit meeting with Eisenhower in Geneva. Soon repudiating Lenin's doctrine of the inevitability of war and advocating that the Communists of the Third World pursue a less doctrinaire revolutionary strategy, he began to travel widely in the outside world. The ideological changes, the warm endorsement of "peaceful coexistence," and a failure to support China's demands for military action against the offshore islands of Quemoy and Matsu (coupled, no doubt, with many other factors) became associated with an increasingly bitter conflict with China—a conflict in which the Soviet Union was charged with conservatism and even counterrevolution.

Yet, despite these aspects of its foreign policy, the Soviet Union often seemed more than willing to create crisis situations in its relations with the West. Beginning in November 1958, Khrushchev issued a series of ultimatums with respect to West Berlin (some with deadlines as short as six months), insisting that the West withdraw its forces and that the city be demilitarized. In 1962, despite repeated American warnings, the Soviet Union attempted to install missiles surreptitiously in Cuba and thereby precipitated a major confrontation which raised the specter of nuclear war.

The variations in foreign policy were reflected even more dramatically in defense policy and expenditures. From 1955 to 1958, the Soviet armed forces were reduced from 5,763,000 men to 3,623,000, and in the latter year the Soviet Union agreed to a suspension of above-the-ground nuclear testing. In January 1960, Khrushchev went further to proclaim an additional reduction of 1,200,000 men in the armed forces, but then in the summer of 1961, the troop cuts were suspended, the military budget was increased by one-third, and nuclear testing was resumed. In 1963 a formal test ban treaty was signed, but military expenditures continued to rise.[71]

The Structure of Power in the Khrushchev Period

No one has denied the ambivalence of policy throughout the Khrushchev era, but in the early 1960s there were major disagreements about the reasons for the ambivalence. One group of scholars spoke of the "underlying consistency of purpose which has informed and guided [Khrushchev's] policies," and it treated the First Secretary as the leader of a liberal or reformist faction dedicated to de-Stalinization, detente, and consumer satisfaction. It saw Khrushchev "fighting an uphill battle . . . against the lively opposition of political forces represented at the top levels of the Soviet regime."[72] (Frol Kozlov and to a somewhat lesser degree Mikhail Suslov were seen as the leaders of the conservative bloc in the Presidium.)

While Khrushchev was acknowledged to be the single most powerful individual in the Soviet Union, these scholars thought him to be subject to defeat, and policy movements in the direction of repression, centralization, and a hard-line foreign policy were generally interpreted as the result of such defeat or of Khrushchev's concessions to ward it off. "Khrushchev's erratic behavior during the summer of 1961, stoking the Cold War one day and dampening it down the next, was more a sign of weakness than of strength," runs one typical example of this type of explanation. "He was not in so secure a position that he could pursue a single and consistent course. He could not ignore the powerful pressures and cross pressures of the internal politics of the Soviet ruling group."[73]

Scholars with such a view—who usually labeled themselves "the conflict school"—argued that Khrushchev's position was particularly weakened in the spring of 1960, in large part because of the impact of the U-2 incident upon his prestige. At the May 1960 plenary session of the Central Committee —held just three days after the downing of the American spy-plane on the eve of a scheduled summit conference with Eisenhower—A. I. Kirichenko, one of Khrushchev's few Presidium supporters in 1957, and four of nine persons elected to full Presidium membership in 1957, A. B. Aristov, N. I. Beliaev, E. A. Furtseva, and N. G. Ignatov, were either removed from the Presidium or demoted to lesser jobs.[74] The demoted members, together with a fifth new member of 1957, N. A. Mukhitdinov, lost their Presidium seats in 1961. These officials—so it was said—were among Khrushchev's closest supporters, and the new Presidium was far more evenly balanced between Khrushchev's associates and opponents, between employees of the Central Committee Secretariat and those of other institutions. (See table 7 for the Presidium membership of December 1962). In fact, the man named to replace Kirichenko as the crucial "second secretary"—the secretary supervising personnel selection—was Frol Kozlov, the reputed leader of the anti-Khrushchev conservative faction.[75]

Table 7 *Members of the Presidium, December 1962*

Member	Year of Birth	Year of Party Entry	Position
N. S. Khrushchev	1894	1918	First Secretary of the Central Committee, Chairman of the USSR Council of Ministers, Chairman of the Central Committee Bureau for the RSFSR
F. R. Kozlov	1908	1926	Secretary of the Central Committee
M. A. Suslov	1902	1921	Secretary of the Central Committee
O. V. Kuusinem	1881	1904	Secretary of the Central Committee
N. M. Shvernik	1888	1905	Chairman of the Control Commission
A. P. Kirilenko	1906	1931	First deputy chairman of the Central Committee Bureau for the RSFSR

Table 7—Continued

MEMBER	YEAR OF BIRTH	YEAR OF PARTY ENTRY	POSITION
N. V. Podgorny	1903	1930	First secretary of the Ukrainian Central Committee
L. I. Brezhnev	1906	1931	Chairman of the Presidium of the Supreme Soviet
A. I. Mikoian	1895	1915	First Deputy Chairman of the USSR Council of Ministers
A. N. Kosygin	1904	1927	First Deputy Chairman of the USSR Council of Ministers
D. S. Poliansky	1917	1939	Deputy Chairman of the Council of Ministers
G. I. Voronov	1910	1931	Chairman of the RSFSR Council of Ministers
AVERAGE	1901	1923	
Candidate member			
L. N. Efremov	1912	1941	First deputy chairman of the Central Committee Bureau for the RSFSR
V. V. Grishin	1914	1939	Chairman of the All-Union Central Council of Trade Unions
K. T. Mazurov	1914	1940	First secretary of the Belorussian Central Committee
V. P. Mzhavanadze	1902	1927	First secretary of the Georgian Central Committee
Sh. R. Rashidov	1917	1939	First secretary of the Uzbekistan Central Committee
V. V. Shcherbitsky	1918	1941	Chairman of the Ukrainian Council of Ministers

Source: 1963 Yearbook, *Bol'shaia sovetskaia entsiklopediia,* p. 19.

Subsequent to these changes in the Central Committee Secretariat, there occurred a major purge in the lower party apparatus. During 1960 and 1961, first secretaries were changed in 57 of the 101 regions in the RSFSR and the Ukraine—in 27 (67 percent) of the 40 most populous of these units. The result of these and other personnel changes was a very substantial turnover within the Central Committee membership. Of the 175 persons named voting members of the Central Committee at the Twenty-Second Party Congress in 1961, only 65 (37 percent) had been voting members of that body at the time of the crisis of June 1957. If one assumed that Kozlov had a key role in the selection of these new members and that many of them were loyal to him, if one assumed that Kozlov led the opposition to Khrushchev, then one might well conclude that Khrushchev's support in this key institution had been undermined.

The opposing explanation for the ambiguities in the policy of the Khrushchev era begins with a quite different image of Khrushchev himself. In this view—that of Merle Fainsod, for example—Khrushchev should not be seen as the leader of some reformist faction, but, instead, should be included among those "essentially conservative transitional figures who undertake to build a bridge from the old to the new." It was conceded that Khrushchev "possessed a willingness to experiment and to strike out in new directions," but it was argued that he did so "without necessarily calculating costs and consequences." When these costs and consequences became apparent, so also did "the limits within which he was prepared to tolerate change." "Like leaders elsewhere who face multiple pressures and impulses, he sought to escape hard choices and found himself responding to events and pursuing policies with contradictory implications." His willingness to strike out in new directions included a willingness to reverse previous positions and policies which no longer seemed satisfactory.[76]

In this interpretation of Khrushchev, the First Secretary was not completely and unreservedly a champion of the consumer, detente, and cultural liberalization, but embodied the inconsistencies of Lenin himself. In this view the "real" Khrushchev was not simply a consumer advocate, but also the man who had defeated Malenkov on the issues of heavy industry and atomic war and who retained these values, at least to some extent. He was the man who not only fought for the publication of *One Day in the Life of Ivan Denisovich,* but who also opposed the publication of Boris Pasternak's *Dr. Zhivago.* He was the man who wrote in his memoirs: "We . . . wanted a relaxation of controls over our artists, but we might have been somewhat cowardly on this score"; the man who wrote about Ehrenburg's *The Thaw:* "We were scared—really scared. We were afraid the thaw might unleash a flood, which we wouldn't be able to control and which could drown us."[77]

Those who held this image of Khrushchev found no need to explain policy ambivalences by Khrushchev's alternate victories and defeats; rather, they attributed them largely to ambivalences within Khrushchev himself and to the flow of events which triggered different responses in him. These scholars suggested that while Khrushchev never achieved the power position attained by Stalin, he had engineered a classic consolidation of power in 1957—a "rise to supreme power" which placed his "leadership . . . beyond challenge."[78] In Merle Fainsod's words, written at the time:

> Many of the basic institutional characteristics of the totalitarian system persist under Khrushchev. He has poured new content into the official ideology, but he remains its final interpreter and brooks no challenge to its doctrinal foundations from any Soviet source . . . Like Stalin before him, Khrushchev monopolizes control of the media of mass communications, saturating the channels of public opinion with party propaganda and permitting no outlets for political programs which challenge his own . . . Like Stalin before him, [he also] tolerates no derogation of his own authority, permits no opposition to raise its head within the party, and insists that the party function as a unit in executing his will.[79]

In the perspective of this interpretation, the removal of Khrushchev's Presidium allies in 1960 and 1961—as well as the Central Committee purge which followed—had much the same political meaning as Stalin's removal of his allies in the 1930s: an attempt by the leader to replace those who had been instrumental in his rise to power with other persons without such memories. The reduction in the number of Central Committee secretaries on the Presidium was seen as an attempt to prevent the Secretariat from dominating the Presidium and thereby to strengthen the position of the one individual (Nikita Khrushchev) who headed the three major collective institutions below the level of the Presidium—the Central Committee Secretariat, the Council of Ministers, and the Bureau of the Central Committee for the RSFSR. Whatever may have been Kozlov's general policy orientation, the fact that he had first been elected a candidate member of the Presidium at the February 1957 Central Committee session that gave Khrushchev his great victory on industrial reorganization suggested to the supporters of this theory that Kozlov was far more likely to be a close supporter of Khrushchev than a political opponent.

Despite the vigor (and often the heat) in the debate about the structure of power in the Khrushchev era, the differences in the opposing positions actually were not as extreme as sometimes appeared. There was general agreement that a basic change in the structure of power had occurred with Stalin's death, and the disagreements arose in defining the extent of that change. As T. H. Rigby (a scholar who emphasized the extent of Khrushchev's power) wrote at the time, "No one either questions on the one hand that Khrushchev occupies a position of special authority in the Soviet leadership (Linden calls him *the* Soviet leader), or suggests on the other that he can do what he likes."[80]

The source of much of the difficulty was that none of the participants in the debate really placed their analysis in a comparative framework or defined clearly how they were using the concept of power. A major dispute on the best way to measure power was taking place in political science in those years, and the foremost American political scientists were defining power in terms similar to those employed by Robert Dahl. ("A has power over B to the extent that he can get B to do something that B would not otherwise do.")[81] They were insisting that power inevitably is (in the words of V. O. Key) "relational" and "situational" in character—that it varies from issue to issue, from case to case.[82] They were arguing that the costs which an action entails must be considered a limitation on the power to impose it.[83]

If the Dahl definition of power is used, obviously Khrushchev was not all-powerful (nor was Stalin), for the definition does not exclude persuasion as an instrument of power. If costs and consequences are a limitation on power, Khrushchev clearly was often aware of such considerations and at times was restrained by them. Just as clearly, scholars such as Merle Fainsod recognized all of this. This recognition was reflected in assertions that the Presidium was "an arena of bargaining in which accommodations and compromises may take place," that "Khrushchev evidenced a willingness to delegate operational authority to his associates and subordinates and to listen to their views," that Khrushchev's judgment "was influenced by the specialized knowledge of his colleagues and a flow of expert advice from below," that he "tried where he could to rest his power on persuasion."[84] But it was not always reflected in language quoted earlier—language which surely sometimes seemed to imply more than was intended.

Similarly, scholars of the "conflict school" were so eager to correct what they believed to be misperceptions in the work of others that they also failed to clarify the meaning of their own statements in comparative terms. They argued that leadership conflict and opposition to the top leader was also a feature of the Soviet political system under Lenin and Stalin (particularly prior to the Great Purge), and at times they implied that Khrushchev's power was analogous to the "limited" power of the leader in these earlier periods. In reality, however, no one believed that a Lenin or a Stalin (even the pre-1937 Stalin) was a first-among-equals in a pure collective oligarchy, and the comparison scarcely suggested a major cleavage with those on the other side in the debate. (Indeed, it is unlikely that Fainsod ever would have assumed that Khrushchev had as much real power as Lenin or the early Stalin.) The need was to distinguish between different patterns of leadership conflict and different patterns in the resolution of such conflict, and, by failing to do so clearly, scholars of the conflict school also used language that implied more than they intended.

Probably the real issue between the different interpretations of Khrushchev's power centered on whether Khrushchev had to obtain a majority of Presidium votes to push through a policy he desired. In stating that "the final power of decision rested with Khrushchev," scholars such as Fainsod were expressing a belief that the first secretary's relationship to the Presidium was not unlike that of an American president to his cabinet. The scholars of the conflict school, on the other hand, treated the Presidium as a body in which each vote was equal and in which a majority vote was decisive.[85] They thought that Khrushchev's ability to shape the agenda and to influence votes was often crucial, but that he still was compelled to obtain a majority in order to enact his policies and that the Presidium members felt reasonably free to vote against him.

Despite the passage of time since Khrushchev's fall from power in 1964 (to be discussed in the next chapter), we unfortunately still know little more about the political process of his time than we knew then. Khrushchev's successors do not even permit scholars to mention his name, let alone analyze the political conflicts in which he was involved, and Khrushchev's own memoirs provide exceedingly little information about post-1957 Presidium politics. The latter do indicate that Khrushchev felt compelled to inform the Presidium of any major decision and to obtain its formal approval, but they suggest that this approval could be obtained very easily at times.[86]

In judging the structure of power in the Khrushchev period, we still must ultimately rely upon our sense of the nature of committee politics and the meaning of different patterns of policy outcomes that emerge from them. To this observer at least, the natural outcome of a divided collective committee is deference to the key individual interests of most of the respective members (logrolling, if you will), compromise on the major issues dividing the committee, and (except in rare cases) gradualism and even conservatism in the change of major policy. Particularly in a committee governed formally by an antifactionalism rule, particularly in such a committee whose members are not selected by an independent electorate and removable only by it, it would seem almost inevitable that policy turmoil would tempt a group with a temporary majority to take advantage of its position and to try to solidify its position by removing its opponents from the decision-making organs. Such a view of committee politics would lead one to conclude that striking policy ambivalence is far more likely to reflect the dominance of an individual who is impulsive, ambivalent, and subject to influence.

To someone with this point of view, policy of the late Khrushchev period simply antagonized too many key groups to have been the product of majority vote on a committee. The military, the local party officials, the industrial administrators, the diplomats, and the educators were merely the most prominent among those who had reason to be unhappy about the policies being followed in the areas of their expertise and self-interest. Most striking of all was the decision to bifurcate the lower party apparatus in the face of the fact that this decision, together with the simultaneous one to amalgamate the economic regions, struck directly and savagely at the power of 30 percent of the voting members of the Central Committee and greatly complicated the work of many more. In 1965, the Georgian party leader, V. P. Mzhavanadze, stated that "members of the party Central Committee with whom I met expressed indignation on this question, told Khrushchev that this would complicate work, that it shouldn't be done, but he did not want to listen to anyone."[87] Apparently he did not have to do so.

The changes that occurred after 1964—the change of policy in directions which major groups could be expected to approve, the end of the frantic reorganizations and policy swings, the major increase in job security for members of the key policy committees—all are strong evidence indeed of the powerful position Khrushchev occupied. To change policy in these directions, the elite had to remove Khrushchev; they presumably could not change policy by majority vote.

But, of course, ultimately Khrushchev was removed. Perhaps in historical perspective this is the most important fact about the Khrushchev era, together with the gradual developments that made it possible. The growth of a sense of personal safety among the top elite, the rise of certain informal "constitutional restraints" on the actions of the leader, an increase in the degree of consultation on top policy decisions (and in the belief that such consultation was required), the opening of a larger number of policy debates to public participation—all of these were features of the Khrushchev era affecting the structure of power within the Soviet Union in the long run, and they should never be forgotten when contemplating Khrushchev's ability to intervene dramatically and decisively in a multiplicity of policy realms. Finally, but by no means least, the establishment of the principle that a First Secretary could be removed peacefully by the means prescribed in the party rules was of crucial significance, and the memory of the result of Khrushchev's dramatic interventions in the policy process is one that no future party leader is likely to lose.

7 | The Return to Normalcy

ALL WESTERN SCHOLARS would agree that the Soviet political system underwent major change with the removal of Khrushchev in October 1964. Of course, awareness of Khrushchev's fate would likely have affected the behavior of any post-1964 party leader, but the change in the relationship between the party leadership and society seems more drastic than would be expected from that factor alone. However, while the new leadership clearly no longer challenged major societal interests or tried to transform society in the way its predecessors had, western scholars have not been able to agree on the basic nature of the change. Some major scholars interpret the Brezhnev regime as a conservative, even reactionary, perhaps even neo-Stalinist one, while others believe that the leadership pushed policy in a cautiously liberal direction. Some speak of the onset of petrification or ossification, but others see movement toward a looser, more pluralistic system.

Lack of historical perspective and the necessary documentary evidence always make it difficult to summarize an era that has not yet passed, and the problems are particularly great when qualified observers differ so dramatically in their interpretations. For these reasons, we will here try to avoid the more controversial issues in conceptualizing the Brezhnev period and will concentrate on developments where some scholarly agreement is possible. Later we will try to sort out the more contentious questions about the way that the Soviet Union is governed today.

The Major Political Actors

In discussing the 1920s and the 1950s, we have been able to discuss a number of Politburo (or Presidium) members as contenders for power and to identify most of them with certain policy positions.* The first highly significant fact about the Brezhnev era is that so little reliable information is available about the policy positions of most Politburo members that no westerner can describe them with any assurance. If Brezhnev did, in fact, strengthen his position by temporary alliances with the liberals or conservatives in the Politburo, if he did put together a clever political program that prevented alliance against him, we simply do not know enough to discuss what happened.

A second highly significant fact about the Brezhnev period is that stability in the inner circle was so great during the first decade of the period that conceivably there were not even contenders for power in the sense that this phrase is used for the 1920s and the 1950s. In October 1964, four men (Leonid Brezhnev, Aleksei Kosygin, Nikolai Podgorny, and Mikhail Suslov) stood out as the major figures within the Presidium; until the removal of Podgorny in May 1977, all four were still Politburo members, and, together with Andrei Kirilenko (also a major Politburo member in 1964), were even more obviously an inner core within the ruling body. Defeats may well have been suffered, but the consequences were far different than they had been in the past.

Immediately after Khrushchev's enforced departure, the party Presidium included ten full members: Leonid Brezhnev (First Secretary), Andrei Kirilenko (First Deputy Chairman of the Bureau of the Central Committee for the RSFSR), Aleksei Kosygin (Chairman of the Council of Ministers), Frol Kozlov (Secretary of the Central Committee, but incapacitated because of a stroke), Anastas Mikoian (Chairman of the Presidium of the Supreme Soviet), Nikolai Podgorny (Secretary of the Central Committee), Dmitrii Poliansky (First Deputy Chairman of the USSR Council of Ministers), Mikhail Suslov (Secretary of the Central Committee), Nikolai Shvernik (Chairman of the Party Control Committee), and Gennadii Voronov (Chairman of the Council of Ministers of the RSFSR).

Over the next eighteen months, three of the original Presidium members were removed: Kozlov in November 1964 because of illness (he soon died), and the two oldest members, Mikoian and Shvernik, in March 1966. Four new voting members were elected: Aleksandr Shelepin (Chairman of the Party-State Control Committee) and Petr Shelest (First secretary of the Ukrainian Party Central Committee) in November 1964, Kirill Mazurov (newly appointed First Deputy Chairman of the USSR Council of Ministers)

---

* In March 1966 the party Presidium was once more called the Politburo, and the First Secretary was renamed the General Secretary. Generally the name appropriate for the year in question will be used in this chapter, but when the reference is to the entire period, the new names will be employed.

in March 1965, and Arvid Pel'she (newly elected Chairman of the Party Control Commission) in March 1966. There were other shifts in position among the existing Presidium members. (For the overall composition of the body after the conclusion of the Twenty-Third Party Congress in March 1966 see table 8.)

Table 8 *Members of the Politburo, March 1966*

MEMBER	YEAR OF BIRTH	YEAR OF PARTY ENTRY	POSITION
L. I. Brezhnev	1906	1931	General Secretary of the Central Committee
A. P. Kirilenko	1906	1931	Secretary of the Central Committee
A. N. Shelepin	1918	1940	Secretary of the Central Committee
M. A. Suslov	1902	1921	Secretary of the Central Committee
A. Ia. Pelshe	1899	1915	Chairman of the Party Control Committee
P. E. Shelest	1908	1928	First secretary of the Ukrainian Central Committee
A. N. Kosygin	1904	1927	Chairman of the USSR Council of Ministers
N. V. Podgorny	1903	1940	Chairman of the Presidium of the Supreme Soviet
K. T. Mazurov	1914	1940	First Deputy Chairman of the USSR Council of Ministers
D. S. Poliansky	1917	1939	First Deputy Chairman of the USSR Council of Ministers
G. I. Voronov	1910	1931	Chairman of the RSFSR Council of Ministers
AVERAGE	1908	1931	
Candidate member			
P. N. Demichev	1918	1939	Secretary of the Central Committee

continued

Table 8—Continued

Member	Year of Birth	Year of Party Entry	Position
D. F. Ustinov	1908	1927	Secretary of the Central Committee
D. A. Kunaev	1912	1939	First secretary of the Kazakhstan Central Committee
P. M. Masherov	1918	1943	First secretary of the Belorussian Central Committee
V. P. Mzhavanadze	1902	1927	First secretary of the Georgian Central Committee
Sh. R. Rashidov	1917	1939	First secretary of the Uzbekistan Central Committee
V. V. Grishin	1914	1939	Chairman of the All-Union Trade Union Committee
V. V. Shcherbitsky	1918	1941	Chairman of the Ukrainian Council of Ministers

Source: 1966 Yearbook, *Bol'shaia sovetskaia entsiklopediia*, p. 18.

The five-man inner core of the post-1966 Politburo—Brezhnev, Kirilenko, Kosygin, Podgorny, and Suslov—were officials who, whatever the conflicts among them, were strikingly similar in background. In 1966, they all were between sixty and sixty-four years of age, and four had joined the party between 1927 and 1931. (The fifth joined in 1921.) All five moved into the political or administrative world sometime after secondary school, but then they all returned to upgrade their education in their mid-twenties. Four of them entered (and completed) an engineering institute and the fifth (Suslov) the Plekhanov Institute of Economics in Moscow. Suslov and Podgorny began their higher education in the mid-1920s, the other three in 1931 during the educational expansion of the First Five-Year Plan. Finally, it should be noted, the five top party leaders were also alike in advancing rapidly in position in the late 1930s, sometimes spectacularly so.[1]

Of the inner five, the man with the broadest range of experience by far was the man who was, in fact, named the First Secretary—Leonid Ilich Brezhnev.[2] Brezhnev had major supervisory experience (and education) in both the agricultural and industrial realms. A Russian by birth, he had been a party leader in four separate republics, including the RSFSR, the Ukraine, and Kazakhstan. He had seven years of political work in the military, part of it dealing with the army and another part with the navy, and for three years he had been Chairman of the Presidium of the Supreme Soviet and had gained the foreign policy exposure associated with that post. Given the diverse responsibilities of a party leader, none of the other potential leaders had nearly as impressive a biography.

Brezhnev was born in 1906 in a metalworker's family, and after working for a few years in the early 1920s, he went to a specialized secondary school (a *technicum*) which prepared specialists in land treatment and reclamation. Upon graduation, he worked in agricultural administration in the Urals, and during the growing tension preceding and accompanying collectivization, he rose to be head of a county (*raion*) agriculture office, deputy chairman of the executive committee of a county soviet, and deputy head of a regional or state (*oblast*) agriculture administration.

Then in 1931, Brezhnev, like many others of his generation, decided to obtain higher education. After a very brief (and almost never mentioned) few months at the Timiriazev Agricultural Academy in Moscow, he returned to his home town in the Ukraine as a metalworker and then entered the Dneprodzerzhinsk Metallurgical Institute. After receiving his engineering degree in 1935,[3] he held a number of minor jobs—an engineering job at the local steel plant, a short stint in the military (probably as a political worker), and the director of a technicum. With the purge he began rising in the Dnepropetrovsk party organization, coming to serve as secretary (but neither the second or first secretary) of the regional party committee, the secretary in charge of the defense industry.

During World War II, Brezhnev was directed to political work in the army and eventually became head of the political administration of a front— and then after the war, head of the political administration of a military district. His performance at this time must have been impressive, for during the period of postwar reconstruction he became regional party first secretary in two industrialized regions in the Ukraine—Zaporozhe from 1946 to 1947 and the more important Dnepropetrovsk from 1947 to 1950.[4] Then for over two years he was transferred to the first secretaryship of the most rural of the Soviet union republics, Moldavia. In October 1952 he received a major promotion, becoming a secretary of the All-Union Central Committee and a candidate member of the party Presidium, but after Stalin's death his career seemed to suffer a serious setback. He was assigned to a relatively minor past —that of deputy head of the political administration of the Ministry of Defense (the deputy head in charge of the navy at that), and he remained there for a year. Both his demotion and subsequent position suggested he may have been the Central Committee secretary in charge of the administrative organs department and therefore the police and military, but that is sheer speculation.

As Khrushchev consolidated his position, however, Brezhnev was one of those from the Ukraine who prospered with him. In February 1954 he was sent to Kazakhstan as Khrushchev's personal representative in supervising his pet Virgin Lands program. At first, he was only second secretary of the Kazakhstan Party Central Committee, but by August he was first secretary and became closely associated with the early success of the program. As a reward, he again returned to Moscow in 1956 to serve as a secretary of the Central Committee and as a candidate member of the party Presidium. In contrast to his predominantly agricultural duties in Moldavia and Kazakhstan, his main responsibility in the Central Committee Secretariat at this time was supervision of heavy industry, the defense industry, and the space program, and in 1958 (after being elected a full member of the party Presidium in 1957) he was also named Deputy Chairman of the Bureau of the Central Committee for the RSFSR, presumably giving him special responsibility for industry in that republic.[5]

When Kirichenko fell into disgrace in early 1960, there were signs that Brezhnev might replace him as "the second secretary," but, in reality, it was Kozlov who assumed that position. In the major shakeup of May 1960 Brezhnev was moved to the Chairmanship of the Presidium of the Supreme Soviet—a post previously filled by a rather inconsequential and elderly member of the party leadership. As an alternative to the "second secretary" slot, this appointment represented a defeat, but for the secretary for industry it was a major promotion. Conceivably it was an attempt to broaden the experience and visibility of an heir apparent, conceivably there is another explanation such as a health problem, but in any case the shift was not a permanent one. After Kozlov's stroke in 1963, Brezhnev was named once more to the Central Committee Secretariat, presumably in large part filling Kozlov's crucial position.[6] When Khrushchev was asked by western newsmen who would replace him as first secretary if he died, the Soviet leader answered "Brezhnev." He was proved right sooner than he anticipated.

A second major member of the post-Khrushchev inner leadership, Aleksei Kosygin, had a much more specialized background.[7] He was born in 1904, and after several years in the Red army during the Civil War, he went to a technicum in the trade field. Then for six years he occupied managerial posts in the consumers' coops of Siberia, during which period (in 1927) he joined the party. Like Brezhnev, he returned to college in 1931, but his choice of an institute—the Leningrad Textile Institute—involved a less drastic career change than Brezhnev's.

Upon graduation in 1935, Kosygin went to work not in the trade network, but in the light industry that produces goods for it. He was appointed a foreman and then a shop head at a Leningrad textile factory, but enjoyed a meteoric rise during the purge. In 1937 he became director of another textile factory and then in 1938 moved quickly to become head of the industrial-transportation department of the Leningrad regional party committee and then chairman of the executive committee of the Leningrad city soviet. In early 1939 Kosygin was named People's Commissar for Light Industry and in 1940 Deputy Chairman of the Council of People's Commissars coordinating the light industries.

Kosygin remained Deputy Chairman of the Council of People's Commissars (later renamed Council of Ministers) for the rest of the Stalin period. His precise duties varied somewhat (from 1943 to 1946 he was also Chairman of the RSFSR Council of People's Commissars and through most of 1948 he was USSR Minister of Finances), but he essentially continued to serve as the top Soviet official in the light industry realm. In March 1946 he became a candidate member of the Politburo and in February 1948 a full member. However, with the death of Zhdanov in 1948 and the launching of the Leningrad Affair, Kosygin seems to have fallen under a cloud because of his link with that city. Khrushchev reported that his life "was hanging by a thread."[8] Although he survived this dangerous period, he apparently never did regain Stalin's full confidence, for when the Politburo was enlarged from ten to twenty-five full members in 1952, Kosygin was the only full member not to retain his seat. (He was demoted to candidate membership.)

Kosygin's position was slow to improve in the Khrushchev period. In the early years he continued his role as the top light industry administrator in the country, but, despite his earlier full membership in the Politburo and the great emphasis placed upon consumer goods in 1953, he even lost his candidate membership in the Presidium named immediately after Stalin's death. While Kosygin regained his candidate membership in the Presidium in 1957 in the large-scale reorganization and expansion of that body, it was not until 1959 that he finally moved to the fore. In that year he became Chairman of the USSR Gosplan (a very powerful post during the early sovnarkhoz years), and the following year his appointment as First Deputy Chairman of the Council of Ministers and his election as a full member of the party Presidium signified that he had become the country's top industrial administrator.

The timing of Kosygin's return to full membership in the Presidium in 1960 could pose some real dilemmas if we assume that the Presidium changes of that year were inspired by a conservative trend. On the face of it, it seems surprising that a conservative faction would be supporting a man so closely associated with light industry or that Khrushchev, the presumed champion of consumer goods, had not been supporting him more vigorously prior to 1960. One obvious explanation, of course, might be that the 1960 changes have often been misinterpreted and that Kosygin's political fate during these years had far less to do with any factional conflicts than with Khrushchev's change in attitude toward heavy and light industry between 1955 and 1960. Such an explanation would be quite congruent with the reputation that Kosygin usually has had in the West—that of a first-class administrator who would not aspire to the top leadership position and who would serve the leader ably without posing a major political threat.

A third member of the inner leadership—Nikolai V. Podgorny—had a much more gradual rise to prominence in Moscow than either Brezhnev or Kosygin.[9] A Ukrainian born in 1903, Podgorny, like Kosygin, had worked in light industry in his early years. He graduated from the Kiev Technological Institute of the Food Industry in 1931, served in managerial posts in the sugar industry in the 1930s, and rose to the post of Deputy People's Commissar for the Food Industry of the USSR in 1940. For some reason, however, his career soon faltered. In 1942 he became director of a Moscow research institute for the food industry, a post of peculiarly minor significance in the critical days of the war.[10] In 1944 he became deputy people's commissar for the food industry of the Ukraine, and two years later he was named permanent representative of the Ukrainian Council of Ministers to the USSR Council of Ministers, a position that almost never is associated with future career advance.

Podgorny's major rise to power began in 1950 with his selection as first secretary of the Kharkov party regional committee. This was a most improbable promotion, first, because the Kharkov first secretaryship was an extremely important party post for a man forty-seven years of age with absolutely no previous experience in party work, and, second, because Kharkov was a major center of heavy industry rather than light industry and Podgorny's background seemed ill-suited for it. Presumably Podgorny had made a very favorable impression upon Khrushchev (the post of representative of the Council of Ministers was in many ways one of liaison between Khrushchev and his Ukrainian organization on the one hand and the central government on the other), and thereafter the fortunes of the two men improved simultaneously.

When Khrushchev succeeded in removing Melnikov as the Ukrainian first secretary in June 1953, Podgorny became the Ukrainian second secretary.

After Kirichenko became a Central Committee secretary in December 1957, Podgorny was named the Ukrainian first secretary, and at the next session of the Central Committee he was elected a candidate member of the Presidium. (In 1960 he became a full member of the Presidium.) In 1963, with Kozlov's stroke, he was promoted into the Central Committee Secretariat, where his work, like Brezhnev's, seemed associated with economic management and personnel selection. (V. N. Titov, Podgorny's second secretary and his successor in Kharkov, was already serving as head of the party organs department for the union republics.)

The fourth figure in the inner party leadership—Mikhail Suslov—is one of the most enigmatic figures among the postwar party officialdom.[11] He was the oldest of the top Brezhnev leaders, born in 1902, and he joined the party a number of years before his colleagues, in 1921. He graduated from the Plekhanov Economics Institute in Moscow in 1928, and, after teaching at Moscow University and the Industrial Academy for three years (being in the latter institute when Khrushchev was its party secretary), he held a staff position in the Central Control Commission—a post which has implied to westerners (probably erroneously) a most unsavory role in the early stages of the purges.

In 1937, Suslov was sent from Moscow to Rostov where he served as one of the regional party secretaries before becoming first secretary of the neighboring Stavropol regional party committee in 1939. During World War II he engaged in military political work in the North Caucasus and was head of the Stavropol partisans (work which conceivably may have brought him into contact with Brezhnev, who was also engaged in political work in the army in that general area). In 1944 Suslov was shifted to the post of Chairman of the Bureau of the Central Committee for Lithuania, a temporary position associated with the consolidation of political control over that area which had been annexed into the Soviet Union only shortly beforehand.

In 1946 Suslov was transferred to other (but unspecified) work in the Central Committee apparatus, but in 1947 he was named head of the propaganda-agitation department of the Central Committee and elected a Central Committee secretary, remaining in the latter post for over thirty years. The extent of his duties in the Stalin period is still somewhat unclear, but, first and foremost, he was the "secretary for ideological questions"—a post that involves responsibility not only for agitation and propaganda but also for cultural affairs in general and even for education. In addition, however, he also seems to have had a special interest in relations with east European Communists, perhaps because of the sensitivity of the ideological element in these relations.

Suslov's postwar responsibilities gave him the reputation of a conservative and even sinister figure within the leadership. His work in Lithuania involved, in part, the deportation of unreliable elements from that newly acquired territory. His movement into ideological work coincided with the Zhdanovshchina and the increased pressure upon the intelligentsia. His involvement in relations with the east European Communists coincided with the establishment of the Cominform, the enunciation of the Two-Camp doctrine, and the tightening of controls in the wake of the Yugoslavian defection. His personal appearance and deportment—which seemed dour and humorless—added to his reputation as a rigid ideologue.

Yet, surprisingly, Suslov survived the Khrushchev years and, in fact, flourished during them. He became a full member of the party Presidium at the May 1955 plenary session of the Central Committee that ratified the reconciliation with Yugoslavia. Now his responsibilities clearly included not only overall supervision of domestic "ideological" affairs but also major responsibilities in the foreign policy realm. (It is symptomatic that in 1954 he became chairman of the Foreign Affairs Committee of one of the houses of the Supreme Soviet.) His speech at the Twentieth Party Congress, as has been seen, also suggested responsibility for personnel selection, but he lost that role by December 1957 at the latest. While westerners usually saw his election to the Presidium as a counterbalance to the simultaneous election of Kirichenko (he was seen as the conservative faction's candidate), Suslov was one of the three Politburo members who gave Khrushchev unwavering support in the struggle with the antiparty group in 1957. Notwithstanding Khrushchev's espousal of peaceful coexistence, his revision of Leninism at the Twentieth Party Congress in 1956, his educational reform, his emphasis upon political participation, and so forth, Suslov remained a major figure in the ideological and foreign policy sphere throughout the Khrushchev period.

Western scholars have tended to explain Suslov's political survival by placing him (together with Kozlov) at the head of a conservative faction which was in constant struggle with Khrushchev.[12] If one is dubious about such a faction (or is simply dubious about Suslov's relationship to it because of his support of Khrushchev in 1957), one is, however, led to suspect that Suslov's policy position was far more complex than is often assumed. Indeed, even general theoretical considerations would lead to the suspicion. A man in charge of educational-cultural-scientific affairs for years is likely to assimilate some of that branch's perspectives (especially in appropriations politics), and a man with a great deal of contact with foreign Communists is likely to develop a more subtle view of the outside world than men with no foreign experience. Suslov may well have opposed some of Khrushchev's harebrained theorizing and some of his inconsistent experimentation; he may well have been relatively conservative on law-and-order and dissidence questions; but he may also have been an ideologue who took Marxist egalitarianism seriously, who had a fairly realistic understanding of the problems of the Communist movement in the western world, and who, in addition, may have become closely allied with Khrushchev during his days in the Industrial Academy. We should keep an open mind on him until more evidence is available.

The man who was to become the fifth member of the inner bureau of the Brezhnev period, Andrei Kirilenko, had at least one distinctive feature in his biography: a close, early association with Brezhnev in the Ukraine. At the time of his seventieth birthday, he was the most sycophantic of the Soviet leaders in his praise of Brezhnev and even used the familiar form of "you" (*ty*) in referring to him instead of the more usual *vy*.[13] He was born in the same year as Brezhnev (1906), joined the party in the same year (1931), and enrolled in an engineering college in the same year (1931), but Kirilenko had not had the rather important regional level administrative experience of a Brezhnev or a Kosygin before entering college. He had been a rank-and-file worker for four years in the 1920s and had only a year or two of low level political work before enrolling in the Novocherkassk Aviation Industry Institute. After graduation, he worked as a design engineer at a Zaporozhe plant for two years. During the purge he became a second secretary of a district party committee in Zaporozhe, then a regional party secretary there, then the second secretary of the regional committee.

During the war Kirilenko served as a member of the political council of an army and later as representative of the State Defense Committee at an aviation plant, but this work did not lead to immediate postwar promotion. When Zaporozhe was liberated, he returned to his old job as its regional second secretary in 1943 and held that post for four years. (When Brezhnev became first secretary in Zaporozhe in 1946, Kirilenko thus came to serve as his first deputy in the party regional committee.) In 1947 Kirilenko became first secretary of the Nikolaev regional committee, and in 1950 he succeeded Brezhnev as first secretary in Dnepropetrovsk. In 1955 he was one of the officials from the Ukraine (although he himself was a Russian) whom Khrushchev transferred to the RSFSR in his consolidation of power. He was selected as first secretary of the Sverdlovsk regional party committee, one of the most important in the Russian Republic.

Kirilenko's political position during the Khrushchev years, like that of many of his associates, was somewhat anomalous. In 1957, in the reorganization and expansion of the party Presidium after the defeat of the antiparty group, he became a candidate member of that body—a very atypical honor for a man in Sverdlovsk, but he was not reelected to the Presidium at the Twenty-Second Party Congress in 1961. The following year, however, his fortunes improved once more, for he was elected a full member of the Presidium and First

Deputy Chairman of the Bureau of the Central Committee for the RSFSR. Perhaps the abrupt changes in his status within a year's period reflect a similar decline and rebound in Brezhnev's fortunes in the early 1960s, but fundamentally they remain unexplained.[14] In any case Kirilenko entered the Brezhnev era as the second-ranking party official in the Russian Republic under Khrushchev's general leadership, and he retained that position, now under Brezhnev, in the first eighteen months after Khrushchev's fall.

The other two voting Politburo members in 1966 who were holdovers from the Khrushchev Presidium were both essentially agricultural specialists.[15] One, Gennadii Voronov, had followed the familiar path of upward mobility in the First Five-Year Plan. The son of a rural teacher, he had been a worker for three years after secondary school, and had entered the Tomsk Industrial Institute in 1932 at the age of twenty-two. However, before graduation, he was directed to the Novosibirsk Institute of Marxism-Leninism in 1936, and his early party career, which began in 1937, was in agitation-propaganda work.

In 1939, Voronov was sent to the Chita regional party committee in eastern Siberia, perhaps as the secretary for ideological questions, but he remained there for sixteen years, rising to the post of second secretary and then first secretary. Chita is not a major industrial center, and Voronov seems to have become absorbed in agricultural questions. In 1955 he actually was appointed a USSR Deputy Minister of Agriculture, and from 1957 to 1962 he served as first secretary of the regional party committee in Orenburg—an important agricultural region. In 1961 he became Deputy Chairman—and soon First Deputy Chairman—of the Bureau of the Central Committee for the RSFSR, functioning essentially as the top party official in charge of agricultural questions for that republic. This post earned him promotion to candidate membership in the party Presidium in January 1961 and to full membership ten months later. In 1962 he was named Chairman of the Council of Ministers of the RSFSR.

The other agricultural specialist in the Politburo was Dmitrii Poliansky, one of the youngest members of the leadership. A true child of the revolution, Poliansky was born on November 7, 1917, in a Ukrainian peasant family. He entered the Kharkov Agricultural Institute in the 1930s and, upon graduation in 1939, worked briefly in the Komsomol and then the military before embarking upon a career in the party apparatus. There is no typical career pattern for a party official, but Poliansky's would come as close to the norm as likely for a party official of the late Stalin and early Khrushchev periods who had a strong orientation toward agriculture and rural affairs. In any case, his biography bespeaks rapid but orderly promotion: head of a political department of a machine-tractor station and first secretary of a district party committee in Siberia (1942–1945), a lower staff official of the Central Committee apparatus (1945–1949), second secretary of the Crimean regional party committee (1949–1952), chairman of the executive committee of the Crimean regional soviet (1952–1954), first secretary of the Crimean regional party committee (1954–1955), first secretary of the Orenburg regional party committee (1955–1957), and first secretary of the Krasnodar regional party committee (1957–1958). (The promotion involved in the last three posts is suggested by the fact that in 1959 the Crimean, Orenburg, and Krasnodar regions had populations of 1,200,000, 1,830,000, and 3,750,000 persons respectively.)

In 1958 Poliansky was called to Moscow to be Chairman of the Council of Ministers of the Russian Republic. Simultaneously he was elected a candidate member of the party Presidium, and two years later he was advanced to full membership. In 1962, he was named Deputy Chairman of the USSR Council of Ministers—the deputy chairman in charge of agriculture—and in 1965 his title was raised to First Deputy Chairman, although his basic responsibilities remained the same. In the new regime, as in the last years of the Khrushchev period, he was the Politburo member who handled direct supervision of the agricultural sphere at the national level.

The four Politburo members who were added to that body after 1964 were a very mixed group. One, Arvid Pelshe, born in 1899, was the oldest person in the top ruling group, and he was the only Old Bolshevik among it, having joined the party in 1915 and having been a deputy to the Petrograd soviet in 1917. A Latvian who had participated in the unsuccessful attempt to establish a Communist regime in that area immediately after the Bolshevik revolution, he moved to the Soviet Union when the effort failed. There he engaged in relatively low level political work in the military and in agriculture, as well as some college teaching in Moscow. (He had graduated from the Institute of Red Professors in 1931.)

With the Soviet seizure of power in Latvia in 1940, Pelshe returned to Riga to work in the Latvian Party Central Committee. In 1941 he became the Central Committee secretary in Latvia for ideological questions, and he held that job for eighteen years. In the aftermath of the 1959 nationalism scandal in Latvia, Pelshe was named the first secretary of the republican central committee. He remained in that post until he was named Chairman of the USSR Party Control Committee—an institution that, more than anything, is the party's supreme court for handling appeals in party expulsions by lower party organs. His simultaneous election to the party Politburo seems a testimony less to the importance of his job than to a desire of the top leadership to maintain a link with the prerevolutionary past and to give representation to the Baltic states—particularly to a Baltic official who had demonstrated special loyalty to the Soviet Union during a local nationalism crisis.

A second newcomer to the Politburo, Kirill Mazurov, also provided representation for a nationality group that had not been receiving it—the Belorussians. This representation was far more than symbolic, for Mazurov held one of the most important posts in the new government, First Deputy Chairman of the USSR Council of Ministers. Mazurov was slightly less than a decade younger than the inner core of the Politburo (he was born in 1914), and he did not join the party until 1940. He graduated from a technicum preparing personnel for the highway system, but after a few years in a district road department and in the army, Mazurov entered Komsomol work. Except for three years in the army and in the partisans during World War II, he spent a decade in the Komsomol, rising to the position of first secretary of the Belorussian Komsomol organization.

In 1947 (the year that he graduated from the Higher Party School by correspondence), Mazurov moved into party work. Within several years he was first secretary of the Minsk city party committee and from 1950 to 1953 he served as first secretary of the Minsk regional party committee. Soon after Stalin's death, he was promoted to the chairmanship of the Belorussian Council of Ministers, and in 1956 he was elected first secretary of the Belorussian Party Central Committee—a post that he held for nine years. In March 1965 Mazurov was appointed First Deputy Chairman of the Council of Ministers. His areas of responsibility seemed rather broad, including heavy industry, transportation, and education.

A third addition to the Politburo, Petr Shelest, brought still another non-Russian to the ruling leadership (this time a Ukrainian) and still another representative of that group of lower and middle level officials who entered college with the expansion of the educational system during the First Five-Year Plan.[16] (The group had a majority of the eleven voting members—Brezhnev, Kirilenko, Kosygin, Pelshe, Shelest, and Voronov—while a seventh member, Podgorny, had several years of engineering education in this period before graduating in 1931.) Shelest was born in 1908, was a worker for five years in the 1920s, became a district Komsomol secretary in 1927 for a year before entering the Communist University and then the Engineering and Economics Institute in Kharkov. He joined the party in 1928. He left college before graduation (perhaps in the temporary mass reduction in the college contingent in 1931–1932),[17] but finished his degree at the Mariupol Metallurgical Institute while serving as an engineer at the local steel plant.

If Poliansky's career pattern is fairly typical for a party official involved in the supervision of agriculture and rural areas, Shelest's has much in common with that of other party officials in urban areas. From 1932 to 1940 (with a year off for military service) he worked in industrial management, rising to the level of plant chief engineer at an important Kharkov enterprise. From 1940 to 1948 he occupied a series of party positions—either party secretary within an important plant or specialized industrial posts within the local party organs—but then from 1948 to 1954 Shelest moved back into industrial administration, this time as director of industrial plants in Leningrad and Kiev —almost surely defense industry plants.

In 1954, Shelest returned to party work as second secretary of the Kiev city party committee. By the end of the year he was second secretary of the Kiev regional party committee, and in 1957 he was named first secretary of that body. In 1962 he became a secretary of the Ukrainian Central Committee (the secretary for industrial questions) and in July 1963 the first secretary in the Ukraine. This latter post brought him election to candidate membership in the party Presidium in December 1963 and to full membership in November 1964.

The fourth newcomer to the Politburo, Aleksandr Shelepin, was the most intriguing of all—or at least so he seemed to western observers.[18] A Russian born in 1918, he was by one year the youngest Politburo member. Unlike seven of his ten colleagues, he had not gone to an engineering institute (or transportation technicum) but had graduated from the Moscow Institute of History, Philosophy, and Literature in 1941. He had had no experience in industrial or agricultural supervision either directly or as a party official, and, unlike nine of his ten colleagues, he had never been first secretary of a regional or republican party committee.

After a short stint as an officer during the Finnish War of 1939–1940, Shelepin had made his career almost entirely within the Young Communist League or Komsomol. He had been Komsomol secretary at the institute, and after returning from the army, he rose rather slowly through the Moscow city Komsomol committee. In 1943 he was named a secretary of the All-Union Komsomol organization and at some point became second secretary. He retained that post until 1952, when he became Komsomol first secretary. In 1958 Shelepin was transferred into party work and made head of the Central Committee's party organs department for the union republics. Later that year he was appointed Chairman of the State Security Committee (KGB).

In 1961, Shelepin returned to party work, this time as a secretary of the Central Committee—presumably the secretary who was responsible for supervising the entire security system. (His old post in the KGB was given to his second secretary—and his successor—in the Komsomol, Vladimir Semichastny.) Then in 1962 with the creation of the Party-State Control Committee, he was named its chairman. As the occupant of this position was both a secretary of the Central Committee and a Deputy Chairman of the Council of

Ministers, Shelepin was the only central official besides Khrushchev to work both in the government and in the party apparatus; after October 1964 he was the only such official.[19]

Almost immediately after the establishment of the new regime, Moscow rumors and western analysts began attributing special importance to Shelepin. His role in the fall of Khrushchev was supposed to have been a critical one because of his presumed control of the secret police, and by the summer of 1965 rumors were suggesting that he would be able to force Brezhnev back into the Chairmanship of the Presidium of the Supreme Soviet and to assume the First Secretaryship himself.[20] However, the bases for all these rumors are most unclear. On the surface at least, Pelshe and perhaps Mazurov were the only Politburo members who seemed less likely than Shelepin to become First Secretary in the near term. In a leadership clearly yearning for a period of stability, Shelepin was the youngest member at forty-seven years of age in 1965; he had not even been a candidate member of the Presidium in the Khrushchev period; he had had none of the coordinating and balancing experience of a provincial first secretary; he had close ties with the unnerving secret police; and he had neither the education nor the experience that would prepare him for leadership of the economy. Under the circumstances, it would have been a real shock if he could have gained more than a small fraction of the votes necessary to defeat Brezhnev. It is difficult to believe that the rumors were more than a result of anxiety, of an exaggerated notion of the importance of Shelepin holding both a party and a governmental post, or perhaps even of a deliberate Brezhnev attempt to discredit him.

The Return to Normalcy

No bill of particulars was ever presented in the Soviet Union to explain Khrushchev's removal, and the immediate cause of this event is still a matter of conjecture.[21] The announcement of a change in leadership stated inaccurately that Khrushchev had resigned for reasons of health, and the criticisms of his rule went little beyond vague statements about his "voluntarism," his "subjectivism," and his harebrained schemes. Indeed, his very name disappeared completely from the media and from the historical literature on the post-Stalin period.

While the nature of the "final straw"—the final policy proposal or action that led his subordinates to remove him—is not known (if, in fact, there was one), the cause of Khrushchev's fall in any broader sense must have been a range of policies that he pursued and the methods by which he made them. As noted, almost every major institutional interest within the elite had reason to be unhappy with the policy being followed and/or the organizational structure in its specialized sphere of activity, and the support for the First Secretary must have been eroded throughout the elite as a whole.

The post-Khrushchev leadership began almost immediately to reverse the Khrushchevian measures which were highly offensive to the various elites. First and foremost, it dismantled most of the former leader's "harebrained" organizational schemes, restructuring the administrative system along lines more congenial to the administrators in each area. The first change came in the organization of the party apparatus, for within six weeks, the Central Committee had met once more to reunite the lower apparatus.[22] The district party committee (*raikom*) was reestablished in the countryside to replace the party committee of the district agricultural administration and the industrial district party committee; the agricultural and industrial regional party committees were reunited into a single regional party committee (*obkom*) and an analogous reunification took place in the regional soviets; the industrial and agricultural bureaus of the all-union and republican central committees were abolished (although the pre-1962 practice of having secretaries and departments specializing on industry and agriculture was retained). Khrushchev's Bureau of the Central Committee for the Russian Republic was not abolished immediately, but in March 1966 it too disappeared.

Perhaps of equal significance, the return of the party apparatus to its former structure was largely accompanied by a return to the status quo in personnel terms. Brezhnev criticized "the unjustified transferring and replacing of personnel" that had occurred under Khrushchev, and he pledged a policy of "respect for personnel."[23] Despite the passage of three years and the presumed earlier loyalty of lower party officials to Khrushchev (or, perhaps even Kozlov, who was Khrushchev's chief assistant for personnel selection in 1961 when many were first selected), fully 76 percent of the regional first secretaries in the RSFSR in the summer of 1965 had held the same post in the summer of 1962, another 4 percent had been first secretary in another region, and still another 11 percent of the old first secretaries either had been promoted or had died. In twelve of the other fourteen republics, the man who was the Central Committee first secretary in late 1961 also occupied this position in the summer of 1965, and in the other two cases the former first secretary had been promoted to a post in Moscow that conferred Politburo membership and, therefore, he must have retained considerable influence in his old republic.[24] Indeed, the return to the status quo ante in the personnel realm included the political rehabilitation of a number of high officials who had been seriously demoted in the last years of Khrushchev's rule.[25]

After the restoration of the party apparatus in its old form, the leadership turned to the reestablishment of the economic administrative system that had existed prior to Khrushchev. In early 1965, the Ministry of Agriculture, which had been stripped of most functions except supervision of agricultural science and spread of technological innovation, was once again placed in charge of agriculture as a whole. Then in October, the complex network of industrial state committees and regional economic councils was abolished, and a system of industrial ministries along the pre-1957 lines was established.[26] Here too there was substantial continuity of personnel. Twelve of the thirty-three industrial and construction ministers appointed in the fall of 1965 had been USSR ministers in 1957, and another ten had risen to the level of deputy minister by that time. Some attempt was made to increase the subtlety of the incentive system for managers and the responsiveness of light industry to consumer demands, and a movement was launched to unite closely allied plants (either plants of similar profile or else large enterprises with their smaller suppliers) into larger firms (*obedinenie*). Nevertheless, the basic structure and operating principles of the planning and administrative system were not changed.[27]

Other organizational changes did occur after the industrial reorganization of 1965, but they were minor in nature. All-Union Ministries of Education and of Preservation of Public Order (later renamed Internal Affairs) were formed in 1966, four new construction ministries were created in 1967, a fifth in 1972, and a new Ministry of Justice in 1970, and in the decade from 1965 to 1975 the number of industrial ministries rose from twenty-nine to thirty-six through the subdivision of existing ministries.[28] Yet, except for this Parkinsonian tendency (also found in a 65 to 70 percent increase in the total number of deputy ministers from 1966 to early 1978), the Brezhnev period basically featured an initial reversal of Khrushchev's organizational innovations and then organizational stability that reversed the Khrushchevian pattern of constant reorganization.

"Normalcy" meant more than a comfortable organizational structure and an end to "permanent purge." It also involved a reversal of the policies most unpopular with the various specialized elites. One of the regime's first acts was to remove the charlatan Lysenko from any position of influence over agricultural or biological science.[29] In education, it cut back sharply on the amount of production training ("shop") required in the schools, and it became less insistent upon giving preference to college applicants with production experience.[30] In its relations with the arts, it tried to reverse the hot-and-cold approach of Khrushchev, and in foreign policy it abandoned the practice of issuing ultimatums (as in the Berlin case) and of taking high risks (as in the Cuban missile crisis). Its advice to foreign Communists in revolutionary or semirevolutionary situations tended to be cautious. In defense policy, the appeals of the military for an increase in the number of the armed forces and of both conventional and strategic weaponry were heeded, but, despite the assertion of many in the West that this increase denoted an extraordinary rise in military power, this action seemed part of a general policy of providing incremental budgetary increases for each major institutional claimant.

In seeking to solidify its rule, the new leadership seemed more eager than Khrushchev to avoid the types of denunciation of the past that might undercut the regime's legitimacy. Khrushchev himself was not criticized except by indirection, and the criticisms of Stalin were muted. Scholars still could discuss most of the shortcomings of the Stalin period in a cautious way (indeed, on balance, the historical discussion was more fulsome and better documented than under Khrushchev), but their freedom to express moral outrage in print was severely restricted. Stalin's "crimes" became Stalin's "mistakes." Biographies of purge victims continued to appear in the press on important anniversaries of their birth, but they seldom elaborated (or, at times, even mentioned) the cause of death. In addition, those who wanted to defend the Stalin period were given a greater freedom than they had had prior to 1964,[31] and in the mass-circulation books of a nonscholarly nature (for example, the basic party history), the more conservative views prevailed.[32] In addition to downplaying criticism of the past, the leaders greatly increased the attention they gave to the party's moment of greatest glory—its leadership of the country in the victory of World War II. In the process patriotic and nationalist themes received greater weight in the legitimatizing propaganda.

In its basic ideology, the new leadership moved sharply away from the Khrushchevian utopian discussion of "withering away of the state."[33] Scholars (but seldom the leaders) continued to speak of the "all-people's state," but the catch phrase of the Brezhnev era was "developed socialism" (*razvityi sotsializm*), with discussion being couched in terms of the impact of "the scientific-technical revolution" upon society and the political system. Great emphasis was now given to a "scientific approach" to decision-making, a phrase which now implied a weighing of alternatives, an understanding of limitations, a reliance upon data and evidence.

Yet, a retreat from Khrushchev's utopianism in language did not involve an abandonment of his endorsement of citizen participation in decision-making, either verbally or in practice. The phrase "developed socialism" was introduced by the same man (Fedor Burlatsky) who was responsible for the phrase "all-people's state,"[34] and a developed socialist system was always said to involve a large degree of political participation. (In fact, the higher education levels produced by the "scientific-technical revolution" were said to increase such participation.) While the new regime was eager to ensure that such citizen units as the voluntary auxiliary police (*druzhinniki*) did not function out of control and that the multiplicity of citizen checking groups worked in a more coordinated fashion,[35] it treated participation as an important and necessary part of the information input required for "scientific decision-making." The use of volunteer (*neshtatnyi*) personnel in administrative work and even of volunteer governmental departments (departments *na obshchestvennykh nachalakh*) continued, and all statistics on citizen involvement showed a much greater percentage increase than did those on the increase in the size of the adult population.

A Struggle for Power?

Judging by the experience of the 1920s and 1950s, "normalcy" in political terms would have entailed a bitter and intense struggle for dominance within the Politburo, and, in fact, the early political moves after Khrushchev's removal did seem to be classic steps in a Brezhnev consolidation of power. However, these steps did not culminate in any denunciation and removal of a Right Opposition, Left Opposition, antiparty group, or the like, and the membership of the top leadership remained far more stable than it had been in the earlier succession periods.

The reasons for the great difference between the succession period of the 1960s and those of the 1920s and the 1950s are far from clear. One possible explanation is that the Politburo members (or at least a strong majority among them) may have agreed at the outset on the need for a common front to prevent the emergence of a single leader and that, as a consequence, no real struggle for power in the traditional sense of that phrase ever occurred. A second possible explanation is that although the entire period was featured by a struggle for personal dominance, Brezhnev simply was unable to consolidate his position—at least not until the Twenty-Fifth Party Congress in 1976.[36] A third possible explanation is that Brezhnev did, in fact, become the dominant figure in the post-Khrushchev Politburo fairly rapidly, but that he chose not to exercise his power in the manner of his predecessors—that for a series of reasons (perhaps including a desire to avoid the selection of younger replacements who might think of themselves as possible successors) he decided not to force out his senior colleagues.

By the assumptions of traditional analyses of Kremlin politics, the most likely serious rival to Brezhnev in the mid-1960s should have been Podgorny.[37] A man with a wide range of experience in supervising light industry, the heavy industry complex of Kharkov, and then the Ukraine as a whole, his job in the Central Committee Secretariat after October 1964 seemed to involve some responsibility for the party apparatus, for he was the man who gave the speech when the apparatus was reunited in November 1964. Moreover, his Kharkov subordinate, V. N. Titov, was the junior Central Committee secretary in charge of organizational party work, and the second secretary of the Ukrainian Central Committee (the secretary in charge of personnel selection in that republic) was yet another man from the Kharkov party organization.[38] If a role in the selection of lower party secretaries is a key to the building of a power base in the Soviet Union, Podgorny seemed well situated.

Or at least Podgorny seemed well situated to pose a challenge to Brezhnev at the end of 1964. A year later his position looked quite different. In April 1965 Titov was removed from the Central Committee Secretariat and sent to Kazakhstan as the republican second secretary, and within three months the Central Committee had published a decision entitled "About Serious Deficiencies in the Work of the Kharkov Regional Party Organization in Party Admission and the Training of Young Communists."[39] The party leadership quite commonly makes a general point or a policy change in the guise of an investigation and decision about the work of one organization or institution, and the Kharkov decision clearly was directed at the overall party admission policy rather than at defects peculiar to that region. However, the choice of this particular organization to criticize was scarcely accidental, and the political import of the choice was very clear. In December 1965, Podgorny himself was moved from his critical slot in the Central Committee Secretariat into the Chairmanship of the Presidium of the Supreme Soviet (replacing Mikoian, who was retired), and in March 1966 his former subordinate was removed as second secretary in the Ukraine. Podgorny and his Kharkov associates all remained in high positions and continued to be members of the party Central Committee, but they were removed from control over personnel selection.

The next potential contender for power to suffer major political reverses was Shelepin. Throughout 1965, his position had been a strange one. On the one hand, he was given considerable prominence in the press, in large part because he was handling a number of foreign policy assignments; on the other hand, there were few indications of his active personal involvement in domestic affairs as Chairman of the Party-State Control Committee. Perhaps his foreign policy responsibilities—which were in no way naturally associated with his formal post—were a central factor in generating the rumors that he was destined for higher office. In fact, it is just as likely that they were a way of diverting his time and efforts away from the political struggle as home. (Of course, his earlier work as KGB head had given him foreign policy expertise, for that institution carries on functions similar to those of the U.S. Central Intelligence Agency as well as internal security ones.) In any case, the Party-State Control Committee was abolished at the December 1965 Central Committee session that removed Podgorny from the Secretariat (it was replaced by a People's Control Committee), and Shelepin lost his post as Deputy Chairman of the Council of Ministers in the process. He remained a secretary of the Central Committee, but now his duties seemed to center on light industry and trade questions—hardly an area of central importance in building a power base.

In July 1967, Shelepin was removed from the Central Committee Secretariat altogether, becoming Chairman of the All-Union Central Trade Union Council—a post even less suggestive of a bright political future. Moreover, a number of men presumed to be closely connected with him suffered major demotion. In September 1966 the top official in the regular police—a man linked with Shelepin both in the Komsomol and the KGB— was replaced by a man just as obviously linked with Brezhnev; in 1967 a former associate in the Komsomol was removed as Director of TASS; in June 1967 the Chairman of the KGB, Semichastny, was removed and directed to a high administrative post in the Ukraine; in July 1967 the first secretary of the Moscow city party committee lost his post after—so the Moscow rumor network persistently reported[40]—attacking Brezhnev's Middle East policy at a Central Committee session; in June 1968 the first secretary of the Komsomol was replaced and several months later was appointed to a quite minor post— Chairman of the State Committee for Physical Culture and Sports; in 1970, two former colleagues of Shelepin in the Komsomol Central Committee were removed from their posts as Chairman of the Television and Radio Committee and Chairman of the State Committee for Publishing.[41]

At the same time that Podgorny's and Shelepin's political position seemed to be weakening, Brezhnev's seemed to become stronger, as former close associates and subordinates from Dnepropetrovsk and Moldavia were moved into key political posts. The Director of the Moldavian Higher Party School under Brezhnev in the early 1950s became head of the important science and education department of the Central Committee, while the head of the Moldavian propaganda-agitation department at that time (and the head of the Secretariat of the Presidium of the Supreme Soviet when Brezhnev was Chairman) became head of the sensitive general department, the department that distributes communications to the Central Committee among the various officials and departments and that handles internal security within the Secretariat.[42] A college classmate of Brezhnev in Dneprodzerzhinsk in the 1930s was named head of the Central Committee Business Office (*Upravliaiushchii delami*), the unit that expends the party's money.[43]

In 1966 Brezhnev seems to have made another major advance when his old second secretary in Zaporozhe (and his successor in Dnepropetrovsk), Kirilenko, assumed the responsibilities of general supervision of personnel selection and of the urban economy that Podgorny had relinquished when he was transferred to the Presidium of the Supreme Soviet. Other critical posts were soon filled by other former officials from Dnepropetrovsk and Moldavia. N. A. Shchelokov, a Brezhnev subordinate *both* in Dnepropetrovsk in the late 1930s and in Moldavia in the early 1950s, became the USSR Minister for the Preservation of Public Order (later renamed Internal Affairs)—the head of the regular police—when that institution was established at the national level in September 1966. Three former Dnepropetrovsk and Moldavia officials became deputy chairmen of the KGB between 1967 and 1970 and were still serving together in that organization in the mid-1970s.[44] A steel plant manager in Dnepropetrovsk under Brezhnev, N. A. Tikhonov, was named Deputy Chairman of the Council of Ministers in 1965 and was promoted to First Deputy Chairman in the summer of 1976. Two other Deputy Chairmen were I. T. Novikov, the top construction administrator in the country, who was a graduate of Brezhnev's Dneprodzerzhinsk Metallurgy Institute,[45] and V. E. Dymshits, the Chairman of the Supply Committee and later director of the energy program, who had been the head of the major construction administration in Zaporozhe when Brezhnev was first secretary. In 1974, still another former Dnepropetrovsk official from the late 1930s, I. V. Arkhipov, became Deputy Chairman of the Council of Ministers, the Deputy Chairman in charge of foreign economic affairs. In addition, V. V. Shcherbitsky, the chairman of the Ukrainian Council of Ministers (and in 1972 the Ukrainian party first secretary) came from Dnepropetrovsk, as did (at least after 1971) a first deputy chairman of the Council of Ministers of the RSFSR and ambassadors to two of the most sensitive posts in the Communist world, Rumania and Cuba.[46]

Over the years the various status symbols suggesting political predominance in the Soviet Union indicated that Brezhnev's strength continued to rise. His name had always come first in lists of Politburo members, for those lists were arranged in alphabetical order and Brezhnev was first within the Politburo by this criterion. However, when Iu. V. Andropov was elected a full Politburo member in 1973, Brezhnev still was listed first, clearly placing himself outside of the alphabetical order. His picture and name appeared prominently in speeches, in scholarly books, on billboards. In some of the major diplomatic moves of the 1970s—for example, a number of the meetings with Henry Kissinger, Willie Brandt, Presidents Richard Nixon and Gerald Ford, and the world leaders at the Helsinki Conference—he alone represented the nation, even when the presence of the head of state (Podgorny) and the head of government (Kosygin) would have seemed imperative for reasons of protocol.

By 1976 Brezhnev was hailed as "a tireless champion of peace and real social justice," an "outstanding fighter for peace and communism," and Central Committee members proclaimed that "all accomplishments—both inside the country and in the international arena—are indissolubly linked with his name."[47] At the Twenty-Fifth Party Congress, one Politburo member (Shcherbitsky) referred to him as the "universally accepted leader [obshche-priznannyi lider] of our party," while a candidate member of the Politburo (Rashidov) called him "the most (samyi) outstanding and most (samyi) influential political figure of contemporary times."[48] Enormous emphasis was placed upon Brezhnev's personal qualities, in particular, upon his "deep humanity, considerateness, and attentiveness to people." As the first secretary of the Lithuanian Central Committee phrased it, Brezhnev is "a man with a great soul in whom is embodied all the best qualities of Man in capital letters."[49]

After the Twenty-Fifth Congress, Brezhnev was given the top military rank, Marshal, and his position as Chairman of the Defense Council was publicly acknowledged for the first time. His seventieth birthday was marked by an outpouring of press articles far greater than Khrushchev received on his seventieth birthday. Then in the summer of 1977 the General Secretary was also named Chairman of the Presidium of the Supreme Soviet, making him head-of-state as well as party leader. The press of the spring of 1978 featured stories about ideological conferences called to organize the study of his memoirs.

Yet, if Brezhnev did become the dominant political figure in the Soviet Union after Khrushchev's fall—and there are no concrete indications that he did not—his consolidation of power was strikingly different from that of Stalin or Khrushchev. In the past, the power of the party leader had seemed to rest in considerable part upon his control of the lower party apparatus and the "circular flow of power" associated with it. If the regional party secretaries were part of the General Secretary's machine and they controlled the selection of delegates to the party congress, then the General Secretary was in a position to control the delegates and the Congress; if the regional party secretaries constituted a large part of the Central Committee membership and the General Secretary had the power to remove them, their ability to challenge him in the Central Committee sessions would seem to be very limited.

The "circular flow of power" theory was never meant to deny the multiple sources of a party leader's support nor to suggest the impossibility of Central Committee members expressing disagreement with the leader (so long as they did not do so in a challenging way) nor even the impossibility of a total collapse of his support. The theory would suggest that the real problem is that of "belling the cat"—of organizing an attack on the party leader—for he presumably he would be in a position to deal with defectors before they gained majority support. However, if someone dared to call an actual vote in the Central Committee, then each member would be on his own. If not bound by considerations of loyalty, each member should be guided by self-interest, which essentially should be a judgment on how he would be likely to fare in each contingent outcome and on how likely each outcome is.

Nevertheless, the circular flow of power theory did hold that the ability to change regional party secretaries was a key element in the General Secretary's power. It corresponded with the fact that both Stalin and Khrushchev did engineer the replacement of many regional first secretaries soon after the death of their respective predecessors and that the new regional secretaries were strong supporters in the party congresses and the Central Committee as each party leader moved against his respective rivals.

In this respect the post-Khrushchev period had a very different appearance. Instead of leading a purge of the local party secretaries, Brezhnev pledged a policy of "respect for personnel," and the new first secretaries selected when the party apparatus was reunited turned out overwhelmingly to be the pre-1962 secretaries. Over 70 percent of the regional (obkom) first secretaries on the 1966 Central Committee and Auditing Commission were already at that level of the hierarchy in the fall of 1961, and another 15 percent of them had become regional first secretaries by the summer of 1963. (Less than one-third of the regional first secretaries named to the central party bodies in 1961 had reached that level at the time of the Twentieth Party Congress in 1956.) Similarly, ten of the fourteen republican first secretaries in 1966 had occupied the same post in 1961, and three of those replaced had been promoted to central posts conferring full Politburo membership (and, presumably, therefore, still had very considerable influence in their old republic).[50] These regional and republican secretaries, it should be noted, had largely been selected in 1961 when Kozlov—allegedly Brezhnev's enemy— was the dominant figure in personnel selection and when Brezhnev's position was thought by some scholars to have been weak.

The low turnover among the provincial party secretaries in the first years after Khrushchev's removal was reflected in great continuity in the membership of the Central Committee elected at the Twenty-Third Party Congress in 1966. Of the full members of the 1961 Central Committee still living at that time, 83 percent were re-elected in 1966, and the percentage would be higher if Khrushchev and a few officials very closely associated with him are excluded. By contrast, less than 50 percent of the still living full members of the 1956 Central Committee had been re-elected to the Central Committee in 1961.

As time passed, more of the old secretaries were removed, died, or—most frequently of all—were promoted, and, as a consequence, the number of regional first secretaries selected after Brezhnev became General Secretary rose steadily. (By the tenth anniversary of Brezhnev's accession, 69 percent of the first secretaries in the RSFSR and the Ukraine were in this category.) At the same time, the size of the voting membership of the Central Committee was also increased substantially, going from 175 in 1961 to 195 in 1966 to 241 in 1971 to 287 in 1976. This expansion of the Central Committee, coupled with removals and deaths among the old members, meant that the proportion of the Central Committee members who had been named to that body since Khrushchev's last party congress in 1961 rose to 55 percent in 1971 and 72 percent in 1976.

Yet, once a person was named a full member, the likelihood of his being demoted to a post that would result in a loss of Central Committee membership still turned out to be quite small. Eighty-one percent of the living full members of the 1966 Central Committee were re-elected in 1971, and an incredible 89 percent of the living full members of the 1971 Central Committee were re-elected in 1976. Each of these percentages would be a point higher if worker-peasant members were excluded from the calculation (the turnover was greater among this group), and, of course, a number of the "removals" are better viewed as natural retirements due to age and health. Of the twenty-two governmental and party officials who were members of the 1971 Central Committee and not re-elected in 1976 (again, it should be emphasized, a most remarkable five-year figure for a group of 216 persons who averaged sixty-two years of age in 1976), 46 percent were 65 years of age or older in the year they lost their Central Committee seat, and another 23 percent were between sixty and sixty-four.

At least until the mid-1970s, there likewise was little evidence that a Politburo member faced much more danger of removal than a member of the Central Committee. To be sure, as was the case with the Central Committee, the ruling Politburo had been expanded in size, for the voting membership had been increased from eleven to fifteen in 1971 with the promotion of three candidate members (V. V. Grishin, D. A. Kunaev, and V. V. Shcherbitsky) and the election of a new member (F. D. Kulakov, the Central Committee secretary for agriculture). However, after the retirement of two holdovers from the Politburo of the 1930s, Mikoian and Shvernik, no one was removed from the Politburo until 1973—nine years after Brezhnev's accession.

To the extent that a General Secretary's power rests on his ability to remove a Central Committee or Politburo member who challenges him, Brezhnev either did not have this power, did not have the need to use it (perhaps because of the object lesson of a few cases such as Egorychev), or did not choose to use it. The question—which we really cannot answer definitively—is the degree to which these different possible answers are accurate.

Probably the most likely explanation for the contradiction between the indicators of Brezhnev's increasing status and his control over personnel selection and the police, on the one hand, and his failure to conduct any significant shakeup of the Politburo or Central Committee during his first decade in office, on the other, is that 1964 brought a "normalization" in the personality of the General Secretary selected as well as in the policies pursued.

Westerners have tended to attribute to Soviet politicians a drive for absolute power—absolute power not only in the sense of total security of their own position but also in an ability to carry out any policy to transform society, whatever the cost. And, surely, the Bolshevik tradition has, in fact, featured great activism and great ruthlessness in pursuing policy goals. Nevertheless, as Khrushchev's fate graphically demonstrated, a ruler's desire for a total ability to carry out any policy can come into conflict with his desire for complete security in his political position.

What is unclear upon reflection is why a party leader would normally be motivated to incur significant personal risk in order to attempt a ruthless and unpopular policy of societal transformation. The type of person who joins a revolutionary movement before it is firmly in power might well be expected to take—or to be oblivious to—such risks, but these risks seem a highly unlikely choice for a person who has risen through the Establishment, occupying a series of bureaucratic positions where success is determined by the ability to balance interests and/or to represent interests in committee politics.

It may well be that the Brezhnev era would be best understood if we ascribed to the General Secretary the type of motivations that we attribute to most politicians in the West. We take for granted that very few leaders seek to alter the political system in a fundamental way—except, perhaps, in response to some major crisis. We often assume that their highest "policy goal" is to be re-elected and that they frequently immerse themselves in foreign relations in order to avoid the conflicts of the domestic sphere where any decision must offend someone. Particularly since Khrushchev's fate served as a fresh reminder both that a General Secretary is secure only so long as the Central Committee will support him against challenge and that the price of defeat can be high, Brezhnev would have been a fool not to be concerned about considerations of personal security.

If Brezhnev's actions and policies are examined in the light of the hypothetical requirements of "electoral" politics vis-à-vis the Central Committee, it is striking how many can be explained in those terms. By guaranteeing Central Committee members a high probability of job security, he gave them a good reason to wonder whether a change of leadership would be in their own personal interest. By expanding the size of the voting membership of the Central Committee 64 percent, he afforded himself the opportunity to create a group within that body who were beholden to him for their promotions. By allowing the specialized state-party-scientific complexes some autonomy in deciding policy questions within their fields of competency and by giving nearly all the complexes a budgetary increase each year, he must have avoided much of the anger that Khrushchev's "voluntarist" and "subjective" interventions clearly provoked.

Perhaps from this perspective, we should think of a very secure consolidation of power by Brezhnev, but one in which he deliberately avoided the type of dominant control of events and society enjoyed by his predecessors. By October 1977, he had held his position for thirteen years—an extremely long tenure by any comparative standards—and nothing in the pattern of policy over that thirteen years would suggest that his basic policy line was challenged and defeated during his period of leadership. It goes without saying, however, that nothing in the world is unchanging. A man of seventy-one in 1977 was not the same as a man of fifty-eight in 1964. His energies, the quality of his arteries (and maybe his judgment), the hopes he represents, the hopes he has frustrated, the quality and energy of his administrative subordinates (especially if they have been aging with him)—all of these can undergo gradual, but drastic change over a thirteen-year period.

The Thrust of Policy

Of course, no political leader can be analyzed solely in terms of a desire to be personally secure in his political position. At a minimum, a leader has to judge which set of policies will maximize his support, and, beyond this, a leader always has other values which to a certain extent have an inevitable impact upon policy, independent of power considerations.

Westerners attempting to summarize the policy thrust of the Brezhnev regime generally have used terms such as "conservative," "ossified," "immobilized," and even "neo-Stalinist," but these characterizations are confusing at best. Words such as "conservative" have many meanings, and if definite standards of comparisons are not specified (and they usually are not in these discussions), writers and readers slip from one meaning to another in their thinking, and quite erroneous assumptions can arise. Such has happened in our understanding of the Brezhnev period.

Certainly it is completely accurate to say that Brezhnev—like Khrushchev before him—was always basically conservative in response to any pressure for fundamental transformation of the one-party system, the socialist command economy, the principle of censorship, and so forth. His response to Alexander Dubchek in Czechoslovakia in 1968 ultimately was much the same as Khrushchev's to Imre Nagy in Hungary in 1956. While he seemed hesitant to institute a drastic intervention in Czechoslovakia—just as he seemed to try to avoid drastic repression of a dissident at home—he was willing, if necessary, to use force to back up his distaste for frontal challenges to party rule.

Similarly, it also is quite accurate to say that Brezhnev and his associates were much more conservative than Khrushchev in their style and rhetoric. They tried in their speeches and actions to convey an image not of flamboyance and permanent revolution, but of sobriety, of sound judgment, of—in their phrase—a scientific approach to decision-making. They were also much more conservative in the way they tackled problems. Policy implementation was no longer featured by a succession of wild campaigns, and the governmental and party machinery were no longer subjected to drastic reorganization almost annually, And, finally, of course, a practice of deferring to specialized elites and of introducing reforms in an incremental way (already discussed as a key element in the return to normalcy) is scarcely likely to be linked with radical policy innovation.

The question, however, is not whether the Brezhnev leadership was radical in its policies, let alone whether it was eager to preside over the dismantlement of the Soviet system. By these tests, virtually all presidential and congressional action in the United States fits in the conservative category, as does that of almost every western government whose country is not in a state of major crisis. If the vast majority of the governments in the industrialized world limit themselves to "the politics of pragmatism . . . to gradual change whether in the direction favored by the left or the right,"[51] the question is whether the movement was to the left or the right in this framework.

If we define "left" or "liberal" as these terms are generally used in American political discourse—as espousal of more egalitarian social welfare policies and of greater individual freedom in the Bill-of-Rights areas—then it seems unquestionably true that, on balance, the trend of policy from the Khrushchev period to the Brezhnev period was actually in a liberal direction rather than a conservative one. In these realms, policy generally represented a further development of trends that began under Khrushchev, but the critical fact is that the trends did continue and that the distribution of income in the late 1970s was more egalitarian than it had been in the mid-1960s and the degree of individual freedom was greater. If we define "liberal" as promoting (or acquiescing in) a diffusion of power, then in some respects the liberalization in the Brezhnev period broke new ground rather than simply involving a continuation of earlier trends.

The liberal direction of policy in the Brezhnev years is most easily documented in the case of social policy. The ratio of the average earnings of the top 10 percent of Soviet workers and employees to the average earnings of the bottom 10 percent declined from 4.4 in 1956 to 3.7 in 1964 to 3.2 in 1970, and a ratio of 2.9 was planned for 1975.[52] (Peter Wiles has calculated an after-tax ratio of 6.7 for the United States in 1968, but the Soviet figure excludes collective farmers.)[53] If the earnings of collective farmers were included in the calculation, the ratios would be higher, but the rate of decline in them would be greater. The same thing would be true if pensioners were included. While the average wages of all workers and employees (collective farmers excluded) increased 57 percent from 1965 to 1976, the total sum expended for pensions rose 143 percent, partly reflecting the inclusion of collective farmers for the first time and partly reflecting the rise in the size of the average pension. (Even with lower pensions given the collective farmer, the size of the average pension rose 57 percent.)[54]

The available wage statistics indicate that the workers did particularly well in the Brezhnev era. From 1965 to 1976, the average wages of the employees of the state and "public" apparatuses rose 25 percent, those of engineering-technical personnel in industry 39 percent, and those of agricultural specialists on state farms 32 percent. By contrast, the wages of industrial workers were up 65 percent and those of construction workers 71 percent.[55]

It was, however, the agricultural sector—long the poorest—that received the lion's share of Brezhnev's war on poverty. Investment in agricultural production, which constituted 14 to 15 percent of total capital investment under Khrushchev, increased steadily under Brezhnev, reaching 20.6 percent by 1974.[56] The rural electrification program was carried through to completion—the proportion of farm homes receiving electricity rising from 74 percent in 1965 to 98 percent in 1971 and 99 percent in 1973. (The total amount of electricity used in agriculture rose four times from 1965 to 1976).[57] The wages of the state farm peasants rose 84 percent—significantly above the rate of increase for the industrial and construction workers—while the earnings of collective farmers rose over 86 percent.[58] Moreover, early in the Brezhnev period, collective farmers were brought under a guaranteed income system and made eligible for state pensions, both for the first time. Agricultural production, on the average, was up substantially.

The liberalization in the political realm after 1964 is not as easy to document and, in fact, a number of western observers would assert that no such development has occurred. However, the pattern of policy outcomes has corresponded closely to that which the various specialized state-party-scientific complexes would prefer, and it is clear that a considerable degree of de facto delegation or diffusion of power to these complexes has taken place. Instead of acting as if they had total knowledge, the leadership has behaved as if they had much to learn, and they have dealt with many policy problems by conducting experiments in individual regions or cities or by introducing them in a piecemeal, incremental manner in an attempt to judge their impact. In this respect at least, the new regime is far indeed from any Stalinist—or even Khrushchevian—inclination toward a concentration of all decision-making in its own hands or prevention of an autonomous development of policy along lines suggested by the specialized elites.

More important for the present argument, the increased deference to specialist perspectives was accompanied by a greater willingness—even eagerness—to have these perspectives formed on the basis of a wide discussion of the policy alternatives. The statistics on political participation rose sharply in the Brezhnev years (as they had under Khrushchev), and the published debates, especially those published in the specialized journals and books, became considerably richer than they had been prior to 1964.

In the process of widening the policy debate, the leadership also pushed back the limits of permissible dissent somewhat. It began to move against open dissenters in a more gingerly and patient manner, often even tolerating the transmission of dissident documents to western correspondents for a matter of months or years before the offender was brought to court. The fact that open dissent was punished in a less summary fashion meant that it became more visible to the West, and, paradoxically, the impression was thereby created that the Brezhnev regime was more repressive than its predecessor, but it was an impression that could be sustained only by a nostalgic misremembering of the Khrushchev years.

In other respects too the new leadership seemed less committed to interference in the private lives of the Soviet citizenry, less committed to the transformation of human nature, more tolerant of individual diversity and freedom. The resurgent antireligion campaign of Khrushchev gave way to a less assertive hostility. The collective farmers, who alone among Soviet citizens had not been given the internal passports necessary for movement in the Soviet Union (a policy that sought to stem the flow of people from the country to the city), now were given an unconditional right to such passports and, therefore, a right to leave the farm.[59] A new divorce law made the dissolution of marriage easier, and the meaningfulness of the reform is indicated by an immediate jump in the divorce rate from a level of 1.3 to 1.6 per thousand population in the late Khrushchev period to a 2.6 to 2.8 level after the decree.[60] In the literary realm, restrictions on novels about slave labor camps and other sensitive subjects remained in force, but those on the publication of light entertainment—for example detective stories, science fiction, and love stories —continued to be gradually relaxed. (Novels about the countryside, often quite frank, came into particular vogue.)

These various statements are, of course, comparative ones, and relate primarily to the direction of trends in policy. Clearly the relationship between the government and the individual remains much more authoritarian than in western parliamentary democracies. Censorship scarcely has withered away, and certain types of dissent do carry with them a very serious risk of prison, especially if persisted in. The diffusion of power is limited by everyone's awareness that the top officials retain quite adequate weapons to deal with subordinates who attempt to use delegated authority "unwisely." Similarly, in social policy, the improvement in living conditions still is limited by the continuing high rates of heavy industry investment and military expenditure, and the egalitarianism has not reached the point promised in the utopian Marxist ideology.

Yet, if the question is the thrust of policy and if the standard of judgment is the performance of political leaders of other industrial countries, there is no question about the direction of social policy. If the Communist regime remained far less tolerant of iconoclasts than the constitutional political systems of the West, this should not obscure the fact that evolution occurred in this sphere and that the direction of that evolution in the Brezhnev period was basically a liberal one, even if of a cautious moderate, and perhaps impermanent character.

The Aging Leadership

Almost immediately after the overthrow of Khrushchev, many western observers began talking of immobilism, of ossification, of petrification in the Soviet political system. The new regime was described as a "government of clerks"—a government which, except perhaps for increased vigor in suppressing dissidence, was marked by "caution and conservatism . . . a dull bureaucratic routine."[61] Analysts soon began emphasizing the advancing age of the ruling group, suggesting for example, that the Soviet leadership was the oldest in the world except for the Chinese.[62]

This line of analysis obviously did catch the change in tone that occurred in the transition from the Khrushchev to the Brezhnev regime, but, in retrospect, it seems a misleading characterization of the developments that occurred in the late 1960s and early 1970s. In the first place, as late as 1971, an attempt to compare a number of groups of Soviet officials with analogous groups in the United States—that is, the party Politburo with a hypothetical American Politburo, the industrial ministers with the chief operating officers of the top one hundred American corporations, the regional party first secretaries with the state governors, the first secretary of the city party committees in the republican capitals with the mayors of the twenty-five largest American cities—found that the average ages in each comparable group were almost identical.[63] In the second place, while terms such as "ossification" are so vague that one can never really prove or disprove their presence, the Brezhnev regime at least met the minimum test of survival for a considerable number of years. Moreover, major industrial and agricultural growth was achieved (more rapid than in the United States, for example), and the various policies which were adopted did seem responsive to the interests and wishes of major groups within society—and in some cases to mass interests.

As time passed, however, certain substantial changes began to take place in the top leadership. The ten-man party Presidium that was left in power after the removal of Khrushchev averaged sixty years of age (with Khrushchev still a member, it had averaged sixty-one years), and the changes in membership introduced in the first year and a half dropped the average age to slightly below fifty-eight years. The four men added to the Politburo in 1971 (V. V. Grishin, F. D. Kulakov, D. A. Kunaev, and V. V. Shcherbitsky) also were very similar in background to other cooptations into the ruling body over the previous fifteen years, and seemed to represent normal rejuvenation. Born between 1912 and 1918 (and, therefore, between fifty-three and fifty-nine years of age in 1971), all had begun their careers in economic work and had sooner or later moved into the party apparatus. All had the experience of serving as a regional or republican first secretary.

After 1971 the pattern of appointments seemed to change. In 1973, at the time of rapprochement with West Germany and the development of fuller detente with the United States, the top three governmental officials in the foreign policy realm were elected to Politburo membership: Andrei Gromyko, the Minister of Foreign Affairs (aged sixty-four in that year), Marshal Andrei Grechko, the Minister of Defense (aged seventy), and Iurii Andropov, the Chairman of the KGB (aged fifty-nine). Then in 1976 the Central Committee secretary for defense, the defense industry, and the police, Dmitrii Ustinov (aged sixty-eight), was promoted from candidate membership to full membership. (When Marshall Grechko died in 1976, Ustinov became Minister of Defense.) The only reasonably young addition to the Politburo during this period was Grigorii Romanov, a man of fifty-three who had risen in the shipbuilding industry in Leningrad and then moved into party work in that city, becoming first secretary of the regional party committee in 1970. He became candidate member of the Politburo in 1973 and a full member in 1976. Other candidate members of Politburo elected after 1971 were sixty-seven years of age (B. N. Ponomarev, Central Committee secretary, in 1972), forty-three years old (G. A. Aliev, first secretary of the Azerbaidzhan Central Committee, in 1976), sixty-six years old (K. U. Chernenko, Central Committee secretary, in 1977), and seventy-six years old (V. V. Kuznetsov, First Deputy Chairman of the Presidium of the Supreme Soviet, in 1977). Of the nine new members and candidate members, only Romanov and Aliev had been a republican or regional first secretary, and Aliev was a career KGB officer recently transferred to party work.

Table 9 *Members of the Politburo, January 1978*

Member	Year of Birth	Year of Party Entry	Position
L. I. Brezhnev	1906	1931	General Secretary of the Central Committee and Chairman of the Presidium of the Supreme Soviet
Iu. V. Andropov	1914	1939	Chairman of the KGB
V. V. Grishin	1914	1939	First secretary of the Moscow city party committee
A. A. Gromyko	1909	1931	Minister of Foreign Affairs
A. P. Kirilenko	1906	1931	Secretary of the Central Committee
A. N. Kosygin	1904	1927	Chairman of the Council of Ministers
F. D. Kulakov*	1918	1940	Secretary of the Central Committee
D. A. Kunaev	1912	1939	First secretary of the Kazakhstan Central Committee
K. T. Mazurov	1914	1940	First Deputy Chairman of the Council of Ministers
A. Ia. Pel'she	1899	1915	Chairman of the Party Control Committee
G. V. Romanov	1923	1944	First secretary of the Leningrad party committee
V. V. Shcherbitsky	1918	1941	First secretary of the Ukrainian party committee
M. A. Suslov	1902	1921	Secretary of the Central Committee
D. F. Ustinov	1908	1927	Minister of Defense
AVERAGE	1911	1933	

* Died in July 1978.

Table 9—Continued

Member	Year of Birth	Year of Party Entry	Position
Candidate members			
G. A. Aliev	1923	1945	First secretary of the Azerbaidzhan party committee
K. U. Chernenko	1911	1931	Secretary of the Central Committee
P. N. Demichev	1918	1939	Minister of Culture
V. V. Kuznetsov	1901	1927	First Deputy Chairman of the Presidium of Supreme Soviet
P. M. Masherov	1918	1943	First secretary of the Belorussian party committee
B. N. Ponomarev	1905	1919	Secretary of the Central Committee
Sh. R. Rashidov	1917	1939	First secretary of the Uzbekistan party committee
M. S. Solomentsev	1913	1940	Chairman of the RSFSR Council of Ministers

Source: 1976 Yearbook, *Bol'shaia sovetskaia entsiklopdeiia*, p. 20; *Pravda*, October 4, 1977, p. 1.

The same pattern of older appointments is often found in additions to the Central Committee Secretariat and especially to the inner core of the Council of Ministers—the deputy chairmen. The new Central Committee secretary for industry selected in 1972 was but forty-eight and the replacement for Ustinov as secretary for the police and the military in 1976 was the same age, but the two other 1976 additions to the Secretariat were sixty-two and sixty-five respectively.[65] The Deputy Chairman of the Council of Ministers appointed in 1973 was fifty-eight years of age, but the Deputy Chairman appointed in 1974 was sixty-seven and the one appointed in 1976 was sixty-six. The Deputy Chairman who was promoted to First Deputy Chairman in 1976 was seventy-one.[65]

At the time that the top appointments in the Soviet political system suddenly began to be made from among men at or past the normal retirement age, a number of the original Politburo members began to be removed, but some of the younger members were affected rather than the oldest ones: Shelest (aged sixty-five) and Voronov (aged sixty-three) in 1973, Shelepin (aged fifty-seven) in 1975, and Poliansky (aged fifty-nine) in 1976. The inner five-man core, who averaged seventy-two years of age in 1976, were all re-elected at the Twenty-Fifth Party Congress in 1976, as was Pelshe (aged seventy-seven).

As a result of the personnel changes—and the lack of personnel changes —in the mid-1970s, the top political leadership two years after the Twenty-Fifth Congress in 1978 had quite a different appearance than it had had in 1966. The most obvious difference was one of age. The inner core of four had, of course, become twelve years older because no change among them had occurred, and the difference between sixty-two years of age and seventy-four is quite substantial. The average age of all the voting members of the Polit-buro rose from fifty-eight to sixty-eight between 1966 and July 1978, of the candidate members of the Politburo from fifty-three to sixty-five, of the voting members of the Central Committee from fifty-six to sixty-one, of the secre-taries of the Central Committee from fifty-five to sixty-five, of the deputy chairmen of the USSR Council of Ministers from fifty-five to sixty-six, of the ministers and state committee chairmen on the Council of Ministers from fifty-eight to sixty-four, and of heads of Central Committee departments from fifty-three to sixty-two.[66]

With the top party and governmental leadership beginning to reach a rather advanced age by any comparative standards, Soviet policy also began to show some signs of real sluggishness. The replacement of the bureaucratic main administrations (glavki) of the industrial ministries by groupings of enterprises called "associations" (ob"edineniia) went much slower than earlier decisions indicated it would, and the new constitution was not introduced until 1977, over a dozen years after first promised. In addition, a number of high level personnel vacancies were filled with incredible slowness. The presi-dency of the Academy of Sciences remained open for six months (and then simply was filled by one of the few academicians on the Central Committee, a man over seventy),[67] the chairmenship of the People's Control Committee and the State Committee for Prices went unfilled for thirteen months, the post of ideological secretary of the Party Central Committee for fifteen months, the chairmanship of the all-Union Trade Union Council for eighteen months, and the chairmanship of the State Committee for Labor and Wages for twenty-three months.

Indeed, one might even make the case that some of the early decisions to change budgetary priorities were allowed to continue in effect for too long, producing in an annual step-by-step process an overall impact that approached the point of irrationality. By 1976, the total investment in agriculture (including supportive industries such as tractor and fertilizer) reached 10 percent of expected national income,[68] while the steady increase in the real defense budget brought expenditures to levels that threatened to produce American defense budget responses that would be counterproductive from the Soviet point of view.[69] The number of hospital beds per capita in the Soviet Union continued its seemingly inexorable rise, the levels coming to exceed western norms by a substantial amount in the face of warnings by Soviet health economists that hospitals were falsifying reports on number of visits and were perhaps acceding to the temptation to keep the beds filled to meet their plan.[70] And these budgetary increases were coming at a time when there were signs of severe pressures on the possibility of maintaining former rates of increase in living standards. Moreover, in the realm of social policy itself, it is conceivable that the disproportionate increases in wages given to workers for such a long period may have produced a ratio of worker/white collar wages that was not optimal for economic growth.

Clearly something seems to have happened within the post-Khrushchev leadership as it was ending the first decade of its rule, and the question is the nature of that change. While many possibilities suggest themselves, the most likely answer is the one that comes first to mind—an aging leader who begins to lose some of the vigor that featured the early years of his administration, who is most comfortable with men of his own generation, and who perhaps fears that younger subordinates in key positions might deal with him as he dealt with his predecessor. The relationship of the General Secretary to the Politburo and the Central Committee will be discussed at considerable length in Chapter 12, but any attempt to explain the changes by a hypothetical stalemate in the Politburo must deal with the fact that the various indicators of a General Secretary's political strength registered a steady and significant increase during this period.

Perhaps an additional explanation for the sluggishness in the Soviet political system in the mid-1970s is a sharp rise in the amount of time Brezhnev devoted to relations with non-Communist countries after 1970. In the first years after the removal of Khrushchev, Brezhnev had a great deal of contact with Communist leaders of the Communist and non-Communist world, but almost none with non-Communist leaders. At late as 1969, he had officially announced meetings with foreigners on ninety-two days, but on only nine of these days was the contact with non-Communists (even counting representatives of leftist Third World regimes, such as Egyptians, Syrians, Algerians, and so forth, as non-Communists). However, the proportion of Brezhnev's foreign contacts devoted to non-Communists rose to 26 percent of the total in 1970, 30 percent in 1971, 43 percent in 1972, 60 percent in 1973 (out of 109 days of contact), and 57 percent in 1974 (out of 100 days contact).[71] These figures declined in later years as Brezhnev's health became worse, but so did his energy for domestic policy.

If one assumes a five-day work week and a month's vacation a year—quite substantial activity for a man in his late sixties—then 100 days constitutes 41 percent of the available work time in a year, and this figure does not include time spent on foreign policy briefings or decision-making with colleagues and subordinates. Some contacts can be sufficiently brief to permit time for a full workday on other subjects, but Brezhnev tended to engage in very long discussions with many of his visitors. It may well be that he, like many American presidents, became fascinated with the conduct of foreign affairs, finding that in that realm a leader usually has more autonomy, less need to antagonize powerful domestic interests (at least if he is careful in his handling of the military), and—by no means least—an opportunity to meet and negotiate with the great of the world. In a one-party, socialist system of the Soviet type, however, the political leadership must make or ratify a far wider range of decisions than in a different type of system, and if a leader becomes absorbed in foreign policy and is unwilling to turn over most of decision-making to younger subordinates, the danger of drift becomes quite real.

By early 1978, however, a major dilemma was becoming clear. There comes a point when the fear to select younger subordinates for the key power positions can produce difficulties and frustrations that increase the likelihood of the very dangers the leader is trying to avoid. Moreover, the older the group of key subordinates who remain when a leader eventually does leave the scene (by whatever means), the greater the political problem which will exist. In particular, the problem of controlling a successor who has every reason to "renew cadres" is a serious one. Brezhnev came to power promising normalcy, and it was a pledge that he kept. The crucial question is whether the steps he took in the mid-1970s will seriously undermine normalcy as the Soviet Union enters a new decade.

The Policy Process

8 | The Individual and the Policy Process

Analyses of western political systems often begin with a discussion of the "input" of proposals and demands from the population and of the institutions (pressure groups and parties) which are seen as the transmission belts or channels for this input. Such, however, has not been the tradition in analyses of the Soviet political system. One reason has been the total absence of competing political parties and autonomous interest group associations, but another has been the widespread assumption that policy initiation in the Soviet Union, particularly in the past, came not from below, but from above—indeed, from the highest levels of the government and the party apparatus.

Yet, one of the great paradoxes of the systems we have called "totalitarian" has been their strong emphasis upon mass participation as well as upon tight central control. The traditional authoritarian dictatorship asked no more from its citizens than political passivity and acquiescence, but the leaders of the Communist party have demanded more. Even under Stalin, they strove for "the total and active involvement of all citizens in the affairs of a rapidly changing and ever more complex society,"[1] and in broad comparative terms the Soviet Union has, in fact, been a "modern participatory state."[2]

In discussing the political process, one of the best-known American theorists, David Easton, defined "demands" (which together with "supports" comprise his definition of "inputs") simply as "an expression of opinion that an authoritative allocation with regard to a particular subject matter should or should not be made by those responsible for doing so." He even included "broad pleas for better government" made to "a fellow-worker between bites of a sandwich on the end of an I-beam" as such input.[3] Gabriel Almond defined "interest articulation" as "the process by which individuals and groups make demands upon the political decision makers."[4]

By Easton's and Almond's definitions, political participation in the Soviet Union clearly has involved "interest articulation" and "the input of demands." To be sure, Soviet citizens have not been able to speak out or participate meaningfully on some questions, but this inability does not necessarily mean an inability to speak out or participate on all questions. Even under Stalin, citizens were strongly encouraged to criticize administrative agencies and to call for change in their action. Even under Stalin, scholars and other professionals advanced major proposals for policy change, and since then this form of participation has broadened into widespread published debate.

It may be argued that this public participation has had little impact upon the Soviet policy process. Western scholars often have contended that " 'popular participation' in the Soviet Union is vastly different than in democratic countries, and indeed in many respects a total inversion."[5] They often maintain that "the democratic state offers the ordinary citizen the opportunity to take part in the political decision-making process as an influential citizen; the totalitarian offers him the role of the 'participant subject.' "[6] They sometimes have insisted that "the Soviet regime increasingly uses political participation to control its people [and] the controls produced by political participation flow in one direction alone."[7]

Whether such assertions are fully justified, however, is a matter on which we should keep a very open mind. Surely they are accurate with respect to forms of participation such as voting in elections, but there are many types of participation, many types of policy, and many ways in which these various types of policy may be influenced. It would be wrong to focus simply on the limitations on public involvement in political decision-making and to ignore the great extent to which this involvement takes place. A discussion of the role of the individual and of the public as a whole must be as integral a part of a discussion of the political process in the Soviet Union as it would be in a discussion of that process in the West.

The Law, the Party, and Freedom of Speech

The degree of real freedom of speech in any country is an extremely difficult matter to discuss. Even court and governmental decisions on the subject invariably leave a rather fuzzy line between speech that is legally protected and that which is prohibited. The variation in the United States Supreme Court's interpretation of the "clear and present danger" rule over the last six decades, let alone its pained efforts to grapple with the definition of pornography and obscenity, illustrate a problem that is universal by its very nature.[8] While Soviet dissidents know the general rules governing free speech in the Soviet Union, they too can never be sure what is permissible in borderline cases.

Even more important, there are many restrictions on free speech short of imprisonment. Except for those persons already in jail, these restrictions result from an individual's fear of the penalties he or she may suffer for expressing forbidden or offensive statements, and, in practice in all countries, penalties are imposed by many individuals, groups, and institutions in addition to a court of law. These penalties can include economic losses, social ostracism, physical violence, harassment, and the like, and they may vary from place to place in a country, depending on the attitudes of local officials and the nature of the social climate. Hence in any country—including the Soviet Union—restrictions on free speech must be a broad and ill-defined network of different types of governmental and nongovernmental restraints of widely varying degrees of intensity. Individuals' willingness to speak out is not limited uniformly, for some will react more strongly to the weaker penalities than others and some may even welcome them as the price for a reputation for courage.

In the Soviet Union the basic law controlling speech has long been that directed at "anti-Soviet agitation and propaganda" (article 70 of the RSFSR Criminal Code.)[9] While the Soviet constitution guarantees "freedom of speech, press, assembly, meetings, and street processions and demonstrations," article 70 prohibits speech which constitutes either "slanderous fabrications which defame the Soviet state and social system," or "agitation or propaganda carried on for the purpose of subverting or weakening the Soviet regime (*vlast*) or of committing particular, especially dangerous crimes against the state." Also forbidden is the "circulating or preparing or keeping, for the same purpose, literature of such content." The maximum penalty for the violation of article 70 is deprivation of freedom for seven years, "with or without additional exile for a term of two to five years."[10]

In 1966, article 70 of the RSFSR Criminal Code was supplemented by article 190. One section (article 190-1) forbids "the systematic circulation in an oral form of fabrications known to be false which defame the Soviet state and social system, and, likewise, the preparation or circulation in written, printed, or any other forms of works of such content." Another section (article 190-3) similarly prohibits "the organization of, and likewise, the active participation in group actions which violate public order in a coarse manner or which are attended by clear disobedience of the legal demands of representatives of authority or which entail the violation of the work of transport or of state and social institutions or enterprises." Violation of this law can be punished by deprivation of freedom for three years.[11]

The real question with laws such as articles 70 and 190 is the manner in which they are interpreted and enforced. For example, India has long had a law very similar in wording to article 70, but for years very severe criticism could be expressed without provoking prosecution. In the Soviet Union, of course, "anti-Soviet agitation and propaganda" includes a far wider range of critical statements. Under Stalin, even the defacement of Stalin's statue could be prosecuted as a weakening of the Soviet regime, and the telling of political jokes fit within the same category. (It should be noted that this did not prevent the circulation of political jokes, and characteristically there was a political joke about the dangers of political jokes: "*Izvestiia* is sponsoring a contest to find the best political joke. First prize is twenty years.") The most private communications could be as dangerous as open speech. Aleksandr Solzhenitsyn's 1945 imprisonment, for example, resulted from a criticism of Stalin included in a private letter opened by the censor.[12]

After Stalin's death, the language of the law affecting freedom of speech was not softened (indeed, the reverse occurred with the addition of article 190), but, in actuality, the law came to be interpreted much more narrowly. According to Soviet scholars of the 1960s, the first step restricting the applicability of article 70 was to make a distinction between (to use traditional western phraseology) "the Soviet state" on the one hand and "the government" or "the leadership" on the other. The law refers to the "Soviet regime" and "the Soviet state," and scholars insist that it not be applied in the case of criticism of the government, its leaders, or their policy.

It has been stated, for example, that the prosecution of a person for criticism of a specific governmental policy would be "a gross infringement of socialist legality." Soviet foreign policy and foreign aid were specifically listed as policies, the criticism of which cannot be considered anti-Soviet agitation.[13] The same is said to be true of criticism of individual state or party leaders: "Even knowingly incorrect (not to speak of critical) statements or condemnations relating to the official or public activity of the leader, to his personal qualities or worth as a man, to his appearance, habits, and tastes, or to his way of life cannot be regarded as anti-Soviet agitation or propaganda."[14]

The second step taken to limit the anti-Soviet agitation and propaganda law was to emphasize the phrase "carried on for the purpose of." Criticism in a personal diary is not covered by the law for there is no intent to spread the "falsehood," and a critical remark provoked by personal difficulties or by delays in the supply system is also exempt, for there is no deliberate intent to subvert the system.[15] (The same reasoning applies to a political joke repeated for reasons of humor.) Moreover, if persons are to be prosecuted, they themselves must know that their "slander" is slanderous. Even the repetition of "Voice of America" accusations is not punishable unless the state proves knowledge and intent. "Decadent, unhealthy, or politically mistaken statements which result from general political illiteracy and backwardness cannot be considered anti-Soviet agitation and propaganda."[16]

The difficulty in proving intent in court may be the major reason for the passage of article 190 in 1966, for the latter does not include "for the purpose of" language. Nevertheless, article 190 does contain a number of the safeguards emphasized during the Khrushchev years. It requires that the circulation of falsehoods be "systematic" and that falsehoods be "known." It too refers to the "Soviet state and social system," not to the current government or its policies. Moreover, in fact, the regime has generally continued to prosecute most of the major dissidents under article 70, and, when it has used article 190, it has tended to employ the section dealing with participation in "group activities that grossly violate public order," that is, participation in demonstrations.

Of course, statements by legal scholars do not guarantee that the law is actually enforced in the manner claimed. However, there are several indications that the cited statements are closely related to court practice. First, western observers have expressed some surprise that the prosecutors in the trials of the dissidents have emphasized the transmission of letters or manuscripts to western publishers or journalists, actions that formally have not been illegal. Such accusations are sometimes treated as evidence of the absence of a rule of law in the Soviet Union. In reality, they may signify the real need of the prosecution to prove the defendant's intention to weaken the Soviet state and its ability to do so only by arguing that the state has been harmed in the international arena. (For this reason, accusations by those such as Iurii Orlov that the Soviet Union was violating the Helsinki Agreement were especially likely to be prosecuted.)

A second indication that the official legal interpretations may be meaningful is the great emphasis placed by the KGB on its educational role. Dissidents report repeated visits by the police before any action is taken, visits in which the agents attempt to persuade them that they are mistaken and that their speech has unhealthy consequences. In part, this practice must be motivated by the hope of collecting useful information, but to a large extent it may be necessitated by the rules of evidence established by the Criminal Code. If the KGB warns a person that certain "decadent, unhealthy, or politically mistaken statements" are indeed "slanderous" and defame the state, then it is much more difficult for the accused to repeat the statements and then to plead ignorance. If the KGB warns a man that his criticisms of the leader seem part of a systematic campaign to defame the state (and such criticism of the leader *is* punishable),[17] then further such statements may be cited as evidence of intent.

An outsider can hardly know precisely the point at which criticism of the "government" and its leader is finally considered systematic criticism of the "state and social system." For example, is it criticism of policy or a criticism of the social system when a person charges that censorship violates the basic principles of the state as enunciated by Lenin and incorporated in the Soviet constitution? In fact, when does acceptable criticism of the Soviet status quo— and, as will be discussed, much is acceptable—become slanderous fabrication? The lines are not clear, and they are likely to vary from locality to locality and from time to time. However, the reluctance to jail persons such as Andrei Sakharov and Aleksandr Solzhenitsyn indicates that far-reaching dissent may be tolerated before legal proceedings are begun.

In practice, the post-Stalin regimes generally have instituted legal proceedings only as a last resort, preferring to use a number of lesser penalties as warnings. The line between acceptable and unacceptable speech is a fuzzy one, but anyone in the vicinity will be given full notice of the precariousness of his or her position. If the warnings are not heeded, the sanctions can be progressively tightened: first, denial of permission to travel abroad, reduced size in the edition of a book or postponement of its publication, loss of administrative post or the possibility of one; then, total rejection of manuscripts, secret police searches of apartments. If the dissident abandons his political activity, he generally is permitted to resume a normal life.

We can take as an example the twenty distinguished scientists, writers, and other intellectuals who in 1967 protested against what they regarded as the unconstitutionality of [article 190] of the RSFSR Criminal Code. As of around early 1971, [only] six had been subjected to reprimands or other relatively mild forms of extrajudicial repression. Even in these cases the action appears to have been taken not for the protest in question but for later acts of protest . . . Most of the signers apparently engaged in little or no further activity objectionable to the authorities and, as a result, suffered no penalties . . . The composer Dmitri Shostakovich . . . a signer, visited the United States as a member of an elite Soviet good will group in 1973.[18]

The secret police have not, of course, withered away in the Soviet Union, and a dissident can reach the point when legal action is taken. If so, there is little, if any, hope of acquittal. All in all, according to the most careful western estimate, approximately 670 persons were sentenced on political grounds between 1960 and 1971.[19] (Contrary to the statements of some westerners, the arrest and jailing of dissidents did not begin with Brezhnev's assumption of power, but was a not unusual occurrence in the Khrushchev era as well.)[20] In the Brezhnev period, the regime has often tolerated the better-known Moscow dissidents for years, but has followed a policy of moving against them systematically, tending to bring up approximately one major case a year. Iulii Daniel and Andrei Siniavsky were brought to trial in February 1966 for publishing critical articles abroad;[21] in January 1967 Alexander Ginzburg and Iurii Galanskov were arrested for compiling and beginning to circulate materials on the Daniel–Siniavsky trial and were tried and sentenced in January 1968;[22] in January 1967 Vladimir Bukovsky was arrested for organizing a public demonstration against the Galanskov arrest and was convicted in September 1967;[23] in August 1968 Pavel Litvinov and others were arrested for staging a demonstration in Red Square against the invasion of Czechoslovakia and were convicted in October;[24] in early 1969 Petr Grigorenko was arrested for a number of activities (including support of the Crimean Tatars) and soon found himself in a psychiatric hospital; in November 1970, not long after the publication of his *Will the Soviet Union Survive Until 1984?*, Andrei Amalryk was brought to trial and convicted;[25] in June 1972 Petr Iakir, son of a prominent general who died in the purges and a major dissident associated with the *samizdat* (self-publication) appearance of the *Chronicle of Current Days,* was arrested, and in August 1973 he and a close associate were tried and convicted; in February 1974, Aleksandr Solzhenitsyn was arrested and then deported.[26] In all these cases, the person involved had a long history of dissident activity, and the actual trial culminated a substantial number of warnings and lesser penalties. Police suppression was not, of course, limited to those Moscow dissidents in touch with western correspondents (a systematic campaign has, for example, been carried out against Ukrainian nationalists),[27] but here too the police seem usually to have moved by steps.

In the mid-1970s, deportation or emigration became an increasingly frequent tool in dealing with dissidents, including many of those arrested earlier. By the end of 1977 Daniel, Siniavsky, Bukovsky, Litvinov, Grigorenko, and Amalryk were all in the West, together with several other prominent dissidents not already mentioned (for example, Zhores Medvedev and Valerii Chalidze). Only Andrei Sakharov among the major dissidents remained active in Moscow, and his position as an academician and his contributions to the construction of the Soviet H-bomb made it awkward for the regime either to arrest or deport him.

The Moscow dissidence movement as a whole increasingly became less a Russian political phenomenon and became more closely associated with the issue of Jewish emigration. Dissidence sometimes now followed the regime's refusal to permit a person to emigrate, and in some cases persons seemed to establish contact with western correspondents in order to overcome regime reluctance to let them leave. The regime's response in individual cases often reflected the current state of Soviet-American relations more than the merits of the particular case. Thus, at the height of Soviet displeasure with the Carter administration's human rights campaign, Anatolii Shcheransky, one of those who had become a dissident after being refused permission to emigrate, was charged with treason and espionage instead of anti-Soviet propaganda, an unprecedented act, and he was finally convicted in 1978 at a low point in Soviet-American relations.

The Law, the Party, and Freedom of the Press

In many ways the legal situation with respect to freedom of the press is similar to that with respect to freedom of speech. The Constitution guarantees freedom of the press, but articles 70 and 190 of the RSFSR Criminal Code contain a clause which extends the limits on oral speech to "the preparation or circulation in written, printed, or any other forms of works of such [proscribed] content."

In one respect, however, the printed word is quite different from that which is spoken. The latter can only be controlled by punishment after the fact or by incarceration of persons who seem likely to speak unacceptable thoughts. (Speech on radio and television is, of course, another matter.) Printed materials, on the other hand, can be controlled through prior censorship, at least if they are produced and/or distributed through orthodox channels.

The Soviet leadership has been quite aware of the possibility of prior censorship and has introduced it in several forms. The publishing industry has been completely nationalized, and it is only the "organizations of the working class" (as defined by the party) that have access to printing presses and stocks of paper. Books are published by publishing houses that are administered either by the State Committee for Publishing, Printing, and Book Trade or by a more specialized institution (for example, the Ministry of Defense or the Academy of Sciences), while newspapers and journals are also the official organ of some political or administrative organization. National newspapers are organs either of the party Central Committee (*Pravda* and five other papers), the government (*Izvestiia*), or an individual ministry or "public institution" (usually a trade union, the Komsomol, or a cultural institution), and the same tends to be true of magazines.

The implications of this type of control over the media have been spelled out with complete clarity by one republican party secretary: "In our country every person who considers himself an artist has the right to create freely and to write what he desires without the slightest restriction. But in similar measure the party and our government enjoy the right of free choice on what to publish."[28] The party leadership attempts to ensure this "right of free choice on what to publish" through a series of measures. First of all, tight control is maintained over the appointment of editors of newspapers, magazines, and publishing houses. These officials are almost invariably members of the Communist party, and their appointment must be approved, if not actually made, by the party organs. Second, the fact that a newspaper or journal is the organ of some institution means that the leaders of that institution can order that it either print or not print some particular article, whether or not the editor desires.[29] Third, the party organs at the various territorial levels—notably the "ideological officials" in them—also issue instructions on what is to be carried in the media. The situation in Armenia is typical: "Each week the leaders of the republican newspapers, of the television and radio, and of Armenpress [the Armenian equivalent of TASS] gather in the propaganda and agitation department of the Armenian Party Central Committee. They are informed in detail about the events of the coming week that require (*podlezhaschchie*) obligatory coverage."[30]

In addition to the systematic governmental and party supervision of the media, the regime has also instituted a formal censorship system to check on the decisions made by the editors and their institutions. Roy Medvedev claims that the top political leadership has the formal right to forbid the publication of any book and that "copies of all publications are automatically sent to the office of the First Secretary for approval."[31] Whether this latter assertion is true or not (and it seems unlikely), there clearly is a governmental censorship office which must formally approve any publication before it may be printed. This office, the Chief Administration for the Protection of State Secrets in the Press, is usually called *Glavlit*—an abbreviation of one of its earliest titles.[32]

The very existence of censorship is a censorable item, and the precise role of Glavlit is difficult to determine. Clearly it compiles lists of types of information that may not appear in print, and its officials are charged with responsibility for enforcing these restrictions.[33] Glavlit is also much concerned about the political implications of pieces of fiction that are to be published. We have many reports from dissident writers about the conflicts they have had with Glavlit, and clearly the censors can show a very detailed interest in the wording of individual passages.[34] There are indications, however, that control over the political contents of party newspapers and magazines is left largely to the editors and to the party officials who supervise them.[35] Certainly the head of Glavlit (since at least 1966, P. K. Romanov) is scarcely a major political figure, for he has not been a member or a candidate member of the Central Committee or a member of the auditing commission and has not held a major political post in the past.[36]

The Development of Policy Debates

As the Soviet dissidents have been able to establish contact with western journalists, the West has come to learn much about them and the sanctions applied against them. Because the values of the dissidents seem similar to our own, because the conflict between the isolated individual and the state has great dramatic interest, the fate of the dissidents has become the focus of intense western interest, and their fate has often been the determining factor in shaping our interpretation of Soviet developments. Their periodic trials, coupled with an unquestioned tightening in the restrictions on moral judgments that may be printed about the Stalin era, have led some western observers to conclude that the fall of Khrushchev signaled a reintensification of repression in the Soviet Union, even the development of neo-Stalinism. Any such assertion should, however, be given careful scrutiny.

In the first place, it has been our knowledge of the repression of dissidence that has increased more than the repression itself. In the Khrushchev era, the transmission of documents to westerners, the holding of dissident press conferences, the staging of demonstrations simply did not occur—and surely because they would have produced a swifter and more drastic governmental response than they have since 1964. Indeed, an examination of the biographies of many well-known dissidents demonstrates that many actually were incarcerated during the Khrushchev period. The fact that the dissidents have had a chance to become well known in the West suggests that the repression, while it clearly exists, has become a bit less severe.

In the second place, prohibition against the expression of some types of ideas does not necessarily mean that no ideas can be expressed. From any long-term perspective, the most noteworthy fact about the expression of ideas in the Soviet Union has not been the continuation of repression of dissidence, but the gradual broadening of open policy debates by those who are willing to work within the system—a broadening which began in the Khrushchev era, but which has continued in the last decade. Not only in practice, but also in theory, the media have become channels that carry increasing amounts of information, criticisms, and policy suggestions. As it was phrased in one Soviet journal,

> Newspapers and journals carry to the leadership the interests and initiatives of the broad masses. They bring public opinion on different questions to light, helping thereby to draw up plans and correct drafts of decisions in correspondence with the desires and needs of the Soviet people. This feedback serves not only to provide information necessary for efficient administration, but is also a direct channel of participation for the toilers in state affairs.[37]

While foreigners have little opportunity to judge Soviet statements about the degree of freedom in oral discussions in the Soviet Union, we can determine for ourselves the degree to which critical remarks can escape the censor's pen and appear in print. Merely by reading a broad selection of Soviet materials, we can easily see that the post-Stalin leadership has been willing to permit a wide-ranging expression of views in a number of public forums—in general newspapers, in magazines, in scholarly journals, in books, and, even more, of course, in more restricted conferences and meetings. By the mid- and late-1960s, the typical situation had become that found in a survey of Soviet social policies: "Every policy discussed in this study has been debated vigorously by specialists and middle-level administrators not only in professional journals, but in the daily press as well."[38] In Soviet debates, the participants do not constantly modify their arguments in a chameleon-like response to changes in the party line. Instead, they "stick tenaciously to their personal theoretical positions over long periods of time."[39] A study of the economic debate revealed that "the representatives of the contending opinion groups elaborate various policy options as rationally as they are able."[40]

In the years prior to Stalin's death, the policy proposals that appeared in the press were almost always very pristine in nature. Authors were not permitted to treat a problem as a whole or to suggest that several interrelated policy measures were required. Indeed, they usually had to write as if they were attacking the alleged sins of a single institution or official rather than overall policy. Even an article that was a de facto appeal for a major change in agricultural policy would be phrased as a criticism of the Ministry of Agriculture. "Objective factors" seldom could be cited as an explanation for some deficiency.[41]

Moreover, the policy suggestions that could be advanced rarely could be supported by the type of factual information that would make them compelling to the reader. Persons could say in print that there was an urgent need to strengthen the feed base for livestock,[42] but they could not present the simple facts that, despite a significant increase in population, the number of livestock was still well below the 1928 level or that the production of grain was below that of 1940.

Increasingly in the post-Stalin period, authors in the Soviet press have not needed to pretend that they are directing their criticisms at individual officials or institutions. Instead, articles now take it for granted that "objective factors" are quite important in determining economic-social relations—that officials and rank-and-file citizens often behave as they do because the basic organizational structure and incentive systems push them in a certain direction. In fact, the articles now tend to concentrate precisely on the objective factors which, in the opinion of the article writer, dictate this or that policy change.

Even though some information is still not publishable because of censorship, authors can now buttress their policy proposals with a considerable amount of documentation. It is symptomatic that articles today are filled with phrases such as "the practice of the advanced farms shows that . . . ," "sociological investigations have shown that . . . ," and (in an article by a county party secretary) "all the more often we use the method of experimentation."[43] Even the results of public opinion polls are now reported as objective factors that necessitate some policy change.[44]

A *Pravda* article authored by a professor at the Timiriazev Agricultural Academy on the mechanization of agriculture is not atypical. The professor sprinkled his article with facts—the percent of price increase in new models of machinery (and the lack of a corresponding increase in productivity), the real ratio between tractors and agricultural machinery on the farms compared with that experimentally shown best, the ratio of engineers to skilled machine operators in agriculture compared to that in industry. He called for a series of interrelated policy changes—an increase in the relative proportion of agricultural machines, an increase in the number of machine operators (and, even more, in the number of engineers and technicians on the farm), a change in the industrial incentive system to give agricultural machinery designers rewards for the creation of economically profitable machines, steps to improve the training of machine operators, and so forth.

The professor did not claim that middle level officials or institutions were to blame for these defects. He did not even mention the Ministry of Agriculture, but stated flatly that past policy was at fault. While acknowledging that the recently adopted Five-Year Plan was moving in the right direction (the number of tractors was to increase by 25 percent as against 65 percent for agricultural machinery), he asserted that even with the new planned rates of production, "the optimal relationship will still not be achieved." His conclusion was expressed very directly. "Consequently, it is extremely indispensable that the plan for the production of agricultural machinery be significantly overfulfilled both through a fuller use of internal reserves and a seeking of additional financial and material resources."[45]

Many western scholars who have come to recognize the existence of policy debate in the Soviet Union still make a sharp distinction between "instrumental" or "within systems" criticisms and those that involve the fundamentals of the system. They assert that the former have been increasingly tolerated by the regime, but that the latter remain strictly forbidden. This distinction does, in fact, have meaning (as has been seen, it is reflected in the official Soviet interpretation of the law against anti-Soviet agitation and propaganda), but it can be extremely misleading.

The question is—what are the "fundamentals of the system"? Take, for example, a 1967 article by R. A. Safarov on the need for increased party responsiveness to information from the population. In this article Safarov dealt with many aspects of information policy, including the need for honesty in reporting in the press. He specifically criticized the fact that the newspapers published only favorable letters at the time of the passage of a new law. The essence of Safarov's article, however, was an appeal for systematic public opinion polling to "find out new public needs, remarks, and proposals on social-political problems." "It goes without saying," he stated, that the polls should be taken on questions of "prime importance," including "all administrative reforms," "legislation connected with the legal status of the individual," "questions connected with the organization and activity of the ruling organs of the state," and public opinion "on individual aspects of the electoral system and on the activity of leading officials." Indeed, he went further to argue that "contradictions between the public will and the law" should be sought out and that measures should be taken "for resolving them through democratic methods appropriate to a socialist state."[46]

From the point of view of any westerner who sees the Soviet political system as a centralized dictatorship, Safarov's article was a major attack on the fundamentals of the system. However, if the Soviet system is seen as basically democratic (as Safarov and many others in the Soviet Union would see it), then his article was simply an appeal for the use of a modern technique that, in his view, would permit the system to function even more responsively. In either case the article was published, and Safarov has continued to write other articles on similar questions. In 1975 he published a book, *Public Opinion and State Administration,* which not only repeated most of the points of his earlier article but also included the results of a public opinion poll showing less than full public satisfaction with the degree to which local government takes public opinion into account.[47]

This example is far from unique. In the post-Khrushchev era there have been few party policies and few aspects of Soviet society that have been immune from attack if the attack is carefully phrased. There has been almost no proposal for incremental change in party policy that has not been published in some form or another. Even on foreign policy and nationalities policy, where actual advocacy of policy change is permitted only in the most veiled terms, scholars have been able to debate the facts of the situation and thereby imply contrasting views of the policy that is required.

In the realm of military strategy, for example, differing views on a number of subjects have appeared in print. Can there be a victor in nuclear war, especially if one side has a preponderance of force? Can an ABM system be an effective defense system? Is there any real possibility of a nuclear war, particularly in Europe? If not, is limited war capability the key to military power? What has the largest payoff in terms of military power—funds directed to basic research and development or those used for improving existing weaponry?[48]

When such a question is too sensitive to be raised directly, Soviet authors have been able to discuss it indirectly by discussing a western debate or by criticizing a position taken in the West. For example, a 1976 book published by a Soviet military publishing house on the relation of science to the military made the following assertion: "Unfortunately in our literature one meets a one-sided approach to this complex problem. It consists in emphasizing that military needs hinder the development of science or cause its lopsided development."[49] In reality, no one in the Soviet Union can publish the type of attack on Soviet military expenditures that is indicated in this statement, so what is the nature of this author's complaint? That those who criticize the American pattern of expenditures on science are making the same point about the Soviet Union in Aesopian language.

Similarly, the reader of the specialized literature on international relations has access to lively debates about the nature of political systems in different parts of the world and in different countries. What is the nature of the forces that shape their respective foreign policies? How progressive are the various types of military dictatorships and one-party regimes in the Third World? What is the best strategy for economic development in nonindustrial countries? (Many Soviet scholars openly express doubt about the desirability of full nationalization in many of these countries.)[50]

The debate with respect to the image of the American political system is typical:

> All Soviet observers of the American scene are united in asserting that a system of class rule prevails in the United States, which they designate by the term "state-monopoly capitalism." Precisely what this term means, however, has been the subject of controversy since the early postwar years. Since 1960, an open polemic has been carried on, as Soviet specialists criticized one another for advancing erroneous views on the character of state-monopoly capitalism in the United States and other countries . . .
>
> Although the debate on state-monopoly capitalism took the form of an academic and even a scholastic exercise, it may be regarded essentially as a political contest to define the adversary in terms that favoured certain broad foreign and domestic policy options which could not be discussed openly . . . Rather than have a perennial "great debate" on foreign policy as such, it was evidently found useful to discuss policy alternatives obliquely by debating the nature of the situation in which policy was being made.[51]

A similar situation has prevailed in the discussion of nationalities policy.[52]

What then are the limits on what may be published in the Soviet Union? In the first place, there are certain fundamentals that Soviet citizens simply cannot explicitly criticize in the media. These include, for example, the principle of the "leading role of the Communist party," the principle of socialism, the work of the central party organs and central party officials, the wisdom of Lenin and Marx, the "peace-loving" character of Soviet foreign policy, and so forth.

In the second place, as the previous discussion makes clear, there are tight controls on the form or tone of what may be said. The Soviet press contains critical statements—often extremely critical in nature—about almost every aspect of the Soviet political system, society, and ideology, but the context in which they are raised, the way in which they are phrased, is all-important. The Soviet citizen can even read the charge that the Soviet Union is a one-party dictatorship or a Russian-dominated empire, that class conflict is disappearing in the West, that the Soviet Union and the United States are converging, but these claims must appear in quotations from western scholars or politicians and the context must be an article or book arguing against them. Nevertheless, it should never be forgotten that, whatever the setting, the charges are printed with great frequency, in all types of media (including the local press), and sometimes in considerable detail.[53]

When Soviet citizens themselves make fundamental criticism of their system—or at least criticism that might be so interpreted—they are not permitted to acknowledge what they are doing. An appeal for basic change in the political system must be explicitly phrased as a proposal aimed at strengthening the democratic character of the system, while an appeal for greater use of market mechanisms must be made in the name of a better functioning socialism. Consequently, Soviet authors must be very careful in "aggregating" their criticisms of major features of the political and social system, for such a comprehensive discussion may give the appearance of an attack on the system as a whole. Thus, Soviet counterparts of nearly all of the points in Michael Harrington's *Poverty in America* have been printed in Soviet sources, many of them quite frequently, but a book containing all of these publishable points simultaneously would not be acceptable, particularly under a provocative title.

In the third place, there are certain policy areas that are considered extremely sensitive. Except in ways indicated earlier, foreign policy questions are difficult to discuss in print, and details of current foreign policy (for example, the proper position of the Soviet Union in the Arab-Israeli negotiations) are virtually impossible. Nationality policy must also be treated with the greatest delicacy, and certain aspects of it—for example, policy with respect to the Jews—seem to be totally forbidden topics. Discussion of the "vices" (with the exception of alcoholism) also tends to be taboo. While the fundamentals of the political and economic system can be criticized in various indirect ways, an article defending the gay life or the drug culture would be prohibited, and one advocating more sexual freedom or pornography could be expressed only in the most veiled terms.

In the fourth place, there are certain types of information on which censorship is maintained. These include not only traditional military matters but also various types of "state and party secrets." The occurrence of a riot is not reported, for example, and comprehensive crime statistics are not made available. Many kinds of economic information (for example, the amount of nonferrous metals produced or, at times, even the state of the harvest) cannot be printed, nor can certain types of social information (for example, comprehensive wage data or the degree of correlation between income and education).

The type of information that is most tightly censored is not that on "defects" in Soviet society (a western observer has relatively little difficulty in collecting an enormous amount of such information from isolated references in Soviet sources), but that dealing with "politics" in the American layman's understanding of that word. The principle of cabinet secrecy that is typical for a parliamentary system has been carried to its ultimate extreme in the Soviet Union. Policy differences among individual Politburo members are never reported, and only the most subtle differences in emphasis in speeches may provide some small clue as to whether a Politburo member is more liberal or conservative in his approach. Even westerners who study these speeches professionally cannot agree on the general policy orientation of such key post-Khrushchev figures as Suslov and Shelepin. The censorship extends to almost any detail about the private lives of the leadership, generally even including the fact that a leader does or does not have a wife or children. Television is beginning to humanize party leaders a bit, but most remain little more than a name and a formal photograph to the vast majority of the Soviet population.

Information about past "politics" often can be as limited as that about the present. Detailed criticism of the Stalin period has become an extremely sensitive subject since Khrushchev's removal, and Khrushchev himself is mentioned even less frequently than his predecessor. Here too, however, the restrictions are not limited to obviously sensitive decisions or evaluations. No memoir, scholarly analysis, or journalistic description of any of the Politburo struggles of the postwar period has been allowed, not even a neutral description, not even a case study of a relatively noncontroversial decision. Except in some of the books on the Lenin period or many memoirs on World

War II, the Soviet reader has almost no chance to gain a sense of the leaders as real people or to learn of top level debates of policy alternatives, and even these books are heavily censored.

Finally, the Soviet leadership exercises a kind of selective censorship by restricting the more radical advocacy of policy change or the more comprehensive criticisms of the status quo to specialized journals and papers. Debate on Soviet military strategy is, for example, limited almost exclusively to the military press. Any Soviet citizen is perfectly free to read specialized journals, but since, in practice, few besides the relevant specialists do so, the transmission of some types of information or policy ideas is basically limited to the particular group working in the particular policy area. Thus, to say that vigorous policy debates now take place in virtually every policy area in the Soviet Union and that these debates have involved carefully phrased criticism of the fundamentals of the system is not to say that policy debates are freely conducted in all Soviet arenas.

The Question of Audience Access

The Soviet leadership behaves as if controlling the nature of the audience that is exposed to an idea is more important than controlling the expression of the idea itself, and it attempts to accomplish this by varying the restrictions on the type of policy suggestions, criticisms, and supporting information that are directed to different types of audience. At one extreme, the greatest freedom of expression seems to be permitted in more or less private gatherings—at a party, with a group of colleagues at work, in a bar. Unfortunately, we in the West have little way of knowing the precise degree of freedom in these settings, but there are a number of indications that quite iconoclastic statements can be made in these circumstances, apparently without serious danger to the speaker.[54] Certainly it would be absolutely wrong to think that the restrictions on publication of ideas also necessarily apply to oral expression. One gains the sense that such matters as the quality of Brezhnev (and earlier, Khrushchev) as a leader or the nature of the Middle East conflict are discussed fairly frequently and that a "public opinion" may form (say, with respect to the Arab cause) that is not always the same as represented in the press.

There are other settings with a relatively narrow audience in which restrictions on expression are also looser. For example, within certain limits discussions in scholarly sessions are rather free-swinging—often, in fact, more "impolite" and unrestrained on a personal level than those in the West. The regime also does not usually seem to impose severe punishment on the transmission of quite radical views directly to the authorities, and it often has even been semitolerant of highly "illegitimate" communications that are confined to the samizdat network with its individual reproductions of documents either by hand or by typewriter.[55]

At the other extreme, the type of activity that has provoked the quickest and most repressive governmental action has been the attempt to reach a larger audience in a more organized, more formal manner—gathering signatures on a petition, distributing leaflets, making a speech in a public square, staging a demonstration, transmitting documents to the West. Thus, at the time of the Soviet invasion of Czechoslavakia in 1968, intellectuals generally could refuse to sign a statement supporting the invasion and not be punished for their refusal, and a protesting telegram which the poet Evgenii Evtushenko sent to Brezhnev and Kosygin likewise went unpunished. Signing a petition, however, certainly risked mild sanctions, while an attempt to organize a demonstration in Red Square brought immediate arrest and conviction in court within two months.[56]

These controls on access of ideas to a mass audience are not limited to "illegitimate" demands. While the party leadership has been quite willing for spokesmen of different viewpoints to seek to build support for their ideas through argumentation in articles and books, it has completely prohibited many types of dramatization of protests that are taken for granted in the United States. Sending a privately organized mass petition or delegation to the local authorities on some local grievances may be permitted,[57] but even on such an issue a person cannot picket an offending administrative agency or hand out a mimeographed complaint. A street demonstration, let alone a sit-in, is likely to be included among those "group actions which violate public order in a coarse manner" and which are prohibited by article 190–3 of the Criminal Code.

The same concern for the nature of the audience is manifested in Soviet publication policy. Almost any Soviet newspaper, magazine, or book that reaches the West can be purchased by a Soviet citizen or read in a major library, but, as already noted, the average citizen in any country, even a well-educated citizen, seldom reads a scholarly journal or the military press. If a particular policy debate is limited to such media, then in practice it will be as invisible to the vast majority of the educated public as if there were a formal, selective censorship aimed at them alone.[58]

Whether a conscious awareness of the possibility of selective censorship is always present or not, there tends to be a strong relationship between the size of audience reached by a Soviet media of communication and the unconventionality of the ideas carried in it. By all accounts, that part of the mass media with the widest audience (television) is the least open to critical information and to demands for major policy change. On the other hand, the freest media are the scholarly books and journals which, while accessible to everyone, are in practice read by only a specialized elite. It is symptomatic that the article advocating public opinion polling mentioned in the last section first appeared in the journal for academics studying questions of state and law. *Pravda* and *Izvestiia,* which reach a broader "attentive public" audience, tend to be more circumspect than the scholarly journals, while the local press (that which is most widely read) tends to be much more cautious.[59]

There often is a similar relationship between the size of the printing for books and journals and the nature of the ideas contained in them. For example, Franklyn Griffiths' dissertation on the Soviet analysis of the American political system distinguishes between four basic images. One group of scholars retain the traditional Stalinist conception of complete subordination of the American government to a unified financial elite (Image I). A second group (with Image II) agree in large part with the first, but they emphasize the existence of conflict within financial capital and therefore see governmental responsiveness to monopoly interests as a more complex process. Scholars with Image III view "the monopolies" as the single most powerful force in the United States, but they see the state as having some independence in the performance of its role and as being responsive at times to other social forces. Those with Image IV downplay the power of the monopolists even further and treat the bourgeoise as a much broader group. They stress the key role of the political elite, particularly those in the executive branch of the government.[60]

In delineating these images of the American system, Griffiths quotes from over fifty books published in the post-Khrushchev period alone, and it is, therefore, possible to use a fairly large sample of books in comparing the size of edition associated with each of these images. As shown in table 10, the more conventional images (I and II) are, on the average, found in books with far larger printings than Image III and especially Image IV. The editions of Image I and II books averaged 70,000 copies, those of III, 19,000 copies, and those of Image IV, 5,400 copies. (If three books with a printing of 200,000 copies and over are excluded, the averages are 27,000, 9,000, and 5,400, respectively.) Not only did authors of more traditional views tend to have their books published in larger editions but also authors sometimes conveyed different images to different audiences.

Journals, too, are subject to the same type of restrictions on circulation. The size of the printing of each issue of many magazines is essentially determined by market forces, but an outspoken journal may be allocated limited supplies of paper and other supplies in order to keep its circulation below the level of potential sales. For example, the literary journal *Novyi mir* was pub-

Table 10 *Size of edition of Soviet books discussing*
American political system, 1965–1969 (in percentages)

IMAGE OF AMERICAN POLITICAL SYSTEM	5,000 AND UNDER	5,001– 10,000	OVER 10,000	TOTAL
Image I and II (N = 16)	13	25	62	100
Image III (N = 19)	42	32	26	100
Image IV (N = 12)	67	33	—	100

Source: The books and the image of the American political system they embody are drawn from the footnotes of Franklyn Griffiths, "Images, Politics, and Learning in Soviet Behavior Toward the United States," Ph.D. diss., Columbia University, 1972, chap. 2. All books published in 1965–1969 mentioned in the dissertation have been included in this analysis, except for two books published by remote republican presses and four books that could not be located. Image I books contain the traditional Stalinist image and Image IV books the most unconventional views. (See the text for a more complete summary.) The size of edition (*tirazh*) was found in the back of each book.

lishing 140,000 copies an issue in 1958 when the liberal Aleksander Tvardovsky became its editor-in-chief. The printing remained at this figure for a year and a half, but then in January 1960 was abruptly cut to 90,000.[61] Despite the fact that the magazine was quickly sold out at the newsstands, it was kept at the 90,000 copies per issue level for three years and then raised only to 113,000 copies in the period 1963–1964. The post-Khrushchev leadership did permit the circulation of *Novyi mir* to rise sharply in 1965 and to reach the 150,000 level in 1966 and 1967, but in the last two years of Tvardovsky's editorship it declined once more, the number of copies per issue averaging 126,000 in 1969. However, when Tvardovsky was replaced by a more conservative editor in 1970, the size of the printing was immediately raised to 160,000.[62]

To repeat, many of these restrictions on the exposure of a mass audience to unconventional ideas are loose ones, and they do not really prevent any determined citizen from obtaining access to unconventional books and journals. Magazines such as *Novyi mir* and *Mirovaia ekonomika i mezhdunarodnye otnosheniia* (World Economics and International Relations—the journal with the most unconventional articles on international affairs) regularly advertise for new subscribers, and in the post-Khrushchev period at least, *Novyi mir* has emphasized that its subscriptions can be taken "without restriction."[63]

The primary limitations appear to be imposed not on the freedom of citizens to obtain the magazine if they wish but on the opportunity of the rank-and-file citizens to become aware of its existence. Thus *Mirovaia ekonomika i mezhdunarodnye otnosheniia* experienced a substantial rise in popularity in the post-Khrushchev era, its circulation in October 1970 (42,000) being double that in early 1964. Yet, as a subscription advertisement in October 1970 issue warned, it remained true that "the journal appears in extremely limited quantity in retail trade."[64] Whatever the reason for this policy (and, of course, many specialized journals are not sold on the newsstand in the West), it means that there is little chance for a potential reader to become interested in the journal through a chance purchase.

Citizen Participation in Political Life

One can imagine a situation in which citizens have the right to participate in the political process but do not actually do so. In fact, this is precisely what often does occur in the Third World and among poorly educated groups in the West. Soviet citizens, too, are frequently said to be politically indifferent and apathetic, and this may well be true in many senses. However, the proportion of the population which is drawn into some form of political participation is very striking indeed.

The most basic type of political participation is simply awareness of the political system, and it is not a type of participation to be taken for granted in a developing nation. Clearly many villagers in countries such as South Vietnam were very slow in even hearing of the national capital of the government, let alone in developing loyalty to it. Even in more industrialized countries, polls have found that, for example, 40 percent of Italian respondents could not name a single political leader in the country and that 62 percent said that they "never follow the accounts of political and governmental affairs."[65]

The Soviet Union has not published poll results on the awareness level of the population, but the vast propaganda effort of the regime surely must have made nearly everyone in the country aware of the political system, the party, its leading figures, and its symbols. Besides attempting to inculcate that information through the schools, the party has recruited many of its members and other activists to serve as part-time propagandists and agitators and to spread its message through talks and face-to-face individual and small group sessions. (In 1975 there were 3.7 million agitators.)[66] Since the face-to-face sessions usually take place at work, they seem particularly well designed to ensure that the most hard-to-reach apathetics do, in fact, become aware, at least in a society in which female participation in the work force is very high.[67]

Participation that involves some input into decision-making is, of course, limited to a narrower group than those who are aware of political affairs. Nevertheless, large numbers of Soviet citizens are engaged in activities that would seem to give them at least the potential of influence on some types of decisions.

First, even the agitation-propaganda work of the party provides ample opportunity for citizen input, for the agitators and the propagandists are supposed to not only make formal speeches or reports but also explain satisfactorily problems which may be leading to disaffection. As a consequence, questions are encouraged, and, in practice, "they concern the most diverse spheres of societal life: politics, the economy, production, living conditions, and so forth," often taking the form of "Why is something permitted?" "Why isn't something done about this?" The agitator and propagandist is supposed to report on sources of dissatisfaction (in fact, to work to remove them if they are local in nature), and the local party organs should have special officials to collate this information and transmit it to higher agencies and to those in a position to correct the situation.[68]

Second, there is considerable popular participation in the simplest sense of Easton's "input of demands"—the making of individual requests, complaints, or suggestions to responsible authorities. One scholar finds that "by the 1960's thousands of citizen demands were pouring to city raion (borough) agencies and organs"—15,000 letters and visits during a six-month period to a single (presumably typical) borough in Leningrad alone.[69] Such communications are not limited to the local level. For example, the USSR Ministry of Health in Moscow received over 64,000 letters and 35,000 visitors in 1969.[70]

If citizens are dissatisfied with the way they have been treated either by government or by their employers, if they have proposals which they think would improve policy or administrative performance, they have the right—in fact, the duty—to appeal to other institutions: the party organs (the primary party organization at the place of work, the local party organs, even the Central Committee in Moscow), the People's Control Committee, the trade unions, the newspapers, even the prosecutor's office and the courts.

Information on the scale of this type of individual activity is available primarily for communications to newspapers; and in this case at least, the activity is widespread. It has been estimated that 60 to 70 million communications a year are sent to all of the Soviet newspapers combined—approximately 75,000 a year to the average central newspaper, 15,000 to 65,000 a year to the average republican or regional newspaper, and 4,000 to 20,000 a year to the average newspaper in the city or district.[71] These figures generally correspond to reports of communications to individual newspapers, although the number of annual communications to the most important national papers (*Pravda, Izvestiia,* and *Sel'skaia zhizn'*) rises to the 400,000 to 500,000 range.[72] The radio and television stations are also sent many letters—in 1966, 439,000 to the central broadcasting studios in Moscow alone.[73] Not all of the communications are relevant to the policy process (for example, 4,847 of the 63,539 communications sent in 1970 to *Gudok*—the newspaper of the railroad industry and trade union—were entries in a chess contest),[74] but a large proportion of them are.

Soviet citizens can and do write directly to political institutions as well. In the five years between 1971 and 1976, 2,000,000 letters were sent to the party Central Committee in Moscow,[75] while in 1974 alone 350,000 were received by all party organs of the Ukraine, including 44,000 by the Ukrainian Central Committee.[76] In 1968, 29,248 written communications were sent to the Azerbaidzhan Party Central Committee, and in both 1969 and 1970 approximately 18,000 were sent to the Armenian Central Committee.[77] In a two-year period in the mid-1970s, 765,000 letters were received by the organs of the People's Control Committee (a checking institution), from 1973 to 1977 over 200,000 were sent to the All-Union Central Trade Union Council, and during this period 2,000,000 letters a year were received by the Central Committee of the Komsomol.[78] Furthermore, when a law is being studied by the Supreme Soviet, citizens will write directly to it (for example, 1,000 letters on a health bill),[79] and when a worker is elected a member of a bureau, he will personally receive letters and visits from other workers.[80]

A third type of political participation—always far more widespread than the earlier images of an "atomized society" suggested—is membership in organized group activity of a kind that can entail potential involvement in various levels of decision-making. Formal group participation begins with membership in the Pioneer organization from the age of ten to fourteen (actually from the fourth through the seventh grade).[81] Sometimes referred to as the equivalent of the Boy Scouts and Girl Scouts (its slogan is even "always prepared"), the Pioneer organization forms its basic units within the school classroom, and nearly all of the children of the appropriate grades are enrolled—a total of 25 million in 1974.[82]

While the Pioneer organization was explicitly created for educational purposes, one of the values that it is supposed to inculcate in its members is an interest in participation in public affairs and services. The Pioneer units have their own meetings, executive council, and elections ("pioneer self-administration"), and to some extent the members help to decide what activities should be undertaken by their organization. Children, it is said, should be encouraged to be organizers and leaders so that their "public activity grows very much."[83]

At the age of fourteen (usually, at the beginning of the eighth grade), Soviet young people may join the Young Communist League—the Komsomol —and 38 million of them were members in 1978.[84] Over the last two decades, the proportion of youth in the Komsomol has been growing steadily, and stood at 34 percent in 1959, 43 percent in 1965, over 50 percent in 1970, and nearly 55 percent in 1974.[85] In 1974, some 30 percent of fourteen-year-olds were Komsomol members, approximately 63 percent of those in the fifteen to seventeen age group, approximately 54 percent of those in the eighteen to twenty-two age group, nearly 40 percent of those in the twenty-three to twenty-five age group, and some 20 to 25 percent in the twenty-six to twenty-seven age group.[86] Some 80 to 90 percent of full-time students of the appropriate age in the high schools, secondary specialized schools, and colleges are members of the Komsomol, well under one-third of those working in the collective farms, approximately 50 percent of those working elsewhere in the economy, and 70 percent of the military troops in the age group.[87]

The primary organization of the Komsomol is located in the place of study or work, not in the district of residence of the member, and it is ideally situated to participate in decision-making in the educational institution or enterprise. In fact, there is every indication that the Komsomol is much more deeply involved in decision-making than the Pioneers. In higher education, for example, "representatives of the Komsomol organizations participate in the work of all leading organs and social associations of the educational institution—the admission, scholarship, living conditions, cultural-mass and sports committees . . . The Komsomol is given the right to participate in the work of the councils of the divisions and the educational institutions."[88]

Because the Komsomol is strictly subordinated to the party both in official doctrine and in practice, because its *vospital'nyi* (training or enlightenment) role is much emphasized, western scholars have usually interpreted participation by the Komsomol in decision-making as a form of political control. That the Komsomol can perform this function cannot be denied, but it surely would be wrong to continue to see the organization in terms of its 1920s role when it was an ideologically committed minority facing "bourgeois" educators and a student body socialized under another regime. Even in the past, the Komsomol also provided a channel through which interested young people could try to affect the detailed conditions in which they studied, worked, and enjoyed themselves, and this function surely has grown in relative importance with the passage of time. Of the 38 million members, 6.5 million serve on "leading committees" of the primary or territorial Komsomol organs, and these persons are in an especially good position to try to influence the administrative decisions.[89] Three and a half million members are enrolled in the Komsomol Searchlight (*Komsomolskii prozhektor*), an organization that checks on deficiencies among the administrators.[90]

The major mass organization for Soviet adults is the trade union, which had an enrollment of 121 million persons in 1978.[91] With certain exceptions (most notably military personnel and policemen) virtually all employed persons in the Soviet Union are trade union members.[92] The trade unions are structured essentially along branch lines (see Chapter 10), and they contain all the employees in the ministries within their respective jurisdictions—not only manual workers, but also white collar, professional, and administrative personnel, up to and including the minister himself. In all, over one-quarter of all trade union members are in white collar jobs.[93]

Like the Komsomol organization, the trade union works under the close supervision of the party organs, and it is not permitted to use such tactics as the strike to further its aims. Nevertheless, the trade union does have a great many responsibilities in the job security, housing, working and living conditions, norm-setting, and "social planning" areas, and employees who want to participate in these types of questions at their place of work have an institutionalized means through which they can do it. Only 4 percent of the chairmen of the trade union organizations of the enterprises or institutions function as full-time trade union officials,[94] the others being drawn from persons with other full-time jobs in the institution.

In all, over one-quarter of the trade union members (28 million in 1968) are listed as "trade union activists"—persons whose participation in trade union work goes beyond mere membership.[95] In 1974, 11.5 million of these activists were said to have been elected to various "leading" positions at the enterprise level or above, while in 1975, 22 million of them were members of specialized commissions of the local trade union committee.[96] The nature of these commissions is, no doubt, suggested by the result of a sociological survey of a number of plants in East Siberia. Twenty percent of the workers participated in the drawing up of the production plans, 10 percent in the re-examination of norms, 37 percent in the distribution of premia, 27 percent in the distribution of housing, 31 percent in hiring-firing decisions, and 26 percent in the distribution of passes to rest homes and resorts.[97] These statistics on trade union activists surely overstate the number of really active persons, but the figures do indicate those who have a somewhat better access and who have shown an inclination to use it at times.

In addition to the trade union organization, the Soviet adult may also participate in other institutions with some role in governmental or administrative decision-making. One of the most notable of these organizations is the People's Control Committee, an organization that has the responsibility for checking on the work of governmental and economic administrators, and that relies heavily on part-time volunteers. As of January 1976, 9,500,000 volunteers had been elected to 659,000 posts and 649,000 groups located in every type of state enterprise and institution, including military units and the central apparatus of the ministries in Moscow, and another 20 million people annually are "drawn into ad hoc mass inspections or consulted informally as technical specialists."[98] Thus, for example, one of every ten employees of the Ministry of Health in Moscow serves in this capacity.[99] In addition, 35,000 persons staff volunteer departments of the People's Control Committee at the district level and above, and 380,000 persons serve on commissions at this above-enterprise level.[100]

Yet another avenue for citizen participation in decision-making is provided by the organizations of "public self-administration." These include such bodies as street committees, apartment house committees, comrade courts for minor offenses, parents' committees at school, voluntary auxiliary police (the *druzhinniki*), sanitary groups and posts, library councils, and so forth, and their total membership was placed at 31 million in 1976.[101] These organizations seem designed primarily to involve the citizenry in activities that would improve the neighborhood or place of work, and they create the opportunity for some citizen input to local administrators. They can also provide a legitimate vehicle for the collective expression of some grievance or for group representation on some local interest. Even in the newspapers one can occasionally read letters from members of a house committee, the chairman of a parents' committee in a school, and so forth.[102]

The fastest growing type of social organization in the Soviet Union is the voluntary society (*dobrovol'noe obshchestvo*). By 1975 some 2,000 of these societies were in existence, many with regional and local units, and they generally have been organized around a hobby or leisure time activity. There are, for example, societies for stamp collectors, dog-lovers, those who want to preserve historical monuments, car enthusiasts, sportsmen of various types, book-lovers, and the like. While the purpose of these societies is not primarily political (except perhaps for some of the conservation societies), clearly they can provide a focus for organized activity on behalf of governmental action which would promote the interest of the respective groups.[103]

In addition to joining formal organizations and societies, Soviet citizens may also participate in various meetings and conferences at their places of work. In the collective farm, this participation is formalized in the character of the institution, for in theory top officials are elected and basic policy determined at a farm meeting. In practice, the kolkhoz is far from autonomous in its actions (including whom it is to "elect" as chairman), but at least meetings are held and the collective farmers discuss "not only production matters, but also village services and the activity of the cultural institutions."[104]

The rest of the economy is explicitly administered from above, but this does not preclude the formation of various collective bodies which have the responsibility of providing advice to the administration and in some cases of making binding decisions. In the educational realm, for example, the schools have a *pedsovet*—a pedagogical council that basically is a teachers' council[105]—while the higher educational institutions have an academic council (*uchenyi sovet*) composed largely of top administrators and important full professors.

However, it is in the spheres of "material production"—notably in the industrial plant, but also in construction, transportation, and so forth—that the number of organizations and meetings are multiplied to their greatest extent. Like other places of work, these enterprises have their party, trade union, and Komsomol organizations with their various committees and subcommittees, and they also have their posts and groups of peoples' control which enroll about one-tenth of their employees. But, in addition, they have general meetings of workers and employees, "permanent production conferences" (which are said to have five and a half million active participants),[106] bureaus of economic analysis, scientific-technical societies and societies of inventors and rationalizers (which have 12 million members, although not all in industry),[107] creative brigades of NOT—*nauchnaia organizatsiia truda* or scientific organization of labor—(which have 453,000 members),[108] public bureaus of technical norming, and so forth.[109] The number of persons who can be drawn into all these forms of "administration of production" can be quite substantial, 64 percent of the employees at sixteen important enterprises studied in one sociological investigation.[110]

Potentially the most significant type of political participation is that which takes place in institutions that are quite explicitly political in nature. Over 16 million persons (over 9 percent of the adult population, some 22 percent of the males between the ages of thirty and sixty) were members of the Communist party in 1978, and 4.0 million of them served in some position within the primary party organization as a member of a committee or a lower level volunteer official.[111] Moreover, in 1959 commissions were established within the primary party organization to assist in the supervision of the administration (*komissiia po kontrol'iu deiatel'nosti administratsii*). The number of such commisions in Ukrainian industrial enterprises rose from 16,000 to 20,000 between 1960 and 1973 and included over 90,000 Communists on the latter date.[112] Finally, a certain number of party members also fulfill the responsibilities of a volunteer *partinformator*—a person who collects information to help the party committees in making their decisions.[113]

Another major type of political participation is associated with the local soviets. Over 2,220,000 persons are selected as deputies to the local soviets, and in 1975 1,776,000 of them served on the soviets' standing committees. (Another 2,611,000 persons worked as volunteer "activists" who assisted the standing committees in their work.)[114] The scale of the work of the standing committees and their participants is suggested by the fact that in 1974 they helped to prepare 465,000 questions for discussion at sessions of the local soviets and another 839,000 questions for discussion by the soviets' executive committees.[115]

Indeed, some citizens are even drawn into various types of executive work within the soviets. The executive committees of the soviets include many important local officials, but 120,000 of their 367,000 members in 1973 were workers and collective farmers and an unknown additional number were rank-and-file white collar employees.[116] In addition, the local soviets also contain a number of wholly volunteer (vneshtatnyi) departments (7,684 of them in 1975, staffed by 66,361 volunteers), and they recruit a much larger number of persons (426,000 in 1975) as volunteer instructors and inspectors for the regular departments and administrative bureaus.[117] Advisory citizen councils may also be attached to departments—for example, the regional education department.[118]

The party organs leading the various territorial subunits of the country also have volunteers to assist them in their work. The ruling committees of these organs contained 416,000 persons in 1975, only 16 percent of them party officials.[119] A wide range of occupations are represented on these committees, and in theory at least, they should not only attend sessions of the committees but should take on assignments between meetings. As in the case of the soviets, the local party organs may also have volunteer (vneshtatnyi) departments and volunteer "instructors" for other departments to supplement the full-time staff.[120] When the party committees meet in plenary sessions, members of the committee, volunteer instructors, and other activists can be gathered together in a commission beforehand to prepare material for the session.[121]

The expansion of citizen participation in direct governmental actions—particularly the creation of volunteer departments and the establishment of volunteer officials—was associated with the Party Program promoted by Khrushchev in 1959 and with his claim that the state was beginning to wither away. His successors no longer emphasize this latter point, and some western scholars assert that citizen participation has become a less significant aspect of Soviet political life since 1964. This judgment seems quite mistaken. It is true that the number of totally volunteer governmental departments has declined somewhat in the last decade,[122] but, as has been seen, even this innovation by Khrushchev has not been abandoned. More important, the actual number of reported participants in nearly all forms of group activity has continued to rise sharply—much faster than the size of the adult population (see table 11). While the reported figures clearly exaggerate the level of meaningful participation, the statistics of the Khrushchev era had the same bias, and there is no reason to doubt the basic direction of the trend.

Finally, of course, it would be wrong to discuss citizen participation without mentioning the existence of illegal participation. One form of such activity, of course, is involvement in the dissident movement. The scale of this activity is very difficult to measure because of its illegality and because of the fuzzy boundary between legitimate protest and illegal dissent. However, by all accounts the number of active dissenters has been small—perhaps between 1,000 and 10,000 at any one time.[123] A second type of illegal participation is in a mass demonstration. Our information on this type of activity is also quite incomplete, but clearly demonstrations of varying intensity do take place periodically—for example, in Tbilisi (Georgia) in 1956, in Temir-Tau (Kazakhstan) in 1959, in Novocherkassk (Rostov region) in 1962, in Erevan (Armenia) in 1965, in Kaunas (Lithuania) in 1972, and so forth. Such demonstrations or riots have been quickly suppressed, but they can involve large numbers of people. Given the memory of the fall of the Polish first secreaty after riots in 1970, this type of participation—and fear of it by the leaders—can be of special importance.

Variations in Participation by Group

Occupation

In such forms of participation as voting in elections or membership in the Pioneers and the trade unions, involvement is virtually universal within the appropriate categories, and hence there can be little variation among social groups in this type of activity—or at least little other than that implied in the statutory requirements for the given type of participation. When, however, Soviet political activities and organizations embrace only a portion of those who are eligible to participate, the different social groups turn out to participate at quite different rates. The variation by social group that is easiest to document is that in Communist party membership, but it is also observable in other types of political activity as well.

The most obvious factor associated with differences in rates of political involvement is occupational status. The relationship begins with the simplest form of participation—general interest in the political sphere and in the outside world. Thus, one study found that 40 percent of the collective farmers surveyed claimed to be interested in concrete information about international life and that this figure rose to 49 percent for workers, 54 percent for students,

Table 11 *Political participation in the USSR, 1954–1976*

Group	1954–1955	Percent Increase 1954–1965	1964–1965	Percent Increase 1965–1970	1970–1971	Percent Increase 1970–1976	1975–1976	Percent Increase 1965–1976
Adult population[a]	120,751,000	18	142,069,501	8	153,237,112	7	163,510,389	15
Party members and candidates[b]	6,864,863	71	11,758,169	19	14,011,784	12	15,694,187	33
Deputies to local soviets[c]	1,536,310	31	2,010,540	3	2,071,333	7	2,210,932	10
Trade union members[d]	40,240,000	74	70,000,000	27	89,000,000	20	107,000,000	53
Komsomol members[e]	18,825,324	20	22,500,000	13	25,500,000	37	35,000,000	56
"Controllers"[f]	Apparently 0	—	4,300,000	86	8,000,000	19	9,500,000	121
Auxiliary police (Druzhiniki)[g]	0	—	5,500,000	27	7,000,000	—	—	—
Activists in "independent organizations"[h]	—	—	20,000,000	25	25,000,000	24	31,000,000	55

[a] The effective adult population is defined here in terms of the number of persons registered to vote in elections. In years when comparable election and census data are available, the adult population as measured by the electoral registration is 2 to 3 percent lower than that as measured by the census. 1954: *Pravda*, March 18, 1954, p. 1; 1965: *Pravda*, March 28, 1965, p. 2; 1970: *Sovety deputatov trudiashchikhsia*, no. 7 (July 1970), p. 7; 1975: ibid., no. 8 (August 1975), p. 20.

[b] 1954, 1965, and 1970: *Partiinaia zhizn'*, no. 14 (July 1973), p. 10; 1976: ibid., no. 10 (May 1976), p. 13.

[c] 1955, 1965, and 1970: N. A. Petrovichev, leading author, *Partiinoe stroitel'stvo*, 3d ed. (Moscow, Politizdat, 1972), p. 403; 1975: *Sovety deputatov trudiashchikhsia*, no. 8 (August 1975), p. 24.

[d] 1954: Petrovichev, *Partiinoe stroitel'stvo*, p. 411; 1965: 1965 Yearbook, *Bol'shaia sovetskaia entsiklopediia*, p. 19; 1970: 1970 Yearbook, *Bol'shaia sovetskaia entsiklopediia*, p. 33; 1975: *Pravda*, March 4, 1976, p. 2.

[e] 1954: Petrovichev, *Partiinoe stroitel'stvo*, p. 415; 1965: 1965 Yearbook, *Bol'shaia sovetskaia entsiklopediia*, p. 18; 1970: 1970 Yearbook, *Bol'shaia sovetskaia entsiklopediia*, p. 31; 1976: *Pravda*, February 28, 1976, p. 6.

[f] 1964: *Kommunist*, no. 13 (September 1964), p. 123; 1971: *Partiinaia zhizn'*. no. 19 (October 1971), p. 41; *Partiinaia zhizn'*, no. 8 (April 1976), p. 27.

[g] 1963: V. E. Poletaev, ed., *Rabochii klass SSSR* (Moscow, Nauka, 1969), p. 425; 1971: F. S. Razarenov, comp., *Narodnomu druzhinniku* (Moscow, Znamia, 1963), p. 115.

[h] 1964: V. M. Chkhikvadze, ed., *Sotsializm i narodovlastie* (Moscow, Politizdat, 1965), p. 86; 1970: *Partiinaia zhizn'*, no. 13 (July 1970). p. 9; 1976: *Pravda*, February 20, 1976, p. 3.

63 percent for engineering-technical personnel, and 61 percent for party-soviet employees. The contrast was even sharper in the proportion of those claiming an interest in commentary on international life: 28 percent of the collective farmers, 29 percent of the workers, 39 percent of students, 40 percent of the engineering-technical personnel, and 55 percent of the party-soviet employees.[124]

The same general occupational pattern is found in actual involvement in political organizations or meetings. As early as young adulthood, one finds that in the more unskilled and semiskilled branches of the economy such as agriculture, transportation, and construction the proportion of employees in the appropriate age groups in the Komsomol ranged from under 33 percent to 38 percent in 1973, but this figure rose to 60 percent of those employed in industry and 72 percent of those in a high-technology ministry such as the Ministry of Oil Refinery and Petrochemicals.[125] Details on the breakdown of Komsomol membership by occupation within these broad branches are very sketchy, but the Komsomol representation seems much higher among professionals than among persons in occupations of lower status. Among engineering-technical personnel, Komsomol representation rises to some 75 to 80 percent in 1970, while among industrial workers it was approximately 53 percent and among construction workers approximately 32 percent.[126] Membership is virtually universal among teachers.[127]

The difficulty we face in teasing out differential rates of participation in the Komsomol by social group reflects the regime's great sensitivity to this question. In comparison with non-Communist countries, the rate of working-class participation in group and enterprise decision-making is probably extremely high, but, given the nature of the ideology, the leadership is reluctant to acknowledge any differentials at all between workers and white collar—or at least any differentials that favor the latter.

As we move to consider less formal organizations than the Komsomol and party (where the rates of membership vary much more by occupation than in the Komsomol), the available national level information is even more sketchy. Nevertheless, a number of sociological studies have looked at activism in specific locales and enterprises, and, while they show some difference by type of activity, they almost invariably reveal a strong correlation between the status of occupation and the rate of participation. Tables 12 and 13, based on a large-scale study of rural youth, show that the difference is not simply one between those in white collar occupations and others but extends to distinctions of status within the broader white collar and "peasant" categories. The same type of differences in participation rates are found within the working class as well. For example, one study of workers in the Urals revealed that 33.1 percent of the least qualified workers took part in public

Table 12 *Occupational background of youthful participants in rural political-social activities (in percentages)*

OCCUPATIONAL GROUP	PARTY KOMSOMOL WORK	TRADE UNION WORK	SELF-GOVERN-MENT WORK[a]	ADMINIS-TRATION AND PUBLIC CONTROL	SOVIETS & SOVIET COMMIS-SIONS
Leaders and specialists	40	57	28	10	32
Other white collar	20	18	12	15	11
Mechanizers (e.g., tractor drivers)	15	6	16	19	22
Workers who service and repair machines	5	2	16	15	4
Construction workers	2	4	3	5	—
Livestock peasants (e.g., milkmaids)	6	—	3	19	20
Peasants with nonmechanical specialty	3	—	5	15	4
Peasants without specialty	4	7	10	2	3
Total	95	94	93	100	96

Source: I. M. Slepenkov and B. V. Kniazov, *Molodezh' sela segodnia* (Moscow, Molodaia gvardiia, 1972), p. 110. Based on a large sociological study of 4,220 youth in fourteen regions and republics, conducted over the 1967–1971 period. Ibid., p. 9.

[a] Work in comrade courts was given as an example of this category of participation.

activities (broadly defined) at the enterprise, in comparison with 46.0 percent of those in middle-skill occupations, and 68.5 percent of those in the most highly skilled jobs.[128]

The more participation entails what westerners would instinctively define as "political" or "policy-oriented" participation, the greater the differentials in rates of participation by status of occupation tend to be. In some low policy-relevant activities such as the voluntary auxiliary police (*druzhinniki*), Soviet scholars privately report that workers are actually represented

Table 13 *Percent of rural youth in political-social activities, by occupational group*

OCCUPATIONAL GROUP	PERMANENT POST OR MEMBERSHIP	EPISODIC INVOLVEMENT[a]	ANY TYPE INVOLVEMENT
Leaders and specialists	46	34	80
Mechanizers (e.g., tractor drivers)	18	25	43
Workers who service and repair machines	10	36	46
Industrial workers in the village	16	28	44
Construction workers	9	21	30
Livestock peasants (e.g., milkmaids)	10	20	30
Peasants with non-mechanical specialty	7	25	32
Peasants without specialty	7	17	24

Source: I. M. Slepenkov and B. V. Kniazov, *Molodezh' sela segodnia* (Moscow, Molodaia gvardiia, 1972), p. 114. Based on a large sociological study of rural youth in a number of regions.

[a] The Russian word translated here as "involvement" actually is *poruchenie,* which *literally* means "assignment." The type of assignments or involvements include those listed in table 12, plus certain other activities such as agitation-propaganda work or leadership roles in local sports clubs.

in greater number than their proportion in the population would indicate. By contrast, only 11 percent of the articles and letters with suggestions for policy change or complaints about the work of individual administrators in *Pravda* and *Izvestiia* in December 1971 and six republican newspapers from December 1974 through February 1975 were workers and foremen. The percentage of workers among the writers of the longer and more significant articles was extremely small (4 percent in *Pravda* and *Izvestiia* and 3 percent in the republican papers), but even among writers of published letters (which tend to be complaints about individual administrators or administrative units), the percentage of workers rose only to 25 and 27 percent, respectively.[129] One could argue that the proportion of letters written by workers is greater than that published, but the head of the letters-to-the-editor department of the railroad newspaper *Gudok* stated in an interview that her editor persistently pressured her to publish more worker letters and that the paper would even rewrite an interesting but poorly written worker's letter to get it included. This situation is probably typical.[130]

A disproportionately great number of white collar employees also participate in party and soviet sessions and committees. Thus, 24 percent of the deputies named to the 1970 Supreme Soviet were workers, but only 12 percent of the reported speakers in the committee (postoiannye komissii) sessions of that convocation (1970–1974) and only 6 percent of the speakers at the formal sessions of the Supreme Soviet themselves were workers.[131] In the local soviets, workers provided 39.9 percent of the deputies in 1973 by Soviet count (which includes sales clerks and state farm "peasants") but only 27.9 percent of the members of the standing committees.[132] They constituted some 28 percent of the party members in 1970, but only 16.7 percent of the members of the committees and bureaus of the primary party organizations.[133]

The advisory committees and councils that are attached to the soviets and party committees are particularly likely to be staffed by elite personnel. A regional department of education council had no member lower in status than a school principal and only one-third of its members at that level; a volunteer school department of a district party committee is likely to be headed by a school principal.[134] Similarly, in the People's Control Committee, two-thirds of the controllers at the enterprise level are workers and peasants, but a majority of the volunteer staff of the supervisory territorial committees of the institution are "highly qualified specialists."[135]

Finally, it should be noted that the illegal dissidence movement has also been white collar in nature. Andrei Amalryk has examined the background of 738 of the signers of letters protesting the Ginzburg–Galanskov trial, and he found the following occupational breakdown among them: academics, 45 percent; persons in the arts, 22 percent; engineers and technical specialists, 13 percent; publishing-house employees, teachers, doctors, and lawyers, 9 percent; students, 5 percent; and workers, 6 percent. If anything, this was the high point of worker participation in dissident activity, for the dissidents were driven to near despair in their efforts to broaden their representation in the working class.

Every piece of evidence suggests that peasant participation in policy-related activities is even lower than that of the worker. They very rarely write letters to newspapers (except Sel'skaia zhizn'—Rural Life), and they seldom are called upon to speak at sessions of the Supreme Soviet. In the 1970–1974 convocation of that body, for example, 13 percent of the deputies were rank-and-file peasants, but only 2 of 159 reported speakers in committee sessions and only one of 234 speakers at the Supreme Soviet were in this occupational category.[137]

The level of peasant participation in lower level soviet and party activities is very difficult to judge because official Soviet usage of the category "collective farmer" includes farm management and technical staff as well as rank-and-file peasants. Nevertheless, few peasants seem to write letters to the newspapers, and the type of sociological study cited in tables 12 and 13 suggests that there is a strong correlation between participation and status of occupation within the countryside, those of lower status having low levels of participation.

We would be remiss, however, if we did not emphasize one point. The evidence certainly suggests that in a system in which the regime seeks to maximize the figures on worker participation, the familiar relationship between occupational status and rate of participation still prevails. It is a fact that should not be forgotten, but from a comparative perspective there is another fact that also must be remembered. There *is* participation by those in blue collar and lower white collar occupations in Soviet political life, and some of this participation is in very important bodies. Workers may be limited to nine votes on the party Central Committee, one spot on the party bureaus in boroughs and cities and half the regions,[138] one or two representatives on the executive committees of regional soviets,[139] and five members on the Presidium of the All-Union Central Trade Union Councils,[140] but these numbers are higher than western norms. A 27.9 percent representation of workers among members of the standing committees of local soviets is very substantial by international standards, and the number of workers on committees at the plant level is probably higher. Nor should it be forgotten that the opinions of lower status personnel can also filter up through general conversations or complaints to propagandists and agitators. When a nonpeasant author writes that "in our opinion the collective farmers with full justice raise the question that each of them should have an average balance of working and free time as in work on state enterprises,"[141] this too is peasant participation at one step removed. The impact of all this participation is still to be discussed—and, to a considerable extent, still to be studied—but as political scientists we should be comparing the Soviet experience with that of other nations, not simply with utopian Marxist images.

Education

To say that participation is correlated with occupation is also, of course, to say that it is correlated with education—at least if higher status occupations generally are staffed by people with higher levels of education. Indeed, when American survey data are analyzed closely, education almost invariably is more strongly correlated with participation than is occupation, and it is very likely that such has also been the case in the Soviet Union in recent years.

Detailed information on the educational background of participants generally is available only for certain specific types of participation. Except in such cases as deputies to the soviets and delegates to party congresses (where those with college education are, not surprisingly, represented in disproportionate numbers), almost the only comprehensive data on this subject pertains to party membership, and here too the differences are great. Of persons thirty years of age and older, 4 percent of those with eighth grade education or less were party members in 1970, compared with 13 percent of those with incomplete secondary education, 24 percent of those with a high school degree, approximately 30 percent of those with incomplete higher education, 36 percent of those with complete higher education, and 49 percent of those with a postgraduate degree.[142]

The other available information on the educational levels of participants comes from survey data. Unfortunately, such studies seldom specify the types of activity considered "participation" or "public activity" for purposes of the questionnaire, but they surely include such things as attendance at production conferences that require little activity. Despite this fact, the differentials by education level are substantial. In one study of Ural workers, 23.8 percent of those with fourth grade education or less took part in public activity, compared with 37.1 percent of those with fifth or sixth grade education, 43.0 percent of those with seventh or eighth grade education, 51.4 percent of those with ninth to eleventh grade education, 60.8 percent of those with specialized secondary education, and 72.3 percent of those with incomplete and complete higher education.[143] The "worker-intelligentsia"—those with higher or specialized secondary education or those with secondary education who are still studying—are invariably found to be the most active group within the working class. In a study of Sverdlovsk plants, workers with ten to eleven years of secondary education participated in "production management" 1.5 times more than those with five to nine years of education, and perhaps more significant, they made 2.8 times as many critical remarks in these settings.[144]

Sex

Like education, sex is a variable that is reported only sporadically in official Soviet statistics on participation, and it is analyzed even less frequently in sociological studies. In this case, however, the difference in participation between men and women is sometimes discussed in general terms in the Soviet press, and occasionally we are also in a position to make a calculation on our own.

Although statistics do not seem to be available, Soviet sources generally agree that girls are more conscientious in their political activity in school than boys and that they remain quite active into young adulthood. It is symptomatic of this general phenomenon that 52.4 percent of all Komsomol members are women and 57.1 percent of all secretaries of primary Komsomol organizations are women.[145] Soviet sources also agree that female participation rates drop sharply with marriage and particularly with the birth of a child and even more with the birth of a second child.[146] Only 24.3 percent of all party members were women in 1976, a figure that (combined with census data) suggests that only some 5 percent of all women between the ages of thirty and sixty are members of the party in comparison with some 22 percent of all men in that age group. However, 31.5 percent of the secretaries of primary party organizations are women.[147]

A number of the available statistics on differentials in participation by sex are similar to those on party membership. For example, 20 percent of the articles and letters with criticisms or suggestions for change that appeared in *Pravda* and *Izvestiia* in early 1975 were written by women, and 24 percent of the speakers in the soviet sessions of the RSFSR regions from 1967 to 1975 were also female. The percentage of women speakers in the republican soviets in 1975 was 20 percent, while that in the city soviets in 1975 stood at 32 percent.[148]

In practice, however, the relative proportion of men and women participating in the decision-making process varies with the type of activity. Soviet scholars privately report that some public organizations are overwhelmingly male in composition (for example, the auxiliary police or *druzhinniki*), while others (for example, library and club councils and the parents' committees in schools) are said to be predominantly female in their active membership. Women also seem heavily involved in trade union work. Almost one-half of the trade union organizations at the enterprise level are chaired by women, and 43 percent of all those in "leading posts" in the trade union organization are women.[149]

There is also considerable variation in male and female participation by policy realm. It is symptomatic that the percentage of women among the letter writers to *Sovetskaia kul'tura* (a newspaper that deals with "culture" both in the literary-artistic and the anthropological sense of the word) stood at 44 percent in early 1975, compared with 20 percent for *Pravda* and *Izvestiia*. It is also symptomatic that in 1967–1975 sessions of the regional soviets in the RSFSR, women comprised only 13.7 percent of the speakers on construction matters, compared with 37.7 percent on health issues, 33.3 percent on cultural ones, and 28.9 percent on education and youth questions.

It is in the top policymaking committees—where participation is far from the voluntary choice of the participants—that the proportion of women is extremely small. Only 3 to 4 percent of the members of the party Central Committee, of the republican party bureaus, and of the regional party bureaus are women, and this figure rises only to 12.5 percent for the members of the executive committees of the regional soviets. (In practice, the women members are often also the worker members.) At this level, however, the differentials in participation rates undoubtedly reflect male attitudes more than the desire of women to participate.

The Impact of Participation

We have examined a multitude of statistics on the participation of Soviet citizens in various aspects of the decision-making process. Unquestionably, many of these figures greatly exaggerate the level of activity—as they do in any country—for many "activists" are far from active and no one has an incentive to purge them from the lists. Yet, the advantage of citing so many of these statistics is that they drive home a point that was an integral part of the totalitarian model, but that often is forgotten: the Soviet Union obviously is a participatory society, with there being a very large number of settings in which citizen participation can take place.

The crucial question is the impact of that participation. After all, many types of political participation that are familiar to westerners are either absent in the Soviet Union or present in only partial form. The Soviet people cannot participate in competitive elections to the legislature; they cannot, with a few exceptions, mainly in the conservation realm, form issue interest groups even on relatively nonsensitive questions; they cannot engage in picketing; they cannot launch a frontal attack on the fundamentals of the system, particularly if they admit what they are doing; they cannot organize factions or parties in an open attempt to change the political leadership. These forms of participation are often thought to be at the heart of mass or group power in the West, and the question is whether the forms of participation that *are* found in the Soviet Union are associated with influence when they are not accompanied by other forms.

Many scholars have strongly emphasized the limitations on political participation in the Soviet Union and have suggested that the types of participation which do exist primarily serve functions of use for the regime. Scholars holding this view would argue that participation in the Soviet Union strengthens the identification of the citizen with the regime and its policy, that it provides the regime with unpaid labor for tasks it considers important, that it supplies the policymaker with feedback information, that it prevents lower level bureaucrats from straying from the party line, that it creates a socially acceptable safety-valve for popular discontent, and so forth.

Clearly, political participation in the Soviet Union does serve the functions enumerated, but this is also true of political participation in the West as well.[150] The question is whether participation also influences decisions at the same time it serves other functions. Unfortunately, this is a question most difficult to answer with certainty, not only because of difficulties in studying the Soviet Union but also because of the inherent difficulties in measuring influence in any setting.[151]

When Soviet refugees are asked their opinion about these questions, they give a variety of answers. Some assert that the citizen is powerless vis-à-vis the party leadership and the bureaucracy, and they describe political participation in the Soviet Union in the most cynical of terms. Others, whatever their view of the overall distribution of influence, talk about settings in which they had some impact on a local matter of importance to themselves or about institutions to which they had been able to complain about a grievance with some success. Some even show real satisfaction with the network of committees and organizations that exist in the Soviet Union, especially at the place of work, emphasizing the point by complaining about the lesser number in the United States.

To a considerable extent, all this refugee testimony is correct, and our evaluation of the impact of political participation in the Soviet Union basically depends upon the standards of judgment that are used. If we ask whether individual citizens without a major administrative or political position and without special expertise normally have the level of influence of persons with these attributes, the answer clearly is "no." An individual letter or complaint about a significant policy is, by itself, most unlikely to affect that policy, and in any case participation in a local factory committee has no relationship to the big decisions on foreign policy, the structure of the political system, or the like.

Even at the local level, it would be totally wrong to see the Soviet Union as some kind of workers' democracy in which all decisions are taken by vote in citizen meetings and in which most important decisions are decentralized to this level. On balance, those participants who have the most influence on local decisions must be those who hold full-time positions in institutions that are directly involved in the decisions. Even the influence of the "participatory institutions" often may reflect the efforts of their full-time employees. When a railroad trade union official in the Soviet Union was asked in an interview about the relative role of his trade union and the people's control groups and posts on the railroads, he answered semicontemptuously, "We have [full-time] staff."

Yet, when we analyze citizen participation in the West, we do not ask whether citizens are omnipotent. We know that an individual's participation in the PTA has no impact on foreign policy or even national education policy and that only a few interested parents even use a school's PTA to influence the decisions of its principal. Those in academia are quite aware of the limitations on the influence of faculty senates and student governments. If we give any serious thought to the subject, we recognize that one individual's vote in national elections or his or her membership dues for a large organization have no impact upon the outcome, and a letter to a congressman by a rank-and-file citizen is little different.[152]

If we attribute influence to citizen participation in the West, what types of possible impacts do we then have in mind? The first is the opportunity for a citizen to complain about some individual grievance or to make some individual request, to have it considered seriously, and to have at least some reasonable chance that it will be acted upon. The second is the opportunity for the citizen to make a policy suggestion or criticism to the relevant authorities and to have it considered or at least counted. The third is the opportunity for the citizen who is seriously interested in a topic to have a real impact on appropriate decisions if he or she is willing to spend the time and effort, perhaps in a leadership role in some kind of collective action. The fourth is the opportunity for "public opinion" to have a collective impact on decisions. One vote or one letter to an official may not matter in itself, but it can be a drop in an ocean whose tides do move things.

If political participation in the Soviet Union is viewed from this perspective, clearly it is not without influence in a number of respects. First, the network of institutions to which a citizen can complain or appeal is extremely large—larger than in a western country—and large numbers of citizens make such appeals and complaints. Obviously many of the complaints do not have an impact, but the party leadership, even under Stalin, has not been motivated to grant lower administrators full freedom of action or freedom from criticism. *Kontrol'* has always involved a regime effort to diffuse citizen dissatisfaction by using local officials as scapegoats, and that effort has no meaning if complaints about these officials are not heeded frequently. Indeed, the draft of the new 1977 constitution specifically included a right to "criticize defects in work" and forbade suppression of criticism, and in response to the discussion of this draft, the following sentence was added to the final version: "Persons who suppress criticism are brought to responsibility" (article 49).[153]

Second, although the right to present suggestions for change to the political authorities has been somewhat restricted, this type of communication has been freer than communication to fellow citizens. As has been seen, the regime not only encourages the input of suggestions on a wide range of subjects, but also collects such information on its own through its agitation-propaganda system and the KGB. The leadership repeatedly insists that all political and administrative institutions carefully analyze their incoming communications and take them into account, and the Central Committee secretary who handles incoming letters has described in some detail the way in which they are systematically studied in his institution.[154]

Third, the individual citizen who is willing to make the effort and work through some committee, bureau, or council surely does have a real chance to affect the decisions of that group or to affect conditions over which it has jurisdiction. The fact that participants, and especially participants in committees and councils, are disproportionately of higher socioeconomic status may be at variance with egalitarian Marxist hopes, but it should not be forgotten in any consideration of the impact of participation. When a professor is on an advisory council, when a doctor is on a public health standing committee of a local soviet, when an engineer is a member of a control commission in a plant, it simply makes no sense to assume that their vigorous suggestions or criticisms are always ignored. Moreover, the Soviet press and interviewed officials both report instances in which the involvement of some worker is said to have affected a particular local decision, and these claims must sometimes be correct. Participation could not perform the functions western scholars hypothesize if citizen efforts were not sometimes rewarded by success.

There also can be considerable incentive for an individual to participate actively on many of the committees. Aside from the possibility of affecting the outcome in a desirable direction, committee participation brings a person to the notice of higher officials. Those who show ability and energy have a real opportunity to be promoted into political or administrative work. Most party officials in particular are likely to have first begun their political career through some sort of part-time participatory work in college or at their place of work, and mid-career promotions of important middle-level officials often follow membership in a party bureau or chairmanship of a standing committee at a higher level and must partially reflect effectiveness in committee politics.

It could be argued, of course, that the great majority of decisions that are susceptible to citizen influence are local, administrative ones which are not very important in any case. Such a normative judgment can neither be proved nor disproved, but at a minimum it should be kept in comparative perspective. In a system in which city and state government is staffed by administrators ultimately responsible to Moscow, local administrative decisions are often equivalent to the questions that are the essence of state and local politics in the West. Even decisions within the plant, college, or apartment house are the type that activists of the late 1960s often strove the most vigorously to influence, and a "minor" tenure decision can seem crucial to the people involved.

As we try to assess the direct impact of individual participation in the

Soviet Union in comparative terms, we face the problem of a real lack of information, for neither Soviet nor western scholars have looked at the question seriously. When this is done, it is most likely that we will find circumstances in which participation has more of an impact in the Soviet Union and other circumstances in which it has less. For example, the freedom to criticize the boss generally seems to be more possible in the Soviet Union, and the type of committee involvement found in the United States in only a few places of work such as the universities seems more universal in the Soviet Union. On the other hand, Soviet citizens seem less able to veto or reshape governmental actions that might infringe upon their comfort and convenience. There certainly is Soviet citizen involvement in committees that discuss neighborhood reconstruction, the location of an expressway, level of air pollution, and the like, but once the decision is made, it is likely to be implemented without delaying actions. However, it should always be remembered that our understanding of the Soviet political process is still at a rudimentary level. We can say that direct citizen participation in the Soviet Union has many of the same characteristics found by sophisticated western political scientists—including major limits on the numbers of people deeply involved and their effectiveness[155]—but the nuances in the similarities and differences are beyond our knowledge.

The type of potential citizen impact about which we have the least knowledge is that of a broader "public opinion," either at a local or a national level. If a consensus forms within a specialized group, within the educated elite as a whole, or within a broader public opinion, are the decision-makers likely to be responsive to it? Are the decision-makers likely to try to anticipate public reaction and act in a way that they think will maximize their support?

It should be recognized that these are questions that we really do not know how to answer in any political system—western as well as Soviet. In any country we see a range of suggestions being made, and we see governmental leaders making decisions that inevitably must, by the nature of things, correspond with some of the suggestions. Does the correspondence between a suggestion and a decision indicate the presence of influence or does it simply represent a coincidence, the decision-makers' own values really having been decisive? Even decision-makers themselves often cannot reliably sort out the factors that led them to a decision, and the measurement of power or influence remains one of the most severe problems for the scholar, regardless of the setting.

In the Soviet Union it is very easy to point to actions that surely would not have been taken in the Stalin and even in the Khrushchev periods had there existed competitive elections. Today it is equally easy to say that competitive elections in the non-Russian republics would produce local political authorities much more responsive to local nationalist feelings, and it is most probable that they would result in the disbanding of the collective farm system throughout the country. As the Brezhnev regime became less eager to undertake broad societal transformation, however, it became much more difficult to judge the extent to which public opinion was influencing policy. Clearly at times it did. The regime responded to educated opinion on the pollution issue more than would be anticipated in a country at the Soviet stage of development, and it increased its affirmative action for workers into college education after the Czechoslovakia unrest in a way that suggested real sensitivity to the dangers of riots.

The overall pattern in which Soviet governmental policy is responsive or not responsive to majority opinion or to elite opinion cannot be ascertained because of the absence of polls on important policy questions, but it is likely to be quite complex. This is a question to which we will return in Chapter 14.

9 | The Individual and the Party

ONE FORM of Soviet political participation quite distinct from that in the West is membership in the Communist party. Lenin's pre-revolutionary insistence that a party member be willing to give more than verbal and financial support was retained in the post-revolutionary period, and admission to the party has been open only to those whom the party accepts. Prospective members must submit recommendations from three members who have been in the party for at least five years; they must have their applications approved by both the bureau and the general meeting of the party organization at their place of work; they must pass through a candidate or probationary stage of one year in length and then must be approved once more by the primary party organization *and* by the bureau of the party organ at the next highest level (usually the district or city party committee).[1] Even after admission, the member still faces the possibility of expulsion for failing to fulfill the duties of membership.

Those who seek and retain membership are explicitly obligated to place themselves completely at the party's disposal. They are obligated to move to any location or any job to which directed, and they must obtain the permission of the local party organization before changing jobs on their own.[2] The stern demands of membership are made dramatically manifest in the party rules. No fewer than ten duties are listed, many of them with a number of subpoints:

(1) To fight for the creation of the material and technical base of communism, to serve as an example of the Communist attitude toward

labor, to raise labor productivity, to take the initiative in all that is new and progressive, to support and propagate advanced experience, to master technology, to improve his qualifications, to safeguard and increase public, socialist property—the foundation of the might and prosperity of the Soviet homeland;

(2) To carry out party decisions firmly and undeviatingly, to explain the policy of the party to the masses, to help strengthen and broaden the party's ties with the people, to be considerate and attentive toward people, to respond promptly to the wants and needs of the working people;

(3) To take an active part in the political life of the country, in the management of state affairs, and in economic and cultural construction, to set an example in the fulfillment of public duty, to help develop and strengthen Communist social relations;

(4) To master Marxist-Leninist theory, to raise his ideological level and to contribute to the molding and rearing of the man of Communist society. To lead a resolute struggle against any manifestations of bourgeois ideology, remnants of a private-property psychology, religious prejudices, and other survivals of the past, to observe the principles of Communist morality and to place public interests above personal ones;

(5) To be an active proponent of the ideas of socialist internationalism and Soviet patriotism among the masses of the working people, to combat survivals of nationalism and chauvinism, to contribute by work and deed to strengthening the friendship of peoples of the USSR and the fraternal ties of the Soviet people with the peoples of the socialist countries and the proletariat and working people of all countries;

(6) To strengthen the ideological and organizational unity of the party in every way, to safeguard the party against the infiltration of persons unworthy of the lofty title of Communist, to be truthful and honest with the party and the people, to display vigilance, to preserve party and state secrets;

(7) To develop criticism and self-criticism, to boldly disclose shortcomings and strive for their removal, to combat ostentation, conceit, complacency, and localism, to rebuff firmly any attempts to suppress criticism, to speak out against any actions detrimental to the party and the state and to report them to party bodies, up to and including the Central Committee of the CPSU;

(8) To carry out unswervingly the party line in the selection of personnel according to their political and work qualifications. To be uncompromising in all cases of violation of the Leninist principles of the selection and training of personnel;

(9) To observe party and state discipline, which is equally binding on all party members. The party has a single discipline, a single law for all Communists, regardless of their services or the positions they hold.

(10) To help in every way to strengthen the defensive might of the USSR, to wage a tireless struggle for peace and friendship among peoples.[3]

Nevertheless, despite many continuities with its prerevolutionary traditions, the Communist party of the Soviet Union has changed radically over the years. The leadership has made membership nearly compulsory for those who want an administrative career, and this policy has had several crucial corollaries which, in turn, have had a major impact upon the nature of the party.

In the first place, while the leadership surely required party membership for entry into the administrative elite in an attempt to create a loyal administrative corps who would share the leadership's basic values, the passage of time has fundamentally changed the nature of the problem. In the 1920s, many administrators and prospective administrators were quite unsympathetic to the revolution, and the installation of a party member as head of an institution or a department served political control functions in the most obvious way. By the 1960s and 1970s, however, administrative candidates for appointment had all been educated within the Soviet system, and, unless a prospective administrator has moved into open dissidence, the regime has great difficulty in judging the real degree of his loyalty in comparison with other candidates.

As political loyalty became a less easy (and less necessary) criterion for making distinctions among the educated population, the leadership's natural desire for an effective administrative system could receive even higher priority in personnel selection. If party membership was to remain a requirement for administrative positions, the leadership had every incentive to ensure that those who would be effective administrators were, in fact, admitted to the party—at least if they manifested the normal loyalty to the system. In practice, the leadership has responded to this incentive with two steps. First, it has generally postponed party admission until the age that candidates have had a chance to demonstrate job competence, and, second, it has admitted a large percentage of those qualified for promotion into the party. Few people now enter the party before their mid-twenties (the average age of party admission was thirty-one in 1966, twenty-seven in 1975), but once that age is reached, the enrollment becomes substantial.

The second consequence of requiring party membership for middle level administrators is a relatively large party, at least if the leadership also wants a large number of workers and peasants in the party for reasons of legitimacy or ideology. As T. H. Rigby has emphasized, industrialization results in an enormous expansion of the number of managerial-professional personnel in any society.[4] There is no way to draw a large proportion of these personnel into the party and to retain a heavy worker-peasant component without permitting the party to grow substantially. In the Soviet Union this process has been hidden to a considerable extent by the postponement of party admission to a later age and by the practice of admitting a relatively low percentage of women into the party, but the proportion of men between the age of thirty and sixty in the party in 1976 was some 22 percent, and the proportion of men of this age with a higher education, over 50 percent.

The increase in the size of the party and the postponement of the age of party admission inevitably has had its impact upon the type of person in the party and upon the nature of the party itself. Unless one assumes an improbable change in human nature, there are limits to the expectations that a mass organization can have of its members and to the demands which it can make upon them. Such an organization can scarcely be thought of as a priesthood or its members as ascetic ideologues. As a result of the change in the nature of the members, the functions of party membership both for the individual and the regime must have become highly complex and subtle.

Trends in Party Membership in the Past

In recent years, party membership trends have been quite regular. The number of party members rises every year, and only a relatively small number of members are expelled. Even changes in the rate of increase in party membership and in its social composition have become incremental in character, and they have tended to be closely associated with the changes in the societal groups from which party members are normally drawn. In the past, none of these generalizations would have been accurate. The size of the party fluctuated enormously from period to period, with years of mass enrollment alternating with years of mass purge. (The Russian word for "purge"—*chistka*—literally means "cleansing.")

Despite Lenin's continued insistence upon a party limited to those willing to support it with activity as well as words, the period after the March and November revolutions saw an immense expansion in the size of the party. The party itself did not have a systematic count of its own membership until 1922, but the official figures of 23,600 members in January 1917, 390,000 members in March 1918, and 732,500 members and candidates in January 1921 are probably sufficiently accurate to give a sense of the manifold increase in membership that occurred during these years. Inevitably the prevailing conditions for admission must have been relatively loose.[5]

In 1921, however, Lenin demanded a widespread purge of the "rascals, bureaucrats, dishonest or wavering Communists, and of Mensheviks who have repainted their 'facade' but who have remained Mensheviks at heart."[6] By 1924, the number of full members had fallen from approximately 567,000 to 350,000—a decrease of 217,000 members in three years (really a decrease of over 382,000 if one includes the 165,000 candidate members in the 1921 count and assumes that they should normally have become full members by 1924). Particularly given the fact that new members had continued to enter the party during these three years, it is obvious that over one-half of the party's members and candidate members at the end of the Civil War had been expelled or had resigned voluntarily by the time of Lenin's death. Indeed, by January 1927, only 263,000 of the pre-1921 full members and only another 54,000 of those becoming full members in the 1921–1923 period remained in the party.[7]

After Lenin's death in January 1924, party membership began to soar once more. The party proclaimed a Leninist Enrollment (*Leninskii prizyv*) both in 1924 and in 1925, and by January 1926 the number of members (including candidates) had risen from 472,000 to 1,079,814, more than doubling in the two-year period. Despite continued expulsions of a significant number of unsatisfactory members (for example, 20,000 in 1925, 25,000 in 1926, 133,000 in 1929–1930),[8] the party continued to grow throughout the twenties. Then during the enthusiasm of the Great Leap Forward of the First Five-Year Plan period, the size of the party doubled once again. The membership rose from 1,677,910 to 3,555,338 in the three years between January 1, 1930, and January 1, 1933.

Both the Leninist Enrollments of 1924 and 1925 and the First Five-Year Plan expansion greatly increased the proportion of party members who were actually employed as workers and peasants. In 1924, only 18.8 percent of the Communists were workers by profession, and a considerably smaller (but undisclosed) number were peasants. In 1927, by contrast, 39.4 percent of the party members were employed as workers and 13.7 percent as peasants.[9] Given the large number of peasants in the country as a whole, party representation in this group remained extremely small, but the proportion of the working class, and particularly the industrial working class, who were party members became quite substantial. Variations in Soviet definitions of workers in these years make exact calculations difficult, but, as table 14 indicates, an estimated 8.4 percent of all industrial workers were Communists in January 1927—and a considerably higher percentage of male industrial workers, especially those in skilled jobs. The proportion of white collar employees working largely for governmental institutions (the *sluzhashchii*) who were in the party was larger than that of the industrial workers, but the reverse was true for the white collar workers as a whole (including the self-employed). For example, in 1928 only 1.2 percent of the "specialists" employed in the economy (those persons with higher and specialized secondary education) were party members, while

Table 14 *Party representation
among various population groups, January 1927*

GROUP[a]	TOTAL NUMBER IN GROUP	COMMUNISTS IN GROUP	PERCENT
Red army	562,000	78,250	13.9
White collar (*sluzhashchii*)	3,441,000	438,832	12.8
Artisans and other white collar[b]	5,614,000	125,425	2.2
Industrial workers	2,560,000	215,559	8.4
Other workers (agricultural excluded)	2,157,000	111,819	5.2
Unemployed	953,000	44,813	4.7
Peasants[c]	20,213,000	116,169	0.6
Agricultural workers	2,560,000	15,765	0.6
Total	38,060,000	1,146,632	3.0

Source: The figures on the number of wage earners and peasant heads of household (*samodeiateli*) come from a commission of the USSR Council of People's Commissars and are found in *Statisticheskii spravochnik za 1928* (Moscow, TsSU SSSR, 1928), pp. 42–43. The party membership figures are from the party census of January 10, 1927, and are found (together with the size of the Red army) in *Itogi desiatiletiia sovetskoi vlasti v tsifrakh 1917–1927* (Moscow, TsSU SSSR, 1928), pp. 18, 22–23, 74. The number of army Communists comes from Rigby, *Communist Party Membership*, p. 241. Since the population figures and those on party membership come from different official sources, it is possible that the definitions of categories are not absolutely identical, but any differences should not significantly affect the results.

a Includes wage earners and peasant heads of household.

b This category includes artisans (*kustari i remeslennye*), of whom only 5,466 of 2,029,500 were party members, students. tradesmen, bourgeoisie of various types, and a few "proletariat" elements (notably servants.) Of the Communists in this category, 28,777 are listed as "junior service personnel" (*mladshii obsluzhivaiushchii personnel*), but it is conceivable that this is an error–that this type of personnel has been distributed among the workers by the compilers of the population statistics.

c The number of working peasants is much higher than this figure on heads of household, and hence the percentage of party members among all peasants is actually even lower than indicated.

only 0.9 percent of the engineers employed in the enterprises were Communists.[10]

During the first years of the First Five-Year Plan, the criteria for selection became even more class oriented. After the first Leninist Enrollment in 1924, a majority of the recruits to candidate membership had, as table 15 demon-

Table 15 Occupation of recruits to candidate membership, 1924–1933

Period	All candidates	Workers		Peasants		White collar	
		Number	Percent	Number	Percent	Number	Percent
Jan.–July 1924[a]	212,330	195,344	92.0	7,000	3.3	9,986	4.7
July 1924–July 1928[b]	902,760	514,152	57.0	153,443	17.0	235,165	26.0
July–Dec. 1928	133,375	97,230	72.9[c]	20,899	15.6	15,246	11.4
1929	297,630	232,027	78.0	44,440	14.9	21,163	7.1
1930	670,529	441,878	65.9	171,484	25.6	57,167	8.5
1931	997,398	630,076	63.2	306,393	30.7	60,929	6.1
1932	762,318	493,037	64.7	226,162	29.7	43,119	5.7

Source: I. N. Iudin, *Sotsial'naia baza rosta KPSS* (Moscow, Politizdat, 1973), pp. 117 and 162, provides figures for the total number of candidates and the number of worker and peasant candidates. Figures for white collar candidates were calculated by subtraction.

a Iudin provides only data on the total number of candidates and the number of worker candidates for the first half of 1924. The figures for peasant and white collar candidates are simply an estimate of the division of the small remainder.

b Iudin provides only a total figure for number of candidates admitted as candidate members from January 1924 to July 1928. The figures for July 1924 to July 1928 have been calculated by subtracting the estimates for the first half of 1924 from these totals. Iudin's figure for the total number of candidates in this period is 6,684 smaller in his discussion of peasants than in his discussion of workers. I have accepted the worker figure, but the difference would mean a variation of only a few tenths of 1 percent in the final figures.

c The rise in the percentage of working-class recruits did not begin in the second half of 1928, but it was not possible to calculate the breakdown between peasant and white collar candidates from Iudin's data until that time. Workers provided 44.4 percent of the recruits for the first half of 1926, 47.0 percent for the second half of 1926, 67.7 percent for 1927, and 69.0 percent for the first half of 1928.

strates, continued to be workers, but a quarter to a third had been persons in white collar positions. Then as the leadership began moving toward a policy of rapid industrialization in 1927, 1928, and 1929, it greatly increased the number of workers admitted into the party. By 1929, the proportion of the candidates who were workers had risen to 78 percent. This figure declined somewhat thereafter, but with the enormous expansion in the total size of the recruitment during the First Five-Year Plan period, the average number of workers admitted as candidate members in *each* of the years 1930, 1931, and 1932 was nearly as large as the total number admitted in the four years from 1925 through 1928.[11]

Despite the continuing movement of worker Communists into white collar jobs, this policy of active recruitment of workers into the party increased the proportion of Communists who were workers by current occupation to a high of 48.6 percent in April 1930, and to 43.8 percent by January 1, 1932.[12] Of all industrial workers as of January 1, 1932, 13.3 percent were reported to be party members,[13] and the percentages were much higher in the larger industrial enterprises. Nine months earlier, 20.5 percent of the workers in such enterprises in the oil industry, 19.8 percent of those in the leather industry, 17.3 percent of those in the metalworking industry, and 16.3 percent of those in the chemical industry were Communists.[14]

Even these figures understate the extent to which the party had become a proletarian one, for many workers were being promoted into administrative work. By 1927, some 270,000 persons who had entered the party as workers were now employed as white collar employees, public officials, military personnel, or college students,[15] while between January 1930 and January 1933 another 666,000 worker-Communists were promoted into work in the state or industrial apparatus or were sent to study.[16] By 1932, 92.1 percent of all party members were either workers or peasants, or had been so when they entered the party.[17]

Undoubtedly, some of those who were workers at the time of their admission into the party had actually come from white collar families and had happened to be workers either because of economic necessity or a desire to "improve" their social standing. Nevertheless, the available education statistics on party members indicate that this was no mass phenomenon. In 1927, only 0.8 percent of all party members had a college degree and another 7.9 percent had a high school diploma. Still another 62.8 percent had completed at least four years of schooling, but 28.5 percent did not even had this much formal education (26.1 percent were listed as home-taught or self-taught, and 2.4 percent as functionally illiterate).[18]

In the early 1930s, major changes began to occur in the nature of party membership. The first of these changes was a sharp increase in the number of peasants admitted to the party, beginning in mid-1930 in the wake of the collectivization decision and continuing until 1933. By mid-1932 only one-fifth of the collective farms had a party cell or an organized group of candidates, but the process of party penetration was at least beginning.[19] Although the leadership also began emphasizing the permissibility and even the desirability of admitting "the best representatives of the intelligentsia" into the party,[20] the statistics of table 15 scarcely suggest a massive recruitment from this stratum in percentage terms. The steady rise in the number of party members in white collar occupations still reflected the upward mobility of those who had joined the party as workers or peasants, not the enrollment of those who already occupied such jobs.

The second change in party admission policy—and the major one—occurred on December 10, 1932, when the Central Committee announced a suspension of all party admission and a mass purge among the existing membership. Within two years the number of members and candidates had dropped by nearly a million and a quarter persons (over one-third of the membership) to 2,358,714. This purge, it should be emphasized, took place before Kirov was assassinated in December 1934, and it seemed little related to a desire to remove former or potential political opposition. Rather, the purge's main target seemed to be collective farmers and new industrial workers who had flocked into the party during the membership drives of the First Five-Year Plan period, and the action was undoubtedly part of the Great Retreat from a number of the Great Leap Forward policies of that period.

The purge of party members did continue after the assassination of Kirov, and at that point its sharpest edge came to be turned more directly against former members of the opposition and then against many of the Old Bolsheviks who supported Stalin himself. Nevertheless, western use of the term Great Purge to refer to the events of 1937–1938 is misleading if it is taken to imply a particularly large number of expulsions from the party during these years. In the entire *three* years from Kirov's death to the low point of membership in January 1938, the number of members and candidates dropped by only 438,000 persons (478,000, if one adds the new admissions during this period), compared with a decline of 1,196,000 members in the previous *two* years. Rigby convincingly estimates that slightly less than 100,000 of this decrease can be assigned to the terrible year of 1937.[21] Indeed, fewer of the Old Bolsheviks were purged in the entire 1934–1938 period than many westerners suggest. In 1927 there were only 9,000 pre-1917 members still in the party and 254,000 members from the 1917–1920 period; by 1939 these figures had fallen to only just under 5,000 and 90,000 respectively, and some of the decline must be attributed to natural deaths over twelve years and to

pre-1934 purges.[22] What occurred during the Great Purge was not any increase in the rate of the purge, but a change in the fate of many who were
expelled.

The prohibition against new party admission lasted from January 1933
until November 1936,[23] and only 40,000 persons were admitted as candidates
between November 1936 and January 1938. From that point onward, however,
the size of the party began to soar once more. By June 1941 party membership
had more than doubled, reaching the highest figure in its history to that date
—3,965,000 members and candidates.[24]

Behind the overall figures showing a return of the party to its former
size (and even beyond), fundamental changes had taken place in the nature
of the membership—changes that have continued to characterize the party
until the present time. The first major difference in the postpurge party
was the age at which people were normally admitted into the party. Admission to the party was legally possible from the age of eighteen, and prior
to the purges of the 1930s, many had, indeed, entered the party when they
were nineteen, twenty, or twenty-one. In 1927 (the last year for which this
information seems to be available in that period), 25 percent of *all* party
members were less than twenty-five years of age,[25] and the situation cannot
have changed much by the time that party admission was suspended in 1933.
(The average age of the party member had increased only slightly, from 31.1
to 32.8, in the six years from 1927 to 1933.)[26] By contrast, only 8.9 percent of
the party members were under twenty-five years of age on the eve of the war,
despite the massive recruitment that had just been completed—a clear indication that most of the new members had been older than that when admitted.[27] The "generation" that was denied party entry through the mid-
1930s was now being admitted, and in the process the youngest adults had
to wait their turn.

The second change in the postpurge party was in the educational and
occupational profile of its membership. In March 1939 the Eighteenth Party
Congress formally abolished all class based distinctions in the rules for party
admission,[28] but this decision simply reflected an earlier change in actual
recruitment practices. While 92 percent of the 1932 party was worker or
peasant in social composition (that is, 92 percent of the members had had
such an occupation when joining the party), this figure had dropped to 65.0
percent by the beginning of 1941.[29] Among the new candidate members admitted between November 1936 and March 1939, only 41.0 percent had been
workers, 15.2 percent peasants, and 43.8 percent white collar,[30] and at least
in Perm, Azerbaidzhan, and Georgia, the percentage of white collar employees
among the new candidates rose to the 60 percent level in 1939 and 1940.[31]

In 1941, 44.4 percent of the party as a whole was still listed as worker by social composition, but neither then nor since has a national figure been given for the number of workers by current occupation. In Perm oblast, however, where 45.6 percent of the members were workers by social origin in January 1941, 20.5 percent were workers by occupation. The comparable figures in Azerbaidzhan were 40.8 percent and 19.6 percent, and in Georgia they were 34.6 percent and 17.7 percent.[32] (The differences primarily reflect variations in the worker and peasant components of the party associated with different levels of industrialization in the respective areas.) If this range of percentages is typical for the nation as a whole—and it should be close— then there were some 700,000 to 800,000 workers by occupation in the entire party at that time. Since there were some 20 to 21 million workers employed in the economy,[33] the proportion of workers who were party members had dropped to the 3 to 4 percent level, even below the 5 to 7 percent range of 1927–1928. By contrast, 20.5 percent of those with higher and specialized secondary education were now members of the party, compared with 1.2 percent in 1928.[34]

With the onset of World War II, the admission policies of the previous few years were once more—if temporarily—modified. In the first months of the war, membership dropped sharply as many Communists were killed or captured, and entry into the party became very difficult. (The requirement of three letters of recommendation from Communists who had known the applicant for at least a year at his place of employment could be next-to-impossible for a person who had just joined an army unit or moved to a defense plant in the hinterlands.) Soon, however, the rules with respect to letters of recommendations and length of candidacy were relaxed, and party admission rose sharply. From June 1941 to January 1946, a total of 5,319,297 persons were admitted to candidate status and 3,615,451 to full membership in the party.[35] Since over three million Communists perished in the war (and others must have been captured), the total membership did not grow as rapidly as the admission statistics would indicate, but by early 1946 it stood at 5,510,862 persons.[36]

During the war, the concentration on recruitment of military personnel as party members meant a return to the policy of admitting younger men and women, and by the end of the war the proportion of Communists under twenty-five years of age had reached 18.3 percent (compared with 8.9 percent four years earlier).[37] Nevertheless, despite the admission of a large number of rank-and-file soldiers during the war (and the proportion of privates and noncommissioned officers among army members had increased from 28 percent in 1941 to 57 percent in the much larger army of 1945),[38] the education level among party members continued to rise. At the beginning of the war,

39.8 percent of the members had at least some secondary education, at the end 57.4 percent. "Not less than one-third of all persons who had finished higher educational institutions" were now party members.[39]

Prior to the war, each period of mass expansion in party membership had been followed by a large-scale "cleansing" of members who were thought to have entered the party unjustifiably during the years of easier admission, and in fact, a fair number of members resigned or were expelled in the immediate postwar period (some 100,000 a year by one estimate).[40] However, the postwar expulsions and resignations constituted a relatively small percentage of the total membership, and they were more than balanced by continued admission of new members. As table 16 indicates, there was some variation in admission policy from year to year in the postwar period (notably a sharp decline in 1948 and 1949 when Malenkov was supervising the party apparatus and a rebound in 1950 and 1951 when Khrushchev took over these responsibilities), but the overall pattern is one of a slowing down in the rate of increase in party membership rather than a purge in the old sense. In 1956 the party was only 30 percent larger than in 1946, an increase of some 3 percent a year, and most of the rise was concentrated in the white collar and specialist categories.

To a considerable extent the slowdown in the growth of the party was the natural result of demographic factors, coupled with an intensification of the prewar tendency to delay party admission until a person was in his middle or late twenties. Given the decision to postpone the age of party admission, the basic age structure of the population virtually dictated a slow growth in party membership in the postwar period, unless the leadership was willing to permit a significant increase in the proportion of society enrolled in the party. The number of persons between the age of twenty-five and thirty-five in the late 1940s (that is, essentially the number of those born between 1915 and 1925) was abnormally small, first, because of the reduced number of births during World War I, and second, because of the concentration of World War II losses in this age cohort. The 1959 census provides the most graphic indication of this fact, for it found only 10,400,000 citizens who had been born in the 1915–1919 period and 11,600,000 from the 1920–1924 period, compared with 19,000,000 persons born between 1925 and 1929. (The number of men in these groups was 4.0 million, 4.5 million, and 8.6 million, respectively.)[41]

As this "trough" in the population statistics passed through the ages of maximum party admission in the late 1940s, a drop in the number of admissions was to be expected in any case. Moreover, of course, it was precisely this age cohort that had provided the large number of young recruits into the party during the war, and hence those in the cohort most inclined

Table 16 *Population in 24–30 age group and party admission, 1946–1975, by sex*

YEAR	NUMBER OF MEN AGED 24–30	AVERAGE NUMBER OF MEN PER YEAR AGED 24–30	NEW MEN CANDIDATES	CANDIDATES DIVIDED BY AVERAGE MEN PER YEAR (PERCENT)
1946	5,680,000	811,000	265,000	33
1947	5,840,000	834,000	200,000	24
1948	6,220,000	889,000	80,000	9
1949	6,790,000	970,000	160,000	16
1950	7,580,000	1,083,000	300,000	28
1951	8,580,000	1,183,000	440,000	37
1952	9,880,000	1,411,000	240,000	17
1953	11,020,000	1,574,000	152,000	10
1954	11,940,000	1,706,000	180,000	11
1955	12,700,000	1,814,000	228,000	13
1956	13,270,000	1,896,000	309,000	16
1957	13,310,000	1,901,000	343,000	18
1958	13,040,000	1,863,000	390,000	21
1959	12,530,000	1,790,000	469,000	26
1960	12,160,000	1,737,000	538,000	31
1961	12,120,000	1,731,000	556,000	32
1962	12,490,000	1,784,000	515,000	29
1963	12,960,000	1,851,000	602,000	32
1964	13,550,000	1,936,000	686,000	35
1965	14,070,000	2,010,000	585,000	29
1966	14,300,000	2,043,000	379,000	19
1967	13,800,000	1,971,000	495,000	25
1968	12,710,000	1,816,000	479,000	26
1969	11,420,000	1,631,000	428,000	26
1970	10,280,000	1,469,000	430,000	29
1971	9,490,000	1,356,000	350,000	26
1972	9,200,000	1,314,000	333,000	25
1973	9,330,000	1,333,000	348,000	26
1974	10,120,000	1,446,000	390,000	27
1975	11,310,000	1,616,000	419,000	26
1976	12,375,000	1,768,000	422,000	24

Source: The number of men and women between the ages of 24 and 30 in each year are extrapolated from the year-by-year breakdowns in 1959 and 1970 presented in *Estimates and Projections of the Population of the U.S.S.R. by Age and Sex: 1950 to 2000* (Washington, D.C., U.S. Department of Commerce, 1973). pp. 15–16. The number of candidates accepted each year are found in (or extrapolated from) *Partiinaia zhizn'*, no. 1 (January 1962), p. 45;

Year	Number of women aged 24–30	Average number of women per year aged 24–30	New women candidates	Candidates divided by average woman per year (percent)
1946	9,160,000	1,309,000	60,000	5
1947	9,240,000	1,320,000	50,000	4
1948	9,700,000	1,386,000	20,000	1
1949	10,480,000	1,497,000	40,000	3
1950	11,300,000	1,614,000	75,000	5
1951	12,270,000	1,753,000	110,000	6
1952	13,250,000	1,893,000	60,000	3
1953	14,050,000	2,007,000	38,000	2
1954	14,510,000	2,073,000	45,000	2
1955	14,800,000	2,114,000	57,000	3
1956	14,840,000	2,120,000	72,000	3
1957	14,420,000	2,060,000	81,000	4
1958	13,760,000	1,966,000	91,000	5
1959	13,040,000	1,863,000	110,000	6
1960	12,600,000	1,800,000	135,000	8
1961	12,510,000	1,787,000	157,000	9
1962	12,890,000	1,841,000	145,000	8
1963	13,310,000	1,901,000	170,000	9
1964	13,900,000	1,986,000	193,000	10
1965	14,450,000	2,064,000	165,000	8
1966	14,660,000	2,094,000	133,000	6
1967	14,120,000	2,017,000	174,000	9
1968	12,990,000	1,856,000	168,000	9
1969	11,690,000	1,670,000	151,000	9
1970	10,490,000	1,496,000	151,000	10
1971	9,730,000	1,390,000	143,000	10
1972	9,480,000	1,354,000	136,000	10
1973	9,600,000	1,371,000	142,000	10
1974	10,420,000	1,489,000	160,000	11
1975	11,580,000	1,654,000	171,000	10
1976	12,725,000	1,818,000	187,000	10

no. 10 (May 1965), p. 9; no. 7 (April 1967), p. 7; no. 14 (July 1973), p. 13; no. 21 (November 1977), p. 26; *Kommunist*, no. 7 (May 1966), p. 4; N. A. Petrovichev, ed., *Partiinoe stroitel'stvo*, 4th ed. (Moscow, Politizdat, 1976), p. 76. The extrapolations on the Stalin period are based on percentages found in a variety of sources on regional party admission.

toward party membership already had ample opportunity to join. Indeed, those who were not in the party might reasonably expect the question: why did you not associate yourself with the party in its time of greatest peril? Under the circumstances, the striking thing about postwar admission to the party is not that it was so small, but that it was so large. If one compares the number of new candidates with the number of men in the twenty-four to thirty age group in the various years (the group moving into the period of concentrated enrollment), one finds the ratio between the two not much lower than during the membership drives of the late 1950s and early 1960s, particularly if the year-to-year variations are smoothed out[42] (see table 16).

For whatever reason, the postwar recruitment into the party was heavily white collar in nature. Some 55 to 60 percent of new candidate members were in white collar positions at the time of their admission, while some 25 percent were workers and some 15 to 20 percent were collective farmers.[43] (Most of the latter group, no doubt, occupied managerial or white collar positions on the farms.) Moreover, of course, some of the members admitted as working class continued to move into white collar work. Judging by regional statistics from Azerbaidzhan, Georgia, and Perm region, somewhat under 20 percent of all party members were workers by occupation toward the end of the Stalin era, and this figure includes subforeman supervisors such as brigade leaders. As in 1940, only some 4 percent of the working class were in the party, compared with some 25 percent of those in the white collar category.[44]

The really low levels of party admission in the postwar period actually came after Stalin's death rather than before it. The number of new candidate members admitted in 1953, 1954, and 1955 were smaller in absolute terms than those enrolled in 1950, 1951, and 1952, but the difference was even more dramatic in relative terms. Those born after 1925—that is, those who were too young to fight in World War II (and, therefore, either to be killed in action or be admitted into the party at that time) were moving into their late twenties in the early 1950s. Hence, as table 16 indicates, the decline in the number of admissions was occurring in the face of a major increase in the size of the pool of eligibles—nearly a doubling of the number of the males in the twenty-four to thirty age group in a decade's time.

With Khrushchev's consolidation of power, the number of persons enrolled in the party began to increase substantially. In the late 1950s this was a fairly gradual process, particularly given the concurrent rise in the number of eligibles, and it was not until 1959 that the proportion of male eligibles admitted exceeded the level of the late 1940s. In the 1960–1964 period, however, the admission drive took on substantial proportions. The party membership, which had risen by only 1,150,000 persons in the nine years from January 1947 to January 1956 (from 6,050,000 members to 7,200,000), rose by

4,550,000 in the next nine years, reaching a size of 11,758,169 by January 1, 1965.

The Khrushchev expansion of the party was not a simple expansion in numbers; it also involved a number of significant changes in the background of those admitted. Some of the changes (for example, that in the proportion of members with at least a high school diploma from 33.9 percent in 1952 to 47.7 percent in 1965) were largely the product of simultaneous changes in the population as a whole; others (for example, the increase in the proportion of women from 19.0 percent in 1952 to 20.2 percent in 1965)[45] may have also reflected a minor change in emphasis in admission policy. But there was one major development that clearly was the result of a deliberate policy decision— a sharp rise in the proportion of workers admitted into the party. In the 1952–1955 period, some 28.3 percent of the new candidates were workers by occupation at the time of their admission (only 23.8 percent in 1952), but this figure increased to 44.7 percent for the 1962–1965 period.[46]

Yet, in broader historical perspective, even the growth in membership in the Khrushchev era could be seen as a belated enrollment of persons who would normally have been admitted into the party in the early and middle 1950s had it not been for the tight membership policy in effect at that time. The average age of admission was thirty-one in 1966,[47] and the 50 percent of the new members who were older than the average were in their mid-twenties a decade earlier. In fact, the average annual proportion of men in the twenty-four to thirty age group enrolled as candidate members in the 1953–1964 period was 23.0 percent—almost exactly the same as (indeed, a fraction smaller than) the 23.5 percent of the 1946–1952 period. Only among the women of this age group did the proportion admitted increase.

Within a year after the fall of Khrushchev, the new party leadership issued a formal decision criticizing the laxity in maintaining admissions standards in the preceding years, and it ordered lower party organs to be more careful in their admission policy.[48] In practice, the number of new admissions to candidate membership, while remaining very high in 1965 (750,000 persons) was sharply reduced to 511,000 persons in 1966. The enrollment of new candidates in the 1967–1970 period did rebound to the 620,000 level on the average, but this figure was still 20 percent lower than the 1960–1964 level. Then the admissions to candidate membership from 1971 to 1975 dropped to an average of 520,000 a year.[49]

At the same time the number of persons who left the party increased steadily during the Brezhnev years. The annual attrition in membership (the difference between the actual number of members in a year and the total of the previous year's membership plus the previous year's admission of new candidates) rose from 150,000 a year in the 1962–1965 period to

195,000 a year from 1966 to 1971, 251,000 a year in 1971 and 1972, and 271,000 a year from 1973 through 1975 (see table 17). Some of this increase is attributable to the aging of the membership and hence a higher mortality rate within the party—perhaps 130,000–140,000 deaths a year in the early seventies compared with some 75,000 a year a decade earlier—but this factor obviously accounts for only about one-half of the attrition in the first half of the 1970s.[50]

The rise in the number leaving the party after 1971 was associated with an exchange of party cards announced by Brezhnev at the Twenty-Fourth Party Congress in 1971 and carried out between March 1973 and February 1975. While the exchange was said to be necessitated by the expiration of the old documents (issued at the previous exchange in 1954), and while it was emphasized that "the exchange of party documents is not a purge," Brezhnev did insist that the exchange should be an "important organizational and political matter," and the Central Committee decision instituting the exchange insisted that "the party organs should ensure that all Communists strictly observe the demands of the program and the rules of the CPSU."[51]

Very little statistical data have been published on the consequences of the exchange of documents, but at the Twenty-Fifth Party Congress in 1975 Brezhnev announced that "around 347,000 persons did not receive new party cards during the period of the exchange." These were persons "who had deviated from the norms of party life, infringed discipline, or lost contact with the party organizations."[52] No details on the composition of this group were given, but some information can be garnered by comparing the overall party statistics in 1973 and 1976. The total number of attritions between 1973 and 1975, exclusive of the estimated number of party deaths in the period, is very close to the figure that Brezhnev gave for the period of exchange of cards alone—a reasonable expectation given the unlikelihood of many explusions in 1975 after the long verification process that had just ended early in the year. An examination of the 1973 and 1976 data on the group composition of the party suggests that the mini-purge affected men much more than women,[53] that it was directed almost exclusively at those with less than a high school diploma, and that the increase above the "normal" attrition rates may have been primarily at the expense of those who joined the party as workers (although perhaps as MTS or sovkhoz workers or perhaps even soldiers) and to a lesser extent those who joined as peasants (see table 17).

A number of western observers have cited these figures on party admissions and expulsions in the 1964–1976 period to suggest that the Brezhnev regime reversed the policy of party admission followed by Khrushchev and that this reversal was part of a general repudiation of Khrushchev's dedication to citizen participation in politics. However, this interpretation encounters serious difficulties. While it is true that the late 1960s did not see

Table 17 *Attrition among party members, 1962–1975, by social composition*

PERIOD	PROJECTED NUMBER OF COMMUNISTS AT END OF PERIOD[a]	ACTUAL NUMBER OF COMMUNISTS AT END OF PERIOD	ATTRITION DURING PERIOD	ATTRITION PER YEAR (PERCENT)
	WHITE COLLAR[b]			
1/1962–1/1966	5,941,296	5,682,291	259,005	1.1
1/1966–1/1971	6,716,073	6,443,747	272,326	0.8
1/1971–1/1973	6,742,968	6,613,496	129,472	1.0
1/1973–1/1976	7,120,956	6,959,766	161,190	0.8
1/1976–1/1977	7,147,691	7,099,196	48,495	0.7
	WORKER[b]			
1/1962–1/1966	4,830,561	4,675,879	163,682	0.8
1/1966–1/1971	6,229,540	5,759,379	470,161	1.5
1/1971–1/1973	6,308,752	6,037,771	270,981	2.1
1/1973–1/1976	6,982,444	6,509,312	473,132	2.3
1/1976–1/1977	6,866,858	6,714,795	152,063	2.3
	PEASANT[b]			
1/1962–1/1966	2,170,143	1,999,139	171,005	2.0
1/1966–1/1971	2,399,509	2,169,437	230,067	1.9
1/1971–1/1973	2,282,968	2,169,764	113,204	2.5
1/1973–1/1976	2,349,436	2,169,813	179,623	2.5
1/1976–1/1977	2,234,488	2,180,485	54,003	2.5

Source: *Partiinaia zhizn'*, no. 14 (July 1973), p. 13; no. 10 (May 1976), p. 14; no. 21 (November 1977). pp. 25, 28.

a The projected number of Communists is calculated by adding the number of members and candidates at the beginning date in the period to the number of candidates admitted in the period. One problem with the methodology is that the social composition of new candidates is given only for those Communists admitted by the territorial party organizations, and thus seems to exclude at least some of the Communists admitted in the army.

b Social composition refers to occupation of a member at the time he or she joins the party, and it remains constant through life. Hence the increased attrition among the worker and peasant category could come from those who were no longer working as workers and peasants. It seems unlikely that workers moving into white collar occupations would have an especially high drop-out rate. However, it is quite possible that much of the peasant attrition comes from tractor drivers or the like who move into the city, become workers, and drop out of political activity in a strange environment.

a continuation in the upward trend in new admissions of the early 1960s, it is highly likely that that trend would have been reversed, regardless of developments in the Kremlin.

The first fact to keep in mind in assessing the party admission policies of the Brezhnev regime is the basic change that occurred in the mid-1960s in the distribution of persons by age within the Soviet population as a whole. Just as the low levels of party admission in the late 1940s must be partly explained by the impact of the two wars on the generation born between 1910 and 1925, just as the Khrushchev upsurge in membership must be partly explained by the fact that the generation born after 1925 avoided participation in World War II, so the slowing down in the growth of the party under Brezhnev must largely be understood in terms of the extremely low birth rates during World War II. Thus, the 1970 census found nearly 25 million persons in both the five-to-nine and the ten-to-fourteen age groups and 25 million persons between the ages of fifteen and nineteen. The thirty-to-thirty-four age group numbered 21 million, but there were only 17.1 million persons between the ages of twenty and twenty-four and 13.8 million in the twenty-five-to-twenty-nine age group.[54] This World War II baby trough began reaching the age of maximum party admission in the mid-1960s, and it remained in this age range for the next ten years. Without a major rise in the proportion of the population drawn into the party, it was inevitable that the size of party enrollment would be affected.

The second fact to recall before speaking of a reversal of party admission policy in 1965 is that the level of party admissions actually remained quite high. In absolute terms the number of admissions was still greater than the norm of the late 1950s, and, particularly prior to 1973, the percentage increase in the size of the party was well above the increase in the size of the adult population. (The adult population, as measured by the number of registered voters, rose 15 percent between 1965 and 1975, while the number of party members and candidates rose 33 percent in the same period.)[55] The number of party members and candidates stood at 16,203,446 in July 1977, an increase of 4½ million since January 1965.[56]

In relative terms—that is, relative to the declining number of eligibles in the twenty-four to thirty age group, the scale of the new enrollment hardly declined at all from the very high rates of the early 1960s—except, perhaps, for a brief period immediately after the 1965 decision on the Kharkov organization. If one looks at the number of Communists among the various age groups in 1965, 1967, and 1973, one finds that among persons eighteen to twenty-five years of age 3.1 percent, 2.2 percent, and 2.5 percent were in the party in the three years, respectively, while 11.0 percent, 11.5 percent, and 11.2 percent of those twenty-six to forty in the same years were party members.

THE INDIVIDUAL AND THE PARTY

There was an increase in the proportion of older persons who were in the party: a rise from 10.7 percent in 1965 to 13.0 percent in 1973 for those between forty-one and fifty and from 5.5 percent to 8.0 percent for those over fifty.[57] However, the latter development seems to represent the aging of a generation with a large number of Communists already enrolled rather than an increase in the number of those over forty recruited into the party. Table 18 shows the continuation of those trends into 1977.

Table 18   *Party representation among age groups, 1977*

AGE GROUP	TOTAL IN AGE GROUP	PARTY MEMBERS IN AGE GROUP	PERCENT OF AGE GROUP IN PARTY
18–25	37,265,000	929,408	2.5
26–30	19,010,000	1,729,738	9.0
31–40	33,520,000	4,134,166	12.3
41–50	33,745,000	4,229,078	12.5
51–60	22,505,000	2,897,398	12.9
61+	32,355,000	2,074,688	6.4
Total	178,400,000	15,994,476	9.0

Source: The population data are extrapolated from *Estimates and Projections of the Population of the U.S.S.R., by Age and Sex: 1950 to 2000* (Washington, D.C., U.S. Department of Commerce, 1973), p. 21. The number of party members by age is found in *Partiinaia zhizn'*, no. 21 (November 1977), p. 31.

The third fact to recall about the admission policy of the Brezhnev regime is that it continued, and, indeed, intensified, the trends toward broadening the social composition of the party that Khrushchev had initiated. The percentage of women in the party, which rose marginally in the Khrushchev years, rose from 20.2 percent in January 1965 to 24.7 percent in January 1977 (in the 1971–1975 period 29.5 percent of the new candidates were women, compared with 21.7 percent in the 1962–1965 period).[58] The proportion of non-Russians in the party, which had actually declined from 38.5 percent in July 1961 to 37.6 percent in January 1965, rose to 39.5 percent in January 1977.[59]

However, the increasing percentage of workers among the new candidates admitted into the party was the most dramatic indication of the continuation of the Khrushchev policy. In 1964, 45.3 percent of the new candidates were workers by occupation, but this figure had risen to 58.6 percent in 1976.[60] Some of this increase has been caused by the transformation of a number of collective farms into state farms (the peasants on the latter are classified as workers)[61] and by the reclassification of certain white collar occupations (notably sales clerk) as working class in 1969,[62] but these factors explain only a moderate proportion of the rise.

While a number of worker-Communists continued to move into white collar positions after joining the party, the later age of party admission and the mass enrollment of the brighter students in college immediately after high school surely makes the upward mobility associated with party membership a much more limited affair than it had been in the 1920s and during the First Five-Year Plan period. Even if many of the worker-Communists have risen into technician and lower managerial positions, the party has still come to develop a strong working-class component in the post-Stalin period, and that situation is considerably more pronounced since 1964.

Consideration of party membership trends over time essentially must be limited to developments that have already occurred, but there is one further fact that deserves mention. The passage of the World War II babies through the normal ages of party admission is a phenomenon that has come to an end. From the mid-1970s onward those knocking on the door of the party were born immediately after the war, and it is a much, much larger group than its predecessors. Either the number admitted into the party must rise fairly sharply, or there will, indeed, be a reversal in the policy on the proportion of Soviet citizens in the party.[63] In October 1976 a new Central Committee decision ("About the Work of Party Organs of Kirgizia in Party Admission and the Training of Candidate Members") indicated a new policy of expanding admissions, but the size of the increase will be the crucial question.[64]

Party Representation by Group

Age

The age distribution among members of the Communist party may not seem of great interest in itself, but, in fact, it is the crucial starting point for any understanding of the real nature of the Communist party today. The basic data available on age distribution are very limited, and they do little more than point to the tendency for the party, while including adults of all ages, to become more middle-aged in its membership with the passage of time. On January 1, 1977, 5.8 percent of the members and candidates were twenty-five years of age and under, 10.8 percent were twenty-six to thirty years old, 25.9 percent were thirty-one to forty, 26.4 percent were forty-one to fifty, 18.1 percent were fifty-one to sixty, and 13.0 percent were over sixty years of age.[65]

The raw figures on the age distribution of party members are less interesting than those on party representation or "saturation" in each age group—figures that are calculated by dividing the total number of members in each age group by the total number of persons in it.[66] As table 18 indicates, this procedure graphically demonstrates how few of those under twenty-six are party members, and it allows us to see that the proportion of Communists is fairly level throughout the middle years of thirty-one to sixty, constituting approximately 12 to 13 percent of all persons of this age.[67] (The proportion of those over sixty who belonged to the party in 1977 was not nearly so great, partly because of the lesser enrollment of the pre-1913 generation in the party originally and even more because of the disproportionate number of women in this age group and the lower levels of party membership among women, especially older women.)

The great difference between the level of party representation in the thirty-one-to-sixty age group and that in the under-thirty and especially in the under twenty-six groups has implications for the way that we conceptualize the party and the party member. In the first place, of course, the low proportion of those under thirty in the party is testimony to the leadership's continuing policy of postponing most party admission until prospective candidates are in the middle to late twenties. Regional statistics indicate that a few people are still admitted into the party in their teens or early twenties (in Perm region, for example, 397—or 0.3 percent of the members and candidate members were twenty years of age or under in 1971),[68] but they are still rare exceptions in comparison with the hundreds of thousands who are admitted each year. Perhaps because of the variations in the size of the age groups passing through their twenties during the 1960s and the 1970s, the average age of party admission had dropped from thirty-one in 1966 to twenty-seven in 1975,[69] but even at this age a person is well advanced on his or her career. Judging by the biographies of the 288 deputies elected to the Supreme Soviet in 1970 or 1974 who had joined the party in 1966 or later, the lowering of the average age of admission occurred after 1970, for those entering the party between 1966 and 1969 did so at the average age of 31.7 compared with 28.8 for those entering in 1970 or later.[70]

The policy of relatively late entry into the party is a crucial one in shaping the nature of the party. Particularly in the past, westerners often distinguished between "Red" and "expert," and argued that "a shrewd and hard-working manager cannot be a convinced, sincere Communist."[71] However, with persons largely being admitted into the party from their mid-twenties to their early thirties, there is no reason to insist upon such a dichotomy. Admission at a later age means that a person's performance can be a critical factor in the decision on whether or not to enroll him, and, in fact, this admission policy has resulted from the regime's desire for evidence of real (rather than just verbal) dedication to the party's goals—evidence that can be manifested in a prospective candidate's performance on the job. As a consequence, party membership is not incompatible with an administrator's being shrewd and hard-working; rather, it is a sign that his superiors think he has such qualities. Indeed, if a person's performance suggests that promotion to a post requiring party membership is warranted, entry into the party can come at a still later age. Of the 1970 and 1974 deputies who joined the party after 1966, 24 percent did so at the age of thirty-five or later, 11 percent of them at the age of forty or later.

A second major implication of the postponement of the usual age of party admission is that we need to be careful in speaking of the elite nature of the party. Only 6 percent of the total Soviet population are party members, but the figure of 12 to 13 percent for party representation among adults between the ages of thirty and sixty leaves a rather different impression. While still constituting a small minority of the age group, this figure is close to that which western political scientists give as the percentage of American adults who are reasonably attentive of political affairs and take some fairly active involvement in them. If we look at the differentials in male-female membership in the party and calculate the percentage of men between the ages of thirty and sixty in the party, the figure becomes even more substantial.

Sex

Throughout Soviet history the percentage of women in the party has been much less than the percentage of men. Only 7.5 percent of the party members were women in 1920, and during the mass enrollments of the 1920s and the First Five-Year Plan period, this figure rose no higher than the 14.7 percent of 1934. The purges of the 1930s had little impact on the proportion of women in the party, but the drawing of more women into administrative and factory work during World War II (and the many deaths among male Communists at the front) increased the female component of the party to roughly the 19 percent level by war's end. There, within a fluctuation of a percentage point or so, the distribution of Communist party members by sex remained frozen for two decades; by January 1965 it was only 20.2 percent.[72]

After the overthrow of Khrushchev, the percent of party members who were women began to grow more substantially, reaching 22.2 percent of the total membership in January 1971 and 24.7 percent in January 1977. The proportion of women among those admitted to candidate membership during the last decade was higher—25.7 percent in the 1966–1970 period, 29.5 percent between 1971 and 1975, and 30.8 percent in 1976.[73] Indeed, because of the higher death rates among male members and apparently a higher purge rate among them in 1973–1974, women came to represent nearly 50 percent of the party's growth from 1972 to 1976. The number of women in the party rose by 483,000 in that period, the number of men by 546,000.[74]

Nevertheless, despite the increase in the representation of women in the party in recent years, the proportion of women who are party members remains quite small in relation to the proportion of men. While there were over 81 million women at least twenty-five years of age in the Soviet Union in early 1976 compared with under 63 million men of that age, there were only 3,800,000 women who were Communists compared with over 11,800,000 men. As table 19 indicates, the consequence is a considerable difference in the party saturation rates among men and women—a difference that has narrowed only slightly in recent years.

So far as can be judged, the small numbers of women in the party result not from any discrimination in party admission policy (if anything, the

Table 19 *Party representation among men and women over 30, 1959–1976*

Year	Population over 30	Party members over 30	Percent in party
		MEN	
1959	33,900,000	5,770,000	17.0
1965	40,500,000	8,170,000	20.2
1970	46,900,000	9,530,000	20.3
1973	50,300,000	9,930,000	19.5
1976	50,700,000	10,140,000	20.0
		WOMEN	
1959	55,500,000	1,400,000	2.5
1965	61,500,000	2,060,000	3.3
1970	67,400,000	2,660,000	3.9
1973	70,800,000	2,970,000	4.2
1976	70,900,000	3,170,000	4.5

Source: Population: "Estimates and Projections of the Population of the USSR by Age and Sex," pp. 15, 16, and 23–27. Party members: *Partiinaia zhizn'*, no. 14 (July 1973), pp. 10 and 19, and no. 10 (May 1976), p. 5. The assumption is made that the age distribution of party members in 1973 (13.1 percent 30 years of age or under) was relevant for the other years as well. The assumption should be accurate enough for real confidence in the basic pattern revealed in the table, but the minor variations in men's saturation between 1965 and 1976 are small enough to be accounted for by variations in the age distribution.

central party organs are likely to be insisting on a reverse discrimination), but from factors that reduce female political participation in general after marriage and especially after the birth of a baby. If a woman holds a full-time job and carries most of the burdens of housekeeping, shopping, and child-raising, she simply has limited time for political activity. And party membership is a form of participation that still retains Lenin's demand for activity—that requires the assumption of further political duties.

Those in the West who have discussed the different rates of party membership among men and women have focused upon the low percentage of women in the party and have concluded—no doubt, correctly—that women in the Soviet Union have less political power than men. For many purposes, however, it is more useful to focus on the percentage of men, for the under-representation of women in the party has inevitably been accompanied by an overrepresentation of the other sex. To say that some 20 percent of all men over thirty are party members—22 to 23 percent of those between thirty-one and sixty—conveys best of all the sense of just how broad the party has become in recent years, just how loose the standards for admission have become. There is no possibility that one-fifth of the male population of any country can be a special ideological priesthood, a group that can arise above occupational and other parochial interests in any single-minded dedication to the party. Twenty percent is a larger figure than could reasonably be assigned for the proportion of politically active persons in the West, and it suggests that—with the exception of a fairly small group of intellectual dissidents—the party has come to incorporate most of the attentive public over thirty—or at least most of the male attentive public.

Education

It is abundantly clear that differences in occupational, income, educational, and most other types of status are strongly associated with party membership—a fact about which the party has been sensitive over the years. The percentage of party members in different income groups has never been published or even hinted at, while the information on the proportion of various occupational groups who are party members is tantalizingly incomplete. In the case of education, on the other hand, we have fairly comprehensive data on educational levels both within the general population and within the party. Thus, it is a simple matter of division to determine that 63 percent of persons with a doctor of science degree were members of the party in 1975, compared with 52 percent of those with a candidate of science degree (really equivalent to a Ph.D.), 32 percent of those with a complete higher education, 13 percent of those with an incomplete higher education, 12 percent of those with a complete secondary education, 6 percent of those with an incomplete secondary education, and 2.5 percent of those ten years of age and over with no secondary schooling.[75]

There is, however, one major difficulty with any such calculation of party saturation within different education groups—a lack of comparability in the ages of those covered in the party statistics and the population statistics. While party members are overwhelmingly above twenty-five years of age, statistics on the population as a whole include persons of all ages. Consequently, some of those listed in the statistical handbooks as having an incomplete secondary education are still teenagers in secondary school, and some—indeed, probably most—of those with incomplete higher education are college students. Such persons obviously distort the results of any calculation in which they are included.

Any reasonable estimate of the proportion of different education groups who are party members must be limited to persons over twenty-five or thirty years of age, but such estimates are complicated by the fact that data on the educational levels of different age groups in the population are published only in the official census and that such data are never published for party members. Yet, as table 20 indicates, even if an extrapolation produces an error of several percentage points, two facts would not be changed: one, a strong correlation between educational level and likelihood of being in the party, and two, a rather high enrollment of those with even complete secondary education, let alone college education.

The most interesting data on party membership among education groups come from an attempt to divide educational figures for party members over thirty into separate statistics for men and women. Such an exercise requires a building of assumption upon assumption as we have no separate age or education distribution data for men and women party members. Nevertheless, assumptions of comparable distributions are most unlikely to produce final errors of over 5 percent in the saturation rates in any one category of men or women, and even a possible error of that magnitude would still leave extremely high figures for the proportion of men with higher and secondary education who are party members. With approximately half of the men over thirty with a college degree being party members and over a third of men over thirty with a high school degree alone being members, we are, indeed, using the word "elite" in a very broad sense if we continue to speak of the party in such terms.

To be sure, such high enrollments in the party of those with higher and secondary education—particularly of those with only secondary education—will be difficult to maintain in the future because of the rapidly rising educational levels of the Soviet population. The post-World War II babies, who began to reach the normal age of party admission in the mid-1970s, are much

Table 20 *Party representation among persons over 30,*
by levels of education, 1970

LEVEL OF EDUCATION	TOTAL IN GROUP	PARTY MEMBERS IN GROUP	PERCENT OF GROUP IN PARTY	PERCENT OF MALES IN GROUP IN PARTY	PERCENT OF FEMALES IN GROUP IN PARTY
Doctor of science[a]	23,600	12,978	55.0	—	—
Candidate of science[a]	224,500	110,131	49.1	—	—
Complete higher education	6,377,000	2,265,000	35.5	52	15
Incomplete higher education	945,000	285,000	30.2	43	13
Complete secondary education	17,097,000	4,033,000	23.6	39	10
Incomplete secondary education	22,915,000	3,037,000	13.3	22	6
Complete and incomplete elementary education	67,495,000	2,556,000	3.8	8	1
Total	114,829,000	12,176,000	10.6	20	4

Source: Total population: *Itogi vsesoiuznoi perepisi naseleniia 1970 goda* (Moscow, Statistika, 1972), III, 6–7, and (for the doctors and candidates of science) *Narodnoe khoziaisto SSSR v 1974 g.* (Moscow, Statistika, 1975), p. 143. Party members: The doctors and candidates of science are given in *Partiinaia zhizn'*, no. 14 (July 1973), p. 17, and the other figures are extrapolated from p. 16 of that issue. It has been assumed that the proportion of party members over 30 was the same in all educational groups. Distribution by sex is an average of several different methodologies using different assumptions. See Hough, "Party 'Saturation' in the Soviet Union," pp. 131–132. The total representation figure should be accurate within several percentage points and that for each sex within five percentage points for those with complete and incomplete higher education and within several percentage points for the others.

[a] The figures for doctors and candidates of science are for 1971 instead of 1970 and include all of the members of those groups—that is, no attempt is made to exclude those 30 years of age or younger. However, 1971 should be little different from 1970, and neither group should include many persons under 30.

better-educated than their elders, and the surge in the number of eligibles, coupled with their higher levels of education, will require a sharp increase in the number of those admitted to the party if the saturation rates are not to drop. Thus far, the party saturation among those with complete higher education (a group for which the age adjustment is not very crucial) has remained essentially level throughout the Brezhnev era, but the test for the figures with respect to secondary education is still to come.[76]

Occupation

In many respects party membership is even more highly correlated with occupational status than with level of education. In many administrative jobs, party saturation is 100 percent (or, occasionally, 99 percent for some ideo-syncratic reason): USSR and republican ministers and deputy ministers, chairmen of district, city, and regional soviets, and heads of administrative bureaus of regional soviets. In many others it is, at most, only a few percentage points below 100 percent: university presidents, directors of significant plants, collective farm chairmen, and army officers above the lowest levels. Paradoxically, the managers of "ideologically sensitive" institutions such as schools, libraries, scientific institutes, and theaters are less likely to be party members than those of "more technical" factories and farms, partly because of the large proportion of women among them. But even here the percentages can be substantial. For example, as early as the 1950s, 79 percent of a sample of school principals who were deputies to local Soviets were found to be party members,[77] and party saturation among leading scientists has risen considerably (see table 21).

What is striking about party representation in the administrative elite is not only the insistence upon party membership for the top economic managers and officials but also the extremely high rates of membership among the more technical, middle level administrative personnel. Thus, in the Leningrad boroughs, 100 percent of the chairmen and deputy chairmen of the executive committees in the late 1960s were members of the party, but the proportion of the heads and deputy heads of departments and heads of the sectors enrolled in the party was almost as high as 95.4 percent.[78] In industry, at least heavy industry, as many as half the senior foremen and three-quarters of the shop heads must be party members. The leadership not only requires party membership for top administrative posts but also is eager that there be a large reserve of party members in the positions from which the top administrators are chosen.

The most difficult judgment to make about party saturation among occupational groups concerns the broader and less elite groups. Obviously,

Table 21 *Academicians and corresponding members of Academy of Sciences in party, by field, 1954 and 1976*

	PERCENT IN PARTY	
FIELD OF SCIENCE	1/1/1954	1/1/1976
Philosophy, law, economics	72	100
Technical, mechanics, electric power	48	79
History	40	90
Geology, earth sciences	40	55
Chemistry	32	67
Physics, mathematics	29	46
Biology	26	52
Literature, language	18	47
Academicians, all fields	33	59
Corresponding members, all fields	39	66

Source: The lists of academicians and corresponding members at any particular time must be compiled from the lists of those who have been elected at electoral sessions of the Academy and those who have died. The former are published in *Vestnik Akademii Nauk SSSR* and, in recent years, in *Izvestiia*, and the biographies of new members are found in the Yearbooks of the *Bol'shaia Sovetskaia Entsiklopediia*. The names of those who have died are listed in the Yearbooks and in the biographical entries of the second and third editions of the *Bol'shaia sovetskaia entsiklopediia*.

Determination of a scholar's field is sometimes somewhat arbitrary in the case of those working on the boundaries of major fields. Since a man can join the party at any age, it is necessary to seek up-to-date biographies, and then a few have, no doubt, become party members after the publication of a biography. These factors, however, should not change the patterns in any significant way.

the educational figures suggest that the professions—particularly those staffed in large part by men—have much larger components of party members than do unskilled occupations employing people without a high school diploma. In fact, Soviet sources in the mid-1960s asserted that nearly half of the agronomists and zootechnicians were party members, as well as 40 percent of the engineers, one-quarter of the teachers, and one-fifth of the doctors.[79] (It is scarcely a coincidence that the rank order of the party saturation among these professions is the same as that of the percentage of women in them: agronomists and zootechnicians, 36 percent; engineers, 40 percent; teachers, 72 percent; and doctors, 74 percent.)[80] There is also variation within general professional groups that seems related to the status of the group as well as its sexual composition. For example, 40 percent of college teachers were party members in 1976, as well as 30 to 35 percent of teachers in secondary specialized educational institutions, 30 percent of those in vocational schools, and 25 percent of those in the general schools.[81]

There are even greater problems in estimating the degree of party saturation among persons with lower status occupations. In the first place, postwar national statistics provide no data on the current "class" of the members, only on the "social composition" of the party (the occupations of the members when they joined the party). Hence if one takes the number of Communists in each social composition group and tries to compare it with the number of persons employed in each category (an exercise which produces an approximate 1970 party saturation of 7 percent for workers, 10.5 percent for collective farmers, and 17 percent for white collar personnel), the results are misleading, for a person who was a worker when admitted to the party is always counted as a worker even if promoted into high administrative work. Suffice it to say that 2,169,764 Communists were listed as collective farmers by social composition in 1973, but only 1,383,475 Communists were in collective farms at that time—and, if Perm region is typical, 8 to 9 percent of this latter number were actually pensioners.[82]

Westerners have emphasized the movement of worker-Communists into white collar work, and, as has been seen, it clearly occurred on a mass scale in the 1920s and the 1930s. In 1932, on the eve of the purge, 2,032,000 Communists (65.2 percent) were workers by social composition, but only 1,370,000 (43.8 percent) were workers by occupation; in 1937, 1,245,000 (62.8 percent) were workers by social composition and only 550,000 (25 percent) were workers by occupation; in Perm region in January 1941, 45.6 percent were workers by social composition (2 percentage points above the national average), but only 20.5 percent were workers by occupation.[83]

In recent years, no national statistics have been published on the number of workers by occupation in the party, but some movement of worker-Communists into white collar positions clearly continues. It has been reported that in three industrial boroughs in Leningrad, for example, 30 percent of the persons who had joined the party as workers in 1965 had become white collar personnel during the next five years.[84] Nevertheless, the later age of party admission and the growing trustworthiness of those with higher education have meant an end to the mass upward mobility of workers *after* entry into the party. Even that which does occur (as in Leningrad) is likely to involve movement into jobs such as technicians or minor managerial posts in industry, jobs from which some reverse mobility can also occur.[85]

The best available indicator of the number of workers by social composition who are still workers by current occupation comes from scattered regional statistics (see table 22). These figures suggest considerable movement out of the collective farmer category, partly because of transformation of

Table 22 *The Azerbaidzhani, Georgian, and Perm party organizations, by social composition and current occupation, 1970*

Category	Number of members, by social composition[a]		Number of members, by current occupation	
AZERBAIDZHAN				
Workers	90,085	(36.1%)	77,194	(30.9%)
Collective farmers	58,212	(23.3%)	35,728	(14.3%)
White collar	101,373	(40.6%)	—	
White collar and others	—		136,748	(54.8%)
GEORGIA				
Workers	83,597	(28.8%)	77,551	(24.7%)
Collective farmers	77,139	(26.6%)	55,968	(19.3%)
White collar	129,455	(44.6%)	135,624	(46.7%)
Students	—		1,315	(0.4%)
All others	—		25,733	(8.9%)
PERM				
Workers	55,723	(43.7%)	40,047	(31.4%)
Collective farmers	16,253	(12.7%)	8,863	(6.9%)
White collar	55,614	(43.6%)	62,782	(49.2%)
Not employed in the economy	—		15,898	(12.5%)

Source: *Kommunisticheskaia partiia Azerbaidzhana v tsifrakh, Statisticheskii sbornik* (Baku, Azerbaidzhanskoe gosudarstvennoe izdatel'stvo, 1970), pp. 28, 32; *Kommunisticheskaia partiia Gruzii v tsifrakh (1921–1970 gg.)* (Tbilisi, Institut istorii partii pri TsK KP Gruzii, 1971), pp. 263–264; *Permskaia oblastnaia organizatsiia KPSS v tsifrakh, 1917–1973, Statisticheskii sbornik* (Perm, Permskoe knizhnoe izdatel'stvo, 1974), pp. 27, 65, 105, 113, 117. (The worker category in Perm was calculated by subtraction.)

a Occupation when entering party.

collective farms into state farms and partly because of movement into the city. They seem to suggest less movement from the worker category into white collar work, but this is a difficult calculation because an undetermined number of the workers who moved up have been "replaced" by peasants becoming workers. The important point, however, is that the ratio between the number of white collar members by occupation and white collar members by social composition is not even remotely in the same range as, for example, in 1932. The era of mass mobility after joining the party seems over.

Determining saturation rates for the broad social categories remains difficult, even if we try to extrapolate from the regional data. If we assume that 28 percent of the party members were workers by current occupation in 1970, 10 percent were collective farmers (which can be calculated on a national level),[86] 17 percent were not employed in the economy (which can be calculated on a national level),[87] and therefore that 45 percent were white collar by occupation (not counting such categories as students and army officers), then we can calculate the following 1970 saturation statistics from census data: workers, 7 percent; collective farmers (including, of course, managerial, professional, and white collar collective farmers), 6 percent if we count those working only in private plot, or 8 percent if we exclude them; white collar, 21 percent.[88] Because of the number of assumptions necessary, no attempt will be made to calculate figures for males over thirty. However, it should not be forgotten that the saturation level can become quite substantial among the most skilled of the male working class. For example, 50 percent of the blast furnace operators (*stalevar*) in the Ukrainian metallurgy industry were party members in 1973.[89]

Nationality

As table 23 indicates, nationality is yet another variable associated with major variation in the likelihood of party membership for an individual. Even among the fifteen nationalities that have their own union republics, the proportion of those over twenty years of age who were in the party in 1970 ranged from 3.5 percent in the case of the Moldavians to 11.6 percent in the case of the Georgians. The number of party members of other nationalities was revealed for the first time in nearly half a century in 1976, but since the total number of each nationality is available only for census years, it is still impossible to calculate the percentages of party membership among these nationalities in any reliable way. Nevertheless, it is clear that the proportion of Jews in the party is well above that of the Georgians—perhaps some 20 percent of those over twenty being party members.[90]

The difficulty with any simple analysis of the variation in party membership by nationality group is that, as table 23 also indicates, the educational levels among the different nationalities vary as much as the levels of party membership. Given the strong correlation between education and party membership, much of the apparent variation in party membership by nationality group really reflects the variation in education. A Georgian with at least a high school education is not three and one-half times as likely to be a

Table 23   *Percent of party members and high school graduates among persons of different nationalities, 1970*

Nationality	Number of nationality at least 20 years of age	Number of party members	Percent party members	Percent with at least high school education[a]
Georgians	1,990,000	230,000	11.6	41
Armenians	1,909,000	215,700	11.3	31
Russians	82,852,000	8,575,100	10.3	26
Azerbaidzhani	1,842,000	189,500	10.3	23
Kazakhs	2,275,000	228,500	10.0	19
Belorussians	5,860,000	480,300	8.2	21
Ukrainians	27,649,000	2,214,100	8.0	24
Kirgizians	586,000	42,800	7.3	19
Uzbeks	3,570,000	257,900	6.9	20
Turkmens	616,000	40,400	6.6	17
Tadzhiks	861,000	53,200	6.2	17
Estonians	727,000	42,600	5.9	24
Latvians	1,036,000	53,800	5.5	24
Lithuanians	1,730,000	88,900	5.1	16
Moldavians	1,518,000	53,800	3.5	11

Source: Nationality: *Itogi vsesoiuznoi perepisi naseleniia 1970 goda* (Moscow, Statistika, 1973), IV, 360–364, 393–404. Party members: Extrapolated from N. A. Petrovichev, ed., *Partiinoe stroitel'stvo* (Moscow, Politizdat, 1970), p. 65, and N. A. Petrovichev, ed., *Partiinoe stroitel'stvo*, 3d ed. (Moscow, Politizdat, 1972), p. 72.

a Based on a total population figure that includes only those persons 10 years of age and over.

party member as a Moldavian high school graduate; rather, the proportion of Georgians with that much education is over three and one-half times as high as the proportion of Moldavians.

Nevertheless, regression analysis can be employed to determine the "typical" relationship between the proportion of a nationality group with complete secondary education and the proportion of it in the party, and then one can look at the individual groups to see which have more or fewer party members than would be expected (or "predicted") for their particular educational level. The results of such an analysis, found in table 24, do indicate variation among nationalities beyond that which their educational levels would normally produce.

Table 24   *Predicted and actual levels of party representation among different nationalities, 1970*

NATIONALITY	PREDICTED PERCENTAGE	ACTUAL PERCENTAGE	PERCENTAGE POINT DIFFERENCE
Kazakhs	7.0	10.0	+3.0
Azerbaidzhani	8.1	10.3	+2.2
Russians	9.0	10.3	+1.3
Armenians	10.4	11.3	+0.9
Belorussians	7.6	8.2	+0.6
Kirgizians	7.0	7.3	+0.3
Turkmens	6.4	6.6	+0.2
Tadzhiks	6.4	6.2	−0.2
Uzbeks	7.3	6.9	−0.4
Ukrainians	8.4	8.0	−0.4
Lithuanians	6.1	5.1	−1.0
Moldavians	4.7	3.5	−1.2
Georgians	13.4	11.6	−1.8
Estonians	8.4	5.9	−2.5
Latvians	8.4	5.5	−2.9

Source: The regression formula for predicted party membership is 1.54 plus .286 times the percentage figure—without decimal point—for those with at least a high school education (see table 23).

Much of the difference between expected and actual percentages of party membership for a nationality can be fairly plausibly explained by historical factors relating to that nationality. Thus, four of the five nationalities with the most abnormally low levels of party membership—Lithuanian, Moldavian, Estonian, and Latvian—were incorporated in the Soviet Union in 1940, and presumably the relative proportion of party members among their older citizens is quite low. The Ukrainian figure too probably results from a disproportionately small party enrollment in the west Ukrainian regions that were seized in 1939. At the other extreme, the relatively high numbers of Russians and Armenians in the party probably reflects the dispersion of members of these nationalities outside their republics (especially into white collar jobs in the cities there). The high figure for the Kazakhs is probably associated with their minority position in their own republic (32.6 percent of the republic's population were Kazakhs in 1970, compared with 42.4 percent for the Russians and 7.2 percent for the Ukrainians)[91] and a political need to enroll them in the party in Kazakhstan in rough proportion to their number in the population.[92] For similar reasons, perhaps, the Azerbaidzhani are enrolled in proportions closer to the Russian, Georgian, and Armenian rates. The relatively low number of Georgians may be associated with the tendency of the Georgians to remain in their republic and for few Russians to move in (96 percent of the Georgians lived in Georgia in 1970 and only 8.5 percent of the republic's population were Russians)[93]—or, maybe, it may simply be associated with a tendency of the leadership to limit enrollment in the union republic nationality that already has the greatest party saturation.

The Primary Party Organization and the Party Assignment

The amount of attention devoted to the differences in party membership over time and across sociological lines obviously implies a belief that membership in the party has some meaning. Of course, the variation by itself suggests that the regime attaches a different type of significance to party membership than to membership in the trade unions or voting in elections where participation is more universal. However, the question remains—what is that significance? What does membership in the party mean so far as involvement in the decision-making process is concerned?

When westerners have analyzed the functions served by party membership, they have, as in their analyses of participation in general, tended to emphasize the functions that membership serves for the regime. Much attention has been devoted to the requirement of party membership for top political and administrative positions—and to the political control functions implied in this requirement. Persons who want upward mobility into the administrative elite—or want simply to remain in this elite—know they must avoid the type of political and religious activity that would be incompatible with party membership now or in the future. Parents who want such mobility for their children feel constrained in any desire to encourage the children to think or act in politically harmful ways.

In talking about party membership for rank-and-file citizens, scholars have emphasized its role in the legitimization process. The party does, after all, call itself the vanguard of the proletariat and the representative of its interests. If all members are professional-managerial personnel, this claim seems particularly hollow, and, hence, the more administrative personnel who are admitted into the party, the greater the pressure to admit a large number of workers and peasants as well.[94]

The leadership made the decision to require party membership for middle level and upper level administrative positions and to admit large numbers of workers and peasants, and surely it is important to explore the reasons for their actions. Nevertheless, institutions and rules that a leadership creates for its own purposes may provide citizens with opportunities that they can take advantage of and use for their own purposes. Any analysis concerned with the decision-making process must focus upon these opportunities and the way in which they are—or are not—used.

From the point of view of an individual, party membership has several potential benefits, even aside from opening up promotion opportunities. First, it can provide politically relevant information that cannot be obtained in published sources. The phrase "party information" has become one of the most fashionable in discussions of party life, and an improvement in the flow of information is said to be indispensable for both scientific decision-making and intraparty democracy. Much of the literature on party information concentrates on the flow of information upwards to higher party officials, but the flow of information downwards is also given considerable attention. The primary party organizations are to be informed about the decisions and work of higher party organizations, members and officials of higher committees are to give reports in the localities, and so forth.[95] In practice, this information often may not be very informative, but at times it must include items not published in the press.

The more important impact of party membership on an individual's life and political role, however, flows from the continuing requirement that a party member "work in one of the party organizations" and that these organizations perform important supervisory responsibilities within the institution in which they are located. With the primary party organization performing control functions, with the party member being required to take on a "party assignment" (*partiinoe poruchenie*), the individual who wants the occupational advantages of party membership is virtually forced to participate in some type of activity relevant to the decision-making process.

The key fact about the primary party organization from a decision-making point of view is that it has been placed not in a "precinct" or other territorial unit,[96] but at the place of work. Formerly a "party cell," the primary party organization is formed in any enterprise or institution in which no fewer than three party members are working, and, as of January 1, 1977, there were 394,014 such organizations in the Soviet Union.[97] All Communists at the place of work are enrolled in the organization and are subject to its discipline, even to the point of needing its approval before changing employment.[98] The members are obligated to meet at least once a month in general session, and they name a secretary and deputy secretary to lead the organization. The election of the secretary must be "confirmed" by the district or city party committee (and "confirmation" can mean a "recommendation" which has great authority behind it).

The primary party organization is an institution whose internal structure and even whose real role varies with the size of the organization. At one extreme, 40.4 percent of the organizations had fewer than fifteen members,[99] and many of them must be rather informal in nature. Higher party officials usually must be little interested in these organizations, and their secretaries are part-time officials who often must be truly elected. The secretaryship sometimes may simply be rotated as an obligation among friends.

At the other extreme, the primary party organization in a giant industrial plant or university can have thousands of members, and its secretary is a full-time official who plays an important role in the politics of the city—an official who frequently is promoted to higher positions within the party apparatus. Moreover, as the organization increases in size, so does the complexity of its structure. Organizations with at least fifteen members elect an executive bureau of from three to nine members to provide direction between meetings of the organization as a whole; those with over three hundred members can have a party committee of from eleven to fifteen members instead of a party bureau;[100] those with over a thousand members can have a widened party committee of approximately fifty members with an inner bureau.

If the primary party organization has over fifty members, suborganizations can be created in the shops, sections, livestock farms, brigades, and departments. In those organizations with party committees (9 percent of the total in 1976), the "shop party organizations," as these subunits are generally called, are themselves given the powers of a primary party organization. (In January 1977, 283,000 of the 414,000 shop organizations had such powers.) Below the level of the shop—or in organizations too small for shop organizations—party groups can be created—nearly 550,000 of them in 1977.[101] The shop party organizations have secretaries as their leading official, but the party groups have only *partgruporgs*—party group organizers. The primary party organization of a huge plant will have a complicated network of such subunits. For example, the Ural Machinery Works (Uralmash) in Sverdlovsk, with 6,500 members in the early 1970s, had 112 party organizations in the shops, departments, and so forth, and a total of 360 party groups.[102] Moscow University, with over 7,000 Communists, had 153 shop organizations and 464 party groups.[103]

The party rules demand that the primary party organizations and their subunits carry out a great number of responsibilities: admission of new members, ideological training of members, mobilization of employees to fulfill the enterprise's major tasks, conducting agitation and propaganda among employees, and leading the struggle against bureaucratic behavior, fraud, and infringement of discipline. However, from a decision-making point of view, the most interesting responsibility of the primary party organization is that implied in the *pravo kontrolia* (right of supervision) assigned to most of the organizations not located in administrative agencies, cultural institutions, or army units.

Western analysts of the Soviet system have manifested considerable confusion over the meaning of *pravo kontrolia*—no doubt, in large part because the official Soviet description of it is sufficiently unclear to have produced confusion among lower officials trying to operate according to its principles. On the one hand, the primary party organizations are instructed to prevent defects, to support innovations of lower officials, to struggle against managerial bureaucratism and to ensure that the right persons are selected for key positions in the institutions (for example, in Moscow University, all teaching appointments).[104] On the other hand, the primary party organizations are also instructed to strengthen the authority of the administrators and to support the principle of one-man management, and they are warned that they should not order the administrators around nor select personnel themselves. Many articles in party journals indicate that managerial and party personnel themselves are not always certain how to reconcile these various injunctions.

Westerners attempting to understand the role of the primary party organization have tended to equate the organization with its secretary, and then have treated the secretary largely as an instrument of higher party control.[105] The confusion in the instructions has itself been called one of the instruments of control. The lack of clear demarcations of authority both legitimates continuing participation by the primary party organization secretaries on any questions they think important and gives them the opportunity to appeal to the provincial party organs if they think necessary. As a consequence, these latter organs are more likely to learn if controversial decisions are being taken at a lower level and are in a position to intervene if they choose.

Although the role of the primary party organization secretary remains a fascinating question from the point of view of administrative theory (and would be particularly fascinating if it could be studied on the spot with sophisticated sociological techniques), it would be wrong to forget the organization as a whole in our discussion of the primary party organization. Whatever the precise meaning of *pravo kontrolia*—and the confusion in Soviet sources must indicate that the meaning varies from locale to locale—the primary party organization provides the institutional framework in which a great many middle and lower level personnel can participate in the decision-making process on a part-time basis.

Indeed, in primary party organizations with fewer than 150 members (and in 1977 only 6.6 percent of the organizations had over 100 members),[106] even the secretaryship is normally a part-time (*neosvobozhdennyi*) position, with the secretary simultaneously holding a full-time job in the enterprise or institution. Except for one or more of the deputy secretaries in the very large organizations,[107] and perhaps the secretaries of a few of the largest shop organizations, all other primary party organization work is part-time in nature. And it is work that involves a great number of people: 2,068,000 serving as secretaries, deputy secretaries, and members of party committees or bureaus of primary party organizations; 1,913,000 as secretaries, deputy secretaries, and members of party committees or bureaus of shop organizations; and nearly 550,000 as party group organizers in 1977.[108]

Of those working within the primary party organization, the secretaries, of course, have the greatest potential for influencing decisions within the enterprise or institution. A number of indicators—most clearly, that of career patterns of officials on the rise—strongly suggest that the status of the secretary of the primary party organization is below that of the institution's chief administrator, but whenever a question of principle (*prinsipial'nyi vopros*) arises, the secretary should at least participate in its discussion. If the secretary cannot persuade the administrator, he or she has the obligation to carry the question to a higher standing party organization for resolution. The same rules apply at the shop level, the appeal to be made to the party committee of the primary party organization.[109]

There are a number of factors that may induce a party secretary not to challenge an administrator, especially one who fulfills his plan. (The fact that the part-time secretary is administratively subordinate to the manager in his regular job must be especially inhibiting.) Nevertheless, the secretaries who want to retain their party position or who want to use it as a springboard to a higher political or administrative position must demonstrate some type of initiative, and this incentive must be a powerful one in organizations of any size. In 1977, 53.7 percent of the secretaries of the primary party organizations had complete or incomplete higher education, and many of these persons must be sensitive about their future career.[110] A sociological study in a large industrial plant found that even the shop secretaries spent two hours a day (only one-half of it during their working hours)—34.7 percent of their free time—on party work.[111] The secretaries of the primary party organizations often must be even busier.

The second category of primary party organization work that has a real potential for influence is membership in the party committee or bureau either at the enterprise or institution level. Relatively little information has been published on the composition of the membership of the committee or bureaus, but that of a construction trust is likely to be rather typical. Its membership include the secretary and a deputy secretary of the party committee (both full-time officials), the head of the trust, three economic leaders of subunits within the trust, two white collar employees (one a quality control engineer), the chairman of the trade union organization, and two workers. (One of these members was also heading the People's Control committee on the trust.)[112] The widening of the party committee in the largest organizations to some fifty members has been justified on the grounds that it permits more workers into the organization's top committee, and the reported cases of widened party committees in industry all indicate a worker component of approximately 50 percent.[113] However, Soviet sources are suspiciously silent about the membership of the inner bureaus of the widened party committees, and the membership of these bodies is probably quite similar to the bureaus in other organizations.

The party committees or bureaus serve, in practice, as the board of directors of the enterprise, except in primary party organizations of administrative agencies. Whatever the relative influence of the enterprise head within this "board" (and it may be very great), the important questions concerning the enterprise are discussed within it. Moreover, the way in which the role of the party secretary is defined ensures—or should ensure—that the director cannot control the agenda. Indeed, in the case of the construction trust just described, all members proposed questions for the agenda, and, since "each 'author' of a proposal supposes that his question is most earthshaking and important," the agenda had to be negotiated, or even decided by majority vote.[114]

The fact that the members of the committee or bureau are subordinated to the manager must, as in the case of the part-time secretary, often restrict their independence, but effective participation on an important committee must be a way of attracting attention and obtaining promotion. Aside from attending meetings, members of the bureaus are called upon to "prepare questions" for the meetings—that is, to conduct some type of inquiry on the question being discussed. In one large industrial plant, even members of the shop organization bureaus spent thirty to forty minutes a day on party work—15.3 percent of their free time, and this cannot be devoid of impact.[115] The status of membership in a party committee must also increase a member's influence in performing his administrative duties. For example, when the quality control engineer on the construction trust party committee complained about output, he could and did speak not only as an engineer but "as a member of the party committee."[116]

The scattered information available on the party group organizers suggests that in industry and agriculture, at least, they are more likely to be workers and peasants, and their role is often described in party journals in more mobilizational terms. Yet, they too can be drawn into the decision-making process: "The party groups, as a rule, take an active part in the preparation of meetings of the primary and shop party organizations, and many questions become the subject of discussion precisely on their initiative. The preparation of individual questions for the general party meeting is sometimes entrusted to one of the party groups."[117] Like the shop party secretaries, the party group organizers at a giant industrial plant spent thirty to forty minutes a day on their party work—12.8 percent of their free time.[118]

Finally, even the rank-and-file party member has a potential impact on decisions greater than the person not in the party. The requirement of a "party assignment"—if not elected party work, then work in the trade union or Komsomol organizations, in self-administration institutions (for example, the comrade courts), or in agitation-propaganda activities—puts a party member in a position to affect conditions at the place of work and/or to transmit complaints to higher officials. Even agitation-propaganda work exposes a party member to questions which "concern the most diverse spheres of life of society: politics, economics, production and living conditions: (why is something permitted? why isn't such and such done?)".[119] Reporting the causes of dissatisfaction to the party committee is a component part of properly functioning "party information." A sociological study in Siberian industrial plants found that party members spent 10.2 percent of their free time on "public affairs," compared with 3.1 percent for persons not in the party,[120] and this distinction must be generally correlated with impact.

Indeed, even participation in general meetings of the primary party organizations may sometimes be of importance. Party spokesmen express repeated concern that many party members are, in fact, not very active and may not even have an assignment. A study of twelve primary party organizations in the Moscow suburb of Khimki, for example, found that 33.5 percent of the members learned about the date of a primary party organization meeting only on the eve of the meeting, that 42 percent never participated in the preparation of a meeting, that 33 percent did not speak even once in a year, and that 40 percent believed that little changed for the better after the discussion of a question.[121] Yet from a comparative perspective, the reverse of these statistics are still very impressive: 58 percent participated in the preparation of a meeting, 67 percent spoke at least once in a year, and 60 percent believed that something did change for the better after a question was discussed.

We cannot, of course, be certain how much impact party membership and participation in the primary party organization by lower employees has upon decisions taken within an enterprise or institution. The usual advantage of full-time officials over part-time ones in the decision-making process must be particularly strong in an institution that is hierarchically structured. But the existence of the primary party organization should at least ensure the institutionalization of a "committee ethos" in the Soviet place of work—the feeling that an administrator cannot simply decide things on his own but must consult with associates and subordinates who have the right and duty to raise questions concerning the performance of their institution. The secretary of the primary party organization should help to overcome one major shortcoming of many committees, namely that even if committees can veto or modify a leader's proposals, they find it much more difficult to institute change if the leader is passive.

Given the inherent nature of committees, the primary party organizations must vary greatly in their impact, depending on the capabilities and inclinations of the members. Nevertheless, in comparative perspective it is not necessary to demonstrate universal activity among the membership to prove that the primary party organization is an institution of importance; it is only necessary to demonstrate that it provides some who are interested with the opportunity to affect decisions in ways they otherwise would not. Surely the primary party organization sometimes must do that, and we should at least entertain the hypothesis that the primary party organization, together with other institutions of participation in the place of work, give Soviet employees as much influence vis-à-vis the chief administrator as in countries such as Yugoslavia where we are more conscious of "workers' control." Certainly it would be premature to make such a conclusion, but if we seek to study the primary party organization as the collective unit described in party theory and focus on the decision-making process rather than on mobilizational functions, we may find that Robert Daniels' phrase "participatory bureaucracy" has more meaning than we have suspected.[122] If we pose the problem in these terms, it is even conceivable that some day the leadership may conclude that western understanding of the operation of "intraparty democracy" at the lower levels is in the Soviet interest, as well as in the interest of the development of political science theory, and we may have an opportunity to study these questions in ways which we can only dream of today.

10 | The Institutional Actors

THE COMMUNIST PARTY is clearly the dominant institution in the Soviet Union. The active participants in the political process are, with the exception of a number of scientific personnel, almost all party members, and the ultimate policymaking organs both in the center and in the lower territorial units are the respective collective party bodies. In functional terms the real cabinet of the Soviet political system is the party Politburo, the real parliament is the party Central Committee, and the real prime minister is the party General Secretary.

Yet, it would be misleading to assert, as some do, that the government and other nonparty institutions simply function as administrative agencies or transmission belts which do more than carry out party policy. To say that "policy is made in the party" is accurate in a certain, very rough sense, but it obscures that fact that the categories of "party" and "government" are overlapping ones in the Soviet Union. The vast majority of party members work full-time for some governmental ministry, and the leading officials of the governmental agencies are members not only of the party but of the leading party organs as well. Five of the fourteen voting members of the party Politburo in May 1978 were officials of the Council of Ministers, while nearly all of the ministers were members or candidate members of the party Central Committee.

As a consequence, the real question is not whether nearly all policy-making takes place within the party broadly defined or whether ultimate authority is possessed by the top party organs. Both of these propositions are surely true. Rather, the question is—where, how, and under what influences is policy within the party actually made?

Whatever the answer to this question, the party in the sense of the party apparatus clearly is not the only institutional actor with a role to play. If the Politburo and the Central Committee are significant in the policymaking process, then so, surely, are those "administrators" who sit on those committees and so too are the large organizations led by those men. In fact, even if the party Secretariat were to have the final say on every important question (and this is most improbable), the executive institutions still would be reservoirs of expertise and centers of specialized interests, and they would still be significant participants in the battle for influence over policy. Even under Stalin, as Fainsod argued, "the party apparatus, the police, the army, and the administrative bureaucracy [vied] with one another for preferment, and the local and departmental interests of different sections of the bureaucracy [exercised] their counterinfluence on the party." That phenomenon can be no less present today, and an understanding of the nonparty institutions is surely indispensable before we can really comprehend the working of the collective party organs and the role of the party apparatus within them.

The Supreme Soviet: The Deputies

The constitution of the Soviet Union declares that the highest organ of state authority is the Supreme Soviet of the USSR. The Supreme Soviet is divided into two chambers—the Council of the Union and the Council of Nationalities. The Council of Nationalities, as its name implies, is designed to provide explicit representation to territories based upon specific nationalities. Thus, each union republic, regardless of size, is divided into thirty-two districts for the Council of Nationalities elections, each autonomous republic into eleven districts, each autonomous region into five districts, and each national district constitutes a single electoral district. In all, the Council of Nationalities contains 750 deputies. The Council of the Union is composed of deputies elected from districts with equal numbers of inhabitants. The Council of the Union elected in 1974 had 767 deputies, but the 1977 constitution specified an equal number of deputies for both houses (article 110) and hence the Council of the Union should decrease to 750 deputies at the 1979 election. (In the past, the elections to both houses were held simultaneously every four years, but the new constitution, in article 90, specified a term of five years for both houses.)[1] Only one candidate—and an approved one—is permitted to run in each district.

The persons elected to the Supreme Soviet are not professional legislators, but perform their duties in conjunction with another, full-time job. Hence, people of a wide range of occupations can be selected as deputies to the Supreme Soviet—not only ministers and national party leaders but also regional political leaders, high military officials, factory and collective farm managers, top scientists and educators, and the like, who could not retain such posts if the Supreme Soviet were in session for a long time.

The majority of Supreme Soviet deputies are, in fact, men and women who hold some type of political, administrative, or supervisory position (see table 25), but in comparative perspective the striking fact about the

Table 25   *Occupations of Supreme Soviet deputies, 1950, 1962, 1974 (in percentages)*

OCCUPATION	1950	1962	1974
Central party official	1.1	1.9	1.7
Regional party official	21.6	15.9	14.2
Central government official	1.4	3.8	6.7
Regional government official	20.3	12.4	7.3
Army officers or police official	7.0	4.6	4.4
Trade union or Komsomol official	2.1	1.2	1.2
Factory and construction employees			
Enterprise manager	2.4	1.4	2.5
Middle management	1.4	1.0	0.2
Foreman	1.4	1.7	0.4
Supervisor	0.8	6.2	6.3
Worker	7.1	11.5	18.1
Agricultural enterprise employees			
Manager or chairman	12.8	8.0	5.6
Middle management or professional	2.9	3.8	3.3
Peasant or link-leader	0.2	15.3	17.6
Cultural figure	3.7	3.1	2.9
Newspaperman	0.2	0.1	0.3
Scientist, college educator, or research designer	6.3	4.5	4.4
Secondary or elementary school educator	4.2	1.8	1.6
Medical personnel	1.1	1.4	1.0
Miscellaneous white collar	0.9	0.3	0.3
Unknown	1.1	0.1	—
Total	100.0	100.0	100.0

Source: 1950: The names of the deputies were printed in *Pravda*, March 15, 1950, pp. 1–4. Their occupations must be ascertained by reading the lists of the nominated and registered candidates carried in the preceding weeks in *Pravda* and *Izvestiia*. 1962: *Pravda*, March 21, 1962, pp. 1–7. 1974: *Pravda*, June 19, 1974, pp. 1–7.

deputies is the high proportion of rank-and-file workers and peasants among them. The Soviet leadership claims that 50.7 percent of the deputies elected in 1974 were workers and collective farmers, but this statistic is an inflated one by western definitions. (All collective farm personnel—including the chairman, middle management, and professionals—are included in the term "collective farmer.") Nevertheless, a substantial and growing number of "real" workers and peasants are elected to the Supreme Soviet. If supervisors below the level of farm brigadier and industrial foreman are included (and they should be by normal western definitions), the proportion of workers and peasants increases from 8 percent in 1950 to 17 percent in 1954 to 33 percent in 1962 to 42 percent in 1974. Approximately another 2 percent of the deputies are nonsupervisory white collar personnel—primarily doctors, teachers, agronomists, and veterinarians.

The regime also strives for broad representation among other groups as well. For example, 31 percent of the Supreme Soviet deputies are women, and 57 percent are non-Russians. The deputies come from 61 different nationalities. A disproportionate number have higher education (50 percent), but 3 percent of the deputies have an incomplete higher education, 37 percent a secondary degree, 12 percent an incomplete secondary education, and 1 percent only an elementary education. All age groups are well represented, with 18 percent being under thirty years of age, 13 percent over sixty, and the rest distributed throughout the middle age brackets.[2]

Yet, for all the variety in Supreme Soviet membership, one fact should not be forgotten. Among the deputies are included the most important political figures in Soviet society. In 1974, there were 227 living voting members of the party Central Committee (of the 241 elected in 1971); 84 percent were selected as deputies to the Supreme Soviet in that year—93 percent if ambassadors, workers, and collective farmer members of the Central Committee are excluded. Similarly, 88 percent of the voting members of the Central Committee elected in 1976 were already Supreme Soviet deputies— 94 percent if the ambassadors, workers, and collective farmers are excluded. All of these figures would be higher if there were not retirements and demotions in the years between the elections.

Moreover, it is precisely the Central Committee members (and others of near-similar status) who seem to dominate the Supreme Soviet. Thus 64 percent of the chairmen of the standing committees and 50 percent of the deputy chairmen selected in 1974 were members and candidate members of the party Central Committee (figures which became 75 percent and 57 percent in 1976), as were nearly 40 percent of the speakers in the Supreme Soviet debates of 1971–1973. By contrast, as can be seen in table 26, only 5 percent of the speakers were workers and subforeman supervisers, and 0.5 percent

Table 26   *Supreme Soviet debates, 1966–1977*

| SESSION | SUBJECT | NUMBER OF PARTICIPANTS | | |
		TOTAL	WORKERS[a]	PEASANTS[b]
7th Convocation				
Aug. 2–3, 1966	Organizational		No debate	
Dec. 15–19, 1966 (4 days)	Plan-budget	49	4	0
Oct. 10–12, 1967	Plan-budget	44	1	0
June 25–27, 1968	Health policy	23	1	0
	Marriage-family	6	1	1
	Foreign affairs	8	1	0
Dec. 10–13, 1968	Plan-budget	44	1	0
	Land legislation	7	0	0
July 10–11, 1969	Foreign affairs	15	1	0
	Criminal law	7	1	0
Dec. 16–19, 1969	Plan-budget	42	4	0
	Health legislation	6	0	0
8th Convocation				
July 14–15, 1970	Organizational		No debate	
	Labor legislation	7	2	0
Dec. 8–10, 1970	Plan-budget	40	3	0
	Water legislation	6	0	0
Nov. 24–26, 1971	Plan-budget	40	4	0
Sept. 19–20, 1972	Conservation	26	0	0
	Status of deputies	6	1	0
Dec. 18–19,1972	Plan-budget	28	2	1
July 17–19, 1973	Education	39	0	0
	Notary public	3	0	0
Dec. 12–14, 1973	Plan-budget	39	2	0
9th Convocation				
July 25–26, 1974	Organizational		No debate	
December 18–20, 1974	Plan-budget	31	2	1
July 8–9, 1975	Conservation of resources	24	3	0

Table 26—Continued

		NUMBER OF PARTICIPANTS		
SESSION	SUBJECT	TOTAL	WORKERS[a]	PEASANTS[b]
December 2–4, 1975	Plan-budget	34	5	0
October 27–29, 1976	Plan-budget	39	6	1
June 16–17, 1977	Forestry and Timber	22	0	0
October 4–7, 1977	Ratification of constitution	83	9	2
December 14–16, 1977	Plan-budget	44	7	2

Source: *Pravda* and *Izvestiia* carries reports on Supreme Soviet sessions the day after they are held. The timing of sessions in a year can be ascertained in the Yearbook of the *Bol'shaia sovetskaia entsiklopediia*.

[a] The worker category includes brigadiers, who are subforeman supervisors who have been workers.

[b] The peasant category includes link-leaders, but not brigadiers. (Since the amalgamation of the collective farms in the 1950s, these officials often supervise units the size of the old collective farm.)

were rank-and-file peasants, even though these categories provide 41 percent of all deputies.

Indeed, there is a high turnover among Supreme Soviet deputies (55.8 percent of the deputies elected in 1974 were named for the first time),[3] and relatively few of the worker and peasant deputies develop sufficient tenure to acquire the contacts and experience that normally are associated with influence. Only 19 percent of the workers and peasants who were elected deputies in 1966 and who were still alive in 1970 were re-elected in that year; only 18 percent of the surviving worker and peasant deputies of 1970 were renamed to the Supreme Soviet in 1974. (This figure stood at 79 percent for those 1966 deputies who were central or republican governmental or party officials or oblast party secretaries, at 82 percent for such officials elected in 1970.)[4] As a result, high officials (defined as those in one of the first six categories in table 25) comprise only 36 percent of all deputies in 1974, but 64 percent of the holdover deputies. While these statistics create further doubt about the impact of the low status deputies, they also mean that the Supreme Soviet contains a large core of the type of officials who could make important decisions if the circumstances were right.

The Sessions of the Supreme Soviet

The actual sessions of the Supreme Soviet are short in length and held infrequently. The Soviet constitution specifies that the Supreme Soviet is to have two regular sessions a year, but even this requirement has not always been met in the post-Khrushchev period. As table 26 indicates, the Supreme Soviet met only once in 1967 and 1971, and it never met more than twice a year. One session, almost invariably held in December, has been devoted largely to the ratification of the plan and budget; the other session usually deals with one or two major pieces of legislation—frequently a codification of the basic laws and principles in a field rather than a change in policy. The sessions usually last for two or three days, but (at least in the last decade) never for more than four days, and each day's session is normally limited to six hours.[5]

Western scholars have generally been quite skeptical about the role of the Supreme Soviet in the policy process. In 1953 Merle Fainsod, for example, concluded that "the role of the Supreme Soviet appears largely ornamental and decorative . . . The proceedings . . . convey the impression of a well-rehearsed theatrical spectacle from which almost all elements of conflict have been eliminated. The slight budget modifications which are initiated by the Supreme Soviet and the occasional criticisms of the performance of lagging ministries give every evidence of being part of a prepared script. Like the elections, the meetings of the Supreme Soviet symbolize national unity."[6]

These words do accurately reflect the role of the Supreme Soviet during the Stalin period. Indeed, in the late Stalin period the Supreme Soviet often met only once a year and then for a budget session often held after the beginning of the year for which the budget was being passed. The description also correctly suggests what is true even today, that the Supreme Soviet bears little resemblance to a western parliament in its work. The absence of opposing parties removes the possibility of confidence votes, and the antifactionalism provision in the party rules prevents the formation of party groups that could challenge the leadership or the piece of legislation being introduced. In practice, no challenge is presented by any individual deputy either, and all bills are passed unanimously by both houses.

Yet, within the basic framework of the Soviet political system, the Supreme Soviet does play a certain role in the policy process, although, to be sure, a lesser role than that of other major institutions. Since the deputies include the major officials of the Soviet system, any policy discussion in this body reaches the top elite directly. In practice, this discussion has become more meaningful in recent years, and the leadership seems to rotate the subject matter of the summer sessions among a broad variety of policy fields in order to maximize this informational function.

The debate which the Supreme Soviet deputies hear (and which the public reads in truncated form in the daily press) is a limited one. The speakers spend much time praising Soviet policy in general and local achievements in particular, but they also voice criticisms of the status quo and propose policy changes. In the summer of 1973, for example, the Supreme Soviet gathered in joint session to discuss education. The three top educational administrators gave reports, and the First Deputy Chairman of the Council of Ministers (K. T. Mazurov, a Politburo member) introduced a bill defining the basic nature of the Soviet educational system. Thirty-nine deputies spoke on the reports, and at least in a portion of the speech, each called for some new governmental action or some change in governmental policy.

At the simplest level, the speakers at the 1973 session of the Supreme Soviet merely appealed for more funds. Some pointed to specific deficiencies in their own locality and asked for help: the allocation of more laboratory apparatus to Lithuanian schools, the construction of a new civil engineering institute in Azerbaidzhan, an increase in the size of the preschool program in Moldavia. Others spoke of educational needs on a countrywide basis—for example, the need for a free textbook program or for a reduction in the size of classes in the elementary school.

In addition, a number of deputies raised more basic policy issues. One proposed preparatory classes for all six-year-olds. (Soviet children start first grade at the age of 7.) Another complained about excessive specialization in the preparation of college students. Still another worried about the "feminization" of the colleges, advocating that admission policies be changed so as to increase the number of boys entering college. (Girls predominate in the regular high schools and, as in the United States, receive higher grades than boys on the average; any preference given to graduates of technical or trade schools or to production workers—as proposed by this deputy—means an increase in the number of boys admitted.) Another deputy stated that more class time should be devoted to lessons (both theoretical and practical) about work—in effect, that there should be a return to the emphasis of the Khrushchev era.

A number of deputies directed their attack (and by name) at a basic Central Committee–Council of Ministers decree of 1966 which provided for the financing of many capital expenditures in higher education through noneducational ministries. Since the heavy industry ministries are those which have the most money and since they naturally favor institutes producing students for their lines of work, it was argued that this policy favors institutes in large industrial centers, particularly engineering institutes. One deputy compared the favored position of the Lvov Polytechnical Institute with that of the Lvov Printing Industry Institute; another complained about the neglect of teachers' colleges under this procedure; another raised the nationality question, suggesting that the uncoordinated decisions of a number of ministries could (and did) lead to an inequitable distribution of investment funds among the republics. All of these speakers appealed for the centralized distribution of investment funds for higher education through the Ministry of Higher and Secondary Specialized Education so that all types of institutions and localities could be treated equally. It was an important challenge not only to a major party decision but also to one of the pillars of support for the supremacy of heavy industry.

The various criticisms and suggestions at the Supreme Soviet had almost no impact on the law under consideration. In fact, nearly all of the provisions of the law were so general that it is difficult to imagine anyone wanting to have much of an impact upon them, and this was not the purpose of the discussion. The intention of the speakers was to try to affect future policy and appropriations, either directly or indirectly. At the conclusion of the session, the First Deputy Chairman of the Council of Ministers stated that "all these proposals and remarks will be attentively examined by the government, and also by the corresponding ministries and departments." That objective, together with the hope of influencing the views of the attentive public, was the point of the whole exercise.[7]

The Presidium of the Supreme Soviet

Perhaps because of the infrequency and brevity of Supreme Soviet sessions, the Soviet constitution also provides for a Presidium of the Supreme Soviet, which "functions as the highest organ of state authority" between sessions. The precise legal relationship between the Presidium and the Supreme Soviet has been the subject of a long (and apparently quite academic) debate among Soviet jurists.[8] Subject to later ratification by the Supreme Soviet, the Presidium has the power to take any action that does not contravene the constitution or change it, including issuing a law, forming and abolishing ministries, ratifying border changes between union republics, and appointing and removing members of the Council of Ministers. Thus, when Khrushchev was removed as Chairman of the Council of Ministers in 1964 and Kosygin was appointed to succeed him, even this action did not require the convening of the Supreme Soviet. In addition, the Presidium has been granted the right to make many crucial decisions without the need for later ratification, including a declaration of war, general or partial mobilization, appointment of the high command of the armed forces, and ratification of treaties.[9]

The 1977 constitution specified that the Presidium of the Supreme Soviet should include thirty-nine members: a Chairman, a First Deputy Chairman, fifteen Deputy Chairmen (one from each of the republics, traditionally the chairman of the Presidium of the Supreme Soviet of the republic), a secretary, and twenty-one other members. In early 1978 the other members included nine of the foremost regional party officials in the USSR (the first secretaries of the four most populous union republics, the two most populous autonomous republics, the Leningrad and Moscow regional party committees, and the Moscow city party committee), the chairman of the All-Union Trade Union Council, the first secretary of the Komsomol, a top scientist, the chairman of the executive committee of the soviet of a national district, the chairman of the Union of Writers of an autonomous republic, a factory director, the Chairman of the Soviet Women's Committee (the only woman to have flown in space), four workers and subforeman supervisors, and a collective farm brigadier.[10]

The Chairman of the Presidium of the Supreme Soviet is usually considered by westerners to be the head of state in the Soviet Union, for his duties include such traditional tasks of this position as signing legislation, receiving the credentials of foreign ambassadors, and so forth. In the past, the Chairman of the Presidium, although a member of the party Politburo, was a relatively minor, often elderly figure within the top leadership and seemed largely to be limited to a symbolic, ceremonial role. The Chairman from 1919 to 1946, M. I. Kalinin, was one of the few sons of a peasant among Stalin's top lieutenants, and with a flowing white beard he had all the appearance of a kindly father.[11] The Chairman from 1946 to 1953, N. M. Shvernik, had been the trade union chairman for nearly fifteen years, while his successor, K. E. Voroshilov, was an increasingly feeble Civil War hero and former People's Commissar of Defense.

With the removal of Voroshilov in 1960, however, the position of the Chairman of the Presidium of the Supreme Soviet began to change radically. Both Leonid Brezhnev, who held the post from 1960 to 1964, and Anastas Mikoian, who held it from 1964 to 1965, were close and powerful associates of Khrushchev, and the Chairman from 1966 to 1977, Nikolai V. Podgorny, clearly was one of the five most important leaders of the post-Khrushchev period. The reason for this change was unclear, but it may have been linked with the much greater tendency of Soviet leaders to travel abroad and to acquire the foreign policy expertise that can be developed by the man who performed the head-of-state functions vis-à-vis foreigners. It may have seemed foolish to be represented abroad by a nonentity and to waste a chance for the inner leadership to increase its information about the outside world at a time when it was rare and valuable.

In 1977 Podgorny was replaced as Chairman of the Presidium of the Supreme Soviet by Brezhnev, and, as in a number of eastern European countries, the posts of party leader and head-of-state were combined in one man. The decision was part of a general increase in the status accorded Brezhnev at the time, but it also insured that the real national leader—the party

General Secretary—would have head-of-state status when meeting with foreign leaders. The new constitution promulgated in that year provided for the first time for a First Deputy Chairman of the Presidium of the Supreme Soviet, presumably to relieve the party leader from many of the day-to-day duties of Chairman of the Presidium. The new First Deputy Chairman, Vasilii V. Kuznetsov, was a seventy-six-year-old who had held the symbolically reassuring post of trade union chairman in the past, but who had also been first deputy minister of foreign affairs for twenty years. He was also elected a candidate member of the party Politburo.[12]

The Presidium as a collective organ is supposed to meet only once every two months,[13] and press reports indicate that, with some variation in both directions, it is convened with that frequency. Its role is more in question. Two of its meetings each year are held on the day before the convening of the Supreme Soviet sessions, and, if not totally formal in nature, they surely must be devoted largely to technical problems related to the organization of the session. Other sessions are engaged, in whole or in part, in pro forma ratification of treaties or receiving reports on foreign visits of the Presidium's chairman or of parliamentary delegations. It is only on such questions as the legal rights and the power of local soviets, the awarding of medals, and the granting of amnesty or citizenship that the Presidium has significant staff, and it is only on these questions and on the codification of legislation that there is no doubt about its major role.

The greatest uncertainty about the role of the Presidium of the Supreme Soviet centers on its relation to the network of standing committees that has been developed since 1966. Formally at least, the Presidium has a major responsibility in selecting the committee chairmen and membership, and it confirms the plans of the committees at the beginning of the year and sometimes hears reports about their sessions. It also can convene temporary commissions to draft or codify various types of legislation.[14] The secretary of the Presidium has claimed that the work in this realm is quite significant:

> The significance of the coordinating function of the Presidium with respect to the commissions has grown to a great extent with the [expansion in the number of] commissions . . . The coordination of the supervisory work of the commissions has . . . substantial significance . . . The Presidium examines the plans of the work of the commissions and generalizes them into an overall plan. In the process, unnecessary duplication is removed, and the maximum amount of mutual connection between the efforts of the commissions are established.[15]

If the standing committees had, in practice, served as the staff of an independent Chairman of the Presidium of the Supreme Soviet and had provided him with some expertise to compete with the resources at the disposal of the Chairman of the Council of Ministers and the General Secretary, the Presidium's role in coordinating their activity might have been extremely important. However, it is by no means certain (or even probable) that this ever occurred. With the General Secretary already having the staff of the Central Committee apparatus at his disposal as well as a number of personal assistants, the standing committees are likely to be of marginal importance as a source of information to him personally. The First Deputy Chairman of the Presidium might try to use the coordinating role of this organ to enhance his knowledge and impact upon events, but such a development is apt to depend upon the selection of a younger official for this post and one more oriented toward internal policy questions.

The Standing Committees of the Supreme Soviet

Perhaps the most interesting development with respect to the Supreme Soviet in recent years has been the expanded activity of the standing committees *(postoiannye komissiia)*. While the last years of the Khrushchev era had witnessed some increase in the role of the committees, the Council of Nationalities had only four committees in 1964 (legislative proposals, budget, foreign affairs, and credentials), and the Council of the Union had five (four counterparts to the Council of Nationalities committees, plus an economic committee). The committees of both houses together contained a total of 219 deputies.[16]

In the post-Khrushchev period, the number of Supreme Soviet committees has been increased several times, and in early 1978 there were fifteen in each house: Agriculture; Conservation; Construction and Building Materials Industry; Consumer Goods; Credentials; Education, Science, and Culture; Foreign Affairs; Health and Social Security; Industry; Planning-Budget; Trade, Consumer Services, and Utilities; Transportation-Communication; Women's Work and Living Conditions and Protection of Motherhood and Childhood; Youth Affairs; and Legislative Proposals (which continues to look at drafts of laws prepared mainly by other committees, but which now deals primarily with law enforcement and matters embodied in criminal and civil law). Except for the Planning-Budget Committees in each house (which have 45 members apiece), each committee has 35 members, and hence the thirty committees of both houses have a total of 1070 deputies.[17]

With 71 percent of the deputies serving as committee members (approximately 80 percent if we exclude deputies such as governmental ministers who are ineligible for membership), the committees obviously contain deputies of all backgrounds. Peasants are, however, disproportionately underrepresented. As indicated in table 27, nearly all committees have a sizable component of regional first secretaries, workers, and peasants (particularly

Table 27 *Occupations of members of standing committees of the Supreme Soviet, 1974 (in percentages)*

COMMITTEE	REGIONAL PARTY OFFICIAL	WORKER	PEASANT	KOLKHOZ-SOVKHOZ OFFICIAL	OTHER
Agriculture	19	3	20	37	21
Conservation	20	24	10	13	33
Construction and building materials	23	33	7	6	31
Consumer goods	23	27	17	9	24
Credentials	21	23	21	10	24
Education, science and culture	13	11	9	4	63
Foreign affairs	18	7	6	9	60
Health and social security	20	21	11	4	43
Industry	16	39	6	9	31
Legislative proposals	30	23	3	6	39
Planning-budget	26	20	7	17	31
Trade, consumer services, and utilities	20	27	11	19	23
Transportation and communication	19	30	9	10	33
Youth affairs	19	21	11	9	40
Average	20.5	22.1	10.5	11.5	35.4

Source: *Izvestiia*, July 26, 1974, pp. 1, 3–5; July 27, 1974, pp. 4–6. For the purposes of this table, the members of, say, the agriculture committee of the two houses are treated as if they were the members of a single large committee. Because of rounding errors, the figures do not always add to 100 percent.

if we include kolkhoz officials among peasants), but there is a real tendency for the specialized committees to contain larger numbers of deputies who work in the area supervised by the committee. Thus, even ignoring regional party first secretaries, 70 percent of the members of both Agriculture Committees work in agriculture or the institutions serving it (for example, the agricultural machinery or fertilizer industries), 54 percent of the Education, Science, and Culture Committees work in those realms, at least 49 percent of the members of the Construction and Building Materials Committees are employed in or supervise these industries, and so forth. In addition, the regional officials on the committees often have a background especially appropriate for the committee to which they have been assigned.[18]

The fact that the members of the Supreme Soviet committees hold a full-time job outside of the Soviet clearly reduces the time they can spend on committee work, and, in practice, the committees typically meet only twice a year. In the first years after the expansion in the number of committees, the committees of the Council of the Union and the Council of Nationalities often met separately, but in recent years the committees of the same name usually have worked together on the same question.[19] One of the two meetings is held late in the year and is devoted to an examination of the sections of the state plan and budget pertaining to the committee's area of specialization. A second meeting concentrates its attention on the detailed examination of one particular question about the work or performance of a ministry or ministries within its sphere of influence. The result of this session is not a law, but nonbinding recommendations on the matter in question—or, at least, nonbinding unless higher authorities confirm them. Finally, on the rare occasion that the Supreme Soviet passes a law in its area, the committee also has the responsibility of examining the preliminary draft of the bill before the session. The secretary of the Presidium of the Supreme Soviet reports that the Planning-Budget Committees of the two houses met 33 and 34 times respectively between 1970 and 1974, implying eight sessions a year for this particular committee.[20]

If the impact of the Supreme Soviet committees in the policy process were to be judged by the results of their relatively few formal sessions, one suspects that the committees would be relatively insignificant. However, in exercising each of their responsibilities, the committees create a "preparatory group" (podgotovitel'naia gruppa), which meets prior to the committee session to examine the question under consideration. These groups spend considerable time in their work, drawing upon outside expertise in the process. The following description, for example, concerns the drafting of the education law debated at the 1973 Supreme Soviet session:

> The suggestion about the expediency of the preparation of this document was introduced to the Presidium of the Supreme Soviet by our predecessor—the Committee on Education, Science, and Culture of the Council of the Union of the USSR Supreme Soviet of the seventh convocation [that

is, of the 1966–1970 convocation]. The Presidium entrusted the Council of Ministers with the working out of the law. Scholars, teachers, lawyers, prominent educators, and representatives of many interested departments and organizations participated in this affair. When the bill was prepared, it was, in accordance with a decision of the Presidium of the USSR Supreme Soviet, published in the press for purposes of discussion and then it was given to the Committees on Education, Science, and Culture, to the Committees on Legislative Proposals, and to the Committees on Youth of both houses for final consideration.

After the publication of the draft of the law, over three hundred suggestions and remarks were sent to the Presidium of the USSR Supreme Soviet. To examine them, the committees formed a joint deputy's preparatory committee into which leaders of the USSR Ministries of Education, of Higher and Specialized Secondary Education, of Justice, and of the State Committee for Vocational-Technical Education also entered. As a result of a detailed analysis of the proposals, it was considered expedient to introduce some changes and additions into the draft of the law.[21]

Similar preparatory groups, which usually seem to contain from five to nine of the committees' deputies, are also formed to examine the questions on which the committees verify the work of the ministries. These questions are not an internal audit of the work of the ministry, but deal with the ministry's performance in the field—for example, tasks in book production, the introduction of new types of building materials, the quality of consumer goods produced by the Ministry of Light Industry, work done to prevent juvenile delinquency, the observance of labor safety on enterprises of the Ministry of Ferrous Metallurgy, of Coal, of Industrial Construction, and of the Food Industry.[22] On this type of question, the preparatory group can demand materials not only from the ministries involved but also from such agencies as the prosecutor's office, the trade union, and the People's Control Committee.[23] The individual members of the group conduct or lead investigations on the subject at hand in their own particular area, and in the process "hundreds and thousands of people" can become involved at times.

Here is a concrete example. At one of its sessions the Committee on Education, Science, and Culture examined the question of the work of the specialized secondary institutions and the way to improve them. Beforehand, the deputies and officials of the republican and local organs studied the situation in more than two hundred trade schools (*technicums*). The conclusions and suggestions which came to the committee from the localities, and also the materials demanded by us from the USSR Gosplan, the

Ministry of Higher and Specialized Secondary Education, and a series of other departments, permitted us to evaluate the situation objectively and to work out concrete recommendations.[24]

Perhaps the most interesting preparatory groups—usually called preparatory committees—are those formed to examine the state budget and plan. There are fifteen of these preparatory committees, eleven of which look at specific sections (*razdels*) of the plan and budget: transportation and communications; construction and the building materials industry; agriculture; health and social security; education, science, and culture; trade, consumer services, and utilities; the fuel and energy industry, metallurgy, and geology; the chemical, petrochemical, timber, and paper industry; the machinery industry; the consumer goods industry; and indicators for conservation and the rational use of natural resources.[25] Another four preparatory committees handle more general questions: one, the summary plans and budgets for the various union republics; a second, the income section of the budget; and a third and fourth, the overall indicators for the plan and budget respectively. Expenditures for defense, the defense industry, and the police apparently do not undergo detailed scrutiny by the Supreme Soviet committees, for the Foreign Affairs and Legislative Proposals Committees are not listed among those which become involved in the examination of the plan and budget.[26]

The preparatory committees for the plan and budget are larger than the preparatory groups which lead committee investigations of the ministries. In 1974, 230 deputies became members of these committees—an average of 15 members per committee,[27] and the members of each committee are drawn from the relevant specialized committees of the two houses, from the two Planning-Budget Committees, and occasionally from a related committee. (For example, members of the Committees for Youth Affairs participate in the preparatory committee on the education plan and budget.)[28] In addition, the preparatory committees also include specialist consultants (in 1973, nearly fifteen per committee) from Gosplan, the State Construction Committee, the State Supply Committee, the Ministry of Finances, the Central Statistical Agency, the State Bank, the Construction Bank, the Central Trade Union Council, and the People's Control Committee, all of whom participate "with the right of a consultative vote."[29]

The work of the joint preparatory committees is conducted over the period of a month from early November to early December. In 1973 the joint preparatory committees averaged nearly five sessions apiece during that period, and the following description of the way the transportation and communications committee functioned seems typical:

Each of its members was assigned a concrete circle of problems connected with the transportation section of the state plan. For a month, these people, together with experienced specialists (consultants of the committee), met with leaders of the ministries, agencies, and Gosplan departments. They examined in all their facets this or that line of the plan—its importance, its indispensability, its priority. The recommendations of the deputies are not an order or a directive. But, nevertheless, in practice, all of the recommendations of the committees are carried out.[30]

The crucial question, of course, is the impact of all these sessions upon the policy outcome. Are the Supreme Soviet standing committees of sufficient importance even to be listed among the significant actors in the Soviet political process, and, if so, what role do they play? Unfortunately, this is a very difficult question to answer, for, incredibly, the regime has revealed exceedingly little information on that aspect of Supreme Soviet activity which almost surely has the greatest claim to "democratic" discussion and exercise of influence.

Clearly, however, any accurate assessment of the role of the standing committees must be a mixed one. On the one hand, the infrequence of the committee meetings, coupled with the fact that many of the members are employed within a ministry supervised by the committees, sharply reduces the ability of the committees to achieve meaningful control over ministerial activity. On the other hand, the length of the preparatory group sessions, the use of outside experts, and the willingness to conduct investigations all strongly indicate that the preparation for committee sessions is far from meaningless. Long studies such as that which the Committee on Education, Science, and Culture conducted on specialized secondary institutions surely must be associated with the development of policy toward those institutions, and, indeed, Brezhnev himself insisted upon the utilization of the results of one such examination of mechanization of the livestock farms which was conducted by the Committee of Industry, Transportation, and Communications in 1968. "The committee did large-scale and very necessary work. It is indispensable to take its proposals into account in the national economic plan."[31]

The work of the preparatory committees on the plan and the budget is especially likely to be a significant stage in the policy process. Given the presence of some fifteen specialists from the top planning-financial institutions in each committee, given the month-long period of work, it is very probable that the preparatory committees are the place where final inter-agency agreement on the details of the plan and budget are hammered out.

For this reason, the claim that "in practice, all of the recommendations of the committees are carried out" is neither surprising nor dubious.

The real difficulty we face is in judging the independent significance of the standing committees and their preparatory subcommittees. Does the presence of deputies in the interagency discussions on the budget and plan sometimes change the outcome? Are the committees—or someone associated with them—able to push the ministries to decisions they would not reach themselves? Or, on the contrary, are investigations such as that on specialized secondary education often really a service to the ministries—and perhaps instigated by them?

Unfortunately, our knowledge about the standing committees and the preparatory groups remains meager. We do not know how their members and leaders are selected, and the occupational data at our disposal are not sufficiently patterned to suggest an answer. Even the committee chairmen are not all members of the party Central Committee (75 percent of the chairmen selected in 1974 were named to the party body in 1976), and (at least in the 1970–1975 period) this figure dropped off to approximately 40 percent for leaders of the preparatory groups and 19 percent for the more active members of the groups. None of the group leaders and only 7 percent of the members were national level officials, while at the other extreme none of the leaders and only 12 percent of the members were workers or rank-and-file peasants (11 percent workers and 1 percent peasants). The great majority of both groups were leading regional officials or enterprise managers.[32]

We also have no information on the method by which topics of committee sessions are chosen—whether by committee consensus, by committee chairman decision, by the initiative of the government or the party organs,[33] or perhaps, by the decision of the Chairman or First Deputy Chairman of the Presidium of the Supreme Soviet. However, in this case there is some variation in pattern from committee to committee that suggests the absence of a single source for all decisions. For example, in the 1970–1974 convocation, the Education, Science, and Culture Committee investigated the situation with respect to trade schools or evening schools three times—the total number of its investigations—while the Transportation–Communications Committee had a policy of rotating its sessions among the different types of transportation.

If the committees and preparatory groups are meaningful actors in the policy process, it is because they give certain individuals the opportunity to mobilize support that otherwise might have been difficult to secure. Surely at times individual deputies do utilize this opportunity and do make an impact upon individual sections of a law or the plan or the actions of a ministry.[34] But the more interesting question is whether the existence of the committees has a systematic impact on policy outcomes.

Three possible types of systematic committee influence suggest themselves. First, of course, the mere bringing together of a variety of people involved in a branch of the economy or affected by it obviously serves informational functions. Testimony of several persons who have been deputies indicates that the discussions at the committee level can be fairly free-swinging, and this must have some indirect long-term impact on policy. Second, it is conceivable (but not really probable) that the committees provide the party leader, as Chairman of the Presidium of the Supreme Soviet, with staff and expertise he otherwise lacks.

Third, the large number of regional officials on the committees may permit some regional bargaining over outcomes in a system that is heavily biased in favor of ministerial considerations. Thus, for example, the chairmen and deputy chairmen of the two Planning-Budget Committees named in 1974 were the chairman of the RSFSR Gosplan, the first deputy chairman of the Ukrainian party organization, the second secretary of the Uzbekistan party organization,[35] and the chairman of the Belorussian Gosplan. The other members included party and governmental officials from every important region in the country. Whether, in fact, regional bargaining takes place (or whether the situation is changing) is something that we do not know. However, it is possible that research on the committees and preparatory groups is much more feasible than we have realized and that many important questions will be answerable in the next few years.

The Council of Ministers

In legal terms the Council of Ministers is a vital institution in the Soviet political system. According to the Soviet constitution, it is "the highest executive and administrative organ of state power" in the country, and its "decisions and orders are binding throughout the territory of the USSR." Since the Supreme Soviet passes a relatively small number of laws, a great deal of major legislation is actually issued by the Council of Ministers, sometimes together with the party Central Committee.

The scale of this "legislative" activity of the Council of Ministers is suggested by an examination of the most important periodic collection of Soviet laws and decisions—*The Handbook of the Party Official (Spravochnik partiinogo rabotnika)*. The decisions selected for this volume are presumably chosen on the basis of their importance for the country, and they cover the widest range of subjects. Of those promulgated from November 1964 through March 1976 dealing with questions of governmental responsibility (for example, the economy, living conditions and wages, education, law-and-order), only 21 were laws of the Supreme Soviet and 86 were decrees of the Presidium of the Supreme Soviet, while, by contrast, 207 were Council of Ministers decisions and another 139 were decisions taken by the Council of Ministers in conjunction with the party Central Committee and/or the All-Union Central Trade Union Council.[36]

In addition to the passage of a series of ad hoc decisions, the Council of Ministers also has a number of statutory responsibilities. It not only must examine the plan as a whole but also is obligated to confirm the material balance of the 274 most important economic items worked out by Gosplan.[37] In addition, it is legally responsible for appointing the USSR deputy ministers and also for confirming the personnel who are members of Gosplan and of the collegia of the ministries.[38]

The actual meaning of all these legal responsibilities and legislative actions is much less easy to define, for the Council of Ministers, literally defined, is an extremely large body, and, as such, can hardly function effectively as a working cabinet. As of early 1978, it contained 106 members: a chairman, two first deputy chairmen, eleven deputy chairmen, sixty-two ministers, twelve chairmen of committees and state committees (sixteen, including those who also serve as deputy chairmen of the Council of Ministers and have already been counted), three additional national administrators (the head of the Central Statistical Agency, the Chairman of the State Bank, and the Chairman of the Agricultural Supply Agency), and the chairmen of the Council of Ministers of the fifteen republics.[39] Over 50 percent of the members of the Council of Ministers (over 60 percent if the republican chairmen are excluded) hold jobs that anyone would consider economic administration, and over one-third head industrial ministries.

While one Soviet textbook asserts that sessions of the Council of Ministers are conducted "regularly,"[40] the size of the Council raises real questions about its actual role as a decision-making body. Press reports seem to suggest that the Council usually is convened once every three months, but the primary purpose of the meetings seems to be for the ministers to hear (and sometimes ratify) a report by the Chairman of the Council of Ministers on plan fulfillment for the previous quarter or year or on the draft plan of the future.[41] Few westerners believe that these sessions of the Council of Ministers are an important part of the Soviet policy process.

However, the Council of Ministers has a smaller body—the Presidium— which surely is a much more important actor in the Soviet political system. The Presidium of the Council of Ministers (not to be confused with the Presidium of the Supreme Soviet) is termed "the working organ of the Council of Ministers," and it is empowered to examine and decide "urgent questions" and to "speak in the name of the government of the USSR."[42] Most of the

"Council of Ministers decisions" printed in such sources as *The Handbook of the Party Official* are undoubtedly Presidium decisions.

For reasons that are not at all clear, the Presidium of the Council of Ministers has been a most shadowy institution. For years officially approved textbooks did not even agree on its membership. Several books stated that "the Chairman, the First Deputy Chairman, and the Deputy Chairmen of the Council of Ministers" were the members; another text specified "the Chairman, the First Deputy Chairman, and also persons personally appointed by the Council of Ministers"; still another spoke of "the Chairman, the Deputy Chairmen, and some other members of the government."[43] A scholar in Moscow in 1975 stated that the Minister of Finances and the Chairman of the People's Control Committee were among the other members, and the executive committee of the regional soviets—the local analogy to the Presidium of the Council of Ministers—almost invariably includes the party first secretary. The 1977 constitution formally recognized the existence of the Presidium and listed "the Chairman of the Council of Ministers and First Deputy and Deputy Chairmen" as its members (article 132), but presumably other officials could be invited if desired.

Clearly the type of officials who sit on the Presidium of the Council of Ministers are very important men. As of early 1978, the Chairman and one of the First Deputy Chairmen of the Council of Ministers (A. N. Kosygin and K. F. Mazurov) were members of the party Politburo, and Kosygin was one of the top four leaders. The Deputy Chairmen included the Chairman of Gosplan, the Chairman of the State Committee for Science and Technology, the Chairman of the State Committee for Construction, the Chairman of the State Committee for Supplies Procurement, the Chairman of the Commission of the Council of Ministers for Economic Ties with Foreign Countries, the Permanent Representative of the USSR to the Council on Economic Mutual Assistance (the agency for coordination of planning in eastern Europe and the Soviet Union), and five top economic coordinators—one for agriculture and the food industry, a second for the defense industries, a third for the machinery industry, a fourth for the energy industries, and a fifth apparently for transportation. The second First Deputy Chairman (N. A. Tikhonov) had been the Deputy Chairman in charge of metallurgy and the chemical industry before his promotion in September 1976, and he seems to continue responsibility for these branches while also providing general coordination to heavy industry as a whole.

Nothing is known about the work of the Presidium of the Council of Ministers, not even the frequency of its meetings. On the surface there should be great overlap in function between the Presidium and the Central Committee Secretariat, but the division of labor between the two committees is obscure. The constitution (article 132) states that the Presidium is a "permanent" organ of the Council of Ministers "for the decision of questions, connected with securing the leadership of the economy and other questions of state administration." The type of Council of Ministers decision that has been published suggests that the Presidium is, in fact, most involved in economic planning and decision-making, and its membership would make it a natural "Economic Bureau," which handles questions just below the level of significance demanded for Politburo consideration.

In addition to its Presidium, the Council of Ministers also has a number of important interdepartmental committees or commissions to handle certain types of questions. The members of these commissions are important officials holding full-time jobs, and one of these members has said in an interview that all commissions also have full-time staff to assist them in the performance of their duties. All of these bodies are mentioned with extreme rarity in Soviet sources, and the manner in which they function or even whether they continue to function at one time or another is shrouded in mystery.

The one commission that has been mentioned in the press in the post-Stalin period has been the Commission for Economic Ties with Foreign Countries, which is headed by a Deputy Chairman of the Council of Ministers.[44] A second commission, headed by the Deputy Chairman of the Council of Ministers in charge of the defense industry, is called the Military-Industrial Commission. It is never mentioned in the Soviet press, but its existence has been confirmed in interviews. It apparently "handles coordination between the Defense Ministry, ministries concerned with military production, and Academy of Sciences institutes engaged in military research and development."[45]

If the structure of 1940 and 1956 still exists, the Council of Ministers also has a Commission for Current Questions (or Commission for Current Matters) which is headed by a major official, perhaps one of the First Deputy Chairmen. In 1940, the commission was headed by a candidate member of the Politburo, Voznesensky and in 1956 it was headed by a full member of the party Presidium, Pervukhin. In 1956, according to a minister at the time, "all disagreements and disputes which arose between the ministries, Gosplan, and other institutions flowed [to this commission]. The number of questions [it handled] was huge, and they often were minor, did not involve conflicts of principle, and really did not demand a decision by the government."[46]

Another very important interdepartmental body is the Defense Council (*Sovet Oborony*). Its existence too was not acknowledged until 1976 when the Soviet press casually indicated that Brezhnev was its chairman. (If the pattern of the Khrushchev years is followed, the General Secretary, who has the rank of Marshal, also has the title of Commander-in-Chief of the armed forces.) The Defense Council was mentioned in the 1977 constitution, its formation listed as one of the responsibilities of the Presidium of the Supreme Soviet, but little is known about its functions other than that implied in its title. A long-time student of the Soviet miliary and participant in the SALT negoiations has asserted that Brezhnev, Podgorny, Kosygin, the Minister of Defense, and the Central Committee secretary handling the military were the only members of the Defense Council in the mid 1970s (although others were said to attend occasionally), but this number seems small by normal Soviet standards for such an important body.[47] A Soviet scholar has stated that two of the First Deputy Ministers of Defense are also members.

Finally, the Council of Ministers has its own apparatus organized in departments (*otdels*) which are structured by branch. Our information on these departments is meager, but, judging by the staff of the RSFSR Council of Ministers,[48] there may be some twenty to twenty-five departments, with their titles not unlike those of the Central Committee departments. Formally the departments are part of the business office (*upravlenie delami*), but, according to Soviet scholars, they really work under the deputy chairman responsible for their branch. Their staff is said to be small (under a dozen persons per department), and their work has been described by one of their former officials is the following terms: "preparation of the drafts of decisions and orders of the all-union government, [and] assistance to the leaders of the country in their complicated work in compiling reports and manuscripts."[49]

The Ministries and State Committees

Whatever the role of the Council of Ministers, its Presidium, or its suborgans as collective organs, the members of the Council and the organizations they head clearly influence policy as separate entities. The Council of Ministers is not just an oversized executive committee; it is also the supervisor of the executive branch of the government. In any realistic sense, it contains not only 106 important men but also tens or even hundreds of thousands of trained civil servants who are employed in the central staffs of the various ministries and state committees—civil servants of the type who have had a major impact on policy throughout the industrial world. Indeed, because virtually all of the Soviet economy is nationalized, such departments are much more numerous than in the West, and the overwhelming majority of Soviet citizens are employed in offices and enterprises administered by them.

The number of ministries and state committees has been quite unstable over time. There were fifty-nine ministries in 1947, forty-eight in 1949, fifty-one in 1952, twenty-five in 1953, fifty-six in 1956, nineteen in 1958 (a time at which industrial ministries had been abolished), and forty-eight in 1966 (a time at which industrial ministries had been re-established).[50] Since 1966 there has been a slow but steady increase in the number of central state agencies, and by the spring of 1978 the government contained sixty-two ministries, sixteen state committees and committees represented on the Council of Ministers, and a number of other committees (for example, Sports and Mine Safety) whose heads do not sit on the Council of Ministers.

The distinction between a ministry and a state committee generally revolves around the institution's responsibilities. A ministry is usually in charge of a single branch, and its orders usually are binding only on its own subunits. Examples are the Ministry of Agriculture, the Ministry of Defense, and the Ministry of the Machine Tool and Instrument Industry. A state committee is an agency whose responsibilities normally cut across a number of branches and whose decrees often relate to other ministries. Examples are the State Committee for Prices, the State Committee for Science and Technology, and the State Committee for Labor and Social Questions. However, there are exceptions to this rule (for example, the State Committee for Television and Radio), and it is most unclear why the People's Control Committee is called a committee instead of a state committee and why the Committee for State Security is listed simply as "attached to" (*pri*) the Council of Ministers instead of being a regular state committee. Soviet scholars themselves are often at a loss to explain these irregularities.

A typical ministry has a minimum of 700 to 1,000 officials; the Ministry of Health was reported to have a staff of 1,000 in 1965 and the Ministry of Energy and Electrification a staff of 2,000 in 1974.[51] In 1965, from 50 to 70 percent of the ministerial officials were said to be party members.[52] These officials are usually organized into a number of specialized administrations (*upravlenie*) and departments (*otdel*). There were at least twenty-eight administrations in a major ministry such as the Ministry of Agriculture in the early 1970s.[53] The administrations and departments are supervised by some five to fourteen deputy ministers, and ultimately by a minister who almost invariably is a member or candidate member of the party Central Committee. (A list of the ministers of each status is found in table 30.) The ministry also has a collegium of its top officials which discusses and makes decisions on major policy questions.[54]

The administrative and staff personnel of the ministries and state committees are highly specialized in both knowledge and expertise. Officials in the Soviet executive are not recruited by formal civil service procedures (for example, by competitive examinations), nor are they guaranteed job tenure. Yet, informally, civil service principles do seem to have permeated the administrative system. Top ministerial officials, as well as junior personnel, generally are the products of the hierarchy in which they are employed (or a closely related one). Their career patterns usually have the specialized, orderly nature that suggests promotion on the basis of performance rather than political criteria. Radical demotion of the kind sometimes found in the Stalin period is now reserved almost exclusively for those who have committed some venal act, unless the person has reached the Politburo level.

Even the cabinet ministers, unlike their western counterparts, are almost never political leaders who are shifted from one ministerial portfolio to another. Indeed, except for ministers promoted to major coordinating committees such as Gosplan or the State Construction Committee or those shifted because of ministerial reorganization, there has not been a single minister in the last twenty years who has been shifted from one portfolio to another. Approximately 20 percent of the ministers or state committee chairmen sitting on the Council of Ministers in 1974 were regional party officials who had been named to head a ministry for which they generally had some professional background.[55] Another 5 percent were professional industrial administrators who were moved to a committee (for example, planning or supplies procurement) thought to require an industrial background. The rest—nearly three-quarters of the total—were specialized professionals who basically had risen through the administrative ranks in the policy areas (usually the ministry or state committee) they currently supervised.[56]

In addition to its central staff, the ministry also contains the personnel of the institutions and enterprises it supervises. The so-called all-union ministry (usually a heavy industry ministry) administers its enterprises directly from Moscow. The others, the union-republic ministries (for example, the Ministry of Education), administer them through a network of territorial offices in the republics, the regions, the counties, and (in nonagricultural ministries) the cities.[57]

Of great importance for the policy process is the fact that scientific personnel constitute a significant part of the de facto ministerial staff, for all the ministries also administer the scientific and many of the educational institutes in their branch. (At least, they do so within the framework of over-all guidance provided by the Ministry of Higher and Specialized Secondary Education and the State Committee for Science and Technology, respectively.) Thus, the Ministry of Agriculture has a research institute on agricultural economics, the Procuracy (the office of the prosecutor general) has an institute on the causes of crime and the measures to prevent it,[58] the State Committee on Prices has one on price formation, and so forth. Similarly, each ministry has educational institutions to prepare the middle level personnel it needs, and some of them have institutions of higher education for this purpose. For example, in 1973 the Ministry of Agriculture had 99 *vuzy* or colleges which it supervised.[59]

The staff of these scientific and educational institutions often work on technical problems, but many also study problems directly relevant to the policy concerns of the ministry or state committee. Indeed, such a study is often their express function. As a result, the top administrators of the major governmental institutions have a great deal of within-house scientific expertise at their immediate disposal if they wish either a policy study or argumentation for use in a policy struggle.

Soviet administrative agencies are told to take a "party" approach in decision-making—that is, an approach which rises above departmental interests to reflect the interests of the nation as a whole. Nevertheless, it is abundantly clear that Soviet administrators continually fall into the trap of "departmentalism."[60] They frequently take policy positions which represent their own interests and the interests of those they represent—or at least these interests as the ministerial officials perceive them, They continually engage in policy conflict with other agencies who represent different interests, conflict which often spills over into the press.

Indeed, not only the ministries as a whole but also their various bureaus and departments function as actors in the policy process. In one such case, the deputy head of the main administration of cotton and fiber crops of the Ministry of Agriculture and the head of the subadministration for fiber crops wrote a long article to defend the interests of the farmers producing flax (and also, of course, the interests of their own unit). First of all, these officials called for increased mechanization in all stages of flax production and for the increased appropriations that would permit this mechanization. Then, in even stronger language, they criticized the Ministry of Light Industry for its procedures in grading and paying for the incoming flax fiber. They flatly charged that the Ministry was underpaying the farmers by over 2.5 million rubles a year (nearly 4 million dollars at the current exchange rate) and then was refusing to permit inspectors from the Ministry of Procurements into their flax storing areas to check out the accusations.[61] Such examples of departmental representation—to be sure, not all so dramatic—can be found in almost every issue of every Soviet newspaper.

Moreover, such articles represent no more than a tiny fraction of the ministerial representation that goes on behind the scenes. In one of the few memoirs published thus far by a postwar minister, the long-time Minister of Finances, A. G. Zverev, repeatedly referred to policy struggles in which he and his ministry took part. The basic conflict in attitude between the financial organs and the state bank—and the struggle between them—is spelled out in detail. ("I strove to neutralize the different fantastic proposals of the bankers.") Zverev also reported at some length on the early postwar efforts of the Ministry of Finances to promote the development of the textile industry and consumer goods production—steps which would have helped to soak up the excess purchasing power and reduce the inflationary pressures that existed at that time. (This was the ministry's "first postwar suggestion to the Council of Ministers.")[62]

Despite the warnings about "departmentalism," there is every indication that party leaders take a certain amount of it for granted—that they agree with those Americans who believe that any worthwhile administrator must be committed to the goals of his or her institution.[63] Zverev clearly did not feel that it was illegitimate to participate in the policy process—nor to admit that he did—and other officials, too, have proudly reported their victories or bemoaned their defeats. One such victory—and the effort it took— was described by the Minister of Construction in the Oil and Gas Industry:

> We raised the question about the development of the fuel branch, about the necessity to seek natural gas. We proved that there are huge reserves of gas in our country. We had to speak out against many recognized authorities; we had, as it is called, to force through our opinion at the price of a not inconsiderable struggle (*probivat' svoe mnenie tsenoi bor'by*).[64]

When officials express dedication to their branch, there is no evidence that they are punished for their position. In one striking case, Z. N. Nuriev, first secretary of the Bashkiria obkom, spoke out with particular vehemence at a plenary session of the Central Committee about the need for Gosplan to give much higher priority to agriculture. He went so far as to insist that the appointment of a special deputy chairman of Gosplan for agriculture was indispensable in achieving this goal, and he had a short exchange with Brezhnev on the subject. It is instructive that these views did not result in the leadership considering Nuriev too departmental for higher agricultural positions. On the contrary, he subsequently was named Minister of Agricultural Procurements and then Deputy Chairman of the Council of Ministers in charge of agriculture.[65] The same attitude is reflected in Khrushchev's response to the possibility that the government may be intimidated by military advocacy: "I don't reproach the military for that—they're only doing their job."[66]

The accommodation of the regime to some degree of departmentalism— indeed, its acceptance of its legitimacy within limits—is also shown in the process by which Central Committee and Council of Ministers decisions are drafted. In the original drafting commissions, the ministries that will be most directly affected by the decision are represented "without fail," and once the draft is completed, it is submitted to all the "interested ministries" for their comments or objections. (The phrases are those of a fairly high Soviet official who was interviewed on the question.) The process takes for granted that ministries will have departmental interests and perspectives and that the higher decision-making bodies should at least be exposed to them.[67]

The point at which the degree of ministerial autonomy in making decisions on the basis of departmental views has become the subject of open debate has been in the relationship of the ministries to the state committees. The existence of committees that deal with such questions as science and technology, labor and wages, supplies procurement, and prices implies the need for a great deal of negotiation and agreement on these subjects between the appropriate state committee and each ministry. Those who advocate greater ministerial independence call for a reduction in the number of questions that must be "cleared" with the state committees; those concerned about ministerial departmentalism demand that the state committees be given added power—perhaps even the power to nullify ministerial decisions.[68] In addition, the recent fascination of Soviet scholars with systems theory may well represent another attempt to impose order upon the centrifugal characteristics of ministerial decisions, but there is little evidence that the systems approach has been seriously introduced.[69]

The State Planning Committee (Gosplan)

Of course, the state committee that has special responsibility for coordinating and controlling the actions of the ministries is the State Planning Committee or Gosplan. In a political system in which the distribution of material resources is more important than the appropriation of money, Gosplan is the closest Soviet equivalent to the American Office of Management and the Budget. It engages not only in long-term planning but also in the extremely detailed compilation of the annual plan.

Soviet planning and appropriation is a two-way process. It begins with directives from the central authorities about changes in priority for the coming year, and each ministry is then asked to submit a detailed plan incorporating proposed appropriations, programs, and (where suitable) output targets that the ministry deems necessary if the goals expressed by the directives are to be met. The ministries make similar requests of their lower units. As a result, a great deal of the planning for each branch takes place within the respective ministries.

The primary function of Gosplan is to reconcile the various ministerial requests within the framework of available resources and regime priorities. It produces four "balances"—one of the overall economy, one of labor resources, one of finance and currency, and one of material resources. The most important is the materials balance. Since the Soviet Union does not have a market economy, the actual distribution of resources (for example, steel, petroleum, machinery, electric energy) is more critical than the financial budget. Supplies are allocated in concrete form, with enterprises and institutions being assigned specific amounts of each item and told the specific supplier. The "balance" is somewhat like a balance sheet which specifies the suppliers and recipients of particular products. In 1973 Gosplan was responsible for working out the balance of what were considered the 1,943 most important items—items which constituted 70 percent of all industrial production in the country. The balances which Gosplan works out do not specify the individual suppliers and recipients; these details are the responsibility of the State Committee for Supplies Procurement and the ministries.[70]

To carry out its functions, Gosplan has two types of internal departments. The so-called "summary" (svodnyi) departments supervise the overall balances, territorial planning, and the like. The branch departments are structured along the same general lines as the ministries, and bear names such as agriculture, building materials and glass industry, culture and education, fisheries, light industry, machinery for the chemical and petroleum industry, trade, petroleum industry, and housing, utlities, and city development. In addition to its departments, Gosplan also has four research institutes, the officials of which not only conduct research and calculations needed in the compilation of the plan but also frequently participate in the published policy debate.

In 1968, Gosplan had ten summary departments and twenty-four branch departments.[71] Historically, the former have had more of a clerical role, and the dominant forces in the organization have been the branch departments and those deputy chairmen who supervise them. (There were sixteen deputy chairmen in 1978, and eleven of them seemed to supervise branch departments.) Like their counterparts in the ministries, the major branch officials in Gosplan are highly specialized in their career development. Indeed, they often come from a ministry in the policy area for which they are currently planning. They often are former high ministerial officials, perhaps a former deputy minister or head of an administration. Thus, in four cases during the Brezhnev era for which biographies are available (the men died and their obituaries were published), the head of the electronics department of Gosplan was a former Deputy Minister of the Radio-technical Industry, the head of the construction and building industry department was a construction engineer with twenty-two years of managerial experience in construction and several years experience as Deputy Minister of the Oil Industry (presumably the deputy minister for construction), the head of an unknown department (presumably the food industry department) was a former Deputy

Minister of the Food Industry, and the head of the foreign trade department had worked in the Ministry of Foreign Trade for twenty years, rising to the post of head of the import administration of the ministry.[72]

In practice, the branch officials in Gosplan tend to serve as the representative, the negotiating agent of their respective ministries in the bargaining process by which a balanced plan is hammered out. In this process, they usually push for the maximum development of their own branch and the maximum allocations of supplies to it. For example, when top officials decided to reduce the production of agricultural machinery in the 1959–1965 plan, the decision produced "categorical objections" from the agricultural machinery department of Gosplan. In the words of the department head (a former Deputy Minister of the Automobile, Tractor, and Agricultural Machinery Industry): "As concerns my position in this question . . . I personally insisted on an increase in the production of the machines."[73] This participation is not limited to the compilation of the annual and five-year-plans, for the 1977 obituary of the head of the agriculture department of Gosplan reported that he had taken "a direct and active part in the preparation of the most important documents of the Central Committee and the Council of Ministers on the development of agriculture."[74]

It is, of course, this type of role in the policy process that led a party official to call for a special Gosplan deputy chairman for agriculture in 1965, and the improvement in the position of agriculture in the Brezhnev era may not be unrelated to the fact that Gosplan soon received both a first deputy chairman and a deputy chairman specializing in that branch.[75] Perhaps the best indication of the position of the Gosplan branch officials is found in their obituaries. Obituaries of important party and governmental officials are usually signed by top officials under whom and with whom they work, including the head and deputy head of the Central Committee department supervising them. The obituaries of Gosplan branch officials are signed both by Central Committee officials handling Gosplan and those in charge of the respective branch.

The Military

In any country, the military is one of the few institutions with the force at its disposal to overthrow the government. There are western observers who contend that the election of the Minister of Defense, Marshal Grechko, to the Politburo in 1973 was symbolic of a major increase in military power in the Soviet Union in the 1970s. For this reason alone, the role of the military as an institutional actor in the Soviet policy process is worth examining.

Yet, in some respects too much emphasis on the military is misleading.

The military is organized into a Ministry of Defense, and the very act of singling it out for special discussion may seem to imply that this ministry is quite unlike the others. This is not true. In no way should it be suggested that only the Ministry of Defense is staffed by professionals, that only that ministry vigorously makes proposals in its sphere of responsibility, and that only that ministry has its ideas reflected in the policy pursued by the party in that sphere. That phenomenon is true of all ministries, and the real question is whether the actual and potential influence of the Ministry of Defense goes well beyond that of other ministries.

In one respect—its size—the Ministry of Defense does seem atypical. Although the exact number of its employees is a closely guarded state secret, there are some four million persons in the armed forces plus an unknown number of civilian employees. An indicator of the scale of the Ministry of Defense is the fact that in early 1978 it had thirteen deputy ministers—twice the number of an average ministry. The responsibilities of these deputy ministers reflect those of the ministry itself (and, of course, its internal structure). Three of the thirteen were first deputy ministers (one of them serving as head of the Warsaw Pact forces and one as head of the General Staff); five were commanders of the major branches of the armed services (the ground forces, the air force, the navy, the strategic rocket forces, and the antiaircraft command), and a sixth was head of Civil Defense. The remaining four deputy ministers had responsibility for some overall ministerial function: research and development (*po vooruzhenii*), construction and quartering, logistics, and inspection.

The most distinctive feature of the Soviet armed forces is the Main Political Administration, which has subunits within each of the five services and in military units down to the company level and which simultaneously functions as a department of the party Central Committee. Westerners often emphasize the political control functions of the political officers vis-à-vis line officers, but the Main Political Administration also supervises many day-to-day activities within the military: political instruction and propaganda work, publication of books and journals (including the ministry's newspaper, *Krasnaia zvezda* or *Red Star*), trade union activities among the ministry's civilian employees, Komsomol activities, sports programs, clubs, libraries, other cultural activities, and so forth. A careful study of the history and current operations of the Main Political Administration demonstrates that the line officers are far more likely to be allied with the particular political officers who "control" them than to be in a conflict situation with them and that the line officers invariably have higher status (and almost invariably higher rank) than these political officers.[76]

The most important fact from our point of view is that the interconnection between the military and political institutions is not a one-way street. The Soviet Union is distinctive in having direct involvement of line military officers in the country's major political institutions. Almost 90 percent of all military personnel are party or Komsomol members. Officers seem to enter the party at a younger age than other college graduates (a sociological study of lieutenants primarily in the twenty-two to twenty-six age range found that 66 percent of them were party members), and party membership seems to become universal for those that are promoted into higher line posts and surely near universal among all officers past their mid-twenties.[77]

Army officers not only join the party but also become involved in higher political activities. Of the 4,998 delegates to the Twenty-Fifth Congress in 1976, 314 were personnel from the army, navy, or border troops,[78] and twenty officers (only one of them a political officer) were named voting members of the party Central Committee in 1976. (An additional ten became candidate members.) Since 1973 the Minister of Defense—in 1978 a civilian, but from 1973 to April 1976 a career officer—has been a voting member of the Polit-buro, and, of course, he has always been a member of the Defense Council. At the local level, an army officer was named a full or candidate member of seven of the fourteen republican party bureaus, and some five to ten officers are regularly named to each of the republican central committees. In all, approximately 6,000 military personnel were members of the com-mittees of the party organs at various territorial levels in 1973.[79]

The same pattern is observable in the selection of deputies to the soviets. Fifty-six military officers (only four of them political officers) were elected to the Supreme Soviet in 1974, and the number of military deputies in the local soviets at that time was put at 13,351.[80] In the past, military personnel did not seem much involved in the detailed work of the Supreme Soviet (only five of the fifty-two officers elected in 1966 were named to a standing com-mittee, only eighteen of the fifty-six military deputies in 1970), but in 1974 twenty-nine of the fifty-four military deputies were on standing committees.[81]

It should be noted, however, that the involvement of the military in civilian life in the Soviet Union is qualitatively different from that often found in China. The boundaries of the sixteen military districts in the Soviet Union do not (with one exception) correspond to those of a single republic or region, but include several such territorial units. For this reason, if for no other, there has been no merging of local party and military positions in the Chinese fashion. At least in the one case on which we have informa-tion—Smolensk in the 1930s—the local commander normally did not even attend the sessions of the regional party bureau meeting to which he had been elected.[82]

The central question, of course, is the meaningfulness of military participation in the political process—the influence that is exercised. In the past a number of western specialists on the military have asserted that the "party and military [are] the two most powerful bureaucracies" in the Soviet Union and that "the relationship between the Communist Party and Soviet military is essentially conflict-prone and thus presents a perennial threat to the political stability of the state."[83] In the Brezhnev era the military has generally had reason to be more satisfied with military policy developments than they were under Khrushchev, and some commentators have speculated that the military now may be even more powerful than suggested earlier. A few have raised the possibility of an actual coup d'etat.

Obviously any discussion of the role of the military is hindered by a lack of information that is peculiar even to the Soviet scene, but several cautionary remarks should be made. In the first place, it surely would be an oversimplification to see some all-out conflict between the party as a whole and the military, particularly one that "presents a perennial threat to the political stability of the state." To be sure, some conflict is almost inevitable between any specialized interest in any society and the political leadership, for the latter has the responsibility of taking many interests into account. However, the party and state leadership includes many engineers with substantial managerial experience in heavy industry and the defense industry (and/or in party work in regions in which such industries are dominant). The image of a "military-heavy industrial complex" conceivably may be somewhat misleading, but at a minimum it points to the fact that the military surely must have allies as well as opponents within the party hierarchy on most policy issues.[84]

In the second place, an important change has occurred within the Soviet military during the last decade. For years the military was dominated by the generation of officers who had had the major role in the Soviet victory in World War II. Not only were these men associated with the aura of this great victory but also most of them had joined the party before many of the political leaders. As late as 1966, the Minister of Defense and 60 percent of the deputy ministers had become party members by 1928—three years before the General Secretary had joined the party—and two-thirds of the commanders of the military districts had entered the party in 1931 or before.

By 1974, however, there had been a fairly complete turnover among the top military officials of the Soviet Union. At that time only the minister, one of fourteen deputy ministers, and two (or perhaps three) of the commanders of the military districts had joined the party by 1931 (or by 1936, for that matter). The new generation generally had become party members during or immediately prior to World War II. They were scarcely young enough to qualify as Young Turks (the deputy ministers averaged sixty years of age in 1974), but it is hard to believe that they had either the political standing or political self-confidence possessed by their predecessors. Moreover, some of the key appointments (most notably, that of the fifty-three-year old chief of staff, V. G. Kulikov) constituted promotions over the heads of men with greater seniority—promotions that suggested not "the work of a senior marshals' club [but] . . . the powerful hand of the Party Secretariat reaching deep into the ranks to make a selection of its own choosing."[85]

Finally, any speculation about a potential military coup d'etat or about party actions taken in response to military compulsion must—particularly in the absence of direct evidence to the contrary—face up to the historical record of the role of the military in modern society. Above all, we should remember that many military coups have occurred in countries in the relatively early stages of industrialization, but almost none in highly developed nations—at least none in industrial nations which have not had a major breakdown of order or a military humiliation. If we contend that civilian authorities in the Soviet Union (and, indeed, in all Communist countries with the possible exception of China) were able to contain any threat of military takeover throughout the early stages of industrialization and that they are beginning to encounter great difficulties now that the country is becoming industrialized, we should realize that we are making a very striking hypothesis in comparative terms.

In actuality, the power or influence of the military seems to stem not from any ability to force through its opinion against Politburo objection, but from its ability to support its requests with technical expertise not possessed by the leadership and especially its ability to appeal to powerful values, emotions, and fears in supporting its policy advice.

> Some people from our military department come and say "Comrade Khrushchev, look at this! The Americans are developing such and such a system. We could develop the same system, but it would cost such and such." I tell them there's no money; it's all been allotted already. So they say, "If we don't get the money we need and if there's a war, then the enemy will have superiority over us." So we discuss it some more, and I end up giving them the money they ask for.[86]

In its technical expertise, however, the Soviet military is not different in kind from a number of specialized groups in society. Indeed, in the West too the "powers [of interest groups] are largely those of partisan analysis [and] they are . . . constrained by the fundamental values of . . . policy makers to whom they appeal."[87] To the extent that the military has a special position, it flows from two facts. First, the very tight censorship on military information and the limitation of debates on military strategy to military journals makes it difficult for civilians, including foreign affairs specialists, to participate in the discussion, even behind the scenes. Second, the decades of emphasis upon heavy industry and the defense industry has drawn many of the most talented people in society into managerial work in these branches and has led to their promotion into top governmental and party positions. As a result, the top governmental officials may have developed many fundamental values in common with the military, and the ability of the military to achieve its aims may not be strongly constrained.

The Academy of Sciences[88]

One of the main features of the Soviet industrialization drive—and probably one of the key factors in its success—has been a major expenditure of funds on the expansion of the educational-scientific network. As a result, the number of persons employed in these spheres has become substantial indeed. By January 1, 1975, there were 2,778 scientific research institutes in the country and 842 institutions of higher education, and the number of "scientific workers" has exploded from 354,000 at the end of 1960 to 1,223,400 at the end of 1975.[89]

Scientific personnel—often called "specialists" in Soviet discourse—clearly play an important role in the Soviet policy process.[90] They not only have certain "defensive" interests as scientists which they try to support,[91] but, more important, they also serve as advocates on policy questions for which their scientific research and expertise is relevant. They sit on commissions and councils, as both professional and volunteer consultants, and they may be drawn into political-administrative work. For example, in 1978 the Ministers of the Radio Industry, of Health, of Finances, and of Higher and Specialized Secondary Education had scientific backgrounds; the head of the science and education department of the Central Committee was a historian; and the Chairman of the State Committee for Science and Technology was an energy scientist. In addition, scientific personnel also take vigorous part in the published policy debates. In December 1971, a month chosen at random to study, they wrote 35 percent of the forty-three long articles in *Pravda* and *Izvestiia* which contained some proposal for policy change and 46 percent of those articles which were devoted almost exclusively to such proposals.

We should not, however, see the scientific-scholarly community as a unified force or group in the Soviet policy process. In the first place, Soviet scholars within a single discipline, economics, for example, can disagree among themselves as frequently as their counterparts in the West. In the second place, as has been seen, many of the educational and scientific institutes are subordinated to the various specialized ministries and state committees, and their scientific personnel frequently identify with the interests and perspectives of their particular branch. Indeed, in large part it is their job to do so—to provide the in-house research (and, no doubt, the within-house "argumentation") which the ministerial officials require.

The only scientific institutes that are not attached to a ministry or state committee are those which belong to the scientific academies. Many of the academies (for example, those of the agricultural, medical, and pedagogical sciences) are closely associated with a specific ministry, but the institutes of the USSR and the republican Academies of Sciences are more varied in their scope. They concentrate their efforts upon basic research, and the areas in which they work are suggested by the names of the four major sections of the USSR Academy of Sciences: (1) Physics and Chemistry, (2) Chemistry and Biology, (3) Earth Sciences, and (4) Social Sciences.[92]

At the end of 1975 there were 246 scientific institutions in the USSR Academy of Sciences, and they employed 41,836 scientific personnel, 53 percent of whom had a degree roughly equivalent to the Ph.D. or better.[93] Another 45,361—45 percent of whom had a higher degree—were employed in the republican Academies of Sciences.[94] The elite of the Academy are the 241 scientists (as of January 1, 1976) elected academicians and the 437 elected "corresponding members."[95] The elections to the Academy are, of course, subject to party influence, but they are far from meaningless. Such powerful figures as the rector of the Higher Party School of the Central Committee, the rector of the Academy of the Social Sciences of the Central Committee, and the deputy head of the international department of the Central Committee have been voted down, and the head of the science and education department of the Central Committee had to wait a decade before being elected a mere corresponding member.[96]

The policy involvement of the Academy of Sciences is as varied as the backgrounds of the scientists working within it. An academician who is a nuclear physicist may write Khrushchev to suggest a nuclear test ban treaty;[97] a computer specialist at the Academy may demand a consolidation of computer units and a movement toward the joint use of computers;[98] a radio astronomer may call for the construction of a big new radio telescope;[99] a thermophysicist may propose the use of hot runoff water from industry for heating purposes;[100] associates of the Institute of State and Law may call for improvement in antialcoholism legislation or a greater importance for the city plan.[101] (The scholars of this latter institute, in fact, have a special role as consultants in the drafting of law on a variety of subjects.)[102]

Nevertheless, there are several major policy areas in which the Academy of Sciences (or a significant segment of it) seems to have a special role. In the first place, of course, the Academy is likely to push for increased expenditures on science and education—and on basic research and classic education at that. In the days when Khrushchev was emphasizing shop training in the schools and a preference in college admission for those with work experience, scholars working in the Academy of Sciences usually spoke out for the traditional academic subjects and for the academically gifted. In the conflict between pure and applied science, the Academy naturally tends to emphasize the need for basic research. At the Twenty-Fifth Party Congress in 1976, for example, the president of the Academy spoke at length on this subject, criticizing "the many specialists and engineers, and industrial officials [who] sometimes incorrectly evaluate basic research [and] say that basic science is science for the scientists and applied research is for everyone else."[103]

In the second place, the Academy is often asked to participate in the planning process. For example, in a study of the early 1970s on "the complex program of scientific-technical development and its social-economic consequences," various Academy institutes were commissioned to prepare 150 "materials."[104] Similarly, the Institute of Economics prepared over thirty reports for Gosplan in the early stages of the preparation of the 1976–1990 long-term plan.[105] Over the years the Institute of Economics has been severely criticized for excessive abstraction in its work and a failure to participate in the planning process as meaningfully as it should. To solve this problem (and it is interesting that this is the way the problem has had to be solved), the leadership has created a number of new economics institutes within the Academy framework, and these institutes have had a considerably larger role in the debate on incentives and on market mechanisms.

In the third place, the Academies of Sciences both in Moscow and in the republics are the institutional center for much of the most vocal and prestigeous support for environmental protection measures in a system with few powerful spokesmen for such issues.[106] With most of the industry-oriented, applied science being conducted by ministerial institutes, the Academy of Sciences has a high proportion of the type of research scientists (notably in biology and geography) who are often most concerned with environmental issues in the West. Not only do individual scientists frequently speak out on this question, but the Academy as a whole can provide institutional support by holding sessions on such subjects as protection of the biosphere.[107]

Finally, the Academy—or at least one element within it—seems to be acquiring a rapidly growing influence on foreign policy questions. There are eight Academy institutes which study either international relations or specific areas of the world: those on the World Economy and International Relations, the Economics of the World Socialist System, the International Labor Movement, Africa, Eastern Studies, the Far East, Latin America, and the USA. The heads of these institutes generally are not scholars with an academic background, but persons with substantial experience in the Central Committee apparatus or the Ministry of Foreign Trade—persons who presumably retain a major policy interest and who presumably are appointed to their post because the leadership wants the institutes to have such an interest. As seen earlier, the articles written by scholars from these institutes do, in fact, often have policy implications, and the institutes are also active participants in behind-the-scenes policymaking. The Institute of the World Economy and International Relations, for example, has been an energetic supporter of expansion of trade between the Soviet Union and the West and has been involved in conflict with other institutes on such questions.[108]

The Trade Unions

In 1978, Soviet trade unions contained 121 million members—virtually every employed person in the Soviet Union with the exception of military-police personnel.[109] To phrase the point more accurately, 121 million Soviet citizens were members of one of the thirty (or perhaps thirty-one) trade union organizations which were subordinated to the All-Union Central Trade Union Council (*Vsesoiuznyi tsentral'nyi sovet professional'nykh soiuzov—*VTsSPS).

As the list of trade unions indicates, the Soviet trade unions are structured along the same branch lines as the ministries: (1) Agriculture and Procurements, (2) Automobile, Tractor, and Agricultural Machinery Industries, (3) Auto Transport and Highways, (4) Aviation Employees, (5) Aviation Industry, (6) Chemical and Oil Refinery Industry, (7) Coal Industry, (8) Communications, (9) Construction and Building Materials Industry, (10) Culture, (11) Defense Industry, (12) Education, Higher Schools, and Scientific Institutions, (13) Electric Stations and the Electrotechnical Industry, (14) Food Industry, (15) General Machinery Industry,[110] (16) Geology, (17) Heavy Machinery Industry, (18) Local Industry and Communal Enterprises, (19) Machinery and Instrument Industry, (20) Medicine, (21) Merchant Marine and River Fleet, (22) Metallurgical Industry, (23) Oil and Gas Industry, (24) Radio and Electronics Industry, (25) Railroad Transport, (26) Shipbuilding Industry, (27) State Institutions, (28) Textile and Light Industry, (29) Timber, Paper, and Woodworking Industries, and (30) Trade and Consumer Cooperatives.[111] In the past there was a secret thirty-first trade union which served the atomic energy industry—the Ministry of Medium Machine-Building—and it may well still exist.[112]

As has been discussed earlier, Soviet trade unions are structured along branch lines, each containing persons who are employed in specified ministries, state committees, and public organizations.[113] Thus, for example, the Trade Union of Education, Higher Schools, and Scientific Workers enlists

only the personnel of the Ministry of Education, the Ministry of Higher
and Specialized Secondary Education, and the Academies of Sciences. A scientist or educator who works in an institute subordinated to another ministry is
a member of the appropriate trade union for that ministry, while, conversely,
a school janitor or other blue collar worker employed by the Ministry of Education belongs to the education trade union.

As a result of this membership policy, there is a close relationship between the branch trade unions and the ministries. Indeed, since administrators as well as workers of a branch are trade union members, top ministerial
officials can be elected to the central committees of the respective trade unions,
and, as a rule, some five to ten of them are.[114] The administrators can even
be members of the Presidiums of these unions. For example, in 1977, the
seventeen-person Presidium of the Education, Higher Schools, and Scientific
Institutions Trade Union included the First Deputy Minister of Education, a
Deputy Minister of Higher and Specialized Secondary education, the deputy
chief scholarly secretary of the Academy of Sciences, the chief scientific secretary of the Academy of Pedagogical Sciences, and the rector of the Moscow
Energy Institute. (In this union at least, the election of deputy ministers to
the Presidium seems to be a new phenomenon, for while these officials were
named to the Presidium in 1972, they had not been on it in 1968.)[115]

The basic unit of the trade union is located in the place of work, and
it is supervised directly by a territorial committee of the branch trade union.
The specialized territorial committees, in turn, are supervised by both the
central office of the branch trade union and a regional (*oblast*) or republican
trade union council which coordinates the activity of all the committees of
the branch trade unions in the area. The chairmen and secretaries (in the
trade union, unlike the party appartus, the secretaries are subordinate officials) formally are all elected by their organization, but the lower committees
are subject to the directives of higher trade union organizations. The lower
trade officials are in the *nomenklatura* of higher trade union committees, and
their selection must be confirmed by these committees.[116] The important
trade union officials at the various levels are surely also in the nomenklatura
of the appropriate party organs, and they normally must be selected from
above by the higher trade union officials in conjunction with appropriate
party officials.[117]

While the major trade union organizations are structured on a branch
basis, the Central Trade Union Council itself is organized along functional
lines. It has the usual central committee and presidium of most Soviet public
organizations, and is led by a chairman, a deputy chairman, a number of
secretaries (ten in early 1978), and a staff which is organized (so far as can
be determined) into some fifteen departments and administrations.[118] The

chairman exercises overall supervision of the trade union, and the deputy chairman too seems to have broad responsibilities. Each of the secretaries may pay special attention to several of the branch trade unions, but their basic responsibility is to oversee the work of one or more of the department heads. In early 1978 each handled one of the following responsibilities: (1) capital construction of trade union buildings, (2) cultural-educational matters, (3) housing and living conditions, (4) labor safety (this secretary also handles trade union work among women), (5) physical culture and sports, (6) relations with trade unions of the Communist world, (7) relations with trade unions of the non-Communist world, (8) resorts and rest homes, (9) wages and economic work, and (10) trade union work in agriculture.[119]

Trade union officials participate in decision-making at all levels. Within the plant they take part in almost all decisions affecting working and living conditions of the employees and are supposed to have a particularly great role in distribution of housing and passes to resorts, in dismissal cases, and in certain social insurance programs.[120] Moreover, of course, trade union officials are among those who advance policy suggestions and criticisms, and such ideas frequently appear in Soviet newspapers and magazines.[121] Behind the scenes, trade unions are one of the "interested organizations" that have representatives on drafting commissions and that are asked to react to the drafts that emerge. The Central Trade Union Council has the official right to name one of its secretaries to the collegium of the State Committee for Prices,[122] and it is quite possible that this right extends to other governmental agencies as well.

Trade unions not only express their opinions on various questions but even make joint decisions with the ministries and other state agencies on these questions. Again and again, Soviet sources use some phrase such as "the Central Committee of the Trade Union, together with the leadership of the branch." Repeatedly it is reported that, for example, "the machinery ministries, together with the Central Committee of our [Machinery Industry] trade union, worked out the 1971–1975 plan for the construction and reconstruction of the [plant] dining halls," and the trade union presidiums frequently meet in joint session with the collegia of the ministries to deal with such questions.[123] Whether jointly with the ministries or not, the trade unions also regularly examine the drafts of the annual and five-year plans and introduce "concrete suggestions" about them.[124]

Just as individual trade unions frequently issue joint decrees with the various ministries, so the All-Union Central Trade Union Council often joins in decisions affecting workers passed by the party Central Committee and the Council of Ministers. In the 1967–1972 period, these joint decisions dealt with such matters as the transfer of workers to a five-day work week, raising wages in the railroad industry, the development of tourism, and improvement of working conditions for machine operators in agriculture.

Less important decisions, such as the details of an insurance system for collective farmers or the rules for awarding bonuses, can be passed jointly by the All-Union Central Trade Union Council and the Council of Ministers. A specialized decision, such as development of research on labor safety, can be issued under the dual authority of the State Committee for Science and Technology and the VTsSPS; a decision ordering an improvement in cultural assistance to the countryside by urban cultural and art institutions may emanate jointly from the VTsSPS and the Ministry of Culture; a decision on the method for establishing piece-work norms may come from the State Committee for Labor and Wages and the VTsSPS.[125]

The fact of trade union participation is simple to document, but the impact of this participation is more difficult to judge. Certainly it is reported —and, no doubt, is true—that trade union suggestions are "attentively examined in the party Central Committee, the USSR Council of Ministers, and Gosplan"[126] and that specific trade union suggestions are accepted by ministries. For example, the Trade Union of the Shipbuilding Industry successfully recommended that workers be shifted periodically from job to job within plants in order to reduce labor turnover, and the VTsSPS was instrumental in having a special section included in the official enterprise annual and five-year plans which included indicators for "social planning."[127]

Yet, there are nagging questions about the relative power of the trade unions in the Soviet policy process. The chairman of the VTsSPS usually has been a member of the party Politburo, and the chairman of the republican trade union organization was in 1976 a member or candidate member of the bureau of the republican Central Committee in thirteen of the fourteen republics with such bureaus.[128] Nevertheless, judging by frequency of election to the republican bureaus over time, the trade union chairman would rank eleventh among civilian officials in the republic, and the chairman of the national VTsSPS ranks no higher.[129] Although the status of the trade union chairmen in the republics appears to have risen substantially in the Brezhnev years,[130] the leadership acted as if the chairmanship of the national trade union was a very low priority post when the incumbent (Shelepin) was replaced in May 1975. The position was left vacant for eighteen months, and the chairman finally chosen in November 1976 had not even been made a candidate member of the Politburo by May 1978.

More important, an examination of the career patterns of top trade union officials creates doubts about the autonomy of their values. Trade union work is not a career on which a young college graduate embarks; it is entered from other work. In recent years a few worker members of the Central Committee have been promoted directly into high trade union work,[131] but the percentage of important trade union officials who began their careers as workers remains relatively small, especially if one excludes persons who were workers for only a year or two before entering the army or going to college (see table 28). Officials of the branch trade unions, including unions at the plant level, predominantly come from professional or lower managerial work. Even those who are former workers tend to go to night school, receive a technician's or engineering degree, and get promoted into staff or line positions before moving into paid trade union work, no doubt after showing their interest and ability in volunteer trade union work beforehand. These officials often return to managerial work when they leave their trade union position.[132]

The chairmen of the national branch trade unions may well have substantial managerial experience. Among the six chairmen named between September 1971 and May 1974, the chairman of the Electric Station and Electrotechnical Industry Trade Union had been head of an electric power substation, the chairman of the Local Industry and Consumers' Services Trade Union had been a deputy minister of consumers' services in Moldavia, the chairman of the Radioelectrical Industry Trade Union had been the head of a laboratory in a factory, and the chairman of the Textile and Light Industry Trade Union had been the director of a textile factory.[133]

The chairmen and the secretaries of the coordinating republican and regional trade union councils usually have had a prior career in party and/or Komsomol work (sometimes with professional or managerial work beforehand) rather than in management, but the chairmen in particular—the persons who represent the trade unions on the party bureaus—are not likely to have held any trade union post before their selection. The same is true of the national leader of the trade union. The last three chairmen of the VTsSPS —V. V. Grishin, A. N. Shelepin, and A. I. Shibaev—all came to their post from party work and had no previous experience in trade union organs. Indeed, Shibaev was in aviation industry management until the age of forty, having reached the level of plant manager.[134]

The available biographical information further suggests that—although trade union work is often associated with low level and middle level upward mobility—this is not a career path which the talented and ambitious can use to rise to the foremost positions in Soviet society. Chairmen of national branch trade unions are almost never moved to other high level work upon completion of the chairmanship, and chairmen of republican trade union councils are also seldom promoted. Of forty-two republican trade union council chairmen who were removed between 1955 and 1972, only five (12 percent) were subsequently named to one of the ten higher ranking republican positions, and only one was transferred to higher trade union work in Mos-

Table 28　*Background of newly appointed trade union officials,*
September 1971–May 1974

NEW POSITION	PERCENT OF NEW APPOINTEES WHO			
	EVER HAD BEEN A WORKER OR PEASANT	HAD BEEN A WORKER OR PEASANT FOR OVER 2 YEARS	HAD HELD A UNION JOB IMMEDIATELY PRIOR TO NEW POSITION	EVER HAD BEEN IN TRADE UNION WORK PREVIOUSLY
Department head or deputy head in VTsSPS apparatus (N=11)	9	0	55	73
Chairman of National Branch Trade Union Council (N=6)	0	0	50	67
Secretary of National Branch Trade Union Council (N=26)	35	27	73	73
Chairman of Republican or Regional Trade Union Council (N=37)	24	7	5	10
Secretary of Republican or Regional Trade Union Council (N=81)	26	10	23	32

Source: Biographies of newly elected officials in "Chronicle" (*Khronika*) section of *Sovetskie profsoiuzy,* various issues from September 1971 through May 1974.

cow. By contrast, 33 percent of the sixty persons occupying the ninth-ranking republican position (party secretary in the capital city or region) and 40 percent of the fifty-three occupants of the twelfth-ranking position (head of the party organs department, or, later, the organizational-party work department, of the republican Central Committee) were promoted to one of these higher status positions.[135] Comprehensive data are not available for lower levels, but ministerial personnel, provincial and city party first secretaries, and managers of important plants almost never have prior trade union experience in their background. By contrast, a significant number have been secretary of the primary party organization in a plant.

A question thus arises about the extent to which trade unions really function more as "company unions." The problem is surely a real one, especially given the absence of the right to strike and the officially recognized responsibility of the trade union to promote productivity. Nevertheless, it should be recalled that even within industry there are often sharp conflicts between managerial officials who occupy line positions and those who are concerned with personnel matters, labor safety, and so forth. If the existence of trade unions were to do no more than increase the leverage of the latter in relation to those who emphasize production, the unions would be of considerable significance. In any case, although the vigor of the trade union defense of workers' interests may be questioned, the causes trade union officials espouse in policy debates in the press are generally those that one would anticipate from trade union officials—better working conditions, stricter observance of labor legislation, less managerial arbitrariness, more labor safety, and so forth. In the major conflict on the degree of wage egalitarianism, the trade unions have been a strong proponent of egalitarianism.

The Komsomol

The Komsomol—the All-Union Leninist Communist Union of Youth (the VLKSM)—can be viewed in several quite distinct ways. On the one hand, the organization surely was established to help promote party values among the younger generation and to mobilize the energies of youth into activities that further party goals; and this surely remains one of its primary functions. On the other hand, in trying to achieve these goals, Komsomol officials inevitably find that the acceptance of regime values by young people and their willingness to participate in socially useful activities depends not only on propaganda activities but also on concrete conditions and policies which are specifically relevant to their lives. As a consequence, Komsomol officials cannot inculcate a Marxist-Leninist world view unless they attempt to represent youth interests in the policy process at least to some extent.

The Komsomol is the youth wing of the Communist party and functions quite explicitly under its leadership. Its structure is closely modeled on the party organization. At the bottom of the pyramid are the primary organizations in all places of work in which there are at least three members. Above the primary organization is the usual tier of district, city, regional, republican, and central organs. At the level of district first secretary or higher, the Komsomol secretaries must be party members, and in many cases they have passed their twenty-eighth birthday—the age at which rank-and-file members are automatically dropped from the organization. The Komsomol first secretary until 1977, E. M. Tiazhelnikov, had been rector of a teachers' college and then secretary of the Cheliabinsk party regional committee for ideological questions before his selection as Komsomol leader in 1968 at the age of forty. His successor, B. N. Pastukhov, had worked exclusively in the Komsomol organization, but he was forty-four years old at the time of his selection.[136]

In May 1978 the central directing apparatus of the Komsomol consisted of a Central Committee of 239 members and 59 candidate members, a bureau of 21 members and 7 candidates, ten secretaries, and approximately a dozen departments with a staff of perhaps some 300 officials.[137] The division of responsibility within the secretariat essentially follows branch lines. One secretary supervised ties with youth organizations in Communist countries,[138] and seven were basically in charge of Komsomol activities within a specific institutional sphere: (1) agriculture, (2) the army and the police (including sports and physical culture questions), (3) cultural institutions (including propaganda and agitation activities), (4) higher and specialized secondary education, (5) industry and trade, (6) general secondary education, and (7) elementary education (this secretary also is chairman of the Pioneer Organization).[139] These secretaries almost always have the education appropriate for their position, and they usually come from lower Komsomol positions that give them special preparation for it. A tenth secretary, who is in charge of personnel selection, also serves as second secretary.

The participation of the Komsomol in the policy process has been formalized by giving it the right to name one of its officials as a member of the collegia of the Ministry of Culture, the Ministry of Higher and Specialized Secondary Education, the Ministry of Education, and the Committee for Physical Culture and Sports, as well as the Presidium of the All-Union Central Trade Union Council and the governing group of the People's Control Committee.[140] On questions in which youth interests are obviously involved, the Komsomol is one of the "interested organizations" called upon to send a representative to the drafting commissions and/or to comment upon the drafts which emerge. One reads that an "initiation group" composed of representatives of the Komsomol, the Ministry of Justice, and Gosplan was formed to draft the rules for student summer work or that the Ministry of Higher and Specialized Secondary Education, together with the student organizations, are working out the rules for research work by students.[141] Similarly, when the Committee on Youth of the Supreme Soviet investigated the degree to which the Ministry of Oil Refineries and Petrochemicals was observing labor laws with respect to the youth, the Komsomol Central Committee apparently investigated conditions on forty-six enterprises and reported the results to the Committee.[142]

The Komsomol newspaper, *Komsomol'skaia pravda,* claims that "the Komsomol widely uses the right of initiative it has been granted to raise this or that question" and that "a whole series of party and state decisions have been taken at the suggestion of the Central Committee of the VLKSM."[143] Wherever the source of initiative, there is no doubt about the number of joint decisions taken by the Komsomol and other institutions—one, for example, on the improvement of tourism and excursions for school children, taken with the Presidium of the VTsSPS, the Ministry of Education, and the State Committee for Vocational-Technical Education; one on establishing a contest for young agricultural mechanizers in the Russian Republic, taken with the RSFSR Ministries of Agriculture and Education and the Agriculture Trade Union; one with the Ministry of Culture and the VTsSPS on improving the library service to major construction projects; one with the Ministry of Education on improving the preparation of history teachers.[144] The Komsomol Central Committee is said to have participated in 250 such governmental decisions from 1963 to 1973.[145]

It is difficult to judge the relative influence of the Komsomol and the ministries with which it normally interacts. Much must depend upon the particular values being defended at a particular time. However, in comparison with the major nonspecialized institutions of society, the Komsomol has not been accorded the status that usually connotes great influence. The Komsomol first secretary has never been a member or candidate member of the party Politburo, and he and his second secretary were the only Komsomol officials to be included among the 426 full or candidate members of the Central Committee elected at the Twenty-Fifth Party Congress in 1976. This figure contrasts not only with eleven deputy ministers of defense on the Central Committee, but also with the six trade union officials named to it.[146] The situation is better at the republican level, for the Komsomol first secretaries are sometimes named candidate members of the republican party bureaus, but in 1976 this was the case in but five of the fourteen republics with such bureaus.

Interrelationships Among the Institutional Actors

The personnel within such institutions as the state bureaucracy, Gosplan, the trade unions, the scientific community, the Komsomol, and also, one might add, within such institutions as the party apparatus, the State Committee for Science and Technology, the People's Control Committee, and so forth have diverse and specialized backgrounds. It is far more likely that a person will be transferred from the Ministry of Railroads to transportation work in Gosplan or the Institute for Complex Transportation Questions or the Railroad Trade Union (or the transportation department of the Central Committee Secretariat or of the People's Control Committee) and back again than that the head of the transportation department in any of these institutions will become the head of its agriculture department (or any other specialized department).

The specialization in the internal structure of the various institutions and in the career patterns of their officials is a fact that deserves the most careful consideration as we attempt to generalize about the Soviet political system. Those who have advocated an interest group approach to the study of the Soviet Union have featured institutions prominently in their lists of important "groups." Yet, if officials dealing with a given policy area within the various institutions have more in common with each other in terms of education and career experiences than they do with many officials within their own institution, then perhaps the most significant interactions, divisions, and alliances cut across major institutions rather than run between them. Perhaps Soviet politics often is better visualized as a conflict among "complexes" (or whirlpools)[147]—a transportation complex, an agricultural complex, perhaps even a heavy industrial-military complex, and so forth. This is a question to which we will return after an examination of another of the most important institutional actors, the Central Committee Secretariat and apparatus.

11 | The Central Committee Secretariat and Apparatus

THE MOST striking feature of the Soviet institutional scene in comparative terms is the role of the extraparliamentary party organs and officials. The Soviet government is parliamentary in form, and many parliamentary systems feature party domination of a weak legislature. Yet, the phrase "party domination" has an institutional meaning in the Soviet Union quite different from its meaning in, say, Great Britain. Normally, in a parliamentary system "the party leadership" of the dominant party is largely synonymous with "the government," consisting of the important leaders of the party who sit in parliament and occupy ministerial positions. While a western party does have an extraparliamentary party organization with its own leaders (for example, the Democratic or Republican National Committees and their chairmen in the United States), these officials generally limit their leadership to fund-raising and organizational activities associated with elections. The committees of the western extraparliamentary party organs usually have a rather minor role in governmental policymaking.

In the Soviet Union, on the other hand, it is not the governmental cabinet or legislature that has the responsibility for reaching final policy decisions, but the top committees of the extraparliamentary party organization (that is, the party congress, the Central Committee, and the Politburo). The party members in the governmental bodies are formally obligated to carry out the decrees of the extraparliamentary party committees, and, in fact, they do so.

Although party members occupying governmental positions often are important leaders within the Politburo, full-time officials of the extraparliamentary party organization also sit on the Central Committee and Politburo. The fourteen-man ruling Politburo contained nine full-time party officials in early 1978, and the inner four of the party leadership at that time contained three top officials of the extraparliamentary party organs—Brezhnev, Kirilenko, and Suslov. Indeed, since the 1920s, the party General Secretary—the head of the staff of the extraparliamentary party organization—has been the real political leader of the country, with the formal head of government—the Chairman of the Council of Ministers—serving as his subordinate.

Involvement of the extraparliamentary party organs in the policy process goes well beyond the role of its leading committees and top officials. The staff of the organization—the Secretariat and the apparatus—have not been limited to propaganda and intraparty organizational work but have participated deeply in policymaking on quite specialized questions. The Central Committee apparatus has been divided into twenty-one or twenty-two departments, nearly all of them dealing with a particular policy area. It is staffed with highly qualified specialists who possess training and experience appropriate for that policy area. For example, in addition to the Ministry of Agriculture within the government, there is an agriculture department within the apparatus of the Central Committee; in addition to the various heavy industry ministries, there is a heavy industry department of the Central Committee. The head of the agriculture department of the Central Committee is a former minister of grain products of the RSFSR, the head of the heavy industry department a former manager of the Norilsk Mining Metallurgical Combine.

The actual role of the Central Committee departments—and of the Central Committee secretaries—has been little discussed in Soviet sources, and it has been the source of considerable confusion in the West. Because of the position of the General Secretary and the repeated Soviet statements about "the leading role of the Communist party," some western scholars write as if the secretaries and departments of the Central Committee monopolize policy initiative in the Soviet system, as if each department dominates the ministries and organizations that it oversees. However, the relationship between the departments of the Central Committee and the various administrative agencies clearly is far more complex than any such image would imply. An understanding of the role of the full-time "institutional actors" of the Central Committee Secretariat and apparatus is crucial before considering the collective party organs.

The Structure of the Central Committee Secretariat and Apparatus

The Central Committee secretaries and the officials of the Central Committee departments are both described as executive agents of the collective party committees, but there is a fundamental theoretical difference between the Secretariat (*sekretariat*) and the apparatus (*apparat*). The party rules stipulate that the secretaries are elected by the party Central Committee, and the Secretariat as such is a small body (eleven members in early 1978) composed of the secretaries who meet essentially once a week to discuss the work of the staff[1] (see table 29). The employees of the apparatus of the Central Committee—of the departments (*otdels*) of the Central Committee—are appointed officials, although the most important of them may well be appointed or confirmed by the Politburo or even the Central Committee. Nevertheless, in practice this distinction between the Secretariat and the apparatus tends to blur, for each secretary has responsibility for one or more departments, and hence the departmental officials work as the staff assistants of the secretaries.

In the first three decades after the revolution, the Central Committee apparatus underwent frequent change,[2] but since 1948 the apparatus has remained quite stable in its fundamental organization and even in most of its details. Basically, the departments have been formed along branch lines, the vast majority of them supervising a group of ministries or other institu-

Table 29   *Central Committee secretaries and their responsibilities, January 1978*

SECRETARY	RESPONSIBILITIES
L. I. Brezhnev	Overall leadership of the country
A. P. Kirilenko	General supervision of the economy and the provincial party organs
M. A. Suslov	General supervision of culture, education, science, and foreign policy
K. U. Chernenko	Secretariat housekeeping; general oversight of bureaucracy
V. I. Dolgikh	Industry, especially heavy industry
I. V. Kapitonov	Lower party apparatus
F. D. Kulakov	Agriculture and food industry (Died—July 1978)
B. N. Ponomarev	Relations with non-Communist countries
Ia. P. Riabov	The military; the defense industry; the police
K. V. Rusakov	Relations with Communist countries
M. V. Zimianin	Culture; education; propaganda; science

Source: 1976 Yearbook, *Bol'shaia sovetskaia entsiklopediia*, p. 20; *Pravda*, October 27, 1976, p. 1. The responsibilities must be inferred from activities reported in the press. Officially, D. F. Ustinov was also still a Central Committee secretary in January 1978, for no formal action ever removed him from the Secretariat when he became Minister of Defense in 1976. However, the 1977 yearbook of the *Bol'shaia sovetskaia entsiklopediia* did not include him in its list of secretaries, and Riabov was assigned precisely the responsibilities that Ustinov had been carrying out.

tions. No Soviet source has given a list of the Central Committee departments in recent years, but a reasonably accurate list can be compiled from scattered references to apparatus officials in the Soviet press.

In May 1978 there were at least twenty-one Central Committee departments: (1) administrative organs, (2) agriculture, (3) chemical industry, (4) construction, (5) culture, (6) defense industry, (7) foreign personnel,[3] (8) general, (9) heavy industry, (10) international, (11) light industry and food industry, (12) machinery industry, (13) organizational-party work, (14) planning and financial organs, (15) political administration of the Ministry of Defense (which also serves as a Central Committee department), (16) propaganda, (17) science and education, (18) socialist countries, (19) trade and consumers's services, (20) transportation and communications, and (21) information (newly created in 1978). In addition, usually reliable indirect evidence suggests the existence of a new twenty-second department which handles foreign aid questions.[4] While there can be some overlap in their duties,[5] each department is generally given responsibility for the supervision of specific ministries or "public organizations" (see table 30).

Table 30 *Central Committee departments and agencies they supervise*

CENTRAL COMMITTEE DEPARTMENT	MINISTRIES, STATE COMMITTEES, AND OTHER INSTITUTIONS
Administrative Organs (Cand CC)[a]	Ministry of Civilian Aviation, A-U[b] (CC)[a]
	Ministry of Defense, A-U (CC)
	Ministry of Internal Affairs, U-R (CC)
	Ministry of Justice, U-R (Cand CC)
	Committee for State Security (KGB), * (CC)
	Procuracy (CC)
	Supreme Court (CC)
	Civil defense units, including DOSAAF
Agriculture[c] (Cand CC)	Ministry of Agriculture, U-R (CC)
	Ministry of (Agricultural) Procurements, U-R (CC)
	Ministry of Reclamation and Water Management, U-R (CC)
	State Committee for Forestry, * (Cand CC)
	All-Union Agricultural Supply Agency, * (CC)
Chemical Industry (Audit C)	Ministry of Cellulose-Paper Industry, A-U (CC)
	Ministry of the Chemical Industry, A-U (CC)
	Ministry of the Oil-Refining and Petrochemical Industry, U-R (CC)

Table 30—Continued

CENTRAL COMMITTEE DEPARTMENT	MINISTRIES, STATE COMMITTEES, AND OTHER INSTITUTIONS
Construction (Audit C)	Ministry of Assembly and Special Construction Work, U-R (CC)
	Ministry of the Building Materials Industry, U-R (CC)
	Ministry of Construction, U-R (CC)
	Ministry of Construction in the Oil and Gas Industry, A-U (CC)
	Ministry of Construction of Heavy Industry Enterprises, U-R (CC)
	Ministry of Industrial Construction, U-R (CC)
	Ministry of Rural Construction, U-R (CC)
	Ministry of the Timber and Wood-Working Industry, U-R (Cand CC)
	Ministry of Transportation Construction, A-U (Cand CC)
	State Committee for Construction, * (CC)
	(Scientific) Academy for Construction and Architecture
	Union of Architects
Culture (Cand CC)	Ministry of Culture, U-R (CC)
	State Committee for Movies, * (Cand CC)
	Writers, artists, composers unions
Defense Industry (Cand CC)	Ministry of the Aviation Industry, A-U (CC)
	Ministry of the Defense Industry, A-U (CC)
	Ministry of the General Machinery Industry, A-U (CC)
	Ministry of the Machinery Industry, A-U (CC)
	Ministry of the Means of Communication Industry, A-U (CC)
	Ministry of the Medium Machinery Industry, A-U (CC)
	Ministry of the Radio-technical Industry, (Cand CC)
	Ministry of the Shipbuilding Industry, A-U (CC)
	(State Committee for the Peaceful Use of Atomic Energy),[d] (Noth)

continued

Table 30—Continued

Central Committee department	Ministries, state committees, and other institutions
Foreign Cadres (CC)	(Ministry of Foreign Affairs), U-R (CC) Ministry of Foreign Trade, A-U (CC) (State Committee for Foreign Economic Ties), * (CC) The extent to which this department becomes involved in decisions other than personnel ones is unclear.
General (Sect CC)	Handles intrasecretariat and intraapparatus housekeeping, the routing of incoming communications, and security for classified documents.
Heavy Industry (Sect CC)	Ministry of the Coal Industry, U-R (CC) (Ministry of the Gas Industry), A-U, (Cand CC) Ministry of Geology, U-R (Cand CC) Ministry of the Iron and Steel Industry, U-R (CC) Ministry of the Non-Ferrous Metallurgy Industry, U-R (CC) Ministry of the Oil Industry, A-U (CC)
Information (Created since 1976)	Probably TASS The department head has been serving as Brezhnev's press secretary.
International (Sect CC)	Handles ties with Communist parties of non-Communist countries Possibly supervises ministries listed under the Foreign Cadres Department, at least in their relations with the non-Communist world.
Light industry and food industry (Audit CC)	Ministry of Fisheries, U-R (Cand CC) Ministry of the Food Industry, U-R (CC) Ministry of the Light Industry, U-R (CC) Ministry of the Meat and Dairy Industry, U-R (CC)
Machinery industry (Cand CC)	Ministry of the Automobile and Truck Industry, A-U (Cand CC)

Table 30—Continued

CENTRAL COMMITTEE DEPARTMENT	MINISTRIES, STATE COMMITTEES, AND OTHER INSTITUTIONS
	Ministry of the Chemical and Petroleum Machinery Industry, A-U (CC)
	Ministry of the Construction, Road, and Communal Machinery Industries, A-U (Cand CC)
	Ministry of Energy and Electrification, U-R (CC)
	Ministry of Energy Machinery Industry, A-U (Cand CC)
	Ministry of the Heavy and Transportation Machinery Industries, A-U (CC)
	(Ministry of the Instrument, Means of Automation, and Control Systems Industries), A-U (CC)
	Ministry of Machinery for Livestock Raising and the Feed Industry, A-U (Cand CC)ᵉ
	Ministry of Machinery for the Light and Food Industries and for Consumer Appliances, A-U (CC)
	Ministry of the Machine-Tool and Tool Industry, A-U (CC)
	Ministry of the Tractor and Agricultural Machinery Industry, A-U (Cand CC)
Organizational-party work (Sect CC)	Local party organs
	People's Control Committee * (CC)
	Party membership records and statistics
	Local soviets
	Komsomolᵉ
	Trade unionsᵉ
Planning and financial organs (Cand CC)	Ministry of Finance, U-R (CC)
	State Committee for Labor and Social Questions * (CC)
	State Committee for Prices, * (Audit C)
	State Committee for Supplies Procurement, * (CC)
	(State Committee for Standards), * (Cand CC)
	State Planning Committee (Gosplan), * (CC)

continued

Table 30—Continued

CENTRAL COMMITTEE DEPARTMENT	MINISTRIES, STATE COMMITTEES, AND OTHER INSTITUTIONS
	State Bank (Gosbank), * (Noth)
	Central Statistical Administration, * (Cand CC)
	(Construction Bank) (Noth)
Political administration of the Ministry of Defense (CC)	Political organs in the armed forces and through them the Ministry of Defense (However, the administrative organs department also has major responsibility for this ministry.)
Propaganda (Sect CC)	State Committee for Publishing, Printing, and Book Trade, * (CC)
	State Committee for Television and Radio, * (CC)
	State Committee for Sports and Physical Culture (Audit C)
	Propaganda-agitation work by party, state, and public organizations
	The political education system within the party
	The newspapers and journals
	Cultural work of the trade unions
Science and Education (CC)	Ministry of Education, U-R (CC)
	Ministry of Health, U-R (Cand CC)
	Ministry of Higher and Specialized Secondary Education, U-R (CC)
	Ministry of the Medical Industry, A-U (Audit C)
	State Committee for Science and Technology * (CC)
	Academy of Sciences (CC)
	Republican ministries of social security
Socialist Countries (Sect CC)	Ties with parties of socialist (Communist) countries
	Possibly supervises ministries listed under the Foreign Cadres Department, at least in their relations with the Communist world.
Trade and Consumers' Services	Ministry of Trade, U-R (CC)
	Consumers' Coops (Cand CC)

Table 30—Continued

CENTRAL COMMITTEE DEPARTMENT	MINISTRIES, STATE COMMITTEES, AND OTHER INSTITUTIONS
(Cand CC)	Republican ministries of consumers' services Republican ministries of the utilities
Transportation- Communications (Audit C)	Ministry of Communications, U-R (Cand CC) Ministry of the Merchant Marine, A-U (Cand CC) Ministry of the Railroads, A-U (CC) RSFSR Ministry of River Transportation Republican ministries of auto-truck transportation

a The words (Sect CC), (CC), (Cand CC), (Audit C), and (Noth) under the names of the Central Committee departments and after the names of the ministries refer to the party status of the occupant immediately after the Twenty-Fifth Party Congress in 1976. Sect CC means that a Central Committee secretary was, in practice, serving as the department head; CC means that the occupant of the post was elected a full member of the Central Committee; Cand CC means that he was elected a candidate member of the Central Committee; Audit C means that he was elected a member of the Auditing Commmission; Noth means that he was elected to none of these bodies.

b The symbols A–U, U–R, and * after the state institutions refer to the legal status of the institution. A–U means that it is an all-union ministry (that is, that it has no subordinate counterparts in the republics); U–R means that it is a union-republican ministry and has such counterparts in at least some of the republics; * means that the given state committee or other agency has a seat on the Council of Ministers. (All ministries have such a seat.)

c In October 1976, three candidate members of the Central Committee—including the head of the agriculture department of the Central Committee and the Minister of Machinery for Livestock Raising and the Feed Industry—were raised to full membership.

d Parentheses indicates a ministry or state committee is probably supervised by the Central Committee department indicated.

e The specialized Komsomol departments and trade unions are supervised by the appropriate specialized Central Committee department.

In addition to the departments enumerated, the Central Committee apparatus also includes a business office (*upravlenie delami*), with such subdivisions as a financial-budgeting department, a capital construction section, a book expediting office (*knizhnaia ekspeditsiia*), a party publishing house department, and an economic (*khoziaistvennyi*), department. The economic department in turn supervises (among others) such units as a "Northern Caucasus group of [rest and relaxation] sanitoria," a repair-construction administration, a retirement home, and a dining facilities section.[6]

The officials who are in direct charge of the Central Committee departments usually have the title of "head" (*zaveduiushchii*), but, in practice, the major supervision of the departments is provided by the Central Committee secretaries. Five of the eleven secretaries actually headed departments themselves in early 1978, but the normal pattern—which also encompasses at least one of the five secretaries who head departments—is for a secretary to supervise several related departments. Thus, the Secretariat is structured along the same branch lines as the apparatus. However, three of the secretaries in the Brezhnev era have occupied a special position. The General Secretary, of course, supervises the entire apparatus, but two other secretaries. Kirilenko and Suslov, have served essentially as first deputy General Secretaries, supervising other secretaries as well as (or in Suslov's case, instead of) departments. Kirilenko has been responsible for those officials supervising personnel selection and the economy (except for agriculture) while Suslov has been handling foreign relations, ideological work, and the educational-cultural sphere. (For the distribution of responsibilities among the secretaries in 1978 see table 29.)

Finally, there are two additional institutions associated with the Central Committee that formally are not part of the Central Committee apparatus but that do contain full-time party officials—the personal assistants of the General Secretary and the Party Control Committee. Of these two, the Party Control Committee seems to be by far the more substantial in size. All officials of the Central Committee apparatus and of the Party Control Committee seem to receive awards on their fiftieth and sixtieth birthdays. From 1967 through 1976, 321 responsible officials of the Central Committee apparatus were so honored and 37 responsible officials of the Party Control Committee, figures that tend to suggest that the latter employs slightly more than 10 percent of the number of persons in the Central Committee apparatus.[7]

The Party Control Committee is assigned responsibility for maintaining party discipline and proper personal behavior among Communists. In practice, the Control Committee tends to concentrate its efforts upon investigations of complaints of "incorrect conduct" among Communists and, even more, upon an examination of appeals of Communists who have been expelled from the party by lower party organs. The Central Committee journal, *Partiinaia zhizn'*, regularly carries Control Committee decisions condemning misconduct by lower officials,[8] but these decisions may create a misleading impression of the center of activity of the committee. A number of indicators —including the age of its chairman and staff—suggest that its more important role is serving as a passive party supreme court which reviews the justice of decisions on expulsions made throughout the country.[9]

The second institution linked to the apparatus—the personal staff of the General Secretary—seems to be a growing institution, or, at least an institution of growing visibility. The only personal assistant of Stalin whose name was made public was A. N. Poskrebyshev—Stalin's "loyal shield-bearer," as Khrushchev called him at the Twentieth Party Congress, provoking laughter in the hall.[10] Khrushchev himself had two assistants who were publicized: G. T. Shuisky (who had been with him since 1941 and whose newspaper background suggested major responsibilities in the speech-writing realm)[11] and A. S. Shevchenko (who seems to have been his assistant for agricultural questions),[12] but he had at least one other assistant who was not mentioned in public, a man named Lebedev who handled cultural affairs.[13] Whatever the actual scale of the personal staffs of Stalin and Khrushchev, only Poskrebyshev seems to have been honored with selection to the Central Committee (in 1952, as a full member), and only Shuisky among Khrushchev's assistants was selected to a leading party organ, and then only to the Auditing Commission in 1961—the third level in status behind full and candidate membership in the Central Committee itself.

By contrast, Brezhnev's major assistant, G. E. Tsukanov, was immediately elected a full member of the Central Committee in 1966, and by 1970 Brezhnev had four other assistants whose names often appeared in the press when he traveled: K. V. Rusakov, his assistant for Communist bloc affairs; A. M. Aleksandrov-Agentov, an assistant for foreign relations with the non-Communist world who apparently concentrated his attention on relations with the United States and arms control; A. I. Blatov, an assistant for relations with other countries in the non-Communist world; and V. A. Golikov, an assistant handling internal affairs, especially agriculture. In 1977 Rusakov was moved from this post and became Central Committee Secretary, and Blatov began handling Communist bloc questions as well. In addition, the press also sometimes mentions I. M. Samoteikin as a research assistant (*referent*) of the General Secretary. His job is said by a highly placed Soviet source to be that of preparing Brezhnev's daily news briefing, but he also often attends meetings with visitors from India or the Middle East. The extent to which these men are deeply involved in policy advising rather than in providing more technical assistance (for example, speech-writing or the drafting of documents) is difficult to judge, but Americans who have had contact with Aleksandrov-Agentov during the Nixon-Ford years gained the impression that he was a major participant in the substance of policymaking. Certainly the status of many of the assistants is rather high. Tsukanov is a full member of the Central Committee (as was Rusakov), while Aleksandrov-Agentov is a candidate member of the Central Committee and Blatov is a member of the auditing commission of the Central Committee.

The Structure of the Central Committee Apparatus

The list of departments indicates considerable specialization within the Central Committee apparatus, but the process is carried still further by the creation of sections (*sektory*) within the departments. So far as can be ascertained, there are some 150 to 175 sections, three to fifteen in each of the departments. The sections, like the departments themselves, usually are organized along branch lines, with one created to correspond to almost every ministry or major type of nonministerial institution. The following list is but a sample of the sections within the departments, and, except perhaps for the propaganda department, it is not even complete for any one of the departments indicated.

Agriculture department
  Land cultivation
  Mechanization
  Procurements
  Reclamations and water economy
  Forestry
  (Agricultural) science and advanced experience
  Sections for certain major USSR territories (for example, the Northern
    Caucasus)

Construction department
  Industrial and transportation construction
  Urban economy (*gorodskoe khoziaistvo*)
  Timber and woodworking industry

Culture department
  Cinematography
  Literature (*khudozhestvennaia literatura*)
  Musical arts
  Theater

International department
  Africa
  Central Europe
  Great Britain and Commonwealth
  Latin America
  Near East
  Southeast Asia
  Scandanavia and Iceland
  United States

Light industry and food industry department
  Fisheries
  Food industry
  Meat and dairy industry

Organizational-party work department
  Individual party card
  Registration of leading personnel
  Party information
  Trade unions and Komsomol organs
  Ukraine and Moldavia
  Baltic Republics and Belorussia
  Central Asia
  Kazakhstan
  Transcaucasia
  Sections for major territories of the RSFSR (for example, Far East oblasts)

Propaganda
  Cultural-enlightenment work (that is, in institutions such as clubs)
  Economic education (extramural education rather than the regular colleges
  Journals
  Mass-political work
  Newspapers
  Party propaganda (that is, the party education system)
  Printing industry and distribution of the press
  Sports and physical culture
  Television and radio

Science and education department
  Economic sciences
  Higher educational institutions
  Philosophy and scientific communism
  Public health and social security
  Schools
  Secondary specialized and vocational-technical education

The departments and sections of the Central Committee are staffed by several types of officials. Most departments are supervised by a head (*zaveduiushchii*), although, as has been seen, this post was actually occupied by a Central Committee secretary in five cases in early 1978. In addition, the departments have a first deputy head and from one to five deputy heads, who normally have responsibility for several sections. The sections in turn are directly led by a head, but only rarely have deputy heads.

Thus, in early 1978 the chain of command within the Central Committee Secretariat and apparatus on questions dealing with the United States would run from General Secretary Brezhnev to Suslov (the secretary in charge of

overall supervision of ideological and foreign policy matters) to B. N. Ponomarev (a Central Committee secretary and head of the international department) to V. V. Zagladin (the first deputy head of the international department) to A. S. Cherniaev (the deputy head of the international department
in charge of Great Britain and the United States) to V. N. Mostovets (the
head of the United States section).

The basic staff members of the departments are given the title "instructor" (*instruktor*), and they are each assigned to a particular section. A
few of the more critical departments (or perhaps secretaries) have a small
number of high level "inspectors" (*inspektory*) for special assignments, and
a larger number of departments have a "group of consultants" (*gruppa
konsul'tantov*) composed of high status and full-time members of the staff
who work on major decisions or projects. In addition, the propaganda department has a lecture group staffed by full-time lecturers (*lektory*), while
the international department includes "research assistants" (*referenty*) among
its staff.[14] (Conceivably this word is always used instead of "instructor" for
this department because of worries about the connotations of the latter.)
Finally, each of the departments also has a "secretariat" (*sekretariat*), which
in this case *is* a secretariat in the American sense of the word "secretary" and
serves as the department's office staff.

The most interesting recent development within the Central Committee
apparatus has been the growth in the number of consultants. In the Khrushchev period only one group of consultants seems to have existed, and, although it was attached to the international departments, it drafted important
political decisions as well and did considerable work on the Party Program.
A number of other departments—for example, agriculture, culture, organizational-party work, planning and financial organs, and propaganda—are
known to have been given consultants' groups, in the Brezhnev period, but
others (including the heavy industry department) are still without one. The
consultants—often men with a scholarly degree—are freed from the daily,
detailed work in which the instructors become immersed, and they may be
assigned the task of preparing major decisions, of leading a year-long study
of a problem, or the like.[15]

While the consultants have broad-gauge responsibilities, the principle
of specialization within the Central Committee apparatus extends down to
the instructor level. Information about the responsibilities of the instructors
can be obtained only through interviews or by inference from the meetings
that they attend or the articles they they write, but a number of examples can
be identified in this way. For instance, in the science and education department there is one instructor who handles medical schools and the education
of doctors, another who is in charge of the Academy of Pedgagogical Sciences

and educational research, and one who deals with the social security system (or at least the Ministry of Social Security of the Russian Republic). The propaganda department has a single instructor who specializes in questions related to the propagation of atheism (and probably policy on religion) and another who seems to deal with county level newspapers.

Some of the departments are also structured in part along territorial rather than branch lines. Thus, the territorial sectors of the organizational-party work department normally include one instructor for each of the country's oblasts and small republics. (However, a single instructor sometimes may handle several adjoining oblasts, at least in the non-Russian republics.) The agriculture department has a similar network of territorial sectors to supplement its branch ones, and its instructors too are likely to handle oblasts within the territory. (For example, there is one instructor who seems to have responsibility for the northern oblasts of Kazakhstan's Virgin Lands.) Finally, a high trade union official has stated in an interview that nearly all of the instructors of the railroad section of the transportation-communications department are each assigned two or three of the country's approximately twenty-five railroads to oversee.

Although many details on the structure and division of responsibility within the Central Committee apparatus can be pieced together from references in the press or from interviews, the overall size of the apparatus remains a closely guarded secret, and Westerners have made estimates ranging from a few thousand to nearly 10,000. No doubt, part of the disparity results from an imprecision in our definition of the Central Committee apparatus. As the staff of the Central Committee, the apparatus, broadly defined, includes the chauffeurs, janitors, secretarial help, clerks, and so forth that are found in any large organization. Indeed, even the employees of the Central Committee newspapers such as *Pravda* might conceivably be considered part of the Central Committee staff. Obviously a definition of the apparatus that includes all or part of the service personnel means an apparatus that is much larger than a definition limited to the "responsible officials"—the instructors and their superiors.

Another part of the explanation for the disparity in estimates may be a widespread misunderstanding in the West about the role of the Central Committee apparatus and hence a widespread failure to appreciate just how small the apparatus may be. The Central Committee sections and departments do not direct the activity of the ministries they oversee, but serve more as a "White House staff" to the General Secretary and the Politburo. Hence they do not require an enormous staff.

Our knowledge about the numbers of instructors in sections in some of the industrial and foreign policy departments is extremely limited, but each piece of information that becomes available points to a section size that often does not exceed a half dozen instructors and that sometimes may be as small as one or two. Sections in some departments conceivably may be larger, but if we assume the existence of 175 sections, each with six instructors, we would arrive at a Central Committee apparatus with some 100 to 125 department heads and deputy heads, 175 section heads, 1,050 instructors, and perhaps 100 to 150 consultants, inspectors, deputy section heads, personal assistants to the secretaries, and so forth—in short, a Central Committee apparatus of some 1,500 responsible officials, not counting those employed in the business office, the lecture group,[16] or the Party Control Committee. A very unreliable article by a man who claims to be a former Central Committee instructor puts the number of full-time responsible employees in the apparatus at just over 900,[17] and, although this figure would imply an average of only three instructors a section, it points in the right direction.

The Background of Central Committee Officials

During the 1920s, officials of the party apparatus were sometimes called *apparatchiki,* and although this term has not been used in the Soviet Union for decades, westerners often still employ it in their descriptions of the Soviet political system. Particularly when coupled with the frequent assumption that Central Committee officials function either as a united interest group or as a unified group of professional politicians standing above the institutional struggle, the word *apparatchik* leaves the impression of a uniform group of men with a "highly professionalized career pattern" and with loyalties "more exclusive" and a commitment "more intense" than among western politicians.[18] Whatever the common interests among employees of the Central Committee Secretariat and apparatus, however, the word is certainly misleading if it suggests officials with similar backgrounds. In practice, the career patterns of the Central Committee staff are as differentiated as the structure of the apparatus itself.

It is true that the top officials of the Central Committee Secretariat who handle "political" matters do, indeed, tend to have a general political background. The General Secretary and the First Deputy General Secretary for personnel and economic questions in 1978 (Brezhnev and Kirilenko) spent years as regional first secretaries in different regions, and the Central Committee secretary who headed the organizational-party work department (I. V. Kapitonov) had a similar career in Moscow, Moscow region, and Ivanovo. Nevertheless, the other Central Committee secretaries tend to have had a more specialized preparation that corresponds with their current duties.

Thus, while Suslov had a fairly broad early career, he has worked in the ideological-foreign policy realm for some thirty years in the Central Committee Secretariat. The secretary who heads the international department (B. N. Ponomarev) worked in the executive committee of the Communist International (Comintern) from 1936 to 1943, and in 1947 he was named head of the Soviet office of the Comintern's successor, the Cominform. At any point in time during the last forty years, Ponomarev was either serving in one of these capacities or was working in the international department of the Central Committee. The secretary in charge of relations with Communist countries (K. V. Rusakov) had been a top administrator in the fish industry until 1957, but for the twenty years before becoming Central Committee secretary he had served in diplomatic work and in the Central Committee apparatus dealing with the Communist world. The secretary in charge of "ideological" questions (M. V. Zimianin) had been Komsomol first secretary, minister of education, and the party secretary for ideology in Belorussia and later chief editor of *Pravda*.

The secretaries who specialize in economic affairs have a far different background. The secretary for agriculture (F. D. Kulakov) and the secretary for industry (V. I. Dolgikh) in early 1978 both held the post of regional first secretary before their promotion into the Central Committee Secretariat, but Kulakov led the party organization in rural Stavropol in the Kuban, while Dolgikh led it in industrialized Krasnoiarsk in Siberia. Before becoming Stavropol first secretary, Kulakov had the classic biography of an agricultural specialist, including work as head of a regional agricultural administration, RSFSR deputy minister of agriculture, and RSFSR minister of grain products. Dolgikh, on the other hand, had twenty years of experience in industrial management, having risen through a number of lower engineering-managerial positions to become director of the Norilsk Mining-Metallurgical Combine near the Arctic Circle in Siberia.

Similarly, the man who bore responsibility for the military and the defense industry through most of the first decade of the Brezhnev regime (D. F. Ustinov) was a former plant manager who became People's Commissar for Armaments in 1941 and remained one of the country's top defense industry administrators for the next twenty-five years (indeed, the top such administrator during most of the Khrushchev period). When Ustinov became Minister of Defense in 1976, his successor (Ia. P. Riabov) was a man who had spent twelve years in managerial work at a major Sverdlovsk industrial plant (reaching the level of shop head) before being transferred to party work. After thirteen years of successively responsible party posts, he was named first secretary of the Sverdlovsk regional party committee. In some ways Riabov's background was even more appropriate than Ustinov's, for supervision of the military in the Secretariat means supervision of the administrative organs department, and that means supervision of the police as well.

This latter responsibility is one for which party work is probably the best training, and party work in Sverdlovsk under Kirilenko presumably meant that Riabov had the added qualification of high political reliability for a highly sensitive job.

The duties of the final secretary (K. U. Chernenko) are not totally clear. Prior to his election as secretary in 1976, he had been head of the general department of the Central Committee—really the secretariat of the apparatus —and apparently his primary (and perhaps exclusive) work is still supervision of this department.[19] Because of the department's responsibility for routing incoming correspondence and complaints and for handling classified documents,[20] the post is a very sensitive one politically, but it apparently does not involve much participation in specialized policymaking as such. For these reasons, Chernenko's background is not unexpected: party work with emphasis upon communication of ideas and an extremely close association with the General Secretary. He engaged in miscellaneous party work for decades, including eight years as head of the propaganda-agitation department of the Moldavian Central Committee (for nearly three years while Brezhnev was first secretary there). Then in 1956 he became head of the mass-political work section of the USSR Central Committee, and, when Brezhnev moved to the chairmanship of the Presidium of the Supreme Soviet, Chernenko followed him as head of the secretariat of the Presidium. In 1965, Brezhnev gave him the same job in the Central Committee apparatus.

The heads of the Central Committee departments have careers that are at least as specialized as those of the secretaries who supervise them. Only five of the fifteen nonsecretarial department heads in early 1978 (and two of the five department heads who were a secretary) were promoted to their present position from within the Central Committee apparatus, and even those five had substantial specialized experience before their first appointment in the apparatus. Thus, the head of the machinery industry department had a decade of engineering-managerial experience at an industrial plant and had risen as high as shop head prior to his appointment as deputy head of Central Committee department; the head of the defense industry had been a director of a branch (*filial*) of a defense plant; the head of the administrative organs department was an army officer with fifteen years in political work in the army; the head of the planning and financial organs department had held a series of supervisory jobs in the Ministry of Light Industry, the Kalinin regional economic council, and the central planning organs over a period of ten years.[21]

All of the 1978 department heads who were appointed from the outside had engaged in party work at some stage of their career, but their backgrounds too were highly specialized. The department heads in the ideological realms tended to have the greatest amount of party work in their backgrounds, but it was overwhelmingly party work in the ideological realm. The head of the culture department had been first secretary of the Minsk regional committee for four years, but he had taught (or been a school principal) for nearly a decade and had thirteen years of work as ideological secretary of the Minsk regional party committee and then of the Belorussian Central Committee. The head of the science and education department had engaged in Komsomol and party work in the countryside from 1929 to 1944, but then he had studied in the Academy of Social Sciences for four years and was trained as a historian. His major book was a history of collectivization. For eight years he was rector of the Higher Party School in Moldavia (overlapping Brezhnev's tenure in that republic), and, after four years of unspecified work in the Central Committee apparatus (but quite possibly involving responsibility for higher party education), he served as deputy rector of the Higher Party School in Moscow for five years.[22] The head of the propaganda department had been Komsomol first secretary, and the head of the information department had been Director of TASS.

Except for the head of the agriculture department (an agronomist whose career centered on party work in three important agricultural regions and the cotton republic of Uzbekistan), the heads of the departments supervising the economy all had major administrative experience in the appropriate branch of the economy before entering party work. The head of the construction department in early 1978 had been head of a construction trust, with sixteen years in construction administration; the head of the light industry and food industry department had worked for fifteen years in light industry, eventually holding the post of head of the textile and sewing industry administration of the Kazakh Ministry of Light Industry; the head of the transportation and communications department had been head of the Gorki Railroad, and prior to that had had a twenty-year administrative career in the railroad industry. The head of the trade and consumer services department was a former first deputy minister of trade in the Ukraine and a former minister of the fish industry in that republic, and the head of the chemical industry department had been a Deputy Minister of the Chemical Industry. The foreign personnel department does not, of course, supervise the economy, but its head had long experience in the foreign policy realm—nineteen years as ambassador to four countries and as a Deputy Minister of Foreign Affairs.[23]

Information about Central Committee personnel below the level of department head is much more scattered, but fairly complete biographies have been found of 205 individuals who held such a position in the period since Stalin's death, and they show the same differentiation in background as is found at higher levels (see table 31). The basic staff members of the departments—the instructors—are not hired directly from college but are drawn from the institutions being supervised by their particular departments. Judging from the available biographies, the average age at which a person has been hired as a Central Committee instructor in the post-Stalin period is thirty-nine. (The thirty-five on whom I have information were all appointed between the ages of thirty-three and forty-six.) The instructors come from a range of middle level positions: first secretary of a district party committee (a very frequent case, especially for the organizational-party work department), head of a construction administration, head of a laboratory of a

Table 31　*Educational background of Central Committee officials below department head, 1953–1976*

TYPE OF DEPARTMENT	TYPE OF EDUCATION (IN PERCENTAGES)				
	ENGI-NEERING	AGRO-NOMICAL	UNIVER-SITY PEDA-GOGICAL SOCIAL SCIENCE	HIGHER PARTY SCHOOL	NONE
Industrial or construction (N = 11)	91[a]	0	0	9	0
Agricultural (N = 15)	0	80[b]	0	20	0
Propaganda-education science-culture (N = 20)	5	0	60	30	5
Organizational-party work (N = 22)	32	9	14	45	0

Source: Biographies found in a wide range of Soviet sources.

[a] This figure includes a graduate from an architectural institute (who works in the construction department) and a graduate of the mechanical-mathematical faculty of Moscow University.

[b] This figure includes a graduate of an engineering-irrigational institute and an institute for the mechanization and electrification of agriculture.

metallurgical research institute, head or deputy head of a department of the Komsomol Central Committee, head of a department of a regional party committee, deputy editor of a regional newspaper. The majority of the instructors are drawn from party work or from among the graduates of the Higher Party School or the Academy of Social Sciences, but even in these cases the appointee usually has had professional or managerial experience outside the party apparatus. (The instructors of the organizational-party work department usually are exceptions.)

Unfortunately, few biographies are available of section heads in departments other than propaganda and organizational-party work, and hence it is impossible to generalize about the diversity among these officials. The section heads in these departments do seem to be young (the average age of first appointment is forty-one), and they tend not to remain in their post for more than five years. Heads of sections in the international department often seem to have longer tenure, and one can also cite a few cases in the industrial departments as well, but we do not have enough information to make firm conclusions. Approximately half of the section heads for whom we have biographies come from outside the Central Committee apparatus, their previous position generally being higher than that of a new instructor. (For example, a disproportionate number would be secretary of a regional party committee instead of a district or county party committee.)

More biographies of deputy heads of Central Committee departments have been published, and it is obvious that these men are substantial figures. First appointed to their position at an average age of forty-four in the post-Stalin period, only 40 percent had risen within the Central Committee apparatus from the position of instructor. Because of their age, many of the outsiders had had a chance to occupy quite significant posts in the administrative system: chairman of the executive committee of the Volgograd regional soviet, chief editor of the journal *Political Self-Education,* head of the Sakhalin steamship line, first deputy chairman of the Kirgizian Council of Ministers, Deputy Minister of the Heavy Machinery Industry. In these cases the biographies were very specialized, and the men involved were assigned to the Central Committee department suggested by their background.

Many of the available biographies of lower Central Committee officials fail to specify the department in which the official is or was employed, and others fail to specify the official's rank. As a consequence, it is impossible to make meaningful statistical comparisons of the occupational backgrounds of lower level officials in the Central Committee apparatus, but there is no doubt about the specialization in career pattern to be found among them. The distinctions in educational background reported in table 31 are an accurate reflection of occupational differences as well.

Responsibilities of the Central Committee Apparatus

As difficult as it is to collect information on the structure of the Central Committee apparatus and the background of its officials, it is even harder to ascertain the precise nature of the responsibilities of that body. Even the role of the Central Committee Secretariat is summarized only briefly in the party rules ("the leadership of current work, chiefly in the realm of personnel selection and in the organization of the verification of fulfillment [of party-state decisions]",[24] and other Soviet sources have a tendency to do no more than quote these words verbatim.

Until recently, nothing was said about the role of the apparatus itself, other than that it assists the Secretariat in the fulfillment of its duties. However, recent Soviet textbooks on party structure are beginning to recognize the existence of the apparatus and to be a bit more explicit in describing its duties:

> The apparatus consists of departments and sections, which are concerned with specific sectors of party work. Direct leadership of these units is carried out by the Secretariat of the Central Committee. The apparatus fulfills assignments of the Politburo and the Secretariat; it collates information which comes into the Central Committee; it helps the Central Committee in the selection and distribution of supervisory personnel; it supervises the fulfillment of decisions; it conducts clerical work and keeps the records of the party members; it administers the party budget, and so forth . . .

> Within the departments . . . are centered the collection of information on a given branch or kind of activity, the study of the condition of things and the developmental trends, the preparation of memoranda and drafts of decisions, and supervision over the execution of party and governmental directives. The departments [also] carry out the duty of instructing (*instruktirovanie*) of the party organizations and departments on all questions within their competency.[25]

Of the various duties of the Central Committee apparatus, that involving the selection of personnel is most formalized. The various political and administrative posts in the country are, of course, formally filled either through appointment by an administrative superior or through election. However, personnel action regarding the most important of these posts (down to the level of chief agronomist on a collective farm, the heads of a shop at a large industrial enterprise, or the secretary of a primary party organization) must also be "confirmed" by a party committee at the district level or higher.[26]

Each committee has a list (*nomenklatura*) of the posts for which it has the right of confirmation.[27] The more important the post, the higher the level of party committee in whose nomenklatura it is located, and the most important posts of all are in the nomenklatura of the Central Committee in Moscow.

The number of posts within the nomenklatura of the Central Committee has never been revealed, but it must be quite substantial. In the industrial realm, for example, the first deputy chairman of the Belorussian regional economic council asserted in an interview in 1958 that ten plant managers and five chief engineers in Minsk were in the nomenklatura of the Central Committee, and five years later the director of the Novo-Baku Oil Refinery said in an interview with some pride that his post was one of those in that category. A Soviet novel has indicated that election of a person to the bureau of a regional party organ, and certainly the election of a secretary, must be approved by the Central Committee,[28] and large numbers of ministerial officials must also be in the nomenklatura of the Central Committee.

Formally party nomenklatura only means that personnel changes with respect to a post must be "confirmed" or approved by a specific party organ, and the official action, be it appointment or election, is the responsibility of another institution or electorate. In fact, party confirmation often must mean no more than that, and at times it probably is a formality. However, the Central Committee clearly has the right to take the initiative in removing an official or selecting a new one. The press frequently refers to provincial party organs that have "removed" or "fired" an official, even when they do not have official authority to do so,[29] and occasionally a similar statement is made about the Central Committee. Thus the history of the Ulianovsk party organization reports that in 1961 "the party Central Committee . . . considered it necessary to free I. D. Iakovlev from the post of first secretary of the regional party committee and recommended that a more experienced party official with higher agricultural and party education be elected to this work."[30] Decisions about a post in party nomenklatura should be made by a collective party organ (for example, the Politburo), but the preparatory work of the departments and secretaries often must be decisive.

The work of a party organ in personnel selection is not limited to posts in its nomenklatura. Lower party committees usually are deeply involved in the selection or removal of an official in the nomenklatura of a higher party committee, and the higher committee may simply ratify a decision actually made by its subordinate. For example, collective farm chairmen are in the nomenklatura of the regional party committees, but the evidence strongly suggests that the district party committees are more likely to lead the negotiations in the selection of new chairmen. The same practice may be followed in the center, with the Central Committee actually being less absorbed in low level personnel work than its nomenklatura suggests. In the past, cases have been reported of provincial party organs which changed occupants of posts in the nomenklatura of the Central Committee without informing it.[31] Of course, a party organ has the right to intervene in any personnel decision not preempted by a higher party organ, and it can petition for change when it cannot make one itself. In addition to its power to order the removal of a corrupt or unreliable lower level official, the Central Committee apparatus can also take part in decisions on the membership of commissions drafting legislation.[32]

Soviet newspaper reports on party work associated with the "selection of personnel" (*podbor kadrov*) make clear that this responsibility is far wider than participation in individual decisions on appointments and removals. "Selection of personnel" also means the establishment and maintenance of general standards and criteria of selection in various categories of personnel, such as efforts to increase the number of college graduates among factory foremen, programs to retrain middle level officials (notably, in recent years, in the field of economics), creation or expansion of a higher education institution to provide more of a certain type of specialist.

The second responsibility of the Central Committee Secretariat and apparatus emphasized in Soviet sources is "the verification of fulfillment" (*proverka ispolneniia*) of party and governmental decisions. The word "instructor" implies an official who tells others how they are deviating from central decisions or how they should fulfill them, and refugees sometimes give much emphasis to this role. One refugee film-maker claims that the Central Committee (presumably the culture department) reviews every film before it can be released, while another depicts the instructor as a "plenipotentiary," a person who can even issue instructions to the first secretary of a republican central committee.[33]

The verification and instructing responsibilities of the Central Committee apparatus need, however, to be viewed with some perspective. If instructors are relaying an instruction from a higher official, their authority is, of course, enormous. Similarly, if they are on an inspection tour, it often must be true that they "are treated like little kings . . . as local officials are anxious to have them write good reports."[34] Nevertheless, two facts should not be overlooked. First, as their biographies show, the lower officials of the Central Committee apparatus are very much middle-range officials in their prestige and power, and they do not have the status to order around republican and regional party first secretaries or USSR ministers or deputy ministers on their own. Second, the staff of the sections is simply too small for them to engage in any systematic and comprehensive inspection of the performance of the vast party-state hierarchy. It is probably symptomatic that in its 205 sessions between 1971 and 1976 (each of which surely dealt with a number of questions), the Secretariat examined only eighty questions involving the verification of decisions already taken.[35]

When the Central Committee apparatus tries to check on the work of the governmental agencies and local party organs and to ensure that they carry out party decisions, it may function in a far more passive and indirect manner than party textbooks suggest. The party rules give each party member the right—in fact, the duty—to report any "action that harms the party and state" to the party organs, "up to and including the Central Committee." The practical consequence of that statutory requirement is a flow of thousands of communications to the Central Committee, and someone must then read them, determine whether the complaints are accurate, and attempt to take corrective action. This responsibility may, in practice, constitute a large part of the apparatus' verification work.

Even in conducting the investigations it does launch, the Central Committee apparatus often operates less as a independent auditor than as an organizer of investigations by others. The major party textbook reports that the practice of organizing temporary commissions (*vremennye komissii*) for the "examination and decision of individual questions" has been and is "widely employed in the activity of all organs of the Central Committee."[36] Apparently these commissions can vary considerably in size. If local party practice is duplicated in the center, a small investigating commission or committee might include a Central Committee instructor, a representative from a relevant ministry or ministries, and perhaps a scholar, and it seems they need not even include the instructor. Soviet historical accounts also sometimes refer to ad hoc investigatory groups called brigades (*brigady*). (One such looked into conditions in Rostov region in 1952 just prior to the removal of the first secretary.)[37] However, the distinction between a commission and a brigade is not clear.

Finally, the Central Committee may also rely entirely upon officials of other institutions in conducting investigations. For example, the People's Control Committee repeatedly organizes nationwide inspections on some problem by its volunteer controllers, and the head of the transportation department of that institution reported in an interview that occasionally such an inspection will actually have been instigated by the transportation-communications department of the Central Committee. The relations between the various Central Committee departments and their specialized counterparts in the Komsomol and the trade unions are very close, and the same should be true of the newspapers of the Central Committee—not only *Pravda*, but also *Rural Life* (*Sel'skaia zhizn'*), *Socialist Industry* (*Sotsialisticheskaia industriia*), and *Soviet Culture* (*Sovetskaia kul'tura*). If there is an indication of a possible trouble spot, the personnel of these institutions can easily be mobilized to look into the situation.

The third major responsibility of the Central Committee apparatus and Secretariat is the one least discussed in Soviet sources, but it may be the most important—"the preparation of memoranda and drafts of decisions . . . the preparation of questions for examination and decision by the plenary session of the Central Committee, the Politburo, or the Secretariat."[38] If the role of the Central Committee apparatus were primarily one of personnel selection and verification of performance, an earlier structure of the apparatus might well be the most appropriate: a distribution of personnel (or cadres) department, an organizational-instruction (or verification of fulfillment) department, and an agitation-propaganda department constituting the core of the institution. However, such an organizational structure is ill-suited for the gathering of information and the drafting of decisions in the various policy realms, and the basic persistence of the present arrangements for three decades may be the best testimony to the seriousness of this defect.

To a considerable extent, "the preparation of memoranda" can be no more than the summarization of the results of an investigation, and even the drafting of a decision can fit within the same category. In actuality, a great many of the published Central Committee and joint Central Committee–Council of Ministers decisions are rather broad statements that deal with an overall policy area such as trade, medical care, or ideological work. They often do little more than formalize existing policy or in several of their sections perhaps give added emphasis to some relatively new trends or developments. A decision will often seem little different from one published on the same subject perhaps four or five years earlier, and more than anything, one gains the impression that a periodic review has occurred—one that conceivably may have entailed a rather extensive staff investigation.

Nevertheless, the phrase "preparation of memoranda" does accurately reflect the fact that much of the apparatus' work is connected specifically with the decision-making process within the Secretariat, the Politburo, and the Central Committee. If these collective bodies are deciding a question, their members want to hear not only a report from the major officials involved but also supporting documentation, an indication of the opinion of other interested institutions, perhaps an independent evaluation and, if the stage of final decision has been reached, a first draft of a decision. This preparation of the documentation is the responsibility of the Central Committee departments.

A number of western scholars have emphasized the role of the Central Committee Secretariat and apparatus in the policy drafting process and have concluded that these institutions are the center of policy initiation in the Soviet political system.[39] We have no conclusive information on this question. There are, however, several indicators that the Central Committee staff often may be reacting to pressures from others or serving as a collector or conduit of ideas and information rather than as an initiator per se.

One reason to suspect a more passive role for the Central Committee apparatus is simply the logic of the Soviet political-administrative system, coupled with several pieces of evidence that the logic is, in fact, at work. The Politburo and the General Secretary are the final arbiters in a system that is a "bureaucracy writ large" without even a market place to resolve conflict. As a consequence, they receive a stream of appeals from institutions that are dissatisfied with decisions at lower levels or that simply want the authority of the Politburo or the party leader behind one of their programs. Lenin himself complained about the tendency for questions to be "dragged" to the Politburo, and a 1957 minister described precisely the same tendency for ministers to advance "minor" matters to the Council of Ministers level in the 1950s.[40] It is difficult to believe that the buck stops there today any more than it did in the 1920s.

A second reason to be cautious in discussing the initiating role of the Central Committee apparatus is that the process by which laws and decisions are drafted in other circumstances in the Soviet Union usually does not involve unilateral initiation. In the various cases on which information is available, several principles seem consistently to be observed. The most fundamental is that the interested (*zainterestnye*) institutions are always consulted. The relevant ministries are always included among such institutions, but trade union and Komsomol officials also report that the opinion of their respective institutions are always asked when the interests of their members are significantly affected by a decision being drafted. Even officials of the People's Control Committee state that they too are given the opportunity to express their views in this process.[41] If the Soviet policy process is to be criticized, it should not be for its lack of consultation, but for, as Brezhnev put it, the fact that "great excesses are permitted with respect to all possible clearances (*soglasovanii*) and collegial discussions."[42]

A second principle of legislation or decision drafting in the Soviet Union is that temporary commissions seem invariably to be created to engage in such activity and that the institutions most directly involved are usually represented on the commissions. Indeed, the initial draft is frequently provided by a major institution in the particular policy realm. Scholars with relevant specialized knowledge are called in as consultants or even as members of the commissions.[43]

The scattered information at our disposal suggests that these basic principles apply in the drafting of Central Committee decisions as well. The party textbook indicates that temporary commissions are created in the central party organs not only for investigatory purposes but also for "the preparation of proposals." "Such a method of preparation and deciding questions," it is said, "permits different points of view to be more fully taken into account, efforts to be coordinated, and subjectivism to be avoided."[44]

In three post-Stalin Central Committee decisions on which concrete information has been found, the commissions, like those on nonparty legislation, were by no means limited to officials of the Central Committee apparatus. The Minister of the Machinery Industry in 1957, N. N. Smeliakov, has written in his memoirs that he was a member of the commission that was established to examine Khrushchev's proposal to create the regional economic councils (sovnarkhozes).[45] A Soviet scholar at the major institute for the study of health organization and economics, the Semashko Institute, stated in an interview that scholars at her institute are invariably consulted on any Central Committee decision dealing with health, and that, indeed, the first draft of a major Central Committee–Council of Ministers decree on the subject was actually written in the institute. A commission that worked in 1977 on a Central Committee–Council of Ministers decision on labor training in schools was chaired by the First Deputy Chairman of the Council of Ministers.

The process of consultation is probably accurately suggested in a Central Committee official's description of the process by which several key 1966 party and state decisions on the treatment of crime were prepared.

> Legal scholars, experienced officials of the law enforcement organizations, the procuracy and the court were recruited into the preparation of the new measures. The necessary sociological investigations were conducted for these purposes, and the experience of other socialist countries in fighting crime was examined. Much was proposed by the workers themselves, by the production collectives. In particular, meetings of officials of the Central Committee, the Moscow city committee, and the Moscow regional committee with workers of a series of important plants were extremely useful.[46]

As a question moves toward final decision, responsible officials from outside the Central Committee apparatus apparently continue to be involved. A member of a visiting Italian Communist party delegation has reported on a 1957 decision to reorganize the staff of the journal *Voprosy istorii* (Questions of History), and the procedure followed is probably fairly typical for an important decision on which a senior Central Committee secretary becomes involved:

> Our own department [Science and Education] is not limited simply to keeping the Central Committee informed on developments in the cultural debate but also takes part in working out the projects and decisions of the Secretariat and the Central Committee. For example, the decision about *Voprosy istorii* was taken after long discussion inside the Secretariat of the Central Committee which was based on a project drawn up by the department. To draw up the project we invited at the start the comrades from the editorial board of the review to the department. Next, in January [1957], we held a bigger meeting, convened by our department and the propaganda department, at which [there] participated not only the editorial board of the review, but also the president and the vice-president of the Academy of Sciences and representatives from the Academy of Scienecs. For two days we had eight- to nine-hour discussions. At the next meeting of the Secretariat, the editors of the review, the comrades of the propaganda department and our department, and finally Comrades Pospelov and Suslov [the Central Committee secretaries for ideological question] all spoke. After this debate, the decision to change the editorial board of the review was approved.[47]

A draft prepared by a commission, even one headed by a Central Committee secretary, need not be approved by those with final decision-making authority; Khrushchev has reported that a recommendation of a 1952 commission on the development of livestock which he headed was totally rejected by Stalin.[48] Nevertheless, a commission report must normally be at least the basis for discussion at the final decision-making stage, and this manner of writing Central Committee decisions must say much about the role of the lower officials of the apparatus. They are the persons who must put together the commissions, organize the necessary meetings, help in the drafting of decisions, and clear the various drafts of top party decisions with the interested officials.

Of course, in trying to ensure that the top leaders become aware of the full range of alternatives, the apparatus officials often need to take the initiative in learning the diversity of views held by knowledgeable persons. They regularly attend major conferences in their fields, the sessions of the standing committees of the Supreme Soviet, and, at least in some cases, the meetings of the collegia of the ministries. They sometimes are named to the editorial boards of journals (for example, the head of the United States section of the international department is on the editorial board of the magazine of the

Institute of the United States and Canada, *SShA*), and thus have an opportunity to be exposed to the views aired in incoming articles. And, finally, they frequently call in scholars for consultation, and they may visit the provinces to gather opinions on a decision being made.[49]

To be sure, even to the extent that the Central Committee officials frequently act more as midwives for the ideas of others, they have some leeway in determining what will survive and prosper. There are choices to be made on which appeals to accept, on which complaints to make the center of an important decision, and on which decision to make. Although staff officials may only have the duty of presenting the range of alternatives objectively or of drafting a decision that will satisfy a number of ministries, they will often be in a position to make a significant impact on the final outcome, and they surely will often be asked by their superiors to take a more decisive role. At a minimum, they can push a controversial position, occasionally even advancing them in print.[50] Yet, whatever the relative influence of the Central Committee officials and those with whom they deal, it is important to understand the constraining factors on their role in the process of policy initiation. The Central Committee departments have many responsibilities, and the size of their staff prevents them from serving as some autonomous policy think tank just as much as it interferes with their being a systematic inspection agency.

The Power of Central Committee Officials

With the Central Committee apparatus structured like a miniature government, staffed by highly trained and experienced personnel, involved in such sensitive questions as personnel selection, inspection of ministerial performance, and the drafting of decisions and policy memoranda, the central question is the relative influence or power of the Central Committee officials and the governmental administrators they supervise. Unfortunately, in this case we not only face the usual problems in measuring power but also must deal with the least discussed and least accessible officials of the inner apparatus. Nevertheless, there are a series of clues about the power relationships between officials of the party apparatus and those of other institutions, and they at least provide some illumination on this crucial question.

The crucial point with which to begin is that both the Central Committee apparatus and the government each have persons of widely different status and power working for them. Thus, the General Secretary is the most powerful individual in the Soviet Union, but his subordinates in the Central Committee Secretariat and apparatus are organized in a hierarchical manner, and most are located at lower levels of the hierarchy. As one "descends" the ladder from secretary to department head to deputy department head to section head to instructor, the decline in power and influence is enormous.

Governmental institutions are also organized in a hierarchy, and the officials at different levels within it vary even more in their power than the staff of the Central Committee. As has been seen, the foremost governmental officials have very considerable standing within the party itself. In early 1978 the Chairman and one of the First Deputy Chairmen of the Council of Ministers, the Minister of Defense, the Minister of Foreign Affairs, and the Chairman of the KGB—all governmental officials—were voting members of the party Politburo, while all of the USSR ministers and chairmen of state committees who had been appointed to their post by the time of the Twenty-Fifth Party Congress in 1976 were voting or candidate members of the party Central Committee.

Whatever the power of the General Secretary, whatever party sources say about the leading role of the party, it transcends all bounds of reason to assume that junior officials of the Central Committee apparatus have a standing that even approximates that of governmental ministers who sit on the Politburo. Indeed, at least in the mid-1930s when a Politburo member suggested a personnel change which was within his jurisdiction but which also was within the nomenklatura of the Central Committee, a firm rule specified that that action should be automatically confirmed by the Central Committee department within twenty minutes. The official reporting this rule in his memoirs cited an example involving a series of appointments of heads of coal mines proposed by Sergo Ordzhonikidze, the People's Commissar for Heavy Industry.[51] Thus, nomenklatura became a complete formality for a top governmental official who was on the Politburo, and whether or not this concrete rule still exists, it must accurately reflect the normal relationship between a Politburo member—whatever his job—and the middle level officials of the party apparatus.

While a person in Kosygin's position obviously is much more powerful than the average official of the party appartus, the real question is the relative standing of the officials below the Politburo level. What is the relative power position of, say, a Deputy Chairman of the Council of Ministers and one of the Central Committee secretaries not on the Politburo, of a Minister and a Central Committee department head, of a deputy minister and a head of a section of a Central Committee department, and so forth? What is the relationship between the Central Committee Secretariat as an institution and the Presidium of the Council of Ministers as a unit?

Of these questions, by far the most difficult to answer relates to the Secretariat and the Presidium of the Council of Ministers as collective institutions. We know almost nothing about the Secretariat except the names of its members and the fact that it met 205 times in the five years between the Twenty-Fourth and Twenty-Fifth Party Congresses, and we cannot even be sure of these two simple facts about the Presidium of the Council of Ministers. Together with the Defense Council, the two institutions constitute the key sub-cabinet committees functioning just below the level of the cabinet itself (the Politburo), but it is most unclear why one question would be referred to one of the bodies, another to the other, and still a third to both simultaneously, as may be the case in joint Central Committee–Council of Ministers decisions. Decisions which relate primarily to institutions administratively independent of the Council of Ministers must be handled by the Central Committee Secretariat, but surely the Secretariat does not limit itself to such questions alone. Perhaps the specific expertise of individual members of the two bodies is sometimes important in determining the agenda. Or perhaps a question will be moved to one forum or the other depending on the judgment of a key Politburo member—even the General Secretary—about the likely effect of the choice of forum on the final outcome.

Our information about the relative standing of different types of Central Committee and ministerial officials is a bit fuller, for we can observe some of the status symbols of the system and can examine the career patterns of officials on the rise. If an official is rising, a move from one job to another is presumably a promotion from a lower status job to a higher status one, and if a particular ranking of jobs is found in enough biographies to reduce the possibility of idiosyncratic factors at work, this indicator should be highly reliable. The various types of evidence indicate a complex overlapping in the status systems (and presumably in the power systems) of the Central Committee apparatus and the governmental administration.

The party General Secretary is, of course, the dominant figure in the Soviet political system, but the Chairman of the Council of Ministers, if not the second-ranking person in the country, is clearly one of the foremost political officials. The post of First Deputy Chairman of the Council of Ministers is usually coupled with membership in the Politburo, and the Deputy Chairmen too are quite powerful figures. The Deputy Chairmen often seem to rank below the Central Committee secretaries in status, but they invariably are members of the Central Committee and certainly seem superior in standing to the nonsecretarial department heads.

The USSR ministers too are important figures in the party, for 73 percent of them were named to full membership in the Central Committee at the Twenty-Fifth Party Congress. Only two heads of a Central Committee department received this honor, if those department heads who served as a Central Committee secretary are excepted. Thus, if we say that, for instance, the head of the construction department of the Central Committee gives policy direction to the Chairman of the State Committee for Construction and to eight of the construction ministers, we are saying that a man deemed worthy of election only to the auditing commission of the Central Committee (a status subordinate even to that of candidate membership in the Central Committee) is superior to men thought worthy of election to voting membership in the Central Committee. With most of the Central Committee department heads in such a status relationship with the ministers they oversee, it is difficult to believe that the general power relationship between the two types of officials is of an opposite character.

The relative status of the middle level officials of the Central Committee departments seems better defined than that of the department heads, for those posts are low enough in the hierarchy to be held by persons in mid-career, and we can sense fairly easily the difference between a career that is still on the rise and one that is not. This indicator, together with others such as the order of signatures on obituaries, suggests that the deputy head of a Central Committee department ranks just below a first deputy minister in standing. For example, the Minister of the Merchant Marine appointed in 1970, T. B. Guzhenko, had risen through engineering posts in the ministry to become the head of several ports and then of the Sakhalin steamship line. In 1960, at the age of forty-two, Guzhenko became head of the personnel administration of the Ministry of the Merchant Marine, and two years later he was named deputy head of the transportation-communications department of the Central Committee, surely the deputy head in charge of water transportation. In 1966 he was appointed First Deputy Minister of the Merchant Marine and in 1970 the Minister.[52] In fact, the available evidence indicates that the status of the deputy head of a Central Committee department is between that of a first deputy minister and a deputy minister. (However, in those cases in which a Central Committee secretary serves as department head, the first deputy head has a status closer to that of the nonsecretarial department head.)

Biographical data also suggests that the position of section head of a Central Committee department ranks below that of deputy minister. When section heads return to the governmental apparatus, they are appointed to a variety of posts, but they never seem to be named to a higher position than deputy minister, a fact which implies that such an appointment is a promotion. (For section heads in the organizational-party work department, future career advancement is likely to be into the territorial party organs, and section heads dealing with the non-Slavic republics are frequently selected as republican party second secretaries.) A Soviet refugee claims that Central Committee instructors are of sufficient stature to aspire to appointment as deputy minister, but I have seen only one biography in which such a promotion had occurred, and the instructor seems a much more junior official than such a claim would imply.[53]

Of course, only the most naive and oversimplified analysis would treat the relative power of various types of Central Committee and governmental officials as being fixed in nature. The power relationship between two individuals or institutions is always situational; it always varies from issue to issue, depending upon circumstances.[54] Even aside from such continual fluctuation, other factors may lead one particular party or governmental official to have a greater or lesser influence than would be typical for his formal post. Thus, whatever the normal relationship between a minister and a Central Committee secretary or department head, the fact that the Minister of Internal Affairs, N. A. Shchelokov, was one of Brezhnev's closest associates over the years must give him a special political strength that other ministers do not possess.[55] Conversely, if an official with high formal status falls into disfavor with the top leadership, then his relationship with his counterparts in the Central Committee apparatus or government must change radically, for his opponents know that in any conflict their appeals to the leadership will likely find support.[56]

Indeed, if the top leaders want, they can structure the contacts to ensure that an official interacts only with a party official of equal or higher status. For example, it has been reported in an interview that during the early Brezhnev years the Central Committee relations with the editor of *Novyi mir*, Aleksandr Tvardovsky, were handled exclusively by the Central Committee secretary, Petr Demichev (a candidate member of the Politburo), while the head of the culture department of the Central Committee dealt with the first deputy editor and lesser departmental officials had contact only with lesser editorial personnel.

Personalistic considerations quite unassociated with high politics also may have a major impact on the relationship between officials of the Central Committee apparatus and those of other institutions. By all outward indicators, O. B. Rakhmanin, the first deputy head of the Central Committee department in charge of relations with Communist countries (the deputy head in charge of relations with Asian Communist countries) should be much more influential in the development of the Soviet Union's China policy than M. S. Kapitsa, the head of the Ministry of Foreign Affairs department in charge of China. The former was elected a member of the auditing commission of the Central Committee in 1971 and a candidate member of the Central Committee in 1976, while the latter has not even been named a deputy minister. Yet, Kapitsa is a long-time Far East specialist in the Ministry of Foreign Affairs,[57] and a well-placed Soviet diplomat reports that he was once Rakhmanin's administrative superior and that he supervised Rakhmanin's dissertation even after Rakhmanin was in the Central Committee apparatus. As a consequence, the diplomat asserted, Rakhmanin has had a tendency to be deferential to his judgment, although he has become somewhat more self-assertive since his dissertation was finally completed. It is impossible to verify this particular assertion, but surely the personality factor often must be crucial in shaping a relationship that is a subtle one by its very nature.

Nevertheless, even in cases when an idiosyncratic factor strengthens the position of either a party or governmental official, the apparatus-government relationship should not be completely one-sided if the Soviet political system is working properly. The major justification for the establishment and maintenance of a costly duplication of men and offices in both the government and the Central Committee apparatus must be prevention of leadership dependence upon a single source of information and advice in the various policy realms. If the leaders exclusively support either apparatus officials or government officials when disputes arise between them, the other would eventually lose heart and cease to function as an alternate source of information and advice. One would think that the leaders would be sensitive to this consideration.

So long as the relationship between the Central Committee Secretariat and apparatus with other institutions does not become frozen, the important point for our purposes is not the precise ranking of the different types of party and governmental officials or the nature of the factors introducing variation in them. What is important is the very fact that the differences are subtle ones and that each hierarchy has important officials whose status and power overlap with that of important officials in the other. This fact alone makes it virtually impossible to conceive of the Central Committee Secretariat and apparatus pre-empting the policymaking role—or the policy initiating role, even in a narrow sense—and of the government simply being limited to the execution of policy. Whatever the exact nature of the Soviet policymaking process, it must be characterized, at least short of the point of final decision, by the type of committee politics familiar to students of large governmental and nongovernmental institutions in the West—a politics that features representation of different interested institutions on the important committees, some attempt to resolve conflicts by adjustment, and the achievement of individual influence in significant part through the ability to maneuver, persuade, and bargain.

The Apparatus-Ministerial Relationship

One of the most persistent themes in western descriptions of the Soviet political system has been conflict between the party apparatus and the government. Sometimes the basic conflicts within the Politburo have been explained in these terms, but at a minimum, analyses of interest group activity almost invariably include the party apparatus and the state bureaucracy among the key groups.

Despite the conflict that must exist between the officials of the Central Committee and governmental hierarchies, it just as surely would be incorrect to see this relationship in purely adversary terms. The very logic of the situation in which the Central Committee officials find themselves often pushes them into representing the interests of those they are supervising. When officials of a department "verify performance" or collect information to "prepare a question," they will be told that more funds and more supplies will improve the situation. Since such an assertion is likely to be true, the officials of the departments will surely make the same point to the party leadership.

This advocacy role of the specialized Central Committee officials can be documented from the articles these men write in the press. These articles are devoted primarily to a summary of current policy and to a criticism of shortcomings of the relevant ministries, but they usually also include a cautious appeal for greater investment in their branch or for better treatment of it by outside ministries and agencies. Thus, the head of the oil and gas industry section of the heavy industry department of the Central Committee was behaving in a typical manner in 1968 when he argued that "it is very important to speed the introduction of new capacity in the oil industry" and that funds should be appropriated for the "integrated automation and tele-mechanization of the production process."[58] The deputy head of the agriculture department of the Central Committee (the deputy head in charge of mechanization questions) was behaving typically when he demanded that the relevant agencies expand the number of types of self-propelled farm machines being produced and that they not raise prices on new models by a greater proportion than the increase in the productivity of these models over old ones (a rule that he suggested was not always being followed currently.)[59]

In practice, each Central Committee department often seems to work together with its ministries as the combined representative of the branch in the appropriations process. For example, in the conflict that flared in the late 1950s over the level of agricultural investment (the conflict in which the head of the agricultural machinery department of Gosplan protested the reduction in the production of agricultural machinery), Khrushchev has testified that the party and ministerial officials specializing in agriculture also functioned as allies:

> At the end of 1959, at the December plenum of the Central Committee of the CPSU, our party worked out new important measures in the agricultural realm . . . I should tell you, when we prepared for this plenum, our agricultural organs—the departments of the Central Committee for the

union republics and for the RSFSR and the ministries of agriculture—worked our fairly broad proposals for the development of all branches of agriculture in the Soviet Union. We rejected these proposals.[60]

The crucial question, of course, is whether to emphasize the conflict or the cooperation between the ministries and the Central Committee department, and, as is usual when we come to crucial questions about the Soviet political system, we again much acknowledge the sparsity of available information. Nevertheless, in this case it seems safe to say that the relationship varies with the type of question involved.

In formal terms the General Secretary is the leader of the Secretariat and the apparatus, and the fact that there was a large turnover of department heads within a few years after both Khrushchev and Brezhnev became head of the Secretariat suggests that the General Secretary has considerable leeway in selecting compatible subordinates in the apparatus. Consequently the Central Committee officials would be expected to be loyal to their own boss in normal circumstances and to take policy positions that would strengthen his political position. Moreover, if the General Secretary has specific ideas for change in a particular policy realm, he perhaps finds it easier to select a Central Committee secretary or department head who is dedicated to these ideas than an enthusiastic minister.

Nevertheless, except during the 1953–1957 period, the major political conflicts in the Soviet political system do not seem to have centered on a struggle between the General Secretary and the top officials in the governmental hierarchy, and in most circumstances—indeed, in most circumstances even during the 1953–1957 period—the Central Committee officials will feel that the greatest contribution they can make to the General Secretary is to ensure that the governmental agencies under their supervision perform their functions as well as possible.

On questions involving the performance of the branch, the essential nature of the relationship of the ministerial and Central Committee officials is likely to depend, first of all, on whether the question is interbranch or intrabranch in character. When the department officials are investigating a complaint about the ministry, making a judgment on a personnel decision, participating in decisions on the course of development of the branch, or simply conveying the will of the General Secretary to a reluctant ministry or institution, a certain conflict of interest or tension is built into the relationship with officials of other institutions. If there is conflict within the branch—say, between empirical sociologists or mathematical economists on the one hand and traditional political economists on the other—the Central Committee officials are almost certain to antagonize someone.

When, however, Central Committee officials deal with problems entailing conflicts of interest with other branches, they are natural allies with officials of "their" ministries, and may well be acting on their behalf. This type of conflict is inherently characteristic of the budgetary and planning process, especially at the level at which top officials in the branch operate, and in a Soviet-type economy, it occurs in hundreds of cases that would be resolved largely by the marketplace in a capitalist economy. The Ministry of Trade's dissatisfaction with light industry's insensitivity to consumer demand on some product, the fish industry's dismay at the building of hydroelectric dams on the Volga River, almost any ministry's desire for the introduction of new types of machinery, the Ministry of Agriculture's demand that more teachers and doctors be sent to the countryside, the Ministry of Light Industry's unhappiness with the quality of flax being delivered by the Ministry of Agriculture, any ministry's wish for a higher pay scale for its employees, the city soviets' frustration at their inability to engage in effective city planning and to provide an equitable distribution of housing to its citizens because of industry's financing and control of much of housing construction, the police's disgust at the Ministry of Trade's reluctance to curb profitable vodka sales, the call by industrial ministries for more applied and less basic research in contrast to the Academy of Sciences' opposite set of priorities—in all of these conflicts the relevant Central Committee departments and sections are likely to be supporting the ministry they oversee and opposing the Central Committee departments and sections (and ministries) on the other side of the issue.

Western scholars studying the Soviet Union have tended to be absorbed with the regime's policy toward the intelligentsia, and in the last two decades they have had increasing access to liberal intellectuals who have formed a strong impression of the role of the Central Committee officials in enforcing this policy. Particularly since neither westerners nor the liberal intellectuals have been much interested in the budgetary process and the way in which funds are acquired for the cultural realm, they have become familiar with the Central Committee officials in a more adversary, intrabranch role. Indeed, since the liberal intellectuals have often tended to be the losers in their battles with the government and the more established cultural authorities in the Union of Writers, westerners often have not been sensitive to the possibility that the Central Committee officials sometimes may be choosing or even mediating between conflicting cultural-literary groups and authorities as much as exercising a control function on their own.

Despite the frequent conflict between the Central Committee officials and those they supervise, westerners clearly should be giving more attention to the cooperative side of the ambivalent relationship between supervisers and supervised. One of the striking features of large-scale organization anywhere is the tendency for those at the top of the organization to spend more of their time as the representative of the organization in its relations with other institutions and the outside environment than as the director of the organization itself. To the extent that this is true of Soviet ministers and Central Committee secretaries and department heads—and to a considerable degree it must be—the cooperative aspect of their relationship is particularly important for the fulfillment of each of their basic roles. With the need for them to work together for a number of years because of the low rates of personnel turnover, with the similarity in background and the movement of personnel back and forth between the party and the governmental hierarchies, one would expect there to be a real tendency for the rivalry between the "controller" and "controlled" to be downplayed and for antagonism and conflicts to be unconsciously, if not consciously, dampened.

Undoubtedly policy conflicts continue to exist within each of the various policy spheres, but conceivably the major battles of this type usually take place at levels below the very top: among scholars, administrative subunits, regions, junior officials of the Central Committee departments, specialized officials of the agencies. In such a case the top specialized officials of the government and party apparatus would be more concerned with trying to reflect any consensus developing within their sphere and to mediate conflicts within it, while representing the sphere in questions that require action by outside agencies.

The most important questions about the Soviet political process center on the relationship of the top leadership to the different policy areas. The overlapping system of party and governmental officials, together with the system of other controlling agencies, seems designed to emancipate the top leadership from domination by the major governmental departments. By appointing personnel with specialized knowledge and experience to the posts in all these institutions, the leadership evidently hoped to obtain independent advisers with sufficient expertise to judge the ministerial reports and proposals and hence to give themselves the ability to judge performance accurately and to decide policy for each branch on the basis of a real freedom of choice.

Yet, the question arises whether the use of specialized personnel in the Central Committee Secretariat and apparatus has not meant the penetration of the values of the specialized elite into the political leadership as much as or more than the enhancement of political control over the policy process— that is, whether the familiar pattern of the regulated coming to dominate the regulators has not developed in the Soviet Union as well as in the West. Even if there is rivalry and tension between individual officials of the Central Committee Secretariat and apparatus and officials of the other institutions— as there is, indeed, between personnel of American regulatory agencies and the industries they regulate—the basic values of the establishment specialists in each of the policy areas may be similar enough to ensure that this tension has relatively little impact on the basic direction of policy.

It should be emphasized once more that our information about the Central Committee Secretariat and apparatus—and about its relations with other institutions—remains far less than we need for confident judgments. Any conclusions on this relationship must remain tentative, all the more so because the relationship must vary from official to official and probably from time to time. Nevertheless, the relationship is a crucial one for our entire conceptualization of the structure of power in the Soviet Union.

12 | The Leading Party Organs

THE RELATIONSHIP between the Central Committee departments and the ministries—even that between the Central Committee secretaries and high governmental officials—is a complex one, and party dominance of the government cannot be equated with party apparatus dominance of the government. The only decisions unconditionally obligatory on the government are those emanating from the collective party organs. The General Secretary may, in fact, have dominated these collective bodies throughout much of Soviet history, but at a minimum, he has placed his most powerful advisers and subordinates on these bodies, and, except for a period in the 1940s and early 1950s, they have been the scene of the most crucial policymaking discussions.

The Party Congress

According to party rules, the congress is the ultimate authority within the party, and given the relationship between the party and governmental institutions, it is, therefore, the ultimate authority in the entire political system. Composed of delegates selected at party conferences in the regions and small republics, a congress is convened once every five years, the date essentially coinciding with the beginning of a new Five-Year-Plan. The congress hears two major reports—the Central Committee report delivered by the General Secretary and one on the new Five-Year Plan (in recent years delivered by the Chairman of the Council of Ministers)—and it approves these reports in essence.[1] At its conclusion, the congress names a Central Committee to govern the party until the next congress. It also selects an auditing commission to oversee party finances and a Chairman of the Party Control

449

Committee, which oversees party morality and expulsions from membership.

In the past the congresses often were comparatively small gatherings (in the early 1920s they included from 408 to 748 voting delegates),[2] and during the crucial years of Stalin's rise to power, a large proportion of the voting delegates (a high of 65.3 percent in 1924)[3] were full-time party officials. With the passage of time, however, the congresses were expanded in size, and the delegates came to include a broader cross section of the Soviet population. At the Twenty-Fifth Party Congress in 1976, for example, 22 percent of the delegates were party officials, but 14 percent were officials of the soviet, trade union, or Komsomol organs, 7 percent were industrial and construction enterprise managers, 5 percent collective farm chairmen and state farm directors, 6 percent military officers, 5 percent literary, artistic, scientific, educational, and health personnel, 26 percent workers, 12.5 percent rank-and-file peasants, brigadiers, and heads of livestock farms, and 3 percent unspecified white collar.[4]

During the 1920s the party congresses were the scene of dramatic factional conflict, but since that time they have been much tamer affairs. The Central Committee and Five-Year-Plan reports have a "state of the union" character, and neither is directly criticized in subsequent discussion by the delegates. All resolutions are passed unanimously. As a consequence, the congress as an institution has generally been described by western scholars as "a rally of the faithful, chiefly significant as a convenient platform from which the leadership proclaims new policies and goals, announces modifications in the rules and program, and obtains formal approval of shifts in the top party command."[5]

Although such a characterization certainly captures much of the essential spirit of a modern party congress, it may be somewhat overdrawn. In the first place, the postwar congresses have lasted for ten to fifteen days, and they do afford speakers with the same type of opportunity to present a pet idea or project to a group of highly influential officials as a Supreme Soviet session does. At the Twenty-Fourth Party Congress in 1971, 276 delegates requested the right to speak on the reports, and 60 received it.[6] For the most part, the congress speakers spend their time reporting on the achievements of the republic, region, ministry, or enterprise they represent and praising party policy, the report being discussed, and the performance of the General Secretary. Yet almost invariably, speakers also criticize Gosplan or a ministry in appealing for additional funds or some policy change. Moreover, even when they praise the main report, speakers choose points to emphasize and thus lend support to a particular policy option or investment priority.

The proposals made by speakers at a party congress are similar to those made at the Supreme Soviet, but they naturally cover a wider range of subjects. The most common appeal is for investment that will benefit the local economy: for example, the reconstruction of coal mines in the Urals, the development and introduction of new agricultural machines to fight wind erosion in Siberia, the exploitation of raw materials in Tadzhikistan, or the reconstruction of the Zavolzhsk Motor Plant in Gorki region. Indeed, at the Twenty-Fifth Party Congress, no fewer than four party officials from the southern regions of the country called for a massive investment program to divert Siberian rivers to the south for irrigation purposes.[7]

A number of speakers at the Twenty-Fifth Congress also dealt with substantive policy issues. The president of the Academy of Sciences spoke at length about the need to support basic research, while several other speakers did appeal for Academy scientists to give more attention to applied research. Another speaker (a Politburo member) called for a strengthening of the economic incentive for managers to introduce technical innovations, while the director of the Magnitogorsk Metallurgy Combine criticized the overloading of "the higher echelon of economic leadership" with minor administrative details. He asserted that many of these details should be decentralized to lower levels. One speaker advocated the restructuring of the relationship between the Ministry of Agriculture and the Agriculture Supply Agency (Soiuzselkhoztekhnika), and another suggested the creation of structural subdivisions within the Council of Ministers to administer interbranch coordination.[8]

Generally the speakers at the party congress only seem interested in influencing future policy, but it is at least conceivable that the debates sometimes affect important political decisions being made at the congress. At the Twentieth Party Congress, Khrushchev's opening speech did not criticize Stalin, but after several speakers raised the question in what may have seemed a threatening manner, the First Secretary returned to the subject with his famous secret speech at the conclusion of the congress. At the Twenty-Second Party Congress, the speeches of the delegates varied considerably in nuance in their denunciation of the members of the antiparty group,[9] and they possibly may have influenced the final decision. The party congresses of the Brezhnev era have not been featured by such dramatic issues, but at the Twenty-Fifth Party Congress several speakers severely attacked the Ministry of Agriculture and these criticisms were followed by the removal of Minister of Agriculture Poliansky from the Politburo. One has a suspicion that some, perhaps most, of these speeches have been managed from the center, but the mere fact that the congress is the supreme authority in theory may make the leadership inclined toward accommodation if it perceives a strong current of opinion running through the delegates.

A second possible role for the party congress centers on the selection of the members of the Central Committee. Formally the congress has the right to elect the Central Committee, and the Central Committee is, in fact, always named at the conclusion of each congress. Nevertheless, from all indications the Central Committee is not selected in open competition on the floor of the congress. The congress delegates are presented with an official slate of candidates (*biulleten' kandidatury*), the number on the slate corresponding to the number expected to be elected. Indeed, two Central Committee members have stated in their memoirs that they themselves had no idea that they were on the list until it was publicly announced at the congress.[10]

The congress delegates have the right to cross names off the list—and to defeat a nominee if he is crossed off by half of them—and in lower party elections they often seem to have the opportunity to do so in some fairly secret manner. At least in the past, a fair number of delegates to the national party congress did cross out names on the list, and at the first congresses after the revolution the number of votes received by each candidate was announced and a rank of popularity thereby revealed. In recent years, however, this situation has changed radically. It has been reported that at least at the Twenty-Second Party Congress in 1962 and the Twenty-Fourth Party Congress in 1971, all of the candidates were elected unanimously.[11] If this is literally true and does not refer to some motion to make the election unanimous by acclamation, the congress delegates must have lost their ability to cross off names with real secrecy, for there were surely a few disgruntled persons among 4,998 delegates.

In any case, since it is highly unlikely that a majority of the delegates will cross out the name of one of the nominees at the present time, the crucial question is the process by which the slate of the Central Committee members presented to the congress has been compiled. How was it decided that the number of voting members was to rise from 175 at the Twenty-Second Congress in 1961 to 195 at the Twenty-Third Congress in 1966 to 245 in 1971 and to 287 in 1976? How was it decided which names would be included on the list?

Western scholars have tended to argue—or simply to assume—that in the post-Stalin period the decision about the composition of the Central Committee is made in the party leadership prior to the congress and that the congress has become an insignificant rubber stamp which confirms the consensus choices of the leadership. This assumption must contain substantial elements of truth. Soviet sources report that the slate of candidates is examined in a preliminary way during the congress by a meeting of representatives (almost surely the first secretaries) of each of the oblast, territorial, and republican delegations,[12] but the slate is most likely drawn up prior to the congress.

The strongest piece of evidence of the consensus nature of the slate of

Central Committee candidates comes from an examination of the type of persons actually selected. As Robert Daniels has emphasized, the Central Committee has in large part come to be an assembly of representatives of institutions and regions rather than of individuals, and hence selection to membership often has an automatic character:

> The unwritten code allocated to each functional hierarchy and to each union republic (and often province) a proportion of seats in the Central Committee corresponding to the imputed status and importance of the particular institution and region . . . There is in practice an organic and automatic connection between this specific set of offices and the Central Committee as a well-defined and quite stable set of leading job slots whose occupants enjoy the elite status conferred by Central Committee membership as long as and only as long as they occupy their respective offices.[13]

It would be a mistake to carry this view to an absolute extreme, for such factors as length of service in the post, ties to the leader, past membership in the Central Committee, or gender do have some impact on the selection process.[14] Yet, it remains true that a knowledgeable westerner who learned beforehand the number of voting members to be named at a congress could accurately predict the names of over 90 percent of the members (or at least of the members other than workers and peasants) simply by following the above rule. Indeed, the chairman of the executive committee of the Leningrad Soviet has reported in an interview that when his predecessor, a Central Committee member, was transferred to another post, he himself has normally been invited to the sessions although not a member, for the information obtained is important in the performance of his job.

Nevertheless, any assumption that the composition of a forthcoming Central Committee rests solely on the consensus of the Politburo members does face a serious problem. The decision on the size of the new Central Committee should be far from automatic, and a Politburo striving to create a Central Committee slate that reflects the balance of forces within the Politburo could presumably manipulate the size to achieve its desired aim. In such a case a new Central Committee should be no more supportive of the General Secretary than the old one. In practice, the congresses have often been associated with a rise in the power and status of the General Secretary. The Central Committee named at the Twentieth Congress in 1956 seems to have been significantly different in political coloration from its predecessor, and even Brezhnev's position—and certainly his status—seems to have become stronger with each congress.

One possible answer to the paradox of a Politburo approving a Central

Committee slate that changes the balance of power is that the party congress may be a more important event than appears on the surface. The old circular-flow-of-power theory assumed that a General Secretary had the ability to build a machine among the regional party secretaries, that these secretaries in turn controlled the delegations sent to the party congress, and that they used their delegations to support the General Secretary at the congress. While there is no evidence of test votes in the contemporary congresses (as there is for the 1920s), perhaps the implicit threat of an appeal to the congress is always in the minds of all the leaders as the Central Committee slate is compiled prior to the congress. That is, perhaps we should consider the possibility that on the eve of a congress the Politburo leaders may already be responding to the realities of power that will be registered in the congress delegations, and that will be made abundantly clear in the preliminary meeting of regional leaders.[15]

The best analogy for such a development—if it has been occurring— is the process by which Conservative party leaders were chosen in Great Britain over an eighty-year period in the second half of the nineteenth century and the first half of the twentieth century.[16] An outsider can see a good deal of struggle for that post over the years, but during that period none broke out at the party meeting that elected the leader. The maneuvering took place well before the meeting, and when the outcome became predictable, all possible contenders united behind the emerging victor in order to present a common front to the delegates, the party rank-and-file, and the electorate. One member of Parliament expressed the guiding philosophy well when he stated, "I think it will be a bad day for this or any party to have solemnly to meet to elect a leader. The leader is there, and we all know it when he is there."[17] It may well be that the party leadership in the Soviet Union has held a similar attitude. If so, we should not forget that recognizing "the leader is there" ultimately reflects the reality of the votes rather than merely the relative charisma of the contenders, and the balance of forces in the congress may be an important part of that reality.

That the congress may be a key event in the struggle for power not only is an interesting point in its own right but also has a number of implications for our understanding of recent Soviet political history. For example, the lengthening of the interval between congresses may be an important factor in evolving relations within the top leadership in recent decades. When congresses were held every year or two prior to the late 1920s, a Central Committee member had every reason to feel insecure in his position. When, on the other hand, a Central Committee member has a tenure of five years (and when the secret police do not terrorize top officials as they did in the late

Stalin period), a General Secretary may feel more hesitant in removing a large number of Central Committee members from their posts or in opposing the fundamental interests of these members. With a longer membership tenure, much more time is available for a coalition of disgruntled or lame-duck Central Committee members to support a challenge to a General Secretary's leadership.

In light of this consideration, Khrushchev almost surely made a major mistake in splitting the party apparatus so soon after the Twenty-Second Party Congress in 1961, for a great many Central Committee members whose role had been drastically reduced by this decision were left on the ruling body for a number of years. In fact, the very timing of the anti-Khrushchev coup may have reflected the realization that a party congress was scheduled for 1965 and that it would name a Central Committee with many new members who had a vested interest in maintaining a bifurcated apparatus.

Similarly, the timing of the congresses may have played an important role in shaping the character of the Brezhnev era. With the "bargain" of October 1964 between the leadership and the Central Committee that there would be "a respect for personnel," the fact that a congress was to be held so quickly (in actuality, in less than seventeen months) after Khrushchev's removal gave Brezhnev little room for maneuver before the election of a new Central Committee. Conceivably Brezhnev may have felt that he had a fairly restricted range of alternatives in choosing a strategy of rule.

The Central Committee

When a party decision is issued between congresses, it almost always is listed as a Central Committee decree—or, more colloquially, a decree of the TsK (Tsehkáw), the abbreviation for *tsentral'nyi komitet*. When a scholar is called to consult with an instructor in one of the Central Committee departments, it is said that he is at the TsK. Such usage is misleading, for the decrees in question seldom actually emanate from the Central Committee, and the consulting scholar certainly never sees that body. The Politburo, the Secretariat, and the apparatus of the Central Committee are informally being given the name of the Central Committee itself.

Properly speaking, the Central Committee is a collective body named at the party congress and mandated to convene in plenary session at least twice a year and serve as the supreme authority in the party until the next congress. Its size has increased steadily over the years, and at the Twenty-Fifth Party Congress in February 1976, 287 persons were named voting members of the Central Committee and 139 candidate or nonvoting members.[18] Although some Central Committee members (6 percent of the full members

Table 32   *Occupations of Central Committee members, 1934–1976*
(in percentages)

INSTITUTION/ OCCUPATION	1934 FULL	1939 FULL	1952 FULL	1952 CAND.	1952 TOTAL	1956 FULL	1956 CAND.	1956 TOTAL	1961 FULL	1961 CAND.	1961 TOTAL
National party apparatus	8.5	10.0	10.5	4.5	7.5	7.5	5.0	6.0	8.5	6.0	7.0
Local party apparatus	32.0	27.0	47.0	19.0	34.0	46.0	31.0	39.0	39.0	35.0	37.0
National government[a]	32.0	31.0	21.0	28.0	24.0	23.0	24.0	23.5	17.0	11.0	14.0
Local government	10.0	4.0	6.5	8.0	7.0	10.0	12.0	11.0	9.0	19.0	14.0
Military[a]	4.0	14.0	4.0	20.0	11.5	4.5	10.0	7.0	8.5	11.0	10.0
Lower foreign affairs[b]	3.0	3.0	1.5	4.5	3.0	4.0	6.5	5.0	6.0	3.0	4.5
Police	3.0	3.0	1.5	6.0	4.0	1.5	1.0	1.0	0	0.5	0.5
Writer-culture	0	3.0	4.0	2.0	3.0	2.0	1.5	2.0	3.0	3.0	3.0
Scientist	3.0	1.5	1.5	2.0	1.5	1.0	1.0	1.0	2.0	3.0	2.5
Trade unions	3.0	3.0	1.0	2.0	1.0	0	2.0	1.0	2.0	0.5	1.5
Worker or peasant	0	0	0	0	0	0	1.0	0.5	2.0	2.5	2.0
Miscellaneous	1.5	1.5	1.0	1.0	1.0	1.0	5.0	3.0	3.0	4.5	4.0
Unknown	0	0	1.0	3.5	2.0	0	0	0	0	0	0
Total number of members	71	71	125	111	236	133	122	255	175	155	330

in 1976 and 9 percent of the candidate members) are officials of the Central Committee Secretariat and apparatus, most have full-time jobs in some other institution.

The Central Committee members are chosen from officials who occupy many of the same types of positions as the Supreme Soviet deputies, a fact that is scarcely surprising since 88 percent of the 1976 voting members had already been selected as Supreme Soviet deputies. However, the Central Committee is a more elite group than the Supreme Soviet. Only 3 percent of its voting members were workers in 1976, and only 0.3 percent were peasants. There were but three plant managers and one collective farm chairman among the voting members of the Central Committee and no other low level white collar personnel. The Central Committee had a narrower social base than the Supreme Soviet by other indicators as well. Only 3 percent of the voting members were women, and only 15 percent were under fifty years of age, 2 percent under forty-five. (The Central Committee has become a much older body in recent years.) In 1971, the last year for which

Table 32—Continued

INSTITUTION/ OCCUPATION	1966			1971			1976		
	FULL	CAND.	TOTAL	FULL	CAND.	TOTAL	FULL	CAND.	TOTAL
National party apparatus	7.0	5.0	6.0	7.0	4.5	6.0	6.0	9.0	7.0
Local party apparatus	36.0	34.0	35.0	33.0	36.0	34.0	36.0	28.0	33.0
National governmenta	22.0	17.5	20.0	25.0	13.0	20.5	24.0	18.0	22.0
Local government	8.0	14.5	11.0	7.0	15.5	10.0	8.0	11.5	9.0
Militarya	7.5	11.0	9.0	8.0	8.5	8.0	7.0	7.0	7.0
Lower foreign affairsb	6.0	1.0	4.0	7.0	2.0	5.0	5.5	3.0	5.0
Police	0.5	0.5	0.5	1.0	1.0	1.0	0.5	3.0	1.5
Writer-culture	1.5	4.0	2.5	1.5	4.5	3.0	2.0	6.5	3.5
Scientists	4.0	1.0	3.0	2.5	4.0	3.0	3.0	3.5	3.0
Trade unions	1.5	2.5	2.0	1.0	2.5	1.5	1.0	2.0	1.5
Worker or peasant	1.5	7.0	4.0	4.5	8.0	6.0	3.5	6.5	4.5
Miscellaneous	3.5	2.5	3.0	3.0	0.5	2.0	2.5	1.5	2.0
Unknown	0	0	0	0	0	0	0	0	0
Total number of members	195	165	360	241	155	396	287	139	426

Source: The membership of the Central Committees through 1966 can be found in Borys Levytsky, *The Soviet Political Elite* (Stanford. The Hoover Institution, 1969), pp. 666–704. The membership of later Central Committees can be found in the Yearbooks of the *Bol'shaia sovetskaia entsiklopediia* following the congresses. Biographies of Central Committee members named from 1961 through 1976 can be found in the same source. Identification of the position of the Central Committee members in other years must be based on a large number of sources. The most reliable and complete are the third edition of the *Bol'shaia sovetskaia entsiklopediia*, the various volumes of *Deputaty Verkhovnogo Soveta SSSR,* and the press at the time.

a Includes the Minister of Defense when he is a civilian; otherwise this official is included in the military category.

b Includes ambassadors and those governmental officials handling foreign affairs who do not hold a ministerial portfolio. (The latter are included in the national government category.)

nearly complete data are available, the voting membership included representatives from twenty-three nationalities, and approximately 38–39 percent of them were non-Russians—a lower percentage than among Supreme Soviet deputies, but a much higher one than among top officials of the Central Committee Secretariat and apparatus.[19]

Except for fifteen or twenty members whose inclusion has more symbolic meaning, the Central Committee now is basically a collection of the approximately 250 most powerful individauls in the country—or at least the occupants of the 250 most powerful posts in the Soviet system. The members of the Central Committee come from both the party apparatus and the governmental hierarchy, from both the various central institutions and the regional centers throughout the country. Over the years the proportion of the Central Committee voting members holding a full-time position in the party apparatus has declined rather substantially, but in 1976, 41 percent still did. Nearly as many—34 percent—were top officials in the central and regional (with four exceptions, republican) governmental apparatus, and this figure does not include the deputy ministers of foreign affairs and of defense.

In comparison with the Central Committees of the late Stalin period, the groups that have shown the most substantial increase in representation in recent decades have been those concerned with foreign relations in one way or another. Seven percent of the 1976 voting members were military officers, while 8 percent were in the diplomatic service or in party or governmental posts supervising some aspect of foreign relations, 5 percent were employed directly in the defense industry, and another 3 to 4 percent (for example, the director of TASS and the chairman of the KGB) supervise organizations with a significant foreign operations section among their subdivisions. In all, a total of nearly 25 percent of the voting members fit within this category.

Election to the Central Committee generally depends far more on the post that a person holds in the Soviet system than on personal characteristics or loyalties. (Of course, the latter may be crucial in obtaining an appointment to the type of post that usually confers Central Committee membership.) This principle of representation of institutions rather than individuals has been observed with sufficient rigor in recent decades that western scholars have normally been able to rely upon Central Committee membership or nonmembership for an institution's or region's top official as an indicator of the relative importance of the institution or region.[20] Soviet sources themselves have begun to speak of the representative character of party committees at all levels in the hierarchy.

The composition of the leading party organs should be sufficiently representative both from a quantitative (numerical) and qualitative point of view. Really authoritative and experienced comrades should be represented on these organs. The membership should include specialists on different problems, branches of knowledge, and directions of work, and from a social point of view the composition of the organs should naturally reflect the social composition of the given party organization within reasonable limits. The observance of these conditions provides a real opportunity for not only general, but all possible specific interests to be taken into account in the working out of different decisions, in the organization of practical work for fulfilling these decisions.[21]

Biographies of the Central Committee members have been published since the early 1960s,[22] and it is not difficult to describe the characteristics of this elite group from many perspectives. But it is almost impossible to describe the work of the Central Committee and the meaning of membership in it. Stenographic reports of Central Committee sessions have not been published since 1965, and even the main report at the sessions is printed only rarely. Hence the scholar—even more than is usually the case—is forced to look at a few "shadows on the wall" and to try to guess what they mean.

The first obvious fact to consider in evaluating the role of the Central Committee is the infrequency of its meetings.[23] One reason that persons with a full-time job elsewhere can become members of the Central Committee is that it often does not exceed the statutory minimum of two meetings a year. In no year in the post-Stalin period has the Central Committee been in session for more than sixteen days (the total for the two plenary sessions in 1955). In the two years from December 20, 1956, through December 20, 1958, the frequency of meetings rose sharply, as the Central Committee was convened eleven separate times for a total of thirty-one days, but in subsequent years the annual number of Central Committee meetings dropped sharply. Counting the session that ousted him in October 1964, the last six years of Khrushchev's term saw the Central Committee meeting only twice in four of the years and three times in the other two, averaging ten days a year in session.

In the Brezhnev period, the Central Committee has assembled even less frequently (see table 33). There were five sessions in the sixteen months between Khrushchev's removal and the Twenty-Third Party Congress in February 1966—seven between October 1964 and March 1966 if the session removing Khrushchev and the postcongress session that elected the Politburo and the Secretariat are included—but these seven sessions lasted for a total of but eleven days. Two of the sessions were three days in length, the other five only one day apiece. The Central Committee met three times more in 1966 after the election session, twice in 1967, and four times in 1968 (Czechoslovakia was the factor leading to an increase). But in four of the next eight years the Central Committee met only twice a year, and in the other four it met three times. In the ten years from 1967 through 1976, a Central Committee session never lasted more than two days, and in 69 percent of the

Table 33 *Topics discussed at Central Committee sessions, 1964–1977*

DATE	TOPIC
October 14, 1964	Removal of Khrushchev
November 16, 1964	Reunification of the industrial and rural party organizations
March 24–26, 1965	Further development of agriculture
	Results of a meeting of foreign Communists
September 27–29, 1965	Industrial reorganization
December 6, 1965	The 1966 plan and budget
	Reorganization of the Party-State Control Committee
February 19, 1966	Draft of the Five-Year Plan
March 26, 1966	The Central Committee report to the Twenty-Third Congress
April 8, 1966	Election of the Central Committee
May 25–27, 1966	Expansion of reclamation
August 1, 1966	First session of the Supreme Soviet (composition of the government)
December 12–13, 1966	Foreign policy
	The 1967 plan and budget
June 20–21, 1967	Policy in the Middle East
	Theses on the Fiftieth anniversary of the revolution
September 26, 1967	The improvement of living conditions
	The 1968 plan and budget
April 9–10, 1968	The international situation
July 17, 1968	The Warsaw meeting of Communist parties
October 30–31, 1968	Agriculture
	Foreign policy activity of the Politburo
December 9, 1968	The 1969 plan and budget
June 26, 1969	International conference of Communist parties
December 15, 1969	The 1970 plan and budget
	Brezhnev report on foreign and internal policy
July 2–3, 1970	Agriculture
July 13, 1970	First session of the Supreme Soviet (composition of the government)
December 7, 1970	The 1971 plan and budget
March 22, 1971	Central Committee report to the Twenty-Fourth Congress

Table 33—Continued

DATE	TOPIC
	Report to the congress on the Five-Year Plan
April 9, 1971	Election of the Central Committee
November 22–23, 1971	The 1972 plan and budget
	Report on international activity of the Politburo
May 19, 1972	The international situation
	The exchange of party documents
December 18, 1972	The 1973 plan and budget
April 26–27, 1973	International activity of the Politburo
December 10–11, 1973	The 1974 plan and budget
July 24, 1974	First session of the Supreme Soviet (composition of the government)
December 17, 1974	The 1975 plan and budget
April 17, 1975	International relations
December 2, 1975	Questions of the Twenty-Fifth Party Congress
	The 1976 plan and budget
December 14, 1975	The draft of the Five-Year Plan
February 20, 1976	Central Committee report to Twenty-Fifth Congress
	Report to Twenty-Fifth Congress on Five-Year Plan
March 6, 1976	Election of Politburo and Secretariat
October 25–26, 1976	The 1977 plan and budget and the Five-Year Plan as a whole
May 24, 1977	The draft of the constitution
October 3, 1977	Ratification of the constitution
December 13, 1977	The 1978 plan and budget

Source: The subject matter of Central Committee sessions are reported in all Soviet newspapers the day after a session. The timing of sessions can be found in the Yearbooks of the *Bol'shaia sovetskaia entsiklopediia*.

cases its length was only one day. In the five years between the Twenty-Fourth and Twenty-Fifth Party Congress (1971–1976), the Central Committee was in session for a total of fifteen days—one fewer than in 1955 alone. The situation did not change in the first two years after the Twenty-Fifth Congress, for from March 1976 to March 1978 the Central Committee met for a total of only five days. (One purely ceremonial one-day session, held in conjunction with the Supreme Soviet, is excluded.)

The second obvious fact about the role of the Central Committee is that, in the Brezhnev period at least, its sessions do not feature the type of debate between central party leaders that took place prior to 1929. In the eleven years from 1966 through 1976, Kosygin, Podgorny, and Suslov were reported to participate in the Central Committee debates only once, and that was in a 1973 session ratifying the raprochment with West Germany and the detente with the United States that had already been announced. Kirilenko, Mazurov, Poliansky, and Shelepin were not listed as Central Committee speakers even once in these ten years. The only Politburo members who are said to have taken part frequently were the party leaders in Moscow, Leningrad, and the major republics, and, as will be seen, their participation simply corresponded to the general practice of having a heavy representation of regional leaders among the speakers. No lists of speakers are published for the sessions which elect the Politburo after the party congresses or which confirm the Council of Ministers every four years after Supreme Soviet elections, and conceivably Politburo members take part in debates there. However, they invariably are one-day sessions and may be very brief.

Indeed, because of the infrequency and the brevity of all the sessions, only a minority of the Central Committee members have had the opportunity to speak in the five-year intervals between congresses.[24] Between the Twenty-Third and the Twenty-Fourth Congresses (1966–1971), 178 speeches were given in the discussions following the reports, and they were delivered by a total of 95 different individuals (92 men and 3 women). Sixty-one of the 95 speakers were full members of the Central Committee, 18 were candidate members, 5 were members of the auditing commission, and 11 were members of neither of these bodies.[25] (The percentage of speeches given by full Central Committee members was higher.) Even counting the reporters, only one-third of the full Central Committee members and 11 percent of the candidate members were able to speak, and 60 percent of these speaking members appeared only once in the five years.

The reduced number of Central Committee meetings from 1971 to 1975 meant an even smaller opportunity for the average member to express his opinions. In those years, 67 speakers gave a total of 92 speeches in the discussions of the reports: 55 full members of the Central Committee, 8 candidate members, 3 members of the auditing commission, and 1 nonmember. Only 24 percent of the full members of the Central Committee and 5 percent of the candidate members spoke as often as once.

The criteria for selecting persons to speak at Central Committee sessions are not altogether clear. Apparently members apply for the right to speak beforehand, and not all of them do so. (For example, at the May 1966 session on water reclamation, Brezhnev complained that only one industrial minister among the members asked for the floor although Brezhnev thought others should have been volunteering to tell how they would be helping in the program.)[26] Either because they make most of the requests or because the leadership wants to hear them or have their names listed as speakers, the party or governmental officials from the republics, the regions, and the city of Moscow dominate the sessions. Together with the Leningrad city party leader, they gave 73 percent of the speeches in the 1966–1971 period and 65 percent of them in the 1971–1976 period. Ministers gave 11 percent and 10 percent of the speeches in the two periods, respectively, and workers and peasants 3 and 10 percent, respectively. The other participants came from a variety of occupations.

As a general rule, regional officials usually seem to receive the right to speak in proportion to the size of their region or republic. The first secretaries of the four biggest republics—the Ukraine, Kazakhstan, Belorussia, and Uzbekistan—speak frequently, and at sessions at which they do not, another major leader from the republic is almost always found among the participants. The leaders of the Leningrad regional and the Moscow city party organizations also often appear. The first secretaries of the smaller republics and the larger regions of the Russian republic speak more infrequently, but again it seems to be the area that is represented as much as the individual leader. When a first secretary is changed between congresses, he may well be given the right to speak before his formal election to the Central Committee after the next congress.

The lists of Central Committee speakers do reveal anomalies that are perhaps associated with the political standing of the officials involved or possibly with their eagerness to speak. The first secretary of the extremely populous Moscow region (third only to the Moscow city organization and the Leningrad organization in number of Communists and containing more party members than eleven of the other fourteen republics) spoke only twice in the 1966–1976 period, and the first secretary of the Turkmen republic (admittedly the smallest in terms of party members) did not speak once in the seven years between his election as first secretary and the end of 1975.[27] The first secretary of the Sverdlovsk regional party committee spoke three times in the 1971–1976 period, but the first secretary in neighboring Cheliabinsk did not speak at all.[28]

The third obvious fact concerning Central Committee sessions is that, beyond their frequency, the general topic being discussed, and the names of the speakers, we really know almost nothing about them. (Indeed, we should even allow for the possibility that there may sometimes have been sessions and speakers not mentioned in the official announcements.) Stenographic reports of the sessions were published in the late Khrushchev years, and at least during this time the speeches seemed of the same general type as were given at the party congresses and Supreme Soviet sessions. The only Central Committee session of the Brezhnev era for which we have a stenographic report—that of March 1965—was featured by considerable frankness in the discussion of agricultural problems,[29] but, of course, criticism was peculiarly easy at this time, for the problems could be and were attributed to the recently deposed leader.

Perhaps the decision not to publish stenographic reports of Central Committee sessions after March 1965 indicates that the sessions continue to be marked by frankness. Moscow rumors did suggest that the first secretary of the Moscow city party committee, N. G. Egorychev, attacked Middle East policy directly at the June 1967 session. In addition, some lower officials who did speak fairly often at Central Committee sessions were subsequently promoted to jobs in policy areas on which they had spoken. The first secretary of the Gorki regional party committee, K. F. Katushev, spoke twice at foreign policy sessions prior to the Czechoslovakian invasion, and then in the last session before the invasion he was elected the Central Committee secretary for relations with Communist countries. A well-placed Soviet scholar relays the report that he had, in fact, taken a hard line toward Czechoslovakia in his speeches. The first secretaries of the Krasnodar and Bashkiria regional party committees were among the speakers at the three Central Committee sessions on agriculture in 1965, 1966, and 1970, and they became top governmental officials in the agricultural realm after 1970. One can imagine that the policy positions they enunciated at these sessions were instrumental in their advancement.

Nevertheless, in subsequently published excerpts from three Brezhnev speeches given at the conclusion of Central Committee sessions (those of May 1966, October 1968, and November 1971), the General Secretary specifically referred to comments made by speakers. He in no way implied that the speakers were actually trying to affect the decision of that Central Committee session, but, like Mazurov at the Supreme Soviet session discussed in Chapter 10, promised that the proposals would be considered in the future. "I want to underline the significance and value of the proposals, thoughts, and remarks made by [the speakers]. On this question only one thing can be said: that the Politburo of the Central Committee, the USSR Council of Ministers, and the ministries will examine the suggestions and remarks in the most attentive way and will take them into account in taking the corresponding decisions." The range of suggestions was not specified, but the sentence following this statement indicates that many of them are the type of request for investment in the local region that are found so frequently in speeches at party congresses and Supreme Soviet sessions: "It is clear that

the requests of all the comrades will not be able to be fulfilled all at once."
Five years later Brezhnev made an almost identical remark in similar circumstances: "But obviously we will have to take existing resources realistic-
ally into account."[30]

The available evidence on the frequency, length, and content of the
Central Committee sessions would suggest that the Central Committee has
played a minor role in the Soviet political system in the Brezhnev period.
On the other hand, the pattern of turnover among Central Committee members (or, rather, lack of turnover among them) and the pattern of major
policy decisions tend to suggest the opposite conclusion. In the past, membership in the Central Committee brought no assurance of job tenure, and
in fact, 70 percent of the Central Committee members in 1934 were killed
in the Great Purge. In the Brezhnev era, by contrast, once a person was named
to the Central Committee, the likelihood of remaining on that body was
very high. As has been seen, 90 percent of the voting members of the 1971
Central Committee still alive in 1976 were reelected in that year, and in the
first two years after the Congress, only 2 percent of the members retired or were
retired ($3\frac{1}{2}$ percent died). Not only did these figures suggest the possibility
that the Central Committee members might be becoming secure enough
to exercise control over the General Secretary, but the policies actually
adopted in the second half of the 1960s and the early 1970s were fairly close
to what might have been expected to emerge from bargaining within the
Central Committee.

There are several possible explanations for this phenomenon. Although
it is unlikely that the Central Committee sessions are frank enough for a
sense of the meeting to be conveyed, Central Committee members do seem
to have some political role outside the actual meeting. An industrial worker
elected to the Central Committee in 1966 reports that he received "materials
of Politburo sessions" several times a month "in order to be kept up-to-date
on current problems and questions of both internal and foreign policy." He
reports that he was called upon to participate in many commissions in which
decisions on the improvement of industrial administration were being worked
out.[31]

It is possible that the leadership not only informs Central Committee
members about Politburo decisions and even deliberations, but also makes
a real effort to elicit their views informally and to be responsive to them.
Brezhnev has stated that regional first secretaries and ministers (all of them
full or candidate members of the Central Committee) send memoranda to
him and that he always reads them "with great attention."[32] It is probable
that these memoranda normally contain requests for investment for the
region or ministry, appeals that decisions by other governmental agencies

be overruled, or policy suggestions relating to the ministry's area of special-ization, but they may also sometimes raise more general policy questions.

The most likely possibility is that Brezhnev tries to gain a sense of Central Committee opinion—or at least Central Committee dissatisfaction—in a more informal fashion and that he simply acts cautiously as a general rule in an attempt to avoid Khrushchev's fate. But, if this is true, if the General Secretary does no more than make an effort to avoid policies that will arouse opposition in the Central Committee, then the Central Committee still is a crucial body in the political system. Since the Central Committee encom-passes representatives from all types of ministries and all regions of the country, a policy that is responsive to a consensus or to the center of opinion in it is going to be responsive to a wide range of interests in the country. In addition, of course, the Central Committee's potential role in any succession crisis always makes it of even more crucial interest in the long run.

The Politburo

Since the early years of the Soviet regime, the party Politburo (or the party Presidium, as it was called from 1952 to 1966) has been the real cabinet of the Soviet system. During the late Stalin period it apparently did not meet often as a collective unit, but even then the persons named to Politburo mem-bership were the dictator's closest lieutenants.

Like the Central Committee, the Politburo has tended to increase in size over the decades. The first Politburo elected in 1919 contained five vot-ing members and three candidates, but by the time of Lenin's death these numbers had risen to seven and three respectively. As Stalin moved to con-solidate his control in the 1920s, he expanded the size of the Politburo, and by February 1934, there were ten full members and five candidate members. The size fluctuated by one or two members from time to time, but except for brief periods (for example, the last five months of Stalin's life and 1957–1961)[33] it remained roughly at the 1934 level for the next three decades. Then, in the Brezhnev era, the number of Politburo members rose again, seeming to stabilize at fourteen to sixteen full members and six to eight candidates in the mid-1970s.

The backgrounds of the members of the Politburo since the 1920s have changed along with the increase in their numbers. Until 1939, all voting mem-bers had been party members since before the revolution, but the number of Old Bolsheviks gradually declined to the point where there has been but one since 1966—Arvid Pel'she. Despite the passing of the old generation, however, the average age of the Politburo voting member has continued to rise: from forty in 1919 to forty-three in 1922, forty-eight in 1934, fifty in

1939, fifty-seven in 1950, fifty-eight in 1957, sixty-one in 1962, fifty-eight in 1966, and sixty-seven in early 1978.

The backgrounds of the Politburo members changed in other respects as well. For example, the Politburo of 1923 contained a minority of Russians among its voting members—three compared with three Jews and one Georgian. The twelve men whom Stalin added in the 1920s and the first half of the 1930s were likewise very mixed in their national background: six Russians, a Ukrainian, a Jew, a Pole, an Armenian, a Georgian, and a Latvian. Undoubtedly, many, if not most, of the non-Russians were thoroughly Russified, but after the Great Purge the Politburo became far more the preserve of those who were even Russian by ethnic origin. Four of the six non-Russian Stalin additions perished during the purge (none of the Russians did, although Kirov and Kuibyshev had died earlier), and the new voting members of the last fifteen years of the Stalin era were overwhelmingly of Russian background: six of the seven selected from 1939 to 1948 and twelve of fifteen named to the enlarged renamed Presidium in 1952. In 1952, nineteen of the twenty-five full members were Russian, ten of the eleven candidate members. To be sure, one extremely prominent figure in the Stalin years continued to speak with a strong Georgian accent, but perhaps Stalin felt uneasy about surrounding himself with too many persons of similar background.

The first post-Stalin Presidium contained eight voting members who were Russian, one who was a Jew (Kaganovich), one who was a Georgian (Beria), and one who was an Armenian (Mikoian), and two of the four candidates were non-Russian by nationality: Bagirov (Azerbaidzhani) and Ponomarenko (Belorussian). While Beria and Bagirov were executed almost immediately and Ponomarenko was removed in 1956, the proportion of non-Russians on the Presidium rose somewhat during the Khrushchev years, standing at 33 percent of the voting members and 67 percent of the candidates in December 1962. (The percentage of non-Russians among the voting members declined to 27 percent with the death of Kuusinen in 1963.) The non-Russians naturally were chosen from those fluent in Russian and loyal to the center, but now all of them except Mikoian had made much of their career within the republic of their nationality. The candidate memberships in particular were used to give direct representation to a number of the republics, for the first secretaries of Belorussia, Uzbekistan, and Georgia were selected as candidate members, together with the chairman of the Council of Ministers of the Ukraine.

Early in the Brezhnev period, the number of non-Russians on the Politburo rose even higher. The Politburo named in March 1966 after the Twenty-

Third Party Congress contained 45 percent non-Russians among its eleven voting members and 63 percent non-Russians among its eight candidates. The 1971 additions to the voting membership essentially maintained the same balance, for two of the new members were Russians, two non-Russians. In the 1970s, however, the national composition became more Russian once again. Three of the five voting members removed were Ukrainian, while four of the five new members were Russian (and the non-Russian, Grechko, subsequently died). As a result, ten of the voting members in early 1977 (71 percent) were Russians, one was Ukrainian, one was a Belorussian, one a Kazakh, and one a Latvian, while five of the candidate members were Russians, one a Belorussian, one an Uzbek, and one an Azerbaidzhani.[34]

A second way in which social characteristics of Politburo members have changed is in the occupation of their fathers. The 1922 Politburo included two members whose parents had a white collar occupation, three whose parents were peasants (and in two cases fairly well-to-do peasants), and two whose parents were workers. The Stalin victory increased the proportion of leaders with working class parentage. The 1934 Politburo included one voting member of white collar origin (his father was an army officer), three of peasant origin, and six of working class origin, while the first post-Stalin Presidium—essentially the old dictator's top lieutenants at the end of his life—included two from a white collar background, one from a peasant background, and six from a working class one.

Khrushchev continued the practice of selecting top lieutenants from working class or peasant strata, but, as befit a man who was emphasizing agriculture, he increased the number of members from peasant homes. The 1962 voting members of the Presidium included one person with white collar parents, four with peasant parents, and seven with working class parents. This trend continued under Brezhnev, and the class origin figures for the voting members in early 1978 stood at two white collar, six peasant, and six working class.[35]

In individual cases, the class origin of a member may have been understated, but in worldwide perspective the top political leadership in the Soviet Union has been striking in the extent to which it has been drawn from those of worker and peasant parentage. The exact significance of this phenomenon is unclear, but it is worth noting that the basic changes in the patterns of social origin have, in fact, tended to be correlated with changes in social policy. Moreover, this factor must also have affected individual relations and behavior within the political elite. One catches a hint of this possibility in Khrushchev's wistful and admiring statement that Molotov "was the city dancer among us . . . and could even play the violin."[36] One suspects that many of the "promoted ones" from the factory bench in the 1930s must have had the fervor, the suspicion of "Chekhov bureaucrats," and the absence of "some subtleties in human relations" that the biographer and assistant of Voznesensky, the Gosplan chairman, reported in one leading Gosplan official.[37]

A third change in the characteristics of Politburo members has been in their level of education. In the early years very few members of the Lenin Politburo had a serious college education. Those who had entered the university had concentrated on revolutionary work and had been expelled fairly quickly. Except for Molotov (who had been expelled from the St. Petersburg Polytechnical Institute in 1912), those who became full members between 1925 and 1937 seem not to have had even this much exposure to higher education.

After the Great Purge, however, new members were increasingly chosen from those who had entered institutions of higher education—usually engineering institutes—in the 1920s and early 1930s after a period of earlier political work. Not all of these men were graduated from college, but the proportion of voting members who had received at least some higher education after 1917 rose to 36 percent in 1950, 50 percent in 1953, 64 percent in December 1957, and 100 percent in 1966 and thereafter.

Nevertheless, the quality of the education received by many of the Politburo members should not be exaggerated. The college experience could be chaotic during the time of the First Five-Year Plan, in any case,[38] and those who were destined for bright political futures usually had earlier political experience. Like a future first secretary of the Stalingrad regional party committee, they must often have missed class with "the ideological flu," that is, missed class to undertake some assignment;[39] like Brezhnev, they normally must have had a series of political jobs in the institute (in his case, at one time or another head of a student detachment to build dikes during a flood, head of a group leading agitation to create a collective farm, director of the institute rabfak, trade union chairman of the institute, party secretary of his class);[40] like one of the characters in a Soviet novel, many must have "graduated with the diploma of an engineer, but not the knowledge of one," as professors felt unable to fail them.[41]

Moreover, many Politburo members did not even complete a full course in a daytime institute. This was true not only of earlier political leaders such as Khrushchev and Malenkov, but, more unexpectedly, of recent additions to the Politburo as well. The members of Brezhnev's generation usually completed an institute of higher education, but those a decade younger frequently had their education disrupted by World War II. Thus, of the six voting members of the 1978 Politburo born between 1914 and 1923, only one (Shcherbitsky) had completed a degree at a daytime institute, and, in fact, only one (Romanov) had a clearly earned degree from a night school. Andropov and Grishin did not complete college, and Mazurov received a correspondence degree from the Higher Party School while Komsomol first secretary in Belorussia and Kulakov one from an agricultural institute at the age of thirty-nine while already RSFSR minister of grain products.

A fourth change in the characteristics of the Politburo members has occurred in their occupational background. The first members, like Lenin himself, had had little vocational experience other than that of a professional revolutionary. Those who were coopted into the Politburo during the Stalin years had had an opportunity to work in responsible posts after the revolution, but career patterns of the twenties and thirties are often difficult to characterize because of the rapid transfer of officials from job to job and even hierarchy to hierarchy. Basically, though, about one-half of the new voting members of the Stalin era (excluding the additions to the expanded Presidium in 1952) had risen through the party apparatus, 30 percent through economic management, and 20 percent through different paths. As tables 3 and 5 illustrate, the number of men on the Stalin Politburo currently employed in the party apparatus was much less than 50 percent. The path to the very top often involved movement into top governmental posts.

During the Khrushchev and early Brezhnev years, the proportion of new Politburo members who had risen through the party apparatus increased substantially. From 1955 through 1971 fully nineteen of twenty-two new members had been first secretary of a republican, regional, or Moscow city party committee either at the time of their entry into the Politburo or, more usually, previously. The biographies of the 1966 members and the 1977 Central Committee secretaries demonstrate that these party officials could have a great deal of prior managerial and governmental experience, but a transfer to party work in early or mid-career was almost always a prerequisite for entry into the leading party organs. Moreover, after 1957, reappointment to a high state position no longer was so necessary for selection as a Politburo member. Full-time party officials began to constitute a majority of the voting members—occasionally a strong majority—and after 1971 the leadership followed a policy on ensuring that a number of regional party leaders—those of the Ukraine, Moscow city, Kazakhstan, and then Leningrad—were included among them.

In 1973 the pattern of new Politburo members coming almost exclusively from positions as present or former provincial first secretaries was broken. The leadership returned to Stalin's practice of having the three major governmental officials in the foreign policy realm on the Politburo, as the Minister of Foreign Affairs, the Minister of Defense, and the Chairman of the KGB were elected full members. Although the last-named official had earlier experience in the party apparatus, the former two were professionals in their respective fields. Then in 1976, the Central Committee secretary for defense, the defense industry, and the police—a long-time defense industry administrator—temporarily added a fourth specialist in this field. (The Minister of Defense died within a month, and the Central Committee secretary was named to replace him.) Nevertheless, as table 9 indicates, a majority of the full Politburo members continued to be full-time party officials.

Unfortunately, it is far easier to summarize the characteristics of members than to describe the way in which they interact once they are on the Politburo. Brezhnev has stated that the Politburo regularly meets once a week, usually on Thursday, in sessions that last from three to six hours.[42] This assertion about the frequency of the meetings is generally confirmed by the report that the Politburo met 215 times in the five years between the Twenty-Fourth Congress in 1971 and the Twenty-Fifth Congress in 1976, at least if cancellations during times of vacations and foreign visits are taken into account.[43]

The nature of the Politburo agenda is shrouded in secrecy. Brezhnev has simply stated that "the most important and urgent questions of internal and foreign policy" are examined, and the best Soviet secondary sources on the party go little further, at least in their discussion of the postwar period.[44] The best information we have on the actual work comes from references to Politburo decisions in speeches that Brezhnev gave to the Central Committee, and these references usually deal only with the nature of the decision.

The only type of Politburo decision-making on which Brezhnev has provided any detail at all has been that involving the annual plan. Clearly the draft plan and budget are examined each year, and at least twice the General Secretary told the Central Committee that the Politburo had done so in "the most attentive manner," in "the most careful manner." In the case of the 1968 plan, he asserted, different variants of the plan were discussed, and the draft proposal by Gosplan was returned for reworking. In 1973, the examination was conducted on a detailed enough level to produce an increase in the construction of grain elevators.[45]

Perhaps because they are the decisions most convenient to mention in public or perhaps because they truly do constitute a large proportion of the Politburo work, the decisions that Brezhnev referred to most frequently were economic ones: the 1965 industrial reorganization; an increase in the production of tractors, trucks, and cars; pay rates for state farm tractor drivers; a reclamation program; the situation in the mineral fertilizer industry; urgent questions of livestock; an increase in the production of mineral fertilizers; a requirement that factories of all industries (including defense) should produce items for agriculture; development of agriculture in Smolensk region;

development of the gas, oil, and refinery industries, including the speeding of the construction of the Tobol Oil-Chemical Combine; improvement of conditions in the Non-Black Earth region; irrigation in the Volga region; improvement of economic management.[46]

Other types of decisions are not mentioned so frequently, but a few examples give some indication of their range: "questions of science and culture" in general, the length of paid vacations for the population, the improvement of scientific-technical potential, the establishment of a new medal entitled Labor Honor.[47] In addition, it has been reported that foreign policy questions occupy a "large place" in the work of the Politburo.[48] Brezhnev has stated that such questions are traditionally placed first on the agenda,[49] and the first deputy head of the international department has written that they "are examined and discussed in detail at practically each session."[50] Westerners have learned of specific sessions held at the time of major negotiations. For example, during the five days of discussions at the Nixon-Brezhnev summit meeting in May 1972, the Americans learned that the Politburo met at least four times.[51] Apparently these meetings were associated with significant changes in Soviet positions during the negotiations.

When a problem is discussed at a Politburo session, the "preparation of the question" ("the preparation of memoranda and of drafts of decisions") is assigned to officials of the Central Committee apparatus. Officials of outside institutions are also regularly invited to sessions when matters of central relevance to them are on the agenda. When the Politburo reached its decision on the expansion of tractor, truck, and automobile production, for example, the Minister of the Automobile Industry presented a report to it,[52] and that practice apparently is quite widespread. One Soviet source reports that the outsiders may even stay for the discussion.

The character of the deliberations as the Politburo moves toward a decision is almost completely unknown. How often do the decisions merely tend to confirm the reports prepared by the Central apparatus, the ministries, and the Politburo members most directly involved? How acrimonious a style of debate is considered permissible? These are questions on which we simply do not have information. Western correspondents have asked the top leaders whether the final outcome is determined by voting, and the answer consistently given in both the Khrushchev and Brezhnev years is that votes are seldom taken and that decisions are reached by some kind of consensus. In 1973 Brezhnev asserted that this occurred 99.99 percent of the time.[53]

Although Soviet statements downplaying the presence of conflict on the Politburo need to be treated with some care, a great many committees do function with little formal voting, and it seems quite likely that such a tradition would have developed in a party in which formal factions are outlawed. Such an assertion, however, says little about how the consensus is reached. Does the minority simply defer to the majority, acknowledging defeat without a formal vote? Are there norms against overriding the strong objections of the minority? Does the Politburo usually defer to the member most expert on a policy question? Is the presumed balance of opinion within the Central Committee as a whole a crucial factor? Does everybody simply defer to the General Secretary when he has a firm opinion? Does the General Secretary often have a firm opinion or is he an instinctive compromiser? These are the crucial questions about the structure of power within the Politburo.

The General Secretary and the Leading Party Organs

In formal party theory, the General Secretary is simply the leader of the executive arm of the Central Committee, the Secretariat. The nature of his role is never discussed in party textbooks, but discussions of the work of the local party secretary—discussions which may, but probably do not, refer to the General Secretary in an Aesopian manner—try with varying emphases to suggest that such officials should exercise initiative in executing policy while not overstepping the bounds of that policy. Lower party officials do imply that the party leader has a very decisive role, for at party congresses in particular, they praise him inordinately and refer to him as head of the Central Committee or head of the Politburo—or, more literally, "the Politburo headed by (vo glave s) the General Secretary of the Central Committee, Comrade Leonid Ilich Brezhnev." Nevertheless, there is no sanction in party theory for the General Secretary having more than one vote on the Politburo or dictating policy to it. There is no suggestion in party theory that a General Secretary has the right to dismiss a Politburo member in the way an American president can fire one of the members of his cabinet.

Even in practice, the general principle of collective leadership within the Politburo seems deeply engrained in the Soviet Union. In the most autocratic days of the Stalin period, the Politburo formally still seemed to operate as if there were collective decision-making and responsibility, and Khrushchev reported in his memoirs, for instance, that executions of high officials such as Voznesensky had to be signed collectively.[54] Stalin's technique for avoiding collective restraints was not to abolish the principle as such, but to intimidate Politburo members into the "correct" collective decision and perhaps even more frequently to conduct business in various subcommittees and at his dacha where he controlled the invitation list.

Under Khrushchev, the principle of regular Politburo (then Presidium) meetings was reestablished, and the Central Committee began to be called into rather long session. At a minimum, Presidium approval had to be obtained for any major action. Thus, when Khrushchev and the delegation flying to Paris for a summit conference with Eisenhower in May 1960 decided to change the approach to be followed, Khrushchev felt required to radio back to Moscow for approval.[55] Even when the party leader was determined to be most arbitrary in forcing through a drastic reorganization, he did so in the form of memoranda to the Presidium which acknowledged its right to make the decisions. (Many of these secret memoranda were published late in the Khrushchev era, and a series that he sent while on a trip to Central Asia provide a fascinating insight into the decision to centralize economic management in the various Central Asian republics into several suprarepublican agencies.)[56] This need to clear actions with the Politburo certainly seems to have continued during the Brezhnev period.

Yet, as the Stalin and Khrushchev cases demonstrate, collective cabinet responsibility need not mean equal distribution of influence within the cabinet, for the collective body may approve a leader's suggestions with little resistance. Even in the Khrushchev era, the Presidium gave its approval to the reversal of strategy at the Paris Conference while the plane was still in the air, and in the Central Asian reorganization Khrushchev was already announcing the likely leading officials of the new organs before he had returned to Moscow and let the Presidium discuss and approve his new idea. Of course, in many other countries as well (Great Britain, for example), the prime minister has become much stronger vis-à-vis the cabinet in the Twentieth Century and is scarcely to be considered a "first among equals."

In the past, western scholars have explained the General Secretray's predominant position in relation to the Central Committee and Politburo in terms of the circular flow of power. According to this theory, the Secretariat's responsibility for executing policy meant the ability to remove local party officials who were not effective in carrying out party policy and the ability to select (or at least confirm) their replacement. As a result, the theory insisted that the regional secretaries had a vital self-interest in pleasing the General Secretary and that they tried to do so not only by executing party policy effectively but also by giving him political support in his battles in Moscow. The theory also suggested that the General Secretary included political loyalty among the most important criteria in selecting lower officials.

The "circularity" in the flow of power resulted from the ability of the local party secretaries to control the delegations to the party congresses and to use their delegations to support the General Secretary and his list of Central Committee members, which not surprisingly included a large number of regional party officials. Thus, the members of the Central Committee, which had the responsibility of controlling the General Secretary, were themselves dependent on him. Anyone who wanted to break the flow of power by organizing against the General Secretary, either in the election of delegates to the congress or in the Central Committee, ran directly into the antifactionalism clause in the party rules unless immediate victory was achieved.

While the circular-flow-of-power analysis was no more than a theory, it did correspond to a number of facts about the Stalin and Khrushchev consolidations of power. In both cases the head of the Central Committee Secretariat emerged victorious in the struggle for power; in both cases a heavy turnover of regional first secretaries occurred early in the struggle for power—a turnover that certainly seemed associated with the General Secretary; in both cases the new regional first secretaries were strong supporters of the General Secretary in the congresses and in the Central Committee.

After Khrushchev's fall, once again it was the leader of the Central Committee Secretariat who became the dominant figure in the next political era. But many phenomena associated with the circular flow of power were not to be observed in the Brezhnev period. The turnover rate among the regional party secretaries became much lower than it had been. Even those secretaries who were removed were almost always given a job that warranted continued membership in the Central Committee. The new regional first secretaries, especially in the Russian Republic, were overwhelmingly promoted from within the region rather than coming from another region or the Central Committee apparatus. One might well argue that the regional secretaries had much less to fear from the General Secretary and that the latter's control over the Central Committee and the Politburo had, therefore, been significantly affected.

The argument has been made earlier that the circular flow of power still was an operative force in the Brezhnev era and that the General Secretary's control over personnel selection remained very great. The quickness with which Podgorny and Shelepin and their supporters were moved out of sensitive positions was impressive, and the phalanx of former officials from Dnepropetrovsk and Moldavia in the crucial control spots in the Central Committee apparatus and the police certainly cannot have been a coincidence. It is hard to believe that the regional party secretaries needed many other object lessons.

Whether this image of Brezhnev's power is correct or not, the simple pattern of events over the dozen years from 1964 to 1976 makes many facts about the relationships within the Politburo relatively clear. In the first place, the scale of the cult of personality in the 1970s leaves no doubt about the identity of the Politburo's leading figure. Level of praise is certainly not identical with level of power, but it should be reiterated that the glorification of Brezhnev came to exceed that given Khrushchev by a considerable margin. The publicity for Kosygin and Podgorny seemed deliberately designed to make their position humiliatingly clear.

In the second place, whether he had the ability to do so or not, Brezhnev obviously did not force through many major policy initiatives over the resistance of his colleagues. In praising him, his subordinates emphasized his modesty, his respect for the opinions of others, and his ability to work with others and weld them into a team. In the words of the first secretary of the Georgian Central Committee, "one of the best qualities of Leonid Ilich is that he does not wrap himself in the mantle of a superman and that he does not try to do everyone's thinking and working for them."[57]

Such testimony is, however, hardly necessary to document that a major, if perhaps temporary, change has occurred in the role of the party leader. The gradualism of policy change, the incrementalism in the appropriations process, and the stability of personnel are evidence enough that Brezhnev has been working within a system of committee politics rather than simply informing a committee, as Khrushchev sometimes was wont to do. Whether he had to or not, Brezhnev often has deferred to the judgments of colleagues and has often tried to put together a program that satisfies as many of them as possible.

This pattern of action has obvious implications for the structure of real influence within the Politburo. Even in the last days of the Stalin period, as Merle Fainsod insisted in 1953, the actual distribution of influence within the ruling party body needed to be understood in specialized terms. The Politburo was not—and is not—composed of a number of undifferentiated "Supreme Court Justices" with some general Politburo perspective. Instead, it has been composed of men who hold important institutional offices and who are responsible for important programs, sectors of the economy, and policy areas. Hence each Politburo member becomes a spokesman for certain specialized interests. (For example, when Molotov was in charge of railroad transport, "he tried to get everything he could for the railroads," according to Khrushchev.)[58] Each Politburo member has a differing degree of expertise and institutional self-interest as each question arises.

Fainsod reported—and accepted—the testimony of a few former Soviet officials that in the late 1930s, "each specialist member of the Politburo acted as a court of first instance on matters under his jurisdiction and presumably disposed of many issues of lesser magnitude without consulting his colleagues":

> According to one highly placed informant familiar with the Commissariat of Foreign Affairs under Litvinov in the late thirties, the Politburo exercised a particularly taut control in that area. When Stalin chose to intervene, his views were invariably decisive. Molotov, the informant reports, played an important role because of his position as chairman of the Politburo subcommittee on foreign affairs. The other members of the subcommittee at that time were Mikoian, who took the lead on questions of foreign trade, and Zhdanov, who before his death exercised

a special responsibility for Comintern (and later Cominform) affairs. The Commissariat of Foreign Affairs, according to this informant, moved along on its own momentum as long as existing Politburo directives covered the contingencies with which it was confronted. If a policy issue arose which could not be disposed of on the basis of past instructions, the Commissar of Foreign Affairs referred the matter to Molotov as chairman of the Politburo subcommittee on foreign affairs. Usually, matters of lesser importance were resolved at this level or in consultation with the full subcommittee. If, in the view of Molotov, the issue was one of major importance, the matter would go on the agenda of the Politburo or would be settled directly in consultation with Stalin. When a full-dress meeting of the Politburo was convoked, the Commissar of Foreign Affairs would report directly to that body with his recommendations. The Politburo would also be supplied with background memoranda prepared by the Foreign Section of the Central Committee Secretariat, which had at its disposal sources of intelligence that were not necessarily available to the Foreign Affairs Commissariat. The Politburo decision, once reached, would be communicated to the Commissariat in the form of a binding directive which the Commissariat would then utilize as a basis for action. In other areas, the Politburo functioned in similar fashion, though not necessarily with such close and immediate attention to detail.[59]

An authoritative Soviet source stated in an interview that permanent Politburo subcommittees do not exist today. However, the increase in the deference to the views of the specialized elites that has marked the Brezhnev period surely translates itself into a more decisive role within the Politburo for the individual members in their areas of special responsibility. It seems likely that they resolve more policy disputes within their policy branch essentially on their own or at least that the General Secretary and the Politburo ratify their decisions more often.

Nevertheless, even today the General Secretary has hardly withered away. Even if he is serving largely as chairman of the board, he still has a major role in selecting subordinates and in setting the general principles of policy and policymaking. Delegation of authority to individual Politburo members in their specialized sphere of influence in the Brezhnev years does not mean that they have the ability to introduce sweeping innovation in their field. The same type of gradualism and "scientific approach" to decision-making is found in almost all policy areas, and this uniformity must be testimony to the influence of the man at the top.

The question for which we still have no answer is the outcome if the General Secretary favors one course of action and a Politburo majority favors another. One assumes that formally decisions are made by a majority and that each member has only one vote, and Soviet scholars sometimes quote with approval a statement made by Lenin's secretary that he sometimes deferred to a majority with which he disagreed.[60] Nevertheless, in a committee that usually functions without formal voting, there is ample opportunity for a chairman to gain "a sense of the meeting" that is very different from that which would be revealed in a vote. Moreover, since it is the Central Committee that has the ultimate authority and the General Secretary's position may be very strong in that body, the other Politburo members may be very reluctant to take a position opposing the General Secretary if the latter has firm views.

The role of the General Secretary is also strengthened by the fact that the type of decision most likely to reach the Politburo level is one that involves conflict among institutions and/or regions. Such conflicts will entail differences among Politburo members as well, and on these questions, there can be no delegation of authority to the specialized members. With a bargaining relationship prevailing among the Politburo members, the General Secretary may well be called upon to resolve the conflict or at least to serve as a broker in working out a mutually acceptable compromise.

It is likely that the General Secretary remains in a position to force through any proposal within reason, especially if he prepares the groundwork beforehand. The real constraints on a General Secretary, besides those that a Central Committee might impose on really radical action(for example, execution of other Politburo members or bargaining away most military might in any unequal SALT negotiations), are the internalized sense of what is improper to do and the fear of accumulated grievances that might eventually provoke the type of action that was successful against Khrushchev.

Ultimately, though, relations within the top leadership are surely too subtle and too varying to be captured adequately in any brief analysis, and they must vary from issue to issue. After 1970 Brezhnev went out of his way to exclude Kosygin and Podgorny from top summit negotiations on foreign policy, even when protocol considerations would dictate their attendance (the Helsinki Conference was the most glaring example). The General Secretary seemed to be trying to create for himself a monopoly of critical information in this realm, and he must jealously guard his prerogatives in it. Similarly, as befits a graduate of a land rationalization school in the 1920s, Brezhnev seems personally involved in the land reclamation program and surely is the major explanation for its very favored position in budgetary allocations. In many other domestic policy areas, on the other hand, the Soviet leader's involvement must be sporadic at best unless a crisis or a serious institutional conflict thrusts a problem on his desk. The role of other individuals on the Politburo must likewise vary with their personality, the success of their programs, the state of their health, and the informal alignments that arise within the top ruling body.

In concluding this section, we should, however, emphasize one point. In the first sixty years of its existence, the Soviet regime has, except for brief transition periods, had four leaders, and each has had—in practice, if not in theory—a very distinctive relationship to the other members of the top political elite. With the passage of time, the probabilities increase that a new change in leadership will occur. If the past is any indication, some of the generalizations made here will then become of little more than historical interest.

Indeed, the situation which prevails during the next succession may well be conducive to formal as well as informal changes in the relations among the top leaders. By choosing—or conceivably being forced—to give long tenure to most Central Committee and Politburo members, Brezhnev will leave a political elite that is very near the age of retirement if he departs from the scene without conducting a major purge. The pressures for rejuvenating the top elite will be strong, especially from those born after the mid-1920s—a group which is much larger than its predecessor because it escaped the annihilation of World War II, which is better educated because it avoided the disruption of its college experience during the war, and which is now reaching the age that is usually deemed appropriate for the foremost positions.

In these circumstances the problem created for the political system is enormous. Presumably the elite has much preferred the "scientific approach" (the deferential decision-making style) of Brezhnev to the arbitrariness of a Stalin or a Khrushchev. Yet, having been exposed to caution and excessive reluctance to remove those of substandard performance for over a dozen years, they are likely to be attracted to a leader who seems to promise somewhat more dynamism and administrative vigor, who even has more charisma. Their dilemma is a serious one. If they select a man of greater dynamism, if he has every reason to rejuvenate the top political and administrative elite sitting on the Central Committee and Politburo, how do they prevent him from building a machine that could emancipate himself from Politburo and Central Committee control? Conversely, if they try to maintain the autonomy of an aging Central Committee, how do they prevent loss of administrative vigor?

One could imagine a number of ways in which the post-Brezhnev leadership might attempt to deal with this problem. However, some methods—for example, limitation of a General Secretary to a single five-year term on the Mexican model—involve radical change in the institutional arrangements within the party. It is a question which deserves our closest attention as the Soviet Union moves to deal with the problem of the succession.

13 | Provincial and Local Politics

THE SOVIET UNION is, as Alfred Meyer has phrased it, "a bureaucracy writ large."[1] All of the country's stores, schools, factories, theaters, and farms are administered through ministerial hierarchies that are ultimately headed by a minister in Moscow. Moreover, Communists in various "public" institutions (and in elected governmental bodies as well) are obligated by the party rules to form a party "fraction" that must carry out the decrees of party organs at their territorial levels. Consequently, even such organizations as the trade unions, the Komsomol, and, of course, the party apparatus—while not part of the governmental machinery—are still part of the overall administrative hierarchy, and, like the state organs, they too are ultimately subordinated to the real cabinet of the country, the party Politburo.

Recognizing the fact that all Soviet institutions are part of a single giant bureaucracy obviously is crucial in understanding the Soviet system, and it has several important implications. On the one hand, public administration becomes an extraordinarily difficult process, for the leadership must attempt to achieve reliability and predictability in the actions of lower officials across a far wider range of activities than is the case in the West. And, they must do so in a country spread over an area the size of the United States, Canada, and Mexico combined, with a population of 255 million people of dozens of different nationalities in 1976 (22 of them numbering at least one million persons at the time of the previous census).[2]

On the other hand, the merging of all institutional life into the governmental sphere also means that many matters become political in the Soviet Union that would not be so considered in the West. One consequence, as westerners have always recognized, is that political leaders have the opportunity to intervene more directly in all spheres of Soviet life; another consequence, which often has not been recognized by westerners, is that the political arena in the Soviet Union is vastly expanded. In all countries bureaucrats often try to influence the policy they are charged with administering, and they try to remove obstacles to that policy created by others, but this tendency must become even more pronounced in a system in which everyone is an administrator.

On the local level in particular, a critical question frequently is the priority to be given the policies and interests of the subordinates of different ministries. Bureaucratic in-fighting becomes very difficult to distinguish in its essential nature, although not in some of its forms, from the phenomenon that we call local politics in the West. Moreover, the variety of committees and councils that are created provide additional opportunity to try to influence the decisions that are made. Indeed, given the breadth of the definition of "political," many of the kinds of citizen involvement in university and business committees and in neighborhood groups and organizations that were strongly advocated by the new left in the United States in the late 1960s have long been a part of the Soviet scene.

The Territorial Subdivisions of the Soviet Union

Like any large country, the Soviet Union is divided into a number of territorial units, which in turn are themselves subdivided into smaller units. The primary division is the union republic, of which there are fifteen. The union republics are largely formed on the basis of a nationality criterion and vary drastically in size and population. The Russian Republic is the size of the original forty-eight American states and Canada combined, while Armenia is only slightly larger than the state of Maryland. Their population in January 1976 ranged from 134,650,000 in the Russian Republic to 1,438,000 in Estonia.

While all of the union republics have a multinational population (see table 34), each is centered primarily upon one of the country's nationalities, and each has two official languages—Russian and that of the major ethnic group of the republic. (The Russian Republic—the RSFSR—has only one official language, except in special "autonomous republics" and "autonomous regions" set aside for non-Russian nationalities within the republic.) Generally speaking, the largest nationalities each have their union republic, but there are exceptions: first, nationalities such as Jews and Germans that are not sufficiently concentrated in one locale, and second, nationalities such as the Tatars and the Bashkirs whose population center is in the interior of the country. In the past the constitution specified that a union republic must

Table 34 *Population of union republics, 1970, by nationality*

Republic	Population	Percent Local Nationality	Percent Russian	Percent Other Nationalities
Armenia	2,491,873	88.6	2.7	8.7
Azerbaidzhan	5,117,081	73.8	10.0	16.2
Belorussia	9,002,338	81.0	10.4	8.6
Estonia	1,356,079	68.2	24.7	7.1
Georgia	4,686,358	66.8	8.5	24.7
Kazakhstan	13,008,726	32.6	42.4	25.0
Kirgizia	2,932,805	43.8	29.2	27.0
Latvia	2,364,127	56.8	29.8	13.4
Lithuania	3,128,236	80.1	8.6	11.3
Moldavia	3,568,873	64.6	11.6	23.8
RSFSR	130,079,210	82.8	82.8	17.2
Tadzhikistan	2,899,602	56.2	11.9	31.9
Turkmenia	2,158,880	65.6	14.5	19.9
Ukraine	47,126,517	74.9	19.4	5.7
Uzbekistan	11,799,429	65.5	12.5	22.0

Source: *Itogi vsesoiuznoi perepisi naseleniia 1970 goda* (Moscow, Statistika, 1972), IV, 12–15.

have a border with a foreign country, allegedly so that it would have a realistic possibility of secession, and perhaps the status of several of the largest autonomous republics will be raised in the future.

According to the constitution, the relationship between the central government and the republics is a federal one. The country is officially called the Union of Soviet Socialist Republics, and the constitution speaks of the union republic as "a sovereign . . . state" (article 76). To emphasize the sovereign nature of the republics, the constitution specifies that each union republic "has the right to enter into direct relations with foreign states and to conclude agreements and exchange diplomatic and consular representatives with them" (article 80). The right to secede from the union is formally recognized.

According to the constitution, the sovereignty of the union republics is restricted only by the "limits indicated in article 73 of the constitution." However, article 73 specifies that the national government has the responsibilities of "establishment of the general principles of organization and activity of the republican and local organs of state authority and administration . . . establishment of the bases of legislation of the USSR and the union republics . . . conducting of a united social-economic policy . . . working out and confirmation of the state plans . . . working out and confirmation of a united state budget . . . general leadership of branches of union-republic significance," and so forth. The sovereignty of the union republics seems to be limited only in all the areas in which they might want to take action. Like all territorial subdivisions in all countries, even the most centralized, the republics do have questions which are delegated to them for resolution, but in this respect the republics are not different in kind from other territorial subdivisions within the country.

The territorial subdivision below the level of the union republic—or at least below the level of the larger union republics—is that of the oblast, the krai, or the autonomous republic. In 1977 there were 120 oblasts, 6 krais, and 20 autonomous republics, and they corresponded roughly to the American state in size. In European Russia their area normally ranges between the size of New Hampshire and that of Indiana, but in Siberia it usually is much larger. (The Yakutia Autonomous Republic, the largest, is twice the size of Alaska.) The autonomous republics are areas like oblasts, based upon a specific nationality (for example, the earlier-mentioned Bashkirs and Tatars), and the krai is essentially an oblast with a relatively small nationality—one might almost say "an Indian reservation"—included within it and subordinate to it.[3] The small nationality units within a krai are simply termed "autonomous oblasts" and ranged from 100,000 to 500,000 in population in 1976, compared with populations of over 500,000 persons in 82 percent of the autonomous republics and 89 percent of the oblasts (97 percent of the oblasts in the RSFSR and the Ukraine).[4] For our purposes, the oblast, krai, and autonomous republic are sufficiently comparable to be treated as identical, and they will be referred to collectively as oblast or region. They are a basic political unit in the Soviet Union, for over the years their party leaders have constituted one of the largest groups selected for Central Committee membership.

The administrative subdivision below the level of the oblast (or of the union republic in areas where there are no oblasts) is rather complex. The oblasts and small republics are all divided into areas called raions, areas that usually are translated as "districts" in English and that are more or less analogous to American counties. The raions in European Russia have averaged approximately 1,000 to 1,500 square miles in recent years, but they were essentially half that size in the 1950s.

In one respect the raion is unlike the typical American county: it has no jurisdiction over the larger or medium-sized cities and towns within the oblast or small republic. The cities of Moscow and Kiev are even administratively independent of the oblast in which they are located and are subordinated directly to the political institutions of their respective republics. In four other cities—Leningrad, Minsk, Tashkent, and Sevastopol—the city government is also subordinated directly to the republican government, but the city party committee is under the direction of the oblast party committee. (Thus, when the top party leaders in Moscow and Leningrad were placed on the Politburo in the mid-1970s, it was the first secretary of the Moscow city committee and the first secretary of the Leningrad oblast party committee who were selected—and appropriately so.)

The other large cities in the Soviet Union (in 1975, all those larger than 60,000 persons) are supervised by the party and governmental institutions of their oblast or small union republic and are not responsible to the local rural raion. The largest cities (in 1975, all but one of those over 225,000 persons and over half of those in the 150,000 to 225,000 range) are in turn subdivided into boroughs—alas, also called raions. In the very largest cities, the population of the urban raions can rise to the 223,000 average of Leningrad and the 286,000 average of Moscow in 1975, but in 56 percent of the cities with borough subdivisions the raions averaged between 90,000 and 130,000 in population in that year and in 80 percent of such cities they averaged between 80,000 and 140,000 persons.

The small towns have their own city soviets, but they are subordinate to the institutions of the rural raion or county instead of to the oblast. (They also have no independent party institutions.) The dividing line at which a town becomes large enough to be administratively independent of the rural raion is a blurred one. On January 1, 1975, 95 percent of the cities in the 40,000 to 60,000 person range were independent of the rural raion, 77 percent of those in the 30,000 to 40,000 range, 51 percent of those in the 25,000 to 29,000 range, 26 percent of those in the 20,000 to 24,000 range, 16 percent in the 15,000 to 19,000 range, and 4 percent of the smaller towns.[5]

Population centers that have not been granted the status of a town (gorod) may be given the status of an "urban settlement" (poselok gorodskogo tipa). The inhabitants of an urban settlement are generally in nonagricultural occupations, and the reason that one population center is given this standing and another is called a city is not clear. The larger the center, the more likely it is to be a city, but, as indicated in table 35, there is considerable overlap between the two categories.

The lowest administrative unit in the rural areas is called the village soviet (sel'skii sovet), and in the past it centered on a rural village. (In Russia, peasants generally did not live on individual scattered farms as in the United States, but in villages of a few hundred persons.) For the first twenty years

Table 35 *Distribution of cities and urban settlements,*
by population, January 1, 1975

POPULATION RANGE	CITIES	URBAN SETTLEMENTS
Under 3,000	71	1,039
3,000 to 5,000	74	976
5,000 to 10,000	263	1,251
10,000 to 20,000	562	422
Over 20,000	1,043	51
Total	2,013	3,739

Source: *Narodnoe khoziaistvo SSSR v 1974 g., Statisticheskii ezhegodnik* (Moscow, Statistika, 1975), p. 32.

after the collectivization drive, each collective farm was essentially limited to an individual village, but after 1950 the regime—led by Khrushchev—moved to amalgamate the farms. As a result, they came to include an increasing number of villages. Eventually the boundaries of the jurisdiction of the village soviet also were, as a general rule, made to coincide with those of the collective (or state) farm, and hence they too came to embrace more than one village.

Subnational Governmental Institutions

The governmental institutions of a union republic and an autonomous republic are very much like those of the national government. The legislature is called the Supreme Soviet, and it has a Presidium to serve as the legislative organ between sessions of the Supreme Soviet. The executive branch is called the Council of Ministers, and the specialized administrative agencies are usually called ministries.

At lower territorial levels, the legislative body is called simply the oblast soviet, the city soviet, the raion soviet, and so forth, and it has no presidium. At this level the administrative unit is called an "administration" (*upravlenie*) or a department (*otdel*) instead of ministry, and the soviet has nothing like a council of ministers that would include all their chiefs. Instead, the top executive body bears the title of "executive committee (*ispolkom*) and includes the heads of only a small proportion of the administrations and departments.

The provincial soviet, while having only a single house or chamber, has many of the features of the Supreme Soviet at the national level: election of

deputies in uncontested elections, Communist party supervision of the nomination process, dominance of the legislative proceedings by the party with
Communist deputies bound by the directives of the local party organs, unanimous approval of all legislation introduced, and so forth.

   Nevertheless, the local soviet seems to have the potential for greater live-
liness and impact than its national counterpart. The soviet sessions are held
only twice a year in the union and autonomous republics, but that number
increases to four times a year in the oblast and six times a year at lower
levels. There apparently is some room for local initiative in the choice of
topics to be discussed, for from July 1968 through the end of 1971 the topic
of public health was discussed at sessions of twenty-seven oblast soviets in
the RSFSR and not discussed in twenty-two.[6] There are also variations in
the patterns of participation in the soviets. From mid-1967 to mid-1971,
the proportion of women speakers in the soviets of the RSFSR oblasts and
autonomous republics ranged from 9 percent in the Tuva Autonomous Republic and 12 percent both in Briansk and Voronezh oblasts to 33 percent
in Novgorod oblast and the Chechen-Ingush Autonomous Republic and 37
percent in Kaliningrad oblast.[7]

   As in the center, the local soviets have standing committees to assist
them in their work. Each union republic had from twelve to seventeen standing committees in 1975, each of ten autonomous republics on which information is available had from nine to thirteen in that year, and each of thirty-
eight such oblasts in the RSFSR had from twelve to nineteen. The titles of
the standing committees are fairly similar to those of the Supreme Soviet
standing committees, and, except for a few committees such as those on
youth, on protection of women and children, and on conservation, they are
structured along branch lines. Nevertheless, the variation in their number
obviously is associated with some variation in the way in which the work of
the committees is subdivided.

   The standing committees, like the soviets themselves, meet much more
frequently than their national counterparts. The head of the socialist legality
and public order standing committee of the Moscow soviet—a scholar at
the Institute of State and Law of the Academy of Sciences—reports that committees at his level meet six times a year and that they require a great deal
of their chairmen's time. A sociological study of raion deputies in Leningrad found that the average deputy spent twenty-two hours a month on
his or her obligations as a deputy, but that 8 percent devoted over forty
hours a month to them and that 2 to 4 percent spent over sixty hours a
month.[8]

   The committees not only engage in the type of oversight activities that
predominate in the nonbudgetary work of the Supreme Soviet standing com-

mittees but also have a much larger role in the legislative process. The greater frequency of local soviet sessions means a greater number of decisions that are passed and that need to be "prepared," and, in addition, the standing committees also prepare questions for sessions of the executive committees. In 1974, they participated in the preparation of over 435,000 questions for sessions of the soviets in the country as a whole and over 839,000 questions for the executive committees.[9] (In that year there were a total of 50,600 soviets in the country.)

In many instances, the standing committee does not prepare a question independently, but instead some of its members take part in the preparatory commission (*podgotovitel'naia komissiia*). According to one Soviet scholar, such commissions are typically chaired by the deputy chairman of the executive committee of the soviet who specializes in the particular policy area, and they include specialists from a number of local institutions. A preparatory commission on a trade question, for example, might include one or two officials from the local planning committee, a top official or two from the administrative bureau handling trade, a representative from the trade union of store workers, and deputies from the appropriate standing committee of the soviet.

In 1977 the average number of deputies in a soviet ranged from 33 at the village level to 78 in the raions, 134 in the cities, and 218 in the oblasts, and over 2,200,000 persons were drawn into these institutions in the country as a whole. The representation of middle-status groups in the local soviets was even higher than in the Supreme Soviet (42.3 percent of the deputies to the local soviets were workers and 56.8 percent of them were not members of the party). With 80 percent of the deputies being named to the standing committees, these bodies too have a membership with a broad social base.[10]

The chairmen of the standing committees of the local soviets—at least at the city level and above—are almost always men and women of higher status occupations, but there is considerable variation from area to area. Thus, excluding the mandate and foreign affairs committees, which are of negligible importance in the republics, Turkmenia had twelve standing committees in 1975 and the Ukraine fifteen. In the Turkmen case, nine of the twelve committee chairmen were heads of departments of the republican party central committee—and the "appropriate" committees at that; in the Ukraine, on the other hand, not a single one of these fifteen standing committee chairmen was a republican party official. More typically, the republican chairmen would include several republican party officials, several scientific or higher education administrators, and a majority who are leaders of party committees or executive committees of soviets in the oblasts, cities, and raions of the republic.[11]

Little comprehensive information has been available on the standing committees at lower levels, but in the relatively few examples at our disposal, the occupations of their chairmen show a similar range. In Primorsk krai, for example, the chairmen of fifteen of the sixteen policy-related standing committees selected in 1977 were chairmen of the executive committees either of the city or the raion soviets, but in Stavropol krai only three of fourteen such committee chairmen had this background and in Khabarovsk krai only two of sixteen. In Stavropol five of the chairmen of policy-related committees were heads of departments of the krai party committee, but none in Primorsk and Khabarovsk. In Khabarovsk—but in no other republic, krai, oblast, or city on which information is available—two workers headed committees: a locomotive engineer the conservation committee and a lathe operator the trade and public eating committee.[12]

At the city level, information on occupations of chairmen of standing committees in 1977 has been found on only three cases, but the pattern in all was similar to that in the city of Izhevsk (population 506,000) in the Mordovian Autonomous Republic: Planning-Budget Committee—head of the planning-economic department of the Izhevsk Metallurgy Works; Industry Committee—director of the knitted goods factory; Consumer Services—director of the Udmurt Services Construction Trust; Health—director of the Second City Pediatrics Hospital; Education—director of a secondary school; Culture—director of the Children's City Library; Trade and Public Eating—head of the local office of a Russian wholesale trade agency; Construction—chief engineer of the Udmurt Civilian Design Bureau; Communal Economy and City Beautification—deputy head of the Northern Urals Sanitation Construction Trust; Transportation and Communications—director of the truck base of the Milk Purchasing Office; Repair and Use of Housing—assistant to the director of the metallurgy works; Socialist Legality and Preservation of Public Order—deputy minister of justice of the Udmurt Republic; Conservation—director of the heating boiler plant; Physical Culture and Sports—dean of the physical education department, Udmurt University; Youth—pro-rector of the mechanics institute.[13]

Whatever the role of the standing committees and the soviets as a whole, it is clear that their real impact on the decision-making process is less on the average than that of the executive officials of the soviet. The top official in the provincial government—as in the center—is the chairman of the republican Council of Ministers, or at lower levels the chairman of the executive committee of the local soviet. The chairman's top lieutenants bear the title of deputy chairman or (in one case) secretary, and the number of these deputy chairmen basically varies with the number of people in the territorial unit. Most raions seem to have two deputy chairmen, but the smaller ones have only one. Small towns are like the raions in their number of deputy chairmen, while a city of a few hundred thousand persons may have three deputy chairmen, a larger city four, and the huge cities even more.[14] The oblasts and autonomous republics in the RSFSR normally have four to five deputy chairmen, and in the union republics the number ranges from five in seven republics to nine in the case of the Ukraine and ten in the RSFSR, with six or seven in the others.[15]

Each of the deputy chairmen supervises a specific group of departments and administrations, the division of responsibility taking place, as is usual in the Soviet political system, along branch lines. The pattern of supervision varies somewhat, depending on the specific experiences of the officials, but in an executive committee of an oblast soviet with four deputy chairmen, one is usually in charge of agriculture, one of construction, transportation, and related industries, one of education, culture, and health, and one of trade, consumer services, and related industries. When there is a fifth deputy chairman, he usually takes responsibility for all industry subordinate to the soviet. In a city with three deputy chairmen, the division of responsibility is usually very similar, except, of course, for the absence of a deputy chairman for agriculture. The secretary of the executive committee must cosign all legislation of the soviet and, in addition to handling housekeeping, may be given responsibility for several substantive departments (typically, sports and physical culture in a larger unit or health, education, and culture in small raions).

The chairman, deputy chairmen, and to a lesser extent the secretary are the major figures of the executive committee, but the executive committee as such is a broader collective body. In the RSFSR in 1975, the executive committees of the oblast soviets usually contained from eight to eleven persons in addition to the full-time inner core. The membership almost invariably included the first secretary of the oblast party committee, the chairman of the executive committee of the city soviet of the oblast capital, and five or six of the heads of the administrations and departments. The administrative officials most often included—although there was variation—were the chairman of the oblast planning committee, the head of the internal affairs administration (the regular police), the head of the finance department, the head of the agriculture administration, and the chairman of the People's Control Committee. In all the cases for which full information is available, a worker was also included among the executive committee members and not infrequently so were a collective farm chairman and a top economic manager (usually the head of a big construction trust or the head of the supply administration of the economic region).[16] The executive committee apparently meets twice a month.

Probably the most knowledgeable Soviet scholar working on the local soviets has written that only the most important questions are discussed by the executive committee as a whole and that "as a rule" even these questions are also "discussed beforehand in a narrower circle of the executive committee—by the chairman, deputy chairmen, and secretary 'in working order' (v rabochem poriadke), as they sometimes say."[17] Yet, if the pattern found in the RSFSR oblasts and capital cities is typical—and it certainly should be—we must not forget that one of the members of the executive committee is almost always the party first secretary of the locality and that the other members include the heads of the most important administrations and departments. It is hard to imagine the first secretary attending a strictly pro-forma meeting of major officials every two weeks—and there is little reason for him to permit this to occur.

In addition to the executive committee (or republican council of ministers), the executive agencies of the local government also include the administrations and departments (in the republics, the ministries and state committees) subordinated to the executive committee. A city with a population of several hundred thousand persons has approximately a dozen such administrative agencies, including, for example, finance, city planning, education, culture, trade, consumers' services, housing, communal economy, and capital construction. A large oblast not only has counterparts to these units but also supervises another thirty or so: four to five in the agricultural and reclamation realm, some half dozen handling different branches of light industry and local industry, perhaps the same number leading various types of construction, and miscellaneous offices such as social security, justice, communications, publishing, television and radio, and so forth. A union republic, in turn, has not only ministries for each of these functions but also additional ones in charge of individual branches of industry.

Although provincial and local governments in the Soviet Union supervise a far wider range of activities than local governments in the West, their power vis-à-vis administrative officials in the region is limited by two factors. In the first place, the administrative officials we have been discussing are subordinated not only to the executive committee or Council of Ministers of the soviet but also to the appropriate department or ministry at the next highest territorial level. Thus, the city education department is subordinated to both the executive committee of the city soviet and the oblast education department. The oblast education department in turn is responsible to both the executive committee of the oblast soviet and the republican ministry of education. The executive committee itself is subordinated to both the local soviet and the executive committee (or Council of Ministers) at the next territorial level. Any such system of "dual subordination" (dvoinoe podchinenie, to use official Soviet language), particularly in a country known for its centralization, obviously reduces the leverage of the local soviets over their subordinates, for the latter can appeal to contravening instructions from ministerial—or "vertical"—supervisors. (The supervision by the soviet and its executive committee is termed "horizontal" in informal Soviet administrative language.)

In the second place, many administrative officials within the respective regions are not subordinated to the soviet in any meaningful way.[18] The enterprises of the all-union ministries (for example, the defense and machinery industries, the railroads, and the airlines) are not responsible to any governmental body at the republican level or below, while most of the rest of heavy industry is in the same category in all but one or two republics (notably the Ukraine). Almost none of the scientific, design, or higher education institutions are supervised by soviets below the republic level (and many of them not even there), and very little light industry or construction is supervised by the soviets below the oblast level (and far from all of it there). Moreover, much of the construction of housing and urban services is financed by the independent institutions, especially the industrial ones. As a result, the plans compiled by the city, oblast, or even republican planning committees cannot deal with the entire economy of their area. The officials of the prosecutor's office and of the secret police (KGB) are also independent of the local soviets.

The Party Organs at the Subnational Level

While party members are enrolled in primary party organizations at their respective places of work rather than at their place of residence, the party organizations in turn are supervised by a hierarchy of party committees that are territorially organized. The most immediate supervisor is the raion or city party committee, for party institutions are not established in the villages, the urban settlements, or the small towns that are subordinated to the raion soviets. Indeed, at times a single party committee is placed in charge of both the rural raion and the raion center whose city soviet is administratively subordinated to the oblast or the union republic. It is symptomatic that in 1976 there were 3,118 rural raiony in the country and 904 cities subordinated to the oblast or the union republic, but only 2,857 rural raion party committees and 815 city party committees. Presumably, 350 of the 904 cities of republican or oblast subordination were supervised by the same party committee that supervised the adjacent raion,[19] whether it bore the title of a raion or city party committee.

Many of the responsibilities of the local party organs *(mestnye partiinye organy)* are of an intraparty nature: collecting party dues, approving the admission of new members, supervising the ideological education of new members, confirming (or selecting) the leaders of the primary party organizations, and so forth. Other responsibilities center upon propaganda and agitation work and control of ideological deviation among the population. In addition, however, the principle that the party committees should dominate the governmental institutions has been extended to the provinces as well, and the local party organs are deeply involved in substantive local decision-making.

The first responsibility of the local party organs in relation to the administrative organs is to ensure that they carry out the decisions of the central party organs and the ministries and fulfill their plans. Beyond that, the local party organs are called upon to provide policy leadership to all the institutions in their area and to coordinate their activities in order to ensure the area's integrated development. To assist the local party organs in the realization of these goals, the party leadership has given them special powers in the realm of personnel selection. The system of party nomenklatura exists in the provinces as well as in the center, and important posts not within the nomenklatura of the Central Committee usually are placed within the nomenklatura of the local party organs at different territorial levels. The importance of the post determines the level of party organ in whose nomenklatura it is located. Before any personnel action is taken with respect to a post in the nomenklatura of a local party organ, that body must give its approval.[20]

The right of nomenklatura formalizes the local party organs' authority over specific personnel decisions, but, in fact, they already have general authority over all institutions within their territory and their decisions are obligatory for these institutions. Indeed, since the local party organs supervise all primary party organizations within their area, they have authority not only over the soviets but also over officials independent of the soviet—for example, those in heavy industry, the railroad, the secret police, the prosecutor's office, and so forth. Only the army units in an area seem quite independent of the local party organs, and even in this case the republican and oblast party first secretaries normally sit on the military councils of the military districts.[21]

The responsibility of the local party organs to serve as "the leading organ" in their territory is not a formal one, nor is it simply the negative duty to act as an auditor to prevent wrongdoing. The local party organs are responsible for political stability, for plan fulfillment of all the enterprises and institutions within their territory, and for the integrated economic development of the area. Far from merely checking on fulfillment of the letter of the law or the plan, they often find themselves in the position of authorizing or requiring some specialized administrator to deviate from his directives or plans so that some other administrative unit has a better chance to carry out its mission.

The internal structure of the local party organs is modeled on that of the central party organs. The highest authority is the congress in the union republic or the conference at lower levels. The congress or conference selects a committee to rule in the interval until the next one is convened—a committee which is called a central committee at the union republic level, but simply the oblast party committee (*obkom*), the city party committee (*gorkom*), or raion party committee (*raikom*) at lower levels. The union republic central committee and oblast party committee averaged approximately 110 voting members in 1976, and the city and raion party committees averaged some 55 voting members.[22] They contain a range of officials analogous to that of the Central Committee in Moscow (see table 36).

The party committee in turn elects an inner ruling committee of seven to fifteen voting members, which is called a politburo at the union republic level and simply a bureau at lower levels. It also elects from three to five secretaries to serve as the party organization's top executive officials, and these secretaries are assisted by an apparatus of full-time officials who are organized into departments *(otdels)*. The size of the secretariats and the apparatus depends on the number of Communists in the party organization—and, therefore, in significant part upon the territorial level of the party organization.

The breadth of the responsibilities of the local party organs is suggested by the structure of their secretariat and apparatus. Normally the central committees of the union republics and the party committees of the oblast party committees have five secretaries: a first secretary, who is the most powerful political figure in the region—the real mayor or governor; a secretary for "organizational questions," who essentially supervises the lower party organs, the police, and the trade unions; a secretary for industry, construction, transportation, and (usually) urban trade; a secretary for agriculture; and a secretary for "ideological questions," who essentially supervises propaganda and agitation work, education, culture, health, and social welfare. One of these secretaries—often the organizational secretary—is given the title of "second secretary."[23]

In practice, the secretaries are in charge of one or more departments, which assist them in their work. As a consequence, the departments too are organized along branch lines. Except for lacking departments handling foreign relations and the political administration of the army, the Ukrainian Central Committees seems to have exactly the same departments as the Central Committee apparatus. A typical republican central committee or the party committee of a fairly large oblast have a somewhat smaller apparatus of some twelve departments: (1) Administrative Organs, (2) Agriculture, (3) Construction and Urban Economy, (4) Culture, (5) General, (6) Information and Foreign Ties,[24] (7) Industrial-Transportation, (8) Light Industry and the Food Industry, (9) Organizational-Party Work, (10) Propaganda and Agitation, (11) Science and Education, and (12) Trade, Financial, and Planning Organs.

Table 36   *Occupational distribution of full members of*
republican Central Committees, 1976

	OCCUPATIONAL DISTRIBUTION IN PERCENTAGES				
OCCUPATION	ESTONIA	GEORGIA	KIRGIZIA	MOLDAVIA	UKRAINE
Central Committee party officials	11.0	14.0	12.0	16.0	10.0
Regional party officials	20.0	23.0	23.0	25.5	25.0
Secretary, primary party organization	0	0	0	0	2.0
Republican governmental official[a]	29.5	20.5	25.0	37.0	17.0
Regional governmental official[b]	5.0	3.0	4.0	2.0	6.0
Military officer[c]	2.5	1.5	1.5	1.0	3.0
Scientist, educator	5.0	4.5	2.5	2.5	5.0
Cultural figure, editor	5.0	5.0	3.0	2.5	2.0
Industrial-construction manager[b]	1.0	3.0	2.5	1.0	5.0
Farm managerial official[d]	5.5	4.5	6.5	1.0	7.0
Worker	8.0	8.0	7.0	3.5	9.0
Peasant[d]	1.0	4.5	5.5	1.0	0.5
Miscellaneous	1.5	1.5	1.5	2.0	1.5
Unknown	5.0	7.0	6.0	6.0	7.0
Total number of members	125	137	125	117	191

Source: The names of members are found in *Sovetskaia Estoniia,* January 31, 1976, p. 1; *Zaria vostoka,* January 25, 1976, p. 1; *Sovetskaia Kirgiziia,* January 19, 1976, p. 1; *Sovetskaia Moldaviia,* February 1, 1976, p. 1; *Pravda Ukrainy,* February 14, 1976, p. 2. The occupations must be ascertained by an extensive examination of the republican press in the months before and after the congress.

a Includes a few republic-wide officials not subordinated to the republican Council of Ministers (for example, the head of the railroad).

b Industrial managerial officials at the regional level are included among the regional governmental officials and those at the republican level are included among the republican governmental officials.

c Includes border troop officials of the KGB and the MVD.

d Low level farm managerial and professional personnel (except link-leaders) are included among farm managerial officials rather than among peasants.

In addition, the Party Commission (the local agency of the Party Control Committee)[25] and the business office (*upravlaiushchii delami*) are sometimes treated as departments in Soviet lists of such bodies.[26]

The secretariats and apparatus of the city and raion party organizations are smaller in size, but are structured along similar lines. The city or urban borough committee normally has three secretaries—one in charge of "organizational questions," one in charge of "ideological questions," and one in charge of industry and construction. The rural raion party normally also has three secretaries—one for organizational questions, one for ideological questions, and one for agriculture. One of the secretaries at this level (almost always the organizational secretary or the secretary for the economy) is given the title and authority of first secretary, and another (usually the organizational secretary or the secretary for the economy) becomes the second secretary.

The average rural raion committee normally has only three departments —organizational, propaganda and agitation, and general. (The general department is in charge of internal business and housekeeping, the routing of incoming letters, and the security of secret documents.) The average city party committee has the same three departments, and an industrial-transportation department as well.[27] A city or raion party committee that supervises both a town of significant size and the surrounding rural raion may have both an industrial-transportation and an agriculture department in addition to the usual three. The departments of the local party organs are led by a "head" (*zaveduiushchii*) and staffed by officials called "instructors."

Westerners have usually estimated the size of the party apparatus at well over 100,000 persons—200,000 responsible workers in one recent estimate[28]— but such figures are surely too high. A series of individual examples suggests that the raion and small city party committees normally have some twelve to twenty responsible workers, while a city in the 300,000 population range has no more than twenty-five to thirty officials.[29] If an average of twenty officials is assumed for the raion and city party committees, one hundred for the oblast committees, and two hundred for the republican central committees, one could reach a total of 100,000, but the estimate for the average raion and city committee is likely to be a bit high.

The 1970 census reports that 146,000 persons were serving as full-time officials in the central and provincial committees of the party, Komsomol, trade union, and other public organizations—87,500 of them leaders of the institutions and their subdivisions and 58,500 of them instructors.[30] Only about one-half of the leaders can have been employed in the local party organs, and even if 40,000 to 50,000 of the instructors work for the local party organs—a reasonable assumption—the staff of the lower party apparatus should have been in the 90,000 range. The number of oblast party committees increased 4 percent between 1971 and 1976 and the number of city and raion party committees 5½ percent. However, even if this implies a 5 percent increase in the size of the apparatus (a dubious assumption), the number of full-time officials of the local party organs should not have become much larger than 100,000.[31]

As is true for the Central Committee apparatus, the specialized officials of the local party organs have very specialized backgrounds. In a survey of 1,620 instructors of city and raion party organs in the RSFSR, Belorussia, Moldavia, and Uzbekistan, 1,478 turned out to have higher education. A detailed breakdown of the type of education among the instructors was not given, but in the borough party committees of Riga, one-third of the instructors were engineers and technicians and one-fourth had a pedagogical education, with the two groups presumably employed in the appropriate departments. Similarly, the Ogreev rural raion party committee employed three engineers, seven agronomists and zootechnicans, and six teachers among its instructors. The instructors in the survey of 1,620 were generally in the thirty to forty age range, and their short tenure suggests a rapid turnover among them. (Over 34 percent had been employed for less than a year, 35 percent from one to three years, and 17 percent from three to five years.) Presumably many were recruited from personnel with specialized professional experience and soon moved back to their specialized career, perhaps to a higher position.[32]

Even the officials of a single department can have a more specialized range of backgrounds than appears on the surface. For example, the ten officials of the agriculture department of the Ulianovsk oblast party committee in 1974 included, among others, a former chief agronomist and a former chief engineer of the oblast agricultural administration (the top governmental institution in the oblast), a man with long experience in the oblast forestry service, a former chairman of a raion planning committee, a zootechnician, and an agronomist from a state farm.[33]

The secretaries too can be drawn from persons with substantial experience appropriate to their specialized position. Only incomplete information is available, but in 1976 the ideological secretaries of the Tadzhik, Kirgizian, Turkmen, and Estonian Central Committees were former Komsomol first secretaries, while the ideological secretary in Latvia had been the minister of higher and specialized secondary education in the republic and the ideological secretary in Lithuania had been the republican minister of culture. The industrial secretary in Latvia had been a plant manager, the industrial secretary of Kazakhstan a minister of construction in the republic, and the industrial secretary of Turkmenia a chairman of the sovnarkhoz (regional economic council), while the agricultural secretary in Lithuania had been the republic's minister of agricultural procurements and the agricultural secretary in the Ukraine a former head of an oblast agriculture administration.[34]

The most powerful official in the locality is the first secretary. He is the foremost representative of the party—in practice, the prefect in the system[35]— and he is responsible for all spheres of activity within the locality. For this reason, almost any background might be considered appropriate for a first secretary and, in fact, a wide variety of career paths do lead to this post. Nevertheless, the preparation of a first secretary tends to be related to the type of locality in which he serves—the nature of its economy and the sensitivity of the nationality question within it (see table 37).

The typical first secretary in an urbanized oblast in the mid-1970s had an engineering degree and had worked for at least five years in technical or managerial posts in industry. He is likely to have become an official of a local party organ—perhaps an official handling industry or first secretary of the borough party committee in which his plant is located—after serving as secretary of the primary party organization in that plant. Once in the party apparatus, the future urban oblast first secretary has tended to remain within the party apparatus in his rise to that position, for the soviet's lack of authority over industry means that a person can obtain broader experience in the supervision of industry as well as other governmental activity only within the party organs.[36] Even in urbanized oblasts, however, the first secretary may be an agricultural specialist (for instance, in Tula in 1974), a former educator and head of the city education department (in Dnepropetrovsk), a man concerned for many years with political control work in non-Russian republics (in Arkhangel'sk), and so forth.[37]

The typical oblast first secretary in a substantial agricultural region is far less likely to be an engineer and far more likely to be an agronomist. (The oblasts with the highest percentage of rural population tend to be small ones outside the Russian Republic, and their preparation and education tends to be somewhat more "political" in nature.) Since the executive committees of the soviet participate in the supervision of agriculture, lower officials can gain experience in more responsible posts in that realm by promotion into soviet as well as party positions, and in fact the oblast first secretaries in agricultural regions often have been moved back and forth between party and governmental positions.

In one such case, the first secretary of the Belgorod oblast party committee graduated from the Moscow Agricultural Academy and assumed a position as chief agronomist of a machine-tractor station in Belgorod oblast. He soon became director of a machine-tractor station and then at the age of twenty-seven was named chairman of the executive committee of the raion soviet. At twenty-nine he was selected as the first secretary of the raion party committee and within a few years first deputy chairman of the executive

Table 37 *Characteristics of first secretaries in oblasts of different levels of urbanization, 1974*

| | | | PERCENT OF FIRST SECRETARIES WHO HAD | | |
PERCENT OF URBAN POPULATION	ENGINEERING OR ECONOMICS DEGREE[a]	AGRICULTURAL COLLEGE DEGREE[a]	AT LEAST 5 YEARS IN TECHNICAL-MANAGERIAL WORK IN INDUSTRY	AT LEAST 10 YEARS CONTINUOUS WORK IN PARTY APPARATUS PRIOR TO BECOMING FIRST SECRETARY	BEEN A KOMSOMOL OFFICIAL
70–90 (N = 35)	80	3	66	54	17
50–69 (N = 49)	31	37	16	39	41
40–49 (N = 29)	7	52	3	38	38
16–39 (N = 33)	6	39	6	36	36

Source: Calculated from the biographies in *Deputaty Verkhovnogo Soveta SSSR Deviatogo Sozyva* (Moscow, Izdatel'stvo "Izvestiia Sovetov Deputatov Trudiashchikhsia SSSR," 1974). The biographies of two first secretaries who died before the publication of this book are also included in the calculation.

a Only three economics degrees are included in the engineering or economics degree category. A few men with degrees in mechanization of agriculture are included within the agriculture category.

498

committee of the Belgorod oblast soviet (surely the deputy chairman for agriculture). At the age of thirty-three he became secretary of the Belgorod oblast party committee (the secretary for agriculture). His next position was chairman of the executive committee of the Belgorod soviet, and in 1971 he was promoted to the first secretaryship of the oblast party committee.[38]

The major problem that the Soviet leadership faces in the selection of oblast first secretaries is that a decreasing number of oblasts are either purely industrial or agricultural in nature. Particularly in the Russian Republic, almost all the populous oblasts that were important suppliers of agricultural products have become industrial centers as well. It was this fact that led Khrushchev to his ill-fated attempt to create independent industrial and rural oblast party organizations in 1962.[39] Sometimes in such oblasts the regime now alternates the preparation of the leader in a change of first secretary, perhaps in the hope that imbalances might be corrected a bit. (Thus, the previous first secretary in Rostov oblast was a plant manager and chairman of a sovnarkhoz, while the present one is a former director of an experimental farm.)[40] Much more frequently, the leadership tries to select persons of different backgrounds for the foremost leadership posts in a locality, thereby maximizing the range of expertise within the inner leadership core.

Far less information is available about the background of party secretaries at lower levels, but what is available suggests that these officials too have a preparation that often is very appropriate for the economies they supervise. The first secretaries of the city party committees in the Russian Republic overwhelmingly have been engineers, and at least early in the Brezhnev period over two-thirds of those who were Supreme Soviet deputies had at least ten years experience in professional-managerial posts in industrial plants, construction, transportation, or higher administrative posts in these realms. The information on post-1966 appointments is too sketchy for any analysis, but it provides no evidence of any drastic change.

In the non-Russian republics, the percentage of city first secretaries who were engineers was much smaller in the past, but it has been growing steadily in recent years (see table 38). Nevertheless, the proportion with long experience in industrial administration remains much lower than in the RSFSR, and the proportion with experience in Komsomol or other "ideological" work is much higher. (Of the Supreme Soviet deputies selected first secretary of non-Russian cities from 1966 through 1974, 52 percent had been Komsomol officials, and another 13 percent had engaged in editorial or educational work.) In the non-Russian areas, sensitivity to the nationality factor and an ability to take it into account without losing political control are crucial needs, and engineers with industrial experience may not have had the best preparation to develop these skills.

Table 38　*Background of first secretaries of
city party committees, 1966, 1970, 1974*

	PERCENT OF FIRST SECRETARIES WHO		
LOCALE OF CITIES	HAD AN ENGINEERING EDUCATION	WORKED AT LEAST 5 YEARS IN INDUSTRY[a]	WORKED AT LEAST 10 YEARS IN INDUSTRY[a]
1966—RSFSR (N = 16)	87	75	69
RSFSR: First appointed after 1966 (N = 7)	86	71	73
1966—Other republics (N = 27)	48	37	30
1970—Other republics (N = 23)	56	35	22
1974—Other republics (N = 17)	76	53	35

Source: *Deputaty Verkhovnogo Soveta SSSR*, published in Moscow by Izdatel'stvo "Izvestiia Deputatov Trudiashchikhsia" after the 1966, 1970, and 1974 elections to the Supreme Soviet. Nearly all of the first secretaries lead party committees in cities with 100,000 population or more. Except in RSFSR after 1966 (where the numbers are too small), the figures refer to persons in the post at that time.

a Industry is shorthand for industry, construction, transportation, and geology.

Information on the rural raion party secretaries is even more sketchy, but fifty-five of the Supreme Soviet deputies of 1966, 1970, or 1974 had held this post sometime in the period after 1965. We should be very careful in our generalizations from this data, for almost 90 percent of the group worked in the autonomous republics or in union republics other than the RSFSR or the Ukraine. Nevertheless, two facts about the group are noticeable. First, the vast majority of the raion secretaries throughout the period have risen through soviet and party work in the rural raions. Second, the younger secretaries have a very different education and career pattern than the older ones. Of the thirty-one secretaries born before 1927, only 19 percent had an administrative job directly in agriculture at the level of kolkhoz chairman or above, and only 11 percent had an agricultural college degree; of the twenty-five secretaries born in 1927 or later, 68 percent had an agricultural degree and

52 percent had been in an agricultural post at the level of kolkhoz chairman or above.[41]

The Relationship of Party and Government at the Subnational Level

The basic governmental and party institutions at the subnational level are structured along much the same lines as those in the center, and the basic relationships among these institutions are also rather similar. The local party organs have been instructed to obtain supremacy in the soviets, and this has meant, first of all, that they should ensure that persons elected to the local soviets are always members or supporters of the party. Only one candidate is permitted in each electoral district, and the local party organs keep a tight control over the nomination process. Nominations to soviets at the lowest levels may sometimes involve spontaneity and local initiative, for often the problem here—as in the West—is finding someone who will carry out civic duties energetically rather than choosing among good alternatives. But the local party organs still have the crucial role in organizing the consultation on candidates and in confirming the final choices.

As in the center, the role of the local party organs goes well beyond ensuring the placement of reliable Communists in the governmental organs. The first secretary of the party committee is the top political figure in the locality instead of the chairman of the executive committee of the soviet, and the most important policy decisions within the locality are made within the bureau of the local party organs rather than within the executive committee of the soviet. The decisions of the party conference, committee, and bureau are binding on all other institutions within the locality. In fact, Soviet newspapers clearly indicate that these decisions can determine who will be the top "elected" officials of the soviet, for they casually report that some party organ "fired" or "freed" the chairman of the executive committee of a soviet from his position.[42]

The local party organ is supposed to "work through" the soviets—that is, its decisions are normally supposed to be incorporated in soviet decisions if the question is within the latter's competency—and the formalities are usually observed, although not always with all due haste. For example, I. T. Frolkin had been referred to as first deputy chairman of the executive committee of the Kaluga oblast soviet in the local press from the beginning of 1975 and had been elected a candidate member of the bureau of the oblast party committee (an event appropriate to his new post), but his formal election as first deputy chairman did not occur until the oblast soviet session of March 27, 1975.[43]

Although local party organs are clearly superior to the soviets (and other institutions as well) within their locality, the relationship between specific party and governmental officials is as complex as it is at the national level. Policymaking power is formally vested in the party committee and party bureau, and these bodies include governmental officials as well as party officials among their members. Except in the case of the Ukrainian Politburo, all the party secretaries at the local level are always elected to the bureau, and they are usually joined by enough lower party officials to give the party apparatus a majority on the bureau. Nevertheless, 43 percent of the voting members of the bureaus of the republican central committees in 1976 worked outside the party apparatus, as did 67 percent of the candidate members (see table 39).

Information on the membership of the bureau of lower party organs is more scattered, but in twelve krais and autonomous republics in the RSFSR in the summer of 1977 the proportion of bureau voting members who worked outside the party apparatus also stood at 43 percent.[44] The bureaus at this level seldom contain a military officer, but nearly all contained the chairman and first deputy chairman of the executive committee of the soviet (or Council of Ministers), the chairman of the trade union council, and the chairman of the KGB as full members, and half contained the chairman of the People's Control Committee. When the bureau is expanded from eleven to thirteen or fifteen, a worker is often added as full member or, even more likely, an industrial or construction official.[45] It rarely was the case in these twelve bureaus, but the editor of the regional newspaper is often a full or candidate member.[46]

The relatively few available examples of city party committees (unfortunately, only two more recent than 1966) suggest a higher percentage of full-time party officials among the full members: the city party secretaries, the head of the organizational-party work department, a borough party secretary or two, and a party secretary either from the military or a local industrial plant. Here too the chairman of the executive committee of the city soviet is always a bureau member, as usually also is the chairman of the people's control committee and one or two other officials from outside the party apparatus (most often, a factory manager, but in Erevan in 1976 the director of a scientific institute).[47] In the Brezhnev era the proportion of bureaus which included a worker among their members increased steadily, and by 1977 all bureaus of city and urban raion committees were said to do so, a development that may reduce the percentage of party officials.[48] In one bureau of a rural raion party committee, the seven full members included the three party secretaries, the chairman of the executive committee of the soviet, the head of the agriculture administration, the chairman of the People's Control Committee, and the chairman of a collective farm.[49]

Table 39 *Occupations of party bureau members
of republican Central Committees, 1976*

OCCUPATION	FULL MEMBERS	CANDIDATE MEMBERS
Central Committee secretary	70	2
Chairman, Council of Ministers	14	0
Chairman, Presidium of Supreme Soviet	14	0
First secretary, capital city or oblast party committee	14	2
First deputy chairman, Council of Ministers	13	3
Chairman, People's Control Committee	8	3
Military officer[a]	7	1
Chairman, Trade Union Council	5	8
Chairman, State Security Committee (KGB)	5	7
First secretary, other city or oblast party committees	3	5
Head of organizational-party work department, central committee	2	9
Deputy chairman, Council of Ministers	1	3
First secretary, republican Komsomol	0	5
Deputy chaiman, Presidium of Supreme Soviet	0	1
Minister of agriculture	0	1
Chairman of executive committee of city soviet	0	1
Rector, agricultural academy	0	1
Director, factory	0	1
Chairman, Collective Farm Council[b]	0	1
Total for the 14 republics	156	54

Source: The names of the bureau members were published after the conclusion of the republican party congresses in January–February 1976 and also were given in the Yearbook of the *Bol'shaia sovetskaia entsiklopediia*. Their occupations were obtained by purusing the republican newspapers both prior to and following the congress.

a Includes one officer of the border guards, which actually are subordinated to the KGB.

b In Moldavia, the Collective Farm Council has replaced the Ministry of Agriculture as the major agency supervising agriculture—an officially approved experiment. The chairman of this Moldavian Council was elected a candidate member of the bureau, and he really is the equivalent of a republican minister of agriculture.

In addition to bureau membership, there is much other evidence that the role of the top governmental officials is far more than that of a meaningless rubber stamp. In 1974, 34 percent of the oblast party first secretaries had once been chairman of the executive committee of an oblast soviet (84 percent of them immediately before first becoming oblast first secretary), and this surely implies that the post entails sufficient responsibility to help prepare a man for the top party job in the oblast.[50] In his study of Smolensk during the 1930s, Merle Fainsod concluded that the oblast party first secretary, the second secretary, and the chairman of the executive committee of the soviet constituted a collective Big Three, and that seems to be the case today.[51] In fact, biographical information indicates that the chairman of the executive committee usually is number two in the trio, and the second secretary number three.[52]

The specialized posts in the local government and party apparatus interlock in status—and presumably influence—in the same way as positions in the USSR ministries and Central Committee departments. In fact, the relative status of the analogous positions seems almost identical. For instance, in the realm of agriculture at the oblast level (where we have a large number of biographies of officials on the rise) it is clear that the secretary for agriculture ranks above the deputy chairman of the executive committee of the oblast soviet for agriculture (but not much above him if the latter has the status of first deputy chairman). The deputy chairman is, of course, superior to his direct subordinate, the head of the agriculture administration of the soviet, but both of these officials have a higher standing than the head of the agriculture department of the oblast party committee.

Similar relationships among secretary, deputy chairman of the executive committee of the soviet, head of administration, and head of department of the party committee seem normal in other policy areas at other territorial levels as well, although sometimes the department head of the party committee may rank a little higher. For example, the head of an industrial-transportation department of the party committee, who supervises all industry—including heavy industry—is a more important official than a soviet official who supervises a single branch of light industry. The same is true of the head of the propaganda and agitation department of party committees with a small number of departments, for he too then has responsibility for a range of activities in the ideological sphere.

The subtleties in the relationships among party and governmental officials at the local level extend well beyond the generalizations just made. Individual personality and expertise must always be a factor in individual influence in political and administrative life throughout the world, but in the Soviet Union this factor must be particularly important because of the regime's strong disposition to combine persons of differing backgrounds in positions of overlapping responsibility. As a result, there is a strong likelihood of some division of authority on the basis of expertise.

Our biographical data on this point are best for the republican level and for members of the Big Three, and the manner in which different specialties can be combined is especially easy to document in this case. Thus, in the Ukraine in 1974 the first secretary and the chairman of the council of ministers were engineers out of the metallurgy and machinery industries, respectively, while the second secretary was an agronomist with great experience in the supervision of agriculture. In Uzbekistan the first secretary had had a career in ideological and editorial work, the second secretary was an engineer with a background in industry and urban party work, and the chairman of the council of ministers was a former agricultural specialist. In Tadzhikistan the first secretary was an agricultural specialist with expertise in cotton growing (in fact, he had once been a USSR Deputy Minister of Agriculture), the chairman of the council of ministers also had an agricultural background with specialization in the mechanization of agriculture, and the second secretary had made his career in industry and in government and party work in the major industrial center of Volgograd. In Kazakhstan, the first secretary was a former head of an ore mining administration, while the second secretary and the chairman of the council of ministers were agricultural specialists (in fact, the second secretary was to become the USSR Minister of Agriculture in 1976). In all these instances, the first secretary was the top authority in the republic—and in the Ukraine, Kazakhstan, and Uzbekistan was even a full or candidate member of the national party Politburo—but the normal "party-state relationship" in industrial and agricultural decision-making must have varied with the background of the key officials in the different republics.[53] A first secretary who is an engineer normally must delegate a good deal of authority on agricultural questions to another member of the Big Three who is an agricultural specialist, and the same must be true of an agronomist first secretary on industrial questions.

Still another factor—indeed, probably the major factor—that complicates the relationship between the governmental and party officials at the subnational levels is the complex system of subordination within which all these officials work. Party theory may speak about local party dominance of the soviets, but the various departments and administrative offices of the latter institutions are also responsible to ministerial lines of command. If a ministry, working under Central Committee and Council of Ministers directives, issues a decree to its local units, the principle of a centralized party would be destroyed if the various local party organs were permitted to institute their own policies and impose them on the local administrators. Even when the local party organs find that a decision would be possible within existing directives, any significant project or program usually requires financial support and investment, and such funds almost always require ministerial approval. A local administrator who disapproves of local party pressure can easily inform his governmental superiors about his reservations.

In addition to dual subordination within the administrative hierarchy, there is also multiple subordination of officials to different local party organs. A factory or a school in a large city may be subject to the directives of a borough party committee, a city party committee, an oblast party committee, and (except in the RSFSR) a republican central committee, and a lower party committee obviously cannot issue a directive to an institution that contradicts the directive of a higher party organ. The situation becomes especially complex because of the system of party nomenklatura. If the director of a factory is in the nomenklatura of the city party committee and the factory chief engineer is in the nomenklatura of the borough party committee, a borough party committee would surely feel constrained in trying to remove a chief engineer who had the confidence of a director who had the confidence of the city party committee.

Finally, of course, the responsibility of the local party organs for the performance of their region tends to make the party officials dependent upon local administrators who can achieve plan fulfillment and who have good enough relations with their ministerial superiors to obtain necessary appropriations. The more an administrator has enough importance to warrant the attention of the top political authorities in an area, the more the political authorities are likely to want to defer to him and to assist him if he is producing results.

The tendency of the local party organs to be dependent upon local administrators is apt to be particularly great in their relationships with the managers of the major heavy industry plants. Not only is the industrial plan an especially important one for a region but the industrial ministries are the source of much of the money for the construction of local housing and service enterprises as well. Moreover, the major industrial plants can be called upon to provide "patronage" (assistance) to other institutions out of their above-plan surplus: equipment for the school or the children's camp or a crew of men to conduct repair work at them, a new barn or a few spare parts for a collective farm, a temporary assignment of workers (even as many as several hundred) to help bring in the harvest or complete a new construction project, a contribution to some city improvement program, and so forth. A Soviet writer expressed the point well when he had a plant manager in his novel reassure his wife about his poor relations with the local raion party first secretary. "He is afraid to fight [me], for he would not be able to take me. His raion is a poor one . . . All its economic base is in [my] hands."[54]

Indeed, one American scholar has concluded that in many Soviet cities—especially in the type of one-industry town that is so prevalent among new Soviet industrial centers—the power of the industrial manager is so great that we should speak of a "company town."[55] This phrase fails to convey the great final authority of the city's party first secretary and the role the city party organ plays in trying to ensure that the plant does provide services to its town, but it still does have a great deal of validity. With the first secretary usually an engineer having managerial experience (and in a one-industry town, surely managerial experience in the major plant), the decisions of the city party organizations are likely to be very responsive to industrial values.

As the local party organs work within the framework of higher directives and plans, as they find themselves dependent upon the various ministries for appropriations and upon their major subordinates for the performance of the area, what, if anything, do they do that warrants their being called the "leading organ" in the region and their first secretary being called a "prefect"?

In the first place, the first secretary and the bureau remain the final authority within their area. There are questions that are decided at each territorial level, and at times the possession of formal authority can be the crucial factor. The role of the local party organs seems particularly great in personnel selection. Except for positions in the party apparatus, posts in the nomenklatura of the party organs are simultaneously in the nomenklatura of another institution, and in these cases the formal right of the party organ is simply one of "confirmation." Nevertheless, a number of interviewed officials insist that the party organs more often are the supervisor with the initiative and the dominant role in personnel selection.

The ministries with units subordinate to the soviets apparently have only a minor role in the selection of their leaders. The first deputy minister of education of the Russian Republic insisted in a 1976 interview that his ministry does not have a formal right of appointment or even confirmation for the heads of the oblast education departments, although they may be consulted informally. Undoubtedly, if the ministry were quite dissatisfied with the head of an oblast education department, it could force him out, for it scarcely is in the interest of local soviet and party officials to have specialized administrators who may have trouble obtaining funds from their "vertical" superiors. The latter can also appeal to the party officials at their level to override lower officials on a personnel question. However, in a field such as education in the RSFSR, career advancement for a local official almost never involves a move to a more important oblast and very seldom to a post in the republican ministry, and this must say a great deal about the relative influence of the ministry and the local political officials in personnel selection.

The role of the local party organs may also be especially great in certain policy areas. They almost surely have the final word in handling any disturbance with political overtones, and they must still have the responsibility of approving or disapproving actions taken by the KGB. Historically, the oblast and raion party committees have had a decisive role in dividing the area's agricultural procurement responsibilities among the subareas or (in the case of the raion party committee) among the farms, and, consequently, they have had a decisive role in determining what crops should be planted. Possibly this role has been declining as the economies of the oblasts and the raions become more complex, but it must still be substantial. One indication of this fact is the continued existence of territorial sections in the agriculture department of the Central Committee to supplement those handling branches of agriculture—a unique arrangement for departments overseeing substantive domestic policy areas.

In the second place, the independence of so many institutions from administrative supervision by local soviets creates a major problem of coordination at the local level. When the directives and regulations of different local administrators come into conflict—and they must as institutional interests become embodied in them—the problem of finding a solution can become great. The normal answer to a nonnegotiable dispute within a bureaucracy is to refer it to the official who is the lowest common supervisor of the disputants. Yet, in any conflict in the Soviet Union involving a representative of an all-union ministry (for example, the director of a machinery plant or a railroad official), there is no common governmental superior short of a Deputy Chairman of the USSR Council of Ministers in Moscow. When the conflict involves trade union or Komsomol officials, no governmental leader at all has the authority to decide it unless it is legal in nature.

The most severe difficulties are found in supplies procurement. The annual plan usually contains the name of the supplier of specific important goods and the amount to be delivered, and it usually indicates the quarter of the year in which a specified quantity of each item should be delivered. Nevertheless, conflicts continuously arise among the recipients, for the timing of a delivery within a quarter or even a month can make a major difference. Such a "minor" decision as to whether to send a particular shipment of bricks to a local hospital construction project or to an industrial plant adding a new shop may determine the fulfillment or nonfulfillment of each's plan.[56]

In western economies, such conflicts about priority in the delivery of supplies or services often are solved by the market place—by an offer of extra payment or a threat to go elsewhere. In the Soviet Union, on the other hand, the financial indices of the plan are not the most important, and the threat to go to another supplier is an impossible one. While a recipient frequently can—and does—obtain faster delivery by agreeing to accept an item of slightly different type or lower quality that the supplier has in stock or can produce with less effort or cost, there is little possibility of extra payment other than an illegal bribe. To resolve such minor conflicts by referring them to a common superior in the Council of Ministers is unthinkable on any but the rarest occasion.

In practice, the local party organs have been given the job of serving as the local "common superior" when the regulations and instructions to officials of different ministries come into conflict or when disputes about priorities in deliveries cannot be resolved by negotiation or compromise. Responsible for the economic performance of the area as a whole and for all institutions within it, the local party organs are ideally placed to judge the relative priority to be given different institutions and projects. Endowed with the authority of the party and subject to removal by the central party organs, they are the natural institution to judge which answer to a dispute would best correspond to the wishes of the party leadership.

If a conflict is a long-term and fundamental one or if it requires substantial appropriations, the ministries become involved and the local party organs are but one of the participants in the negotiations. Moreover, even a local party decision on a less fundamental dispute can be appealed to a higher party organ. However, the number of short-term problems flowing to the local party organs is large, and the administrative system simply could not function if a large proportion of local party decisions were being appealed. As a consequence, the actual authority of the local party organs must be great in these cases. Their power is limited more by fear of the consequences of a bad decision (for example, plan nonfulfillment by a major enterprise or major ministerial dissatisfaction at the violation of a directive) than by direct restrictions.

Indeed, in one situation the coordinating power of the local party organs has been informally institutionalized. The conflicts among institutions are especially severe in construction, both because of an excessive amount of construction in relation to resources and because of the multiple subordination of different construction trusts, subcontractors, and suppliers. If a construction project is a significant one, the normal answer to this problem is the creation of a special staff (*shtab*) for the project to coordinate the activities of the organizations involved. Each of these staffs is headed by an official of the local party organ, and it directs the scheduling of activities in a detailed manner.[57]

The coordinating role of the local party organs has several important implications for the nature of the party-state relationship in the localities and for the nature of the party apparatus itself. The scale of party activities in industry and economic development is so large that the local party organs may spend a large proportion of their time on them, and the soviets may be left with more leeway in other policy realms under their supervision than we have assumed. In addition, to the extent that this responsibility leads to the recruitment of engineers with managerial experience into party work, it tends to enforce the dedication to industrialization that long has been a feature of the Soviet Union. In 1976, 46 percent of the delegates to the Twenty-Fifth Party Congress were elected from oblasts and small republics that in 1974 were headed by first secretaries with technical and/or managerial experience in industry, construction, or transportation, and another 3 percent came from oblasts headed by engineers without such experience.[58] Few changes in first secretary had occurred between 1974 and 1976, and there is no indication that they affected these statistics in any significant way.

The nature of the party organs' work makes it quite impossible for local party officials to be unbending ideologues intent upon enforcing the letter of central decrees. If the party officials are to be successful, they must have a keen sense of how and when to bend the rules, and surely they create far fewer grievances if they learn to bargain out conflicts instead of relying on fiat. With oblast first secretaries the major sources of recruitment for the central leadership, the habits and skills developed by the successful officials at this level have a significance far beyond the functioning of the administrative system.

The Patterns within Subnational Politics

The importance of the nationality issue obviously makes republican politics very different from the politics of a city or rural raion in the Russian republic. The politics of a national capital such as Moscow must be different from those of a one-industry city. The politics of Central Asia, where people of the local nationality have a relatively low level of education on the average, are different from the politics of Armenia and Georgia, where the education levels are much higher.[59]

Nevertheless, a few generalizations can be made about the political process at the local level. The first is that much of the politics in all the subnational territorial units involves the petitioning for funds from above. Standard operating funds (such as teachers' salaries) are often distributed by formula, but new projects of any significance must be financed on an individual basis by the relevant ministry. As a consequence, a significant part of the activity of the major local officials consists of attempts to obtain more money or supplies for local administrators.

Many of the appeals for funds appear in the press or in speeches to the Supreme Soviet, the party congress, the Central Committee, or other conferences, but this activity is only the visible shadow of a much larger behind-the-scenes effort. Indeed, sometimes when Soviet scholars explain the division of responsibility among different specialized officials in a locality, they do so in terms of who it is that handles negotiations with different higher officials. The head of an oblast administrative department, it is said, usually makes the case to the republican ministry, the deputy chairman of the executive committee of the oblast soviet usually deals with Gosplan, and the specialized party secretary may make an appeal to specialized higher party officials. The head of a department of a local party organ may spend a great deal of time corresponding with other regions to try to speed up supplies deliveries (and, of course, responding to such appeals from other areas).[60]

The practice of allocating money from above to individual projects must have further implications for the local political process. If the regime made a block grant to each soviet (or gave them an independent tax source), then the top local officials would have to choose how to divide it, and the various administrators would become competitors with each other in pushing their project. With local administrators being forced to appeal to their ministerial superiors, they compete more with their counterparts in other regions than with their colleagues. The top local officials can support nearly all of their subordinates, at least at this initial stage of the appropriations process. As a consequence, the alignments that arise in this aspect of the budgetary process resemble those found in American competition for defense industry contracts. All local officials—including those of the local party organs—are likely to unite behind the local administrator seeking investment funds, supplies, a more favorable price for its product, or an easier plan.

The competition for funds in the appropriations process usually is a micropolitical affair: it often centers on individual projects or even small additional amounts of money and supplies, and it frequently involves individual plants, administrative departments, soviets, and local party organs. However, there is also a competition for funds that has a broader policy content. When Ukrainian officials support the development of Ukrainian coal and Russian Republic officials push investment in the Tiumen oil fields in Siberia, the struggle transcends mere bureaucratic politics to become an important political issue. The same was true of the conflict over investment for the opening of the "virgin lands" in the east versus reclamation work in the western regions, and it is also true of the developing battle over the investment implications of the growing urban population in Central Asia.[61]

A second generalization that can be made with complete assurance is that the concrete indicators of social services show enormous variation from republic to republic, from oblast to oblast, and from city to city, both in the level of services and in the rate of their growth. For example, the proportion of children in the RSFSR up to age six who were enrolled in day-care institutions in 1970 ranged from 10 percent in the Dagestan autonomous republic to 70 percent in the Komi autonomous republic, and the number of hospital beds per 10,000 population ranged from 78 in the Dagestan autonomous republic to 145 in Kemerovo oblast and 165 in Magadan oblast. From 1965 to 1973, the number of hospital beds increased by 2 beds per 10,000 population in Kaliningrad oblast, but by 45 beds per 10,000 population in Kurgan oblast, with the increase in the other RSFSR oblasts between these two extremes.[62] The increase in the number of square meters of housing per capita in the oblast capitals in the Russian Republic from 1962 to 1970 ranged from 4 percent at one extreme to 53 percent at the other.[63]

Some of the variation in social service indicators is associated with factors that are officially built into national policy (for example, more hospital beds and day-care centers in urban areas), and some of the variation in growth in services is associated with different rates of urbanization or with a central desire to equalize services somewhat. Much of the variation, however, is of a more random nature, and in the case of hospital beds at least it was considerably more random in the early 1970s than it was in the early 1960s.[64] The only reasonable explanation for these random differences is that they are produced by something in the local political scene.

We really do not have the information to determine the factors that lead to major regional differences in outcome. In the case of the hospital beds, performance proved to better, on the average, in oblasts in which health was discussed in the soviet and in oblasts in which there had been a change in party first secretary, chairman of the executive committee of the soviet, and/or head of the health department. In the case of the day-care centers, performance was better, on the average, in oblasts in which a higher proportion of the speakers in the soviet sessions were women. These "political factors" are simply ones on which information was available, and they likely are not the most important at work. Yet, they are suggestive of the type of local political influences that have a much greater impact in the Soviet political system than assumed in our images of a totally centralized system.

If we could engage in a detailed case study of a local government in the Soviet Union, it is highly probable that we would arrive at many of the same conclusions that Robert Dahl did in his study of New Haven.[65] To a considerable extent, an active and skilled local political leader may well have a major impact, especially in initiating and coordinating the effort to bring together various outside funds and local interests to launch some project. Normally, however, the decision-making process is likely to be rather specialized and compartmentalized, and the greatest influence is likely to be exercised by those most directly involved in a policy area. Citizens (especially those in the professional and managerial strata) who take a special interest in a subject and who are willing to work in the relevant committees and councils have a real possibility of affecting the outcome. None of these hypotheses is meant to imply that the fate of a Soviet republic, oblast, or city is wholly in the hands of the local leaders or citizenry, but that is a universal in modern society.[66]

The third generalization to make about the political process at the subnational level is that it also features a politics concerning the degree of autonomy to be permitted each level. At one extreme, this type of politics involves a continuous marginal conflict about the amount of money local agencies can spend without approval, about the amount that they can shift from one section of the budget to another on their own, about the number of personnel that can be appointed or fired without higher approval, about the degree to which ministries should establish fixed formulae for the providing of services, and so forth. At the other extreme, this politics can involve such major steps as Khrushchev's creation of the sovnarkhozs and the expansion of the authority of the republics in industrial planning and management, or dissident agitation for a fundamental change in the independence of the republic.

Certain types of struggle for greater autonomy or centralization seem particularly important in the last decade. For example, the struggle over economic reform has centered more on the relative autonomy to be given the industrial plant managers in investment and pricing decisions than on the authority of local political authorities. Nevertheless, radical economic reform would have implications for the subnational political process. It should reduce the number of supply conflicts which the local party organs have to solve, but, on the other hand, the devolution of investment decisions to the plant level should increase the impact of the local party organs upon them—at least so long as the powers of the local party organs were not redefined in a major way. Moreover, any economic reform that entailed the use of market mechanisms rather than direct administrative control in the operation of agriculture would, of course, drastically change the role of the agricultural officials both of the soviets and the local party organs.

Another major dispute about local autonomy—and clearly the most vocal one involving the local governmental institutions directly—centers on the use of the industrial ministries as a conduit for funds for the construction of much of the country's urban housing and communal services. At least since the mid-1950s, the major newspaper and magazine of the Presidium of the Supreme Soviet (*Izvestiia* and *Sovety Deputatov Trudiashchikhsia*) have carried countless articles complaining about the Balkanization of the city that occurs when each major plant provides housing and services to its own workers in its own district.[67] Effective city planning and equity in the distribution of services are said to be extremely difficult to achieve in these circumstances.

(The soviet finds it difficult to control an enterprise which has the purse strings in its hands, and the latter may, in practice, dictate the location of its new construction and provide its workers with better housing and services than other city residents receive.) Local soviet officials have continuously demanded that all housing and "social" funds be allocated to them directly so that they can use them according to a comprehensive plan and distribute them equitably among all residents.

In 1958 and 1967 the Central Committee and the Council of Ministers issued decrees—very similar decrees, in fact—which supported the principle of comprehensive soviet control of all housing and services in the city, but which called for gradualism and included many ambiguous and even contradictory clauses.[68] Although the Soviet press of the mid-1970s contains many of the same complaints that appeared in the 1950s and 1960s, it does seem that some change has occurred: the soviet must approve any new land use and apparently often now does so with more bite; those enterprises with small appropriations for housing construction now usually turn them over to the soviet in return for the appropriate number of flats in the new apartment house instead of building their own house over a long period of time; new coordinating institutions (notably the "directors' council") have been established under local party leadership to pool and coordinate expenditures. But the calls for more radical change continue, and the issue is far from settled.

Still another major dispute involving local autonomy—that on the autonomy of the republics—is surely the most important in the Soviet Union, and for that reason it is subject to the greatest restrictions in the Soviet press. In the modern world a country's most serious political problems often flow from the presence of ethnic minorities, especially minorities that have a distinct language and sufficient size and geographic concentration to make secession a thinkable alternative. The problems often come to a head when a significant number of the members of the minority acquire enough education to feel entitled to top jobs held by the dominant ethnic group—and when they acquire enough education to organize effectively.[69] Merely on the basis of worldwide experience, one would expect the Soviet Union—regardless of the nature of its political system or the policies it follows—to face this problem in particularly severe form because of the multiplicity of its minorities.

Aside from any struggle for autonomy, the nationality question is an implicit part of any political conflict involving republics. For example, any investment proposal regarding a republic implicitly raises an issue of equity among the republics, and sometimes spokesmen for projects raise it quite explicitly. An official speaking in the Supreme Soviet asserts that the practice of financing the construction of higher educational institutions through industrial ministries could lead to inequities for some republics. Central Asian economists attack the propriety of shipping Central Asian cotton to textile plants in central Russia rather than developing more such plants in Central Asia.[70] A scholar in Moscow contends that it is unfair that the RSFSR is the only republic not to have its own republican Academy of Sciences,[71] and, in doing so, he reflects a widely held (but not widely expressed in print) opinion among Russians that too high a proportion of investment is made in the borderlands.

The nationality struggles that go on behind the scene are far more difficult to discern, but they cover many concerns. Some dissidents propose virtual independence for their republics, while Brezhnev asserted that the discussion on the new constitution included the suggestion that the union republics be abolished altogether.[72] Other than the investment questions, the most important "normal" conflicts relate to language use and to the hiring of members of the local nationality. The great nationality scandal of the Khrushchev era rose precisely from this problem, for a number of high Latvian officials opposed further expansion of Latvian heavy industry on the grounds it would require the importation of Russian workers and lead to the further dilution of the proportion of Latvians in the republic.[73] This particular movement was ended by a purge of the top officials, but the issue does not die. In Armenia a local citizen reported that the Erevan subway was being built in the early 1970s with imported Russian workers, but that they were being housed in a tent city so that they would not be tempted to stay after the subway was finished. In Central Asia the concern about the growing educated urban population can lead, another Soviet citizen reports, to the thought that too many local jobs are held by outsiders.

The cutting edge of the nationality issue at the present time seems to be the language to be used in work and study. A multilingual state such as the Soviet Union obviously needs a common language of discourse, for, even leaving aside the Russians, nationalities such as the Estonians, Latvians, and Lithuanians cannot communicate among themselves unless one of their languages or an outside one is taught in the schools of each. Russian certainly is a natural lingua franca for that area of the world, but the crucial question is whether Russian is simply the language for conversing with outsiders or whether it is the major language of work and study for everyone—or at least everyone in the professional and managerial strata—in the republic.

As the politics of Quebec demonstrates, the "working language" issue can be explosive. It not only is a natural symbolic issue but also is closely associated with the issue of upward mobility and preference in hiring. If engineering, science, as well as other subjects are taught in Russian in a republic's elite universities and institutes, then those raised in Russian-speaking homes are going to have a natural advantage. If the instruction is in the native language, Russians will be at a major disadvantage—if they can understand at all. The same is true for the language used within the bureaucracy and in business committee meetings. Obviously the top republican officials who deal with Moscow and other republics need an excellent knowledge of Russian, and those in industry have a particular need to be able to read directives and communications. Nevertheless, a person who has a native's understanding of the language used in business meetings is going to have an advantage over a person who is unsure whether he has caught every subtlety, and this factor may well be reflected in hiring and promotion policies.

The Soviet regime consistently has followed several policies with respect to language. It has given parents the option of sending their children to elementary and high schools with instruction either in Russian or in the native language. (In the latter schools the students take Russian as one of their subjects—as a foreign language, so to speak.) Both Russian and the local language are recognized as official languages of communication in each republic, but if committees include Russians who do not know the local language, the committees' working language will by necessity be Russian. In at least one case—the bureau of the republican party central committee—the regime follows an appointment policy that ensures that this will be the case. At least one of the bureau members is a Russian sent from outside the republic and rotated back to the Russian Republic before having a chance to become too assimilated.[74] In the vast majority of the cases in the last fifteen years, this man has been the Central Committee second secretary, but the KGB chairman, a top military officer, or another official can also serve this function.

The provision of school instruction in the local language and the requirement of the use of Russian as a working language in the bureaus of the republican central committee are but two very basic principles for a language policy in a multilingual country. They leave a great many issues unresolved. It appears—but is by no means certain—that the central issues in the Soviet Union in recent years have arisen in the education realm. What is the language of instruction at the college level where specialized classes may not have sufficient students to make parallel courses conducted in separate languages an economical solution? Should students in the Russian-language elementary and secondary schools be required to take instruction in the native language?

The significance of these two issues goes far beyond the students being taught. If Russian parents believe that their children will not be able to enter local institutes because of the language of instruction, many will be inclined to move to areas where this problem does not exist. The requirement that Russian children take courses in the local language may not be so burdensome to those who have long made a home in the republic and plan to remain, but it can be a powerful disincentive for those who might want a temporary job in the republic or who might want to move there after their children are already in school.

In the late Stalin period, both of these questions seemed to be answered in favor of the Russians. Apparently the language of instruction in the major institutes and universities in the non-Russian republics was usually, perhaps always, Russian, while the Russian children going to Russian-language schools in, say, Turkmenia did not have to learn the Turkmen language. In the late 1950s the regime seems to have given the republics more leeway in requiring courses in the local language,[75] but in the tightening of controls over the republics in 1959, it explicitly damned (and removed) the party first secretary in Azerbaidzhan who did require Russian children to take Azerbaidzhani.[76] The course of developments in the Brezhnev era in this respect is unclear, but there are pieces of evidence—notably referring to the republic of Armenia—which suggest increasing reliance upon and insistence upon the local language.

American studies of the nationalities have tended to focus on individual republics and to be more concerned with demonstrating the fact of central control than with exploring variations in the precise degree of control and de facto autonomy. As a consequence, it is extremely risky to try to generalize about trends in this area, and it may well be that there is considerable difference from republic to republic. Certainly Armenia and Georgia appear far more dominated by persons of the local nationality than do a number of the Central Asian republics, and the degree of republican influence on the content of the policies they administer may vary in like manner.[77]

Although our knowledge about state and local politics in the Soviet Union is meager, we remain with the certain fact that the different statistical indicators of social services and standard of living show enormous variations from republic to republic, from oblast to oblast within a republic, and from city to city. It seems likely that there must also be at least some variations in policies that cannot be quantified. These variations must be associated with local political or individual influences of some type, and if we are sensitive to the need to explore them, the future may permit a such fuller understanding of this question.

14 | The Distribution of Power

T HE CRUCIAL QUESTION about Soviet political institutions concerns the way in which they function—particularly, the type of relationship that institutions develop among themselves and with the population. Such an analysis, unfortunately, is difficult and subtle, for formal rules and structures are not always an accurate indicator of the essential nature of a political system. American and British political institutions are very different in structure, but the observer has a sense that the underlying political systems are similar in nature; on the other hand, American institutions are very similar to those which have existed at various times in the Philippines and many Latin American countries, but the political systems are quite different. If we think of a political system in this broad sense, how do we conceptualize the Soviet system and the distribution of power within it?

It is difficult to describe any political system in terms of elite-mass relations, power relationships within the elite, and the degree of pluralism within the system. For this reason the effort to analyze the distribution of power in the Soviet Union has inevitably been marked by controversy, and generalizations of any nature arouse disagreement. Therefore, it seems appropriate to consider the major scholarly controversies concerning the Soviet political system as part of an effort to illuminate the problem of describing the Soviet System.

The Totalitarian "Model"

Scholars have always debated the nature of the Soviet political system, but in the early 1950s the vast majority of westerners at least agreed on how the system should be labeled. The Soviet system was called a totalitarian one, and the arguments concerned the way such a system should be defined and the nature of its inner dynamics. Despite variations and vagueness in definitions of the concept of totalitarianism, much of its essential meaning is expressed in the word itself: a totalitarian political system is one that seeks total control over society and the citizenry—and that achieves it to a considerable extent.

Probably the best-known and most widely accepted attempt to define a totalitarian system was made by Carl Friedrich and Zbigniew Brzezinski in their *Totalitarian Dictatorship and Autocracy*. The definition centers on institutional features.

1. An official ideology, consisting of an official body of doctrine covering all vital aspects of man's existence to which everyone living in that society is supposed to adhere, at least passively; this ideology is characteristically focussed and projected toward a perfect final state of mankind—that is to say, it contains a chiliastic claim, based upon a radical rejection of the existing society and conquest of the world for the new one.

2. A single mass party led typically by one man, the "dictator," and consisting of a relatively small percentage of the total population (up to 10 percent) of men and women, a hard core of them passionately and unquestioningly dedicated to the ideology and prepared to assist in every way in promoting its general acceptance; such a party being hierarchically, oligarchically organized and typically either superior to, or completely intertwined with, the bureaucratic government organization.

3. A system of terroristic police control, supporting but also supervising the party for its leaders, and characteristically directed not only against demonstrable "enemies" of the regime, but against arbitrarily selected classes of the population; the terror of the secret police systematically exploiting modern science, and more especially scientific psychology.

4. A technologically conditioned, near-complete monopoly of control, in the hands of the party and its subservient cadres, of all means of effective mass communication, such as the press, radio, and motion pictures.

5. A similarly technologically conditioned, near-complete monopoly of control (in the same hands) of the effective use of all weapons of armed combat.

6. A central control and direction of the entire economy through the bureaucratic coordination of its formerly independent corporate entities, typically including most other associations and group activities.[1]

While Friedrich and Brzezinski's definition is often treated as the best summary of the totalitarian model, its static and descriptive nature does not fully capture the dynamics that most scholars attributed to such a system. The cohesion of the model stemmed from its assumptions about the motivations of the totalitarian leaders—above all, from the assumption that the leaders were seeking total power either for its own sake or, more usually, as a means to transform man and society to conform with their ideological images of a perfect society.

> Unlike most dictatorships of the past and present, the totalitarian movements wielding power do not aim to freeze society in the status quo, but on the contrary institutionalize, or plan to, a revolution which mounts in scope, and frequently in intensity, as the regime stabilizes itself in power . . . Totalitarianism . . . subverts . . . direct restraints immediately after the seizure of power, but, unlike traditional dictatorships it proceeds, once entrenched, to pulverize all existing associations in society in order to remake that society and subsequently, even man himself, according to certain "ideal" conceptions. In time it even attempts, not always successfully, to overcome the natural restraints on political power. Without doing so, totalitarianism can never achieve the isolation of the individual and the mass monolithic homogeneity that are its aim. Only with both of them (the paradox between them is more apparent than real) can the existing pluralism be transformed, into an active unanimity of the entire population which will make the transformation of society, and ultimately man, possible.[2]

In a sense, the Friedrich-Brzezinski six-point definition specified the organizational requirements for the achievement of total control.

Yet, for all its popularity as a description of the Stalin era, the totalitarian model always had certain shortcomings. Even as a descriptive model, it had a basic contradiction at its core. The drive to transform society, to remake man, and to keep the administrators from becoming a privileged elite implies the continuing use of radical reformers against established authority. In practice, it requires the toleration of a consideration amount of disorder. The First Five-Year Plan period had this character, as did—so far as a nonspecialist can judge—the periodic cultural revolutions in China. The drive to achieve total political control, on the other hand, suggests restraints on the wild radicals, for such persons may well be disrespectful of all authority. This aspect of the model implies (or at least it did in the Soviet Union) the reestablishment of authority and authority figures, even many of a traditional nature. It suggests rigidity in structure rather than constant transformation.

The totalitarian model gained plausibility as a depiction of the Stalin regime because the policies of the First Five-Year Plan period could be cited as evidence of a determination to transform society while the rigid controls in the late Stalin period could be cited as evidence of the authoritarian features. In the process, however, the conservative nature of most of the Stalin period— the immobilism of the Stalin regime in the dictator's last years—was obscured from view.

As a predictive tool, the totalitarian model had other limitations. To state, for instance, that without overcoming restraints "totalitarianism can never achieve the isolation of the individual and the mass monolithic homogeneity that are its aim" was to treat totalitarianism as an actual entity with its own inner laws. In the process, it was easy to forget that the leaders were human beings with individual interests and values and easy to assume they would always act in accordance with the interests of the system or the party.

> Those in charge of the Soviet society have assumed that economic and social development in all its aspects can be purposefully steered by man in the direction of an ideal solution . . . To be less totalitarian [there would have to be] some degree of withdrawal on the part of those in charge from their commitment to total social and economic engineering . . . It is doubtful that as long as the party remains in power the tendency of the regime to stress unattainable goals will vanish. Indeed, it is these goals, inherent in the current ideology, which justify to the population the sacrifices which the party's domination involves. Thus, as long as the party continues to hold its successful grip on the instruments of power, we can expect it to continue stressing first the long-range goals of an ultimate utopia, and then the consequent sacrifices to achieve them, even though possibly at a diminishing rate of effort.[3]

In taking for granted that the leader would want to maximize his power and transform society, this analysis did not really explain why this would continue to be true, especially in the case of the leaders of postrevolutionary generations. Above all, the model failed to pinpoint the existence of a potential conflict between a leader's determination to transform society at all costs and his desire to maximize his power in the sense of making himself secure in his position. As Khrushchev was to discover, and perhaps as Stalin himself already realized, a policy of active transformation is certain to create powerful enemies. Why should it be assumed that future leaders would be motivated to take such risks?

In looking at the long-term dynamics of the system, the totalitarian model was especially weak in gliding over the implications of the succession. It was easy enough to imagine how Stalin could have developed an ability to terrorize the elite, for the elite might not have realized what was happening before it was too late. But why should the post-Stalin elite be expected to permit history to repeat itself when death removed the dictator from the scene? To an extent that was not realized, Stalin himself was the cornerstone in the structure he erected.

Finally, in both descriptive and predictive terms, the totalitarian model did not say enough about the policy process, for the scholars working within the tradition of the model primarily studied the techniques used by the leader to maintain power. This neglect of the policy process can be explained in several ways. Most important, no doubt, was the lack of information about policymaking in the Stalin period, but perhaps equally significant may have been an unconscious realization that the policy process cannot be very important when policy is so frozen.

Yet, as a long-range proposition, it clearly was unrealistic to suppose that a future dictator would not want information and advice on the best way to achieve policy goals, particularly on such complex matters as industrial growth. The emphasis upon overlapping governmental, party, police, and military hierarchies pointed in the right direction, but if the implications of the need for information had been explored more fully, there might have been more of a tendency to hypothesize a need for debates among specialists, policy research, and the diffusion of influence. Stalin's reluctance to engage in policy innovation may well have resulted from his instinctive understanding of its consequences, but at some point his successors were likely to become dissatisfied with the immobilism of the postwar period and be forced to face the political implications of innovation.

Western Models of the Post-Stalin Period

With the death of Stalin, fundamental changes occurred in the nature of the Soviet political system. Thus, four of the six points in Friedrich and Brzezinski's definition of a totalitarian system became less descriptive of the Soviet system: the ideology became less rigid and less optimistic about the perfectability of man; the dictator no longer dominated his subordinates in the way that Stalin had, and the party came to assume more of a mass character, at least among men past the age of Komsomol membership; the role of the secret police was sharply restricted, and arbitrary terror disappeared as citizens no longer had a reason to fear arrest without reason or warning; the centrally controlled means of communication became more open to iconoclastic ideas, and the partial raising of the Iron Curtain permitted even more unorthodox ideas to reach many citizens. In spheres not well covered by the definition, there was an opening-up of the policy process with a wider consideration of policy alternatives and a greater effort to achieve Marxist goals in social policy. Khrushchev in particular seemed infused with much of the

Great Leap Forward spirit of the First Five-Year Plan period—and, paradoxically, of the totalitarian model.

The Friedrich-Brzezinski definition continued to point to features of the Soviet political system that were significantly different from the political systems of the West. However, if the definition could be saved only by making it loose enough to cover both the Stalin and post-Stalin regimes, as well as the even less restrictive political systems in eastern Europe, it was inevitable that questions would be raised about its usefulness. Moreover, the failure of the totalitarian model to predict the direction of post-Stalin developments suggested that the model had failed to capture the driving mechanism of the system.

As dissatisfaction with the totalitarian model increased, a number of new models or conceptualizations were advanced as full or partial substitutes. One set of models—the "directed society models"—were published for the most part in the mid-1960s and incorporated much of the activism and commitment to change manifested by Khrushchev during his tenure as first secretary. The scholars proposing these models believed that many of the features of the totalitarian model continued to be relevant for an understanding of the post-Stalin system, but they sought to modify the model to take account of post-1953 changes. They retained the image of a society that was being directed by the political leaders and even incorporated it in the labels they used (for example, "administered society," "command society," "ideological system," "monist system," and so forth).[4] Yet, they saw movement in a more rational and less rigid direction as well as less reliance on terror. One article discussing "the administered society" was subtitled "totalitarianism without terror,"[5] and this phrase is not an unfair characterization of the essence of most of the directed society models.

A second group of models, which became most prominent in the post-Khrushchev period, generally treated the Soviet Union in much more conservative terms. The scholars developing these models contended that power in the Soviet Union is now exercised less by a single dictator than by a group of officials, and they labeled the Soviet Union an oligarchy, an elite dominated system. Like the directed society models, the elite models depicted a passive—or quiescent—society, tightly controlled from above, and there could be great overlap between the two models if the elite theorists spoke of a relatively narrow ruling elite that retained some sense of historical mission.

Nevertheless, most of those arguing for an elite model followed Trotsky and later Milovan Djilas in emphasizing a much broader ruling group, namely the bureaucracy. In this case, the motivation of the elite—and the purpose for which society was said to be dominated—was not ideologically inspired transformation but the preservation of privilege. Indeed, scholars speaking of oligarchical rule in the Soviet Union have frequently had such a jaundiced view of the Soviet bureaucracy that they have spoken of the political system as petrified or immobilized.

Two other groups of scholars—those calling themselves the "conflict school" and those associated with the interest group approach—were much more assertive in proclaiming their break with the totalitarian model. These schools contained persons with a wide range of views (in fact, in some cases far more traditional views than found among some of the scholars in the first two groups), but they were united in their dissatisfaction with the lack of attention to the policy process in the totalitarian model. They attacked the notion (most clearly found in the work of Hannah Arendt)[6] that the Soviet Union was an atomized society, and they denied that the party and the leaders were united in their policy views. The totalitarian model they attacked was sometimes a caricature of that found in the best scholarly literature, but it was a caricature that had already been created by many secondary observers who had been describing the Soviet Union as a totalitarian state.

Scholars employing the conflict and interest group approaches agreed that groups exist in the Soviet political system, that they initiate policy proposals, and that conflict among them is widespread. The two schools, however, emphasized different kinds of political conflict, and their basic images of the essential character of Soviet politics were quite dissimilar. The conflict school treated the Soviet policy process primarily as one featuring conflict between factions based on personalistic ties to important Politburo leaders. The policy process often took on the appearance of Oriental court politics, the power implications for one's faction determining the policy position one took and the relative strength of the factions determining the outcome.[7]

The scholars adopting the interest group approach, on the other hand, concentrated their attention far more on bureaucratic or occupational groups. While recognizing the obvious existence of a political struggle for power that involved central and regional political leaders, they focused their attention upon the continuing published debates in various policy areas. On the surface at least, these debates are far easier to link with different institutional interests than with a factional struggle, and interest group scholars tended to accept the debates largely on face value as an autonomous—although, of course, censored—expression of these interests. (The scholars of the factional conflict school, by contrast, would be more inclined to believe that persons advancing positions in the press might be acting as surrogates for top leaders who could not speak in their own names.) The interest group scholars tended to see bureaucratic conflict as being at the heart of the Soviet policy process on all but the most overarching questions, but their analysis became ambiguous in the treatment of the power of the interest groups.[8]

A number of scholars who in broadest terms still work within the framework of the interest group approach, fearing that the very word "group" conjures up images of a united group that the most vehement denials cannot completely erase,[9] have proposed the use of different language and imagery. The first was Franklyn Griffiths, the coeditor of the major book on interest group theory, who advocated that scholars focus upon "tendencies" instead of upon "groups." A tendency, in Griffiths' definition, is "a pattern of articulation [that is, an expression of views] associated with a loose coalition of actors operating at different levels of the political structure, whose articulations tend in the same direction but are unlikely to be fully aware of the common thrust and consequences of their activity."[10] In contrast to most of those speaking of interest groups, Griffiths insisted that the important tendencies cannot be specified or listed beforehand, for they are too ephemeral and varied. They can be discovered in a particular case only by examining the debate that is taking place.

The present author, while agreeing completely with Griffiths that the political alignments in any country are varying and ill-formed in nature, has, nevertheless, felt it desirable to generalize about the patterns that seem to emerge most frequently, for otherwise comparison of the structure of power in different countries is very difficult.[11] The model of interactions that has seemed most suggestive to me is one sometimes proposed in the study of the United States—one that Ernest Griffiths has labeled "whirlpools," that Theodore Lowi has described and condemned as "interest group liberalism," that most Americans would be familiar with from the phrase "military-industrial complex" if it were assumed that analogous complexes existed in all policy areas.[12]

The assumption of these models is that the political conflicts in the United States tend to be compartmentalized, with the debate in such policy area (or "whirlpool") being largely limited to those whose careers are associated with it, those most directly affected by the decision, and a few who have developed a special interest in it. It is assumed that meaningful participation in agricultural policymaking, for example, is largely limited to the farm organizations, officials in the federal and state departments of agriculture, the agricultural committees in Congress, political leaders from agricultural regions, and scholars working within the field. In interbranch conflict, those in the whirlpool or complex are seen as usually uniting against those in competing whirlpools or complexes. Thus, instead of the type of conflict discussed in the civics textbooks (that is, the checks and balances between the Congress and the executive branch), one finds the Defense Department and the Armed Forces and Armed Services Committees of Congress normally allied against other such combinations—say, the Office of Education and the committees of the two houses handling education. Scholars using this line of analysis usually argue that policy in each policy realm tends to reflect the major societal interests within the complex—a point that has been used either to praise the pluralistic nature of the system or to damn its domination by vested interests.

If such an analysis were applied to the Soviet system, the scholar would focus on analogous policy areas, predict a number of "tendencies" within each area, but suspect that they would largely be limited to the confines of the complex. Any hypothesis about frequent conflict between the party apparatus and the state as such would arouse considerable doubt, for it would be expected that the key alliances in extrabranch conflicts would cut across such institutions as the party apparatus, the governmental bureaucracy, the planning organs, the trade unions, the scientific community, the Komsomol, and so forth. If the analysis were pushed to the extreme, it might be suggested that Soviet Union has moved toward the model of "institutional pluralism."

> [In a system marked by institutional pluralism] one can speak of "complexes" . . . and of "whirlpools" . . . of specialized party, state, "public," and scientific personnel working within the respective policy areas. The definition of goals formally remains the responsibility of the party leadership, but except for ensuring that the Marxist goals in social policy are pursued, the leadership is not to act with "voluntarism"—that is, it generally should follow the advice of the specialized "complexes" or "whirlpools" in their respective policy areas, limiting itself to a mediation of the conflicts that arise among them. In practice, policy-making power informally comes to be delegated to these complexes.[13]

Obviously these various approaches to the visualization of the Soviet political system are not mutually exclusive, and scholars working primarily within one will usually incorporate insights from the others, if only as qualifications to their basic generalizations. Indeed, the debates about the nature of the Soviet political system sometimes remind one of the story of the blind men who tried to understand the nature of an elephant by touch and who fell into disagreement because one had handled the tusk, another a foot, another the tail, and so forth. Scholars using the different approaches have often focused on different aspects of the political process and, therefore, have inevitably arrived at different generalizations about the essentials of the system.

Thus, the directed society models clearly are useful in pointing to the unquestioned authority of the top political officials in the Soviet Union over all spheres of life, the placing of the most important posts in all institutions within the nomenklatura of the party Central Committee, and the highly centralized nature of the formal political and administrative structure. It now seems misleading to use the word "totalitarian" in descriptions of the contemporary Soviet scene (the leader simply is not striving for the type of total control connoted by that word), but obviously the political system is quite authoritarian in its suppression of organized opposition, its maintenance of censorship, and its restrictions on political discussion.

Similarly, those speaking of oligarchical or elite rule are surely right in suggesting that Brezhnev does not have as much real freedom of action as did Stalin, and that, at a minimum, there has been a considerable diffusion of actual influence within the top decision-making collective. In addition, assertions about the unequal distribution of power between the top elite and the masses are also accurate. A high-level or even middle-level administrator clearly has a greater impact on decision-making than an average worker or peasant. Finally, the elite models of the Soviet political system also correctly highlight the fact that bureaucratic institutions as a whole often have an impact that transcends that of their individual members. The continuation of a number of Soviet policies is most easily explained as the product of the vested interests of the bureaucracies most directly involved.

Nevertheless, it is not enough merely to label the Soviet system an elite-dominated one and to leave the analysis at the level. Power is distributed unequally in all countries, and simply to document that some elite in the Soviet Union has more power than the masses does not really say anything about the differences and similarities between it and other countries. Moreover, such broad assertions do little to alert us to the possibility of a subtle evolution in the power relationship between state and society at a time when the basic institutions remain stable on the surface. The Soviet Union has undergone considerable change over the last quarter of a century, but since the elite had greater power than the masses both at the beginning and the end of this period, a focus on this fact alone leaves us poorly placed to understand the dynamics of the system.

Perhaps most important of all, the directed society and elite-domination models retain one major weakness of the totalitarian model: they say little about the process by which goals and policy are formulated. The directed society models in particular take the values and goals of the directing leadership for granted and really are models of the administrative side of the political system. The elite-domination models have much the same character. In speaking of rule by a large bureaucracy as a whole, they implicitly raise the possibility that the process of policy information may be a complex one, but generally they obscure this point with their emphasis upon the authoritarian nature of the system.

This neglect of the policy process was always a serious weakness in the totalitarian model, but the weakness becomes especially severe in models which deal with a postrevolutionary generation of leaders. Such men may be less fixed in their ideas, and the process of policy formation may be crucial in shaping the contents of the policy that is adopted. If society is being "directed" from a center that is responsive to major societal interests, then the Soviet political system is far different in character than earlier models have suggested.

While the directed society and elite-domination models focus on the manner in which the Soviet Union is controlled, the interest group and conflict approaches really are more concerned with another aspect of the political process: the way in which decisions are reached. Indeed, little effort would be required to wed these approaches with either the directed society or elite-domination models. One could see an interest group struggle for influence in which the advocacy of policy positions only provided information for the benefit of the leadership rather than involving the exercise of pressure or power. (Brzezinski and Huntington's *Political Power USA/USSR* comes close to such a position.)[14] One could posit a bureaucratic interest group struggle which excluded other interests from the policymaking process as the mechanism by which bureaucratic domination is maintained. One could describe a directed society in which the content of policy is determined by a struggle of Politburo factions that are largely independent of major societal interests. (Much of the literature of the factional conflict school has tended toward such an image of the Soviet political system.)

Thus, the basic insights of the interest group and factional conflict approaches about the presence of conflict in the Soviet policy process should be seen as a valuable supplement to other models and should not be considered controversial. The words "interest group" and "faction" are not used by Soviet officials and scholars in their descriptions of the normal working of the Soviet system, but unquestionably that system features political behavior which corresponds to western definitions of those terms. The Dnepropetrovsk-Moldavian group linked with Brezhnev is a political faction by any reasonable definition, while the ministries, like many other Soviet institutions, certainly are interest groups by the classic western definition of such groups: "any group that, on the basis of one or more shared attitudes, makes certain claims upon other groups in the society for the establishment, maintenance, or enhancement of forms of behavior that are implied by the shared attitudes."[15] Moreover, the Soviet system clearly has featured conflict among these various types of groupings—even during the petrification of the late Stalin years.

The major reason that the assertions of the interest group school and the faction school have, in fact, been the center of controversy is that other propositions are often included with—or simply read into—their more basic generalizations. Attempts are made to specify the actual nature of the group structure or the factional conflict at a particular time, and the available information, all recognize, can be spare. Focus on specific groups and factions may seem to imply—despite the original theorists' repeated contentions to the contrary—that the meaningful conflict within the system occurs between the groups and factions, not within and across them.

Most basically, of course, when scholars advocate research on conflict within society or justify their own such research, they almost inexorably are implying that that conflict is very important for the functioning of the political system. Especially since the scholars involved have been attacking the totalitarian model vigorously, the reader frequently gains the impression that the exercise of power is being attributed to the contending forces. The careless reader may incorrectly think that the description of the political process leaves no place for the political authorities and that the Soviet political system is being treated as identical with systems in the West. Even accurate statements about the specific nature of the conflict or any implications that power has been diffusing in the Soviet Union are bound to be controversial.

The Nature of Policy Initiative

One reason the various western models and generalizations about the informal political process come into conflict is that they often refer to different aspects of that process. Perhaps the most useful way to try to sort out the differences among the models and preserve their respective insights is to analyze the political processes by stages. The natural starting point is the process by which people try to initiate new policies or modify old ones.

The first classic attempt to analyze the process of policy initiative in the Soviet Union was made by Brzezinski and Huntington in their *Political Power USA/USSR*. In a section entitled "Trickle Up and Bubble Down," Brzezinski and Huntington argue that policy initiatives in the United States "bubble up" from the middle-level officials, but that in the Soviet Union the "top leaders play an active role in policy generation." In fact, they

suggest, "the initiative in formulating most important policy measures probably rests with the Central Committee Secretaries and the departments of the
central apparat."

A leadership imbued with over-all goals derived from ideologically
affected long-term perspectives has inherently a different conception of its
role from that of a leadership that is guided by a tradition of pragmatic
day-to-day reaction to events seen basically as part of a spontaneously un-
folding reality. In the former case, to shape reality initiative must be
monopolized by the leaders; in the latter case, initiative can impose itself
on the leaders.[16]

Unfortunately, this language, taken out of context, may suggest far more
than Brzezinski and Huntington had in mind, for they were using a much
narrower definition of policy initiative than the casual reader is likely to
assume. They were generalizing only about the process by which the final
decision is initiated, for they refer to a considerable amount of societal input—of "bubble up"—in the early stages of policymaking. "Undoubtedly,"
they assert, "ideas and proposals do drift up the party and governmental
hierarchies." In the case of the 1958 education reform, for example, Khrushchev's speech was said to mark "the beginning of the process of policy initiative," but there still was mention of "several years of growing difficulties and
discontent during which the specific groups directly involved presumably
tried to make their complaints heard."[17] Furthermore, Brzezinski and Huntington clearly did not mean their generalizations to apply to decisions other
than the most important, and they surely would agree that some decisions
that would be labeled policy decisions in the West are initiated within the
ministries and perhaps are even adopted on their authority alone.[18]

Unquestionably, the Politburo members and the Central Committee
apparatus do have the power to initiate decisions, and they must at times use
their power. Indeed, at least according to the testimony of Soviet officials,
many of the most important decisions are initiated in their final stages by
the General Secretary himself, often in a written memorandum (zapiska).
This point is especially easy to document for the Khrushchev era, for many
of the First Secretary's memoranda—including many that were secret at the
time of the decision's adoption—came to be published in Khrushchev's
selected speeches and articles.[19] In the Brezhnev era, we must rely on Soviet
officials who give the General Secretary credit for some decisions, but at the
Twenty-Fifth Party Congress alone these decisions included the reclamation
program, the Non-Black-Earth development program, the specialization policy in agriculture, and specific decisions relating to the development of

Armenia, Georgia, Turkmenia, and Yakutia.[20] In the latter cases Brezhnev may be given credit he does not deserve, but the decisions on the three union republics came shortly after the removal of a republican first secretary and perhaps the General Secretary was really being given credit for that personnel change.

Yet, while the party leader certainly can have a brainstorm—and some of Khrushchev's decisions had precisely that appearance—the initiation process in any wider sense surely must include the stream of proposals and pressures impinging upon the leadership and the apparatus. Or, rather, we should say that it must include the many flows of proposals and pressures coming from a variety of directions. This is the basic insight of those who advocate an interest group approach, and it is difficult to contest it.

If policy initiation in the Soviet Union is defined in these broader terms, then probably the most serious criticism to be made of the interest and factional conflict schools is that neither conveys a sufficient sense of the degree to which this kind of policy initiation is often an individual phenomenon. An observer may see the group interests being promoted in the various proposals being advanced and the group perspective reflected in a particular individual's views. But it is still individuals who write letters and articles, who complain to political officials, governmental administrators, and even agitators and propagandists.

There is a temptation to link individuals with the initiation of complaints of limited significance about the work of specific administrators and to see the more complex policy solutions emanating from bureaucratic group and 'interest aggregation" institutions. However, such a view is probably quite misleading. As one reflects upon the policy process in the United States, one is struck by the proportion of the major policy innovations that originate from the academic community, from the policy related institutes and firms, and from persons who move back and forth between them and the government.

A similar pattern seems to appear in the Soviet Union as well. Scholars write a high proportion of the articles in *Pravda* and *Izvestiia,* as well as in the more specialized journals,[21] and even ideas emanating from heads of bureaucratic institutions may actually be more individual than institutional in character. This is the essential insight of those speaking of the role of the specialist in the Soviet political process,[22] but it would be wrong to think that this phenomenon is limited to the Soviet Union.

Agenda-Setting and the Building of Support

The major potential contribution of the factional conflict and interest group schools to our understanding of the Soviet political system (or any political system) centers on their ability to explain how ideas and proposals become the subject of serious discussion and how support is generated for them. Questions can be decided intelligently only if a substantial number of people turn their attention to them and weigh the merits of the possible solutions. Yet, there is a real limit to the number of ideas that can be handled by the human mind, especially since these minds are also concerned with the problems of day-to-day life. The number of ideas and suggestions that appear in print—let alone that are uttered to a more restricted audience—are far too vast to be seriously considered on the agenda of decision-making, and a society must have mechanisms to focus on a narrower range of them.

To a considerable extent, of course, many of the central items on the agenda in any country are really set by events. If a war breaks out between Israel and Egypt, or an Egyptian president visits Israel, no sophisticated political science theory is needed to predict that it will be a top priority item on the agenda both in the United States and the Soviet Union, regardless of the political system. Similarly, a severe drought, an Arab oil embargo, an outbreak of active ethnic dissidence, or a sharp rise in the rate of inflation will affect not only the agenda but also the support accorded different policy alternatives. Nevertheless, crisis and semicrisis events are only a small part of political life, and even in those cases there are alternatives to be defined and decisions to be reached. The full range of the problems that might be considered in modern industrial society is immense and the full range of possible solutions is even greater.

One development in the modern world that alleviates this problem is the compartmentalization of decision-making among specialized elites, for the number of questions on which any one decision-maker must focus is thereby reduced. A second development is the tendency for society to delegate the setting of the agenda to a relatively small number of authoritative spokesmen and to pay special attention to ideas they raise, support, or denounce. While certain individual intellectuals, columnists, and institutional actors play this role in the West, some of the most important of these authorities are the leaders of parties and organized interest groups, who devote great effort to building support for ideas beneficial to themselves and the groups they try to represent.

In the Soviet Union there can be no competing political parties or even open factions within the Communist party, and the law prohibits the formation of voluntary associations intended to promote the legal or economic interests of their members. The questions remain: How is attention narrowed to a manageable range of alternatives? How is support built for the different alternatives? What types of alliances tend to be formed most often in the struggle to achieve policy goals?

The answers to these questions will depend in large part on the level of our analysis. The setting of the agenda and the building of support extends from the first substantial efforts to focus public or governmental attention on a proposal (what David Easton would call the reduction process)[23] to the movement of that proposal toward a final vote in Congress or the Politburo or a final decision by the General Secretary or President. Obviously these processes are going to be very different in character.

If we are talking about the setting of the final agenda for the most important decisions in the Soviet Union, then we are referring to questions decided by the General Secretary and Politburo. This agenda must basically be set by the top Politburo leaders and Central Committee secretaries (and perhaps their personal assistants) on the basis of suggestions made by the Central Committee departments, the governmental agencies, the top regional leaders, and leading scholars. The alliances within the Politburo must be based on a number of factors, especially in a period of transition, but similarity in philosophical orientation and/or in the basic interests of the branch being supervised by the respective members must be of fundamental importance.

Such a level of analysis, however, is rather formalistic in nature, and it contributes little to a meaningful comparison of the Soviet political system with others. What really interests us is how the key political decision-makers become convinced that a proposal should be on the agenda, and how they come to support this alternative rather than another. Are these decisions made autonomously on the basis of the ideology and values of the decision-makers, or do they reflect societal pressures of various types?

This question has not been much analyzed in our study of the Soviet system. The traditional view is that the party leadership has defined the agenda of discussion and has vigorously used the secret police and censorship to enforce its definition. Persons are said to enter the leadership only via cooptation—compatibility with the existing leadership being a key criterion of selection. The most extreme version of this interpretation would contend that only the top political elite has been able to use the press to mobilize support for its own preferences. A more moderate version would acknowledge the regime's increasing willingness to open up the press to debate on specific policy questions, but it would treat this development as part of the leadership's efforts to inform itself, to receive feedback information. The regime's sensitivity about citizen efforts to build support for their ideas would be much emphasized.

Obviously the traditional understanding of the Soviet political system does capture large elements of truth, but it would be wrong to assume that the nature of a political situation in any country can be defined solely in terms of the leadership's aims. Despite the efforts of the Soviet leadership to limit the agenda, its decision to permit debates implies a willingness to let others try to organize support for their ideas, at least in a verbal way. Its desire to be exposed to information about societal shortcomings and to proposals for improvement implies a willingness to let others influence the setting of the agenda, at least as long as the proposals do not become too threatening. And regardless of the regime's desires, nothing could prevent some of those affected by a policy from attempting to influence it in whatever manner they can.

If we ask how these efforts to focus attention on a relatively few proposals and to generate support for them are organized, we find ourselves very close to the heart of the real disagreement between the scholars associated with the interest group approach and those associated with the factional conflict approach. The interest group scholars have suggested that those working in the same institution or in the same occupation are likely to develop a sense of common interests, that those in the significant administrative posts have been able to use their official positions to define issues of importance to their unit, and that they have been able to use these positions (and especially their membership in the committees of the system) to bargain for these interests as they see them. With the policy relevant cleavages seen in institutional and occupational terms, the policy relevant alliances also tend to be seen in these terms, the representatives of institutions with common interests supporting them jointly in the committees.

The factional conflict scholars would not deny that such efforts at interest definition and representation take place in the Soviet Union, but they pay relatively little attention to this phenomenon. Rather, they suggest that the final outcome will be little affected by such representation and bargaining unless the institutional leaders associate themselves with one of the leading Politburo figures and his faction. In this view, an idea becomes important because a faction finds it useful to advance and support it. The way to build meaningful support for an idea, therefore, is to cement relations with one's faction, to gain the support of that faction for one's own proposal, and to try to promote the victory of that faction over its opponents.

A Factional or an Institutional-Branch Policy Process?

As we consider the arguments of the interest group and factional conflict schools, we should recognize that any modern political system features efforts by both factional and institutional or occupational groups to control the agenda and to organize support for their respective interests. In the United states, for example, ad hoc committees and organizations are formed to support and oppose a great variety of specific ideas, and a large number of sector and occupational interests become represented not only by interest group associations but also by the administrative and legislative agencies dealing with the policy areas that affect them. Scholars and commentators with divergent values have emphasized the importance of the politics involving these groups, especially those of a branch and occupational nature, and V. O. Key, probably the foremost political scientist of his generation, was not alone in insisting that "in the alliances of pressure politics those between administrative agencies and private groups are often extremely significant in the determination of courses of action."

> Pressure politics among the activists takes something of the form it would take if there were no election or no concern about the nature of public opinion; that is, those immediately concerned make themselves heard in the process of decision . . . The process of politics among the activists is governed to some extent by the expectation that all entitled to play the game shall get a fair deal (or at least a fair hearing before their noses are rubbed in the dirt).[24]

Despite such assertions, a number of politically relevant "factional" groupings are also visible in the United States. The most obvious are the Democratic and Republican parties and the subfactions that appear most clearly when governmental posts are filled at the time of a change of administration. The Watergate hearings revealed two groups within the White House staff centering on John Mitchell and H. R. Haldeman, while the weeks immediately after President Carter's victory in 1976 brought to the surface a rather intense conflict between his top political adviser, Hamilton Jordan, and the head of the transition team, Jack Watson. In addition to these types of factional activity, one can also see rather loose groupings such as "liberals" and "conservatives" that are partly—but only partly—associated with the party struggle.

No doubt, a balanced view of the American political system would see both the factional and interest group activity as important in setting the agenda and building support for ideas—and it would also, no doubt, give great weight to the role of the media. Nevertheless, when scholars such as Key emphasize the importance of the politics centering on the alliances between administrative agencies and pressure groups, when Brzezinski and Huntington insist that the processes of power acquisition and policymaking are often quite separate in the United States,[25] they are suggesting in effect that the factions, especially those associated with parties, are not as important in defining the agenda or in building support for ideas as much party theory has maintained. The man-on-the-street who dismisses "campaign oratory" as irrelevant is making much the same point.

In the Soviet Union, too, there is unmistakable evidence for the existence of factional and bureaucratic-occupational interest group activity. Any westerner who reads Soviet printed debates cannot fail to gain a sense of a very recognizable political process centered on administrative institutions. Officials of these institutions at all levels are constantly advancing proposals for change, and, if the role and responsibilities of the various institutional units are properly understood, the proposals of their respective officials normally turn out to correspond to the interests of the institution as a westerner would define them. Moreover, the practice of ensuring representation from the same major institutions and branches on the important party and governmental committees and on legislative drafting commissions also creates a strong impression that the institutional actors play a critical role in the system—that they are the ones who have interests and ideas that need to be incorporated in decisions.

Conversations with Soviet officials lead in the same direction. These persons habitually and easily refer to the point of view (*tochka zreniia*) of, say, plant managers or financial officials. When they are asked why they send articles to the press instead of simply to high officials, they give two reasons—first, that an article reaches a number of officials instead of just one, and, second, that it increases the awareness of common problems among those in a similar situation and mobilizes them to act. The strongest evidence that this latter phenomenon is occurring is the fact that the greatest number of complaints about the grievances of those in various ministries and trade unions are found in the specialized journals and magazines of the respective institutions. Since this type of newspaper and magazine is read almost exclusively by those within the group, the primary purpose of these complaints must be to try to build a sense of common group interest and perspective.

Contemporary Soviet ideology freely acknowledges diversity of interests within Soviet society,[26] but factions within the party still are strictly forbidden. As a consequence, neither Soviet scholars nor political leaders may recognize the existence of factional political activity, let alone discuss its nature, unless they are condemning in a one-sided manner those defined as factionalists in the past. Still, there can be no question about the existence of factional activity. Even in the late Stalin period, Fainsod, who analyzed the Soviet system as totalitarian, described the informal organization of the party as approximating "a constellation of power centers, some of greater and some of lesser magnitude and each with its accompanying entourage of satellites." He asserted that careers are made by "clinging to the coattails of the great lords of communism" and that "cliques rise and fall in the Soviet hierarchy depending on the fortunes of their patrons." Indeed, he quoted Stalin himself to document the existence of personal entourages:

Most frequently officials are selected not according to objective criteria, but according to accidental, subjective, narrow, and provincial criteria. Most frequently so-called acquaintances are chosen, personal friends, fellow townsmen, people who have shown personal devotion, masters of eulogies to their patrons, irrespective of whether they are suitable from a political and a businesslike standpoint . . .

Take, for example, Comrades Mirzoian and Vainov. The former is secretary of the regional party organization in Kazakhstan; the latter is secretary of the Yaroslavl regional party organization. These people are not the most backward officials in our midst. And how do they select officials?

The former dragged along with him to Kazakhstan thirty or forty of his "own" people from Azerbaidzhan and the Urals, where he formerly worked, and he placed them in responsible positions in Kazakhstan.

The latter dragged along with him to Yaroslavl a dozen or so of his "own" people too, and he also placed them in responsible positions. Consequently, Comrade Mirzoian has his own crew. Comrade Vainov also has his.[27]

In recent decades the size of the entourage accompanying a middle-level official seems much smaller than Stalin suggests for the 1930s, and it now may usually be limited to a few personal assistants. Yet, the movement of a man into a top Politburo post does bring promotion for a number of officials associated with him earlier in his career—or at least, to phrase the point in the most favorable light, officials whose excellence of performance he had had an earlier opportunity to observe at close range. Khrushchev's rise provided career advancement to a number of his former subordinates in the Ukraine, while Brezhnev's election as First Secretary brought similar good fortune to a sizeable group of officials from Dnepropetrovsk and Moldavia.

Conversely, the defeat of a major Politburo figure can have disastrous political consequences for those closely associated with him. Fourteen members and candidate members of the Central Committee elected in 1961 had been engaged in Komsomol work sometime between 1948 and 1958, a period when Shelepin was second secretary (the secretary for personnel selection) and then first secretary of the All-Union Komsomol organization.[28] In 1976 one of this group was still on the Central Committee. The problem was not the advanced age of these men or any general pattern of removing members from the Central Committee (see table 40). The top leadership also must not have believed that Komsomol work disqualified one for a top political position, for those 1961 Central Committee members who had been in Komsomol work in the 1937–1947 period did extremely well in the Brezhnev years. The associa-

Table 40 *Full and candidate members of 1961 Central Committee
still on 1976 Central Committee, by organizational affiliation*

Organizational affiliation in 1961 or in earlier career[a]	All 1961 members still alive in 1976		Living members, excluding those over 70 and off the Central Committee	
	Average age	Number still on Central Committee	Average age	Number still on Central Committee
Dnepropetrovsk party organization	63	6 of 6	63	6 of 6
Belorussian party organization	64	7 of 8	64	7 of 8
Leningrad party organization	63	6 of 8	62	6 of 7
Kharkov party organization	68	5 of 9	67	5 of 7
Top foreign policy officials[b]	70	8 of 11	69	8 of 9
Industrial-construction officials in central or regional government[c]	69	19 of 27	68	19 of 23
RSFSR obkom first secretaries[d]	63	33 of 57	63	33 of 55
Ukrainian party organizations other than Kharkov or Dnepropetrovsk	64	7 of 18	63	7 of 17
Moscow city and regional party organization	61	7 of 16	61	7 of 16
Non-slavic republican party organizations	63	10 of 35	62	10 of 31

Table 40—Continued

ORGANIZATIONAL AFFILIATION IN 1961 OR IN EARLIER CAREER[a]	ALL 1961 MEMBERS STILL ALIVE IN 1976		LIVING MEMBERS, EXCLUDING THOSE OVER 70 AND OFF THE CENTRAL COMMITTEE	
	AVERAGE AGE	NUMBER STILL ON CENTRAL COMMITTEE	AVERAGE AGE	NUMBER STILL ON CENTRAL COMMITTEE
In Komsomol sometime between 1948 and 1958	55	1 of 14	55	1 of 14
In Komsomol sometime between 1937 and 1947 but not later	61	14 of 18	61	14 of 18

Source: The list of 1961 Central Committee members and their biographies are found in the 1962 Yearbook of the *Bol'shaia sovetskaia entsiklopediia*. However, many of these biographies are incomplete, and they have been supplemented from other sources A good source for this purpose is Borys Levytsky, *The Soviet Political Elite* (Stanford, Calif., Hoover Institution on War, Revolution and Peace, 1970.)

a Affiliation with a regional party organization means that the person has held a post in the party apparatus within the region. There is some overlap in the categories. For example, the Moscow and Leningrad first secretaries are included among the RSFSR obkom first secretaries, and the Tula first secretary is included both in the latter category and in the figure for Dnepropetrovsk, the province where he worked previously. The former Komsomol officials in particular are likely to be found in other categories as well.

b Top officials in both the Central Committee apparatus and Secretariat and the governmental agencies in Moscow. Ambassadors—who generally were old party officials on the way out and who had extremely low political survival rates—are not included.

c Given the abolition of the industrial ministries, this is an imprecise category, but it includes the chairmen of state committees in the industrial-construction realm, the chairmen of regional economic councils, and former industrial administrators whose responsibilities in the planning organs or the Council of Ministers essentially centered on industrial planning or administration.

d This figure includes only men working as obkom (regional) first secretaries at the time of the Central Committee election in 1961. unlike other categories, in which past work also qualifies a person for inclusion in the category.

tion with Shelepin almost surely explains the removal of so many of the younger officials with Komsomol backgrounds.

A connection with a top Politburo official other than the top winner or the top loser may also have an impact on future career success. The "expected" political survival rate for officials near fifty years of age on the 1961

Central Committee is probably close to the 60 percent figure for the obkom first secretaries of the RSFSR, for a variety of top leaders of different factions were responsible for their selection at one time or another, and these pressures probably canceled out each other. The proportion of 1961 Central Committee members of other categories still on that body in 1976 varied enormously in either direction, and the differences seem far more related to ties with a Politburo leader than to other factors. Thus, the officials from Belorussia (Mazurov's region), from Leningrad (Kosygin's region), from Kharkov (Podgorny's region), and, of course from Dnepropetrovsk were much more successful than the average, especially if we correct for the higher age of the Kharkov officials. The same is true of the top foreign policy officials (Suslov's main area of responsibility in 1961) and the top industrial and construction officials (the area of responsibility both of Kosygin as First Deputy Chairman of the Council of Ministers and of Brezhnev as the Central Committee secretary for industry from 1956 to the summer of 1960).

By contrast, the officials from the Moscow party organization, from the Ukraine outside of Kharkov and Dnepropetrovsk, from the non-Slavic republics, and especially from the Komsomol in recent years fared far less well than the average. The Moscow figure is somewhat surprising given the presence of three former Moscow party officials (Grishin, Demichev, and Kapitonov) on the Brezhnev Politburo and Central Committee Secretariat, but one of Shelepin's close supporters (Egorychev) was prominent in the city organization and perhaps the Moscow organization itself was split into factions. The Ukrainian statistic is close to that for the RSFSR obkom first secretaries, especially when three Kievan officials including Shelest are excluded, and, except for the Kievan officials, may also reflect the multiplicity of factional influences on their selection. The figure for the non-Slavic republics, on the other hand, must at least partly reflect the fact that Kirichenko and then Kozlov had special responsibilities for these areas and that in 1958 and 1959 the heads of the party organs department of the Central Committee for the union republics were Shelepin and then Semichastny, Shelepin's second secretary in the Komsomol and his successor as Komsomol first secretary.

Many scholars would cite such evidence to demonstrate a faction-dominated policy process, but it is not clear that these alliances are closely related to the policy process. After all, despite the factional conflict between John Mitchell and H. R. Haldeman in the Nixon administration, the two men seem to have had similar policy views. Moreover, if there had been an American Politburo, both surely would have loyally voted to support President Nixon's proposals, regardless of their own views. Hamilton Jordan professes few policy interests.[29] One could at least imagine that Soviet factional activity too is concerned almost entirely with the acquisition of position and has relatively little policy content.

The relationship of factional activity to the policy process is, unfortunately, another of those questions about the Soviet Union on which very little information is available, and we must therefore rely on minor clues and even our feelings about the nature of the system. One thing that can be said with great assurance is that the views of the General Secretary have been of great importance in the Soviet system. At least thus far, a change in General Secretary had had a profound and quick impact not only on a number of maor policies but also on the basic way in which decisions are reached.

Nevertheless, factional defeat in the Soviet Union no longer means that the top figures in the faction, let alone any middle-level figures, are removed from all influence on decision-making. Thus, among those most closely associated with Shelepin and removed from Central Committee membership in the Brezhnev years are officials who still were named Chairman of the State Committee for Sports and Physical Culture, Deputy Minister of Education, First Deputy Chairman of the State Committee for Vocational-Technical Education, and deputy chairman of the Ukrainian Council of Ministers (the deputy chairman for transportation). If the policy views of the Shelepin faction were totally at odds with those of the Brezhnev faction, it is difficult to believe that these officials would have been given these jobs. Certainly a liberal Democrat in the United States would hardly put Reagan Republicans in responsible positions in educational decision-making, nor would the reverse take place.

The pattern of appointments and removals in many specialized policy areas over the last few decades—including to a considerable extent an important policy area such as industry[30]—often seem little related to factional changes in the leadership. Frequently, the impression is created of Weberian career patterns with promotion based in large part on specialized competence. Even within the party apparatus, changes in republican or regional first secretaries are generally not followed by immediate wholesale changes among other political leaders in the republic, unless the change is accompanied by major scandal.

What is most unclear is whether the lower officials who become linked with a top leader share his policy orientation. That is, it could be hypothesized that a regional or republican leader with a "liberal" approach toward most questions selects subordinates of like views and that, therefore, his promotion into the top leadership is really the victory of a liberal entourage associated with him. More important, it could be hypothesized that those associated with more liberal—or conservative—regional leaders see their future career success dependent upon the victory of their policy orientation and build alliances with others throughout the country with a similar orientation. In this view, a good deal of the political activity in the country—behind the scenes, if not in the press—might be directed toward advancing and supporting ideas that will increase the appeal of a faction.

In my opinion, such hypotheses about the Soviet political system would be basically misleading. A range of views from quite reactionary to quite liberal surely are found among Soviet officials on major issues. Undoubtedly, when a regional first secretary selects an official such as a city first secretary, he is not likely to to be comfortable with a person of radically different views. (The same need not be true of specialized subordinates.) But these statements do not necessarily imply a consciousness of the need for political alliance along philosophical lines or the existence of a politics that centers on such alliances.

The evidence casting doubt on a factionally centered policy process is subtle and difficult to discuss in brief terms. Certainly the unquestioned fact that both Stalin and Khrushchev chose and kept as their most trusted subordinates men who, upon their own accession to top leadership posts, turned out to differ with the old leader on major policy questions demonstrates the absence of complete policy unity within a faction. It is also suggestive that the sensitive foreign policy realm provides almost no evidence of factionally inspired personnel change in the most important posts, except for the removal of Molotov and Shepilov. Indeed, the highest foreign policy officials of 1977—Suslov, Gromyko, and Ponomarev—were top subordinates to Molotov in the late 1940s and leading officials in the Khrushchev era as well.

Other possible evidence that the policy process is not factionally centered includes the failure of the pattern of promotions and demotions after Khrushchev's removal to correspond to the composition of the liberal and conservative factions hypothesized at that time. One might also point to the major role of the regional first secretaries—to act first of all as administrative officials, the prefects of the system—and suggest that their administrative ability, political loyalty, and willingness to follow orders are more significant criteria in their selection than their policy views.

If this evidence is accepted, one still could emphasize the key role of the General Secretary in setting the basic policy balance in the country, if nothing else by determining that it reflect a collective judgment. One would suggest, though, that his faction and that of other leaders are more like a personal entourage than a group of likeminded persons whom he to some extent represents. The process of acquiring a leadership post would be seen essentially as one of maneuvering to impress those with the ability to coopt, of building a broad network of contacts, of trying to get a position that could be used to build a power base, and of developing the range of experiences and the type of reputation that might impress colleagues when the decision to select a new General Secretary must be made. One suspects that the best—and most usual—strategy for a political hopeful in the Soviet Union, especially one at middle levels of the system, would be to refrain from policy controversy or even a policy stance and to try to acquire the stance of a sound and progressive moderate as those terms would be defined by the Soviet establishment.

In this view of the Soviet political process, the antifaction rule is fairly effective in curbing the formation of any substantial network of alliances along philosophical lines among regional and other middle-level political officials. The nature of censorship—especially the restriction of the more sensitive debates to specialized journals—strengthens the tendency for the policy relevant alliances to remain compartmentalized within specialized "whirlpools" even more fully than occurs in the West, with the selective censorship making it difficult to appeal through the press for outside allies. As a consequence, this view would emphasize the importance of institutions—ministries and their subunits, trade unions and other "public organizations," regional party and governmental units, and scientific institutes—in defining which problems are most important and which solutions are the reasonable policy alternatives.

There obviously also exists an intellectual community—especially in Moscow, but to a lesser degree in other major cities—whose members, though employed in various institutions, communicate socially. A few members of this community become dissidents, but most are key members of a broader establishment. The process by which this community focuses on issues (the newspaper *Literaturnaia gazeta* surely is an important part of the process for at least one wing of the community) and the degree to which their deliberations help define the broader alternatives for political leaders are far from clear. This process may be quite important, even to the extent of identifying persons with ideas who can be recruited into the Central Committee apparatus, the personal staff of the leaders, or other policy sensitive posts, but we know little about it.

The Diffusion of Power

In any country, the final policy outcome can be fundamentally determined by the nature of the proposals that reach the agenda and the quality of the support that is mobilized behind them. Yet, leading political authorities are charged with the responsibility of making decisions—of making an "authoritative allocation of values." These authorities may and do seek to avoid such responsibility by innumerable stratagems, but, in the words of

President Truman, the buck ultimately stops at their desks. Even when they are not called upon to make an actual decision, the results of the bargaining at lower levels may be shaped by assumptions about the likely outcome if the question were referred to higher authorities.

On one level of analysis, the structure of decision-making power generally is one of the simpler questions of political science. Final authority usually needs to be incorporated in formal rules and hence is readily observable. Even when some documents attribute enormous power to institutions that exercise it only in formal terms (those asserting that the Supreme Soviet is the supreme legislative body in the Soviet Union, for example), other documents can make the real situation quite clear. Particularly in a parliamentary system, the relation between the leader and the rest of the cabinet is always a subtle question, but here too one can gain a fairly good sense of the relative strength of the leader.

At this level, the Soviet system is a parliamentary system of a special type. The Central Committee serves as the parliament of the system—the institution to which the cabinet (the Politburo) and the leader are responsible. Since the Stalin years, the leader must at least discuss every major decision with the Politburo, and the General Secretary cannot remove a Politburo member without the agreement of the Central Committee. Nevertheless, the independence of the Central Committee is sharply reduced by the administrative subordination of its members to the political leaders in their everyday jobs. The General Secretary's key role in selection of personnel for these posts has historically been a major factor in his power with relation to the Central Committee.

Whatever the division of power among the Central Committee, the Politburo, and the General Secretary, some combination of these party officials obviously has unlimited authority to make any decision that it deems desirable. No institution can declare its decisions unconstitutional and so far as can be judged, there are no checks and balances of the American type within the top party organs themselves. Despite the federal nature of the political system, the central party organs can override any local decision or intervene on any local question.

In analyzing the Soviet political system, many American scholars have, however, drawn conclusions of too sweeping a nature from these facts. Mindful of the comparison with the institutional conflicts built into the American system, they have forgotten that most of the statements about the formal power of political institutions in the Soviet Union are true of any parliamentary system with a disciplined majority party.

Consider, for example, the situation in Great Britain. The country has no Supreme Court to declare an act of Parliament unconstitutional, and, indeed, no written constitution limiting the authority of Parliament at all. Within the Parliament, the cabinet and the prime minister have a great ability to work their will on legislative policy. The members of Parliament are in the "nomenklatura" of the central party authorities, for the latter must confirm the local party organization's choice of nominee at each election and hence can deny the party nomination to a recalcitrant legislator at the next election. In practice, the members of Parliament generally can be counted upon to support the position of their party's leadership in a parliamentary vote. Even if it were assumed that the party leadership would not or could not use this authority to abolish opposing parties and that it will remain responsive to the electorate, one still could speak about the lack of formal restraints on a tyranny of the majority—a possibility that has concerned many political philosophers over the centuries.

When we define the American and British political systems as constitutional in nature, we are not referring to the ultimate legal power of the highest governmental authorities. We are not denying—or certainly should not be denying—the ability of these governments to take almost any action if a majority of the officials in the decisive positions in government are united. In World War II the British Parliament was able to postpone the elections beyond the legally required deadline. Despite its institutional checks and balances, the American government was able to place loyal, native-born Japanese-Americans in concentration camps for the duration of the war, for the Supreme Court was unwilling to state that the action was an unconstitutional denial of due process. For decades the American government was totally unwilling to enforce the constitutionality guaranteed voting rights of blacks in the South, or to deprive states of congressmen when blacks were denied voting rights as provided in the Fourteenth Amendment.

Similarly, when we talk about a pluralistic diffusion of power in Great Britain and the United States, we are not talking merely about group ability to exercise power directly against a united leadership. All such analyses of the American and British systems are based on a definition of power that admits of its exercise through anticipation of the reaction of others (for example, the electorate), direct action, the control of economic resources, strength of personality, political reprisals, the invoking of legal authority, the use of force, and so on. We have been willing to speak of the "power" of Henry Kissinger in American foreign policy from 1968 to 1976 or the "power" of trade unions in Great Britain, even though neither had authority to compel the president or the Parliament to take action.

Moreover, virtually all leading American theorists on power—and certainly all those who have analyzed the American system as pluralistic—have vigorously denied that power is some concrete entity that can be "stored in a keg." They have insisted that power inevitably is situational and relational—that the power relationship between two individuals, let alone between groups or between the government and the masses, is always varying, depending on the issue and the particular circumstances.

In short, to state that a government is limited or that power is diffused within a political system means that power is diffused in practice, that government acts in a limited way in practice, and that political leaders who violate the rules of the game are likely to suffer unpleasant consequences. To say that a system is a constitutional one means, in large part, that the rulers have assimilated constitutional norms and that they feel internal psychological pressures both to respond to societal demands and to refrain from certain types of action. These norms obviously need not be embodied in a written constitution or enforced by a Supreme Court, for the British political system with its unwritten constitution is clearly as "constitutional" as the American system.

In discussing the distribution of power in the Soviet Union, we have often forgotten the way in which we define our concepts in analyzing the West, and we often use quite different criteria in making our judgments. We have asked whether the Politburo has the legal authority to take action, and, since the Soviet political system has the form of a parliamentary government, we naturally and correctly have said that it does. We have treated power in absolute, nonsituational terms, speaking of the party's "monopoly of power" or saying that control of the party apparatus is the only power resource in the Soviet Union. As Alfred Meyer has stated,

> In dealing with the Communist world, our notions of what a political system is and does have been suspended. For describing that world we have used concepts and models reserved for it alone or for it and a few other systems considered inimical. Thus one might almost say that the Communist world was analyzed outside the framework of comparative political science. Or else we used one set of concepts for Communist countries and another for the rest of the world. Most American political scientists would reject the elitist models of Pareto, Mosca, and Michels and would criticize a sociologist like Mills for seeking to apply them to the United States. Yet have not most studies of the Communist world described Communist states in the crudest Paretan terms as the rule of self-appointed elites striving to perpetuate themselves and structuring the entire system to this purpose? And I stress the crudeness of these interpretations, which neglect most of the subtleties and sophistication of both Mosca and Pareto.[31]

When judgments about the distribution of power in the Soviet Union are based on such definitions and then compared with judgments about the distribution of power in the West that are predicated on different definitions, the comparisons that emerge inevitably are extremely dissimilar in nature.

If we are concerned with understanding the "real" or informal distribution of power in the Soviet Union in comparative terms, then we must at least ask the same questions that we do in the West to see if the same political phenomena exist. And if we do this, one conclusion does indeed emerge with inescapable clarity: there has been a major diffusion of power in the Soviet Union in recent decades, especially since the removal of Khrushchev.

This diffusion of power has been labeled in varying ways by different scholars. Even in the late Khrushchev period, scholars sometimes asserted that "the Soviet system has lost some of its freedom to mold the society, especially since it can no longer entirely disregard the complex industrial and urban interests, which have developed considerable institutional and group cohesion."[32] At other times, particularly during the Brezhnev years, scholars have talked about petrification or stagnation in the political system.[33] Still others have spoken about the power of the Soviet interest groups or the trend toward a more pluralistic system.[34] I have tried to describe this diffusion of power as movement toward "institutional pluralism.."[35]

The word "pluralism" has been given many meanings over the years, but it has generally been used to describe the type of political system found in the West—and even then only by those persons who do not believe that the western democracies are elite or class dominated. Indeed, the word first came to prominence in the early part of the twentieth century, when it was associated with British political philosophers who were trying to deny the state as much sovereignty as it was exercising in western democracies. Consequently, the application of the pluralism label to the Soviet system, however modified or qualified, is bound to provoke objections from some.[36]

At a minimum, the type of pluralism that exists in the Soviet Union clearly is different in important respects from that in the West, and some modifying adjective like "institutional" must be used to emphasize these differences. The word "institutional" in this context should not be taken to imply that institutions are the only actors in the political process. Institutional pluralism means only that the legitimate political process must take place within an institutional framework, and perhaps the phrase "institutionalized pluralism" would convey the meaning better. Our discussion of policy processes (see Chapter 8) shows the Soviet system as a highly participatory one for the individual as well as for the institution. The distinctive feature of individual participation in the Soviet Union is that people must work through official channels. They cannot picket, hand out leaflets, speak on the street corner, or the like; they cannot form interest groups around issues; they cannot organize competing political factions or parties.

It has seemed useful to employ the word "pluralism" to describe the Soviet Union because the leading American political scientists of the 1950s and 1960s began defining that term in ways that deemphasized competitive elections and confrontation politics. The phenomena that they treated as the essential characteristics of pluralism were of a type that at least theoretically could be found in a country without western style elections. These characteristics include a population conditioned to make moderate demands and to think of politics as "the art of the possible"; a society and bureaucracy that contains a number of different specialized interests, none completely dominant; a bargaining mentality within the elite; a political leadership that is accommodating and "responsive" and serves as a broker facilitating agreements among competing interests; decisions that feature "steady appeasement of relatively small groups" rather than majority rule;[37] resolution of any major conflict through gradual adjustments in the balance of policy; a budgetary process marked by incrementalism. In fact, the development of precisely such political phenomena seems to distinguish the Brezhnev regime from its predecessors.

To state that the Soviet Union now is characterized by a type of pluralism serves several useful purposes. First, it reminds us that the changes that some see as evidence of petrification of an ideological system could also be cited as evidence of evolution toward a more western system. Second, it raises a crucial theoretical question that has been given insufficient attention by political scientists: what aspects of pluralism (the above-mentioned features emphasized by political scientists or the right to take more dramatic actions and to vote in elections) are associated with the consequences that we associate with pluralism. What is the actual impact of confrontation politics, interest groups formed on issues, and competitive elections upon "who gets what" in a society?

Whatever objections might be made to the label "pluralism," however, one fact should not be obscured. Whether scholars speak of the growing difficulty of transforming society, of oligarchical petrification, of power for interest groups, or of institutional pluralism, they all agree on at least one basic point, namely, that actual power is now not as concentrated in the top political leadership as it once was and has diffused downward to some extent.

The Distribution of Power

To say that power has diffused does not reveal who has received it, and an examination of the actual distribution of power can take place on many levels. One possibility is simply to look at the formal legal arrangements that determine the location of ultimate authority. Another is to try to appraise the power of the government in relation to the individual, especially the individual who is opposed to the government. A third possibility is to attempt to ascertain the distribution of influences that determine the content of decisions, regardless of how repressive they are for the individual.

The formal distribution of power in the Soviet Union has already been discussed. Ultimate power is concentrated within the top committees of the Communist party, and the relationship of the General Secretary to those committees is similar in form to that of a prime minister to a cabinet and a legislature in a parliamentary system in which one party has a strong and disciplined majority. The restraints, when they exist, are informal in nature.

The power of the government as it touches on the individual is a difficult subject to analyze in any country. In principle, laws are meant to be enforced, and in every modern government a complex system of police, courts, and prisons evolves to ensure that government will have an enormous imbalance of power in relation to any individual who chooses to violate its laws. If we speak of the power of the government toward the individual, we really mean, first, that there are channels of appeal through which an individual can seek the help of governmental agencies to overturn a punishment by another governmental agency, and second, that government cannot (or will not) interfere with the freedom of the individual to engage in certain types of activities. Westerners would almost invariably include among these activities the rights to criticize government and to try to replace governmental leaders in some orderly, prescribed manner.

By these criteria, particularly the second, Soviet government clearly is far more powerful than the Soviet citizen and the relationship is more heavily weighted against the individual than it is in the West. The Soviet leadership is quite open in proclaiming its intention to punish those who persistently "slander" the political and social system, who form unauthorized political action groups, or who use factions or parties to attempt to replace the leadership. Moreover, when the political leadership agrees to suppress a dissident, there is no court or other institution to protect the individual.

The system is an authoritarian one in terms of political freedom. It would be wrong, however, not to mention two types of restraints on government that have developed in recent decades. The Soviet Union does have review procedures that provide a check on arbitrary actions by lower officials. While secret police officials sometimes seemed a law unto themselves in the Stalin period,[38] the post-Stalin regimes have strengthened political controls over the police. This probably has meant that a fairly substantial review process exists to watch over the actions of local KGB agents and institutions. Even if local party officials take an action against an individual—as when Kaluga officials began making it impossible for Solzhenitsyn to work and live in the region—an appeal to Moscow can override them.

Even at the national level, the KGB is subject to the supervision of the administrative organs department of the Central Committee and one of the Central Committee secretaries. And beyond the possibility of an appeal on any KGB action, it is likely that police action against dissidents known to the West must be cleared with higher political authorities. The fate of a Solzhenitsyn or a Sakharov is probably decided by the Politburo as a collective body.

Moreover, some informal restraints on the government's interference in political freedom seem to be developing. The criticism of governmental leaders and policy is not supposed to be punishable, and criticism of the social system as a whole is not legally punishable unless it is persistent. Many types of criticism of society and policy that would have been considered dissent twenty-five or even fifteen years ago have now become quite legitimate.

The third way of looking at the distribution of power in the Soviet Union is to explore the location of the sources of influence on policy, whatever its content. If we use the word "power" in the way it normally is defined in the West, we should realize that power cannot be totally centralized in any system, even the most repressive one. In an ultimate sense, political power usually is exercised by a societal group as a leader anticipates some unfortunate consequence if he does not take some action. Such a consequence is not limited to loss of votes at the next election. The possibility of a riot or revolt, the belief that a goal will not be met or that a program will fail, the threat of apathetic or misdirected performance in the economic sphere—all of these consequences are caused by societal groups and give them power, even if there are no spoken threats. In this sense no sizable group in any society is totally powerless. In this sense even the Russian peasants of the early 1930s had enough power to preserve their private plots in the midst of the collectivization drive.

An attempt to generalize about the patterns within the informal distribution of power in the Soviet Union is fraught with danger, quite aside from the problems of obtaining necessary information. There is a fundamental methodological problem to begin with, for we really do not know how to measure power reliably in any political system. In fact, since power is not a concrete thing but a relationship that varies with the situation, there is something inherently dubious about making summary statements that inevitably have to treat power as a more static phenomenon.

Probably the safest generalization about the distribution of power in the Soviet Union is that it must vary with the policy area. In the spheres of foreign and defense policy, one gains the impression of deep leadership involvement and of participation limited to specialists. Even the civilian foreign policy specialists seem to receive extremely little information about Soviet defense decisions except that which they read in western sources. In the transportation realm, on the other hand, one has the sense of little leadership involvement, fairly wide debate in the media, and domination by the major interest group, the railroads. In the realm of wages, it is unclear who is making policy, but one gains the sense of real responsiveness to workers and peasants.

A second reasonably safe generalization is that the strongest political actors below the leadership level (or, conceivably, the factional level) are "vertical" or branch, not regional, officials. Whether one wants to emphasize the role of the ministries, the Secretariat and departments of the Central Committee, or a specialized complex cutting across these and other institutions, one is talking about a type of politics that is different from, say, Yugoslavia, where bargaining among republics seems to dominate. Obviously, regional interests and regional bargaining do have a significant place in the Soviet political system, but in relative terms they are less important.

The strength of specialized branch interests is increased not only by the centralized nature of the system but also by the nature of Soviet censorship. The more that debates tend to be limited to more specialized forums, the more difficult it is for outside perspectives to be brought to bear on them and for outside interests to influence the final outcome.[39] The Soviet leaders have increased the freedom of specialized officials to debate incremental changes in almost all policy areas, presumably in large part because they want expert advice that is worked out in a collective way. As they come to realize that specialist advice is not merely "scientific" but also self-interested, they may develop the fear that their interests and those of the community are not being served in an optimal manner and may feel the need for a wider airing of the central issues involved.

The absence of competitive elections is another factor that weakens the relative power of regional interests. Such elections at the republic level would obviously increase the support behind a number of nationality sensitive issues (for example, the content of historical textbooks) and force a change in many of these policies. But, especially if the electoral system were to feature single-member districts, there almost surely would be added pressure for a more equitable territorial distribution of resources among the regions, and particularly into the small towns and rural areas. (The comparison of the development of the rail and road networks in the United States and the Soviet Union is a fascinating one.)

A third relatively safe generalization about the distribution of power is that among the specialized branch interests those associated with industrial growth have been in a position of special power. To a considerable extent, this phenomenon seems associated more with the stage of economic development than with the type of political system, for in the early years of rapid industrial growth in the United States the major industrial interests were dominant and such issues as environmental ones received less attention than in the Soviet Union today.

In addition, however, the basic ideological drive of the Communist party was associated closely with the need to industrialize, and the incentives that Stalin established to attract the best personnel to heavy industry were highly successful in creating a powerful group that would push for continued high priority for the industrial branch. Indeed, managerial personnel from heavy industry and the defense industries were named to the highest political and governmental positions. The college graduates who were moved into the administrative elite after the Great Purge came overwhelmingly from the engineering institutes, and by the late 1940s approximately 40 percent of the Politburo members were of this background. In early 1978, nine of the thirteen First Deputy Chairmen and Deputy Chairmen of the USSR Council of Ministers were engineers who had been high officials in heavy industry and construction (and a tenth one had plant level experience), and five of the eleven Central Committee secretaries were graduates of heavy industry engineering institutes (although one worked in light industry). Of the first secretaries of the twenty-five most populous regions (krais, oblasts, or autonomous republics) in March 1976, 60 percent were heavy industry or defense industry engineers (usually with years of experience in managerial positions) or had worked for at least ten years in management in heavy industry.[40]

A leadership intent on controlling industry has reason to recruit persons with the knowledge to do so. More important, a leadership intent on coopting the best talent with administrative experience would want to turn to that sector to which the best talent had been attracted originally. But talent is accompanied by values, and officials who in their youth and middle years had justified their role in life in terms of the country's need for rapid industrial growth and a stronger defense capacity may well carry this psychological baggage with them as they rise to higher positions. This is the crux of the argument that there is a dominant "military-heavy industrial complex" in the Soviet Union. The charge has large elements of validity to it, especially if many of the most talented segments of the scientific community and of the working class are recognized as part of the "complex."

A fourth generalization that one would like to make about the distribution of power concerns that which prevails among different societal classes or strata, but this is the most difficult judgment of all. Obviously the average college graduate, the average middle level administrator, let alone the average top official, has more power than the average worker or the average peasant, but these observations are true of every political system in the world. The only relevant question is the pattern of inequality in the Soviet Union as compared with other countries.

Most westerners discussing a diffusion of power in the Soviet Union in the last decade have talked about diffusion to elite groups within the bureaucracy or simply to the bureaucracy or the New Class as a whole. There has been a widespread impression that Khrushchev's "populism" entailed some increase in the power of the masses in relation to the bureaucracy, but that the Brezhnev era has seen a reversal of this trend and a restrengthening of the position of the professional and managerial elite. That this should occur has been thought to be natural by westerners, for they have argued that power for the broad masses depends on the existence of competitive elections and the right to organize groups. As Seymour Martin Lipset has expressed the point, "the underprivileged can impress their concerns on the social system only in a policy in which they are free to organize in unions, parties, cooperatives, and the like . . . The primary weapons of the lower strata of the exploited classes are the ability to organize, to strike, to demonstrate, and to vote rulers out of office."[41]

Such assumptions should, however, be scrutinized very carefully. In the post-Stalin years, the managerial and professional strata have gained considerably more autonomy in their working life, and the reduction in the power of the secret police has benefitted them more than other groups. Yet, in the last quarter of a century, the trends in wage and social welfare policy have been strongly in favor of the low-income groups, including for the first time the peasants, and these trends have been continuing in the Brezhnev era as well. By the mid-1970s, the distribution of income, including especially income associated with property, was almost surely more egalitarian in the Soviet Union than in the United States. Moreover, the top 15 to 20 percent of the Soviet population generally have not been able to acquire exclusive suburbs and exclusive neighborhood schools to anywhere near the same extent as their American counterparts, and many of the restrictions of the system (for example, those on travel abroad, on the acquisition of expensive imported goods, and even on many kinds of free expression) are felt more sharply by those with the money for luxuries and with higher education.

Perhaps such facts say little about the relative power of the top and lower strata in the Soviet Union in comparative terms and may simply reflect the more egalitarian and authoritarian values of the leaders, but it could at least be argued that they do reflect responsiveness to power as well. Income is, after all, something which can be used to achieve a great many other values, and it should be highly prized by everyone. It somehow seems unreasonable to say that the Soviet professional and managerial elite has been gaining more power than the rest of the population but that they have not used it to gain a larger share of national income.

The distribution of income in the Soviet Union—and the statistics on worker involvement discussed earlier—deserve greater consideration by political science theorists. It may be that in a country with an educated population but without the type of legitimization provided by elections, the leadership feels under more pressure to respond to mass resentment—especially mass urban resentment—at elite privileges with concrete policy actions. Emigrants from the Soviet Union report that the 1968 unrest in Czechoslovakia was quickly followed by a more vigorous affirmative action program forcing all institutions of higher education and all departments within them to admit more workers, peasants, and their children. By any reasonable definition of the term, "power" was a factor in this decision and many others like it.

Whatever our final conclusions about the distribution of power among different strata of the Soviet population, it is absolutely clear that we should not be speaking as if there were some sharp line between some elite which shares in political power and a mass which has none. If we were to try the impossible task of ranking people by their relative power, we would find some continuum or spectrum of power with tiny and almost imperceptible gradations as we moved up and down our ranking between the most powerful and the least. Or, perhaps, we would find a series of continuums.

Although the study of power is said to be the central subject of political science, our knowledge of the comparative distributions of power in different countries and our understanding of the factors associated with these differences are still in an extremely rudimentary stage. Even such issues as the impact of competitive elections have been judged more on the basis of long-held assumptions than empirical analysis. The wisest course would be to avoid definitive conclusions and hope that the Soviet experience will be one of the factors stimulating renewed attention to fundamental theoretical issues.

The Development of Constitutional Restraints?

Everyone would agree that the Soviet political leadership has not exercised power as determinedly in recent years as in the past. Everyone should agree—but they do not—that the regime has become more tolerant of individual iconoclasm, including political dissent, than it was in the Stalin era or even the Khruschchev years. The question is—do these developments simply reflect the personalities and values of the present leaders (or perhaps a temporary impasse among them) or do they represent a basic change in the nature of the political system?

If one were to argue that the Soviet political system has changed in a fundamental way, one might suggest that unwritten constitutional restraints of the type found in Great Britain are slowly beginning to develop in the Soviet Union. If so, the restraints that would be most likely to be developing are on the ability of the leader to execute political opponents, to override expert knowledge and the interests of major societal groups, and to restrict individual freedom beyond a certain point. If they are developing, they probably are still primarily of a psychological nature—the development of deeply felt norms in the leadership and the elite that certain things are improper and even repulsive in a fundamental sense. Conceivably, however, institutional restraints are also beginning to develop in the Soviet Union. If membership in the Central Committee reflects appointment to certain high positions, if these appointments come to be determined more by promotion from within than by outside interference, if the leader's ability to remove Central Committee members is severely restricted, the Central Committee would be far more independent of the General Secretary and in a far better position to control him.

If we had access to information on the inner workings of the Soviet system, we might be able to make fairly good judgments about the reasons for the more limited exercise of leadership power seen in recent years. Yet, ultimately only time is a reliable test of the durability (or even existence) of institutional and constitutional restraints in any country. To deserve the labels of "institutional" and "constitutional," the restraints must persist for sufficient time for political actors to be certain that it is not rational to contravene them and, indeed, for these actors to reach the point where the thought of challenging the restraints never seriously enters their minds. Because of the extremely low personnel turnover rates of the post-Khrushchev period, the test of the next succession should be an excellent one, but its outcome is one that can be discussed only in the context of a broad consideration of the Soviet future.

15 The Future of the Soviet System

As CHICHIKOV, the leading character in Nikolai Gogol's nineteenth-century novel *Dead Souls,* was riding through the Russian countryside in his three-horse troika, he began thinking of Russia as a troika and musing about the direction of its historical development:

> The horses fly like a whirlwind, the spokes of the wheels are blended into one revolving disc, the road quivers, and the pedestrian cries out—halting in alarm—and the troika dashes away . . . And, Russia, art not thou too flying onwards like a spirited troika that nothing can overtake . . . What is the meaning of this terrifying onrush? What mysterious force is hidden in this troika, never seen before . . . Russia, whither flyest thou? Answer![1]

To a large extent, Chichikov's question has been central for those interested in the Soviet Union. Textbooks on the Soviet Union—unlike most of those on western governments—invariably end with a discussion of the future, and many of our models center not on the Soviet present but on the presumed future course of Soviet development: Is the Soviet Union rationalizing, petrifying, converging, becoming more pluralistic, losing its dynamism, or what? The question of the Soviet future has been of equal interest not only to Russian area specialists but also to theorists of democracy and political development and to those who comment on and shape foreign policy toward the Soviet Union.

Yet, despite all the effort devoted to thought about the Soviet future, the predictive record has really been less successful than one would have expected. The early assumptions, based on the experience of the French Revolution, were that there would be a quick collapse of the regime in the face of counterrevolution, and NEP later was seen as the first major step in a convergence of the Soviet Union and the western democracies. This view became especially popular after Stalin defeated Trotsky on what was thought to be the issue of world revolution versus the building of socialism in one country.

In the Stalin era the general assumption during World War II was that victory in the war and the need for reconstruction would lead to a continuation of the wartime "reconciliation" between the Soviet regime and its people. The disillusionment associated with the absence of such a development was then expressed in the totalitarian model, which was put forward in its fullest form precisely at the end of the Stalin period as the Soviet Union was on the threshhold of an era of greater freedom.

At the very end of the Khrushchev period scholars offered a proliferation of variants of the directed society model, all of which reflected the First Secretary's dynamism and dedication to change. These models tended to be more static than predictive, but clearly they were meant as models of the system rather than of Khrushchev's personal regime, and scarcely suggested the type of change—either the overthrow of Khrushchev or the kind of regime that would be established afterwards—that was imminent. Even those writers who were adopting the factional conflict variants of the directed society model were not forecasting that the leading members of "Khrushchev's faction"—Brezhnev, Podgorny, and Kosygin—would be the center of the effort to replace the First Secretary.

The fall of Khrushchev in 1964 brought more fragmented predictions, but few indeed caught the combination of conservative style and moderate liberalism in policy toward social questions and some aspects of civil liberties that was to mark the rest of the 1960s and the 1970s. The Brezhnev period had neither the appearance of the continuing permanent revolution which some foresaw nor the open factional conflict which others expected. Least of all did a regime that survived, prospered, and produced moderately liberal policy for over a decade appear to be an ossified one run by hidebound clerks.

When scholars have often been so unsuccessful in their predictions of the Soviet future, when academics specializing on the western countries (who have immeasurably more information on public opinion and political conflicts than specialists on the Soviet Union) generally eschew prediction, when many consider long-range planning by the State Department's Policy Planning Board largely irrelevant because of the impossibility of taking all contingencies into account, the temptation is extremely strong to hypothesize that our fascination with predicting the Soviet future reflects our lack of knowledge of that system rather than our knowledge of it. The temptation is equally strong to break with tradition and to write a book without a concluding chapter on the future.

Nevertheless, general interest in the Soviet future remains strong, especially within the United States government, and if others are analyzing the subject, one can hardly resist making his own contribution to the dialogue. Moreover, many of the questions about the present (for example, whether the changes in the Brezhnev period reflect the personality of the General Secretary or are "constitutional" changes in system, whether the system has "legitimacy," and so forth) are most easily raised in a discussion of the future. The predictive record of Soviet studies should, however, be kept clearly in mind, and any analysis of the subject—regardless of who makes it—should be considered highly speculative. Indeed, since prediction tends to contain some type of deterministic assumption, especially when a single course of development is being predicted rather than a probabilistic outcome in a series of cases, the possibility always exists that the whole exercise is a dubious one. Chance may have a significant role in shaping societal development in any country, the Soviet Union not excluded.

Past Predictions and the Problem of "System"

Perhaps the best way to try to avoid mistakes in predicting the Soviet future is to ask what has led to miscalculations in the past—to discover whether there has been a consistent reason for our forecasting difficulties. If this question is asked, at least part of the answer becomes perfectly obvious: time and time again we have simply taken the present situation as we have seen it and assumed that present trends can be projected into the future.

Prediction of the future on the basis of present developments is not, of course, unique to Soviet studies. Generals proverbially plan for the last war, and few of the major American social scientists of the early 1960s predicted the riots among minorities and youth in western nations. In fact, in realms such as long-term weather forecasting or stock market analysis, prediction on the basis of present trends is often considered the technique with the highest probability of success.

In Soviet studies, however, the normal tendency to predict the future on the basis of the present has been greatly strengthened by the fascination of scholars with building "models" of the Soviet "system." This development has been a natural one, for the Soviet experience has seemed sufficiently strange that we have felt a need to try to understand and summarize it in some easily intelligible and consistent manner. Models do introduce structure into the chaos of information about the Soviet Union, and in their emphasis upon the interconnections between phenomena—or the common causes of them—they are a major aid to memory. The Soviet leaders themselves have reinforced the pressures toward such a mode of analysis by embodying their preferences in ideological orthodoxy and by insisting that their particular definition of the political system was the only thinkable contemporary expression of Marxism-Leninism.

Yet, the very reasons that produce an interest in models are precisely the reasons that they are so dangerous. The attempt to find interconnections and common causes may uncover interconnections and common causes that do not exist. In retrospect, one of the most striking features of the Soviet political system has been the impact of the values and personality of the leader, not only on policy but also on the very way decisions are made. By being intent on summarizing the essential nature of the "system" as a whole, we have often been led to assume that the idiosyncracies of each leader are actually the fundamentals of the system. By concentrating on the organizing principles of the system as we have seen them, we have neglected many phenomena that do not fit the model.

Most important for our purposes, a focus upon "system" can also create great problems for the analysis of the future. Of course, any attribution of leader characteristics to the system as a whole leaves us particularly ill-placed to foresee changes that might be produced by the removal of the leader alone, but the problem goes much deeper. If one thinks of the existence of a system as a whole, it sometimes is difficult to think of one aspect of the system changing without a transformation of the system as a whole. However, it should not be forgotten that in the mid-1950s the machine-tractor stations in agriculture often were treated as a fundamental reflection of ideology and therefore virtually impossible to replace without a total change in system. Aspects of Soviet society that we now take for granted as inherent parts of the system may also disappear with as little impact on other characteristics of it.

The danger of focusing on the system as a whole in analyses of the future becomes particularly great when our definition of the system is not precise. Consider, for example, the historical question: Was the Soviet political system in 1952 a stable one over the near and medium term? Obviously that system was stable in the sense that the Soviet leaders were not to be confronted with the problem of widespread riots either then or in the coming decade. It was also stable in the sense that the basic political institutions and the primacy of the Communist party and of Marxism-Leninism remained basically unchanged for at least a quarter of a century.

Despite these continuities, the Soviet political system in 1952 seldom was analyzed simply in terms of its institutional features. The system was described as one of absolute one-man rule, arbitrary police terror that virtually atomized society, an ideology so all-encompassing as to define the nature of genetics and linquistics and so rigid as to permit a deviationist the option of open recantation at best, a leadership with an inner compulsion to transform man and society in conformance with the dictates of the ideology. That system turned out to be very unstable, disappearing in large part soon after Stalin himself left the scene. What then do we want to conclude about the stability of the Soviet political system of 1952? The necessity for choice in our definition of political system—and the difficulty in making it—illustrates the dangers of the analysis.

If we try to predict the evolution of the Soviet "system" in the future, it is particularly vital that we specify what it is that we are discussing, for some features of that system are likely to prove very durable, regardless of the future course of events. The Soviet Union has an authoritarian political system, but it has a constitution and a set of party rules that correspond in large part to western conceptions of democracy, and it pledges allegiance to an ideology promising the establishment of full democracy and individual freedom. It glorifies a "founding father" who emphasized the absolute correctness of his basic views and advocated authoritarian means to achieve them, but who portrayed the future in most utopian terms in *State and Revolution*.

Because of the ambiguous nature of the Soviet political tradition, any future evolution is highly likely to retain the framework of the present system in one sense or another. At one extreme, a major movement toward western-style democracy surely would be carried out under Lenin's slogan "All Power to the Soviets," and any abolition of censorship would be undertaken in the name of the Soviet constitution. At the other extreme, a return to a more authoritarian and repressive system (probably even a military coup) would be justified on the grounds of ideological purity and struggle against capitalist elements. The establishment of a one-party system with more competitive elections within the party would be justified by the earlier-quoted Lenin statement that "Of course, it is permissible (especially before a Congress) for different groups to organize in blocs (and so is it to canvass for votes)."

Thus, the really significant debates on the fundamentals of the Soviet system are not likely to center on the question suggested by Solzhenitsyn (that is, whether to repudiate Marx and Lenin), but on which aspect of Marx and Lenin to emphasize. With even the most radical evolution apt to have such a character, more subtle evolution will be even less clear-cut in its impact upon the institutional characteristics of the system and will be even more difficult to analyze. It is a danger we should always keep in mind when we talk loosely about the stability or evolution of "the system."

Evolution Toward a Constitutional Democracy?

When westerners ask about the evolution of the Soviet system, the question they usually have in mind involves change of the most radical kind. Will the Soviet Union become a constitutional democracy like the United States? Will the dissidents soon be ruling Russia?

Especially in the absence of comprehensive public opinion polls or even comprehensive contact with members of the Soviet upper stratum, there is really only one way to judge the likelihood of a total collapse of the regime. We essentially must take our general notions about the sources of stability and instability in political systems and then compare what we know about the Soviet Union against these generalizations. Unfortunately, however, when we try to engage in such an activity, the answers do not point in the same direction.

Most of the basic conclusions of political scientists about the sources of political stability would suggest that the fundamentals of the Soviet political system should have powerful support. The Communist regime came to power in a great social revolution, and its symbols and much of its general ideology seem to have been attractive to large numbers of workers and peasants. Unlike the situation after the 1789 revolution in France, a large portion of the losing Russian elite in 1917 either emigrated or were killed in the Civil War. While collectivization and repression eroded many early sources of support, the party did come to be associated with a highly successful industrialization program and especially with restoration of the nation's position in the international area and with achievement of historic national goals. After victory in World War II, the party also became associated with a steadily rising standard of living and an apparent solution to the problems of unemployment and inflation that came to plague western economies in these years.

Probably most important of all, rule by the Communist party was accompanied by upward mobility for a large percentage of the Soviet people. In the 1920s and early 1930s an astonishing proportion of the skilled working class was promoted into administrative or professional positions, either directly or after having been sent to college (usually engineering institutes). As has been seen, some 230,000 persons admitted into the party as workers had enjoyed such mobility by 1927, and another 666,000 had a similar experience between 1930 and 1933 alone. And these figures do not include those workers who were promoted before entering the party or without entering the party at all. When one compares the number of the upwardly mobile in these years with the number of skilled industrial workers under thirty years of age, one has the impression that this subclass must have been liquidated through promotion—that as many as 50 percent of them may have been affected. Small wonder that this category of people was given a special name: the *vydvizhentsy,* the pushed-forward ones.

Westerners tend to think that upward mobility ceased after the Great Purge of 1937–1938, but this is simply not true in the definition of mobility that is meaningful to people: Is my job of higher status than that of my father? Industrialization in all countries brings an enormous expansion in the number of professional-managerial and skilled labor jobs that the population finds desirable, and there must be upward mobility into these jobs, for the old elites do not have enough offspring to fill them, even neglecting the possibility of downward mobility among these offspring. Table 41 indicates the scale of the expansion of desirable jobs produced by rapid industrialization in the Soviet Union, and the above average death rates and emigration among the old upper stratum, coupled with the below average birth rates in the urban white collar families, meant that an especially high proportion of the new jobs had to be filled from below. The continuation of low birth rates among the new elites (one-child families have been common) perpetuated this situation.

Much of the intergenerational mobility comes early in adult life, especially at the time that working class and peasant youth go through secondary specialized and higher educational institutions into white collar jobs. However, college admission is much more restricted in the Soviet Union than in the United States, and this leaves room for more mobility for those who begin their careers as workers and peasants and move into technician, professional, or lower administrative-political positions as they take night courses as adults. Moreover, the various programs for upgrading skills at work provide many opportunities for movement from unskilled and semiskilled into skilled labor jobs.

Those of working class and peasant origins not only have the opportunity to move into white collar strata in general but also have considerable access to the "power" positions in the political and economic hierarchies. There are many pieces of evidence suggesting that the children of the elite primarily aspire to (and obtain) jobs of a professional and cultural nature: scientist, college teacher, journalist, diplomat, and so forth. An elite mother may be heard speaking of the post of plant manager as one "beneath" her son, especially since the route to it requires engineering and lower administrative work in the factory rather than staff work in a ministry or in a research or design institute. As a result, such jobs are often open to children of lower white collar, worker, or peasant families. For example, in 1977 the director of the Magnitogorsk Metallurgy Combine reported that 192 of the 200 leading personnel of the Combine (chief specialists and heads of shops and departments) had begun their career as workers.[2] Undoubtedly a number of these workers were children of white collar parents who were employed as workers for only a short time, but the chance for social mobility to this type of post is very great.

Entry into political work has much of the same character. In one oft-quoted, but rather ambiguous, statement, Brezhnev remarked in 1971 that "over 80 percent of the present secretaries of republican central committees and of oblast and krai party committees, as well as of chairmen of the republican Council of Ministers or executive committees of the krai and oblast soviets, began their activity as workers and peasants, as did around 70 percent of the USSR ministers and chairmen of state committees."[3] A large-scale 1974–1975 study of the party apparatus of twenty-nine city and raion party committees in seven republics discovered that 82.6 percent of the personnel had come (were *vykhodtsy*) from the working class and the peasantry. Of those employed in the city and urban raion party apparatuses, 65.2 percent were workers and collective farmers by social origin (that is, presumably had a father with such a job), while this figure rose to 79.8 percent in the rural raion committees. A total of 56.3 percent of those in the survey had been a worker or collective farmer in their first job.[4]

The upward mobility and improvement of living standards, it should be emphasized, are not limited to the Russians. For many years—even decades—a number of western scholars have emphasized the dangers to long-range stability posed by the multinational character of the country. There is much to be said for this point, for rising education levels among ethnic or religious minorities have often been associated with a great increase in unrest in other parts of the world. Yet, in most cases of strongest discontent—for example, in the 1960s and the 1970s, the French in Quebec, the Catholics in Northern Ireland, the Blacks in the United States—many of the minority who actually receive higher education find their path into high status jobs blocked—often unfairly by objective standards—by members of the majority group. Nothing is more explosive than throttling the chance for advancement for a significant-sized group that is educated, ambitious, and talented enough to organize resistance.

In the Soviet Union, the regime has from the beginning not only permitted but even promoted the movement of members of local nationalities into college, into the party, and into higher status jobs within the republic. It has dealt with nationalist opposition harshly, but the rewards for talented individuals who avoid such activity are high. This combination of stick

Table 41 *Persons in occupations of different status levels, 1939–1970*

TYPE OF OCCUPATION	1939	PERCENTAGE CHANGE 1939–1959	1959	PERCENTAGE CHANGE 1959–1970	1970
Higher education white collar[a]	4,860,000	+67	8,115,000	+82	14,790,000
Lower education white collar[a]	6,720,000	+58	10,650,000	+51	16,030,000
Skilled labor (light industry excluded)[b]	7,470,000	+145	18,330,000	+63	29,860,000
Skilled labor in light industry[b]	2,125,000	+36	2,900,000	+25	3,625,000
Medium skilled labor[c]	6,550,000	+78	11,680,000	+3	11,975,000
Higher skilled labor in agriculture[d]	2,690,000	+30	3,500,000	+12	3,925,000
Least skilled labor[e]	9,935,000	+5	10,450,000	−23	8,075,000
Unskilled labor in agriculture[d]	32,075,000	−5	30,365,000	−38	18,680,000

Source: *Itogi vsesoiuznoi perepisi naseleniia 1959 goda, SSSR* (Moscow, Gosstatizdat, 1962), pp. 161–166; *Itogi vsesoiuznoi perepisi naseleniia 1970 goda* (Moscow, Statistika, 1973), VI, 14–23, 620–632. The table is based on the detailed occupational categories in the census. The occupations were ranked by the number of persons in them with a given education level in 1959 (1970 in the case of those in white collar occupations). The occupations were divided into three main groups—white collar ("mental work" in the Soviet census), blue collar outside of agriculture ("physical work" in the Soviet census), and "physical labor" in agriculture. Each of these major groups was then subdivided on the basis of the education level of the occupations within it, and the most highly educated blue collar worker group

564

was further subdivided between light industry (textiles, sewing, food industry, leather industry, shoe industry, leather industry, and waitresses) and other industries. The occupational categories were then held constant for all three years, and the number of persons in the different occupations within the category were totaled for each of the years. The assumption is made that in a general sense the occupations with persons of higher levels of education in them turn out to be the occupations with high status, especially if adjustments are made for two low-paid groups, the lower education white collar occupations (usually clerical and technician) and the workers in light industry. In fact, the listings of occupations produced by this methodology do correspond generally to one's impressions of occupational status. The phenomenon of the expansion of higher status jobs during industrialization is a universal one, and the methodology is adapted from the work of three leading western sociologists: Bernard A. Blishin, Otis Duncan, and Joseph Kahl.

ª Includes those occupations in the "mental work" category in which at least 10 percent of the persons in them had complete higher education in 1970. (I would have preferred to use 1959 data, but it was not available.) Three occupations (sales clerks, beauty operators, and photographers) were listed in "mental work" in the 1959 census, but were transferred to physical work in the 1970 census. I have kept to the 1959 designation throughout.

ᵇ Includes those occupations in the "physical work" category in which at least 40 percent of the persons in them had at least incomplete secondary education in 1970. The definition of light industry is given in note a, the exclusion of the occupations transferred in 1970 is discussed in note b.

ᶜ Includes those occupations in the "physical work" category in which between 25 and 39 percent of the persons in them had at least incomplete secondary education in 1959.

ᵈ Includes those occupations in the agricultural "physical labor" category in which at least 30 percent of the persons in them had at least incomplete secondary education in 1959. These included heads of livestock sections, brigadiers, link-leaders, lowest level bookkeepers, and tractorists and other mechanizers. (The latter occupation had risen from 45 percent of the category in 1939 to 81 percent of it in 1970.) Heads of livestock sections ("fermy") were transferred to the "mental labor" category in the 1970 census, but I have kept them in the "physical labor" category throughout for consistency.

ᵉ Includes those occupations in which less than 25 percent of the persons in them had at least incomplete secondary education in 1959.

and carrot has proved highly effective in the past, and it may continue to be so for longer than we anticipate, especially if the republics gradually receive more de facto autonomy on middle level decisions.

We see in the Soviet Union, therefore, a country whose political system is associated with a great increase in national power and the achievement of national goals, with upward mobility for the ambitious and the talented, and with steadily rising standards of living (indeed, even progressively greater egalitarianism in income distribution) for the masses. That is scarcely the classic description of a country on the verge of revolution, even leaving aside the question of police repression.

Why then might one even contemplate the possibility of fairly rapid movement toward a constitutional democracy in the Soviet Union? The main reason on theoretical grounds would be the existence of a strong worldwide correlation between the level of industrial development in a country and the presence of classic democratic institutions such as competitive elections. The most industrialized countries are almost all constitutional democracies, while democratic political forms are found only infrequently in the least industrialized countries.[5]

Many social scientists have insisted that this tendency for the most industrialized countries to have classic democratic institutions is not a chance phenomenon. For example, Talcott Parsons, probably the foremost American sociologist of this century, includes "the democratic association with elective leadership and fully enfranchised membership" among the "evolutionary universals" of societal development.[6] In a society with a great deal of specialization of labor, he argues, universal suffrage and competitive elections are vital for reasons both of legitimacy (the need to recognize the equality at one basic level of those performing all of society's tasks) and of effectiveness (the need for a mechanism to integrate the different specialized perspectives). The theoretical argument in favor of a future democratization of the Soviet Union is not simply one that can be deduced from Parsons' line of analysis; it is one that he himself made directly. "In the long run [the Soviet system's] legitimacy will certainly be undermined if the party leadership continues to be unwilling to *trust* the people it has educated . . . To trust the people is to entrust them with a share of political responsibility."[7]

Karl Deutsch, a former president of the American Political Science Association, made a similar argument about the democratizing impact of education, but he emphasized its psychological consequences.

> Industrialization requires mass education as well as a large expansion of higher education . . . A good deal of research shows that in general people with little education prefer to be told only one side of a prob-

lem. When presented with two conflicting views, they tend to become confused and angry . . . Better educated people tend in most countries to feel angry and insulted when presented only one side of an issue. They want to hear all sides and make their own decisions.[8]

British sociologist Frank Parkin goes further and suggests that Marx's description of constitutional democracy as "bourgeois democracy" has at least one grain of truth to it.[9] He suggests that constitutional democracy has been peculiarly advantageous to those in the top 10-15 percent of the population—a group in modern society that would include most of the business-managerial-professional stratum. This group is likely to include a disproportionate number of those who entertain the unorthodox thoughts that are protected by constitutional guarantees of free speech as well as those who aspire to political power and participation. In addition, the vote may be particularly important in giving the various elements of the elite a base of power that guarantees pluralism within the elite.

Which line of theoretical analysis is then likely to be most successful in predicting the future of the Soviet political system—that which points to the presence of the usual sources of stability in the Soviet Union or that which links industrial development with the rise of western-style constitutional democracy?

As we try to answer this question, we should begin by recognizing that we are operating in the realm of pure conjecture. The experience of a number of countries strongly suggests that Communist regimes are very stable in countries in early stages of industrialization, at least if the party came into power on its own, but we simply have no evidence about Communist regimes in more advanced industrial states.

In my opinion the likelihood of a dissident victory and the development of a full constitutional democracy in the Soviet Union in the near future is not very great unless some zero-growth economic crisis occurs or the political systems of eastern Europe collapse. Although the experience of countries such as Hungary, Czechoslovakia, and Spain demonstrates that the forces antagonistic to an authoritarian regime can surface quickly in the right political circumstances, political systems that have been successful in maintaining the nation's independence, territorial integrity, and power position have hardly ever collapsed in the modern world. In these respects the Communist regime in the Soviet Union has been especially successful.

Moreover, besides the presence in the Soviet Union of the general phenomena usually associated with political stability, there are two specific features of the Soviet scene that also mitigate strongly against near-term evolution toward a multiparty democratic system. The first of these has been the regime's policy of requiring party membership for virtually all upper level administrators and a large proportion of middle level administrators. As has been seen, this policy has not resulted in an administrative system staffed by ideologues, but at least it surely has created a professional and administrative stratum that, whatever its hopes for democratization, must have concern about the consequences of an anti-Communist revolt on a personal level. A post-Communist regime in Russia could not function without former party members serving in important administrative and even political posts, but undoubtedly there would be investigations and commissions to distinguish between "good" Communists and "bad" ones, and many careers would be ruined. Few in significant administrative posts can feel entirely secure in the face of such a prospect, and the willingness of the upper and middle strata to try to crush any Hungarian-type revolution in the Soviet Union is likely to be quite widespread.

A second factor complicating any evolution toward constitutional democracy is the relationship between democratization and Russian nationalism in the Soviet Union. The most direct interconnection between the two phenomena flows from the multinational character of the Soviet Union and the system of alliances in eastern Europe. Even if a Russian prefers democratization for himself personally, he must know—perhaps unconsciously—that such a development might well produce a major decline in the world position of Russia. The Communist regimes of eastern Europe surely would not survive the establishment of constitutional democracy in the Soviet Union, and the political line that certainly would be most fruitful in elections in nearly all these countries would be an anti-Russian one. It is difficult to imagine the Warsaw Pact and the Comecon surviving much longer than the Communist regimes.

The likelihood of the Soviet Union itself surviving as a territorial unit in the wake of democratization is much more difficult to judge. The control of Moscow over the non-Russian borderlands dates from well before the Bolshevik revolution, and, as a result, the economy of the entire country has become well integrated and the population in each republic has become multinational in character. Because of these factors, national independence would produce short-term turmoil, even if the Russians did not try to use force to "maintain the Union." In these circumstances, many persons in the borderlands might well vote for a looser federation rather than complete independence. Nationalities such as the Armenians who have had unhappy relations with neighbors (the Turks in the Armenian case) might be particularly loathe to break all ties with the Russians, but those such as the Latvians, Estonians, and Lithuanians who have had a relatively recent experience of national independence might be especially likely to choose the opposite path.

Yet, whatever the ultimate consequences of democratization, the establishment of a multiparty system would, at a minimum, surely result in the creation of nationalist parties in all the republics. Americans, who are aware from their own history of the strength of the issues and emotions that led the North to fight a long and costly war to prevent self-determination for the South and to keep those states in the Union, can well imagine the normal Russian reaction to the thought of the loss of so much of the country. Nationalism has become no less potent a force in the twentieth century than it was in the nineteenth.

Russian nationalism also works against an evolution toward constitutional democracy in a more subtle way. One of the great debates among the Russian intelligentsia in the late nineteenth century concerned the necessity of Russia following a western line of development. In practice, Russia did undergo western style rapid industrialization and urbanization with the creation of large-scale factory units, but it certainly did not do so with western capitalist mechanisms. Russia created a new political and economic system that not only brought great military power to itself but also served as a model that other countries adopted. In a sense, Moscow did become a Third Rome.

When dissidents propose the establishment of a constitutional democracy, they are, in practice, calling for the abandonment of a system that Russia created and for its replacement by a system associated with Russia's foremost adversary. Moreover, because of the censorship and the access dissenters have been given to western newsmen, the dissidents' positions become known to Russians almost exclusively through western channels of propaganda, and thus they become even more strongly linked with the United States in the public mind. It is a factor to which we should be more sensitive, for it may be a major one in preserving the present system.

To be sure, the political evolution of a country is not something which always takes place gradually under "normal" conditions. Unexpected crises occur, and the alternatives that present themselves at such times can be very different from those only a few weeks or months earlier. For example, if the Soviet Union came to face simultaneous revolts in a number of countries in eastern Europe and they began to spread to some of the republics inside the Soviet Union, then a democratic federation might seem the preferable choice, even to an ardent Russian nationalist. The same might be true if nationalist movements inside the Soviet Union successfully took up terrorist tactics and were able to sustain them for a long period. Similarly, the rise of a new General Secretary who tried to use the power of his office to institute terror or some highly unpopular policy might convince the elite that democratization was vital for their own safety. And, of course, if the Soviet Union becomes involved in a nuclear war, or even if a country or terrorist group employs a nuclear device anywhere in the world, the political consequences in the Soviet Union (and elsewhere) are incalculable.

While such possibilities—and others like them—must each individually be of fairly low probability, collectively the chance that something "unexpected" will take place is fairly significant. The Soviet regime faces many problems. In the economic sphere, the tempo of economic growth has been rising at progressively lower rates, and the transition from fossil fuels to other sources of energy is likely to produce severe shocks to all economic systems.[10] In the demographic sphere, the proportion of non-Europeans within the Soviet population has risen from 11.5 percent in 1959 to 17 percent in 1977, and by the end of the century the differentials in birthrates among ethnic groups are likely to ensure that almost 40 percent of the teenagers and young adults will be non-Europeans, most of them Central Asians.[11] In the political sphere, the problem of ensuring timely leadership successions while maintaining controls on the leader has not been solved, and the next succession may be particularly troublesome. The Soviet political elite will have to demonstrate great skill to handle all these problems successfully.

Within-Systems Evolution

An expression of doubt about the total collapse of the Soviet system should not, however, terminate all thought of change within that system. One of the most consistent facts about the Soviet system has been very substantial within-system change after the accession of a new leader to power. Although the next succession conceivably could be different in this respect, it likely will, depending upon its timing, involve a major generational change in the leadership echelon and a major turnover among the top administrative elite. To conclude that a change in General Secretary, combined with a change in generation in the top elite, is going to be associated with complete stability in the nature of the system for the first time during a Soviet transition is to make assumptions about the institutionalization of the Soviet system that seem to me unwarranted.

If the Soviet political system is to undergo some type of change, what is likely to be its nature? In the absence of any meaningful knowledge of the views of top contenders and those involved in the selection process, the most reasonable way to try to predict major political developments in the future is to try to judge the changing weight of social forces in the country and to assume that developments are most likely to be responsive to them. If we attempt to make such an assessment, then it seems to me that the preponderance of pressure is in the direction of liberalization. Complete freedom of speech is likely to be frightening to many for nationalist reasons, and strong reliance on market mechanisms is likely to be even more frightening because of a fear of inflation. Nevertheless, liberalization in the sense of a relaxed censorship and freer debates, more access to Western culture and consumer goods, more tolerance of iconoclasts, and greater freedom to travel abroad— in short, movement towards a system like Hungary today—are goals that seem to command fairly strong support within the professional-managerial strata— within the much-maligned "bureaucracy."

Public opinion polls on sensitive attitudes have not been published in the Soviet Union, but there are a number of reasons to believe that the balance of support for authoritarianism vs. liberalization has been shifting in a major way over the last few decades. It should never be forgotten that authoritarianism had a good deal of support in key urban strata in the 1920's and the 1930's. After the mid-1920's, the party became a party of up-ward-mobile workers and peasants—and poorly educated ones at that. If Erich Fromm and others are right that the insecurity associated with great societal flux and a shattered world-view produces tendencies towards author-itarianism and a desire to "escape from freedom," such tendencies must have been very strong in Russia in the first decades of the Twentieth Century.[12]

In such circumstances many urban Soviet citizens must have found some security in the growing authoritarianism of the party, in the growing rigidity and simplicity of doctrine, and even in the awesome figure of Stalin. There must have been many who were eager to blame all difficulties on kulaks, on bourgeois specialists, on "speculators," and so forth, and who must have applauded the idea that they should be smashed. The idea that sacrifices were necessary to save Russia from foreign attack must have had great appeal, and those with a more sophisticated knowledge of Marxism must have found Preobrazhensky's argument about the necessary relation-ship between rapid industrial growth and a squeezing of the population in early stages of "accumulation" congenial. (Those enjoying upward mobility and improving living standards must have found it all the more convincing since it relieved any guilt feelings about the sufferings of others.) It certainly would be wrong to suggest that the worst aspects of Stalinism were no more than a response to the psychological needs of the time, but it also would be wrong to ignore the psychological climate that existed.

With the passage of time, however, the sense of what is appropriate and required must have changed in many respects. Educational levels have risen enormously, and most of those born in the Soviet period—especially those born after the mid-1920's—have had more stable life-patterns. The propensi-ties towards authoritarianism in key urban sectors must have been reduced. Moreover, those with higher levels of education in the Soviet Union not only must have some of the attitudes about being presented a range of views that

Deutsch attributed to them, but they also would benefit disproportionately from such products of liberalization as travel abroad, Western consumer goods, and the like. Constitutional restraints on the leadership would be most likely to protect their position.

Perhaps of equal importance, the upper strata surely have become less confident about the legitimacy of repression of other classes. The early justifications for repression tended to be time-limited in nature. In *State and Revolution,* Lenin had referred to "the present type of people who destroy without reason" in speaking of the need to postpone full communism; Preobrazhensky had argued that the early states of industrialization were particularly difficult ones and that socialism would have to feature some of the more unpleasant features of capitalism until the economic base for communism was built; Stalin's impassioned defense of high tempos centered on the imminent dangers of capitalist encirclement and the need to catch up within ten years. Today none of these arguments is as relevant as it was in past. Marxism-Leninism was a doctrine promising freedom and democracy on a scale not seen in the West, and, as the ideological arguments in favor of postponing these promises lose force, those pushing for a freer society find that the basic ideology of the system is a powerful tool to which they can appeal.

The possibility must be admitted, of course, that a change in upper stratum attitudes will produce no response from the political leadership other than fear and increased repression. However, it should be emphasized once again that the children of the political-administrative elite overwhelmingly enter those professions that tend to be most sympathetic to some liberalization and Westernization. As the average age of those occupying the important administrative posts has risen in the 1960's and 1970's, the proportion with children who have become young adults obviously has been increasing. The older generation not only must be subject to socialization from the young, but also be aware that any major increase in repression would affect their own.

The greatest threats to a liberalizing trend would seem to be short-term ones. Older members of the Soviet elite treat the younger members of the elite—especially those born after 1926–1927 who avoided the disruptions of World War II—as more confident, less cautious, and better educated than they themselves, and this latter generation would be especially unlikely to be associated with a more repressive policy. Yet, no man born after 1923 presently sits on the Politburo. As an aging leader or generation tries to hold on against pressures for change within the party, it conceivably may take some frightened defensive steps, but the natural course of action for *any* leadership seeking to consolidate power is to accommodate itself to major social forces rather than to resist them.

The Problem of the Succession

As the length of the Brezhnev regime extends beyond a dozen years, the situation at the top of the Soviet political system looks increasingly fragile. Rumors about Brezhnev's health multiply, and, despite the removal of five Politburo members between 1973 and 1977, the leader gives the impression of a man drawing more into himself and a comfortable group of associates of his own age. He seems to have followed a conscious policy of preventing any person of the right age and set of experiences from occupying a post that would provide a natural base for succeeding to the leadership.

With no natural successor, with a top leadership near seventy years of age, with the Central Committee sixty-one years old on the average, the possibility of a troubled succession is substantial. In a broader sense the succession involves the passing of a whole generation from the scene as much as simply one man. This process could take many forms, especially depending upon the length of Brezhnev's own tenure, but, unless the present General Secretary launches a major renewal of personnel himself or outlives his generation, the disappearance of the generation from political dominance will have to occur during the uncertainties of the succession itself.

Given the existing personnel selection, the basic problem with a post-Brezhnev succession remains the circular flow of power and the institutional controls on a General Secretary. If a new General Secretary, especially a younger and more vigorous one, is able to conduct a full-scale removal of the type of official who sits on the Central Committee and to replace them with persons loyal to himself, is he not going to be in a particularly good position to emancipate himself from Central Committee control? If the Central Committee members are concerned about their own position, will they elect a man interested in change?

A second problem centers on the dominance of the personal Brezhnev entourage of so many key power positions within the party apparatus and government. As has been discussed earlier, the top General Committee secretary for the economy and organizational matters, four of the deputy chairmen of the USSR Council of Ministers, the heads of the science and education and the general departments of the Central Committee (as well as the head of the Business Office), the Minister of Internal Affairs, three deputy chairmen of the KGB, and the first secretary of the Ukrainian Central Committee had direct early career connections with Brezhnev, and the number associated with him indirectly or at later stages of their career is much greater. Those with direct early ties are, of course, a rather old group, and they would be the natural target for early removal when their patron leaves the scene.

In such a situation, one can imagine the Brezhnev inner group making a concerted—even desperate—effort to maintain their position by having one of their own, presumably Kirilenko, named as General Secretary. Such a move might work out very well if Kirilenko agreed to serve as an innovating transitional figure, but if he chose to maintain the status quo in terms of policy and personnel, it would surely produce great strains within the party hierarchy.

A third problem flows from the length of Brezhnev's rule and the tendency for his regime to lose vigor in the mid-1970s. Since 1924, the Soviet Union has had only three leaders, in contrast with, for example, ten presidents in the United States. With the exception of Malenkov in the first week after Stalin's death, the man named General Secretary or First Secretary at the beginning of the succession has remained in power for at least a decade. In the case of Brezhnev and, even more, Stalin, the result was growing rigidity in the latter part of the period; in the case of Khrushchev, it was a policy of increasingly volatile and erratic nature.

As members of the Soviet political echelon have pondered the history of their country, they must have been struck by the thought that the political system would have functioned much better if the party leader had always been removed after, say, eight years—the American constitutional limit. However, with no possibility of earning a large sum of money from memoirs, with no chance to speak out on major political issues, and without even a guarantee of meaningful freedom of movement, no sensible General Secretary will consider voluntary retirement before it is absolutely necessary.

A fourth problem in the succession arises from an extremely complicated international situation. The success of Euro-Communism poses an enormous question of how to react, all the more so since those in eastern Europe can surely ask why a Communist program that is legitimate in Italy is not legitimate in their country. The change in leadership in China may raise the choice of a reconciliation with that country, particularly after a change in leadership in the Soviet Union permits the Chinese to blame difficulties on the old leaders. And, finally, of course, with the major capitalist adversary, the United States, emphasizing the gulf between the two countries in values and making improvement in trade relations dependent upon change in internal policy, those who want to promote liberalization within the system in the Soviet Union face the danger that their program will be perceived as giving in to American pressure, as a betrayal of Russian national dignity.

It is difficult to explore in detail how the problems of the succession might be resolved. Much will depend upon the accidents of health: How long will Brezhnev live and what will have happened to other Politburo members in the interval? There is too great a likelihood that any specific scenario will be irrelevant because chance happenings like a coronary attack or some event in the outside world will redirect developments. What is worth emphasizing, however, is that, barring some resolution before Brezhnev's departure, the four problems of the succession are of such scale to present a really major challenge for the Soviet political elite. In the past we have regularly talked about succession crises, but, in practice, the transitions have not actually deserved that characterization. The next transition has the potential to be a true crisis and to result in more radical change, at least in later stages, if not immediately. For example, a constitutional limit upon the length of the tenure of the party leader—perhaps five years as exists in Mexico—would alleviate many of the problems that have been discussed, and there is a good chance that some such rule will be adopted sometime in the next decade. But whatever is done, the Soviet system needs some mechanism that would promote a more frequent change in the national leader and would ensure the possibility of rejuvenation of the administrative elite without weakening all controls on the party leader. The difficulties of the next transition may well be the occasion—or provide the pressure—for an attempt to deal with these problems.

Conclusion

We began the chapter with Chichikov's question "Russia, whither flyest thou?" and we end by acknowledging that the answer remains largely obscured by the dust of the Russian troika, if not other traffic. It should be emphasized once more that the scholarly record of prediction has been extremely poor, and if the ideas presented here were to become the conventional wisdom, one has the uneasy feeling that that would almost surely guarantee that they are wrong.

But perhaps the most important point to make in conclusion is that the job of the scholar is not to predict, but to understand. To be sure, understanding should be an aid to prediction, but the future still depends on such a complex interaction of accidents of personality, of the health of leaders, of unexpected crises, of responses to them that inevitably must be made with insufficient information and in the heat of emotion, and of events in countries quite outside the knowledge of a specialist on the country about which a prediction is being made. Ultimately it may be little more than chance that makes one prediction come true and another fail.

The Soviet future should not be looked upon simply as something to predict; it should also be seen as the source for additional data for our understanding of the Soviet system and the processes of political development. Too many of the generalizations of social science theory are based upon western and even Anglo-American experience, and too many of our theories of development are based on little more than the ideological belief that our western system is destined to be the final stage of historical development. The Communist countries—if they are not treated simply in ideological terms—provide the opportunity to test our theories and generalizations and to reexamine many of our assumptions. It is with the excitement of the opportunity for discovery rather than with the certainties of our models that we should await future developments in the way the Soviet Union is governed.

Notes

1. The Origins of Bolshevism

1. "Doklad o revoliutsii 1905 goda" (Lecture on the 1905 Revolution), in V. I. Lenin, *Polnoe sobranie sochinenii* (Moscow, Gospolitizdat, 1962), XXX, 328.

2. Strictly speaking, the leader of Russia bore the title of emperor by the nineteenth century, but there seems little reason to break with the normal conventions and I will continue to speak of the tsar.

3. Quoted in B. H. Sumner, *Survey of Russian History* (London, Duckworth, 1944), pp. 67–68.

4. Ibid., p. 67.

5. See ibid., p. 104.

6. Alexander Gerschenkron, *Economic Backwardness in Historical Perspective* (Cambridge, Mass., Harvard University Press, 1962), p. 236.

7. See Gerald T. Robinson, *Rural Russia Under the Old Regime* (New York, Longmans, Green, 1932).

8. Richard Pipes, *Russia Under the Old Regime* (New York, Charles Scribner's Sons, 1974), pp. 171–190, esp. 177–178.

9. For a history of the process by which this decision was taken, see Terence Emmons, *The Russian Landed Gentry and the Peasant Emancipation of 1861* (London, Cambridge University Press, 1968).

10. See Theodore Von Laue, *Sergei Witte and the Industrialization of Russia* (New York, Columbia University Press, 1963).

11. Witt Bowden, Michael Karpovich, and Abbott Payson Usher, *An Economic History of Europe since 1750* (New York, American Book Co., 1937), p. 607.

12. The oil industry lagged behind, and indeed the volume of production of petroleum dropped from 632 million poods (a pood equals 36 pounds avoiridupois) in 1900 to 561 million poods in 1913. In the same period, pig iron increased from 177 million to 283 million poods, iron and steel from 163 million to 246 million, coal

from 1,003 million to 2,214 million, and cotton consumption from 16.1 million to 25.9 million. P. I. Lyashchenko, *History of the National Economy of Russia to the 1917 Revolution* (New York, Macmillan Co., 1949), p. 688.

13. Ibid., p. 674.

14. See S. Frederick Starr, *Decentralization and Self-Government in Russia, 1830–1870* (Princeton, Princeton University Press, 1972).

15. A discussion of these changes can be found in William H. E. Johnson, *Russia's Educational Heritage* (Pittsburgh, Carnegie Press, 1950), and Patrick L. Alston, *Education and the State in Tsarist Russia* (Stanford, Stanford University Press, 1969).

16. Although the amount of land available to the peasantry increased between 1877 and 1905, it failed to keep pace with the peasant's fecundity. The average size of household allotments declined from 35.6 acres in 1877 to 28.1 acres in 1905. Robinson, *Rural Russia Under the Old Regime*, p. 94.

17. Richard G. Robbins, *Famine in Russia, 1891–1892* (New York, Columbia University Press, 1975).

18. V. R. Leikina-Svirskaia, *Intelligentsiia v Rossii vo vtoroi polovine XIX veka* (Moscow, Mysl', 1971), p. 70. Quoted and discussed in Pipes, *Russia Under the Old Regime*, pp. 262–263.

19. Bertram D. Wolfe, *Three Who Made a Revolution* (New York, Dial Press, 1948), p. 33.

20. The most vigorous spokesman for the view that the bureaucracy—or at least many in the bureaucracy—often pushed innovation rather than simply throttling it is Starr, *Decentralization and Self-Government*. A sharp attack on the notion of a "good" society and a "bad" bureaucracy is also found in Robbins, *Famine in Russia*.

21. This point is much emphasized in Richard Pipes, *Struve: Liberal on the Left, 1870–1905* (Cambridge, Mass., Harvard University Press, 1970), esp. pp. 29–30, 84–86, 95.

22. An excellent discussion of this movement can be found in Franco Venturi, *Roots of Revolution: History of the Populist and Socialist Movements in 19th Century Russia* (New York, Knopf, 1960), pp. 497–506.

23. Ibid., pp. 633–708.

24. Richard Pipes, *Social Democracy and the St. Petersburg Labor Movement, 1885–1897* (Cambridge, Mass., Harvard University Press, 1963), p. 8.

25. For a discussion emphasizing the creation of a police state in Russia after 1881 see Pipes, *Russia Under the Old Regime*, pp. 281–318.

26. The standard biography of Plekhanov is Samuel H. Baron, *Plekhanov: The Father of Russian Marxism* (Stanford, Stanford University Press, 1963).

27. The first statement is from the 1887 program of the group, the second from G. Plekhanov, *O zadachakh sotsialistov v bor'be s golodom v Rossii* (Geneva, 1892), pp. 38–39.

28. Pipes, *Struve*, p. 51 n. 30.

29. Ibid., pp. 104ff.

30. "Chto delat' " (What Is To Be Done), in Lenin, *Polnoe sobranie sochinenii*, VI, 60.

31. Friedrich Engels, "Speech at the Graveside of Karl Marx," in Robert C. Tucker, ed., *The Marx-Engels Reader* (New York, W. W. Norton, 1972), p. 603.

32. Carl Schurz, *The Reminiscences of Carl Schurz* (New York, The McClure Company, 1907), I, 140.

33. Richard Pipes, "The Origins of Bolshevism: The Intellectual Evolution of Young Lenin," in Richard Pipes, ed., *Revolutionary Russia* (Cambridge, Mass., Harvard University Press, 1968), pp. 26–52.

34. Quoted in Wolfe, *Three Who Made a Revolution*, p. 121.

35. Still probably the best such psychological study is Leopold H. Haimson, *The Russian Marxists and the Origins of Bolshevism* (Combridge, Mass., Harvard University Press, 1955).

36. N. K. Krupskaia, *Vospominaniia o Lenine* (Moscow, Gosudarstvennoe izdatel'stro, 1931), pp. 6–7.

37. Baron, *Plekhanov*, pp. 66–68.

38. "Chto delat'," in Lenin, *Polnoe sobranie sochinenii*, VI, 30.

39. Ibid., pp. 40, 38. The italics are Lenin's.

40. Ibid., p. 30. The tense of the sentence has been changed. The italics are Lenin's.

41. Ibid., pp. 28, 127.

42. "Letter to P. G. Smidovich (August 2, 1902)" and "Letter to the Moscow Committee of the RSDRP (August 24, 1902)," XLVI, 210, 212.

43. "Chto delat'," ibid., VI, 112.

44. These four paragraphs have been assembled from statements taken out of order from the letter. "Pis'mo k tovarishchu o nashikh organizatsionnykh zadachakh," ibid, VII, 21, 8, 9, 10, 16, 21, 22. The italics are Lenin's.

45. "Chto delat'," ibid, VI, 135, 127.

46. Ibid., VI, 178 and n.

47. "Pis'mo k tovarishchu," ibid., VII, 18–19.

48. *Vtoroi s" ezd RSDRP*, [*Iul'-Avgust 1903 goda*], *Protokoly* (Moscow, Gospolitizdat, 1959), p. 265.

49. "Shag vpered, dva shaga nazad," in Lenin, *Polnoe sobranie sochinenii*, VIII, 254–255, 259n.

50. Ibid., p. 249; "Chto delat'," ibid, VI, 140; *Vtoroi s"ezd*, pp. 276–278.

51. "Shag vpered," in Lenin, *Polnoe sobranie sochinenii*, VIII, 254; *Vtoroi s"ezd*, p. 265.

52. *Vtoroi s"ezd*, p. 464.

53. Ibid., pp. 277–278.

54. Krupskaia, *Vospominaniia o Lenine*, p. 96.

55. Baron, *Plekhanov*, pp. 189–192.

56. "Kak chut' ne potukhla 'Iskra'?" in Lenin, *Polnoe sobranie sochinenii*, IV, 334–352.

57. See the discussion in J. L. H. Keep, *The Rise of Social Democracy in Russia* (Oxford, Clarendon Press, 1963), pp. 107–111.

58. *Vtoroi s"ezd*, p. 263.

59. Ibid, pp. 22, 36, 54–56.

60. Ibid., p. 167.

61. Ibid., p. 275.

62. Krupskaia, *Vospominaniia o Lenine*, p. 95.

63. "Shag vpered," in Lenin, *Polnoe sobranie sochinenii*, VIII, 265 and n.

64. "Letter to M. N. Liadov," November 10, 1903, ibid., XLVI, 323. See also "Rasskaz o II s"ezde RSDRP" (Account of the Second Congress of the RSDRP), ibid., VIII, 16–17.

65. I owe this point to Leopold Haimson, who refers to the Lydia Dan archive in the Columbia University Menshevik Archive.

66. This point is emphasized in Leonard Schapiro, *The Communist Party of the Soviet Union*, 2d ed. (New York, Random House, 1971), p. 54.

67. *Komsomol'skaia pravda*, July 5, 1928, p. 4. I owe this reference to Sheila Fitzpatrick.

68. *Vtoroi s"ezd*, p. 169; Leon Trotsky, *Nashi politicheskie zadachi* (Geneva, Izdatel'stvo Rossiskoi sotsial-democraticheskoi partii, 1904), p. 54.

69. A good description of Lenin during this period is found in Nikolay Valentinov (N. V. Volski), *Encounters with Lenin* (London, Oxford University Press, 1968), esp. pp. 111–151. Valentinov suggests that Lenin was torn between an impulse to compromise and an impulse to strike back.

70. George Vernadsky, *A History of Russia* (New Haven, Yale University Press, 1944), p. 195.

71. Robinson, *Rural Russia Under the Old Regime*, p. 182.

72. Ibid., p. 183.

73. Ibid., p. 194.

74. Lyaschenko, *History of the National Economy of Russia*, p. 747. Donald Male states that the figure given by Lyashchenko is generally accepted. However, the number of peasants who remained in the commune is a controversial subject, and the speed with which many seemed to return to it after the revolution even suggests that some may have departed only on paper. D. J. Male, *Russian Peasant Organization Before Collectivization* (London, Cambridge University Press, 1971), pp. 18–21. See also Dorothy Atkinson, "The Statistics on the Russian Lend Commune, 1905–1917," *Slavic Review*, 32 (December 1973), 773–787. A brief description of the agricultural progress that occurred in these years is found in Sergei Pushkarev, *The Emergence of Modern Russia, 1801–1917* (New York, Holt, Rinehart, and Winston, 1963), pp. 264–270.

75. "Pobeda kadetov i zadachi rabochei partii," (The Victory of the Kadets and the Tasks of the Workers' Party), in Lenin, *Polnoe sobranie sochinenii*, XII, 326.

76. See Wolfe, *Three Who Made a Revolution*, p. 121.

77. "Dve taktiki sotsial-demokratii v demokraticheskoi revoliutsii," in Lenin, *Polnoe sobranie sochinenii*, XI, 37.

78. Ibid., p. 89.

79. Ibid., p. 90.

80. "Otnoshenie sotsial-demokratii k krest'ianskomu dvizhenii" (Social Democracy's Attitude Toward the Peasant Movement), ibid., XI, 222.

81. For a description of the various intra- and interfactional conflicts of these years see Schapiro, *The Communist Party of the Soviet Union*, pp. 72–142.

82. The calculation is that of David Lane and is found in his *The Roots of Russian Communism* (Assen, Netherlands, Van Gorcum, 1969), pp. 13–15. In subsequent pages Lane used these biographies in an attempt to compare the social background of the Bolsheviks and Mensheviks.

83. Adam B. Ulam, *The Bolsheviks* (New York, Macmillan Co., 1965), p. 218.

84. Lane, *Roots of Russian Communism*, p. 13.

85. Ibid., pp. 52–58.

86. N. N. Popov, *Outline History of the Communist Party of the Soviet Union* (New York, International Publishers, 1934), I, 237–238.

87. Wolfe, *Three Who Made a Revolution*, p. 478.

88. This paragraph is drawn from a two-part article by Leopold Haimson, "The Problem of Social Stability in Urban Russia, 1905–1917," *Slavic Review*, 23 (December 1964), 619–642, esp. 627, 629–632, and 24 (March 1965), 1–22, as well as from his "Reply" to critics, 24 (March 1965), 47-56, esp. 49–51.

89. Lenin's classic analysis of this question is found in his pamphlet, "Imperialism—The Highest Stage of Capitalism," which is available in many editions.

90. Pushkarev, *The Emergence of Modern Russia*, p. 395.

91. Merle Fainsod, *How Russia Is Ruled* (Cambridge, Mass., Harvard University Press, 1953), p. 47.

92. Moshe Lewin, *Lenin's Last Struggle* (New York, Random House, 1968), pp. 17–18.

93. "Chto delat'," in Lenin, *Polnoe sobranie sochinenii*, VI, 38–39.

94. "Letter to V. A. Noskov (August 4, 1902)," ibid., LXVI, 212–215; "Pis'mo tovarishchu," ibid., VII, 22–23.

95. For example, see the discussion of his relationship with Bukharin in Stephen F. Cohen, *Bukharin and the Bolshevik Revolution.* (New York, Alfred A. Knopf, 1973), pp. 22–42.

2. The Road to Power

1. The appropriate references will be found in the other notes to this chapter.

2. Russia had not adopted an adjustment in the calendar made in the West in the Middle Ages, and by 1917 its calendar was thirteen days behind the western. Thus, November 7 in the West was October 25 in Russia. Since the Soviet regime quickly adopted the western calendar, I am using the western dates, but the reader who wants to read more about the revolution should be warned that most of the specialized literature (except for Chamberlin) makes the opposite choice and hence places the various events of 1917 on different dates than given in this chapter.

3. The phrase is from Philip Selznick, *The Organizational Weapon* (New York, McGraw-Hill, 1952).

4. These generalizations really apply to the revolution in Russia. In the non-Russian areas of the Russian empire, the situation was much more complex as the nationality question interacted with the class one.

5. V. P. Semennikov, ed., *Nikolai II i velikie kniaziia* (Moscow-Leningrad, Gosudarstvennoe izdatel'stvo, 1925), p. 122.

6. For a description of the meeting by one of the participants (and leading chroniclers of the revolution) see N. N. Sukhanov, *The Russian Revolution, 1917*, edited, abridged, and translated by Joel Carmichael (London, Oxford University Press, 1955), pp. 57–73.

7. V. V. Shulgin, *Dni* (Belgrade, Novoe vremia, 1925), p. 179.

8. These conditions included political amnesty, civil liberties, and freedom to organize trade unions and to strike; abolition of all caste, religious, and national limitations; replacement of the police by a people's militia; local self-government; the convocation of a constituent assembly; protection of the military units that took part in the revolution from loss of arms or removal from Petrograd; and the guarantee of general civil and political rights to soldiers on condition that they maintain strict military discipline in service. P. N. Miliukov, *Istoriia vtoroi russkoi revoliutsii* (Sofia, Rossiisko-Bolgarskoe knigoizdatel'stvo, 1921), I, part 1, 47.

9. A. Shliapnikov, *Semnadtsatyi god* (Moscow-Leningrad, Gosudarstvennoe izdatel'stvo, 1925–1927), II, 236.

10. "Rezoliutsiia vserossiiskogo soveshchaniia sovetov rabochikh i soldatskikh deputatov," in N. Avdeev, *Revoliutsiia 1917 g., Khronika sobytii*, 2d ed. (Moscow, Gosudarstvennoe izdatel'stvo 1923–1926), I, 198.

11. *Partiinaia zhizn'*, no. 19 (October 1967), p. 8.

12. William Henry Chamberlin, *The Russian Revolution 1917–1921* (New York, Macmillan Co., 1935), I, 117.

13. "Manifesto of the Russian Social-Democratic Labor Party 'To All Citizens of Russia'," in V. I. Lenin, *Collected Works* (New York, International Publishers, 1929), XX (2), 378–379.

14. N. N. Popov, *Outline History of the Communist Party of the Soviet Union* (New York, International Publishers, 1934), I, 352.

15. Ibid.

16. L. Kamenev, "Without Secret Diplomacy," translated in Lenin, *Collected Works*, XX (2), 380.

17. "Letter to A. M. Kollontai, March 16, 1917," in V. I. Lenin, *Polnoe sobranie sochinenii* (Moscow, Gospolitizdat, 1964), XLIX, 399.

18. "Letter to A. M. Kollontai, March 17, 1917," ibid., p. 402.

19. That the Germans would permit such a trip in time of war was attributed to their hope that Lenin's antiwar position, if enunciated inside Russia, would weaken the Russian war effort. This incident, more than any other, led to the suspicion and charge that Lenin was a German agent.

20. Quoted in Chamberlin, *The Russian Revolution*, I, 117.

21. "Doklad na sobranii Bolshevikov-uchastnikov vserossiiskogo soveshchaniia sovetov rabochikh i soldatskikh deputatov" (Speech Delivered at a Caucus of the Bolshevik Members of the All-Russian Conference of the Soviets of Workers' and Soldiers' Deputies), in Lenin, *Polnoe sobranie sochinenii*, XXXI, 108–111.

22. E. H. Carr, *The Bolshevik Revolution, 1917-1923* (New York, Macmillan Co., 1951), I, 81.

23. L. Kamenev, "Our Differences," translated in Lenin, *Collected Works,* XX (2), 380–381.

24. "Pisma o taktike" (Letters on Tactics), in Lenin, *Polnoe sobranie sochinenii,* XXXI, 132.

25. "O zadachakh proletariata v dannoi revoliutsii" (On the Tasks of the Proletariat in the Present Revolution), ibid., p. 114.

26. "Pisma o taktike," ibid., p. 133.

27. Ibid., pp. 133–134.

28. "O dvoevlastii" (On Dual Power), ibid., p. 145.

29. "Zadachi proletariata v nashei revoliutsii" (The Tasks of the Proletariat in Our Revolution), ibid., p. 155.

30. "Doklad o tekushchem momente i ob otnoshenii k vremmenomu pravitel'stvu 14 (27) Aprelia" (Report on the Present Situation and the Attitude Toward the Provincial Government), in Lenin, *Polnoe sobranie sochinenii,* XXXI, 244.

31. At the party conference in early May, the membership was announced to be 80,000 persons, and Soviet calculations in the 1960s put the figure in excess of 100,000. I. I. Mints, *Istoriia velikogo oktiabria* (Moscow, Nauka, 1968), II, 32. However, calculations in the 1920s put the number in the 40,000 to 46,000 range. T. H. Rigby, *Communist Party Membership in the U.S.S.R.* (Princeton, Princeton University Press, 1968), p. 61. As Rigby points out, it was difficult even to define a party member in these hectic times, and the higher figure may not simply represent inflation in local reports but also a looser definition of a member and even a difficulty in differentiating between a Bolshevik and a Menshevik in some local organizations that had never split.

32. Chamberlin, *The Russian Revolution,* I, 148.

33. Ibid., I, 152–153.

34. Marc Ferro, *The Russian Revolution of February 1917* (Englewood Cliffs, N.J., Prentice-Hall, Inc., 1972), pp. 123–125.

35. Merle Fainsod, *Smolensk Under Soviet Rule* (Cambridge, Mass., Harvard University Press, 1958), pp. 27–28.

36. Ferro, *The Russian Revolution of February 1917,* pp. 123–125, 115, 119–120.

37. Ibid., p. 123.

38. Oliver H. Radkey, *The Agrarian Foes of Bolshevism* (New York, Columbia University Press, 1958), pp. 358.

39. A. V. Shestakov, "Krest'ianskie organizatsii v 1917 godu," in V. P. Miliutin, ed., *Agrarnaia revoliutsiia* (Moscow, Gosudarstvennoe izdatel'stvo, 1928), II, 116–117.

40. Radkey, *The Agrarian Foes of Bolshevism,* pp. 374–385, 439–442. John L. H. Keep, *The Russian Revolution: A Study in Mass Mobilization* (London, Weiderfeld & Nicolson, 1976), pp. 153–247.

41. The word "moderate" is always a relative term. Those with more middle-class or liberal leanings (for example, those likely to support the Kadets) considered many of these "moderate" socialists to be wild radicals. On the other hand, Soviet historians, in recognizing that the workers were supporting the Mensheviks more than the Bolsheviks at this time, state that "a petty bourgeois wave engulfed a significant stratum of the proletariat." Mints, *Istoriia velikogo oktiabria,* II, 416.

42. Ferro, *The Russian Revolution of February 1917,* pp. 112–121.

43. Mints, *Istoriia velikogo oktiabria*, II, 416–417.

44. Ferro, *The Russian Revolution of February 1917*, p. 217.

45. Chamberlin, *The Russian Revolution*, I, 159.

46. Ibid., 155.

47. Mints, *Istoriia velikogo oktiabria*, II, 649–654.

48. For an excellent discussion of the June and July unrest in Petrograd (particularly the relations between the Central Committee, the Petrograd city committee, and the Military Organization of the Bolshevik party) see Alexander Rabinowitch, *Prelude to Revolution* (Bloomington, Indiana University Press, 1968).

49. Ibid., p. 229.

50. Mints, *Istoriia velikogo oktiabria*, II, 672. See *Shestoi s"ezd RSDRP (Bolshevikov)* [August 1917], *Protokoly* (Moscow, Gospolitizdat, 1958), p. 36.

51. Merle Fainsod, *How Russia Is Ruled* (Cambridge, Mass., Harvard University Press, 1953), p. 69.

52. Ibid., p. 68–69. The Lenin quotation is from "Odin iz korennykh voprosov revoliutsii" (One of the Fundamental Questions of the Revolution), in Lenin, *Polnoe sobranie sochinenii*, XXXIV, 204. Quotations marks have been used in this paragraph because Fainsod has sometimes been accused of interpreting the Bolshevik revolution as the product of a tightly organized, conspiratorial party. See n. 107 for a further long quotation in the same vein from the first edition of *How Russia Is Ruled*.

53. *Shestoi s"ezd*, p. 295. Fourteen said that they began work in the Bolshevik organization in 1915, 1916, and 1917, and eight did not answer, presumably because they were in the process of joining at the time.

54. See Stephen F. Cohen, *Bukharin and the Bolshevik Revolution* (New York, Alfred A. Knopf, 1973), pp. 49–52.

55. For a discussion of this matter on a member-by-member basis see Robert Vincent Daniels, *The Conscience of the Revolution* (Cambridge, Mass., Harvard University Press, 1960), pp. 45–50.

56. Chamberlin, *The Russian Revolution*, I, 155.

57. Ibid., 202.

58. For a good description of the steps leading to the Kornilov affair see Alexander Rabinowitch, *The Bolsheviks Come to Power* (New York, W. W. Norton & Company, 1976), pp. 94–128.

59. Chamberlin, *The Russian Revolution*, I, 203.

60. Ibid., pp. 277–280. See also Keep, *The Russian Revolution*, pp. 358–381.

61. Radkey, *The Agrarian Foes of Bolshevism*, pp. 429–430.

62. Quoted in Chamberlin, *The Russian Revolution*, I, 281.

63. Rabinowitch, *The Bolsheviks Come to Power*, pp. 168–172, 342 n. 4.

64. "Bolsheviki dolzhny vziat' vlast'" (The Bolsheviks Must Assume Power), in Lenin, *Polnoe sobranie sochinenii*, XXXIV, 239–240. The italics are Lenin's.

65. "Marksizm i vosstanie" (Marxism and Insurrection), ibid., XXXIV, 247.

66. Ibid., p. 244.

67. Ibid., p. 245.

68. Those present at the meeting were Trotsky, Kamenev, Rykov, Nogin, Stalin,

Sverdlov, Bubnov, Bukharin, Lomov, Kollontai, Dzerzhinsky, Uritsky, Joffe, Shaumian, Sokolnikov, and Miliutin.

69. Leon Trotsky, *The History of the Russian Revolution* (New York, Simon and Schuster, 1932), III, 133.

70. *Protokoly tsentral'nogo komiteta RSDRP, Avgust 1917-Fevral' 1918* (Moscow, Gospolitizdat, 1958), p. 55.

71. See the discussion in Isaac Deutscher, *The Prophet Armed: Trotsky, 1879–1921* (London, Oxford University Press, 1954), pp. 289–314. Rabinowitch basically accepts the Trotsky version of the story (*The Bolsheviks Come to Power*, pp. 287, 313), but Robert V. Daniels, both in *Red October* (New York, Charles Scribner's Sons, 1967) and in a private communication of July 15, 1976, expresses the strongest belief that this version is "based on Trotsky's lies afterwards to make his record look more aggressive."

72. Daniels, *Red October*, p. 56.

73. "Iz dnevnika publistista" (From a Publicist's Diary), in Lenin, *Polnoe sobranie sochinenii*, XXXIV, 263.

74. "Krizis nazrel" (The Crisis Has Matured), ibid., XXXIV, 280–283. All the italics are Lenin's.

75. Ibid., XXXIV, 340–350, 385–390.

76. "Krizis nazrel," ibid., XXXIV, 281.

77. The information about the circulation of Lenin's letter is from Mints, *Istoriia velikogo oktiabria*, II, 923–924, n. 23. The Daniels statement is from a private communication of July 15, 1976.

78. Quoted in Trotsky, *History of the Russian Revolution*, III, 137.

79. "Doklad" (Report), in Lenin, *Polnoe sobranie sochineniia*, XXXIV, 391–392.

80. *Protokoly TsK RSDRP*, pp. 83–86.

81. Ibid., pp. 124–125. An excellent sense of the divisions and hesitancy among Petrograd leaders can be gained from Daniels, *Red October*, pp. 89–96.

82. The Kamenev statement is published in Lenin, *Collected Works*, XXI (2), 261.

83. "Pis'mo k chlenam partii Bol'shevikov" (Letter to Bolshevik Party Members), in Lenin, *Polnoe sobranie sochineniia*, XXXIV, 420.

84. "Pis'mo v tsentral'nyi komitet RSDRP (b) (Letter to the Central Committee of the R.S.D.R.P.), ibid., XXXIV, 423, 427.

85. *Protokoly TsK RSDRP*, pp. 106–108.

86. Ibid., p. 119.

87. Daniels, *Red October*, pp. 64–72.

88. Quoted ibid., p. 73.

89. Ibid., p. 118.

90. "Resolutions of the Pre-Parliament," in James Bunyan and H. H. Fisher, *The Bolshevik Revolution, 1917–1918* (Stanford, Stanford University Press, 1934), pp. 91–92.

91. "The Proposal of Dan, Gotz, and Avxentiev," ibid., pp. 93–94.

92. Daniels, *Red October*, p. 106. For the note to Sverdlov see "Pis'mo Ia. M. Sverdlovu," in Lenin, *Polnoe sobranie sochinenii*, XXXIV, 434.

93. Mints, *Istoriia velikogo oktiabria,* II, 954.

94. Daniels, *Red October,* p. 118. Mints also makes much of this fact. *Istoriia velikogo oktiabria,* II, 1107, n. 39.

95. Quoted in Daniels, *Red October,* p. 217.

96. Ibid., p. 144.

97. "Pis'mo chlenam TsK" (Letter to Members of the C.C.), XXXIV, 435–436.

98. "K grazhdanam Rossii" (To the Citizens of Russia), in Lenin, *Polnoe sobranie sochinenii,* XXXV, 7.

99. "Proclamation of the Congress on the Assumption of Power," in Bunyan and Fisher, *The Bolshevik Revolution,* p. 122.

100. Trotsky, *History of the Russian Revolution,* III, 324.

101. According to Trotsky, the name originated in a conversation between himself and Lenin. For the story see Leon Trotsky, *Lenin* (New York, G. P. Putnam's Sons, 1925), p. 132.

102. Leon Trotsky, *My Life* (New York, Charles Scribner's Sons, 1930), p. 337.

103. See Deutscher, *The Prophet Armed,* pp. 322–324, and Keep, *The Russian Revolution,* pp. 253–256.

104. John Keep, "October in the Provinces," in Richard Pipes, ed., *Revolutionary Russia* (Cambridge, Mass., Harvard University Press, 1968), pp. 180–216. See also Keep, *The Russian Revolution,* pp. 358–381.

105. Keep, "October in the Provinces," p. 187.

106. Quoted in Daniels, *Red October,* p. 100.

107. Fainsod, *How Russia Is Ruled* (1953), p. 86.

108. Oliver Henry Radkey, *The Election to the Russian Constituent Assembly* (Cambridge, Mass., Harvard University Press, 1950).

109. The election returns by district are provided ibid., pp. 78–80, and the percentages here and subsequently are calculated from this table. In the northern district of Olonets, there were only two candidates on the ballot—one SR and one Menshevik–with each voter having two votes. Ibid., p. 17. n. g.

110. In addition to the statistics, ibid., p. 80, see pp. 34–35.

111. Ibid., pp. 35–37, 80.

112. Ibid., pp. 23–29, 51–69.

113. "Comment," in Pipes, *Revolutionary Russia,* pp. 218–219.

114. Chamberlin, *The Russian Revolution,* I, 286–287.

3. The Establishment of the Soviet Regime

1. "Dve taktiki sotsial-demokratii v demokraticheskoi revoliutsii" (Two Tactics of Social Democracy in the Democratic Revolution), in V. I. Lenin, *Polnoe sobranie sochinenii* (Moscow, Gospolitizdat, 1964), XI, 44–45.

2. Ibid.

3. V. I. Lenin, *State and Revolution,* chap. V, sec. 4. Because of the wide availability of this work in various editions and collections, I am citing the section number rather than the page number in any particular edition. It, together with all the relevant notes, is found in Russian in Lenin, *Polnoe sobranie sochinenii,* XXXIII.

4. *State and Revolution,* chap. III, sec. 3.

5. Karl Marx, *The Civil War in France* (New York, International Publishing, 1962).

6. Lenin *State and Revolution,* chap. III, secs. 2, 3; chap. V, sec. 2. For a fuller discussion of Lenin's prerevolutionary views on these subjects see Barrington Moore, *Soviet Politics—The Dilemma of Power* (Cambridge, Mass., Harvard University Press, 1950), pp. 38–58, and Jeremy R. Azrael, *Managerial Power and Soviet Politics* (Cambridge, Mass., Harvard University Press, 1966), pp. 12–27.

7. *Protokoly TsK RSDRP (b)* [Avgust 1917-Fevral' 1918] (Moscow, Gospolitizdat, 1958), p. 55. At this meeting the Bolshevik Central Committee adopted the following resolution: "Considering that on the basis of the experience of previous negotiations the compromisers have been conducting these negotiations not with the goal of forming a unified Soviet government but with the goal of splitting the ranks of the workers and soldiers, of disrupting the Soviet government, and of winning over the Left Socialist Revolutionaries to the policy of compromising with the camp of the bourgeoisie, the Central Committee resolves: to allow party members . . . to take part in the last attempt of the Left Socialist Revolutionaries to form a so-called uniform government with the aim of a final unmasking of the impossibility of such an attempt and a final cessation of further negotiations on the subject of forming a coalition government." Ibid., p. 130.

8. Quoted in Leon Trotsky, *The Stalin School of Falsification* (New York, Pioneer Publishers, 1937), pp. 110, 112.

9. *Protokoly TsK RSDRP,* p. 136.

10. Ibid., p. 135.

11. James Bunyan and H. H. Fisher, *The Bolshevik Revolution, 1917–1918* (Stanford, Stanford University Press, 1934), p. 375.

12. Ibid., p. 85.

13. Ibid., pp. 93–94.

14. "Rech' o rospuske uchreditel'nogo sobraniia na zasedanii VTsIK, 6 (19) ianvaria 1918 g." (Speech on the Dissolution of the Constituent Assembly, Delivered at a Meeting of the All-Russian Central Executive on January 6/19 1918), in Lenin, *Polnoe sobranie sochinenii,* XXXV, 240–242.

15. "Tezisy ob uchreditel'nom sobranii" (Theses on the Constituent Assembly), ibid., p. 166.

16. *Tretii vserossiiskii s"ezd sovetov rabochikh, soldatskikh i krest'ianskikh deputatov* [January 23–31, 1918] (St. Petersburg, 1918), p. 85.

17. Ibid., pp. 93–94.

18. The richest source on the history of the drafting of the 1918 constitution is G. S. Gurvich, *Istoriia sovetskoi konstitutsii* (Moscow, Izdatel'stvo sotsialisticheskoi akademii, 1932). This volume contains the texts of all proposals submitted to the committee and provides a revealing analysis of the debates within the drafting group.

19. *Vos'moi s"ezd RKP (b)* [Mart 1919 goda], *Protokoly* (Moscow, Gospolitizdat, 1959), pp. 428–429.

20. Quoted in Edward Hallett Carr, *The Bolshevik Revolution, 1917–1923* (New York, Macmillan Co., 1951), I, 219.

21. Text published in *Izvestiia,* no. 239 (November 29/December 12, 1917), p. 1.

22. Leon Trotsky, *Sochineniia* (Moscow, Gosudarstvennoe izdatel'stvo, 1925, 1927), III, part 2, 138.

23. Reported in *Nash vek,* no. 21 (December 23, 1917/January 5, 1918), p. 3.

24. The best treatment of the Civil War remains William H. Chamberlin, *The Russian Revolution, 1917–1921* (New York, Macmillan Co., 1935), 2 vols.

25. D. Fedotoff White, *The Growth of the Red Army* (Princeton, Princeton University Press, 1944), p. 51.

26. See Stanley W. Page, "Lenin, the National Question, and the Baltic States, 1917–19," *The American Slavic and East European Review,* VII, no. 1 (February 1948), 15–31.

27. For a comprehensive discussion of the Soviet efforts to regain control of the borderlands see Richard Pipes, *The Formation of the Soviet Union* (Cambridge, Mass., Harvard University Press, 1954).

28. "Otchet tsentral'nogo komiteta 18 marta" (Report of the Central Committee, March 18 [1919]), in Lenin, *Polnoe sobranie sochinenii,* XXXVIII, 137. For good discussions of the opposition parties in these years see Oliver Henry Radkey, *The Sickle Under the Hammer* (New York, Columbia University Press, 1963), Leonard Schapiro, *The Origin of the Communist Autocracy* (London, London School of Economics and Political Science and G. Bells and Sons, 1955), and William G. Rosenberg, *Liberals in the Russian Revolution: The Constitutional Democracy Party, 1917–1921* (Princeton, Princeton University Press, 1974).

29. "Politicheskii otchet tsentral'nogo komiteta R.K.P. (b) 27 marta" (Political Report of the Central Committee of the RCP (b), March 27 [1922]), in Lenin, *Polnoe sobranie sochinenii,* XLV, 95.

30. While the formation of various types of agricultural communes was encouraged at this time, the Bolsheviks were far too preoccupied with other questions to worry about agricultural reorganizations that might further antagonize the peasants. See Robert G. Wesson, *Soviet Communes* (New Brunswick, N.J., Rutgers University Press, 1963).

31. Adam B. Ulam, "The Historical Role of Marxism and the Soviet System," *World Politics,* VIII, no. 1 (October 1955), 28–29.

32. Sheila Fitzpatrick, *The Commissariat of Enlightenment* (London, Cambridge University Press, 1970), p. 138.

33. Carr, *The Bolshevik Revolution,* II, 110.

34. It fell to Trotsky to provide a frank rationalization for the militarization of labor in the Soviet state. He declared, "We are now advancing towards a type of labour socially regulated on the basis of an economic plan which is obligatory for the whole country, i.e. compulsory for every worker. That is the foundation of socialism . . . And once we have recognized this, we thereby recognize fundamentally—not formally, but fundamentally—the right of the workers' state to send each working man and woman to the place where they are needed for the fulfillment of economic tasks. We thereby recognize the right of the state, the workers' state, to punish the working men or women who refuse to carry out the order of the state, who do not subordinate their will to the will of the working-class and to its economic tasks . . . The militarization of labour in this fundamental sense of which I have spoken is the

indispensable and fundamental method for the organization of our labour forces." Quoted ibid., 215.

35. "O prodovol'stvennom naloge" (The Tax in Kind), in Lenin, *Polnoe sobranie sochinenii*, XLIII, 219.

36. Paul Avrich, *Kronstadt 1921* (Princeton, Princeton University Press, 1970), p. 13.

37. Seth Singleton, "The Tambov Revolt (1920–1921)," *Slavic Review*, XXV (September 1966), 499. Also see Oliver K. Radkey, *The Unknown Civil War in Soviet Russia* (Stanford, Hoover Institute, 1976).

38. See Avrich, *Kronstadt 1921*, for a full account of the revolt. The resolution is found on pp. 73–74.

39. *Desiatyi s"ezd RKP (b)*, [*Mart 1921 goda*], Stenograficheskii otchet (Moscow, Gospolitizdat, 1963), p. 468.

40. "Doklad o zamene razverstki natural'nym nalogom 15 Marta" (Report on the Substitution of a Tax in Kind for the Surplus-Grain Appropriation System, March 15 [1921]), in Lenin, *Polnoe sobranie sochinenii*, XLIII, 59.

41. Carr, *The Bolshevik Revolution*, II, 302.

42. T. H. Rigby, *Communist Party Membership in the USSR, 1917–1967* (Princeton, Princeton University Press, 1968), pp. 52, 59–63.

43. Quoted in Jeremy R. Azrael, *Managerial Power and Soviet Politics* (Cambridge, Mass., Harvard University Press, 1966), p. 118.

44. Ibid., p. 68–69.

45. Fitzpatrick, *The Commissariat of Enlightenment*, esp. pp. 59–68.

46. The most convenient source for the various arguments in the debate is *Sed'moi ekstrennyi s'ezd RKP (b)* [*Mart 1918 goda*], Stenograficheskii otchet (Moscow, Gospolitizdat, 1962). The fullest discussion of the negotiations is found in John W. Wheeler-Bennett, *Brest-Litovsk, The Forgotten Peace* (London, Macmillan and Co., 1938), and an excellent short account is found in Carr, *The Bolshevik Revolution*, III, 9–42. For a good summary of Bukharin's views, see Stephen F. Cohen, *Bukharin and the Bolshevik Revolution* (New York, Alfred A. Knopf, 1973), pp. 62–69.

47. Quoted in Wheeler-Bennett, *Brest-Litovsk*, p. 188.

48. The German general wrote in his diary, "It is the most comical war I have ever known. We put a handful of infantry men with machineguns and one gun on to a train and push them off to the next station; they take it, make prisoners of the Bolsheviks, pick up a few more troops, and go on. This proceeding has, at any rate, the charm of novelty." Quoted ibid., p. 245.

49. Robert V. Daniels, *The Conscience of the Revolution* (Cambridge, Mass., Harvard University Press, 1960), pp. 87–91.

50. Ibid.

51. *Vos'moi s"ezd*, pp. 144–159.

52. For a summary of these events see "Primechaniia," in V. I. Lenin, *Sochineniia*, 2d ed. (Moscow, Partizdat, 1932), XXIV, 750–751. They are also, of course, reported in *Vos'moi s"ezd*.

53. *Deviatyi s"ezd RKP (b)* [*Mart-Aprel' 1920 goda*], Protokoly (Moscow, Gospolitizdat, 1960), pp. 50–53, 47, 57.

54. "Zakliuchitel'noe slovo po dokladu tsentral'nogo komiteta 30 Marta" (Concluding Remarks on the Report of the Central Committee, March 30 [1920]), in Lenin, *Polnoe sobranie sochinenii,* XL, 262.

55. Quoted in Daniels, *The Conscience of the Revolution,* p. 121. A good discussion of the Workers' Opposition and the debate on the role of the trade union can be found on pp. 119–136.

56. Quoted ibid., p. 132.

57. *Desiatyi s"ezd,* p. 399.

58. "Krizis partii," in Lenin, *Polnoe sobranie sochinenii,* XLII, 243.

59. "Zakliuchitel'noe slovo po otchetu TsK RKP (b) 9 Marta" (Concluding Remarks on the Report of the CC of the RCP (b), March 9 [1921]), ibid., XLIII, 43.

60. "Pervonachal'nyi proekt rezoliutsii X s'ezda RKP (b) o sindikalistkom i anarkhistskom uklone v nashei partii" (First Draft of the Resolution Adopted by the Tenth Congress of the RCP (b) on the Syndicalist and Anarchist Deviation in our Party), ibid., pp. 94, 96.

61. "Doklad ob edinstve partii i anarkho-sindikalistskom uklone 16 Marta" (Speech of March 16 [1921] on Party Unity and the Anarcho-Syndicalist Deviation), ibid., p. 101.

62. "Pervonachal'nyi proekt rezoliutsii X s"ezda RKP (b) o edinstve partii" (First Draft of the Resolution Adopted by the Tenth Congress of the RCP (b) on Party Unity), ibid., pp. 89–92.

63. Ibid., p. 92.

64. *KPSS v rezoliutsiiakh* (8th ed.), II, 281. Lenin in a speech at the Eleventh Congress reported that the motion failed by three votes. See "Zakliuchitel'noe slovo po politicheskomu otchetu TsK RKP (b) 28 Marta" (Concluding Remarks on the Political Report of the CC of the RCP (b), March 28, [1922]), in Lenin, *Polnoe sobranie sochinenii,* XLV, 129.

65. *Odinnadtsatyi s"ezd RKP (b) [Mart-Aprel' 1922], Stenograficheskii otchet* (Moscow, Gospolitizdat, 1961), p. 102.

66. Ibid., pp. 199–200.

67. "Politicheskii otchet tsentral'nogo komiteta RKP (b) 27 Marta" (Political Report of the Central Committee of the RCP (b), March 27, [1922]), in Lenin, *Polnoe sobranie sochinenii,* XLV, 88–89.

68. "Zakliuchitel'noe slovo po politicheskomu otchetu TsK RKP (b) 28 marta," ibid., p. 120.

69. *VKP (b) v resoliutsiiakh,* I, 538.

70. Merle Fainsod, *How Russia Is Ruled,* 2d ed. (Cambridge, Mass., Harvard University Press, 1963), pp. 147–148, 160. For a comprehensive survey of the scholarly literature of the 1950s and 1960s that concludes that the entire scholarly community saw "an unbroken continuity between Bolshevism and Stalinism," see Stephen F. Cohen, "Bolshevism and Stalinism," in Robert C. Tucker, *Stalinism* (New York, W. W. Norton & Company, 1977), pp. 3–29. The validity of this charge depends on one's definition of Stalinism. If Stalinism means a Third Revolution and an authoritarian system, then this reading of the literature is quite correct; if Stalinism means all the personal tyranny, all the irrational excesses, and all the purges of the Stalin

period, then nearly all the major scholars followed Fainsod in emphasizing the importance of Stalin's personality in creating a number of discontinuities with the Leninist tradition.

71. Adam B. Ulam, *The Bolsheviks* (New York, Macmillan Co., 1965), p. 477.

72. Theodore H. Von Laue, *Why Lenin? Why Stalin?* (Philadelphia, J. B. Lippincott Co., 1964), p. 202.

73. Moshe Lewin, *Lenin's Last Struggle* (New York, Random House, 1968), pp. 17–18.

74. Ibid., p. 134; Cohen, *Bukharin and the Bolshevik Revolution,* pp. 137–138. In his biography of Lenin, Louis Fischer moved toward the same point much more tentatively: "One cannot escape a faint suspicion . . . that had he lived even he might have changed . . . In his last testament . . . there is a thread that seems to lead to the conclusion that he knew something was wrong." *The Life of Lenin* (New York, Harper & Row, Publishers, 1964), p. 657.

75. Lewin, *Lenin's Last Struggle,* pp. 134–135.

76. Quoted in Cohen, *Bukharin and the Bolshevik Revolution,* p. 138.

77. Lewin, *Lenin's Last Struggle,* pp. 88–89. The quote within the quote is from Pipes, *Formation of the Soviet Union,* p. 276, and refers to the structure of the legislative organs.

78. Edward Hallett Carr, *The Interregnum, 1923–1924* (New York, Macmillan Co., 1954), p. 5.

79. This is a point made in private communication by Leonard Schapiro.

80. Karl Mannheim, *Ideology and Utopia* (New York, Harcourt, Brace, and Company, 1936), pp. 173–177.

4. The Choices and Struggles of the 1920s

1. The men who became Politburo members as Stalin consolidated his power are: A. A. Andreev, V. Ia. Chubar, L. M. Kaganovich, S. M. Kirov, S. V. Kosior, V. V. Kuibyshev, A. I. Mikoyan, V. M. Molotov, G. K. Ordzhonikidze, P. P. Postyshev, Ia. E. Rudzutak, and K. E. Voroshilov. The biographies of these men—and of many Central Committee members over the years—can be found in Borys Levytsky, *The Soviet Political Elite* (Stanford, The Hoover Institution on War, Revolution, and Peace, 1970).

2. For a list of the signers of the Platform of the Forty-Six see Edward Hallett Carr, *The Interregnum, 1923–1924* (New York, Macmillan Co., 1954), pp. 370–373. The average age cited is based on information about some 50 percent of the signers.

3. "Pis'mo k s'ezdu" (Letter to the Congress), in V. I. Lenin, *Polnoe sobranie sochinenii,* 5th ed. (Moscow, Gospolitzdat, 1964), XLV, 343–348. A convenient translation of this document can be found in Robert C. Tucker, *Stalin as Revolutionary, 1879–1929* (New York, W. W. Norton and Co., 1973), pp. 270–271.

4. Thus, an article by a perceptive journalist of the time simply took for granted that "his race will bar Trotsky from ever succeeding to Lenine's post." Ernestine Evans, "And After Lenine?" *The Century Magazine,* 105, no. 2 (December 1922), 263. For a recent discussion of this point see Joseph Nedara, *Trotsky and the Jews* (Philadelphia, The Jewish Publication Society of America, 1972), chap. 11. In all of the

antiregime uprisings of 1921—the Petrograd and Moscow strikes, the peasant revolts, and Kronstadt—anti-Semitic slogans had been raised. Paul Avrich, *Kronstadt 1921* (Princeton, Princeton University Press, 1970), pp. 15, 36, 46, 178–180, 197.

5. Edward Hallett Carr, *Socialism in One Country* (New York, Macmillan Co., 1958), I, 143–144. Good short biographies of Trotsky, Stalin, Bukharin, Kamenev, and Zinoviev are on pp. 139–186.

6. Evans, "And After Lenine," p. 262; William Henry Chamberlin, "Who's Who in Soviet Russia," *The Atlantic Monthly*, 134 (October 1924), 547.

7. Stephen F. Cohen, *Bukharin and the Bolshevik Revolution* (New York, Alfred A. Knopf, 1973), p. 226; Carr, *Socialism in One Country*, I, 176–177; Robert V. Daniels, *The Conscience of the Revolution* (Cambridge, Mass., Harvard University Press, 1960), p. 173.

8. N. N. Sukhanov, *The Russian Revolution 1917* (London, Oxford University Press, 1955), p. 230.

9. Isaac Deutscher, *The Prophet Unarmed* (London, Oxford University Press, 1959), p. 94.

10. Sukhanov, *The Russian Revolution 1917*, p. 229. The English version merely reads "central," but the original Russian word is "tsentral'neishii." Nikolai Sukhanov, *Zapiski o revoliutsii* (Berlin, Izdatel'stvo Z. I. Grzhebina, 1922), II, 265–266.

11. Tucker, *Stalin as Revolutionary*, pp. 169, 183, 270.

12. Sukhanov, *The Russian Revolution*, p. 229.

13. Ulam is one leading scholar who evaluates Stalin essentially in these terms, calling him a "skillful politician" in 1917 and "a superb one" by the mid-1920s. Adam Ulam, *Stalin* (New York, The Viking Press, 1973), p. 273. A few western correspondents actually picked Stalin as the likely successor before the event. For example, Walter Duranty in January 1923 referred to Stalin as "one of the most remarkable men in Russia and perhaps the most influential figure here today." *The New York Times*, January 18, 1923, p. 3.

14. Leon Trotsky, *Stalin* (New York, Harper and Brothers, Publishers, 1941), p. 247.

15. Ibid., p. 247.

16. The evidence on these questions is very weak if one is limited to western sources. Much research has been done on the establishment of the dictatorship and Lenin's struggles with the various oppositions, but next to nothing has been done on how Lenin organized his administration, let alone how he organized his "White House staff." I am indebted to Sheila Fitzpatrick for the point about Molotov. T. H. Rigby has a forthcoming book on the subject.

17. At the Eleventh Party Congress in 1922, Lenin had stated, "What can we do . . . to get to the bottom of all those Turkestan, Caucasian, and other questions? . . . We have to have a man to whom any national representative can go and explain in detail what the problem is. Where can we find him? I don't believe that Preobrazhensky could name any candidate other than Comrade Stalin." *Odinnatsatyi s"ezd RKP(b)* [*Mart-Aprel' 1922*], *Stenograficheskii otchet* (Moscow, Gospolitizdat, 1961), p. 122.

18. There were disagreements, and a good catalogue of them can be found in Roy A. Medvedev, *Let History Judge* (New York, Alfred A. Knopf, 1971), chap. 1.

19. Daniels, *Conscience of the Revolution*, p. 70.

20. Tucker, *Stalin as Revolutionary*, p. 223.

21. Evans, "And After Lenine," p. 264.

22. Ibid., pp. 262, 264.

23. Tucker, *Stalin as Revolutionary*, pp. 108, 158–163.

24. This point is emphasized in Adam B. Ulam, *The Bolsheviks* (New York, Macmillan Co., 1965), pp. 553–571.

25. Tucker, *Stalin as Revolutionary*, pp. 270–271.

26. Deutscher, *The Prophet Unarmed*, p. 79. Cohen calls them a "hyphenated entity." *Bukharin and the Bolshevik Revolution*, p. 255.

27. Daniels, *Conscience of the Revolution*, p. 174.

28. Medvedev, *Let History Judge*, p. 42. This image, like many which arose in the bitterness of the struggle for power, may be quite wrong—a point that Stephen Cohen raises in private correspondence: "Kamenev was admirable and superior in many ways. I wonder if their relationship wasn't different or more complex."

29. Carr, *Socialism in One Country*, I, 153.

30. Quoted in Tucker, *Stalin as Revolutionary*, p. 271.

31. E. H. Carr has reported that "no other Bolshevik leader was denounced even by his worst enemies, in terms of such searing contempt," and the characterizations that westerners have made of him include "vain and obtuse," "despicable," "a weak man and a demagogue liable to be carried away by his own oratory," and "unscrupulous and cowardly." Carr, *Socialism in One Country*, I, 155–158; Leonard Schapiro, *Origins of the Communist Autocracy* (London, London School of Economics and Political Science and G. Bells and Sons, 1955), p. 174. Again, however, we must face the fact that Zinoviev was considered one of the three top leaders, and one would think that he had some redeeming characteristics.

32. *Desiatyi s"ezd RKP (b)*, [*Mart 1921 goda*], *Stenograficheskii otchet* (Moscow, Gospolitizdat, 1963), p. 402. Lenin ranked first, Tomsky third, Stalin sixth, Rykov seventh, Trotsky tenth, and Bukharin twelfth. This ranking was distorted by the trade union issue at the Congress, but Zinoviev's and Kamenev's position was still striking.

33. As he did throughout the testament, Lenin took away with his left hand what he gave with his right. He coupled this statement with the following: "But his theoretical views can only with great doubt be considered fully Marxist, for there is something scholastic in him (he never studied, and I do not think he has ever fully understood, dialectics)." Quoted in Tucker, *Stalin as Revolutionary*, p. 271.

34. The standard biography of Bukharin is Cohen, *Bukharin and the Bolshevik Revolution*, and the foregoing material is drawn from pp. 3–44 of that book. For a much less sympathetic treatment of Bukharin, see Carr, *Socialism in One Country*, I, 162–173.

35. Cohen, *Burkharin and the Bolshevik Revolution*, p. 84.

36. Carr, *Socialism in One Country*, I, 168. In private communication, Cohen

vigorously rejects this characterization, particularly the phrase "extreme right," arguing that there were others (including Rykov) to the right of Bukharin.

37. Quoted ibid., p. 172.

38. See Cohen, *Bukharin and the Bolshevik Revolution,* p. 151.

39. Jay B. Sorenson, *The Life and Death of Soviet Trade Unionism* (New York, Atherton Press, 1969), p. 93.

40. Daniels, *Conscience of the Revolution,* pp. 156–159.

41. Cohen, *Bukharin and the Bolshevik Revolution,* p. 228.

42. *Odinnatsatyi s"ezd,* p. 398. See also p. 500, and for Trotsky's views see pp. 133–134.

43. Leon Trotsky, *My Life* (New York, Charles Scribner's, 1930), pp. 478–479.

44. Quoted in Max Shachtman, *The Struggle for the New Course,* published in one volume with his translation of Leon Trotsky's *The New Course* (New York, New International Publishing Company, 1943), p. 54.

45. Carr, *The Interregnum,* pp. 368–369. The entire platform is translated on pp. 367–373.

46. Reprinted in Trotsky, *The New Course,* p. 25.

47. Carr, *Socialism in One Country,* II, 196.

48. I. I. Korotkov was a department head at the time of the Twelfth Congress and may have been so earlier. The identification of the occupations of the Central Committee members is based primarily on material in Levytsky, *The Soviet Political Elite.*

49. Actually this is an impressionistic statement, and much more study of the career patterns of the leading prerevolutionary komitetchiki is needed.

50. *Deviatyi s"ezd RKP (b) [Mart-Aprel' 1920 goda], Protokoly* (Moscow, Gospolitizdat, 1960), p. 32. Quoted and discussed in Leonard Schapiro, *The Communist Party of the Soviet Union,* 2d ed. (New York, Random House, 1971), p. 247.

51. *KPSS v rezoliutsiiakh* (8th ed.), II, 73.

52. "Doklad tsentral'nogo komiteta 29 Marta 1920 g." (Report of the Central Committee, March 29, 1920), in Lenin, *Polnoe sobranie sochinenii,* XL, 237–238.

53. *Izvestiia tsentral'nogo komiteta rossiiskoi kommunisticheskoi partii (bol'shevikov),* no. 29 (March 7, 1921), p. 7. Hereafter cited as *Izvestiia Tsk.*

54. See Molotov's organizational report to the Fourteenth Party Congress in *XIV s'ezd vsesoiuznoi kommunisticheskoi partii (b) [18–31 dekiabria 1925], Stenograficheskii otchet* (Moscow-Leningrad, Gosudarstvennoe Izdatel'stvo, 1926), p. 89.

55. A good summary of the organization of the Secretariat (and changes in it within our period) can be found in Schapiro, *The Communist Party,* pp. 249–255. An extremely detailed description of the work of local Jewish sections (*evsektsii*), although not of its central office, is provided by Zvi Y. Gitelman, *Jewish Nationality and Soviet Politics* (Princeton, Princeton University Press, 1972).

56. Carr, *Socialism in One Country,* II, 199–200.

57. *KPSS v rezoliutsiiakh* (8th ed.), II, 398–399.

58. *Deviatyi s"ezd,* p. 255.

59. Daniels, *Conscience of the Revolution,* p. 103.

60. Ibid., p. 168.

61. A report of the Central Committee for the period March 1922 to April 1923 stated: "The period of broad mobilizations, upon which main attention was focused two to four years ago, has now been succeeded by the epoch of all-around accounting of party forces, the training and promotion of new cadres of party workers, and intensified direction by the party in all matters of assigning party workers." *Izvestiia TsK*, no. 4 (52) (April 1923), p. 45.

62. Ibid., no. 3 (51) (March 1923), p. 28.

63. This was made completely explicit only in the party rules confirmed in August 1922. *Programmy i ustavy KPSS* (Moscow, Politizdat, 1969), pp. 267–268. For the 1919 rules see pp. 245–258. Until 1961, all further versions of the party rules contained this provision, for many years also demanding that all bureau members be confirmed as well. See ibid., passim.

64. *Izvestiia TsK*, no. 3 (51) (March 1923), p. 28.

65. Ibid., p. 51.

66. Quoted by Trotsky at the Thirteenth Congress in 1924. The validity of the quotation was not challenged. *Tridnatsatyi s"ezd RKP(b) [Mai 1924], Stenografiche-skii otchet* (Moscow, Gospolitizdat, 1963), pp. 148–149.

67. *Dvenatsatyi s"ezd RKP(b) [17–25 Aprelia 1923 goda], Stenograficheskii otchet* (Moscow, Gospolitizdat, 1968), p. 64. Jurisdiction over personnel selection in the administrative apparatus did not have the same significance as this jurisdiction with respect to a party post. Lower administrative officials also were responsible to their administrative superiors, and personnel action for a given post normally required agreement between the governmental and party organ with responsibility for this post. See Schapiro, *The Communist Party*, p. 321.

68. The Trotsky quote is from Carr, *The Interregnum*, p. 295. The figures are from *Dvenatsatyi s"ezd*, p. 421, and *Desiatyi s"ezd*, p. 762. No such statistic is given in the stenographic report of the Eleventh Congress.

69. A. I. Mikoian, *V nachale dvadtsatykh* (Moscow, Politizdat, 1975), pp. 140–141.

70. *Pravda*, December 7, 1923, p. 5.

71. See, for example, Max Eastman, *Since Lenin Died* (London, The Labour Publishing Company, 1925), pp. 40–50.

72. Trotsky, *The New Course*, p. 25.

73. *Pravda*, December 18, 1923, p. 4.

74. I. V. Stalin, *Sochineniia* (Moscow, Gospolitizdat, 1947), VII, 380.

75. Ibid., VI, 14–15.

76. Ibid., pp. 44–45.

77. *KPSS v rezoliutsiiakh* (8th ed.), II, 507–515.

78. The statistics on voting delegates comes from *Tridnatsatyi s"ezd*, p. 711, while those on Central Committee members were calculated from a number of sources, including Levytsky, *The Soviet Political Elite*.

79. A good summary of this question can be found in Carr, *The Interregnum*, pp. 7–9.

80. Richard B. Day, *Leon Trotsky and the Politics of Economic Isolation* (Cambridge, Eng., Cambridge University Press, 1973), p. 72.

81. Ibid., p. 101.

82. The classic summary and analysis of the debate has been provided by Alexander Erlich, first in "Preobrazhenski and the Economics of Soviet Industrialization," *Quarterly Journal of Economics,* LXIV, no. 1 (February 1950), 57–88, and then in *The Soviet Industrialization Debate* (Cambridge, Mass., Harvard University Press, 1960). For a criticism of this formulation see James R. Millar and Alec Nove, "A Debate on Collectivization: Was Stalin Really Necessary?" *Problems of Communism,* XXV (July-August 1976), 50–52.

83. Quoted in Carr, *Socialism in One Country,* I, 205. The quotations in the previous pages come from pp. 202–204.

84. This tends to be Cohen's explanation. *Bukharin and the Bolshevik Revolution,* pp. 165, 184–185.

85. Carr, *Socialism in One Country,* I, 206.

86. Ibid., pp. 244–245.

87. Cohen, *Bukharin and the Bolshevik Revolution,* pp. 168–173.

88. Carr, *Socialism in One Country,* I, 204–205.

89. Quoted in Cohen, *Bukharin and the Bolshevik Revolution,* p. 165.

90. Ibid., pp. 173–184.

91. Quoted in Carr, *Socialism in One Country,* I, 244.

92. Ibid., I, 259–260.

93. Ibid., I, 195, 199–201, 244; II, 57–59.

94. Ibid., I, 287, 299.

95. Stalin, *Sochineniia,* VII, 128–132.

96. Carr, *Socialism in One Country,* I, 348–351; Day, *Leon Trotsky and the Politics of Economic Isolation,* pp. 108–111.

97. Carr, *Socialism in One Country,* I, 348.

98. Stalin gave the speech in May 1925. "Last year production of the metal industry consisted of 191 million prewar rubles. In November of last year the plan for the 1924/25 fiscal year was put at 273 million prewar rubles. In January of this year, this plan, in view of its lack of correspondence to the actual growth of the metal industry, was changed and reached a sum of 317 millions. In April of this year this higher plan again turned out to be unwarranted, in view of which it had to be raised to 350 millions. Now they tell us that even this plan was insufficient, for it will have to be widened further, reaching 360–370 millions." *Sochineniia,* VII, 129.

99. See Daniels, *The Conscience of the Revolution,* pp. 253–254.

100. "Stalin first enunciated the doctrine of Socialism in One Country at the end of 1924. Trotsky did not reply until late in 1926, almost two years later. In the meantime Zinoviev and Kamenev . . . loudly challenged the supposed Leninist orthodoxy claimed for the new theory. Trotsky gave no public indication that he shared such misgivings. In fact, his first inclination was to support Stalin rather than the Zinoviev opposition." Day, *Leon Trotsky and the Politics of Economic Isolation,* pp. 3–4.

101. Many sources date the takeover with the naming of Uglanov as party secretary in Moscow in September 1924. For example, see Daniels, *Conscience of the Revolution,* p. 254, including n. 2. Fainsod and Carr suggest that Uglanov was a Kamenev-Zinoviev man who soon defected to Stalin's side. Fainsod, *How Russia Is*

Ruled (1953), p. 164, and Carr, *Socialism in One Country*, II, 22, 52. Uglanov had been a Petrograd party secretary before being transferred to Nizhnii Novgorod (presently Gorki) and then to Moscow. Mikoian, the party leader in Nizhnii Novgorod at the time, asserts in his memoirs that Stalin had sent Uglanov to Nizhnii Novgorod in 1922 because he could no longer work with Zinoviev. (Mikoian describes the incident that led to the conflict between Zinoviev and Uglanov.) Mikoian, *V nachale dvadtsatykh*, pp. 144–148.

102. *XIV s"ezd*, p. 186.

103. Ibid., pp. 274–275.

104. Edward Hallett Carr and R. W. Davies, *Foundations of a Planned Economy, 1926-1929* (London, Macmillian Co., 1969), I, 278, 314.

105. Alec Nove, *An Economic History of the U.S.S.R.* (London, Allen Lane, Penguin Press, 1969), p. 151. A good short discussion of the relation of prices to the economic difficulties of the time can be found on pp. 129–142. The importance of the imbalance of prices in this period was first emphasized in Jerzy F. Karcz, "Thoughts on the Grain Problem," *Soviet Studies*, XVIII (April 1967), 399–435.

106. This is drawn from Carr and Davies, *Foundations of a Planned Economy*, I, 322, 843–897.

107. *Pravda*, November 26, 1929, p. 2.

108. Nove, *Economic History of the U.S.S.R.*, pp. 154–156.

109. Carr, *Socialism in One Country*, II, 224. This statement refers specifically to Stalin's struggle with Zinoviev and Kamenev, but it corresponds to his views on Stalin's consolidation of power as a whole.

110. Fainsod, *How Russia Is Ruled* (1953), pp. 156–166.

111. The phrase "circular flow of power" comes from Robert V. Daniels, "Soviet Politics Since Khrushchev," in John W. Strong, ed., *The Soviet Union under Brezhnev and Kosygin* (New York, Van Nostrand-Reinhold Co., 1971), p. 20. Daniels presents such an interpretation of Stalin's rise to power not only in this article but much more fully in his *The Conscience of the Revolution*.

112. Tucker, *Stalin as Revolutionary Leader*, pp. 292, 303.

113. Azrael, *Managerial Power and Soviet Politics*, pp. 78–90.

114. Cohen, *Bukharin and the Bolshevik Revolution*, pp. 327–328.

115. All of these quotations come from *Pravda*, December 21, 1929, which devoted seven of its eight pages to articles about Stalin–all of a character suggested by the quotations.

5. The Years of Transformation and Petrification

1. There are, of course, exceptions: for example, John A. Armstrong, *Politics of Totalitarianism* (New York, Random House, 1961), Seweryn Bialer, *Stalin and His Generals* (New York, Pegasus, 1969), Robert F. Miller, *One Hundred Thousand Tractors* (Cambridge, Mass., Harvard University Press, 1970), and Adam B. Ulam, *Stalin* (New York, The Viking Press, 1973).

2. See, for example, Stalin's article in *Izvestiia*, July 28, 1927. For a fuller discussion of the war scare see Alfred G. Meyer, "The War Scare of 1927," *Soviet Union*, no. 1 (1978), and John P. Sontag, "The Soviet War Scare of 1926-27," *Russian Review*,

37 (January 1975), 66–77. The danger of war remained a recurrent theme after 1927. Sheila Fitzpatrick, "The Foreign Threat During the First Five Year Plan," *Soviet Union*, no. 1 (1978).

3. Louis Fischer, *The Soviets in World Affairs*, 2d ed. (Princeton, Princeton University Press, 1951), II, 741.

4. See Merle Fainsod, *Smolensk Under Soviet Rule* (Cambridge, Mass., Harvard University Press, 1958), pp. 238–241.

5. Edward Hallett Carr and R. W. Davis, *Foundations of a Planned Economy, 1926–1929* (London, Macmillan Co., 1969), vol. I, part 2, pp. 584–590.

6. This discussion of the Cultural Revolution is based upon Sheila Fitzpatrick, "Cultural Revolution in Russia, 1928–1932," *Journal of Contemporary History*, 9, no. 1 (1974), 33–53, and Sheila Fitzpatrick, "Cultural Revolution as Class War," in in Sheila Fitzpatrick, ed., *The Cultural Revolution in Russia, 1928–1931* (Bloomington, Indiana University Press, 1978). For a vivid example of the campaign in one university see Fainsod, *Smolensk Under Soviet Rule*, pp. 343–358.

7. Fainsod, *How Russia Is Ruled* (1953), p. 103.

8. This discussion is based on the detailed analysis in M. Lewin, *Russian Peasants and Soviet Power* (London, George Allen and Unwin Ltd., 1968), pp. 446–481.

9. Fainsod, *Smolensk Under Soviet Rule*, p. 245. A good summary of the collectivization drive as a whole in the regime is provided on pp. 242–251.

10. "Golovokruzhenie ot uspekhov," *Pravda*, March 2, 1930, p. 1; reprinted in I. V. Stalin, *Sochineniia* (Moscow, Gospolitizdat, 1949), X 191–199.

11. Leonard E. Hubbard, *The Economics of Soviet Agriculture* (London, Macmillan Co., 1939), p. 118.

12. *Sotsialisticheskoe stroitel'stvo SSSR, Statisticheskii ezhegodnik* (Moscow, Ts-UNKhU Gosplana SSSR, 1936), p. 278.

13. Miller, *One Hundred Thousand Tractors*, pp. 43, 50.

14. Jerzy F. Karcz, "From Stalin to Brezhnev: Soviet Agricultural Policy in Historical Perspective," in James R. Millar, ed., *The Soviet Rural Community* (Urbana, University of Illinois Press, 1971), p. 54.

15. Alec Nove, *An Economic History of the U.S.S.R.* (London, Allen Lane, Penquin Press, 1969), p. 186.

16. Winston S. Churchill, *The Hinge of Fate* (Boston, Houghton Mifflin, 1950), p. 498.

17. I. Ia. Trifonov, *Likvidatsiia ekspluatatorskikh klassov v SSSR* (Moscow, Politizdat, 1975), pp. 302–310; N. A. Ivnitskii, *Klassovaia bor'ba v derevne i likvidatsiia kulachestva kak klassa* (Moscow, Nauka, 1972), pp. 247–260. These books provide many citations for those who would like to explore this question further, and in themselves they clearly indicate that, contrary to some assertions in the West, substantial work on the history of collectivization has continued in the post-Khrushchev era.

18. Ivnitskii, *Klassovaia bor'ba v derevne*, pp. 298–299, 318–319, 326, and Trifonov, *Likvidatsiia ekspluatatorskikh klassov*, p. 371, 379. A nice discussion of the variations in Soviet figures on this matter can be found on pages 298–299 of the former. For a description of the exiles working on the construction of the Magnito-

gorsk Metallurgy Combine see John Scott, *Behind the Urals* (Boston, Houghton Mifflin, 1942), p. 85.

19. Frank Lorimer, *The Population of the Soviet Union* (Geneva, League of Nations, 1946), pp. 133-137, 140.

20. See Dana Dalrymple, "The Soviet Famine of 1932-34," *Soviet Studies*, XV (January 1964), 250–284.

21. Karcz, "From Stalin to Brezhnev," p. 44. Net marketings equal gross marketings minus grain which was returned to the rural sector (for example, grain sent to peasants in non-grain-producing areas).

22. Alec Nove, *Economic Rationality and Soviet Politics, or was Stalin Really Necessary* (New York, Frederick A. Praeger, 1964), pp. 26, 27, 32.

23. The basic problem is that goods can be added together only in money terms and that prices can change over time. In trying to control for price fluctuation, one normally uses the prices of a given year, but prices do not all move at the same speed or even in the same direction. In particular, new items have a tendency to be very expensive at first and then to drop in price as production difficulties are ironed out and quantity rises, while this pattern is not observed in items that have been produced for some time. Imagine a country that produces 100 washing machines and 100 color television sets in 1960. Imagine that the washing machines cost $200 in 1960 and $250 in 1970, but that the color television sets cost $1000 in 1960 and only $500 in 1970. Finally, imagine that the production of washing machines had risen to 115 items in 1970 and that of color television to 500. At 1960 prices, total production rose from $120,000 in 1960 (100 x 200 plus 100 x 1000) to $523,000 in 1970 (115 x 200 plus 500 x 1000) or 336 percent. At 1970 prices it rose from $75,000 (100 x 250 plus 100 x 500) to $278,750 (115 x 250 plus 500 x 500) or 268 percent. There is no a priori reason to choose one set of prices over the other, and the problem relates not only to types of goods but also to models. The problem becomes especially great in the early stages of industrialization when a high proportion of production is in new items. For a discussion of this question of the "index problem" in the Soviet context see Abram Bergson, *The Real National Income of Soviet Russia Since 1928* (Cambridge, Mass., Harvard University Press, 1961), pp. 182–187.

24. *Narodnoe khoziaistvo SSSR 1922–1972* (Moscow, Statistika, 1972), pp. 136–141.

25. James R. Millar, "What's Wrong with the 'Standard Story'?" in James R. Millar and Alec Nove, "A Debate on Collectivization: Was Stalin Really Necessary?" *Problems of Communism*, XXV (July-August 1976), 54.

26. Karcz, "From Stalin to Brezhnev," pp. 42–46.

27. Millar, "What's Wrong with the 'Standard Story'?" p. 55. Millar's contribution to the Millar-Nove debate (his rejoinder as well as his opening attack on the standard story) is the most comprehensive statement of the revisionist position available, while Nove's rebuttal joins the issue squarely. The published version of the debate also contains footnotes which will lead the reader to other contributions in the longer-running discussion.

28. David Granick, *The Soviet Metal-Fabricating Industry and Economic De-*

velopment: Practice Versus Policy (Madison, University of Wisconsin Press, 1967).

29. This point is made in Gail Warshofsky Lapidus, *Women in Soviet Society* (Berkeley, University of California Press, 1978).

30. 1928 and 1940: *Narodnoe khoziaistvo SSSR v 1974 g., Statisticheskii ezhegod-nik* (Moscow, Statistika, 1975), p. 559; 1933: *Zhenshchiny i deti v SSSR, Statisticheskii sbornik*, 2d ed. (Moscow, Gosstatizdat, 1963), p. 100.

31. Boris Nicolaevsky, *Power and the Soviet Elite* (New York, Frederick A. Praeger, 1965), pp. 3–97. The quotations are from pp. 91 and 92.

32. See, for example, Stephen F. Cohen, *Bukharin and the Bolshevik Revolution* (New York, Alfred A. Knopf, 1973), pp. 342–347. In *How Russia Is Ruled*, Merle Fainsod treated the Seventeenth Congress as a triumph for Stalin. He quoted the leader's statement, "At this Congress . . . there is nothing more to prove and, it seems, no one to fight," and he gave no indication that he believed Stalin's assertion to be misleading. (1963 ed., pp. 157–158, 195.) Near the end of his life, however, Fainsod had concluded—to quote from notes on a talk he gave at Columbia University in November 1971—that "Stalin's victory was not quite as easy as we, in the past, have assumed it was." He still felt there were more questions than answers about the 1929–1934 period, but seemed to associate himself with the view that Kirov posed a challenge for Stalin and that the Seventeenth Congress represented a defeat for the Soviet leader. Merle Fainsod, "Stalin and the Role of the Party," University Seminar on Communism, Columbia University, November 10, 1971.

33. See Roy Medvedev, *Let History Judge* (New York, Alfred A. Knopf, 1971), pp. 142–143, 155–156 for the evidence on this point.

34. *XVII s"ezd vsesoiuznoi kommunisticheskoi partii (b), Stenograficheskii otchet* [January 26–February 10, 1934] (Moscow, Partizdat, 1934), pp. 7, 251, 259, 351, 379, 525, 566.

35. Nicolaevsky, *Power and the Soviet Elite*, pp. 31–32, 76.

36. Ibid., p. 44. The italics are in the original.

37. Medvedev, *Let History Judge*, p. 156. For a skeptical view of this testimony see Adam B. Ulam, *Stalin* (New York, The Viking Press, 1963), p. 374, n. 14.

38. Medvedev, *Let History Judge*, p. 156.

39. Ibid., pp. 156–157. S. V. Krasnikov, *S. M. Kirov v Leningrade* (Leningrad, Lenizdat, 1966), pp. 187-188.

40. The term Great Retreat comes from the title of a book describing Soviet policy in the early 1930s. Nicholas S. Timasheff, *The Great Retreat* (New York, E. P. Dutton and Co., Inc., 1946).

41. Franz Borkenau, *The Communist International* (London, Faber Ltd., 1938), pp. 380–385. The authors of a recent Soviet book discussing this question assert that the initiative for change came from European Communists, that Stalin was doubtful but let the issue be debated through 1934 and only gradually became convinced himself. B. M. Leibzon and K. K. Shirinia, *Povorot v politike Kominterna* (Moscow, Mysl', 1975), pp. 90–106.

42. "Novaia obstanovka—novye zadachi khoziaistvennogo stroitel'stva" (New Conditions—New Tasks in Economic Construction), in I. V. Stalin, *Sochineniia* (Moscow, Gospolitizdat, 1951), XIII, 72.

43. Merle Fainsod, "The Structure of Development Administration," in Irving Swerdlov, ed., *Development Administration* (Syracuse, Syracuse University Press, 1963, pp. 1–24.

44. Abram Bergson, *The Structure of Soviet Wages* (Cambridge, Mass., Harvard University Press, 1944), p. 117, reports that the average salary of the white collar worker in industry was 172 percent of that of the blue collar worker in 1928, but 192 percent in 1934.

45. Murray Yanowitch, "The Soviet Income Revolution," *Slavic Review*, XXII (December 1963, 688, reports a steady decline in differentials after 1932. Sheila Fitzpatrick, *Education and Social Mobility in the Soviet Union 1922–1934* (London, Cambridge University Press, 1979) suggests that Stalin (and western scholars taking his speech literally) exaggerated the actual amount of wage egalitarianism that had taken place during NEP and the First Five-Year Plan period.

46. In 1932 it was decreed that absentees could be deprived of ration cards and living quarters, but these penalties were frequently evaded by enterprises desperate for labor. As war approached, even stricter rules of discipline were instituted. In December 1938, all wage earners were provided with "labor books" containing a full record of their employment. No worker could be hired except upon presentation of his book, which remained with the enterprise as long as he was employed by it. A decree issued in June 1940 forbade workers to change employment without the express permission of management and made departures without authorization punishable by imprisonment. Even tardiness of more than twenty minutes became subject to a heavy penalty. Solomon M. Schwarz, *Labor in the Soviet Union* (New York, Praeger, 1952), pp. 86–129.

47. One-man management was not an innovation of the industriaization drive, but insistence upon its enforcement became stronger. See Jerry F. Hough, *The Soviet Prefects* (Cambridge, Mass., Harvard University Press, 1969), pp. 81–86.

48. David Granick, *Management of the Industrial Firm in the USSR* (New York, Columbia University Press, 1954), and Joseph S. Berliner, *Factory and Manager in the U.S.S.R.* (Cambridge, Mass., Harvard University Press, 1957). Despite the publication dates of these books, both are based almost exclusively upon data relating to the 1930s.

49. Alex Inkeles, *Social Change in Soviet Russia* (Cambridge, Mass., Harvard University Press, 1968), p. 159.

50. T. H. Rigby, *Membership in the Communist Party, 1917–1957* (Princeton, Princeton University Press, 1968), p. 409.

51. Fainsod, *How Russia Is Ruled* (1963), pp. 109–110. See Sheila Fitzpatrick, "Culture and Politics under Stalin: A Repraisal," *Slavic Review*, 35 (June 1976), 211–231, as well as the various essays in Fitzpatrick, *Cultural Revolution in Russia, 1928–1931*.

52. Fitzpatrick, *Education and Social Mobility in the Soviet Union*, chap. 9.

53. Salomon M. Teitelbaum, "Parental Authority in the Soviet Union," *American Slavic and East European Review*, IV (December 1945), 54—69. H. Kent Geiger, *The Family in Soviet Russia* (Cambridge, Mass., Harvard University Press, 1968), pp. 51-55, 88—96.

54. Stalin, *Sochineniia*, XIII, 38–39.

55. *Pravda*, June 9, 1934, p. 1.

56. Fainsod, *Smolensk Under Soviet Rule*, pp. 262–263; Jerry F. Hough, "The Changing Nature of the Kolkhoz Chairman," in James R. Millar, *The Soviet Rural Community* (Urbana, University of Illinois Press, 1971), pp. 104–106.

57. Karcz, "From Stalin to Brezhnev," p. 54.

58. This argument is made in Kendall Bailes, *Technology and Society Under Lenin and Stalin* (Princeton, Princeton University Press, 1978).

59. Fainsod, *How Russia Is Ruled* (1963), pp. 104, 107, and 111.

60. Bailes, *Technology and Society Under Lenin and Stalin*.

61. I owe this point to George F. Kennan. Also see Daniel Yergin, *Shattered Peace* (Boston, Houghton Mifflin Company, 1977), p. 31.

62. In 1930 the assignment department had subsections for heavy industry, light industry, transport, agriculture, foreign cadres, financial-planning-trade, soviet administration, and accounting. The culture and propaganda department had subsections for such areas as the schools, science, and literature, while the organization-instruction department had subsections for party work in industry, transportation, agriculture, and the universities. Except perhaps for the culture and propaganda realm, these sectors apparently were not deeply involved in such activities as decree drafting, writing of policy memoranda, and so forth. V. K. Beliakov and N. A. Zolotarev, *Organizatsiia udesiatevaet sily* (Moscow, Politizdat, 1975), p. 52.

63. *XVII s"ezd*, pp. 561–562, 672, 676.

64. "O reorganizatsii kul'tprop TsK VKP (b)," *Partiinoe stroitel'stvo*, no. 11 (June 1935), p. 47.

65. For a full discussion of the reorganizations see Fainsod, *How Russia Is Ruled* (1963), pp. 190–200.

66. Rigby, *Membership in the Communist Party*, p. 116. I. F. Petrov, ed., *Kommunisticheskaia partiia—um, chest', i sovest' nashei epokhi* (Moscow, Mysl', 1969), pp. 221–222.

67. *Narodnoe khoziaistvo SSSR, 1922–1972*, p. 345.

68. Iu. V. Arutiunian, "Kollektivizatsiia sel'skogo khoziaistva i vysvobozhdenie rabochei sily dlia promyshlennosti," in R. P. Dadykin, ed., *Formirovanie i razvitie sovetskogo rabochego klassa (1917–1961 gg.)* (Moscow, Nauka, 1964), p. 110.

69. Fitzpatrick, *Education and Social Mobility*, chap. 10.

70. See Crane Brinton, *The Anatomy of Revolution* (New York, Prentice-Hall, Inc., 1938), pp. 52-53, 56-57, for a discussion of desertion of the intellectuals and a loss of self-confidence among the ruling class as key elements in revolution, and, therefore, key developments for a leadership to avoid.

71. Gregory Bienstock, Solomon Schwarz, and Aaron Yugow, *Management in Russian Industry and Agriculture* (Ithaca, Cornell University Press, 1948), p. 117.

72. M. Riutin, "Rukovodiashchie kadry VKP(b)," *Bol'shevik*, no. 15 (August 15, 1928), 27.

73. "Pis'mo D. I. Kurskomu" (Letter to D. I. Kursky), in V. I. Lenin, *Polnoe sobranie sochinenii* (Moscow, Gospolitizdat, 1964), XLV, 189.

74. Anton Ciliga, *The Russian Enigma* (London, Labour Book Service, 1940).

75. See n. 18.

76. This point is discussed at length in Fainsod, *How Russia Is Ruled* (1953), p. 366.

77. See, for example, Medvedev, *Let History Judge,* pp. 157–166, and Robert Conquest, *The Great Terror* (New York, Macmillan Co., 1968), pp. 44–50.

78. A rather convincing statement of this position (one which takes into account the evidence and arguments of Medvedev and Conquest) can be found in Ulam, *Stalin,* pp. 375–388.

79. *History of the Communist Party of the Soviet Union (Bolsheviks) Short Course* (New York, International Publishers, 1939), p. 326.

80. The information about the prosecution of the Zinovievites is drawn from Conquest, *The Great Terror,* p. 58.

81. Rigby, *Communist Party Membership,* p. 204. The membership figures (which include candidates) come from pp. 52–53.

82. See Fainsod, *How Russia Is Ruled* (1953), pp. 313–314.

83. A stenographic report of the trial is available. *Report of Court Proceedings, The Case of the Trotskyite-Zinovievite Terrorist Centre, Heard before the Military Collegium of the Supreme Court of the USSR, August 19–24, 1936* (New York, Howard Fertig, 1967).

84. For a translation and discussion of this trial see Robert C. Tucker and Stephen F. Cohen, eds., *The Great Purge Trial* (New York, Grosset & Dunlap, 1965).

85. The count is that of A. I. Todorski, head of the educational institutions administration of the People's Commissariat for Defense at the time. Medvedev, *Let History Judge,* p. 213. For another count—different in detail, but pointing in the same direction—see F. Beck and W. Godin, *Russian Purge and the Extraction of Confession* (New York, The Viking Press, 1951), p. 106. Medvedev's book contains a great deal of information on those in other categories removed during the Great Purge.

86. *Kommunisticheskaia partiia sovetskogo soiuza v rezoliutsiiakh i resheniiakh s"ezdov, konferentsii i plenumov TsK,* 8th ed., (Moscow, Politizdat 1971), V, 303–312. Translated in Robert H. McNeal, ed., *Resolutions and Decisions of the Communist Party of the Soviet Union* (Toronto, University of Toronto Press, 1974), III, 303–312.

87. Beck and Godin, *Russian Purge and the Extraction of Confession,* p. 38.

88. The three were M. M. Litvinov, L. M. Kaganovich, and K. M. Voroshilov.

89. Arthur Koestler, *Darkness at Noon* (New York, Macmillan Co., 1941). Koestler's hero, Rubashov, apparently was modeled on Bukharin.

90. Nicolaevsky, *Power and the Soviet Elite,* p. 102.

91. Conquest, *The Great Terror,* p. 532.

92. Ibid., pp. 534–535.

93. B. Ts. Urlanis, *Istoriia odnogo pokoleniia* (Moscow, Mysl', 1968), pp. 200-205. The hypothesis that most of the 1926–1939 "excess deaths" resulted from collectivization tends to be supported by Urlanis' failure to give mortality figures for his group during the 1930–1934 period. "Since the generation of 1906 passed through these ages [from 25 to 30] in difficult years, the growth in the mortality rates

for this generation was somewhat higher than [the norm]." Ibid., pp. 199-220. Urlanis' choice of the 1906 group to study was a shrewd one from the point of view of publishability, for, as he notes, both Brezhnev and Kirilenko were born in that year.

94. George F. Kennan, *Soviet Foreign Policy, 1917–1941* (Princeton, D. Van Nostrand Company, Inc., 1960), p. 89.

95. George F. Kennan, *Russia and the West under Lenin and Stalin* (Boston, Little, Brown, and Co., 1961), pp. 315–316.

96. Fainsod, *How Russia Is Ruled* (1953), p. 441. It should be noted, however, that Stalin did not rely on this technique in the first years of his rule. Thus, 63 percent of the voting members of the 1934 Central Committee had been Central Committee members nine years earlier in 1925 (42 percent had been full members in 1925, 21 percent candidate members), and another 14 percent had been named to that body in 1927. (The 1934 members were almost all still in high positions in 1937.) For a treatment of the removal of one of these long-time party secretaries in these terms see Fainsod, *Smolensk Under Soviet Rule*, pp. 59–60.

97. Nicholas V. Riasanovsky, *A History of Russia*, 2d ed. (New York, Oxford University Press, 1969), p. 547.

98. *Voprosy istorii*, no. 5 (May 1970), pp. 13-15. The Politburo held joint sessions with the State Defense Committee and the Supreme Headquarters.

99. Bialer, *Stalin and His Generals*, pp. 339–341, contains a great deal of information on the Supreme Headquarters in particular. See also Armstrong, *The Politics of Totalitarianism*, pp. 113–135. A new and most insightful treatment of the high politics of the Supreme Headquarters is found in Timothy J. Colton, *Commissars, Commanders, and Civilian Authority: The Structure of Soviet Military Politics* (Cambridge, Mass., Harvard University Press, 1979).

100. Armstrong, *The Politics of Totalitarianism*, pp. 136–137.

101. Alexander Dallin, *German Rule in Russia, 1941–1945* (London, Macmillan Co., 1957), p. 663.

102. Rigby, *Communist Party Membership*, pp. 215–231.

103. Ibid., pp. 260, 239. See pp. 236–272 in general.

104. Alexander Werth, *The Postwar Years* (New York, Taplinger Publishing Co., 1971), p. 12.

105. Hough, *The Soviet Prefects*, pp. 47–49, 175–176.

106. See Vera Dunham, *In Stalin's Time* (New York, Cambridge University Press, 1976).

107. For the text of the resolution on abuses see Vladimir Gsovski, *Soviet Civil Law* (Ann Arbor, University of Michigan Press, 1948), II, 487–497; for that on the Council of Kolkhoz Affairs see *Sobranie postanovleniia SSSR*, nos. 13 and 14 (1946).

108. *Pravda*, September 19, 1947, p. 1.

109. *Sovietskaia Rossiia*, February 6, 1968, p. 1. Quoted and discussed in Hough, "Changing Nature of the Kolkhoz Chairman," pp. 106–108.

110. *Pravda*, October 6, 1952, p. 4.

111. *Current Digest of the Soviet Press*, II (April 15, 1950), 12.

112. N. S. Khrushchev, *Stroitel'stvo kommunizma v SSSR i razvitie sel'skogo khoziaistva* (Moscow, Gospolizdat, 1962), I, 97–98.

113. Karcz, "From Stalin to Brezhnev," p. 62.

114. Leonard Joel Kirsch, *Soviet Wages* (Cambridge, Mass., MIT Press, 1972), p. 3.

115. *Narodnoe khoziaistvo SSSR, 1922–1972 gg.*, p. 350. E. V. Klopov, V. N. Shubkin, and L. A. Gordon, eds., *Sotsial'noe razvitie rabochego klassa SSSR* (Moscow, Nauka 1972), p. 143.

116. Robert Feldmesser, "Equality and Inequality under Khrushchev," *Problems of Communism*, IX (March-April 1960), 31–39.

117. I. V. Stalin, *Sochineniia*, ed. Robert H. McNeal (Stanford, The Hoover Institution on War, Revolution, and Peace, 1967), III, 2.

118. Harold Swayze, *Political Control of Literature in the USSR, 1946–1959* (Cambridge, Mass., Harvard University Press, 1962), pp. 36–41. For these decrees see *KPSS o kulture, prosveshchenii, i nauke, Sbornik dokumentov* (Moscow, Politizdat, 1963), pp. 216–227.

119. See the discussion in Armstrong, *Politics of Totalitarianism,* pp. 173–187.

120. *KPSS o kulture,* p. 220.

121. Swayze, *Political Control of Literature,* pp. 54–82. The quotations are from pp. 59, 71, 75.

122. Stalin's "Economic Problems of Socialism," was published in *Pravda*, October 3 and 4, 1952, and was translated in Leo Gruliow, ed., *Current Soviet Policies* (New York, Frederick A. Praeger, 1953), pp. 1–20. For the attacks and recantations see *Voprosy ekonomiki*, no. 12 (December 1953), pp. 102–116, which is translated in *Current Digest of the Soviet Press*, V, no. 3 (January 28, 1953), 3, and *Izvestiia*, January 23, 1953, p. 3.

123. The rise of Lysenko is analyzed in one of the most important books of the last decade: David Joravsky, *The Lysenko Affair* (Cambridge, Mass., Harvard University Press, 1970).

124. For a general discussion of this problem, see Fitzpatrick, "Culture and Politics under Stalin."

125. *Pravda,* January 13, 1953, p. 1, 4.

126. *Kommunist,* no. 1 (January 1953), pp. 46–58.

127. Nikita S. Khrushchev, *Khrushchev Remembers,* ed. and trans. Strobe Talbott (Boston, Little, Brown and Co., 1970), pp. 308–310.

128. Ibid., p. 297.

129. Ibid., p. 299.

130. Ibid., pp. 308–310.

131. Ibid., p. 311.

132. Milovan Djilas, *Conversations with Stalin* (New York, Harcourt, Brace, and World, Inc., 1962), pp. 76–77.

133. Khrushchev, *Khrushchev Remembers,* p. 614.

134. Fainsod, *How Russia Is Ruled* (1953), pp. 456–458; Robert Conquest, *Power and Policy in the U.S.S.R.* (New York, St. Martin's Press, 1961), chap. 6.

135. Examples may be found in Bialer, *Stalin and His Generals*. For one notable example see pp. 459–461.

136. In the post-Stalin period, as scholars began attacking the totalitarian model, they sometimes referred to *How Russia Is Ruled* as an example of a book which neglected conflict in the Soviet political process. For this reason, it seems appropriate to use quotation marks very liberally in this section rather than simply to incorporate Merle Fainsod's words directly and anonymously into the text as is done in many other places in this edition. Despite the 1953 publication date, the words quoted in this section unquestionably were written before Stalin's death and were meant to refer to the system existing at that time as well as that of 1953.

137. Translated in Gruliow, *Current Soviet Policies*, p. 7.

138. Fainsod, *How Russia Is Ruled* (1953), p. 287.

139. Robert C. Tucker, *The Soviet Political Mind* (New York, Frederick A. Praeger, 1963), pp. 27–35.

140. Khrushchev, *Khrushchev Remembers*, pp. 614–615.

141. Ibid., pp. 610–611.

142. Fainsod, *How Russia Is Ruled* (1953), pp. 201, 276.

143. Ibid., pp. 351, 328.

144. Ibid., pp. 328, 478, 351.

145. Ibid., p. 352.

146. Miller, *One Hundred Thousand Tractors*, pp. 90–91, 385, n. 56. For a discussion of the work of legal scholars in this period see Peter H. Solomon, Jr., *Soviet Criminologists and Criminal Policy: Specialists in Policy Making* (New York, Columbia University Press, 1978).

147. The month of December was selected for comparability with a study of the Soviet press of late 1947. Alex Inkeles and Kent Geiger, "Critical Letters to the Soviet Press," *American Sociological Review*, 17 (December 1952), 694–703, and 18 (February 1953), 12–23. A month late in the Stalin period was wanted, and December 1951 was chosen over December 1952 because discussion of the recent Nineteenth Party Congress might make the latter date atypical. From a general perusal of the Soviet press of these years, December 1951 seems, in fact, to have been a fairly average month.

148. *Pravda*, December 10, 1951, p. 2; December 25, 1951, p. 3; December 26, 1951, p. 2; *Izvestiia*, December 8, 1951, p. 2; December 11, 1951, p. 2; December 20, 1951, p. 2.

149. *Pravda*, December 21, 1951, p. 2; *Izvestiia*, December 30, 1951, p. 2; December 22, 1951, p. 2; December 12, 1951, p. 2; *Pravda*, December 12, 1951, p. 2; December 8, 1951, p. 2; *Izvestiia*, December 29, 1951, p. 2.

150. Many of these proposals are translated in Gruliow, *Current Soviet Policies*, pp. 36–52.

151. These articles are translated in *The Current Digest of the Soviet Press*, V, no. 2 (February 21, 1953), 33; no. 4 (March 7, 1953), 14; no. 8 (April 4, 1953), 25.

152. Alex Inkeles, *Public Opinion in Soviet Russia* (Cambridge, Mass., Harvard University Press, 1951), p. 202. See, in general, the discussion on pp. 196–222.

153. Fainsod, *How Russia Is Ruled* (1953), p. 325.

6. The Revitalization of the System

1. Lazar Volin, *A Century of Russian Agriculture* (Cambridge, Mass., Harvard University Press, 1970), p. 323.

2. For the "doctors' plot" see Robert Conquest, *Power and Policy in the USSR* (New York, St. Martin's Press, 1961), pp. 154–191.

3. Khrushchev's secret speech is reprinted in Nikita S. Khrushchev, *Khrushchev Remembers*, ed. and trans. Strobe Talcott (Boston, Little, Brown, and Co. 1970), pp. 559–618. See also pp. 306–312.

4. The biographies of these officials can be found in Borys Levytsky, *The Soviet Political Elite* (Stanford, The Hoover Institution on War, Revolution, and Peace, 1970). See also Walter Duranty, *Stalin and Company* (New York, William Sloane Associates, 1949).

5. Bernard Bromage, *Molotov* (London, Peter Owen Limited, 1956).

6. For the Bureau of Culture see V. S. Akshinsky, *Kliment Efremovich Voroshilov*, 2d ed., (Moscow, Politizdat, 1976), p. 235. According to Khrushchev, Stalin thought Voroshilov was an English spy—or said he did—and essentially removed him from policymaking at the end. Khrushchev, *Khrushchev Remembers*, p. 308.

7. Kermit E. McKenzie, "Anastas Ivanovich Mikoian," in George W. Simonds, *Soviet Leaders* (New York, Thomas Y. Crowell, 1967), pp. 50–74. For Mikoian's position at the end of the Stalin era (a very poor one) see Khrushchev, *Khrushchev Remembers*, pp. 280–281, 309–310.

8. Martin Ebon, *Malenkov, Stalin's Successor* (New York, McGraw-Hill, 1953).

9. Conquest, *Power and Policy in the USSR*, 79–94; Khrushchev, *Khrushchev Remembers*, p. 313.

10. Edward Crankshaw, *Khrushchev* (London, Collins, 1966); Lazar Pistrak, *The Grand Tactician* (New York, Frederick A. Praeger, 1961); Konrad Keller, *Khrushchev* (New York, Frederick A. Praeger, 1961); Khrushchev, *Khrushchev Remembers*.

11. See Hough, *The Soviet Prefects*, p. 55 and esp. p. 370, n. 40, and Jerry F. Hough, "The Changing Nature of the Kolkhoz Chairman," in James R. Millar, ed., *The Soviet Rural Community* (Urbana, University of Illinois Press, 1971), pp. 108–110.

12. Thaddeus Wittin, *Commissar: The Life and Death of Lavrenty Pavlovich Beria* (New York, Macmillan Co., 1972).

13. Khrushchev, *Khrushchev Remembers*, pp. 318–320, 322, 338–339.

14. Ibid., p. 246.

15. A list of the delegates to the Twentieth Party Congress was published at the end of the stenographic report of the congress, and the party organization which had selected the delegate was given after his or her name. By counting the number of delegates from each organization, one can arrive at the size of the delegation from each.

16. For an English translation see Ilya Ehrenburg, *The Thaw* (Chicago, Henry Regnery Company, 1955).

17. Khrushchev, *Khrushchev Remembers*, p. 324.

18. *Pravda*, March 10, 1953, p. 3. Both the original and doctored photos are reprinted in Leo Gruliow, ed., *Current Soviet Policies* (New York, Frederick A. Praeger, 1953), p. 254.

19. A few observers suggested that Malenkov voluntarily chose the chairmanship of the Council of Ministers, assuming that it, rather than the Secretariat, would be a stronger base of power in the struggle for the succession. However, it seems highly improbable that a man with a quarter of a century's experience in the Central Committee Secretariat (most of it dealing with personnel questions) would have made such a major misjudgment about the structure of power in the Soviet Union.

20. Khrushchev, *Khrushchev Remembers*, pp. 322–341.

21. *Pravda*, July 10, 1953, p. 1.

22. See Harold Berman, *Justice in the USSR: An Interpretation of Soviet Law*, rev. enl. ed. (Cambridge, Mass., Harvard University Press, 1963), 66–74.

23. *Pravda*, March 13, 1954, p. 2.

24. Richard Mills, "The Formation of the Virgin Lands Policy," *Slavic Review*, 29 (March 1970), 58–69.

25. *Izvestiia*, June 13, 1954, p. 3.

26. *Pravda*, February 3, 1955, p. 1.

27. Ibid., February 9, 1955, p. 1.

28. Nikita S. Khrushchev, *Khrushchev Remembers, The Last Testament* ed. and trans. Strobe Talbott (Boston, Little, Brown and Co., 1974), pp. 12–13.

29. During World War II, Stalin had visited Teheran and Potsdam, but at the time each city was in a quite special category because of the war.

30. *Pravda*, July 4, 1957, p. 2.

31. Joseph S. Berliner, *Factory and Manager in the USSR* (Cambridge, Mass., Harvard University Press, 1957), p. 302.

32. The names of the organizational secretaries are found in Grey Hodnett and Val Ogareff, *Leaders of the Soviet Republics, 1955–1972* (Canberra, Australian National University, 1973).

33. Herbert S. Dinerstein, *War and the Soviet Union*, rev. ed. (New York, Frederick A. Praeger, 1962), pp. 28–62.

34. Quoted *ibid.*, pp. 170–173. The order of the sentences has been changed slightly. The word "fear" was italicized in the original.

35. Walter Z. Laqueur and George Lichteim, eds. *The Soviet Cultural Scene* (New York, Frederick A. Praeger, 1958); Hugh McLean and Walter N. Vickery, eds., *The Year of Protest—1956* (New York, Vintage Russian Library, 1961).

36. The RSFSR did not have a republican party organization and the Karelo-Finnish Republic was changed from a union republic to an autonomous republic during this period and is included among the RSFSR regions.

37. No suggestion is made that all of the delegates from a region would necessarily be beholden to the local first secretary. For example, Khrushchev's opponents in the Presidium were delegates from Moscow. However, clear-cut Khrushchev supporters (for example, the Procurator General, who had come from the Ukraine) were sometimes elected delegates from areas not included in this count, and it is assumed that this type of exception canceled each other out.

38. For the text of Khrushchev's secret speech see Khrushchev, *Khrushchev Remembers,* pp. 559–618.

39. *Pravda,* October 18, 1961, p. 9.

40. *XX s"ezd Kommunisticheskoi partii sovetskogo soiuza, Stenograficheskii otchet* (Moscow, Gospolizdat, 1956), I, 532.

41. *Pravda,* October 27, 1961, p. 10.

42. Speech of E. A. Furtseva, ibid., October 22, 1961, p. 3.

43. Ibid., December 19, 1958, p. 2.

44. Ibid., October 25, 1961, p. 3.

45. Ibid., p. 3.

46. Ibid., p. 3.

47. See T. H. Rigby, "Khrushchev and the Resuscitation of the Central Committee," *Australian Outlook,* XIII (September 1959), 179.

48. *Pravda,* July 4, 1957, pp. 1–2.

49. Ibid., October 29, 1961, p. 6.

50. Ibid., November 3, 1957, p. 1.

51. Timothy J. Colton, "The Zhukov Affair Reconsidered," *Soviet Studies,* XXIX (April 1977), 185–212.

52. *Bakinskii rabochii,* July 11, 1959, p. 2; February 17, 1960, p. 5. The same issue also arose in Latvia and is discussed in the sources listed in n. 53.

53. Michael J. Widmer, "Nationalism and Communism in Latvia: The Latvian Communist Party Under Soviet Rule," Ph.D. diss., Harvard University, 1969, pp. 200–232, 527–559. Juris Dreifelds, "Latvian National Demands and Group Consciousness Since 1959," in George W. Simmonds, ed., *Nationalism in the USSR and Eastern Europe in the Era of Brezhnev and Kosygin* (Detroit, University of Detroit Press, 1977), pp. 136–156.

54. The counts are based on Hodnett and Ogareff, *Leaders of the Soviet Republics.*

55. For decisions expressing the change, see *Spravochnik partiinogo rabotnika,* 2d ed. (Moscow, Gospolitizdat 1959), pp. 311–314, 547–549, 595–599.

56. Jerry F. Hough, "A Harebrained Scheme in Retrospect," *Problems of Communism,* XIV (July-August 1965), 26–32.

57. *Pravda,* August 2, 1957, pp. 1–2.

58. *The New York Times,* May 21, 1961, p. 1.

59. *Pravda,* January 21, 1961.

60. These figures include income from both farm wages and the private plot. David W. Bronson and Constance B. Krueger, "The Revolution in Soviet Farm Household Income," in Millar, *The Soviet Rural Community,* pp. 214, 241.

61. *Narodnoe khoziaistvo v 1972 g., Statisticheskii sbornik* (Moscow, Statistika, 1973), p. 516.

62. Sidney I. Ploss, *Conflict and Decision-Making in Soviet Russia* (Princeton, Princeton University Press, 1965), pp. 272–277.

63. Nicholas DeWitt, "Upheaval in Education," *Problems of Communism,* VIII (January–February 1959), 25–34; Joel J. Schwartz and W. R. Keech, "Group Influence

and the Policy Process in the Soviet Union," *American Political Science Review,* 62 (September 1968), 840–851.

64. Philip P. Stewart, "Soviet Interest Groups and the Policy Process: The Repeal of Production Education," *World Politics,* 22 (October 1969), 29–50.

65. *Pravda,* November 2, 1961.

66. *Spravochnik partiinogo rabotnika* (2d ed.), pp. 550–554.

67. Abraham Brumberg, ed., *In Quest of Justice* (New York, Frederick A. Praeger, 1970), pp. 464–474.

68. All Soviet books and journals contain a small paragraph at the end which includes technical information about that issue. One of the pieces of information presented is the size of the edition (the *tirazh*).

69. Priscilla Johnson, *Khrushchev and the Arts* (Cambridge, Mass., MIT Press, 1965), pp. 2–5.

70. Ibid., p. 1. This book contains a large number of the documents of this campaign.

71. Michel Tatu, *Power in the Kremlin* (New York, The Viking Press, 1969), pp. 68–79.

72. Carl Linden, "Khrushchev and the Party Battle," *Problems of Communism,* XII (September–October 1963), 27–28. See also Robert C. Tucker, "The 'Conflict' Model," ibid., XII (November–December 1963), 59–61.

73. Carl A. Linden, *Khrushchev and the Soviet Leadership, 1957–1964* (Baltimore, John Hopkins University Press, 1966), p. 116.

74. In addition, very clear and convincing "Kremlinological" signs indicated that the position of another of Khrushchev's 1957 supporters, Anastas Mikoian, had seriously weakened during the spring. See Tatu, *Power in the Kremlin,* pp. 79–84.

75. Actually ten persons had been elected to the Presidium in 1957, but since one of them (Zhukov) was also removed in that year, he is excluded from the calculation. There is no formal post of second secretary, but Kozlov was listed second among the secretaries, contrary to what alphabetical order would have dictated. *Pravda,* November 3, 1961.

76. Merle Fainsod, "Khrushchevism in Retrospect," *Problems of Communism,* XIV (January–February 1965), 1–10.

77. Khrushchev, *Khrushchev Remembers, The Last Testament,* pp. 78–79.

78. Fainsod, *How Russia Is Ruled* (1963), pp. 120, 173.

79. Ibid., pp. 580–581, 583.

80. T. H. Rigby, "The Extents and Limits of Authority," *Problems of Communism,* XII (September–October 1963), 37.

81. Robert A. Dahl, "The Concept of Power," *Behavioral Science,* 2 (July 1957), 202–203.

82. V. O. Key, Jr., *Politics, Parties, and Pressure Groups,* 4th ed. (New York, Thomas Y. Crowell Co., 1958), pp. 4–5.

83. John C. Harsanyi, "Measurement of Social Power, Opportunity Costs, and the Theory of Two-Person Bargaining Games," *Behavioral Science,* 7 (January 1962), 67–80.

84. Fainsod, *How Russia Is Ruled* (1963), pp. 337–338, 174.

85. For example, see the detailed analysis of votes in Tatu, *Power in the Kremlin*, p. 157.

86. The most interesting incident reported in the memoirs involved the decision to cancel the Paris summit conference with Eisenhower in 1960. This decision, Khrushchev states, was actually made on the plane on route to Paris, a Presidium decision being reversed in the process. The new decision was cleared with the Presidium, which gave its approval. Khrushchev, *Khrushchev Remembers, The Last Testament*, pp. 450–452.

87. *Plenum tsentral'nogo komiteta Kommunisticheskoi partii sovetskogo soiuza* [24–26 marta 1965 goda], *Stenograficheskii otchet* (Moscow, Politizdat, 1965), p. 89.

7. The Return to Normalcy

1. The biographical information in this section comes from a number of sources. The major ones are the series of *Deputaty Verkhovnogo Soveta SSSR*, published by the Izvestiia publishing house after each election since 1958 and the 1961, 1966, 1971 yearbooks of the *Bol'shaia sovetskaia entsiklopediia*. A convenient English-language source is Borys Levytsky, *The Soviet Political Elite* (Stanford, The Hoover Institution on War, Revolution, and Peace, 1970).

2. John Dornberg, *Brezhnev, The Masks of Power* (New York, Basic Books, 1974). The first Soviet biography of Brezhnev is *Kratkii biograficheskii ocherk, Leonid Ilich Brezhnev* (Moscow, Politizdat, 1976). In addition, the various Soviet newspapers carried a number of articles about different aspects of his life in December 1976 just prior to his seventieth birthday. See also *Leonid I Brezhnev: Pages From His Life* (New York, Simon and Schuster, 1978). Two volumes of memoirs, *Malaia zemlia* and *Vozrozhdenie* were published in 1978.

3. *Izvestiia*, December 14, 1976, p. 5.

4. The responsibilities of a first secretary are manyfold, as a 1947 *Pravda* editorial reminds us. "The Central Committee [in its decision] noted that the Zaporozhe regional party committee has not understood the political significance of the construction project [the reconstruction of the Zaporozhe Steel Plant] and that the obkom first secretary, comrade Brezhnev, leads the construction site superficially. The regional committee officials say that they are devoting much attention to agriculture. And so it should be . . . But does this mean that a most important reconstruction site can be neglected? Not in any case." *Pravda*, April 19, 1947, p. 1. *Vozrozhdenie* is Brezhnev's memoirs on this period and deals with this issue.

5. Information on these specific points comes from *Bol'shaia sovetskaia entsiklopediia*, 3d ed. (Moscow, Sovetskaia entsiklopediia, 1971), IV, 18.

6. Nikolai Podgorny was elected to the Central Committee Secretariat at the same time, and the division of responsibilities between the two men is not clear.

7. Grey Hodnett, "Alexei Nikolaevich Kosygin," in George W. Simmonds, ed., *Soviet Leaders* (New York, Thomas Y. Crowell Co., 1967), pp. 40–50.

8. Khrushchev, *Khrushchev Remembers*, p. 257.

9. Grey Hodnett, "Nikolai Viktorovich Podgorny," in Simmonds, ed., *Soviet Leaders*, pp. 75–82.

10. This point is emphasized ibid., p. 77.

11. Grey Hodnett, "Mikhail Andreevich Suslov," in Simmonds, ed., *Soviet Leaders,* pp. 108–115.

12. See, for example, Carl A. Linden, *Khrushchev and the Soviet Leadership, 1957–1964* (Baltimore, John Hopkins University Press, 1966), pp. 110–112, 134–138, 143–144.

13. *Pravda,* October 15, 1976, pp. 1–2.

14. See the discussion in Michel Tatu, *Power in the Kremlin* (New York, The Viking Press, 1969), pp. 220–225.

15. Their views are discussed in Werner G. Hahn, *The Politics of Soviet Agriculture, 1960–1970* (Baltimore, John Hopkins University Press, 1972).

16. Grey Hodnett, "Pyotr Efimovich Shelest," in Simmonds, ed., *Soviet Leaders,* pp. 95–103.

17. Sheila Fitzpatrick, *Education and Social Mobility in the Soviet Union* (London, Cambridge University Press, 1979), chap. 9.

18. Robert M. Slusser, "Alexander Nikolaevich Shelepin," in Simmonds, ed., *Soviet Leaders,* pp. 87–95.

19. Shelepin's subordinates in the Party-State Control Committees in the republics and provinces were also both a party secretary and a deputy chairman of the appropriate soviet. Most high officials are also deputies to the Supreme Soviet, and a few sit on the Presidium of the Supreme Soviet.

20. See Grey Hodnett, "Succession Contingencies in the Soviet Union," *Problems of Communism,* XXIV (March–April 1975), 8, n. 23.

21. A speculative discussion is found in Martin Page, *The Day Khrushchev Fell* (New York, Hawthorn Books, Inc., 1965).

22. *Pravda,* November 17, 1964, p. 1.

23. Ibid., March 30, 1966, p. 8.

24. In December 1965, one republican first secretary (Zarobian of Armenia) was removed and demoted, but even he became a Deputy Minister of the Electrotechnical Industry.

25. D. A. Kunaev, who was demoted from first secretary of the Kazakhstan Central Committee to chairman of the Council of Ministers, was returned to his former post; V. V. Shcherbitsky, who was demoted from chairman of the Ukrainian Council of Ministers to first secretary of the Dnepropetrovsk regional party committee, was likewise restored to his old position; V. V. Matskevich, the top agricultural administrator in the country prior to 1960, who was moved to the second ranking job in the Virgin Lands program, was named Minister of Agriculture; I. V. Kapitonov, who was moved from first secretary in Moscow to the similar position in the much less important Ivanovo region, was named a Central Committee secretary; T. I. Sokolov and N. N. Rodionov, the Kazakh party leader for the Virgin Lands territory and the Central Committee second secretary, respectively, who were reduced to low level provincial jobs, became first secretaries of important regional committees.

26. *Pravda,* September 28, 1965, pp. 1–4; October 1–3, 1965.

27. Karl Ryavec, *Implementation of Soviet Economic Reforms* (New York, Frederick A. Praeger, 1975).

28. The Central Intelligence Agency periodically issues a *Directory of Leading Soviet Personnel* in three volumes, and they are very useful in following changes in organization as well as in personnel.

29. David Joravsky, *The Lysenko Affair* (Cambridge, Mass., Harvard University Press, 1970), pp. 173–186; Zhores A. Medvedev, *The Rise and Fall of T. D. Lysenko* (New York, Columbia University Press, 1969), pp. 221–243.

30. Philip P. Stewart, "Soviet Interest Groups and the Policy Process: The Repeal of Production Education," *World Politics*, 22 (October 1969), 29–50.

31. See, for example, the incredible discussion of collective leadership during the years of the Great Purge in P. A. Rodionov, *Kollektivnost'—vysshii printsip partiinogo rukovodstva*, 2d ed. (Moscow, Gospolitizdat, 1974).

32. Sidney Ploss, "Soviet Party History: The Stalinist Legacy," *Problems of Communism*, XXI (July–August 1972), 32–41.

33. Roget Kanet, "The Rise and Fall of the 'All-Peoples' State: Recent Changes in the Soviet Theory of the State," *Soviet Studies*, XX (July 1968), 81–93.

34. See the discussion of this point in Jerry F. Hough, *The Soviet Union and Social Science Theory*, (Cambridge, Mass., Harvard University Press, 1977), p. 112.

35. This question is discussed in William Jones, "Maintaining Public Order: The Militia and the MVD in the Post-Khrushchev Era," Ph.D., Duke University, 1977.

36. This argument is advanced in Grey Hodnett, "Succession Contingencies in the Soviet Union," *Problems of Communism*, XXIV (March-April 1975), 8.

37. Tatu, *Power in the Kremlin*, pp. 499–503.

38. N. A. Sobol.

39. *Partiinaia zhizn'*, no. 15 (August 1965), pp. 23–25.

40. *The New York Times*, June 29, 1967, p. 7; July 12, 1967, p. 21.

41. The police official (minister for the preservation of public order in the RSFSR) was V. S. Tikunov, the first secretary of the Moscow party committee was N. B. Egorychev, the first secretary of the Komsomol was S. P. Pavlov, the Chairman of the State Television and Radio Committee was N. N. Mesiatsev, the Chairman of the State Committee for Publishing was N. A. Mikhailov, and the director of TASS was D. P. Goriunov. All of their biographies can be found in *Deputaty Verkhovnogo Soveta, Sed'moi sozyv* (Moscow, Izdatel'stvo "Izvestiia sovetov deputatov trudiashchikhsia SSSR," 1966).

42. The head of the science and education department was S. P. Trapeznikov, and the head of the general department was K. U. Chernenko. For a discussion of the general department see Leonard Schapiro, "The General Department of the CC of the CPSU," *Survey*, 2 (Summer 1975), 53–65.

43. G. S. Pavlov. In addition, Brezhnev's leading personal assistant, G. E. Tsukanov, also came out of Dneprodzerzhinsk.

44. S. K. Tsvigun, V. M. Chebrikov, and G. K. Tsinev. Their biographies can be found in the 1971 yearbook of the *Bol'shaia sovetskaia entsiklopediia*.

45. Novikov was graduated in 1932, three years before Brezhnev, but such differences may not have been crucial at that time, when the students were already in their twenties and members of the party.

46. N. F. Vasil'ev, V. I. Drozdenko and N. P. Tolubeev, respectively.

47. *XXV s"ezd Kommunisticheskoi partii Sovetskogo Soiuza* [24 fevralia-5 marta 1976 goda], *Stenograficheskii otchet* (Moscow, Politizdat, 1976), II, 132.

48. Ibid., I, 137, 177.

49. Ibid., I, 420.

50. These figures differ from those on p. 253, first, because they refer to a period some six months later, and, second, because many refer to those on a committee in 1966 (when there were expanded committees) rather than to survivals.

51. Seymour Martin Lipset, *Revolution and Counterrevolution* (New York, Basic Books, 1968), p. 244.

52. Peter Wiles, *Distribution of Income: East and West* (Amsterdam, North-Holland Publishing Company, 1974), p. 25 and table 4; G. S. Sarkisian, *Uroven', tempy i proportsii rosta real'nykh dokhodov pri sotsializme* (Moscow, Ekonomia, 1972), p. 132. Incidentally, Wiles draws his data from Sarkisian, pp. 125, 126, 132.

53. Wiles, *Distribution of Income*, p. 48, table 8.

54. *Narodnoe khoziaistvo SSSR za 60 let* (Moscow, Statistika, 1977), pp. 472, 521, 654. The average pension was calculated by simply dividing the number of pensioners into the total pension expenditures.

55. Ibid., pp. 472–473.

56. Ibid., p. 437. In relative terms, the agricultural investment was largely diverted from housing, whose share of total investment dropped from 18.3 percent in the last Five-Year-Plan of the Khrushchev period to 13.9 percent in 1976. (However, urban living space rose from 10.0 square meters of useful space per capita in 1965 to 12.2 square meters in 1976.) Calculated from ibid., pp. 7, 496.

57. Ibid., p. 160.

58. One Soviet source asserted that the wages of the average collective farmer were 68 percent of those of the state farm peasant in 1965 and 75 percent of them in 1974, and this figure is calculated on that assumption. *Partiinaia zhizn'*, no. 20 (October 1975), p. 16. It is not clear whether the private plot income of the collective farmer is included in these figures. *Narodnoe khoziaistvo SSSR za 60 let* p. 472.

59. *Pravda*, December 25, 1974, p. 1; December 26, 1974, p. 3.

60. *Narodnoe khoziaistvo SSSR za 60 let* p. 77; *Narodnoe khoziaistvo SSSR v. 1964 g., Statisticheskii ezhegodnik* (Moscow, Statistika, 1965), p. 41.

61. Zbigniew Brzezinski, "Victory of the Clerks," *New Republic*, 151 (November 14, 1964), 17.

62. Zbigniew Brzezinski, *Between Two Ages* (New York, The Viking Press, 1970), p. 169.

63. Jerry F. Hough, "The Soviet Union–Petrification or Pluralism?" *Problems of Communism*, XXI (March–April 1972), 40.

64. The secretary for industry was V. I. Dolgikh and the secretary for the police, the military, and the defense industry was Ia. P. Riabov; the other 1976 additions were K. U. Chernenko and M. V. Zimianin. Their biographies can be found in the 1971 Yearbook of the *Bol'shaia sovetskaia entsiklopediia*.

65. Z. N. Nuriev, I. V. Arkhipov, N. V. Martynov, and N. A. Tikhonov. See ibid. A younger man, K. F. Katushev, aged fifty, was named Deputy Chairman of the

Council of Ministers in 1977, but he already had been a Central Committee secretary for nine years.

66. Those heads of Central Committee departments who are also Central Committee secretaries are included with secretaries, not in the figures on department heads.

67. A. P. Aleksandrov.

68. Gregory Grossman, "An Economy at Middle Age," *Problems of Communism,* XXV (March–April 1976), 20.

69. Albert W. Wohlstetter, "Racing Forward? Or Ambling Back?" *Survey,* 22 (Summer–Autumn 1976), 163–217.

70. *Sovetskoe zdravookhranenie,* no. 3, 1974, p. 16.

71. These counts are based on listings in an annual U.S. government publication, *Appearances of Soviet Leaders* (Washington, D.C., Government Printing Office).

8. The Individual and the Policy Process

1. Howard Swearer, "Popular Participation: Myths and Realities," *Problems of Communism,* IX (September–October 1960), 42.

2. Gabriel A. Almond and Sidney Verba, *The Civic Culture* (Boston, Little, Brown and Co., 1965), p. 3.

3. David Easton, *A Systems Analysis of Political Life* (New York, Wiley, 1965), pp. 38–39, 80–81.

4. Gabriel A. Almond and G. Bingham Powell, *Comparative Politics: A Developmental Perspective* (Boston, Little, Brown, and Co., 1966), p. 73.

5. Swearer, "Popular Participation," p. 42.

6. Almond and Verba, *The Civic Culture,* p. 3.

7. Zbigniew Brzezinski and Samuel P. Huntington, *Political Power USA/USSR* (New York, The Viking Press, 1964), p. 93.

8. See, for example, Martin Shapiro, *Freedom of Speech: The Supreme Court and Judicial Review* (Englewood Cliffs, N.J., Prentice-Hall, Inc., 1966).

9. An identical statute can be found in the criminal codes of the other republics, but the numbering is different. By convention, it is the RSFSR code to which western scholars and commentators always refer.

10. Harold J. Berman and James W. Spindler, trans., *Soviet Criminal Law and Procedure,* 2d ed. (Cambridge, Mass., Harvard University Press, 1972), p. 153.

11. Ibid., pp. 180–181.

12. David Burg and George Feifer, *Solzhenitsyn* (New York, Stein and Day, 1972), pp. 51–56.

13. V. I. Kurlianski and M. P. Mikhailov, eds., *Osobo opasnye gosudarstvennye prestupleniia* (Moscow, Gosiurizdat, 1963), p. 126.

14. Ibid., p. 123.

15. M. V. Iuretskii, *Osobo opasnye gosudarstvennye prestupleniia* (Moscow, Gosiurizdat, 1965), pp. 76–77.

16. Kurlianski and Mikhailov, *Osobo opasnye gosudarstvennye prestuplentiia,* p. 130.

17. Ibid., p. 123.

18. Frederick C. Barghoorn, "The Post-Khrushchev Campaign to Suppress Dissent," in Rudolf L. Tokes, ed., *Dissent in the USSR* (Baltimore, Johns Hopkins University Press, 1975), p. 63. The petition in question and the names of the signers are found in Pavel Litvinov, comp., *The Demonstration in Pushkin Square* (Boston, Gambit, 1969), pp. 14–15. Barghoorn expresses his debt to Peter Reddaway for research on this point.

19. The estimate is by Boris Lewytzkyji and is printed in *Opposition in der Sowiet-Union* (Munich, 1972), p. 39. Quoted in Barghoorn, "The Post-Khrushchev Campaign," p. 85.

20. Abraham Brumberg, ed., *In Quest of Justice* (New York, Frederick A. Praeger, 1970), pp. 464–474.

21. The case and trial are described in Max Hayward, *On Trial* (New York, Harper & Row, Publishers, 1966).

22. The case and trial are described in Pavel Litvinov, comp., *The Trial of the Four* (New York, The Viking Press, 1972).

23. The case and trial are described in Litvinov, *The Demonstration in Pushkin Square*.

24. The case and trial are described in Natalia Gorbanevskaya, *Red Square at Noon* (New York, Holt, Rinehart, and Winston, 1972).

25. For a discussion of Grigorenko and Amalrik see Abraham Rothberg, *The Heirs of Stalin* (Ithaca, Cornell University Press, 1972), pp. 289–312.

26. Iakir: *New York Times,* June 22, 1972, p. 2; April 29, 1973, p. 4; August 28-September 7, 1973 (various articles). Solzhenitsyn: ibid., January 15–19, 1974 and February 10–15, 1974 (various articles).

27. B. R. Bociurkiw, "Soviet Nationalities Policy and Dissent in the Ukraine," *World Today,* 30 (May 1974), 214–226.

28. *XXIII s"ezd Kommunisticheskoi partii Sovetskogo Soiuza: Stenograficheskii otchet* (Moscow, Gospolitizdat, 1966), I, 422.

29. See the discussion of the relationship of *Novyi mir* to the Union of Writers in Zhores A. Medvedev, *Ten Years After Ivan Denisovich* (New York, Alfred A. Knopf, 1973). The discussion illuminates not only the legal requirements but also the reluctance to act through flat directives.

30. *Kommunist* (Erevan), March 6, 1973, p. 3.

31. Medvedev, *Ten Years After Ivan Denisovich,* p. 9.

32. An excellent bibliography about Glavlit is provided in Martin Dewhirst and Robert Farrell, *The Soviet Censorship* (Metuchen, N.J., Scarecrow Press, 1973), pp. 153–165. The book also provides refugee testimony about Glavlit. See also Mark W. Hopkins, *Mass Media in the Soviet Union* (New York, Pegasus, 1970), pp. 78–79, 95–96, 122–129, 134–135. For a very interesting attempt to tease information from the censorship numbers on central newspapers see John H. Miller, "The Top Censorship Team? A Note," *Soviet Studies,* XXIX (October 1977), 590–598. See also *Sobranie postanovlenii pravitel'stva CCCP,* no. 19 (1966), p. 397.

33. See Dewhirst and Farrell, *The Soviet Censorship,* p. 56, and *Washington Post,* July 19, 1973, for lists of censorable items. It should be noted, however, that the

lists change from time to time, and some formerly forbidden items are now publishable. Translations of western works give an especially good opportunity to see what type of statements are unacceptable. See B. E. Lewis, "Soviet Taboo," *Soviet Studies,* XXIX (October 1977), 603–606.

34. Dewhirst and Farrell, *The Soviet Censorship,* pp. 76–95.

35. See Medvedev, *Ten Years After Ivan Denisovich,* pp. 18–19, n. 4.

36. Dewhirst and Farrell, *The Soviet Censorship,* p. 164. *Prominent Personalities in the USSR* (Metuchen, N.J., Scarecrow Press, 1958), p. 523.

37. *Zhurnalist,* no. 12 (December 1975), p. 44.

38. Robert J. Osborn, *Soviet Social Policies: Welfare, Equality, and Community* (Homewood, Ill., Dorsey Press, 1970), p. 14.

39. Grey Hodnett, "What's in a Nation?" *Problems of Communism,* XVI (September-October 1967), p. 3.

40. Richard Judy, "The Economists," in H. Gordon Skilling and Franklyn Griffiths, eds., *Interest Groups in Soviet Politics* (Princeton, Princeton University Press, 1971), p. 245.

41. These conclusions are based on a detailed examination of *Pravda* and *Izvestiia* in late 1951 and early 1952. Further results of this examination will be reported later in this chapter.

42. See, for example, *Izvestiia,* February 21, 1953, p. 2.

43. Ibid., December 1, 1971, p. 2; December 2, 1971, p. 2; December 6, 1971, p. 2.

44. *Izvestiia,* December 3, 1971, p. 3; December 25, 1971, p. 2.

45. *Pravda,* December 1, 1971, p. 2.

46. R. A. Safarov, "Vyiavlenie obshchestvennogo mneniia v gosudarstvenno-pravovoi praktike," *Sovetskoe gosudarstvo i pravo,* no. 10 (October 1967), pp. 46–54.

47. R. A. Safarov, *Obshchestvennoe mnenie i gosudarstvennoe upravlenie* (Moscow, Iuridicheskaia literatura, 1975). When persons in Kalinin oblast (the site of a major study by the Institute of State and Law) were asked, "To what degree do you consider that the executive committees, the departments, and administrative bureaus take in the opinion of the population into account?" 6.9 percent answered "fully", 55.9 percent "partly" (*otchasti*), 11.4 percent "they don't," 22.3 percent "it is difficult to answer," and 4.3 percent did not answer. Ibid., p. 121. His views were then published in the Central Committee journal, *Kommunist* no. 12 (August 1977), pp. 29–40.

48. Thomas W. Wolfe, "Soviet Military Policy After Khrushchev," in Alexander Dallin and Thomas B. Larson, eds., *Soviet Politics Since Khrushchev* (Englewood Cliffs, N.J., Prentice-Hall, Inc., 1968), pp. 23–40; Roman Kolkowicz, "The Military," in Skilling and Griffiths, eds., *Interest Groups,* pp. 131–170.

49. V. M. Bondarenko, *Sovremennaia nauka i razvitie voennogo dela* (Moscow, Voenizdat, 1976), p. 49.

50. Elizabeth Valkenier, "New Soviet Views on Economic Aid," *Survey,* no. 76 (Summer 1970), pp. 24–29.

51. Franklyn Griffiths, "Images, Politics, and Learning in Soviet Behavior Toward the United States," Ph.D. diss., Columbia University, 1972, p. 72.

52. Hodnett, "What's In a Nation?"

53. See the discussion in Jerry F. Hough, *The Soviet Union and Social Science Theory* (Cambridge, Mass., Harvard University Press, 1977), pp. 197–198.

54. See, for example, William Taubman, *The View From Lenin Hills* (New York, Coward-McCann, 1967), pp. 8, 12–13, 168–171, 182.

55. For a discussion of *samizdat* see Julius Telesin, "Inside 'Samizdat,'" *Encounter* (February 1973), pp. 25–33.

56. Rothberg, *The Heirs of Stalin,* pp. 235–250.

57. For example, residents of an apartment house may write a joint letter to the newspaper to call for repairs. See, for example, *Izvestiia,* November 14, 1971, p. 4. An authoritative spokesman has said that this is permissible if all other avenues have been exhausted, but did so in the context of mentioning that a city party committee had called such an action "incorrect and harmful in Soviet conditions" and had punished a Communist who had done it. G. Shitarev, *Leninskii stil' v rabote i normy partiinoi raboty* (Moscow, Moskovskii rabochii, 1969), p. 37.

58. The relationship between the nature of the idea or information and the size and nature of the audience is not a purely Soviet phenomenon. The freedom of the U.S. Communist party to publish does not mean equality with the Democratic and Republican parties in access to a mass audience. The reader of the *New York Times* receives both a type and a quantity of critical information not generally available to the reader of the *New York Daily News,* and the reader of the *Wall Street Journal* receives in-depth reporting on the defects of the American economic system not found either in the *Times* or the *Daily News.* We tend to explain this phenomenon in terms of market forces and reader demand, and it would be wrong to ignore these factors in the Soviet Union as well.

59. When asked why central journals had numerous articles about the difficulties of economic reform at the Rostov Agricultural Machinery Works in 1966 and 1967 while the local Rostov newspaper *Molot* ignored these problems to concentrate on the benefits of the reforms, one of the editors of *Molot* acknowledged in an interview the existence of a "division of labor" (*razdelenie truda*) between central and regional newspapers on such questions. The regional press, he stated, serves more of a mobilizational role, while the central newspapers are more the vehicle for debate. Again, it may be worth noting that scholars have found local American radio and television stations to be more conservative than the national networks, and American newspapers more conservative in reporting local developments than national ones. Some of the factors at work in the United States are surely also present in the Soviet Union.

60. Griffiths, "Images, Politics, and Learning," chap. 2.

61. Some scholars have seen May to June 1960 as a watershed in Soviet history, a liberal Khrushchev being defeated by a conservative coalition at the time, largely because of the U-2 incident (see Chapter 6). The timing in the reduction in the *Novyi mir* circulation is one of the pieces of evidence suggesting some difficulty in that interpretation.

62. As in the case of books, the size of the edition (*tirazh*) is given on the last page of each issue of a magazine. Medvedev claims that the subscription list of *Novyi mir* rose 40,000 in 1969. If true, the decline presumably came in newstand copies. Medvedev, *Ten Years After Ivan Denisovich,* p. 121.

63. See *Novyi mir*, no. 10 (1964), p. 288, for what I believe is the first use of that phrase.

64. *Mirovaia ekonomika i mezhdunarodnye otnosheniia*, no. 10 (1970), back cover.

65. Almond and Verba, *The Civic Culture*, pp. 54, 58–59.

66. *Partiinaia zhizn'*, no. 10 (May 1976), p. 23.

67. See Inkeles, *Public Opinion in Soviet Russia*, pp. 67–131, and Jerry F. Hough, *The Soviet Prefects* (Cambridge, Mass., Harvard University Press, 1969), pp. 126–140.

68. A. Beliakov and I. Shvets, *Partiinaia informatsiia* (Moscow, Politizdat, 1970), pp. 50, 83.

69. James H. Oliver, "Citizen Demands and the Soviet Political System," *American Political Science Review*, LXIII (June 1969), 466–467.

70. *Meditsinskaia gazeta*, July 24, 1970, p. 1.

71. *Zhurnalist*, no. 12 (December 1975), p. 45.

72. Hopkins, *Mass Media in the Soviet Union*, pp. 303–304; *Pravda*, January 8, 1973, p. 1; *Sel'skaia zhizn'*, May 8, 1976, p. 1.

73. Hopkins, *Mass Media in the Soviet Union*, p. 304.

74. *Gudok*, January 9, 1971, p. 2.

75. *Voprosy istorii KPSS*, no. 11 (November 1977), p. 37.

76. *Pravda*, July 25, 1975, p. 2.

77. *Bakinskii rabochii*, March 11, 1971, p. 5; *Kommunist* (Erevan) February 27, 1971, p. 5. When a first secretary is changed and announces an anticorruption program, there may be a flood of complaints about wrongdoing. In such a situation in Azerbaidzhan, the number of communications rose from the 30,000 level indicated to 81,961 in 1970.

78. *Kommunist*, no. 18 (December 1976), p. 36; *Pravda*, March 22, 1977, p. 5; *Molodoi kommunist*, no. 8, 1976, p. 42. Citizens can also visit institutions with complaints or suggestions. For example, the institutions of the People's Control Committee received 765,000 visits in the two-year period. Party institutions receive far fewer visitors–for example, only 5,125 visits to the Leningrad regional party committee in 1973, 100 a week–and a foreigner moving from a district soviet to a district party committee (often in the same building) moves from an area filled with people to one relatively empty. For Leningrad, *Partiinaia zhizn'*, no. 9 (May 1974), p. 27.

79. *Meditsinskaia gazeta*, December 12, 1969, p. 1.

80. This point was discussed in an interview by P. N. Masharakin, a worker at the Ural Machinery Works and a member of the bureau of the Komsomol Central Committee, during a 1974 visit to the United States on a delegation. He receives a number of letters addressed to him personally.

81. Pupils in the first through third grade are enrolled as Octobrists, a group that is run by the Pioneers. However, the Octobrists do not seem to have much of a formal organization or much political participation in almost any sense of the term.

82. *Uchitel'skaia gazeta*, August 27, 1974, p. 3.

83. V. N. Khanchin and B. E. Shirvindt, eds., *Pionerskaia rabota v shkole* (Moscow, Prosveshchenie, 1972), p. 172. See also N. G. Ogurtsov and V. P. Aleksandrova,

Vospitanie obshchestvennoi aktivnosti uchashchikhsia (Minsk, "Narodnaia Asveta," 1972), esp. pp. 81–82, 146.

84. *Komsomol'skaia pravda,* April 26, 1978, p. 7.

85. *Slavnyi put' leninskogo komsomola* (Moscow, Molodaia gvardiia, 1974), II, 469, 530. The 1974 percentage was calculated from *VLKSM, Nagliadnoe posobie* (Moscow, Molodaia gvardiia, 1975), p. 12, and *Narodnoe khoziaistvo SSSR v 1973 g., Statisticheskii ezhegodnik* (Moscow, Statistika, 1974), p. 33. The calculation is complicated by the fact that only 38.2 percent of all Komsomol admission takes place at age fourteen, with 44.2 percent occurring from fifteen to seventeen, and 16.8 percent (perhaps readmission) from eighteen to twenty-three. *VLKSM, Nagliadnoe posobie,* p. 77.

86. Calculated from *Narodnoe khoziaistvo SSSR v 1973 g.,* p. 33 and *VLKSM, Nagliadnoe posobie,* p. 77.

87. Students: *Narodnoe khoziaistvo SSSR v 1973 g.,* pp. 566, 679, and 687; *VLKSM, Nagliadnoe posobie,* pp. 17–20. Assuming that only day students are included in the Komsomol figures, 94 percent of students of higher education institutions were Komsomol members on January 1, 1974, as were 87 percent of those of secondary specialized institutions and some 76 percent of those of the eighth to tenth grade in the regular secondary schools. Only 62 percent of the students in vocational schools were Komsomol members at that time. The percentage calculated for students of higher educational institutions is confirmed in *XVI s"ezd vsesoiuznogo leninskogo kommunisticheskogo soiuza molodezhi [26–30 maia 1970], Stenograficheskii otchet* (Moscow, Molodaia gvardiia, 1971), I, 360. Employed in the economy: *Komsomol'-skaia pravda,* January 20, 1973, p. 1; army: *Slavnyi put' leninskogo komsomola,* II, 673; collective farms: *Molodoi kommunist,* no. 12 (1974), p. 26; I. M. Slepenkov and B. V. Kniazev, *Molodezh' sela segodnia* (Moscow, Molodaia gvardiia, 1972), p. 22. These sources place the number of young collective farmers at six million and the number of collective farmers in the Komsomol at two million. However, the latter figure presumably includes students on the farms, and the number of Komsomol among working collective farmers must be much lower. It should be emphasized that comparison of Komsomol statistics with those on a category of citizens is not an exact exercise, for the definitions in the two different sources may not be identical. Nevertheless, the percentages should be accurate within tolerable limits.

88. *Kommunist,* no. 11 (July 1973), p. 39.

89. *VLKSM, Nagliadnoe posobie,* p. 87.

90. B. A. Ruchkin and M. V. Sturov, eds., *Osnovy komsomol'skogo stroitel'stva* (Moscow, Molodaia gvardiia, 1977), p. 371. A discussion of the Komsomol Prozhektor is found on pp. 371–378.

91. *Trud,* April 27, 1978, p. 2.

92. Collective farmers were enrolled in 1977 and 1978.

93. *Sovetskie profsoiuzy,* no. 8 (April 1972), p. 72.

94. I. O. Snegereva and L. S. Iavich, *Gosudarstvo i profsoiuzy* (Moscow, Profizdat, 1967), p. 55.

95. V. E. Poletaev, ed., *Rabochii klass SSSR* (Moscow, Nauka, 1969), p. 413.

96. *Pravda,* June 9, 1974, p. 2; *Sovetskie profsoiuzy,* no. 5 (March 1975), p. 34.

97. *Sovetskie profsoiuzy,* no. 4 (February 1975), p. 17.

98. The 1976 membership figure is provided in *Partiinaia zhizn',* no. 8 (April 1976), p. 27, and that on the number of groups and posts in *Kommunist,* no. 18 (December 1976), p. 26. The figure on ad hoc participation was provided in an interview given Professor Jan S. Adams and reported in her paper "Public Inspectors in the Mid-1970s," American Association for the Advancement of Slavic Studies, St. Louis, Mo., October 6–9, 1976. For a thorough discussion of the Committee of People's Control see her *Citizen Inspectors in the Soviet Union, The People's Control Committee* (New York, Praeger Publishers, 1977).

99. *Meditsinskaia gazeta,* November 14, 1975, p. 1.

100. *Kommunist,* no. 18 (December 1976), p. 27.

101. *Pravda,* February 20, 1976, p. 3.

102. For example, *Sovetskaia Moldaviia,* January 27, 1975, p. 1, contained a letter, signed by the chairman of the parents' committee and eighteen teachers, complaining about a school bus.

103. See the discussion of the "Armenian Car-Lovers' Society," in *Kommunist* (Erevan), February 23, 1975, p. 2.

104. *Sovetskaia Rossiia,* February 15, 1973, p. 2.

105. For a discussion of a pedagogical council which dealt with the case of a student expulsion and took a divided decision (19 to 16) in favor of expulsion, with the Komsomol organization objecting, see *Sovetskaia Belorussiia,* June 28, 1972, p. 2.

106. *Ekonomicheskaia gazeta,* no. 39 (September 1977), p. 5.

107. *Sovetskie profsoiuzy,* no. 4 (February 1975), p. 17.

108. Ibid., no. 9 (May 1975), p. 37.

109. See the general discussion in *Ekonomicheskaia gazeta,* no. 31 (July 1975), pp. 4–6 of the insert section.

110. N. I. Alekseev, "Ob uchastii trudiashchikhsia v upravlenii proizvodstvom," *Voprosy filosofii,* no. 2 (February 1972), p. 25.

111. *Partiinaia zhizn',* no. 21 (November 1978), p. 39.

112. V. I. Polurez, *Deiatel'nost' KPSS po povysheniiu effektivnosti promyshlennogo proizvodstva i usloviiakh razvitogo sotsializma* (Kiev, Vishcha shkola, 1974), p. 39. See the discussion in *Partiinaia zhizn',* no. 8 (April 1976), pp. 57–63.

113. *Partiinaia zhizn',* no. 1 (January 1967), p. 62; no. 14 (July 1975), pp. 36–39.

114. *Sovety deputatov trudiashchikhsia,* no. 5 (May 1975), pp. 28, 30.

115. Ibid., p. 30.

116. Ibid., no. 5 (May 1973), pp. 74–75.

117. Ibid., no. 5 (May 1975), p. 29.

118. *Narodnoe obrazovanie,* no. 8 (1972), p. 19.

119. *Partiinaia zhizn',* no. 10 (May 1976), pp. 19, 21.

120. For a volunteer school department of a party district committee see ibid., no. 13 (July 1975), p. 49.

121. Z. I. Kliucheva, "Proverka ispolneniia—sostavnaia chast' organizatsionno-partiinoi raboty," in I. I. Pronin and S. A. Smirnov, eds., *Zhiznennaia sila leninskikh printsipov partiinogo stroitel'stva* (Moscow, Politizdat, 1970), p. 243. For a discussion

of similar commissions preparing the meetings of the primary party organizations see V. I. Pavlov, "Pervichnye organizatsii—osnova partii," ibid., p. 294.

122. The number of totally voluntary soviet departments in the RSFSR declined from 6,212 on January 1, 1964, to 5,037 in 1969, but had rebounded a bit to 5,230 in 1972. Ts. A. Iampolskaia, *Obshchestvennye organizatsii i razvitie sovetskoi sotsialisticheskoi gosudarstvennosti* (Moscow, Nauka, 1965), p. 82; N. P. Bannykh, *Uchastie obshchestvennosti v deiatel'nosti ispolkomov mestnykh sovetov* (Moscow, Iuridicheskaia literatura, 1972), p. 53.

123. Theodore Friedgut, "The Democratic Movement: Dimensions and Perspectives," in Tokes, *Dissent in the USSR*, pp. 123–128.

124. V. I. Brovikov and I. V. Popovich, *Sovremennye problemy politicheskoi informatsii i agitatsii* (Moscow, Mysl, 1969), p. 29.

125. The Ministry of the Oil Refinery and Petrochemical Industry figures are in *Komsomolskaia pravda*, March 7, 1974, p. 2. The other statistics have been derived through extrapolation. The Komsomol totals are found in *Politicheskoe samoobrazovanie*, no. 6 (June 1974), p. 40, and the total number employed in each branch is published in *Narodnoe khoziaistvo SSSR v 1973 g.* (Moscow, Statistika, 1974), pp. 574–575. The assumption was made that the age distribution among employees in agriculture, transportation, construction, and industry was the same in January 1974 as it had been in 1970. *Itogi vsesoiuznoi perepisi naseleniia 1970 goda*, vol. VI, 448–458.

126. For Komsomol workers in industry and construction, *VLKSM, Nagliadnoe posobie*, pp. 60 and 62; for Komsomol members among the engineers and technicians, *Molodoi kommunist*, no. 5 (1970), p. 62; for the number of persons in various occupations and the age distribution among them, *Itogi vsesoiuznoi perepisi naseleniia 1970 goda*, VI, 14–23 and 448–458. The figure for engineers and technicians might be quite wrong, for it is not clear which census categories are covered by "engineers" and "technicians" in Komsomol statistics, and I have had to make several assumptions that may not be correct.

127. According to p. 32 of the 1970 Yearbook of the *Bol'shaia sovetskaia entsiklopediia*, 500,000 teachers were in the Komsomol at that time. My extrapolation from census data put the total number of teachers at 480,000.

128. M. T. Iovchuk and L. N. Kogan, eds., *Dukhovnyi mir sovetkogo rabochego* (Moscow, Mysl', 1972), p. 177.

129. It is sometimes difficult to distinguish between an article and a letter, but in those cases in which a heading was not provided in the newspaper, length was taken as the distinguishing characteristic.

130. The interview took place in July 1973.

131. The percentage of workers among deputies was obtained by count from the biographical directory, *Deputaty Verkhovnogo Soveta, Vos'moi sozyv* (Moscow, Izdatel'stvo "Izvestiia," 1970), the percentage among speakers at Supreme Soviet sessions from reports of them in *Izvestiia*, and the percentage among speakers at committee sessions from *Vedomosti Verkhovnogo Soveta SSSR* and *Izvestiia*. (The latter count excluded sessions of the foreign affairs committees which have little relationship to decision-making—and few worker participants—and it is incomplete because the speakers at a number of the sessions are not reported.)

132. *Voprosy istorii KPSS,* no. 3 (March 1976), pp. 33, 37.

133. 1970 Yearbook, *Bol'shaia sovetskaia entsiklopediia,* p. 30.

134. *Narodnoe obrazovanie,* no. 8 (1972), p. 19; *Partiinaia zhizn',* no. 13 (July 1975), p. 49.

135. *Kommunist,* 18 (December 1976), p. 27.

136. Andrei Amalryk, *Will the Soviet Union Survive Until 1984?* (New York, Harper and Row, 1970), pp. 15–16.

137. See n. 131.

138. *Kommunist,* no. 14 (September 1977), p. 54.

139. In the fifteen executive committees of regional soviets of the RSFSR in 1975 and 1977 for which complete information is available on the occupations of the members, 12 percent were workers.

140. The members of the Presidium were listed in *Trud,* March 26, 1977, p. 1. The occupations of members must be identified through a reading of the newspaper over the months.

141. *Pravda,* December 7, 1974, p. 2.

142. See table 20 of Chapter 9.

143. Iovchuk and Kogan, *Dukhovnyi mir sovetskogꙋ rabochego,* p. 178.

144. Iu. E. Volkov, "Socio-Political Activeness of the Masses and the Impact of the STR on Its Development," paper presented at the VIII World Congress of Sociology, Toronto, Canada, August 17–24, 1974.

145. *VLKSM, Nagliadnoe posobie,* pp. 26, 88.

146. *Pravda,* September 5, 1975, p. 2; I. M. Slepenkov and B. V. Kniazov, *Molodezh' sela segodnia* (Moscow, Molodaia gvardiia, 1972), p. 115.

147. *Partiinaia zhizn',* no. 10 (May 1976), p. 20.

148. See the discussion in Jerry F. Hough, *The Soviet Union and Social Science Theory* (Cambridge, Mass., Harvard University Press, 1977), pp. 142–143, 148.

149. Ibid., pp. 143, 147–148.

150. D. Richard Little, "Mass Political Participation in the U.S. and the U.S.S.R.: A Conceptual Analysis," *Comparative Political Studies,* 8 (January 1976), 437–460.

151. See Hough, *The Soviet Union and Social Science Theory,* pp. 203–221.

152. Mancur Olson, *The Logic of Collective Action* (Cambridge, Mass., Harvard University Press, 1965).

153. The draft version of the constitution was published in *Pravda* and *Izvestiia,* June 4, 1977, and the final version in October 8, 1977, of these newspapers. All Soviet newspapers and journals carried discussion of the constitution in most of their issues between these two dates.

154. *Voprosy istorii KPSS,* no. 11 (November) 1977, p. 37.

155. The classic pluralist analysis of this question in recent years is Robert Dahl, *Who Governs?* (New Haven, Yale University Press, 1961).

9. The Individual and the Party

1. In party organizations with over 1,000 members, the shop organizations may be given the right to admit new members, and the party committee of the overall organization may be given the right to confirm the decision. The requirements for

admission are found in the party rules. An English version can be found in *The Current Digest of the Soviet Press, XIII* (December 20, 1961), 1–8, with changes ibid., XVIII (May 4, 1966), 9, 43.

2. *Partiinaia zhizn'*, no. 11 (June 1974), pp. 70–72. In practice, the obligation is not always observed. Articles in the Soviet press repeatedly contain examples such as the following: "Sometimes we meet with cases when party members put their personal interests above all and seek all possible reasons to refuse to leave Kiev for another place, and what is particularly disturbing is that the party committees often agree with this even when there is no respectable reason for the party member's refusal." *Pravda Ukrainy*, February 19, 1974, p. 3. See also Jerry F. Hough, *The Soviet Prefects* (Cambridge, Mass., Harvard University Press, 1969), pp. 169–170.

3. With a few exceptions, I have relied upon *The Current Digest* translation cited in n. 1.

4. T. H. Rigby, *Communist Party Membership in the USSR* (Princeton, Princeton University Press, 1968), pp. 522–523.

5. Unless otherwise noted, the figures in this section are drawn from Rigby, *Communist Party Membership*, esp. pp. 52–54, which give the number of members and candidates for every year from 1917 to 1967. However, in recent years party historians have not been confident enough about the division between full members and candidate members in 1921 to publish separate figures in their table of membership, but they do confirm the overall figure of 732,000 members and candidates in 1921. *Partiinaia zhizn'*, no. 14 (July 1973), p. 9. The March figure is that given at the time and presently said to be confirmed by studies, but calculations made by the Statistical Departments of the Central Committee in the early 1920s put the figure in January 1918 at 115,000. As during the revolution itself, the divergencies may reflect the strictness in the definition of a member as much as inflation in reporting. Rigby, *Communist Party Membership*, pp. 61–62.

6. "O chistke partii" (About the Party Purge), in V. I. Lenin, *Polnoe sobranie sochinenii* (Moscow, Gospolitizdat, 1962), XLIV, 124.

7. Calculated from table 13 in A. Bubnov, "VKP(b)," *Bol'shaia sovetskaia entsiklopediia* (Moscow, "Sovetskaia entsiklopediia," 1930), XI, 537, table 13.

8. Rigby, *Communist Party Membership*, pp. 127, 179.

9. Ibid., p. 116.

10. For specialists, ibid., p. 409; for engineers, I. P. Barmin, *Iz opyta raboty KPSS i Sovetskogo gosudarstva po sozdaniiu kadrov sovetskoi intelligentsii* (Moscow, Izdatel'stvo Moskovskogo universiteta, 1965), p. 9.

11. I. N. Iudin, *Sotsial'naia baza rosta KPSS* (Moscow, Politizdat, 1973), p. 117.

12. Rigby, *Communist Party Membership*, pp. 116, 184.

13. V. Vlasov, "Rost i kachestvennoe ukreplenie riadov partii," *Partiinoe stroitel'stvo*, no. 16 (August 1932), p. 5.

14. G. Peskarev, "Dinamika rosta i problema regulirovaniia sostava partii," *Partiinoe stroitel'stvo*, no. 17 (September 1931), p. 38.

15. *Sotsial'nyi i natsional'nyi sostav VKP(b)* (Moscow-Leningrad, Gosudarstvennoe izdatel'stvo, 1928), pp. 57, 59. Precise figures are given for the movement of worker-Communists out of this category, but not all moved into these white collar

categories. Some of the categories in the Soviet source (for example, unemployed) are not precise in their social implications, and hence the estimate here is made in round figures.

16. Iudin, *Sotsial'naia baza rosta KPSS*, pp. 129–130.

17. Rigby, *Communist Party Membership*, p. 116.

18. *Partiinaia zhizn'*, no. 14 (July 1973), p. 16.

19. Rigby, *Communist Party Membership*, pp. 188–189.

20. Ibid., pp. 190–192.

21. Ibid., pp. 211–212.

22. Bubnov, "VKP(b)," p. 537.

23. There did exist "groups of sympathizers" at this time, and entry into these groups (on the recommendation of two party members) was not closed. Over 200,000 had been admitted by the end of 1934, and this number had risen to 400,000 by 1936. These groups "played a large role in the preparation of a reserve for [later] entry into the party." V. K. Beliakov and N. A. Zolotarev, *Organizatsiia udesiateriat sily* (Moscow, Politizdat, 1975), p. 74.

24. V. Beliakov and N. Zolotarev, *Partiia ukrepliaet svoi riady* (Moscow, Politizdat, 1970), p. 145.

25. Rigby, *Communist Party Membership*, p. 354.

26. Beliakov and Zolotarev, *Partiia ukrepliaet svoi riady*, p. 35.

27. Ibid., p. 158.

28. Rigby, *Communist Party Membership*, pp. 100–101, 221–224.

29. Beliakov and Zolotarev, *Partiia ukrepliaet svoi riady*, p. 143. 43.7 percent of the members were listed as workers, 22.2 percent as peasants.

30. Rigby, *Communist Party Membership*, p. 223.

31. In Azerbaidzhan the percentage of white collar personnel among the new candidates was 52.0 percent in 1939 and 59.4 percent in 1940, in Georgia it was 60.0 percent in 1939 and 58.1 percent in 1940, and in Perm region it was 62.8 percent in 1939 and 62.7 percent in 1940. *Kommunisticheskaia partiia Azerbaidzhana v tsifrakh, Statisticheskii sbornik* (Baku, Azerbaidzhanskoe gosudarstvennoe izdatel'stvo, 1970), p. 123; *Kommunisticheskaia partiia Gruzii v tsifrakh (1921–1970 gg.)* (Tbilisi, Institut istorii partii pri TsK KP Gruzii, 1971), pp. 97, 103; *Permskaia oblastnaia organizatsiia KPSS v tsifrakh, 1971–1973, Statisticheskii sbornik* (Perm, Permskoe knizhnoe izdatel'stvo, 1974), p. 41.

32. *Permskaia oblastnaia organizatsiia KPSS v tsifrakh*, pp. 27, 64, 102, 107, 115; *Kommunisticheskaia partiia Azerbaidzhana v tsifrakh*, pp. 26–31; *Kommunisticheskaia partiia Gruzii v tsifrakh*, pp. 99, 104.

33. In the first quarter of 1940, 19,629,000 workers were employed in the economy, and this figure must have increased to 20 to 21 million by 1941. S. L. Seniavsky and V. P. Telpukhovsky, *Rabochii klass SSSR, 1938–1965* (Moscow, Mysl', 1971), p. 305.

34. Rigby, *Communist Party Membership*, p. 409.

35. Beliakov and Zolotarev, *Partiia ukrepliaet svoi riady*, pp. 147–148.

36. The number of deaths is found ibid., p. 150. As John Armstrong and T. H. Rigby have noted, if the wartime admissions are added to the 1941 figure for party

membership and the wartime party deaths are then subtracted, the resulting figure is larger than the 1946 membership figures. Rigby, *Communist Party Membership*, pp. 251, 275, n. 3; John Armstrong, *The Politics of Totalitarianism* (New York, Random House, 1961), pp. 40, 370, n. 3. They speculate that captured Communists may not be included.

37. Beliakov and Zolotarev, *Partiia ukrepliaet svoi riady*, p. 138.

38. Rigby, *Communist Party Membership*, p. 254.

39. Beliakov and Zolotarev, *Partiia ukrepliaet svoi riady*, p. 158.

40. Rigby, *Communist Party Membership*, p. 281.

41. *Itogi vsesoiuznoi perepisi naseleniia 1959 goda, SSSR* (Moscow, Statistika, 1962), p. 50.

42. Since over 80 percent of new admissions in the immediate postwar period were men (despite the much larger number of women alive in the 1915–1925 age cohort), the variation in the number of men has to be a more sensitive indicator of the number of eligibles. After 1960, however, the difference between the number of men and women of this age essentially disappears.

43. In the 1952–1955 period as a whole, 28.3 percent of all new candidates were workers, 15.8 percent were collective farmers, and 55.9 percent were white collar and others. N. A. Petrovichev, ed., *Partiinoe stroitel'stvo*, 3d ed. (Moscow, Politizdat, 1973), p. 81. Figures from Azerbaidzhan, Georgia, and Perm suggest that these figures are also roughly accurate for the 1950 to 1952 group. *Kommunisticheskaia partiia Azerbaidzhana v tsifrakh*, p. 124; *Kommunisticheskaia partiia Gruzii v tsifrakh*, pp. 169, 173, 179; *Permskaia oblastnaia organizatsiia KPSS v tsifrakh*, p. 47.

44. *Kommunisticheskaia partiia Azerbaidzhana v tsifrakh*, p. 32; *Kommunisticheskaia partiia Gruzii v tsifrakh*, pp. 160, 175; *Permskaia oblastnaia organizatsiia KPSS v tsifrakh*, pp. 27, 103, 109, 115–116. The figures on social groups within the working population as a whole come from S. L. Seniavsky, *Izmeneniia v sotsial'noi strukture sovetskogo obshchestva, 1938–1970* (Moscow, Mysl', 1973), pp. 416–417.

45. Education: *Partiinaia zhizn'*, no. 10 (May 1965), p. 11; no. 14 (July 1973), p. 16. Women: ibid., no. 10 (May 1965), p. 13; no. 14 (July 1973), p. 16.

46. Ibid., no. 14 (July 1973), p. 13. These figures are for admission by the territorial party organizations. An earlier source had given 27.2 percent for the 1952–1955 period, without specification of any limitations. (The difference presumably involves admission within the army.) Ibid., no. 19 (October 1967), p. 11.

47. *Voprosy istorii KPSS*, no. 8 (August 1976), p. 27. Actually, the cited figure is thirty for the average age of admission to candidate membership, and I have simply assumed that admission to membership comes a year later.

48. For a discussion of this decision ("About Serious Deficiencies in the Work of the Kharkov Oblast Party Organization in Party Admission and the Training of Young Communists") see Chapter 7.

49. *Partiinaia zhizn'*, no. 10 (May 1976), p. 13.

50. For a calculation of the deaths in the party in the Khrushchev era see Rigby, *Communist Party Membership*, pp. 310–311. My rough estimate was calculated by taking the age-specific mortality figures published in *Naselenie SSSR, 1973* (Moscow, Statistika, 1975), p. 142, and applying them to the groups of Communists of different

ages published in *Partiinaia zhizn'*, no. 14 (July 1973), p. 19. (The Communists of different ages were divided between men and women before the different mortality rates for each were applied.) If Communists of advancing years and/or failing health tend to drop out of the party, then the actual number of deaths would be correspondingly lower.

51. *Pravda*, March 31, 1971, p. 10; *Partiinaia zhizn'*, no. 11 (June 1972), p. 5, and no. 5 (March 1973), p. 8.

52. *Pravda*, February 25, 1976, p. 7.

53. In 1973 there were 3,408,000 women and 11,412,000 men in the party. In the next three years, 480,000 women and 1,150,000 men were admitted as candidate members. Without any attrition, there would have been 3,888,000 women and 12,562,000 men in the party in January 1976. In actuality, there were 3,794,000 women and 11,845,000 men—a shortfall of 94,000 women and 712,000 men. I would estimate 46,000 female deaths and 400,000 male deaths in the period, leaving resignations and expulsions at 48,000 and 317,000, respectively—a ratio of men to women twice that in the party as a whole.

54. *Itogi vsesoiuznoi perepisi naseleniia 1970 goda* (Moscow, Statistika, 1972), II, 12–13.

55. See table 11 of Chapter 8.

56. N. A. Petrovichev, *Partiinoe stroitel'stvo*, 4th ed. (Moscow, Politizdat, 1976), p. 62.

57. For the age distribution of party members see *Partiinaia zhizn'*, no. 10 (May 1965), p. 13; no. 19 (October 1967), pp. 9, 16; no. 14 (July 1973), p. 19. The age distribution of the population in 1965 and 1967 is extrapolated from 1959 and 1970 census data in *Itogi vsesoiuznoi perepisi naseleniia 1970 goda*, II, 12–13. The age distribution of the population in 1973 comes from *Narodnoe khoziaistvo SSSR v 1972 g.* (Moscow, Statistika, 1973), p. 34. In 1965 the age categories were actually eighteen to twenty-five, twenty-six to thirty-nine, forty to forty-nine, and fifty and over.

58. *Partiinaia zhizn'*, no. 10 (May 1965), p. 13; no. 10 (May 1976), p. 14; no. 21 (November 1977), p. 32.

59. Ibid., no. 1 (January 1962), p. 49; no. 10 (May 1965), p. 12; no. 21 (November 1977), p. 31.

60. Ibid., no. 21 (November 1977), p. 25.

61. Because of this development (and because of the decline in the number employed in agriculture), the number of collective farmers among the new candidates declined from 15.8 percent in 1952–1955 to 15.0 percent in 1962–1965 to 11.2 percent in 1971–1975. Ibid., no. 14 (July 1973), p. 13; no. 10 (May 1976), p. 14.

62. *Itogi vsesoiuznoi perepisi naseleniia 1970 goda*, VI, 4.

63. See the discussion in Hough, *The Soviet Union and Social Science Theory*, pp. 133–135.

64. *Partiinaia zhizn'*, no. 20 (October 1976), pp. 9–11.

65. Ibid., no. 21 (November 1977), p. 30.

66. The word "saturation" is T. H. Rigby's term for the proportion of Communists in a given sociological group. Rigby, *Communist Party Membership*, p. 200.

67. These figures must be approximate because data for the age distribution of the total population must be extrapolated.

68. *Permskaia oblastnaia organizatsiia KPSS v tsifrakh*, p. 96.

69. *Voprosy istorii KPSS*, no. 8 (August 1976), p. 27.

70. The biographies are published in the quadrennial *Deputaty Verkhovnogo Soveta* (Moscow, Izdatel'stvo "Izvestiia," 1970, 1974).

71. Albert Parry, *The New Class Divided* (New York, Macmillan, 1966), p. 159.

72. Petrovichev, *Partiinoe stroitel'stvo* (1972), p. 87.

73. *Partiinaia zhizn'*, no. 10 (May 1976), pp. 16, 14; no. 21 (November 1977), p. 26.

74. Unfortunately, the 1976 collection of party statistics, published ibid., gave the total party membership as of February 1976, the eve of the Twenty-Fifth Party Congress, but then provided sociological data on the party as of January 1976. Only the number of women in the party is published, so the number of men must be determined by subtraction, and for the January 1, 1976, enrollment figure, one needs to go to another source: for example, Petrovichev, *Partiinoe stroitel'stvo* (1976), p. 62.

75. Figures for those of different educational levels is found in *Narodnoe khoziaistvo SSSR v 1974 g., Statisticheskii ezhegodnik* (Moscow, Statistika, 1975), pp. 39, 143. The educational distribution within the party is extrapolated from *Partiinaia zhizn'*, no. 14 (July 1973), pp. 16–17, and no. 10 (May 1976), p. 15.

76. Hough, *The Soviet Union and Social Science Theory*, pp. 135–139.

77. Rigby, *Communist Party Membership*, p. 437. In general, see pp. 324–348 and 412–453 for a thorough discussion of party saturation among occupational groups.

78. B. D. Levin and M. N. Perfil'ev, *Kadry apparata upravleniia v SSSR* (Leningrad, Nauka, 1970), p. 197.

79. Rigby, *Communist Party Membership*, p. 439. It should be noted, however, that all Soviet statistics on party and Komsomol membership among professionals must be treated with great care. There is a difference between party saturation in engineering posts (which at times are filled by nonengineers—the so-called *praktiki*) and party saturation among engineers with diplomas (who may not be working in an engineering post). Soviet sources refer to either group as engineers and usually do not specify which definition they have in mind. Consequently, when a westerner has to calculate saturation, he is often reduced to guessing which denominator to use.

80. *Itogi vsesoiuznoi perepisi naseleniia 1970 goda*, VI, 167–168.

81. *Voprosy istorii KPSS*, no. 1 (January 1977), p. 15.

82. *Partiinaia zhizn'*, no. 14 (July 1973), pp. 15, 21. *Permskaia oblastnaia organizatsiia KPSS v tsifrakh*, p. 112.

83. 1932: Rigby, *Communist Party Membership*, p. 116; 1937: Iudin, *Sotsial'naia baza rosta KPSS*, p. 130. Iudin states that 62.8 percent of the members were workers by social origin and that the number of workers by social origin exceeded the number of workers by occupation by 700,000 persons. There were 1,920,002 members and candidates in January 1937, and the figures of 1,245,000 and 550,000 are easy to calculate from Iudin's information. However, in his 1921–1933 tables (pp. 128 and 164) Iudin always excludes Communists in the army from his data, and, as a result, his social origin figures (but not his occupation figures) are slightly different from those in Rigby's tables on p. 130. (The difference should, incidentally, be useful for

calculating data on Communists in the army.) If Iudin follows the same practice for 1937, then my calculations may be incorrect, but the error should not be more than a few tens of thousands. Perm: *Permskaia oblastnaia organizatsiia KPSS v tsifrakh,* pp. 27, 64, 101, 105, 117. The figure is produced by subtracting the number of white collar employees by occupation and the number of collective farmers by occupation from the total number of Communists employed in the economy.

84. T. H. Rigby, "Soviet Communist Party Membership Under Brezhnev: A Rejoiner," *Soviet Studies,* XXIX (July 1977), p. 452. Rigby draws his data from *Partiinaia organizatsiia i rabochie Leningrada* (Leningrad, Lenizdat, 1974), p. 66.

85. For example, in 1970 3.8 percent of workers had complete or incomplete higher education or complete secondary specialized education, and this figure rose to 5.5 percent for workers in the basic metallurgy and machinery industry occupations and to 8.5 percent for the basic workers in the chemical industry. *Itogi vsesoiuznoi perepisi naseleniia 1970 goda,* VI, 62–627. The percentage for workers was determined by subtracting those with such education in agricultural "physical labor" from those in "physical labor."

86. Petrovichev, ed., *Partiinoe stroitel'stvo* (1976), p. 359.

87. The figure of those employed in the economy can be calculated from the agricultural data ibid., pp. 348, 359.

88. I have used the calculation of the total number of workers, collective farmers, and white collar employees in the population as a whole from Seniavsky, *Izmeneniia v sotsial'noi strukture sovetskogo obshchestva,* p. 425.

89. V. I. Polurez, *Deiatel'nost' KPSS po povysheniiu effektivnosti promyshlennogo proizvodstva v usloviiakh razvitogo sotsializma* (Kiev, Vishcha shkola, 1974), p. 21.

90. The number of Jews in the party was published for the first time in decades in *Partiinaia zhizn',* no. 10 (May 1976), p. 16. The saturation rate for 1970 must be extrapolated from party data on "other nationalities" in Petrovichev, *Partiinoe stroitel'stvo* (1970), p. 65, and Petrovichev, *Partiinoe stroitel'stvo* (1972), p. 72, and from census data on the total number of Jews in *Itogi vsesoiuznoi perepisi naseleniia 1970 goda,* IV, 9, 373. The details of the extrapolation are described in Jerry F. Hough, "The Number of Soviet Jews in the Communist Party," *Soviet Studies* (forthcoming).

91. *Itogi vsesoiuznoi perepisi naseleniia 1970 goda,* IV, 13.

92. Thus, on January 1, 1971, 34.6 percent of the members of the party organization in Kazakhstan were Kazakhs—very close to the 32.6 percent of Kazakhs in the republic. V. A. Kadeikin, ed., *Voprosy vnutripartiinoi zhizni i rukovodiashchei deiatel'nosti KPSS na sovremennom etape* (Moscow, Mysl', 1974), p. 177.

93. *Itogi vsesoiuznoi perepisi naseleniia 1970 goda,* IV, 9, 13.

94. Rigby, *Communist Party Membership,* pp. 522–523. See pp. 1–48 and 510–525 for a more extended discussion of functions served by Communist party membership.

95. See, for example, A. Beliakov and I. Shvets, *Partiinaia informatsiia* (Moscow, Politizdat, 1970).

96. There are exceptions to this rule. In places where there are too few members to form a primary party organization, one or two members may be enrolled in a

territorial organization. Moreover, pensioners may be enrolled in a territorial party organization at their apartment house complex.

97. *Partiinaia zhizn'*, no. 21 (November 1977), p. 36.

98. Every Soviet citizen has the right to change jobs with two weeks notice, and party members are no different in this respect. What they risk is expulsion from the party if they exercise this right without approval.

99. *Partiinaia zhizn'*, no. 21 (November 1977), p. 37.

100. *Spravochnik sekretaria pervichnoi partiinoi organizatsii,* 3d ed. (Moscow, Politizdat, 1969), p. 159.

101. Statistics in this paragraph are from *Partiinaia zhizn'*, no. 21 (November 1977), p. 36.

102. A. M. Korolev, *V nogi s zhizn'iu* (Moscow, Politizdat, 1974), p. 226.

103. *Partiinaia zhizn'*, no. 20 (October 1976), p. 32.

104. Ibid., p. 36.

105. Hough, *The Soviet Prefects*, pp. 86–97, provides such an example.

106. *Partiinaia zhizn'*, no. 21 (November 1977), p. 37.

107. In the large organizations there are three deputy secretaries: one for organizational and political work, one for coordination of the various supervisory (*kontrol'*) activities of organizations within the enterprise, and one for agitation and propaganda work.

108. *Partiinaia zhizn'*, no. 21 (November 1977), pp. 36, 39.

109. Hough, *The Soviet Prefects*, pp. 94–95.

110. *Partiinaia zhizn'*, no. 21 (November 1977), p. 40.

111. T. M. Novikova, "Obshchestvennaia rabota v strukture biudzheta vremeni partiinykh aktivistov," *Sotsiologicheskie issledovaniia*, no. 1 (1976), pp. 149, 151.

112. N. Borodin, "Partiinyi komitet—kollektivnyi rukovoditel'," in V. M. Tatarinov, ed., *Zakon partiinoi zhizni v deistvii* (Kuibyshev, Kuibyshevskoe knizhnoe izdatel'stvo, 1965), p. 42.

113. I. N. Iudin, *Nekotorye voprosy organizatsionno-partiinoi raboty* (Moscow, Politizdat, 1973), p. 134; *Partiinaia zhizn'*, no. 21 (November 1976), p. 52.

114. Borodin, "Partiinyi komitet," p. 43.

115. Novikova, "Obshchestvennia rabota," pp. 149, 151.

116. Borodin, "Partiinyi komitet," p. 10.

117. V. P. Shan'gin, ed., *Sputnik partgruporga* (Moscow, Politizdat, 1975), p. 4.

118. Novikova, "Obshchestvennia rabota," pp. 149, 151.

119. Beliakov and Shvets, *Partiinaia informatsiia*, p. 50.

120. Novikova, "Obshchestvennia rabota," p. 150.

121. I. E. Ponomarev, "Sotsiologicheskie issledovaniia v rabote gorkoma partii," in N. N. Bokarev, ed., *Sotsiologicheskie issledovaniia v partiinoi rabote* (Moscow, Institut sotsiologicheskikh issledovanii, 1973), pp. 66–67. It was said that these figures increased after a campaign to activate the primary party organizations in Khimki, but I have used the earlier figures as more typical of the country as a whole.

122. Robert V. Daniels, "Soviet Politics Since Khrushchev," in John W. Strong, ed., *The Soviet Union Under Brezhnev and Kosygin* (New York, Van Nostrand-Reinhold Co., 1971), pp. 22-23.

10. The Institutional Actors

1. The Soviet constitution of 1977 is available in many sources, but its original publication was in *Pravda and Izvestiia*, October 8, 1977. The constitution is translated in *The Current Digest of the Soviet Press*, XXIV (November 9, 1977), 1–13. This translation has the further virtue of indicating the differences between the final version and the original draft published in June.

2. *Deputaty Verkhovnogo Soveta SSSR, Deviatyi sozyv* (Moscow, Izdatel'stvo "Izvestiia," 1974), pp. 3–4. The statistic on the percentage of non-Russians is based on a count from the individual biographies.

3. Ibid., p. 3.

4. These figures are based on a personal count from the biographies of the deputies. D. Richard Little also emphasizes the distinction between "permanent members" and "transient members," the latter group containing "most of the worker and peasant deputies. "Soviet Parliamentary Committees After Khrushchev: Obstacles and Opportunities," *Soviet Studies*, XXIV (July 1972), 44. However, Professor Little asserts that only 6 of the 480 deputies elected to the Council of Union for the first time in 1966 were re-elected in 1970 while every 1962 deputy who was re-elected in 1966 was also re-elected in 1970. By my count, the number of deputies newly elected to the Council of Union in 1966 and re-elected in 1970 was not 6 but 143. Moreover, 30 percent of the deputies elected both in 1962 and 1966 (80 of 267 deputies by my count) were not re-elected in 1970. Deputies who died are excluded from the calculation.

5. V. I. Vasil'ev and F. I. Kalinychev, eds., *Nash narodnyi parlament* (Moscow, Gospolitizdat, 1966), p. 45. This source says that the Supreme Soviet usually meets from 10:00 A.M. to 2:00 P.M. and from 4:00 P.M. to 6:00 P.M.

6. Fainsod, *How Russia Is Ruled* (1953), p. 325.

7. The debate is reported in *Zasedaniia Verkhovnogo Soveta SSSR vos'mogo sozyva, Shestaia sessiia [17–19 iulia 1973 g.], Stenograficheskii otchet* (Moscow, Izdatel'stvo Verhovnogo Soveta, 1973). The Mazurov quotation is from p. 303.

8. See the discussion in Peter Vanneman, *The Supreme Soviet: Politics and the Legislative Process in the Soviet Political System* (Durham, N.C., Duke University Press, 1977), pp. 188–195.

9. See articles 119, 121, and 122 of the 1977 constitution.

10. In 1974 there were twenty members. Their names are listed in *Izvestiia*, July 27, 1974, p. 4, their occupations ibid., June 19, 1974. At that time Brezhnev was a simple member, but he was removed when he became Chairman and the scientist elected in 1974 died in 1977. In December 1977, three men—a scientist and the trade union and Komsomol leaders—were elected to bring the total to twenty-one. *Pravda*, December 15, 1977, p. 1.

11. Prior to the introduction of the 1936 constitution, Kalinin's post was actually Chairman of TsIK (the Central Executive Committee), but this committee had several hundred members and at that time was really the closest equivalent to the Supreme Soviet.

12. For Brezhnev's election, *Izvestiia*, June 17, 1977, p. 1, and for Kuznetsov's,

October 7, 1977, p. 1, and October 8, 1977, p. 2. For the importance of the foreign relations role, ibid. June 18, 1977, p. 1.

13. B. V. Shchetinin and A. N. Gorshenev, *Kurs sovetskogo gosudarstvennogo prava* (Moscow, Vysshaia shkola, 1971), p. 391.

14. M. P. Georgadze, ed., *Verkhovnyi Sovet SSSR* (Moscow, Izdatel'stvo "Izvestiia," 1975).

15. Ibid., p. 134.

16. V. P. Antonova and A. I. Filatova, *Sovetskoe gosudarstvennoe pravo* (Moscow, Iuridicheskaia literatura, 1969) pp. 493–496. See D. Richard Little, "Soviet Parliamentary Committees After Khrushchev," *Soviet Studies.*

17. In 1974 there were but fourteen committees, and the lists of their members are found in *Izvestiia,* July 26, 1974, pp. 1, 3–5; July 27, 1974, pp. 4–6. The Women's Work and Living Conditions and Protection of Motherhood and Childhood Committee was formed in October 1976, and its members were listed then. Ibid., October 31, 1976, p. 3. The figure of 1,070 total committee members is confirmed in *Voprosy istorii KPSS,* no. 11, 1977, p. 31.

18. For example, the chairman of the Transportation and Communications Committee of the Council of the Union in 1974, I. E. Klimenko, was first secretary of the Smolensk regional party committee, but he graduated from the Rostov Engineering Institute for the Railroad Industry and worked for seven years in that industry before entering party work. V. M. Kavun, the chairman of the Agriculture Committee of the Council of Union, is chairman of the Vinnitsy oblispolkom, but is an agronomist with seventeen years experience as a collective farm chairman.

19. The existence of joint sessions make Soviet counts of the number of sessions unreliable. For example, the statistics published in Georgadze, *Verkhovnyi Sovet SSSR,* pp. 136–137, on the Education, Science, and Culture Committee of the Council of the Union are not the same as those cited in *Pravda,* May 21, 1974, p. 3.

20. Georgadze, *Verkhovnyi Sovet SSSR,* p. 136.

21. *Pravda,* May 21, 1974, p. 3. For another description of the legislative process with respect to Supreme Soviet laws see S. G. Bannikov, "Zakonodatel'naia initsiativa Verkhovnogo Suda SSSR," *Sovetskoe gosudarstvo i pravo,* no. 3 (1974), pp. 16–17. For a good general discussion see Georgadze, *Verkhovnyi Sovet SSSR,* pp. 195–223.

22. These were among the questions discussed in 1975. A short report of each committee session is found in *Vedomosti Verkhovnogo Soveta SSSR,* in *Izvestiia,* and (in many cases) in the appropriate specialized paper.

23. *Sovetskoe gosudarstvo i pravo,* no. 11 (November 1975), p. 4.

24. *Pravda,* May 21, 1974, p. 3.

25. This latter section was introduced into the budget for the first time in 1974. *Izvestiia,* December 5, 1974, p. 2.

26. Georgadze, *Verkhovnyi Sovet SSSR,* p. 253.

27. Ibid., p. 254. In 1973, when there were only fourteen joint preparatory committees, 162 deputies participated. A. Shitikov, "Vos'moi sozyv," *Sovety deputatov trudiashchikhsia,* no. 5 (May 1974), p. 9. In 1975 the Committee for the Plans and

Budgets of the Union Republics contained 18 deputies, a fact which probably denotes that the four general committees are larger than the more specialized ones. *Izvestiia*, November 22, 1975, p. 2.

28. *Pravda*, May 21, 1974, p. 3.

29. Georgadze, *Verkhovnyi Sovet SSSR*, p. 255. The number of specialists is given in Shitikov, "Vos'moi sozyv," p. 9.

30. *Politicheskoe samoobrazovanie*, no. 6 (June 1974), p. 125. *Gudok*, December 5, 1973, p. 3. In December of recent years *Izvestiia* has carried a number of reports on the work of the joint preparatory committees.

31. L. I. Brezhnev, *Voprosy upravleniia ekonomikoi razvitogo sotialisticheskogo obshchestva* (Moscow, Politizdat, 1976), p. 179.

32. The reports on committee sessions in *Izvestiia* and *Vedomosti Verkhovnogo Soveta SSSR* often include the name of the leader of the preparatory group and the names of those who spoke at the session. The latter generally seem to be drawn from other members of the group, and the figure given is actually of reported speakers at the group sessions. (The percentages are based on the identification of 60 leaders and 213 speakers.) For the leaders and members of the preparatory groups, the percentage of Central Committee membership was calculated as of the time of the respective sessions.

33. Thus, the heads of the departments in the apparatus of the party Central Committee generally are members of an appropriate Supreme Soviet standing committee (and in the case of the Legislative Proposals, Agriculture and Foreign Affairs Committee is a committee chairman as of 1977). However, judging by published reports, no Central Committee department head has served as leader of a preparatory group or preparatory committee since June 1969 when the head of the machinery industry department headed the preparation of a question on the electrification of agriculture.

34. An individual deputy may, of course, also have an impact outside the framework of the committee structure simply by raising some local problem before a ministry. See, for example, Iu. Iu. Pitra, "Predstavliaia svoi okrug," *Sovety deputatov trudiashchikhsia*, no. 5 (May 1974), pp. 23–26. Georgadze, *Verkhovnyi Sovet, SSSR*, p. 168, provides four examples of ministerial decisions taken on deputy initiative to improve conditions in the local district. When one checks out the names he gives with the lists of occupations of deputies, it turns out that three were workers appealing about a question concerning their enterprise and the fourth was a writer.

35. In 1976, this official, V. G. Lomonosov, was named Chairman of the State Committee for Labor and Social Questions. Such a promotion suggests another possible role for the committees: exposure of regional officials to national policy-making processes and to national leaders, and preparation of some of them for work in the capital. However, there is less movement than one might expect from committee chairmanships and leadership of preparatory groups into central posts in the policy area being overseen.

36. *Spravochnik partiinogo rabotnika*, 6th to 16th eds. (Moscow, Politizdat, 1966–1976). Of the joint decisions, 112 were issued jointly with the party Central

Committee alone and twenty-seven with the Trade Union Council alone or with the Central Committee and the Trade Union Council together.

37. I. Kalinin, "Uluchshenie balansovoi raboty i voprosy soversherstvovaniia planirovaniia," *Planovoe khoziaistvo*, no. 8 (August 1973), pp. 16–18.

38. Aleksei I. Lepeshkin, *Sovetskoe gosudarstvennoe pravo* (Moscow, Iuridicheskaia literatura, 1971), p. 555; N. S. Koval' and B. P. Miroshnichenko, *Planirovanie narodnogo khoziaistvo SSSR*, 2d ed. (Moscow, Vysshaia shkola, 1968), p. 97.

39. The number of deputy chairmen of the Council of Ministers and the number of ministries change quite frequently, and, consequently, so does the size of the council. For a current list see the latest yearbook of the Great Soviet Encyclopedia (*Ezhegodnik Bol'shoi sovetskoi entsiklopediia*).

40. B. V. Shchetinin and A. N. Gorshenev, *Kurs sovetskogo gosudarstvennogo prava* (Moscow, Vysshaia shkola, 1971), p. 391.

41. *Izvestiia*, January 18, 1977, p. 1; April 22, 1977, p. 1; October 20, 1977, p. 1. In 1977 a June session was even more ceremonial—a joint session with the Politburo and the Presidium of the Supreme Soviet to hear a Brezhnev report. Ibid., June 25, 1977, p. 1.

42. Shchetinin and Gorshenev, *Kurs sovetskogo gosudarstvennogo prava*, p. 391; Ia. N. Umansky, ed., *Sovetskoe gosudarstvennoe pravo* (Moscow, Vysshaia shkola, 1970), p. 396; S. S. Kravchuk, ed., *Gosudarstvennoe pravo SSSR* (Moscow, Iuridicheskaia literatura, 1967), p. 470.

43. Umansky, *Sovetskoe gosudarstvennoe pravo*, p. 396; Lepeshkin, *Sovetskoe gosudarstvennoe pravo*, p. 546; Kravchuk, *Gosudarstvennoe pravo SSSR*, p. 470; Shchetinin and Gorshenev, *Kurs sovetskogo gosudarstvennogo prava*, p. 391.

44. See the biography of M. A. Lesechko, 1966 Yearbook of the *Bol'shaia sovetskaia entsiklopediia*, p. 599.

45. To the best of my knowledge, Soviet printed sources have never mentioned this commission, but its existence is acknowledged by Soviet officials in a position to know. The quotation is from Raymond L. Garthoff, "SALT and the Soviet Military," *Problems of Communism*, XXIV (January–February 1975), 29. In 1940 there was a Council of the Defense Indutsry attached to the Council of People's Commissars (as the Council of Ministers was then called), and it apparently was a predecessor to the Military-Industrial Commission. V. V. Kolotov, *Nikolai Alekseevich Voznesensky* (Moscow, Politizdat, 1970), p. 144.

46. For 1940, ibid., p. 145; for 1956 (and the quotation about it), see N. N. Smeliakov, *S chego nachinaetsia rodina* (Moscow, Politizdat, 1975), pp. 176–177.

47. Garthoff, "SALT and the Soviet Military," p. 29. The reference to Brezhnev as Chairman of the Defense Council is found in *Pravda*, May 9, 1976, p. 1, and the reference to Khrushchev as Commander-in-Chief is in Nikita S. Khrushchev, *Khrushchev Remembers: The Last Testament*, ed. and trans. Strobe Talbott (Boston, Little, Brown, and Co., 1974), pp. 12–13.

48. Officials of the departments of the RSFSR Council of Ministers are awarded medals on their fiftieth and sixtieth birthday, and their names and often the names of their departments are printed in *Vedomosti Verkhovnogo Soveta RSFSR*.

49. Kolotov, *Nikolai Alekseevich Voznesensky*, p. 313.

50. Fainsod, *How Russia Is Ruled* (1963), p. 393; the 1958 and 1966 Yearbooks of the *Bol'shaia sovetskaia entsiklopediia*, pp. 6 and 20–21 respectively.

51. Ministry of Health: *Meditsinskaia gazeta*, November 26, 1965, p. 1; Ministry of Energy and Electrification: *Pravda*, November 2, 1974, p. 2. In 1966 it was stated that forty-six ministries and state committees (of the sixty-five that existed at that time) had more than 500 Communists apiece in them. It was also stated that 50 to 70 percent of the ministerial staff normally were party members, and hence it is possible to calculate a 700 to 1,000 person minimum figure for two-thirds of these central bodies. *Partiinaia zhizn'*, no. 24 (December 1966), pp. 26, 30.

52. *Partiinaia zhizn'*, no. 24 (December 1966), p. 26.

53. In a number of industrial ministries, the administrative bureaus have now been replaced by *ob"edinenie*, sometimes translated as associations, but it is not clear that the difference is a major one from an administrative point of view. The Moscow telephone directory is an excellent source for the internal structure of most ministries.

54. See I. L. Davitnidze, *Kollegii ministerstv (Pravovoe polozhenie i organizasiia raboty)* (Moscow, Iuridicheskaia literatury, 1972).

55. For example, the Minister of the Iron and Steel Industry, I. P. Kazanets, is a metallurgical engineer who worked for fifteen years in lower engineering and administrative posts at two major steel plants. His last jobs at the plant level were party ones, and he then became party first secretary in a city and later a region that are centers of the iron and steel industry. After five years of top party-state work in the Ukraine, he was named to his present ministerial position. The Minister for Construction in the Oil and Gas Industry, B. E. Shcherbina, had been regional first secretary for twelve years in Tiumen', the center of the major new Soviet oil field, while the minister of culture at that time, E. A. Furtseva, was a former first secretary of the Moscow city party committee with earlier experience in Komsomol and party work oriented toward educational and cultural questions.

56. The biographies of nearly all the ministers and state committee chairmen can be found in the 1971 Yearbook of the *Bol'shaia sovetskaia entsiklopediia*, pp. 577–643. See also the 1977 Yearbook, pp. 582–627.

57. The annual Yearbook of the *Bol'shaia sovetskaia entsiklopediia* indicates which ministries are all-union and which union-republic in its enumeration of the current members of the Council of Ministers. See table 30 of Chapter 11.

58. For an excellent discussion of the role of the scholars of this institute in the policy process see Peter H. Solomon, Jr., *Soviet Criminologists and Criminal Policy: Specialists in Policy Making* (New York, Columbia University Press, 1978).

59. *Ekonomicheskaia gazeta*, no. 35 (August 1973), p. 15.

60. For such a complaint see ibid., no. 2 (January 1974), p. 5.

61. *Sel'skaia zhizn'*, January 24, 1973, p. 2. For a follow-up report see ibid., July 13, 1973, p. 2.

62. A. G. Zverev, *Zapiski ministra* (Moscow, Politizdat, 1973), pp. 161, 181–186.

63. See Aaron Wildavsky, *The Politics of the Budgetary Process* (Boston, Little, Brown, 1964). For a further discussion of this point in the Soviet context see Hough, *Soviet Prefects*, pp. 175–177.

64. *Komsomol'skaia pravda,* November 6, 1973, p. 2.

65. *Plenum tsentral'nogo komiteta Kommunisticheskoi partii Sovetskogo Soiuza [24–26 marta 1965 goda], Stenograficheskii otchet* (Moscow, Politizdat, 1965), pp. 97–98. *Deputaty Verkhovnogo Soveta* (1974), p. 328.

66. Khrushchev, *Khrushchev Remembers: The Last Testament,* p. 540.

67. The best western discussion of this type of commission is found in Solomon, *Soviet Criminologists and Criminal Policy.*

68. A pro-ministerial article is A. S. Petrov, "Ekonomicheskaia reforma i tendentsii organizatsii otraslogo upravleniia promyshlennost'iu," *Sovetskoe gosudarstvo i pravo,* no. 3 (1971), p. 21; an article opposing this position (and this article) is V. S. Pronina, "Osobennosti kompetentsii gosudarstvennykh komitetov Soveta Ministrov SSSR," ibid., no. 5 (1974), pp. 53–61. Ministers also speak out on this issue. *Ekonomicheskaia gazeta,* no. 13 (March 1974) p. 4.

69. For a discussion of the flirtation with systems theory see Paul Cocks, "The Policy Process and Bureaucratic Politics," in Paul Cocks, Robert V. Daniels, and Nancy Whittier Heer, eds., *The Dynamics of Soviet Politics* (Cambridge, Mass., Harvard University Press, 1976), pp. 156–178.

70. Of these 1,943 items, 274 must be confirmed by the Council of Ministers. The balance of 17,484 less important items is worked out by the State Committee on Supplies Procurement, and some 40,000 lesser items by the ministries. Kalinin, "Uluchshenie balansovoi raboty i voprosy sovershenstvovanie planirovaniia," pp. 16–18.

71. A list of the departments is contained in Koval' and Miroshnichenko, *Planirovanie narodnogo khoziaistva SSSR,* 2d ed., pp. 97–98.

72. Electronics: A. I. Bobrov, *Planovoe khoziaistvo,* no. 11 (1974), p. 153. Construction: B. M. Platonov, *Pravda,* January 22, 1966, p. 4. Food industry: *Pravda,* August 10, 1971, p. 6. Foreign Trade: M. M. Gusev, *Izvestiia,* March 7, 1974, p. 4. However, some Gosplan officials do spend virtually their whole career in Gosplan. See *Planovoe khoziaistvo,* no. 6, 1977, p. 160, for the obituary of such a man, the head of the agriculture department.

73. *Plenum tsentral'nogo komiteta,* March 24–26, 1965, p. 150.

74. *Planovoe khoziaistvo,* no. 6 (1977), p. 160.

75. The first deputy chairman was T. I. Sokolov, and the deputy chairman was N. P. Gusev. In 1976 Sokolov was replaced by P. A. Paskar', the chairman of the Council of Ministers of Moldavia, an agricultural specialist who had experience in supervising the experiments in agricultural organization in that republic. *Deputaty Verkhovnogo Soveta* (1974), p. 343.

76. Timothy J. Colton, *Commissars, Commanders, and Civilian Authority: The Structure of Soviet Military Politics* (Cambridge, Mass., Harvard University Press, 1979).

77. 1976 Yearbook of the *Bol'shaia sovetskaia entsiklopediia,* p. 68.

78. *XXV s"ezd Kommunisticheskoi partii Sovetskogo Soiuza [24 fevralia-5 marta 1976 goda], Stenograficheskii otchet* (Moscow, Politizdat, 1976), I, 298. In 1966, 352 of the 4,943 delegates to the Twenty-Third Party Congress were of this category.

XXIII s"ezd Kommunisticheskoi partii Sovetskogo Soiuza [29 marta-8 aprelia 1966], *Stenograficheskii otchet* (Moscow, Politizdat, 1966), I, 279, 283.

79. Timothy J. Colton, "Civil-Military Relations in Soviet Politics," *Current History*, 67 (October 1974), 162. The bureaus can be found in the Yearbooks of the *Bol'shaia sovetskaia entsiklopediia*, the occupations of the members in the republican newspapers or in the semiannual journal *Current Soviet Leaders* (Mosaic Press, Oakville, Ontario).

80. *Krasnaia zvezda*, May 16, 1974, p. 3.

81. The counts have been made by the author, and they exclude the two cosmonauts elected in 1966 and 1974 and the single one named in 1970.

82. Merle Fainsod, *Smolensk Under Soviet Rule* (Cambridge, Mass., Harvard University Press, 1958), p. 68.

83. Roman Kolkowicz, *The Soviet Military and the Communist Party* (Princeton, Princeton University Press, 1967), pp. 7, 11.

84. This is the central theme of Colton, *Commissars, Commanders, and Civilian Authority*. The same point is made in William E. Odom, "The Party Connection," *Problems of Communism*, XXII (September–October 1973), 12–26. There are also divisions within the military. See Roman Kolkowicz, "The Military," in H. Gordon Skilling and Franklyn Griffiths, ed., *Interest Groups in Soviet Politics* (Princeton, Princeton University Press, 1971), pp. 145–153.

85. Odom, "The Party Connection," p. 21.

86. Nikita S. Khrushchev, *Khrushchev Remembers*, ed. and trans. Strobe Talbott (Boston, Little, Brown, and Co., 1970), p. 572. This point is discussed in Colton, "Civil-Military Relations in Soviet Politics," p. 61.

87. Charles E. Lindblom, *The Policy-Making Process* (Englewood Cliffs, N.J., Prentice-Hall, Inc., 1968), p. 68. See also pp. 64–65.

88. This discussion is limited to the Academy of Sciences; the points made could be repeated almost verbatim for the universities (in contrast to the more specialized educational institutions).

89. *Narodnoe khoziaistvo SSSR v 1974 g., Statisticheskii ezhegodnik* (Moscow, Statistika, 1975), p. 691; 1965 Yearbook of *Bol'shaia sovetskaia entsiklopediia*, p. 79; *Narodnoe khoziaistvo SSSR v 1975 g., Statisticheskii ezhegodnik* (Moscow, Statistika, 1976), p. 165.

90. See Donald D. Barry, "The Specialist in Soviet Policy-Making: The Adoption of a Law," *Soviet Studies*, XVI (October 1964), 152–165, and Solomon, *Soviet Criminologists and Criminal Policy*.

91. Zbigniew Brzezinski and Samuel P. Huntington, *Political Power USA/USSR* (New York, The Viking Press, 1965), p. 196.

92. *Bol'shaia sovetskaia entsiklopediia*, 3d ed. (Moscow, Izdatel'stvo "Bol'shaia sovetskaia entsiklopediia," 1970), I, 316. For the position of the Academy see V. A. Dozovtsev, "Akademiia nauk SSSR: pravovoi status, organy upravleniia, i funktsii," *Sovetskoe gosudarstvo i pravo*, no. 11 (1974), pp. 19–26.

93. *Narodnoe khoziaistvo SSSR v 1975 g.*, p. 167.

94. Ibid., p. 146.

95. 1976 Yearbook of the *Bol'shaia sovetskaia entsiklopediia*, p. 77.

96. The elections are held every two years in even-numbered years, and in recent years *Izvestiia* has published the names of the nominees as well as of those elected. The three cases of rejected candidates come from the 1974 elections. The nominees were listed in *Izvestiia*, November 1, 1974, pp. 3–4, the election results ibid., November 28, 1974, p. 5. The elections of the science and education department (S. P. Trapeznikov) is reported in *Izvestiia*, December 26, 1976, p. 2, and was extraordinarily delayed by past Soviet standards. Moscow rumors persistently reported his rejection in the past.

Elections to other academies also can have a meaningful character. For example, in 1968 Trapeznikov was nominated as an academician of the Academy of Pedagogical Sciences and the deputy head of the science and education department of the Ukrainian party Central Committee (Kobzar) was nominated as a corresponding member. Neither was elected, although at the meeting announcing the results, Trapeznikov was said to have withdrawn. *Uchitel'skaia gazeta*, January 4, January 6, and February 6, 1968.

97. Andrei D. Sakharov, *Sakharov Speaks* (New York, Alfred A. Knopf, 1974), pp. 30–34; Khrushchev, *Khrushchev Remembers: The Last Testament*, pp. 68–71.

98. *Pravda*, December 22, 1973, p. 3.

99. Ibid., August 29, 1975, p. 3.

100. Ibid., February 21, 1977, p. 2.

101. *Sovetskoe gosudarstvo i pravo*, no. 2 (1973), pp. 41–48, and no. 9 (1973), pp. 64–72.

102. *Vestnik Akademii Nauk SSSR*, no. 10 (1976), pp. 3–11.

103. *XXV s"ezd Kommunisticheskoi partii Sovetskogo Soiuza [24 fevralia-5 marta 1976 goda]*, *Stenograficheskii otchet* (Moscow, Politizdat, 1976), I, 218.

104. *Planovoe khoziaistvo*, no. 3 (March 1973), p. 38.

105. *Sovetskoe gosudarstvo i pravo*, no. 10 (1973), p. 154.

106. There is no equivalent to the Environmental Protection Agency in the Soviet Union, and responsibility for enforcing antipollution laws is spread among a number of organizations. It is symptomatic that pollution questions (at least water pollution questions) are handled in the Central Committee apparatus by the forestry section of the agriculture department.

107. *Vestnik Akademii Nauk SSSR*, no. 9 (1973), pp. 3–51.

108. For the development of this institute and the views associated with it see William Zimmerman, *Soviet Perspectives on International Relations* (Princeton, Princeton University Press, 1969). *Wall Street Journal*, November 20, 1973, p. 1, contains a journalistic report on its activity, including the assertion that western diplomats believe that the institute has "considerable clout" in the foreign policy process.

109. *Trud*, April 27, 1978, p. 2.

110. For a discussion of the Ministry of General Machinery, which produces rockets, see Karl F. Spielman, "Defense Industrialists in the USSR," *Problems of Communism*, XXV (September–October 1973), 54.

111. For a number of years, the total number of publicly acknowledged trade

unions stood at twenty-five, and the list (with the name of the chairman of each) could be found in the latest yearbook of the *Bol'shaia sovetskaia entsiklopediia*. However, in 1977 the Aviation and Defense Industry Trade Union and the Machinery Industry Trade Union were each split into three separate unions, while the Oil, Chemical, and Oil Refinery Industry Trade Union was split into two. *Trud,* February 10, 1977, p. 1, February 19, 1977, p. 1, and March 2, 1977, p. 1.

112. Edwin B. Morrell, "Communist Unionism: Organized Labor and the Soviet State," Ph.D. diss., Harvard University, 1965, p. 314–317.

113. Normally it is easy to judge which ministries are associated with the various trade unions from reports in the trade union newspaper *Trud,* especially reports of the meetings and congresses of the specialized unions. According to an interview, the officials of the party and Komsomol apparatus, as well as the generalized trade union officials, are enrolled in the Culture Trade Union.

114. Ts. A. Iampol'skaia, "Vzaimodeistvie obshchestvennykh organizatsii i gosudarstva pri formirovanii ikh organov," *Sovetskoe gosudarstvo i pravo,* no. 12 (December 1970), pp. 25–26.

115. *Uchitel'skaia gazeta,* February 15, 1977, p. 1. The other members are the chairman, three secretaries, and two department heads of the Central Trade Union, four chairmen of republican and regional committees of the trade union, the editor of *Uchitel'skaia gazeta,* and a rank-and-file teacher. For the memberships of the Presidium in 1968 and 1972 see ibid., January 13, 1968, p. 1, and February 12, 1972, p. 2.

116. For a discussion of nomenklatura in the trade unions see Morrell, "Communist Unionism," pp. 179–181.

117. See the discussion in Hough, *The Soviet Prefects,* pp. 159–161.

118. It has been possible to identify a capital construction administration, a tourist council, a business office, and thirteen departments: (1) culture-mass work, (2) financial, (3) general, (4) housing and living conditions, (5) international, (6) juridical, (7) labor safety, (8) organizational-instruction, (9) physical culture and sports, (10) relations with trade unions of socialist countries, (11) social insurance, (12) socialist competition and production-mass work, and (13) wages and economic work.

119. The responsibilities of most of the secretaries can be easily determined by the nature of their speeches and articles.

120. Emily Clark Brown, *Soviet Trade Unions and Labor Relations* (Cambridge, Mass., Harvard University Press, 1966); Mary McAuley, *Labor Disputes in Soviet Russia* (Oxford, Clarendon Press, 1969).

121. For example, articles by national trade union officials advocating changes in the planning and financing of labor safety measures and in the incentive system in agriculture can be found in *Sovetskie profsoiuzy,* no. 3 (February 1973), pp. 37–38, and no. 5 (March 1973), pp. 13–15.

122. G. A. Ivanov and A. Sh. Pribluda, *Planovye organy v SSSR* (New York, Ekonomika, 1967), p. 76.

123. Ibid., no. 6 (March 1973), p. 26. In 1966 the Ministry of the Heavy, Energy, and Transportation Machinery Industry issued twelve joint decisions with the

Machinery Industry Workers Trade Union, and in 1965 the chairman of the Health Employee Trade Union was actually named to the collegium of the Ministry of Health. Davidnidze, *Kollegii ministerstv*, pp. 107, 66.

124. *Kommunist*, no. 14 (September 1973), p. 52.

125. The last example comes from *Sotsialisticheskii trud*, no. 6 (1975), p. 99, and the next to last one from *Sel'skaia zhizn'*, January 13, 1974, p. 3. The other examples are found in *Spravochnik partiinogo rabotnika*, 8th through 12th eds. See the discussion in my article in Arcadius Kahan and Blair Ruble, eds., *Industrial Labor in the USSR* (Elmsford, N.Y., Pergamon Press, 1979).

126. *Kommunist*, no. 14 (September 1973), p. 52.

127. *Sovetskie profsoiuzy*, no. 14 (September 1973), p. 52, and no. 21 (November 1976), p. 35.

128. The membership of the republican bureaus is reported in the Yearbooks of the *Bol'shaia sovetskaia entsiklopediia* under the entries on the respective republics.

129. Lists of all important republican officials from 1955 to 1972 (including the names of all bureau members) are printed in Grey Hodnett and Val Ogareff, *Leaders of the Soviet Republics, 1955–1972* (Canberra, Australian National University, 1973). The ranking was determined by giving two points for full membership of a post in a republican bureau and one point for candidate membership and then adding the totals for all the republics. The top seven officials are the five secretaries of the Central Committee, the chairman of the Council of Ministers, and the chairman of the Presidium of the Supreme Soviet. The eighth is the first deputy chairman of the Council of Ministers, the ninth is the first secretary of the capital city or regional party committee, the tenth the chairman of the People's Control Committee, and the chairman of the KGB and the head of the organizational-party work department of the Central Committee tied for twelfth.

130. In 1966, one of the trade union chairmen was a full member and eight were candidate members; in 1971, three were full members and seven were candidates; in 1976, five were full members and eight were candidates. The names of the bureau members and of the trade union chairmen are found in the Yearbooks of the *Bol'shaia sovetskaia entsiklopediia* in the sections on the respective republics.

131. A. V. Viktorov became a secretary of the VTsSPS in 1975, while A. Ia. Rybakov became chairman of Machinery and Instrument Industry Trade Union in 1977.

132. For example, the chairman of the trade union of the Sverdlovsk Railroad in 1973 became deputy head of the railroad. *Gudok*, August 9, 1973, p. 1, and August 24, 1973, p. 3.

133. For biographies of central trade union chairmen see *Sovetskie profsoiuzy*, no. 20 (October 1973), p. 48 (Electric Stations and Electric Industry); no. 3 (February 1973), p. 44 (Local Industry); no. 9 (May 1972), p. 47 (Radiotechnical Industry); no. 22 (November 1971), p. 48 (Textile and Light Industry).

134. Grishin was second secretary of the Moscow regional party committee, Shelepin a secretary of the Central Committee, and Shibaev the first secretary of the

Saratov regional party committee. Their biographies are found in a wide variety of sources, including the 1971 Yearbook of the *Bol'shaia sovetskaia entsiklopediia*.

135. See n. 129.

136. Tiazhelnikov's and Pastukhov's biographies are found in *Deputaty Verkhovnogo Soveta SSSR* (1970), pp. 450, 338. For the change in leadership see *Komsomol'skaia pravda*, May 28, 1977, p. 1. Tiazhelnikov became head of the propaganda department of the party Central Committee.

137. *Komsomol'skaia pravda*, April 26, 1978, p. 7. In a 1974 interview it was stated that the working youth department had a staff of twenty-one in addition to the department head—two deputy heads, one responsible organizer, and eighteen instructors. A few departments—notably the Komsomol organs department (the personnel department)—may be larger, but the working youth department should be fairly typical in size.

138. It has been stated in an interview that all relations with youth organizations of the non-Communist world—including Communist organizations of these countries—are handled by the Committee of Youth Organizations.

139. The list of Komsomol secretaries is found in each Yearbook of the *Bol'shaia sovetskaia entsiklopediia*, and their responsibilities are easy to deduce from *Komsomol'skaia pravda*. The Chairman of the Pioneers was elected a Komsomol secretary for the first time in resent years in 1977. *Komsomol'skaia pravda*, June 22, 1977, p. 1.

140. Trade union: *Trud*, March 26, 1977, p. 1. People's Control Committee: Jan S. Adams, *Citizen Inspectors in the Soviet Union: The People's Control Committee* (New York, Praeger Publishers, 1977), p. 157. Collegia: *Politicheskoe samoobrazovanie*, no. 10 (1975), p. 132.

141. *Sotsialisticheskaia zakonnost'*, no. 4 (1973), p. 62; *Kommunist*, no. 11 (July 1973), p. 43.

142. *Komsomol'skaia pravda*, March 20, 1974, p. 2.

143. Ibid., October 28, 1973, p. 1.

144. These examples are taken from *Dokumenty TsK VLKSM* (Moscow, Molodaia gvardiia, 1973).

145. *Politicheskoe samoobrazovanie*, 10 (1975), p. 132.

146. In addition to Tiazhelnikov and Pastukhov (see n. 136), Z. G. Novozhilova, the secretary for secondary schools (the only woman secretary at that time) was elected a member of the Auditing Commission.

147. Ernest S. Griffith, *The American System of Government*, 4th ed. (New York, Frederick A. Praeger, 1965), pp. 102–103.

11. The Central Committee Secretariat and Apparatus

1. In the five years between the Twenty-Fourth and Twenty-Fifth Congresses in 1971 and 1976, the Secretariat met in 205 sessions—an average of 41 meetings a year. *Voprosy istorii KPSS*, no. 12 (December 1976), p. 33.

2. For a description of these changes see Fainsod, *How Russia Is Ruled* (1963), pp. 190–208. Soviet sources are beginning to write about the Central Committee apparatus in the pre-Purge period. See, for example, N. A. Zolotarev and P. I.

Kotel'nikov, eds., *Organizationno-partiinaia rabota. Iz istorii partiinogo stroitel'stva,* 2d ed. (Moscow, Politizdat, 1973), and V. K. Beliakov and N. A. Zolotarev, *Organizatsiia udesiateriat sily* (Moscow, Politizdat, 1975).

3. In western discussions this is often called the "Travel Abroad Department," but the Russian title is *otdel zagranichnykh kadrov. Vedomosti Verkhovnogo Soveta RSFSR,* no 45 (November 17, 1965), p. 994.

4. Soviet obituaries of important persons are usually signed by those with whom the deceased worked, including a top official or two of the appropriate Central Committee department. In late 1977 the obituary of a high official of the State Committee for Foreign Economic Ties included A. S. Shcherbakov in the place in the list of signers usually reserved for the Central Committee department heads. (Shcherbakov had been Ambassador to Vietnam during the war, and at the Twenty-Fifth Congress he was listed as deputy head of of a Central Committee department.)

5. Obviously, the propaganda department supervises agitation-propaganda work in all ministries. Other than this example, the most important overlap is likely to come in supervision of institutions that cut across branch lines—for example, the trade unions, the Komsomol, Gosplan, the People's Control Committee, and newspapers. There are special Central Committee sections which supervise these institutions, but the specialized subsections of the institutions really work under the appropriate specialized departments of the Central Committee. For example, the working youth department of the Komsomol has closest connection with the industrial departments of the Central Committee, the agriculture department of Gosplan has close connections with the agriculture department of the Central Committee, and the foreign departments of newspapers such as *Pravda* and *Izvestiia* receive their guidance from the international departments of the Central Committee.

6. These various offices were mentioned in lists of officials who received an award on their fiftieth or sixtieth birthday. The lists are published almost weekly in *Vedomosti Verkhovnogo Soveta RSFSR.*

7. Most of the names were found ibid., but a few received awards from the USSR Supreme Soviet and their names were listed in *Vedomosti Verkhovnogo Soveta SSSR.* This methodology may exaggerate the size of the Party Control Committee somewhat. Most officials of the Central Committee apparatus leave before they reach their fiftieth birthday, while officials of the Party Control Committee may well be older and therefore receive awards in higher proportion. (Officials at the level of department head and above were excluded from the calculations.)

8. See, for example, *Partiinaia zhizn',* no. 20 (October 1966), p. 59; no. 24 (December 1976), p. 55; no. 3 (February 1977), p. 50.

9. For a discussion of the Party Control Committee in the past see Paul Maupin Cocks, "The Politics of Intra-Party Control: The History and Institutional Role of Control Organs in the CPSU and the CPC," Ph.D. diss., Harvard University, 1969. For a discussion of the work of the lower organs of the Party Control Committee (the party commissions) see *Aktivnye pomoshchniki partiinykh komitetov* (Moscow, Politizdat, 1974).

10. Leo Gruliow, ed., *Current Soviet Policies—II* (New York, Frederick A. Praeger, 1957), p. 182.

11. Shuisky's biography can be found in the 1962 Yearbook of the *Bol'shaia sovetskaia entsiklopediia,* p. 622.

12. Sidney Ploss, *Conflict and Decision-Making in Soviet Russia* (Princeton, Princeton University Press, 1965), p. 202.

13. Information about Lebedev was received in an interview with a former high Soviet cultural official, who, unfortunately, had forgotten his first name and patronymic.

14. For three examples see *Vedomosti Verkhovnogo Soveta RSFSR,* no. 42 (October 16, 1975), p. 763; *Bakinskii rabochii,* October 27, 1974, p. 1; and *Sovetskaia Tatariia,* May 26, 1977, p. 1.

15. The title "consultant" is found in the lists of medal winners and in an occasional press reference, but the function of the group was described in interviews with two former Central Committee officials.

16. I have identified seventeen Central Committee lecturers in the press in 1975, 1976, or 1977, and this number may represent approximately half the total number. Important provincial officials also have paid lecturers—three to four in the republican and regional committees in 1966. *Partiinaia zhizn',* 19 (October 1966), 48.

17. A. Pravdin, "Inside the CPSU Central Committee" (An interview conducted by Merwyn Mathews), *Survey,* 20 (Autumn 1974), 95. Pravdin (a pseudonym) puts the size of the service staff at 2,400. The problem with the article is suggested by the treatment of the organizational-party work department (always referred to as the organizational department in the article). The staff of the department is said to number sixty—which seems highly improbable given the number of regions and republics it covers, let alone its many other functions—and then it is said to have inspectors and instructors to cover all the major ministries and enterprises—officials that I most seriously doubt it has and that would expand its size well beyond the 100 to 150 level that I would estimate. In speaking of an organizational department specialized by ministry, Pravdin seems to be going back to the type of verification of fulfillment department that was abolished in 1948. Ibid., pp. 95, 99–100.

18. Zbigniew Brzezinski and Samuel P. Huntington, *Political Power USA/USSR* (New York, The Viking Press, 1965), p. 163.

19. After his election as Secretary, Chernenko wrote articles on oversight (*kontrol'*) in general and attended conferences on the subject. To some extent this is a natural responsibility for a man in charge of handling complaints to the Central Committee about other institutions, but he seems to have been given responsibility for such institutions as the People's Control Committee which previously had been under the responsibility of other departments and secretaries.

20. Leonard Schapiro, "The General Department of the CC of the CPSU," *Survey,* 21 (Summer 1975), 53–65.

21. V. S. Frolov, I. D. Serbin, N. I. Savinkin, and B. I. Gostev.

22. The head of the culture department is V. F. Shauro, the head of the science and education department is S. P. Trapeznikov, and the head of the propaganda department is E. M. Tiazhel'nikov. The biographies of Shauro and Trapeznikov illustrate the type of career connections frequently found in the top party elite.

Shauro was engaged in ideological work in the Central Committee in 1947 when he was sent to Belorussia at the same time as M. T. Iovchuk, deputy head of the propaganda administration of the Party Central Committee. In 1970, Iovchuk, after two decades of teaching and research work in philosophy, was given a major promotion to the rectorship of the Academy of Social Sciences. In 1947 both men were working under the direction of M. V. Zimianin, the ideological secretary in Belorussia—a situation that was duplicated in 1977 when Zimianin was named ideological secretary of the Central Committee. In 1947 Mazurov had just moved from first secretaryship of the Belorussian Komsomol into low level work in the Belorussian Party Central Committee, and he was to be first secretary both of the Minsk regional committee and the Belorussian Central Committee when Shauro was the ideological secretary in each body. Finally, it might be mentioned that the present Minister of Foreign Trade, N. S. Patolichev, was Belorussian party first secretary from 1950 to 1956.

    Trapeznikov had been head of the agriculture department of the Penza regional party committee from 1942 to 1944—a time at which Kulakov (the late Central Committee secretary for agriculture) was a district party secretary in that region. (Kulakov became Trapeznikov's successor as department head in 1944 and worked in Penza region until 1955.) Chernenko (the present Central Committee secretary supervising the general department) was sent to Penza in 1945 and worked as a regional party secretary there until 1948. In 1948 he was sent to Moldavia as head of the agitation-propaganda department of the republican central committee—the same year that Trapeznikov was named rector of the Moldavian Higher Party School, which is, of course, supervised by the agitation-propaganda department, and in 1950 both became Brezhnev subordinates.

    23. V. A. Karlov, I. N. Dmitriev, F. I. Mochalin, K. S. Simonov, Ia. I Kabkov, V. V. Listov, and N. M. Pegov.

    24. *Pravda*, November 3, 1961, p. 2.

    25. N. A. Petrovichev, ed., *Partiinoe stroitel'stvo*, 3d ed. (Moscow, Politizdat, 1972), pp. 184–185.

    26. For example, the nomenklatura of a district party committee in Amur oblast included the head of a mine, the director and chief engineer of an electric station, and the chief engineer of a mining field. The relatively low level of the positions in the nomenklatura of this party committee is suggested by the fact that 60 percent of their occupants were under forty years of age in 1975, 16 percent under thirty. *Amurskaia pravda*, April 1, 1975, p. 2.

    27. A general discussion of nomenklatura and its role in personnel selection can be found in Jerry F. Hough, *The Soviet Prefects* (Cambridge, Mass., Harvard University Press, 1969), pp. 114–116, 150–170, and Bohdan Harasymiw, "*Nomenklatura*: The Soviet Communist Party's Leadership Recruitment System," *Canadian Journal of Political System*, 2 (December 1969), 493–512. The word "nomenklatura" is a generic one and refers to the list of positions over which any institution has the formal right of appointment or confirmation. For example, a ministry has its nomenklatura, as does a city soviet, various higher trade union organizations, and so forth. *Sovety deputatov trudiashchikhsia*, no. 2 (February 1974), p. 82. Edwin B. Morrell,

"Communist Unionism: Organized Labor and the Soviet State," Ph.D. diss., Harvard University, 1965, pp. 179–181.

28. Fedor Panferov, *Volga-Matushka reka* (Moscow, Sovetskii pisatel', 1954), pp. 29–32, 164, 181, and 217.

29. Jerry F. Hough, "The Soviet Concept of the Relationship between the Lower Party Organs and the State Administration," *Slavic Review*, 24 (June 1965), 216; Hough. *The Soviet Prefects*, p. 155.

30. *Ocherki istorii Ulianovskoi organizatsii KPSS* (Ulianovsk, Privolzhskoe knizhnoe izdatel'stvo, Ulianovskoe otdelenie, 1972), II, 347.

31. *Partiinaia zhizn'*, no. 9 (May 1959), p. 26.

32. Peter H. Solomon, Jr., *Soviet Criminologists and Criminal Policy: Specialists in Policy Making* (New York, Columbia University Press, 1978). For example, the deputy head of the organizational-party work department (N. S. Perun, presumably the deputy head supervising the local soviets) was made a member of a commission working on the legal rights of the regional soviets. *Vedomosti Verkhovnogo Soveta SSSR*, no. 44 (November 3, 1976), p. 753.

33. Pravdin, "Inside the CPSU Central Committee," p. 98.

34. Ibid., p. 98.

35. *Voprosy istorii KPSS*, no. 12 (December 1976), pp. 33, 36.

36. Petrovichev, *Partiinoe stroitel'stvo* (1972), p. 166.

37. D. I. Dubonosov, *Vo glave trudovogo pod"ema mass* (Rostov, Izdatel'stvo Rostovskogo Universiteta, 1967), p. 66.

38. Petrovichev, *Partiinoe stroitel'stvo* (1972), p. 184; V. I. Snastin, ed., *Partiinoe stroitel'stvo* (Moscow, Mysl', 1972), p. 140.

39. Brzezinski and Huntington, *Political Power USA/USSR*, p. 204.

40. N. N. Smeliakov, *S chego nachinaetsia Rodina* (Moscow, Politizdat, 1975), pp. 176–177.

41. This statement is based on interviews with two high officials of the People's Control Committee and on Jan S. Adams, *Citizen Inspectors in the Soviet Union: The People's Control Committee* (New York, Praeger Publishers, 1977), pp. 192–195.

42. Leonid I. Brezhnev, *Ob aktual'nykh problemakh partiinogo stroitel'stva*, 2d ed. (Moscow, Politizdat, 1976), p. 274.

43. By far the best discussion of these principles—and their application in a particular policy realm—is found in Solomon, *Soviet Criminologists and Criminal Policy*.

44. Petrovichev, *Partiinoe stroitel'stvo* (1972), p. 166.

45. Smeliakov, *S chego nachinaetsia Rodina*, pp. 196–197. Smeliakov was one of the first to write about the sovnarkhozes after the publication of Khrushchev's note on the subject. *Pravda*, April 3, 1957, p. 2. It seems to be quite usual for the early press articles on a decision to come from this source.

46. *Partiinaia zhizn'*, no. 17 (September 1966), p. 15.

47. *Problemi e realta dell' URSS* (Rome, 1958), p. 75.

48. Khrushchev, *Khrushchev Remembers*, pp. 610–611.

49. See, for example, *Sovetskaia Belorussiia*, November 21, 1962, p. 2.

50. N. Lobachev, V. Efimov, "Planovye pokazateli v mekhanizme khoziaistvo-

vaniia," *Kommunist*, no. 16 (November 1975), pp. 23–32. The occupation of the authors was not given, but Lobachev was deputy head of the planning and financial organs department of the Central Committee. A note was attached to the article to the effect that "a series of questions raised in the article have a provisional character," and, in fact, a number of rather important changes were proposed in the economic incentive system.

51. A. Chuianov, *Na stremnine veka* (Moscow, Politizdat, 1976), pp. 40–41. Presumably this rule applied primarily to posts that generally were handled by the departments. If Ordzhonikidze wanted to change a really important official, he surely would have consulted with Stalin.

52. 1971 Yearbook of the *Bol'shaia sovetskaia entsiklopediia*, p. 590.

53. Pravdin, "Inside the CPSU Central Committee," p. 100. The one exception was V. A. Slastenenko, who moved from the post of instructor of the propaganda department to that of deputy chairman of the State Committee for Publishing, Printing, and Book Trade. *Zhurnalist*, no. 10 (October 1975), p. 73, and *Sovetskaia Moldaviia*, January 8, 1976, p. 3.

54. In the words of V. O. Key, Jr., power is not "a substance that could be poured into a keg, stored, and drawn upon as the need arises." *Politics, Parties, and Pressure Groups*, 4th ed. (New York, Thomas Y. Crowell Co., 1958), pp. 4–5.

55. Before World War II, Shchelokov was chairman of the executive committee of the Dnepropetrovsk city soviet, while Brezhnev was secretary of the regional party committee. When Brezhnev became Moldavian first secretary in the early 1950s, he called Shchelokov to Moldavia to serve as the First Deputy Chairman of the Council of Ministers of the republic. Shchelokov is the only man to have served under Brezhnev both in Dnepropetrovsk and Moldavia.

56. For such a case involving A. M. Rumiantsev, the vice-president of the Academy of Sciences, see Pravdin, "Inside the CPSU Central Committee," p. 99.

57. As early as 1957, Kapitsa was already serving as deputy head of the Far Eastern Countries Department of the Ministry of Foreign Affairs. *Pravda*, September 20, 1957, p. 1. For a partial biography see *Diplomaticheskii slovar'* (Moscow, Politizdat, 1971), II, 25.

58. *Ekonomicheskaia gazeta*, no. 51 (December 1968), p. 8.

59. *Pravda*, March 1, 1975, p. 3.

60. N. S. Khrushchev, *Stroitel'stvo kommunizma v SSSR i razvitie sel'skogo khoziaistva* (Moscow, Gospolitizdat, 1963), IV, 109.

12. The Leading Party Organs

1. The congresses also hear other reports—notably those of the chairmen of the auditing commission and the mandate committee—but these do not play an important part in the proceedings.

2. L. A. Apollonov, *Verkhovnyi organ leninskoi partii* (Moscow, Politizdat, 1976), p. 66.

3. *Tridnatsatyi s"ezd RKP(b)* [*Mai 1924 goda*] *Stenograficheskii otchet* (Moscow, Gospolitizdat, 1963), p. 711.

4. *XXV s"ezd Kommunisticheskoi partii Sovetskogo Soiuza [24 fevralia-5 marta 1976]*, *Stenograficheskii otchet* (Moscow, Politizdat, 1976), I, 293—299.

5. Fainsod, *How Russia Is Ruled* (1963), pp. 217–218.

6. Apollonov, *Verkhovnyi organ leninskoi partii*, p. 167.

7. The various proposals are found in *XXV s"ezd*, I, 154, 241, 312, 358, 142, 180, 339, 348.

8. Ibid., pp. 218, 157, 427, 136, 362, 247, 157. For a similar survey of suggestions made at the Twenty-Third Congress in 1966, see Jerry F. Hough, "The Party Apparatchiki," in H. Gordon Skilling and Franklyn Griffiths, eds., *Interest Groups in Soviet Politics* (Princeton, Princeton University Press, 1971), pp. 60–61, and for a survey of those made at the Nineteenth Congress in 1952 see Jerry F. Hough, *The Soviet Prefects* (Cambridge, Mass., Harvard University Press, 1969), pp. 258–259.

9. Michel Tatu, *Power in the Kremlin* (New York, The Viking Press, 1967), pp. 151–157.

10. N. S. Patolichev makes such an assertion about his election in 1941 in *Ispytanie na zrelost'* (Moscow, Politizdat, 1977), p. 114, and S. A. Antonov about his election in 1966 in *Svet ne v okne* (Moscow, Politizdat, 1977), p. 196.

11. For 1962, A. I. Sidorov, *Verkhovnyi organ KPSS* (New York, Mysl', 1964), p. 142; for 1971, Apollonov, *Verkhovnyi organ leninskoi partii*, p. 188.

12. Apollonov, *Verkhovnyi organ leninskoi partii*, pp. 185–186. According to Medvedev, the meeting of this group during the Eighteenth Party Congress in 1939 provided a dramatic semipublic setting for Stalin's announcement that the former People's Commissar for Internal Affairs, Ezhov, had fallen from favor. Roy A. Medvedev, "New Pages from the Political Biography of Stalin," in Robert C. Tucker, ed., *Stalinism* (New York, W. W. Norton & Company, 1977), pp. 218–219.

13. Robert V. Daniels, "Office Holding and Elite Status: The Central Committee of the CPSU," in Paul Cooks, Robert V. Daniels, and Nancy Whittier Heer, eds. *The Dynamics of Soviet Politics* (Cambridge, Mass., Harvard University Press, 1976), pp. 79–80, 78.

14. For example, the following positions whose occupants were full members of the Central Committee in 1971 were not so represented in the Central Committee of 1976, despite the substantial increase in the number of full members in the latter year and the very low rates of turnover in the Central Committee between the two years: the Ministries of Radiotechnical Industry and of Transportation Construction; the first secretaryships of the Ivano-Frank, Tuva, and Ural regional party committees; the second secretaryship of the Turkmenia Central Committee; the first deputy chairmanship of the USSR Party Control Committee and the chairmanship of the Ukrainian Party Commission; the first secretaryship of the Novosibirsk city party committee; the chairmanship of the Georgian Council of Ministers; the ambassadorships in India and Mongolia; and the Leningrad Military District.

15. There is testimony that a number of party Presidium members did make such a response when Khrushchev proposed making his secret speech to the Twentieth Party Congress. Apparently they questioned the wisdom of this action and acceded only when Khrushchev threatened to ask the congress to decide whether it wanted to hear him. Tatu, *Power in the Kremlin*, pp. 143–147.

16. This analysis rests on R. T. McKenzie, *British Political Parties* (New York, St. Martins Press, 1955). I am endebted to Professor Ronald Rogowski of Duke University for the point.

17. Ibid., p. 34.

18. Because of deaths among its members, the Central Committee is almost always smaller than it was at the time of the congress at which it was elected. For example, the Central Committee of 241 voting members selected in 1971 had been reduced by death to 225 by 1976.

19. Generally the nationality of Soviet officials is indicated only in the various volumes of *Deputaty Verkhovnogo Soveta SSSR*. The figure given is an approximate one because information on the nationality of nineteen Central Committee members was not found and was guessed at on the basis of last name. However, the percentage of non-Russians cannot be lower than 37 percent or higher than 45 percent, and in practice it cannot vary more than a point from the 38–39 figure. The breakdown is extremely likely to be 62 percent Russians, 19 percent Ukrainians, and 29 percent other nationalities. The nationality breakdown of the full and candidate members in 1961 was almost identical to that of the full members in 1971, but in 1952, 72 percent of the full and candidate members were Russians, 7 percent Ukrainians, and 21 percent other nationalities. Although the percentage of "other nationalities" rose, that of nationalities from the Transcaucasus fell from 6.5 percent in 1952 to 3 percent in both 1961 and 1971. Seweryn Bialer, *Soviet Political Elite: Concept, Sample, Case Study*, Ph.D. diss., Columbia University, 1966, p. 188. (This dissertation contains a wealth of data on other characteristics of Central Committee members.)

20. For a pair of articles that attempted to make such deductions from the membership of republican central committees as well as the All-Union Central Committee see Jerry F. Hough, "The Soviet Elite: I, Groups and Individuals," *Problems of Communism*, XVI (January–February 1967), 28–35; "The Soviet Elite: II, In Whose Hands the Future?" ibid., XVI (March–April 1967), 18–25.

21. N. I. Kolchenko, "Sochetanie kollektivnosti s personal'noi otvetstvennost'iu —vazhneishii printsip partiinogo rukovodstva," in P. A. Rodionov, ed., *Problemy partiinogo stroitel'stva* (Moscow, Izdatel'stvo politicheskoi literatury, 1972), p. 139.

22. In 1962, 1966, 1971, and 1977, biographies of voting and candidate members of the Central Committee, as well as of members of the Auditing Commission, were published in the yearbook of the *Bol'shaia sovetskaia entsiklopediia*.

23. The best source for the dates and subject matter of Central Committee sessions from 1953 to 1971 is *Kommunisticheskaia partiia Sovetskogo Soiuza v rezoliutsiiakh i resheniiakh s"ezdov, konferentsii, i plenumov TsK*, 9th ed. (Moscow, Politizdat, 1971–1972), vols. VI–X. It even gives precise dates for some plenary sessions that were not published at the time (for example, those that dealt with the Beria and Zhukov removals). The yearbooks of the *Bol'shaia sovetskaia entsiklopediia* contain information about more recent sessions.

24. The names of the speakers at the Central Committee sessions are listed in a communiqué printed in central newspapers immediately after the sessions.

25. In the May 1966 session, five of the speakers were agricultural scientists and

lower agricultural officials not on the Central Committee. Subsequently, the only nonmembers to speak were regional party officials who had been elected to their post after the congress and who were taking the "place" on the Central Committee that their post would formally give them at the election of the new Central Committee after the next party congress.

26. L. I. Brezhnev, *Voprosy agrarnoi politiki KPSS i osvoenie tselinnvkh zemel' Kazakhstana* (Moscow, Politizdat, 1974), pp. 164–165.

27. The approximate number of party members in each region and republic can be calculated by counting the number of delegates each is permitted to elect to the party congress. The names of the delegates, together with their party organization, were published at the end of the second volume of the stenographic report of the Twenty-Fifth Congress.

28. Sverdlovsk was Kirilenko's former region, and in October 1976 its first secretary, Ia. P. Riabov, was named Central Committee secretary in charge of the police, the military, and defense industry.

29. For a discussion of this Central Committee session and a summary of the criticisms made at it see Solomon Schwartz, "Agriculture: The Curtain is Lifted," *Problems of Communism*, XV (March–April 1966), 12–20.

30. L. I. Brezhnev, *Voprosy upravleniia ekonomikoi razvitogo sotsialisticheskogo obshchestva* (Moscow, Politizdat, 1976), pp. 134, 330. See Brezhnev, *Voprosy agrarnoi politiki*, p. 207, for the 1968 remark.

31. Antonov, *Svet ne v okne*, p. 224.

32. Brezhnev,*Voprosy upravleniia ekonomikoi razvitogo sotsialisticheskogo obshchectva*, pp. 476–477.

33. At the Nineteenth Congress the name of the Politburo was changed to Presidium, and the latter contained twenty-five full members and eleven candidates. However, a secret inner bureau was named with the former number of members. For a discussion of this point, see Nikita S. Khrushchev, *Khrushchev Remembers*, ed. and trans. Strobe Talbott (Boston, Little, Brown, and Co., 1970), 279–282. The 1957 Presidium named after the removal of the antiparty group included fifteen full members and eight candidates.

34. The nationality of the Politburo members is found in Borys Levitsky, *The Soviet Political Elite* (Stanford, Calif., The Hoover Institution on War, Revolution, and Peace, 1969), esp. pp. 745–757, but also in individual biographies in specific cases.

35. Except in the case of Bulganin (who subsequently was revealed to be of white collar origin), I have relied on Levitsky, *The Soviet Political Elite*, for information on the social origin of Politburo members.

36. Khrushchev, *Khrushchev Remembers*, p. 290. "Molotov . . . was the city dancer among us. He had grown up in an intellectual family, and as a university student, he had been at many student parties and knew how to dance the way students did. He loved music and could even play the violin. In general he was a very musical person. I'm not an expert in this, in fact I'm a pretty bad judge, but in my eyes Molotov was a first-class dancer."

37. V. V. Kolotov, *Nikolai Alekseevich Voznesensky* (Moscow, Politizdat, 1974), pp. 233–235. This man was no more than a single individual, but the author went out of his way to identify him with those promoted from the industrial workers.

38. Sheila Fitzpatrick, *Education and Social Mobility in the Soviet Union* (London, Cambridge University Press, 1979).

39. A. S. Chuianov, *Na stremnine veka* (Moscow, Politizdat, 1976), p. 39.

40. *Pravda,* December 11, 1976, p. 3; *Izvestiia,* December 14, 1976, p. 5.

41. Fedor Panferov, *Volga-Matushka Reka* (Moscow, Sovetskii Pisatel', 1954), pp. 184–186. The long relevant passage on this character's education is translated in Hough, *The Soviet Prefects,* p. 365, n. 11.

42. *New York Times,* June 15, 1973, p. 3.

43. *XXV s"ezd,* I, 91.

44. N. A. Petrovichev, ed., *Partiinoe stroitel'stvo,* 3d ed. (Moscow, Politizdat, 1972), p. 162.

45. L. I. Brezhnev, *Ob osnovnykh voprosakh ekonomicheskoi politiki KPSS na sovremennom etape* (Moscow, Politizdat, 1975), I, 99, 244; II, 349.

46. Ibid., I, 72, 110, 190, 195, 350, 425; II, 69–70, 77, 197, 207, 351, 382. Brezhnev, *Voprosy agrarnoi politiki KPSS,* p. 223.

47. Brezhnev, *Ob osnovnykh voprosakh ekonomicheskoi politiki,* I, 188, 248; II, 207, 360.

48. *Voprosy istorii KPSS,* no. 12 (December 1976), p. 67.

49. *New York Times,* June 15, 1973, p. 3.

50. Vadim Zagladin, "Neuklonnaia volia k miru," *Novoe vremia,* no. 51 (December 17, 1976), p. 5. Quoted in Ben Fischer, "The Soviet Political System and Foreign Policy-Making in the Brezhnev Era," paper presented to the National Convention of the AAASS, October 14, 1977, Washington, D.C.

51. Raymond L. Garthoff, "SALT and the Soviet Military," *Problems of Communism,* XXIV (January–February 1975), 29. Several other instances are discussed in Fischer, "The Soviet Political System and Foreign Policy-Making."

52. Brezhnev, *Ob osnovnykh voprosakh ekonomicheskoi politiki,* I, 110.

53. *New York Times,* June 15, 1973, p. 3. The same norm has been enunciated for the functioning of the bureaus of the lower party organs. "First of all, the bureau should try to work out a decision that is correct in principle. For this purpose it is sometimes necessary even to adjourn so members of the bureau can think through the question, study the materials and opinions of comrades more deeply. In such cases the decision is usually taken unanimously." *Partiinaia zhizn',* no. 13 (July 1974), p. 73.

54. Khrushchev, *Khrushchev Remembers,* p. 256.

55. *Khrushchev Remembers,* pp. 451–452.

56. N. S. Khrushchev, *Stroitel'stvo kommunizma v SSSR i razvitie sel'skogo khoziaistva* (Moscow, Gospolitizdat, 1963), VII, 179–286. See Jerry F. Hough, "Enter N. S. Khrushchev," *Problems of Communism,* XIII (July-August 1964), 28–33.

57. *XXV s"ezd,* I, 186.

58. *Pravda,* May 11, 1962, p. 1.

59. Fainsod, *How Russia Is Ruled* (1953), p. 282.

60. L. A. Slepov, "Osnovnye cherty leninskogo stilia partiinogo i gosudarstven-

nogo rukovodstva," in I. I. Pronin and S. A. Smirnov, ed., *Zhiznennaia sila leninskikh printsipov partiinogo stroitel'stva* (Moscow, Politizdat, 1970), p. 222–223.

13. Provincial and Local Politics

1. Alfred E. Meyer, *The Soviet Political System* (New York, Random House, 1965), p. 458.

2. The total population of the USSR and its major territorial subdivisions on January 1, 1976, is found in *Narodnoe khoziaistvo SSSR v 1975 g.* (Moscow, Statistika, 1976), pp. 16–21, and the number of persons of each nationality is given on pp. 32–35.

3. Primorsk krai on the Pacific coast has no such nationality units within it, and it is unclear why—except for historical reasons—it is called a krai instead of an oblast.

4. *Narodnoe khoziaistvo SSSR v 1975 g.*, pp. 16–21.

5. A list of all cities and raions in the Soviet Union, organized by republic and oblast, is published in the periodically issued book, *SSSR: Administrativno-territorial'-noe delenie soiuznykh respublik* (Moscow, Izdatel'stvo "Izvestiia Sovetov deputatov trudiashchikhsia SSSR"). The population of cities over 15,000 persons on January 1, 1975, is provided on pp. 636–650 of the 1974 edition, and a list of cities with urban raions—and the number of raions in each city—is found on pp. 629–635 of that volume.

6. For a discussion of this question see Jerry F. Hough, *The Soviet Union and Social Science Theory* (Cambridge, Mass., Harvard University Press, 1977), p. 167. There actually were fifty-six oblasts in the RSFSR, but this information was available for only forty-nine of them.

7. Ibid., pp. 140–141, 156–157.

8. B. K. Alekseev and M. N. Perfil'ev, *Printsipy i tendentsii razvitiia predstavitel'-nogo sostava mestnykh sovetov* (Leningrad, Lenizdat, 1976), p. 120. See pp. 166, 186, 200, 222, 254, and 280 for a breakdown of these figures by sociological variables such as age, education, and sex.

9. *Sovety deputatov trudiashchikhsia*, no. 5 (May 1975), p. 30.

10. *Izvestiia*, June 25, 1977, pp. 1–2. K. F. Sheremet, ed., *Sovety deputatov trudiashchikhsia i razvitie sotsialisticheskoi demokratii* (Moscow, Nauka, 1976), p. 67. The latter provides a comprehensive discussion of the local soviets and is an excellent introduction to the subject.

11. The names of the republican standing committees and their chairmen were published in the various republican newspapers after the first Supreme Soviet session following the 1975 elections. The occupations of the chairmen can be ascertained from the list of the deputies published immediately after the elections.

12. *Krasnoe znamia* (Primorsk), May 24, and June 29, 1977; *Stavropol'skaia pravda*, June 1, and June 25, 1977; *Tikhookeanskaia zvezda* (Khabarovsk), June 5, and June 28, 1977. "Policy-related" committees include all committees but the mandate one.

13. *Udmurtskaia pravda*, June 26, 1977. The occupations of the chairmen of the Izhevsk standing committees are also known for 1975. Six of the committees had the same chairman as in 1975: Education; Trade and Public Eating; Construction; Transportation and Communications; Repair and Distribution of Housing; and Youth.

The chairman of a seventh committee, the Industry Committee, was director of the knitted goods factory and had been chairman of the Consumer Service Committee in 1975. The other chairmen had been: Planning–Budget—deputy head of the Udmurt Statistical Administration; Industry—deputy director of the Izhevsk Defense Plant; Health—head of a department at the medical institute; Culture—a director in the local theater; Communal Economy—director of a concrete factory; Socialist Legality and Preservation of Public Order—a judge; Conservation—chief doctor of the city sanitation station. Ibid., June 26, 1975.

14. While in Moscow in 1976 and 1977 I examined newspaper reports of "election" sessions of the city soviets of eleven RSFSR oblast capitals in 1975 and of twelve such sessions of city soviets held in 1977 in the autonomous republics and krais of the RSFSR. (Current copies of these newspapers, but not those of the regular oblasts, are available in Lenin Library in Moscow.) All the capital cities had at least three deputy chairmen, and, although there were exceptions, the fourth deputy chairman tended to be added when the city's population rose over 500,000. In the Chuvash and Karelian autonomous republics and in Primorsk krai, the names of the deputy chairmen of the executive committees of the soviets of the raiony and small cities were published. Five of the city soviets had one deputy chairman, and eight had two; seven of the soviets of the rural raiony had one deputy chairman, and forty-seven had two; eight of the soviets of the urban raiony had one deputy chairman, and two had two.

15. In fifty-one oblasts and autonomous republics of the RSFSR in 1975, four had three deputy chairmen, twenty-three had four, twenty had five, and two had six. The number (and names) of the deputy chairmen of the councils of ministers of the union republics are given in the 1976 Yearbook of the *Bol'shaia sovetskaia entsiklopediia* in the entries on each republic.

16. The names of the members of the executive committee are published in the report of the soviet session immediately following an election. However, the occupations of the members are almost never given at that time, and must be sought in the list of deputies and their occupations published previously. (Often the names of the deputies are published twice, first at the time of the registration of candidates and then at the time of the election, and in these cases their occupations usually are given only in the first list.) The union republics and autonomous republics have broad councils of ministers instead of executive committees. These councils of ministers, too, have inner presidiums, but their membership is as obscure as that of the Presidium of the USSR Council of Ministers. (In the one case that I have seen, the Central Committee second secretary joined the chairman and deputy chairmen of the Council of Ministers. *Sovetskaia Kirgiziia*, April 18, 1963, p. 1.)

17. I. A. Azovkin, *Mestnye sovety i sistema organov vlasti* (Moscow, Iuridicheskaia literatura, 1971), p. 133.

18. In a few respects the local soviets have jurisdiction over all institutions in their territory. For example, the city health department can issue sanitation regulations that are obligatory for all institutions, while any institution that makes a land-use decision must have it approved by the local soviet.

19. 1976 Yearbook of the *Bol'shaia sovetskaia entsiklopediia*, pp. 13, 14.

20. See the discussion in Jerry F. Hough, *The Soviet Prefects* (Cambridge, Mass., Harvard University Press, 1969), pp. 114–116, 150–170.

21. See Chapter 10.

22. The number of party committees at each level and the total number of committee members (both voting and candidate members) and members of the auditing commissions were published in *Partiinaia zhizn'*, no. 10 (May 1976), p. 19. By dividing the total membership by number of committees one obtains a figure of 180 members for the republics and oblasts and 90 for the cities and raions. In the union republics, about 60 percent of these members are voting members of the central committees, and that percentage has been used in calculating the figures cited here.

23. In thirteen krais and autonomous republics of the RSFSR on which it was possible to obtain information in the summer of 1977, there was much more variety in the specialty of the secretary selected as second secretary. Four of the second secretaries handled organizational questions, four handled industry and construction, and three handled agriculture. Two had a mixed set of responsibilities (either industry or construction coupled with certain aspects of the organizational responsibilities)— a useful reminder of the fact that the first secretaries have considerable leeway in deciding how to distribute functions among their subordinates.

24. This department clearly is responsible for dealing with visiting foreign Communists and for supervising such agencies as Intourist and the Society for Cultural Ties with Foreign Countries. The reason for the word "information" in the title is quite unclear, but the transmission of intraparty information is handled by the information section of the organizational-party work department.

25. For a description of the work of the party commissions see *Aktivnye pomoshchiki partiinykh komitetov* (Moscow, Politizdat, 1974).

26. Such is the case in the list of departments of republican central committees and regional party committees published in N. A. Petrovichev, ed., *Partiinoe stroitel'stvo*, 3d ed. (Moscow, Politizdat, 1972), pp. 176–177.

27. Ibid., pp. 180, 183.

28. Robert H. McNeal, "Paying for the Party," *Survey*, 22 (Spring 1976), 64.

29. In 1966 Vladimir oblast had twenty-two city and raion party committees and 415 responsible officials in them, an average of 19 a committee. *Partiinaia zhizn'*, no. 12 (June 1966), p. 11.

30. *Itogi vsesoiuznoi perepisi naseleniia 1970 goda* (Moscow, Statistika, 1973), VI, 259.

31. For the number of party organs in 1971 and 1976 see *Spravochnik partiinogo rabotnika, 1976*, p. 462.

32. The data for this paragraph come from D. M. Kukin, ed., *Voprosy raboty KPSS s kadrami na sovremennom etape* (Moscow, Mysl', 1976), pp. 104, 158.

33. G. Vorobev and V. Loskutov, "Sel'skokhoziaistvennyi otdel obkoma partii," *Partiinaia zhizn'*, no. 15 (August 1974), pp. 31–40.

34. The names of the secretaries are found in the 1976 Yearbook of the *Bol'shaia sovetskaia entsiklopediia* under the entries for the respective republics, and their specialty can be easily ascertained by purusing the major newspaper in the republic. The earlier posts of the secretaries indicated can be found in Grey Hodnett and Val

Ogareff, *Leaders of the Soviet Republics, 1955–1972* (Canberra, Australian National University, 1973) through the use of the index, with the exception of the Ukrainian secretary (N. M. Borisenko), whose biography is printed in *Deputaty Verkhovnogo Soveta SSSR* (1974).

35. Hough, *The Soviet Prefects.*

36. The biographies of the relatively few managerial personnel who reach the level of obkom first secretary should not lead us to the inference that the transfer of a manager to party work is usually permanent. On the contrary, most such officials return to managerial positions in a relatively short time.

37. I. Kh. Iunak, A. F. Vatchenko, and B. V. Popov. *Deputaty Verkhovnogo Soveta SSSR* (1974), pp. 506, 89, 359.

38. M. P. Trunov. See the 1971 Yearbook of the *Bol'shaia sovetskaia entsiklopediia*, p. 633, and *Deputaty Verkhovnogo Soveta SSSR* (1974), p. 440.

39. William J. Conyngham, *Industrial Management in the Soviet Union* (Stanford, Calif., Hoover Institute Press, 1973); Jerry F. Hough "A Harebrained Scheme in Retrospect," *Problems of Communism*, XIV (July-August 1965), 26–32.

40. M. S. Solomentsev and I. A. Bondarenko. See *Deputaty Verkhovnogo Soveta SSSR* (1974), pp. 413, 73.

41. These statistics are based on the biographies, ibid. (1966), (1970), and (1974).

42. *Kommunist* (Erevan), February 23, 1975, p. 1; *Sovetskaia Kirgiziia*, June 26, 1976, p. 2.

43. *Znamia* (Kaluga), March 28, 1975, p. 1. Many earlier issues of this newspaper contained matter-of-fact references to Frolkin's position.

44. In most regions, one can determine the membership of the bureau by examining the signatures at the conclusion of the obituaries of important regional officials. The names of bureau members come first, usually in alphabetical order. Their occupations can be determined by reading the newspapers over several months. There is the possibility of error in this methodology, but it should be minimal, especially if several obituaries with a comprehensive list of signatures are published. For a list of the members of seven bureaus of oblast party committees in 1966 see Hough, *The Soviet Prefects*, p. 333.

45. In 1977, half of all obkom bureaus contained workers. *Kommunist*, no. 14 (September 1977), p. 54.

46. *Zhurnalist*, no. 3 (March 1976), p. 7, for a list of editors on bureaus.

47. *Kommunist* (Erevan), January 10, 1976, p. 1.

48. *Kommunist*, no. 14 (September 1977), p. 54.

49. *Partiinaia zhizn'*, no. 2 (January 1967), p. 36.

50. These calculations are based on the men who were first secretary at the time of the 1974 elections to the Supreme Soviet. With the exception of two men who died, their biographies can be found in *Deputaty Verkhovnogo Soveta SSSR* (1974).

51. Merle Fainsod, *Smolensk Under Soviet Rule* (Cambridge, Mass., Harvard University Press, 1958), p. 93.

52. Either the chairman or the second secretary may be promoted directly to the post of first secretary, and these two positions are, in fact, very typical paths to the top. However, sometimes a man on the rise will move from second secretary to chairman of

the executive committee and then first secretary, and presumably the chairmanship is a promotion, for the reverse path is almost never observed. For two examples at the oblast level see the biographies of N. S. Priezzhev and V. N. Ptitsyn in *Deputaty Verkhovnogo Soveta SSSR* (1974); for an example at the city level see the biography of A. I. Ali-zade, ibid. (1966), and for one at the raion level see the biography of D. L. Gelashvili, ibid. (1970).

53. These officials are: in the Ukraine—V. V. Shcherbitsky, A. P. Liashko, and I. K. Lutak; in Uzbekistan—Sh. R. Rashidov, V. G. Lomonosov, and N. D. Khudai-berdyev; in Tadzhikistan—D. Rasulov, R. Nabiev, and A. I. Shitov; in Kazakhstan—D. A. Kunaev, V. K. Mesiats, and B. A. Ashimov. Ibid. (1974).

54. V. Dudintsev, *Ne khlebom edinym* (Munich, Izdatel'stvo TsOPE, 1957), p. 27.

55. William Taubman, *Governing Soviet Cities* (New York, Frederick A. Praeger, 1973), esp. pp. 54–72.

56. Hough, *The Soviet Prefects,* pp. 214–217, 224–234.

57. Ibid., 193–194.

58. The numbers of delegates from each region must be counted from the list of delegates to the Twenty-Fifth Congress in *XXV s"ezd Kommunisticheskii partii Sovet-skogo Soiuza [24 fevralia-5 marta 1976 goda]*, *Stenograficheskii otchet* (Moscow, Politiz-dat, 1976), II, 329–596, and the biographies are found in *Deputaty Verkhovnogo Soveta SSSR* (1974). The cities of Moscow and Kiev are not subordinated to the surrounding oblasts, and they elect deputies to the party congresses independently. They are counted as oblasts in this calculation.

59. John A. Armstrong, "The Ethnic Scene in the Soviet Union: The View of the Dictatorship," in Erich Goldhagen, ed., *Ethnic Minorities in the Soviet Union* (New York, Frederick A. Praeger, 1968), pp. 3–49.

60. Hough, *The Soviet Prefects,* 217–224.

61. Grey Hodnett, "Technology and Social Change in Soviet Central Asia: The Politics of Cotton Growing," in Henry W. Morton and Rudolf L. Tokes, *Soviet Politics and Society in the 1970s* (New York, Free Press, 1974), 60–117.

62. See the discussion in Hough, *The Soviet Union and Social Science Theory,* pp. 155, 165.

63. Jerry F. Hough, "Soviet Urban Politics and Comparative Urban Theory," *Journal of Comparative Administration,* 4 (November 1972), 316.

64. Hough, *The Soviet Union and Social Science Theory,* pp. 160–169.

65. Robert A. Dahl, *Who Governs?* (New Haven, Yale University Press, 1961).

66. For example, the issues on which Dahl concentrated were the launching of a local development project (in significant part with federal funds), the location of a new school and its relationship to park land, and the choosing of minor governmental officials. Clearly many of the most crucial questions of the development of New Haven —and all cities—are determined by decisions of the federal government, the state government, industrial corporations, and the like. Dahl, *Who Governs?*

67. Taubman, *Governing Soviet Cities,* contains many quotations from such articles. See Robert J. Osborn, *Soviet Social Policies* (Homewood, Ill., Dorsey Press, 1970), p. 223.

68. "O razvitii zhilishchnogo stroitel'stva v SSSR," in *KPSS o rabote sovetov, Sbornik dokumentov* (Moscow, Gospolizdat, 1959), pp. 492–508; "O merakh po dal'-neishemu uluchsheniiu raboty raionnykh i gorodskikh sovetov deputatov trudiash-chikhsia," *Pravda*, March 14, 1971, p. 1.

69. Karl Deutsch, *Nationalism and Social Communication* (New York, Wiley, 1953).

70. Hodnett, "Technology and Social Change in Soviet Central Asia," pp. 96–102.

71. Aleksandr E. Lunev, *Teoreticheskie problemy gosudarstvennogo upravleniia* (Moscow, Nauka, 1974), pp. 181–182.

72. *Pravda*, October 5, 1977, p. 2.

73. See n. 53 of Chapter 6.

74. On January 1, 1977, the average length of tenure of the republican second secretaries was four years, compared with nearly twelve years for the republican first secretaries. The predecessors of the second secretaries had held their post for an average of six years, compared with tenures of eight, nine, ten, nineteen, and thirty-four years for the six first secretaries removed in the last decade.

75. Nicholas DeWitt, *Education and Professional Employment in the U.S.S.R.* (Washington, Government Printing Office, 1961), pp. 556–574, p. 563 for the language question.

76. *Bakinskii rabochii*, February 17, 1960, p. 5; July 11, 1959, p. 2.

77. Armstrong, "The Ethnic Scene in the Soviet Union."

14. The Distribution of Power

1. Carl J. Friedrich and Zbigniew Brzezinski, *Totalitarian Dictatorship and Autocracy* (Cambridge, Mass., Harvard University Press, 1956), pp. 9–10.

2. Zbigniew Brzezinski, "Totalitarianism and Rationality," *American Political Science Review*, L (September 1956), 752–753.

3. Ibid., pp. 760–761.

4. Allen Kassof, "The Administered Society: Totalitarianism Without Terror," *World Politics*, 16 (July 1964), 558–575; T. H. Rigby, "Traditional, Market, and Organizational Societies and the USSR," ibid., pp. 539–557 (see also his later "Politics in the Mono-Organizational Society," in Andrew C. Janos, ed., *Authoritarian Politics in Communist Europe: Uniformity and Diversity in One-Party States* [Berkeley, University of California Press, 1976]); Zbigniew Brzezinski and Samuel P. Huntington, *Political Power USA/USSR* (New York, The Viking Press, 1964); George Fischer, *The Soviet System and Modern Society* (New York, Atherton Press, 1968).

5. Kassof, "The Administered Society: Totalitarianism Without Terror."

6. Hannah Arendt, *The Origins of Totalitarianism* (New York, Harcourt-Brace, 1951).

7. Carl A. Linden, *Khrushchev and the Soviet Leadership* (Baltimore, John Hopkins University Press, 1966); Sidney I. Ploss, *Conflict and Decision-Making in Soviet Russia* (Princeton, Princeton University Press, 1965).

8. The major book on the subject is H. Gordon Skilling and Franklyn Griffiths, eds., *Interest Groups in Soviet Politics* (Princeton, Princeton University Press, 1971).

9. A typical example of the refusal of a critic to take such denials into account is William E. Odom, "A Dissenting View on the Group Approach to Soviet Politics," *World Politics*, 29 (July 1976), 542–567.

10. Franklyn Griffiths, "A Tendency Analysis of Soviet Policy-Making," in Skilling and Griffiths, eds., *Interest Groups in Soviet Politics*, p. 358.

11. See the discussion in Jerry F. Hough, *The Soviet Union and Social Science Theory* (Cambridge, Mass., Harvard University Press, 1977), pp. 204–205.

12. Ernest S. Griffith, *The American System of Government*, 4th ed. (New York, Frederick A. Praeger, 1965), pp. 102–103; Theodore Lowi, *The End of Liberalism* (New York, Norton, 1969).

13. Jerry F. Hough, "The Man and the System," *Problems of Communism*, XXV (March-April 1976), 14.

14. Brzezinski and Huntington, *Political Power USA/USSR*, p. 196.

15. David Truman, *The Governmental Process* (New York, Alfred A. Knopf, 1951), p. 33.

16. Brzezinski and Huntington, *Political Power USA/USSR*, pp. 203–209.

17. Ibid., pp. 206–207.

18. For documentation of the role of the relevant ministries and scholars attached to them in policymaking in the criminal justice realm see Peter H. Solomon, Jr., *Soviet Criminologists and Criminal Policy: Specialists in Policy Making* (New York, Columbia University Press, 1978).

19. N. S. Khrushchev, *Stroitel'stvo kommunizma v SSSR i razvitie sel'skogo khoziaistva* (Moscow, Gospolitizdat, 1962–1964). See, for example, vol. I, 85–100 (the Virgin Lands proposal); IV, 137–150 (a report on a trip to Astrakhan); VII, 163–177 (the bifurcation of the party apparatus); VII, 249–286 (thoughts on a Central Asian trip); VIII, 114–124 (a proposal on mineral fertilizers).

20. *XXV s"ezd Kommunisticheskoi partii Sovetskogo Soiuza [24 fevralia-5 marta 1976 goda], Stenograficheskii otchet* (Moscow, Politizdat, 1976), I, 165, 187, 262, 339, 348, 390, 404; II, 107.

21. In a number of cases the individuals may be transmitting ideas discovered in other countries rather than developing them themselves, but from the point of view of the Soviet system they are still initiating agents. (Sometimes one has the impression that developments in the United States are actually one of the most important sources of policy initiation in the Soviet Union.)

22. Solomon, *Soviet Criminologists and Criminal Policy*.

23. David Easton, *A Systems Analysis of Political Life* (New York, Wiley, 1965), pp. 128–149.

24. V. O. Key, Jr., *Public Opinion and American Democracy* (New York, Alfred A. Knopf, 1967), pp. 524–543, esp. pp. 527 and 537.

25. Brzezinski and Huntington, *Political Power USA/USSR*, pp. 191–193.

26. George Breslauer, "The Soviet System and the Future," *Problems of Communism*, XXV (March-April 1976), 69.

27. I. V. Stalin, *Sochineniia*, ed. Robert H. McNeal (Stanford, Calif., Hoover Institution on War, Revolution, and Peace, 1967), I, 230–231. Quoted in Fainsod, *How Russia Is Ruled* (1953), p. 201.

28. Shelepin became secretary of the All-Union Komsomol in 1943 and second secretary at some time between then and 1952. Even if 1948 is not the year in which he became responsible for personnel selection, the previous Komsomol officials are likely to have been removed by him. Shelepin became Komsomol first secretary in 1952.

29. *The Washington Post*, January 26, 1977.

30. Jerry F. Hough, *The Soviet Prefects* (Cambridge, Mass., Harvard University Press, 1969), pp. 175–176.

31. Alfred G. Meyer, "The Comparative Study of Communist Political Systems," *Slavic Review*, 26 (March 1967), 11.

32. Brzezinski and Huntington, *Political Power USA/USSR*, p. 75.

33. Robert Conquest, "Immobilism and Decay," *Problems of Communism*, XV (September-October 1966), 35–37; Zbigniew Brzezinski, "Reflections on the Soviet System," ibid., XVII (May-June 1968), 44–48.

34. Philip Stewart, "Soviet Interest Groups and the Policy Process," *World Politics*, 22 (October 1969), 50.

35. Hough, *The Soviet Union and Social Science Theory*, pp. 10–12, 22–24.

36. Joseph LaPalombara, "Monoliths or Plural Systems: Through Conceptual Lenses Darkly," *Studies in Comparative Communism*, 8 (Autumn 1975).

37. Robert A. Dahl, *A Preface to Democratic Theory* (Chicago, University of Chicago Press, 1956), pp. 27–28, 133, 146.

38. It may be that our views are somewhat exaggerated in this respect. Khrushchev, the former first secretary of the Stalingrad obkom, and the former first secretary of the Yaroslavl obkom all report in their memoirs that even in 1938–1939 the regional NKVD officials gave them lists of "guilty" persons to approve. All these men mentioned such instances to report that they had refused to approve. In the Stalingrad case the local NKVD officials appealed the decision to Moscow, but the first secretary's decision was allowed to stand. Earlier in the purge, most officials probably would (or at least should) have been afraid to object, but perhaps in more normal times the local party officials exercised fairly substantial control over the secret police. Nikita S. Khrushchev, *Khrushchev Remembers*, ed. and trans. Strobe Talbott (Boston, Little, Brown and Co., 1970), pp. 109–110; A. Chuianov, *Na stremnine veka* (Moscow, Politizdat, 1976), pp. 45–48; N. S. Patolichev, *Ispytanie na zrelost'* (Moscow, Politizdat, 1977), pp. 87–88.

39. E. E. Schattschneider, *The Semi-Sovereign People* (New York, Holt, Rinehart, and Winston, 1960), pp. 2–18.

40. 1977 Yearbook, *Bol'shaia sovetskaia entsikopediia*, pp. 582–627.

41. Seymour Martin Lipset, "Introduction to the Anchor Edition," *Political Man* (New York, Anchor Books, 1963), xxii–xxiii.

15. The Future of the Soviet System

1. Nikolay Gogol, *Dead Souls* (New York, Alfred A. Knopf, 1927), p. 78. Those using other editions can find the extended quotation easily, for it is the last paragraph of Book One.

2. *Trud*, October 12, 1977, p. 2.

3. *XXIV s"ezd Kommunisticheskoi partii Sovetskogo Soiuza [30 marta-9 aprelia*

1971], *Stenograficheskii otchet* (Moscow, Politizdat, 1971), I, 124. It is unclear whether these figures refer to father's occupation or the first job of the official or a combination of both.

4. D. M. Kukin, ed., *Voprosy raboty KPSS s kadrami na sovremennom etape* (Moscow, Mysl', 1976), pp. 152–153. The 82.6 percent includes those who were workers or collective farmers either by social origin or first job, but the other figures indicate a major overlap in the two categories. "Collective farmer," unfortunately, includes professional and managerial personnel of collective farms, although not of state farms. Over 82 percent of the *vykhodtsy* have higher education, and 11 percent are currently in correspondence schools. Ibid., p. 159.

5. Seymour Martin Lipset, *Political Man* (Garden City, N.Y., Doubleday & Company, 1960), chap. 2.

6. Talcott Parsons, *Sociological Theory and Modern Society* (New York, The Free Press, 1967), p. 514.

7. Ibid., p. 518.

8. Karl W. Deutsch, *Politics and Government* (Boston, Houghton Mifflin Co., 1970), p. 305.

9. Frank Parkin, *Class Inequality and Public Order* (New York, Frederick A. Praeger, 1971).

10. Central Intelligence Agency, *Soviet Economic Problems and Prospects* (Washington, D.C., U.S. Government Printing Office, 1977).

11. See the discussion in Jeremy Azrael, "Emergent Nationality Problems" (Santa Monica, Rand Corporation Paper R–2172–AF, 1977), pp. 3–8.

12. Erich Fromm, *Escape from Freedom* (New York, Farrar and Rinehart, 1941).

Index

661